Studies in Diversity Linguistics

Chief Editor: Martin Haspelmath
Consulting Editors: Fernando Zúñiga, Peter Arkadiev, Ruth Singer, Pilar Valenzuela

In this series:

ISSN: 2363-5568

A grammar of Yakkha

Diana Schackow

language
science
press

Diana Schackow. 2015. *A grammar of Yakkha* (Studies in Diversity Linguistics 7).
Berlin: Language Science Press.
This title can be downloaded at:
http://langsci-press.org/catalog/book/66
© 2015, Diana Schackow
Published under the Creative Commons Attribution 4.0 Licence (CC BY 4.0):
http://creativecommons.org/licenses/by/4.0/
ISBN: 978-3-946234-11-1 (Digital)
       978-3-946234-12-8 (Hardcover)
       978-3-946234-13-5 (Softcover)
ISSN: 2363-5568

Cover and concept of design: Ulrike Harbort
Typesetting: Diana Schackow, Sebastian Nordhoff, Lennart Bierkandt, Felix
Kopecky
Proofreading: Slavomir Čéplö, Christian Döhler, Joseph Farquharson,
Constantin Freitag, Tom Gardner, Eitan Grossman, Andreas Hölzl, Charles Ka
Shing Ko, Linda Lanz, Timm Lichte, Michelle Natolo, Stephanie Natolo, Conor
Pyle, Benjamin Saade, Aviva Shimelman, Aaron Sonnenschein, João Veloso
Fonts: Linux Libertine, Arimo, DejaVu Sans Mono
Typesetting software: XƎLATEX

Language Science Press
Habelschwerdter Allee 45
14195 Berlin, Germany
langsci-press.org
Storage and cataloguing done by FU Berlin

Freie Universität Berlin

Contents

Contents

Contents

Contents

Acknowledgments

This grammar is a revised version of my doctoral dissertation at the University of Zürich, which I have submitted in January 2014 and successfully defended in February 2014. It would not exist in its present form without the support of various people and institutions. First of all, I am very grateful to Prof. Novel Kishor Rai for suggesting Yakkha as a language to work on for my doctoral dissertation and for establishing the contact to the Yakkha community in 2009.

None of this work would have been possible without the generous support and the overwhelming hospitality of so many people from the Yakkha community. I would like to thank from all my heart Kamala Jimi (Linkha), who opened her home to me and my husband Lennart. She became our friend and also my most important Yakkha teacher. This grammar owes much to her enthusiasm. My deepest gratitude also goes to Magman Linkha and Man Maya Jimi, who took the time to work with me and share their native speaker intuitions with me. Kamala Linkha, Magman Linkha and Mohan Khamyahang also painstakingly went through each record of my lexical database and offered corrections and additions where appropriate.

Many people were so kind to let me record and archive their speech, thus creating the basis for my linguistic analyses. धेरै धन्यबाद् to Prem Kumari Jimi, Kamala Jimi (Koyongwa), Kamala Jimi (Linkha), Ram Kul Bahadur Jimi, Dhan Kumari Jimi, Ganga Ram Jimi, Sita Linkha, Magman Linkha, Lanka Maya Jimi, Om Bahadur Jimi (Koyongwa), Desh Kumari Jimi, Padam Kumari Jimi, Chom Bahadur Jimi, Kaushila Jimi, Man Bahadur Khamyahang, Hasta Bahadur Khamyahang, Man Maya Jimi, Bhim Maya Jimi, Mohan Khamyahang and his mother. Many thanks also go to Magman Linkha, Ajaya Yakkha and Shantila Jimi for letting me incorporate their written stories into my database.

I would also like to thank everyone in the Kirant Yakkha Chumma (Indigenous Peoples Yakkha Organization) for their trust and their interest in my work and also for practical and administrative support, especially in the early phase of the project, in particular Kamala Jimi (Koyongwa), Indira Jimi, Ramji Kongren and his family in Dandagaun, and Durgamani Dewan and his family in Madi Mulkharka. Heartfelt thanks also go to Dhan Kumari Jimi, Dil Maya Jimi, Nandu

Jimi and their families for their hospitality. I am very grateful to Kaushila Jimi, Sonam Jimi and Vishvakaji Kongren in Kathmandu for their spontaneous help, and to the teachers at Shree Chamunde Higher Secondary School and Ram Kumar Linkha for taking an interest in my work.

I wish to express sincere appreciation to Balthasar Bickel for sharing his insights and expert knowledge on Himalayan languages and on Kiranti languages in particular. This thesis has also greatly benefited from numerous discussions with Martin Haspelmath, whose comments gave me new perspectives on various topics throughout this work.

I would like to thank my colleagues and friends at the MPI EVA and the University of Leipzig for linguistic discussions and shared enthusiasm: Iren Hartmann, Katherine Bolaños, Eugenie Stapert, Kristin Börjesson, Lena Terhart, Swintha Danielsen, Falko Berthold, Sven Grawunder, Alena Witzlack, Zarina Molochieva, John Peterson, Netra Paudyal and Robert Schikowski. I have also benefited greatly from the ELDP language documentation workshop held at SOAS in March 2012. Conversations with colleagues at conferences and other occasions have also been valuable, especially with Mark Donohue, Martin Gaenszle, Kristine Hildebrandt, Gwendolyn Hyslop, Eva van Lier, Tom Owen-Smith and Volker Gast.

Special thanks go to An Van linden, Mara Green, Alena Witzlack, Iren Hartmann, Katherine Bolaños, Lennart Bierkandt, Falko Berthold, Tom Owen-Smith and Tyko Dirksmeyer for their comments on individual chapters, to Hans-Jörg Bibiko for automating the dictionary clean-up to the greatest extent possible, and to Lennart Bierkandt, additionally, for elegantly formatting the kinship charts and numerous diagrams, and for levelling the LaTeX learning curve for me. Of course, I take responsibility for any mistakes or omissions in this work.

My work on Yakkha has been funded by a graduate scholarship from the State of Saxony (2009–2012) and by an Individual Graduate Studentship from the Endangered Languages Programme ELDP (2012–2013, Grant No. IGS 154). The field trip in 2011 was financed by a travel grant from the German Academic Exchange Service DAAD. I would also like to thank Bernard Comrie, director of the Linguistics Department at the Max Planck Institute for Evolutionary Anthropology (MPI EVA) for hosting my ELDP project and also for financing my field trips in 2009 and 2010. The MPI EVA provides ideal conditions for such work, and my thesis has benefited greatly from the resources at this institution and from discussions with colleagues and guests of the department. I thank Claudia Büchel and Julia Cissewski in Leipzig as well as Sascha Völlmin in Zürich for being so incredibly helpful in all administrative matters.

I am very thankful to Martin Haspelmath for offering me the opportunity to publish my work at Language Science Press, to three anonymous reviewers for their valuable comments and suggestions, to Sebastian Nordhoff for managing the publication process and, last but not least, to the numerous proofreaders, who did a wonderful job.

My heartfelt gratitude goes to my family and my friends in Germany, Nepal and elsewhere, especially to my mother for her support during all these years, and to Laxminath, Rita and the whole Shrestha family in Kathmandu. Without Laxminath's efforts, my spoken Yakkha skills would probably be better now, because my Nepali skills would have been much worse. This work is dedicated to the memory of Belayati Shrestha.

Finally, I thank Lennart (again): for making those Nepal journeys "our" journeys.

Abbreviations

Linguistic abbreviations

1,2,3	person (1>3: first acting on third person, etc.)	GEN	genitive
		GSR	generalized semantic role
A	most agent-like argument of a transitive verb	HON	honorific
		HORT	hortative
ABL	ablative	REP	reportative marker
ADD	additive focus	IGN	interjection expressing ignorance
AFF	affirmative		
ALT	alternative	IMP	imperative
AUX	auxiliary verb	INCL	inclusive
BEN	benefactive	INF	infinitive
B.S.	Bikram Sambat calendar, as used in Nepal	INIT	initiative
		INS	instrumental
CAUS	causative	INSIST	insistive
CL	clause linkage marker	INT	interjection
COM	comitative	IRR	irrealis
COMP	complementizer	ITP	interruptive clause linkage
COMPAR	comparative	LOC	locative
COMPL	completive	MDDL	middle
COND	conditional	MIR	mirative
CONT	continuative	NATIV	nativizer
COP	copula	NSG	nonsingular
CTMP	cotemporal (clause linkage)	NC	non-countable
CTR	contrastive focus	n.a.	not applicable
CVB	converb	n.d.	no data
DU	dual	NEG	negation
EMPH	emphatic	Nep.	Nepali
ERG	ergative	NMLZ	nominalizer
EXCL	exclusive	NPST	non-past
EXCLA	exclamative	OPT	optative
G	most goal-like argument of a three-argument verb	P	most patient-like argument of a transitive verb

POL	politeness	REP	reportative
PL	plural	RESTR	restrictive focus
PLU.PST	plupast	S	sole argument of an intransitive verb
PRF	perfect tense		
POSS	possessive (prefix or pronoun)	SBJV	subjunctive
		SEQ	sequential (clause linkage)
PROG	progressive	SG	singular
PST	past tense	SIM	simultaneous
PST.PRF	past perfect	SUP	supine
PTB	Proto-Tibeto-Burman	T	most theme-like argument of a three-argument verb
PURP	purposive		
Q	question particle	TAG	tag question
QUANT	quantifier	TEMP	temporal
QUOT	quotative	TOP	topic particle
RC	relative clause	TRIPL	triplication
RECIP	reciprocal	V2	function verb (in complex predication)
REDUP	reduplication		
REFL	reflexive	VOC	vocative

Abbreviations of kinship terms

B	brother	M	mother
BS	brother's son	MB	mother's brother
BD	brother's daughter	MF	mother's father
BW	brother's wife	MM	mother's mother
e	elder	MZ	mother's sister
D	daughter	S	son
F	father	W	wife
FB	father's brother	y	younger
FF	father's father	Z	sister
FM	father's mother	ZS	sister's son
FZ	father's sister	ZD	sister's daughter
H	husband	ZH	sister's husband

1 Introduction

1.1 Aims of this grammar

This work is the first comprehensive description of the Yakkha language (ISO-639: ybh), a Kiranti language spoken in Eastern Nepal. The primary focus of this work is on the dialect spoken in Tumok village.

The grammar is intended to serve as a reference to scholars interested in linguistic typology and comparative studies of Tibeto-Burman and Himalayan languages in general, and also as a foundation for members of the Yakkha community to aid future research and activities aiming at documenting and preserving their language.

The grammar is written in a typological framework. Wherever possible I have tried to incorporate a historical perspective and comparative data in explaining how a particular subsystem of the grammar works. For the sake of reader friendliness and to ensure long-term comprehensibility, the analyses are not presented within any particular theoretical framework, and terms that strongly imply a particular theory have been avoided as far as this was possible.

Preparing a grammar can be a simultaneously satisfying and frustrating task, both for the same reason: the sheer abundance of topics one has to deal with, which makes grammars very different from works that pursue more specific questions. Necessarily, a focus had to be set for this work, which eventually fell on morphosyntactic issues. Verbal inflection, transitivity, grammatical relations, nominalization, complex predication and clause linkage are dealt with in greater detail, while other topics such as phonology, the tense/aspect system and information structure leave much potential for further research. Since this is the first grammatical description of Yakkha, I have decided to include also the topics that are analyzed in less detail, in order to share as much as possible about this complex and intriguing language.

1.2 How to use the grammar

1.2.1 Structure of the book

Following the well-established traditional order, I will provide some background on the langauge and its speakers (Chapter 2), and treat the most important grammatical aspects of the language successively: phonology (Chapter 3), morphology (Chapters 4–10), syntax (Chapters 11–16) and, albeit briefly, discourse-structural particles and interjections (Chapter 17). §1.5 in this chapter provides a typological overview and highlights the main features of Yakkha by means of simple examples. Appendices contain (a) three narrative texts and (b) charts with the complex kinship terminology. The book also includes a subject index and an index to the grammatical morphemes found in Yakkha, in order to make the information on particular topics easily accessible.

1.2.2 Orthography and transliterations

The orthography used in this grammatical description does not represent the phonetic level, because it is impractical to note down every phonetic difference and individual variation, especially since a phonetic analysis is not the major goal of this work. The orthography does not represent the phonemic level either, because Yakkha has a complex system of morphophonological rules, so that the pronunciation may show considerable deviations from the underlying forms. This is the reason why I use a representation on the allophonic level, including allophones that are the result of voicing, assimilations and other morphophonological operations. Most examples in Chapter 3 on the phonology are supplemented by the underlying forms (in slashes), in order to demonstrate the morphophonological processes.

While the orthography employed here is based on IPA, some deviations have to be noted: following the common orthographic traditions found in descriptions of Tibeto-Burman languages, the symbol <y> is used for the palatal approximant (IPA: [j]), <c> is used for the alveolar fricative (IPA: [ts]), and <ch> stands for its aspirated counterpart (IPA: [tsʰ]). Aspirated consonants are written <ph>, <th>, <kh>, <wh>, <mh>, <nh>, <ŋh>. Geminated consonants are written with double letters, e.g., [mm] or [ss]. Yakkha has several prefixes that have the phonemic value of an unspecified nasal. The nasal assimilates to the place of articulation of the following consonant. I do not use a special character for the nasal, but write it as it appears, i.e., as [m], [n] or [ŋ]. If the underlying form is provided, it is written /N/.

Nepali lexemes, used for instance when referring to sources of loans, are provided in the International Alphabet of Sanskrit Transliteration (IAST). Common place names are generally not transliterated, but provided in a simplified orthography that is generally found in local maps.

Yakkha does not have a writing tradition, but over the last few decades a few written materials have been published locally (cf. §1.4), using the Devanagari script, with varying orthographies. Devanagari is not ideal for Yakkha because it does not have a grapheme for the glottal stop, but a number of solutions have been used in these language materials, such as writing <?> or using the grapheme for a central vowel <अ> together with a *virām* <ः> (indicating that the inherent vowel should not be pronounced in the Devanagari script). Devanagari is not used in this book, but I have used the option that incorporates <?> into Devanagari in the Yakkha-Nepali-English dictionary that has been composed alongside this grammar.[1]

1.2.3 Glossing and further conventions

The purpose of the glosses is to facilitate understanding the examples, which necessarily entails a simplification of the facts. The labels used in the glosses do not represent analyses. This is particularly important with regard to the person inflection. As is typical for Kiranti languages, an inflected form cannot be neatly segmented into straightforward form-function correspondences (though from a Kiranti perspective, the verbal inflection of Yakkha can be considered as rather simple). To provide an example, the transitive person marking on the verbs has labels such as '1pl.A' (for the marker *-m*) in the glosses, so that the reader can identify the reference of a marker in a particular person configuration. The actual distribution of these markers is likely to be more narrow or wider than the gloss labels suggest (cf. §8.2). But glossing the above-mentioned marker with '1/2pl.A>3.P', for instance, would result in cryptic glosses that make reading the examples a rather cumbersome task.

Categories that have no corresponding overt marker, such as the subjunctive, are represented in square brackets, e.g., [SBJV]. This may have two reasons: either the morpheme is zero, or the morpheme got deleted in the surface form due to morphophonological processes. The nominative, which is also zero, is never written in the glosses. It is implied when a noun appears without an overt case marker.

---

[1] Cf. http://dianaschackow.de/?nav=dictionary.

The category labels are congruent with the Leipzig Glossing Rules,[2] with Yak-kha-specific category labels added where necessary. All abbreviations are listed on page xv. Language-specific morphological categories such as the Past Subjunctive mood or the Ablative case are capitalized, to distinguish them from universal categories.

When kinship terms are used in the glosses, they are abbreviated according to common practice: lower case *e* and *y* stand for 'elder' and 'younger', upper case *M* stands for 'mother', *F* stands for 'father', *Z* stands for 'sister', *B* stands for 'brother', *W* stands for 'wife', *H* stands for 'husband', *S* stands for 'son', *D* stands for 'daughter'. Combinations of them are read like possessive phrases, e.g., *FeZH* stands for 'father's elder sister's husband'.

In the texts, and in some of the Nepali literature cited, the Bikram Sambat (also Vikram Samvat) calendar is used. This is the official calendar in Nepal, and it is 56.7 years ahead of the solar Gregorian calendar. Sources using this system have "B.S." written behind the year.

The Yakkha examples that are provided in this grammar contain references to the corpus, in square brackets. Examples without such references are from elicitations that have not been recorded.

1.2.4 Notes on terminology

1.2.4.1 Nominalization

Nominalization is a versatile strategy in Sino-Tibetan languages, and its functions reach well beyond the classical uses of nominalization, which has given rise to the term *Standard Sino-Tibetan Nominalization* (Bickel 1999c). Since also relative clauses, complement clauses and main clauses can be noun phrases structurally, the reader should note that this work employs a very liberal understanding of the term nominalization, as is commonly found in works on Sino-Tibetan languages. Alternatively, one could have made up new labels for each function of a nominalizer, such as *attributivizer, complementizer, factuality marker*, but then, the functional connection between these uses would have been obscured, especially since grammars are rarely read chronologically. I found that this use of the term puzzled readers and hearers who are not familiar with Sino-Tibetan languages. Still, I decided to retain the label *nominalization* in this work also for the less canonical uses of nominalization, in order to keep functional and historical connections maximally transparent.

---

[2] Cf. http://www.eva.mpg.de/lingua/resources/glossing-rules.php.

A similar issue is the employment of case markers in clause linkage. I retained the case labels also when these markers attach to (not necessarily nominalized) clauses as clause linkage markers. Especially if one case marker is highly multifunctional in clause linkage, it is futile to find new labels for each function (the comitative marker =*nuŋ* is an example, see Chapter 14.7).

1.2.4.2 Generalized Semantic Roles (GSRs)

I have analyzed Yakkha argument structure and grammatical relations by looking at how generalized semantic roles (GSR) are realized and aligned in morphology and syntax, following the methodology of Bickel (2011a) and Witzlack-Makarevich (2010). GSRs are defined by their semantic properties and they are always determined in relation to a particular predicate. For instance, the most agent-like argument (A) of *mokma* 'hit' is the hitter, and the most patient-like argument (P) is the hittee. The sole argument of an intransitive verb is the S argument. Analogously, one can identify the most goal-like argument (G) and the most theme-like argument (T) of three-argument constructions. The identification of GSRs purely follows semantics, and is determined regardless of how the arguments are realized in morphology and syntax. For instance, the most agent-like arguments of experiential predicates such as 'love' and 'be disgusted' (i.e., the experiencers) are realized as possessors in one particular verb class in Yakkha.

Such an approach is necessary because Yakkha does not have a dominant alignment type, and thus, a morphologically and syntactically consistent notion of subject and object cannot be determined. In converbal constructions, S and A align, while in case marking and in some complement constructions S and P align. Nominalization and relativization constructions present a mixed picture. Marginally (only in verbal person marking and in complement clauses), the privileged argument can also be determined by reference and by information structure. The most bewildering diversity of alignment types is found in the verbal person marking.[3]

The Yakkha verb, if transitive, shows agreement with both arguments. To identify the respective morphology, I use the terms *(transitive) subject agreement* and *(transitive) object agreement*. It should be kept in mind that these labels do not imply any particular formally unified behavior, neither with respect to case and person marking nor with respect to the choice of pivots in any construction. In the glosses, the labels A and P are used, since in the standard frame of argument

---

[3] This diversity is not random and has parallels in the related languages, cf. §8.2.

realization markers referred to by A index A arguments and markers referred to by P index P arguments. This need not be the case, however, as some experiencer arguments might be realized as P morphologically, e.g., in experiential verbs such as *khikma* 'taste bitter to someone' (cf. Chapter 11).

1.3 Data sources

1.3.1 Fieldwork

The material used to write this grammar was collected during four field trips between 2009 and 2012, amounting to roughly one year altogether. I have spent most of the time in Tumok (Nepali: Tamaphok) village, with occasional visits to the surrounding villages Waleng (Nepali: Madi Mulkharka), Mamling, Yaiten (Nepali: Dandagaun), Hombong and to the market town Mudhe Saniscare. Tumok is a night's and half a day's bus ride away from Kathmandu (via Dharan, Dhankuta and Hile). One gets off the bus in Mudhe Sanischare and walks down to Tumok village for another hour or two.[4]

During the first field trip in 2009 Kamala Koyongwa travelled with me, helping me in many ways. From the first year on I stayed with Kamala Linkha, a teacher at the Shree Chamunde Higher Secondary School in Tumok, who became my friend and also my main Yakkha teacher, simply by sharing her everyday life with me. She never grew tired of explaining her language and aspects of Yakkha life to me. Magman Linkha, a teacher at the same school, has provided me with numerous beautifully-told narratives. He also helped me to check transcriptions and dictionary entries, patiently answering my many questions. Since he is himself engaged in various activities aiming at documenting and preserving his cultural heritage, he was also my most important source regarding sociolinguistic and ethnographic questions. In 2010, Kamala's niece Man Maya Jimi, a student who also works in adult literacy education programs, started working with me and proved to be a patient and thoughtful consultant in elicitations, transcriptions, translations and dictionary checks. In Kathmandu, I also had several valuable elicitation sessions with Kaushila Jimi and her son Sonam as well as with Visvakaji Kongren.

During the early trips (2009 and 2010) I recorded texts from various genres (legendary and autobiographical narratives, spontaneous conversations, songs,

---

[4] Alternatively, one may take a domestic flight to Tumlingtar and try to catch a bus or a jeep there, but since the transport situation was not reliable in Tumlingtar in 2009 and 2010, I resorted to making the journey to the east by bus in my later field trips (2011 and 2012).

Figure 1.1: My main Yakkha teachers: Kamala Linkha, Man Maya Jimi, Magman
Linkha

pear stories, procedural descriptions) and tried to gather as much language data
as possible while living in the village. In total, I recorded utterances from 22
different speakers. The youngest person recorded was 16 years old, the oldest
people were above 60 years. To each person recorded I have explained the purpose of the recordings and my plan to archive them online. Their consent is
mostly found as part of the recordings, usually at the end of the files. After an-
alyzing the data in Germany, I used the later trips (2011 and 2012) mainly for
refined elicitations and data checking, with the consultants mentioned above in
Tumok and in Kathmandu.

In the elicitations, relying on nonverbal stimuli in the natural environment
proved to be much more productive than prepared questionnaires or audiovi-
sual stimuli. The only stimuli that I have used were the Pear Story (Chafe 1980)
and the Cut and Break Clips (Bohnemeyer, Bowerman & Brown 2010). Questionnaires that were used included the questionnaire from the Leipzig Valency
Classes Project (Max Planck Institute for Evolutionary Anthropology), the questionnaire from the project on referential hierarchies in three-participant constructions (University of Lancaster) and the Questionnaire for Transitivizing/De-
transitivizing Verb Systems (by Johanna Nichols). The other topics were elicited
with questionnaires compiled by myself and on the spot when certain topics
came up during transcriptions and checks of the lexical data. Elicitations on
clause linkage in 2012 were partly undertaken together with Lennart Bierkandt
for a co-authored paper (Bierkandt & Schackow submitted).

1.3.2 The corpus

The structure and content of the current Yakkha corpus is displayed in Table 1.1. The corpus contains 3012 clauses and roughly 13.000 annotated words. The texts are transcribed and annotated audio-recordings of roughly 3 hours length. The audio recorder used is an Olympus Linear PCM Recorder LS-11. The texts of the genre *legacy data* are only available in written form, using Devanagari script. They are taken from school books (Jimi, Kongren & Jimi 2009; 2010) and from narratives that originated in a workshop organized in 2012 by the Mother Tongue Center Nepal (Yakkha 2012a; Yakkha 2012b; Linkha 2012). I have transliterated them into the orthographic representation used in this work, with slight adjustments where the orthographies used were rather impractical, for instance when they lumped together the voiceless and voiced consonants or /r/ and /l/ (which is the case in the above-mentioned school books). Researchers using the corpus should be aware of the fact that many neologisms are used in written Yakkha that are not (yet) established in the spoken language.

The texts are labelled as follows: a unique identifier, followed by an underscore and a three-letter genre code, followed by an underscore and the number of the text from that particular genre. For example, a text coded '12_nrr_03.wav' is the twelfth recording in total and the third text of the genre 'narrative'; '12_nrr_-03.txt' is the corresponding text file. These labels (including the record number) are provided when the examples are from the corpus; when no such label is

Table 1.1: Content of the annotated Yakkha corpus

GENRE	NUMBER OF RECORDINGS	RECORDS (roughly corr. to clauses)
narratives	8	488
conversations	5	1336
pear stories	4	225
songs	3	40
legacy data (written)	5	595
texts on tradition and material culture	3	328
	28	**3012**

Table 1.2: Text genres and codes

CODE	GENRE
nrr	narrative
cvs	conversation
sng	song
mat	description of material culture
tra	description of traditions
pea	pear story
par	elicited paradigm
leg	legacy data (written)

provided, the examples are from elicitations or from unrecorded spontaneous speech. The applications used for annotation and time alignment were Toolbox[5] and ELAN.[6]

The genre codes are displayed in Table 1.2. The entire corpus is accessible online via the Endangered Languages Archive (ELAR).[7]

1.3.3 The lexical database

The lexical database[8] contains 2429 entries, all checked with at least two speakers. It contains grammatical, semantic, phonological and ethnographic notes as well as botanical terms (relying on the Nepali translations given in Manandhar (2002) and occasionally Turner 1931). One may also browse for parts of speech and for semantic categories, if one is interested in particular semantic domains like body parts, kinship, spatial orientation, colour terms etc. A digital community version

---

[5] Toolbox is free software developed by SIL, see http://www-01.sil.org/computIng/toolbox/index.htm.

[6] ELAN is free software developed by the Language Archive of the Max Planck Institute for Psycholinguistics in Nijmegen, see Wittenburg & Sloetjes (2008); URL: http://tla.mpi.nl/tools/tla-tools/elan/

[7] http://www.hrelp.org/archive/. The annotations in this work may, in a few cases, deviate from the annotations in the archived corpus, as upon closer inspection during the analyses some minor adjustments were inevitable. The examples as they are analyzed and annotated in this work represent the most recent state of analysis.

[8] Archived at the Endangered Languages Archive (ELAR) together with the corpus, see http://www.hrelp.org/archive/.

of the dictionary (using Lexique Pro),[9] with the Yakkha entries in Devanagari, can be found online.[10]

1.4 Earlier studies on Yakkha language and culture

Material on the Yakkha language that is available beyond local sources is exceedingly rare. The oldest source is a wordlist in Hodgson (1857). A chapter in the Linguistic Survey of India provides a brief introduction and some Yakkha texts that were collected with Yakkha speakers who had migrated to Darjeeling (Grierson 1909: 305–315).[11]

More recent works on the language are a glossary (Winter et al. 1996), a Yakkha-Nepali-English dictionary (Kongren 2007b), two articles about the inflectional morphology, both based on the same verbal paradigm collected by Gvozdanović (Gvozdanović 1987; van Driem 1994) and an article by myself on three-argument constructions (Schackow 2012b).

Research on cultural and political aspects has been undertaken by Subba (1999) and by Russell (Russell 1992; 1997; 2000; 2004; 2007; 2010). Recently, two M.A. theses on aspects of Yakkha culture have been completed in Nepal, one thesis on culture and adaptation by Rai (2011) and one thesis on kinship terms by Linkha (2013). Ethnographic introductions in Nepali can be found by Kongren (2007a) and by Linkha (2067 B.S.), the former containing also some English chapters. Further locally available materials in Yakkha and Nepali are a collection of poems (Dewan et al. 2059 B.S.) and a collection of thematically ordered wordlists and articles on the Yakkha traditions (Linkha & Dewan 2064 B.S.). For a more detailed bibliography of the works on Yakkha that were published in Nepali the interested reader is referred to Rapacha, Yalungcha & Tumyahang (2008).

1.5 Typological overview of the Yakkha language

The following brief overview is intended for the reader who is not familiar with Kiranti languages or other Sino-Tibetan languages in general. It provides basic information on the most important features of the language.

---

[9] See http://www.lexiquepro.com/.

[10] See http://dianaschackow.de/?nav=dictionary. Even though the database has been carefully checked, it is likely that further corrections and additions will be made in the future.

[11] This source and Russell (1992) use a spelling <Yakha>, but the correct spelling is <Yakkha>, since the first syllable is closed by /k/. In contemporary sources, also in Devanagari, the language name is always written as <Yakkha>.

1.5.1 Phonology

Yakkha has five vowel phonemes (/i/, /e/, /a/, /o/ and /u/). Diphthongs are rare and can mostly be traced back to disyllabic structures. The basic distinctions in the consonant phonemes, according to the place of articulation, are bilabial, alveolar, retroflex, palatal, velar and glottal. Plosives, the affricate and the bilabial glide have an aspirated and an unaspirated series. The maximal syllable structure is CCVC. Complex onsets originate in disyllabic structures too; they consist of sequences of obstruent and lateral, rhotic or glide. The syllable coda is mainly restricted to nasals and unaspirated plosives. The morphophonological processes are manifold and very complex in Yakkha, with each rule applying to its own domain (discussed in §3.5). A feature located at the boundary between phonology and morphology is a process of copying nasal morphemes in the verbal inflection (discussed in §3.5.8). This process is typical for Kiranti languages.

1.5.2 Word classes

Morphology and syntax clearly distinguish nominal and verbal classes in Yakkha (see Chapters 5 and 8). Word classes appearing in the noun phrase are demonstratives, pronouns, quantifiers and (marginally) numerals (see Chapter 4). Numeral classification exists, but it plays only a very marginal role. The verb shows complex inflectional morphology, resulting in hundreds of possibilities of inflection for each verbal stem.

Less clear is the distinction of adjectives and adverbs, as many of them derive from verbal roots. However, the salience of reduplication and rhyming patterns in noun-modifying and verb-modifying lexemes justifies treating them as separate word classes (see Chapter 6). Rhyming and reduplications, often combined with ideophones, almost exclusively feature in the classes of adjectives and adverbs in Yakkha.

Other word classes constitute closed classes, such as conjunctions, postpositions, interjections and discourse-structural particles (see Chapters 16 and 17). The postpositions are partly derived from relational nouns.

1.5.3 Nominals

Yakkha nouns can be simple or compounded out of several nominal roots. There are several nominalizers in Yakkha, some deriving nouns (-*pa* and -*ma*), some constructing noun phrases (-*khuba*, -*khuma* and =*na*/=*ha*).

Nouns can be inflected by possessive prefixes, alternatively to using possessive pronouns (compare (1a) and (1b)). The possessive prefixes are very similar in form to the possessive pronouns. Case and number markers are clitics;
they attach to the whole noun phrase. Yakkha has an unmarked nominative, an
ergative/instrumental =ŋa, a genitive =ka, a locative =pe, an ablative =phaŋ, a
comitative =nuŋ, and further markers with less central functions, mainly from
the comparative domain. Argument marking shows reference-based and word
class-based alternations (discussed in §5.2 for the ergative case and in §11.2.2 for
three-argument constructions).

(1)   a.   *a-paŋ=be*
           1SG.POSS-house=LOC
           'in my house'
      b.   *ak=ka   paŋ=be*
           1SG.POSS=GEN   house=LOC
           'in my house'

1.5.4 Verbs

The inflected verb indexes agents and patients of transitive verbs and expresses
many grammatical categories (tense/aspect, mood, polarity (see (2)). This example also shows the above-mentioned process of nasal copying; suffix -*m* appears
twice in the suffix string. Person (including clusivity), number and syntactic role
marking interact in intricate ways in the person marking paradigm (see §8.2). As
example (2) shows, the Yakkha verb is mainly suffixing; there is only one prefix
slot.

(2)   *n-dund-wa-m-ci-m-ŋa-n=ha.*
      NEG-understand-NPST-1PL.A-NSG.P-1SG.A-EXCL-NEG=NMLZ.NSG
      'We do not understand them.'

Yakkha has a very productive system of complex predication, where several
verbal roots are concatenated to yield a more specific verbal meaning (discussed
in Chapter 10). In complex predicates, the first verb carries the lexical meaning,
while the second verb adds a further semantic specificiation, for instance regarding aktionsart, the spatial directedness of the event, or the affectedness of some
argument. In (3), the second verb carries a benefactive notion, adding a beneficiary argument to the argument structure of the lexical verb. Complex predicates
trigger recursive inflection, as shown here by the imperative marker -*a*, that ap-

pears twice (treated in detail in Chapter 10). Predicates can also be compounded by a noun and a verb (see Chapter 9).

(3)　　*ka*　*katha*　*lend-a-by-a-ŋ.*
　　　　1SG　story　exchange-IMP-V2.GIVE-IMP-1SG.P
　　　　'Tell me a story.'

1.5.5 Syntax

Yakkha phrase structure is overwhelmingly head-final, with the nominal head at the end of the noun phrase, and with the verb being the final constituent of the clause (see (4a)). In complex clauses, the subordinate clause generally precedes the main clause (see (4b)). Nominalizers and markers of clause linkage can follow the verb. Permutations of the word order are possible (see Chapter 12); they follow discourse requirements. Arguments are frequently dropped, resulting in a low referential density.

(4)　a.　*raj=ŋa*　　*u-ma*　　　　　　　*kheps-u=na.*
　　　　　Raj=ERG　3SG.POSS-mother　hear[PST]-3P=NMLZ.SG
　　　　　'Raj heard his mother.'
　　b.　*tumok=pe*　　*tas-u-ŋ=hoŋ*　　　　　　　*a-phu*
　　　　　Tumok=LOC　arrive[PST]-3P-1SG.A=SEQ　1SG.POSS-elder_brother
　　　　　chimd-u-ŋ=na.
　　　　　ask[PST]-3P-1SG.A=NMLZ.SG
　　　　　'When I arrived in Tumok, I asked my elder brother (about it).'

The argument structure in Yakkha distinguishes several valency classes, which are discussed in Chapter 11. The basic distinction is that between intransitive and transitive verbs, which is also reflected in two different verbal inflectional patterns. There is a class of labile verbs, mostly showing an *inchoative/causative* alternation. Experiential predicates predominantly occur in a construction that treats the experiencer as the metaphorical possessor of a sensation or an affected body part (the Experiencer-as-Possessor Construction, see (5)).

(5)　a.　*a-pomma=ci*　　　　　*ŋ-gy-a=ha=ci.*
　　　　　1SG.POSS-laziness=NSG　3PL-come_up-PST=NMLZ.NSG=NSG
　　　　　'I feel lazy.'
　　b.　*ka*　　　　*nda*　*a-luŋma*　　　　*tuk-nen=na.*
　　　　　1SG[ERG]　2SG　1SG.POSS-liver　pour-1>2[PST]=NMLZ.SG
　　　　　'I love you/I have compassion for you.'

The argument structure can be modified, by means of derivations (causative), complex predication (benefactive, middle, reflexive), and an analytical construction (reciprocal), as shown in (6). Both the reflexive and the reciprocal construction make use of a grammaticalization of the verbal root *ca* 'eat'.

(6) a. *kiba=ŋa   hari   kisi-met-u=na.*
         tiger=ERG   Hari   be_afraid-CAUS-3.P[PST]=NMLZ.SG
         'The tiger frightened Hari.'

    b. *nda   (aphai)   moŋ-ca-me-ka=na.*
         2SG   (self)   beat-V2.EAT-NPST-2=NMLZ.SG
         'You beat yourself.'

    c. *kanciŋ   [...]   sok-khusa   ca-ya-ŋ-ci-ŋ.*
         1DU   [...]   look-RECIP   eat.AUX-PST-EXCL-DU-EXCL
         'We (dual, excl) looked at each other.'

Furthermore, morphologically unmarked detransitivizations are possible (marked only by a change in the person marking morphology). In this way, both antipassive and passive constructions may occur in Yakkha, sometimes leading to ambiguities. In (7), the person morphology on the verb is intransitive in both examples, signalling a third person singular subject of an intransitive verb, although *khemma* 'hear' is clearly transitive, and in most cases is inflected transitively (compare with (7c)). While (7a) is a passive structure, (7b) is an antipassive. Unmarked antipassives (the morphosyntactic demotion of a generic or unspecific object) are wide-spread in Kiranti languages, but unmarked passives are, to this point, only known in Yakkha. The more frequent structure is, however, the antipassive, which is not surprising given its older nature.

(7) a. *ceʔya   kheps-a-m=ha.*
         matter   hear[3SG]-PST-PRF=NMLZ.NC
         'The matter has been heard.'

    b. *Dilu   reɖio   khem-meʔ=na?*
         Dilu   radio   hear[3SG]-NPST=NMLZ.SG
         'Does Dilu listen to the radio (generally)?'

    c. *pik=ŋa   kiba   kheps-u=na.*
         cow=ERG   tiger   hear[PST]-3P=NMLZ.SG
         'The cow heard the tiger.'

Yakkha does not have a dominant grammatical relation, both reference-based and role-based (ergative, accusative) alignment patterns are found, depending on the particular construction. Especially the verbal person marking system shows an incredible heterogeneity of alignment types, which is, however, not unusual in a Kiranti-wide perspective (see Figure 8.2 on page 228).

Nominalization is a core feature of Yakkha syntax (discussed at length in Chapter 13). The nominalizers have a wide range of functions, from nominal modification/relativization and complement clauses to marking independent clauses. The nominalizers -*khuba* and -*khuma* construct noun phrases (and relative clauses) with the role of S or A, while the nominalizers =*na* and =*ha* are almost unrestricted with regard to which participant they can relativize on (see (8)). The only relation not found with relative clauses in =*na* or =*ha* is A, which results in syntactic ergativity for relative clauses, since S and P are treated alike by this relativization and differently from A. The nominalizers =*na* and =*ha* are also frequently used to nominalize independent clauses, with the function of structuring information on the text level (see Chapter 13.3.3).

(8) a. *heko=ha=ci*   *mok-khuba* *babu*
       other=NMLZ.NSG=NSG beat-NMLZ boy
       'the boy who beats the others'
    b. *nna* *o-hop*   *wa-ya=na*   *siŋ*
       that 3SG.POSS-nest exist-PST[3SG]=NMLZ.SG tree
       'that tree where he has his nest'

Complement constructions show long-distance agreement, distinguishing various subtypes, each with its own configuration of person and case marking (see Chapter 15). There are two basic types: infinitival complement clauses and inflected complement clauses (see (9)). In this particular example, the same complement-taking verb *miʔma* acquires two separate meanings, depending on whether the embedded structure is infinitival or consists of an inflected verb.

(9) a. *ka* *kheʔ-ma* *mit-a-ŋ=na.*
       1SG go-INF   think-PST-1SG=NMLZ.SG
       'I want to go.'
    b. *nda*   *cama* *ca-ya-ga=na*   *mi-nuŋ-nen=na.*
       2SG[ERG] rice   eat-PST-2=NMLZ.SG think-PRF-1>2=NMLZ.SG
       'I thought you ate the rice.'

Adverbial clause linkage has three major types: infinitival clauses (see (10a)), converbs (see (10b)) and inflected adverbial clauses (see (10c)). The subtypes of these three basic types are discussed in detail in Chapter 14. Further conjunctions can connect clauses on the text level, such as *khaʔniŋgo* 'but' and *nhaŋa* 'and then, afterwards'.

(10) a. *uŋci=ŋa   men-ni-ma=ga   cum-i.*
          3NSG=ERG   NEG-see-INF=GEN   hide-1PL[PST]
          'We hid, so that they would not see us.'

      b. *o-pomma   ke-saŋ   ke-saŋ   kam*
          3SG.POSS-laziness   come_up-SIM   come_up-SIM   work
          cog-wa.
          do-NPST[3SG.A;3.P]
          'He does the work lazily.'

      c. *ka   kucuma   khas-a=nuŋ*
          1SG[ERG]   dog   be_satisfied[3SG]-SBJV=COM.CL
          pi-ŋ=ha.
          give[PST;3.P]-1SG.A=NMLZ.NSG
          'I fed the dog sufficiently (in a way that it was satisfied).'

2 The Yakkha language and its speakers

This chapter provides basic information on the geographic (§2.1) and cultural-historical background of the Yakkha language (§2.2), a genealogical classification of Yakkha as a member of the Kiranti language family (§2.3), and its sociolinguistic (§2.4) context. The reader should note that the following observations are not made by a trained anthropologist. An in-depth anthropological study is beyond the scope of this introductory chapter (see §1.4 for existing anthropological studies).

In this chapter, the term Kiranti can indicate both ethnic and linguistic affiliations. It refers to a group of roughly 30 ethnically and linguistically distinct, yet related, communities in eastern Nepal. The internal structure of the Kiranti group is complex, and linguistic classifications may deviate from ethnic classifications, cf. §2.2 below.

2.1 Geographical context

Nepal can roughly be divided into three geographical zones: the Himalayan range in the north, the middle hills (the Mahabharat range, stretching parallel to the Himalayan range) and the plains in the south (the Tarai). The Himalayan range is home to speakers of Tibeto-Burman languages. The plains are mostly inhabited by speakers of Indo-Aryan languages. Furthermore, a few Austroasiatic languages, one Dravidian language and an isolate (Kusunda) are spoken in Nepal. Speakers of Kiranti languages, including Yakkha (see Figure 2.1), inhabit the hilly area between the Likhu river in the west and the border with Sikkim in the east, with elevations between 1,500m and 2,700m. Kiranti settlements can also be found in the plains and in India (Darjeeling, Sikkim).

The Yakkha region (i.e., the area inhabited by people who consider themselves Yakkha ethnically)[1] is located in the Koshi zone of the Eastern Development Region, in the south of Sankhuwa Sabha district and in the north of Dhankuta district (see the map in Figure 2.2). Within the region in Eastern Nepal commonly

---

[1] If the region were defined by linguistic criteria, it would be much smaller; see §2.4.2.

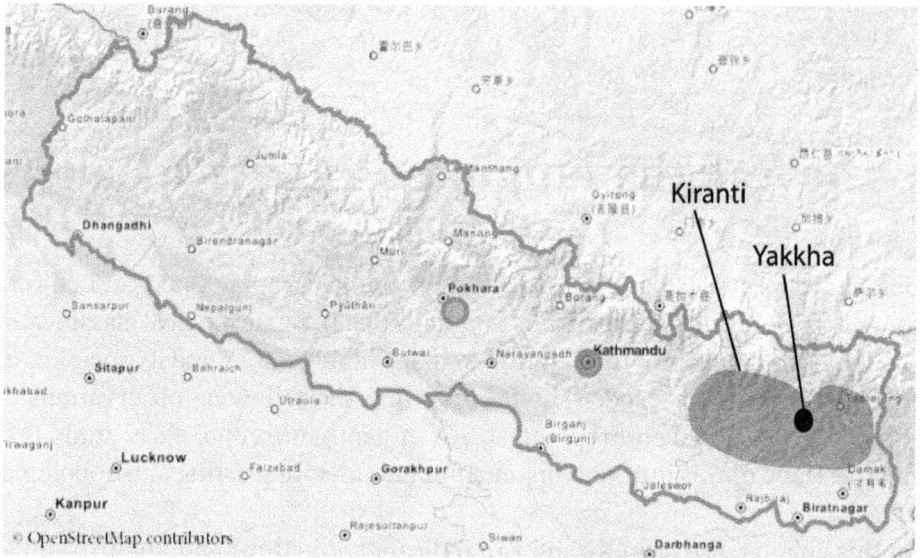

Figure 2.1: Location of the Yakkha region within Nepal (OpenStreetMap: http://www.openstreetmap.org, accessed on 28 March 2015)

known as *Kirant* ('Kiranti area'), the Yakkha region belongs to the *Pallo Kirant* 'Far Kiranti area', located on the east of the Arun river.

The core Yakkha region contains the following Village Development Committees (VDCS):[2] Canuwa, Marek Katahare and Dandagaun in Dhankuta district, and Tamaphok (Tamfok in the map), Mamling, Ankhinbhuin, Madi Mulkharka, Madi Rambeni, Baneshwor, Chainpur, Kharang, Wana (Bana in the map), Siddhakali, Siddhapokhari and Syabun in Sankhuwa Sabha district. The Yakkha region is also known as the *Tin Thum* ('The Three Regions'): the *Das Majhiya* in the south, the *Panch Majhiya* in the middle and the *Panch Kapan* in the north (Kongren 2007a: 86), a distinction originating in the tax system that was enforced under the Gorkha rule in the 18th century. The language is only spoken by parts of the Yakkha population, being replaced by Nepali in almost half of the geographic area inhabited by Yakkha people. Curiously, the language proficiency decreases drastically towards the north of the Yakkha area (Magman Linkha, p.c.), contrary to the expectation that greater distance to the main roads and thus greater isolation should have had a positive effect on the preservation of a language.

---

[2] Nepal is administratively divided into 5 development regions, 14 zones, 75 districts and 3,913 village development committees (VDCs). Each VDC contains several villages and is further divided into numbered wards.

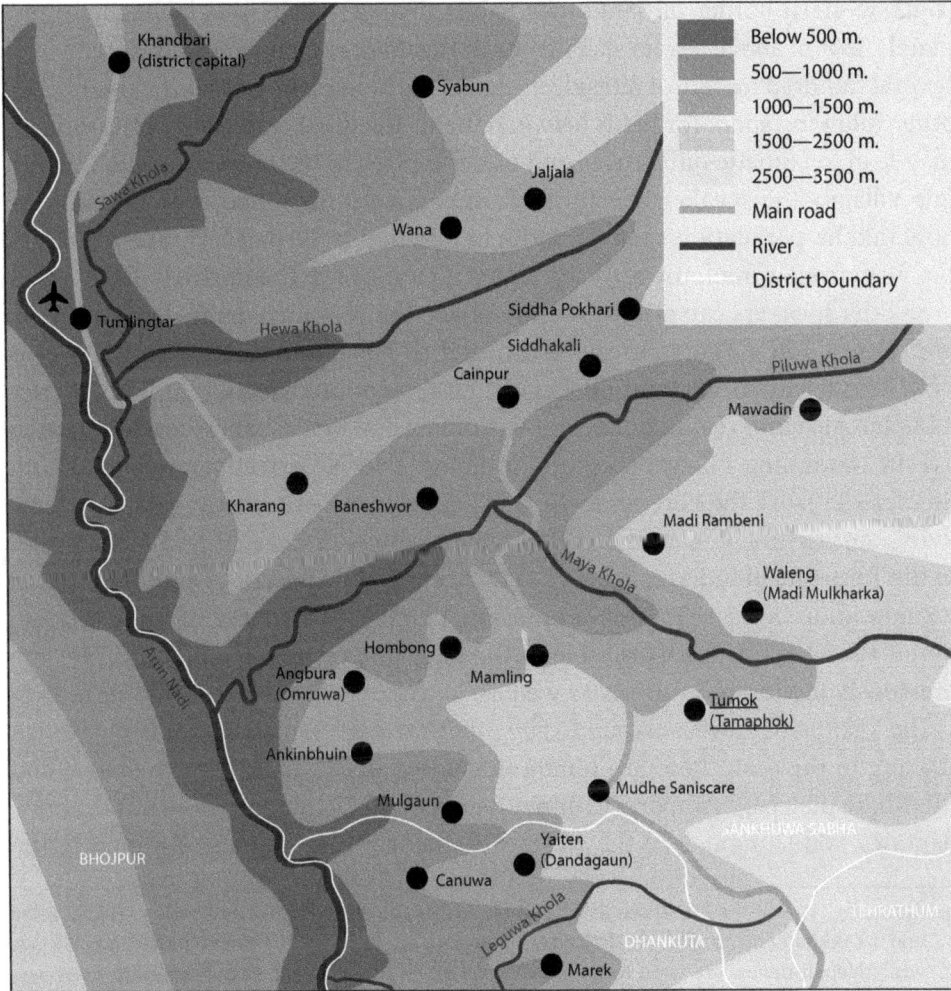

Figure 2.2: Map of the Yakkha region, drawn by the author

Yakkha has at least four dialects (see §2.4.1 below). The focus of this work is on the Tumok dialect, named after the village where it is spoken (27.208°N, 87.384°E), in Tamaphok VDC.[3] Tumok lies on the south-western slopes of the Maya Khola valley.[4] The Maya Khola flows north-west into the Piluwa Khola, which is a tributary of the Arun river (the main river in the region, partly flowing along the south-western border of Sankhuwa Sabha district). Tumok is located approximately 1500m above sea level. Villages in this hilly region generally spread over several hundred meters of altitude, because the houses are not built close to each other, allowing space for fields between them. The great extension of the villages may lead to climatic differences and to differences in the crop cycle even within one village. The speaker density in Tumok is very high, and even parts of the non-Yakkha population speak Yakkha in addition to Nepali.[5] Figure 2.3 shows the view from Tumok towards the Himalayan range in the north.

Yakkha speakers can also be found outside the core area defined above. There are about 80 households in the south-east of Dhankuta district, in Mudhebas VDC, Kuruletenupa VDC and Bodhe VDC (Magman Linkha, p.c.). In Ilam district, a Limbu-speaking region bordering with India, Yakkha speakers are reported to live in Namsaling village, speaking a dialect that is perfectly intelligible with the Yakkha from the core area. Nowadays there are also many Yakkha people living outside the hills, in the city of Dharan (Sunsari district) and other places in the Tarai and in India (especially in Darjeeling and Sikkim). A common reason for migration is the search of land or employment. Of course, Yakkha are also found elsewhere in the world due to the high rate of Nepali emigration for the previously mentioned reasons as well as education.

The Yakkha region is surrounded by other Kiranti languages. Going clockwise, starting in the east, these are Limbu (including the Tamarkhole, Phedappe and Chatthare dialects). Athpare, Chiling, Belhare and Chintang follow in the south, Bantawa and Dungmali in the west, Mewahang, Lohorung and Yamphu in the

---

[3] Tamaphok is also the Nepali name of Tumok. Many Yakkha villages have both a Nepali name and a Yakkha name. Impressionistically, Yakkha names are used to refer to particular villages, while Nepali names are used to refer to VDCs (which are in general conglomerations of several villages). This is also the case, e.g., for Waleng (Nepali: *Madi Mulkharka*), Yaiten (Nepali: *Dandagaun*) and Angbura (Nepali: *Omruwa*).

[4] *kholā* is a Nepali word for 'little river'.

[5] Among the non-Yakkha population, it is more common to speak Yakkha for members of castes that were perceived as "low" (according to Hindu social law) than for members of so-called "high" castes. Despite changes in the legal system, these distinctions still play a role in social practice and thus, it is more attractive for members of discriminated groups to learn Yakkha, while members of "high" castes often do not know any Yakkha, even after having lived in the area for decades.

Figure 2.3: Tumok at the end of the rainy season, Sept. 2012

north. This geographical classification has to be understood in an idealized sense. Most of the villages in Nepal are ethnically and linguistically diverse, so that one may also find Sherpa, Gurung, Tamang, Newari and Parbatiya (Nepali speaking) households in the Yakkha region.

2.2 Cultural and historical background

2.2.1 Kiranti

Kiranti (also Kirāt, Kirāta, Kirãti) nowadays refers to a set of roughly 30 communities speaking related languages, who inhabit the Himalayan foothills in Eastern Nepal and share key cultural practices, including nature worship and a body of oral knowledge, myth and ritual in which the veneration of ancestors plays a major role (known as *Munthum* in Yakkha). Within these parameters, however, there is considerable heterogeneity of cultural practices, beliefs and origin myths, and shifting ethnic and linguistic affinities do not seem to be uncommon (Yakkha itself being a prime example, as will be explained further below).[6]

---

[6] Although this is commonly overlooked in current politics in Nepal, present-day ethnic distinctions are the product of several waves of migrations and millenia of mutual influence in

We have very little historically verified knowledge about the Kiranti people.[7] The term Kiranti comes from Sanskrit *kirāta* and dates back to Vedic texts such as the Atharvaveda, which is considered the oldest Veda after the R̥gveda (van Driem 2001: 594). It is generally accepted by Nepali and foreign historians alike that kings known as Kiranti (or Kirāta) must have ruled over central Nepal before they were overthrown by the Lichhavis early in the first millenium CE (Whelpton 2005: 13). However, the well-documented history of Nepal unfortunately only begins with the Lichhavi dynasty, so that it is not at all clear whether the ancient Kirantis were the forefathers of the Kiranti people who currently live in eastern Nepal. One should note that in the old Indian texts the term *kirāta* had a much broader reference, applying to Tibeto-Burman hill peoples in general (Whelpton 2005; Schlemmer 2003/2004). The self-designation Kiranti in the present sense came to be used only with the advent of the Gorkha kings, when a common Kiranti identity began to evolve under Hindu dominance (Gaenszle 2002: 340). Before that era, there was no common feeling of being Kiranti: clan affinities were most important, and autonyms such as Khambu/Khombo (for the Rai) and Yakthumba (for the Limbu) were used among the Kiranti groups.

Present-day Kiranti legends trace the groups' origins to a variety of locales, from Tsang in Tibet to Varanasi in the Gangetic plains (see van Driem 1987: xix for Limbu), or places in the Tarai (see Gaenszle 2012: 34 for Mewahang).[8] It is

the Himalayan contact zone of Indosphere and Sinosphere (terms from Matisoff, e.g., Matisoff 1990b). The perception of distinct "pure" and time-stable ethnic and linguistic groups presents a highly idealized picture that does not do justice to the complex social reality of a multi-ethnic country like Nepal. Most current ethnic identities have been shaped by mixing with other groups or by adapting to other groups in one way or another, and these processes are, of course, continuing in the present.

[7] The work of renowned Limbu historiographer Iman Singh Chemjong (1967), widely perceived as the major source on Kiranti history among the Kiranti people, uses the available sources (both western scholarly work and indigenous chronicles) with few epistemological criticisms, and does not provide sufficient evidence to be called historical in the academic sense. It is rather to be seen as an attempt to anchor Kiranti culture in the deepest past possible and the widest area possible, with evidence spanning large parts of Eurasia from Greece to Cambodia (Schlemmer 2003/2004: 125). Despite its methodological shortcomings, Chemjong's work must be praised for its contribution to the acknowledgement and recognition of a distinct and unique Kiranti culture (see also Gaenszle 2002: 340).

[8] The Yakkha legends I recorded are about their ancestors' deeds and journeys in the area where present-day Yakkha people live. My own materials do not contain myths regarding a prior place of origin. This does not imply that there are no such myths. I have recorded only eight narratives, which is probably not even close to representative of what is still out there, un-recorded. In general, the Kiranti groups have a strong concern for the past and vibrant oral traditions in which origins and migrations are recalled for many generations (Gaenszle 2000; 2002).

not known when and how the ancestors of the Kiranti groups entered Nepal, but it is very likely that they came at least 2000 years ago from the east (van Driem 2001; LaPolla 2001; Gaenszle 2002). Kiranti languages show striking similarities with rGyalrongic languages spoken in the South of China and with the extinct Tangut language, especially with regard to hierarchical patterns in the person marking system (see, e.g., DeLancey (1981); Ebert (1990); LaPolla (2007); Jacques (2012a), and also §8.2 and §15.1.7 of this work), although direct contact between these groups has not been proven.[9] Another argument for migration from the east is that those Tibeto-Burman groups that have entered Nepal via the north, such as the Tamangs for instance, show a close relation to Tibetan culture and Tibetan Buddhism (LaPolla 2001), while Kiranti culture is clearly distinct from Tibetan culture.[10]

The Kiranti peoples' more recent history has been described in various sources (Caplan 1970; Pradhan 1991; Gaenszle 2002; Schlemmer 2003/2004; Whelpton 2005) and will only be briefly summarized here. As a nation state, Nepal was founded by Pṛthvī Nārāyaṇ Śāha (1723–1775), the king from Gorkha[11] who conquered the area known as Nepal today. Seen as a hero by Nepali nationalists, for the ethnic minorities his name stands for the suppression of their cultures and languages. Local groups confronted the king and his successors with strong armed resistance, but eventually Gorkha rule was established. The Kiranti region, bordering British-ruled Sikkim in the East, was critical to maintaining the Gorkha rule, and in order to keep the Kiranti groups loyal, they were given a privileged status and a certain degree of autonomy. In a system known as *kipāt*, land rights were reserved for Kiranti people who owned the land by virtue of their ethnic affiliation. Local headmen were appointed to collect taxes. The titles given to them (Rai, Subba, Jimdar) are still reflected in contemporary Kiranti surnames. Later, the Gorkha kings changed their strategy and sought to control and assimilate the Kiranti region. Kiranti groups were officially incorporated into the caste system (as *matvāli jāt*, 'drinking caste'), and the state encouraged Hindu

---

[9] There is a scholarly debate as to whether these similarities are Proto-Tibeto-Burman (and got lost in the other languages) or whether the groups showing hierarchical patterns in person marking form a separate branch of Tibeto-Burman (see, e.g., van Driem 1991; LaPolla 2001; DeLancey 2010; Jacques 2012a; LaPolla 2012). The debate boils down to the still unsettled question of whether Proto-Tibeto-Burman had person marking morphology or not, and it will probably only be settled once more data on Tibeto-Burman languages are available.

[10] To provide a culinary example: fermented soybeans (*kinama* in Yakkha) are an integral part of the Kiranti cuisine. While this dish is not widely cherished outside the Kiranti sphere in Nepal, it is widespread in Northeast India (e.g., in Nagaland), and also known from Thailand, Burma, Korea and Japan (Tamang 2010).

[11] Gorkha is a district in the Western Development Region of Nepal.

settlers to move east. They were allowed to take control of land previously held by Kiranti people, thus systematically undermining the *kipāt* system. Brahmanic values became more influential, Nepali was propagated as the national language and attempts to express and preserve one's ethnic identity were suppressed as threats to the nation state. On an everyday level, obviously some expression of 'Kiranti-ness' must have continued, because distinct Kiranti cultural practices are still present nowadays (see also the observations made by Russell 2004).

Hindu dominance began to erode only recently, with the 1990 constitution, in which Nepal's multi-ethnic and multi-lingual social reality was officially acknowledged for the first time (Article 4), and more so since the end of the monarchy in 2006. Currently, a new and strong sense of a common Kiranti identity is emerging, which can be attributed to the recent climate of rising ethnic consciousness (over the last two decades). The different Kiranti groups (Limbu, Rai, Yakkha, Sunwar) now share a newly-built temple in Sāno Hāttiban in the south of Kathmandu and they celebrate festivals together that were originally celebrated separately, on village level.[12] The mythical king Yalambar has undergone a revival as the legendary founder of the Kiranti dynasty, an iconic figure representing an idealized glorious past. A recently built and newly-renovated statue of Yalambar in the market town Mudhe Sanischare in Sankhuwa Sabha district may illustrate the perspective that Kiranti people themselves have on their origins (see Figure 2.4).[13]

Another iconic figure for Kiranti identity is the 18th-century Limbu scholar Te-ongsi Sirijunga Xin Thebe (Sirijanga) from Sikkim, who is celebrated as the initiator of an ethnic awakening and as the creator of the Limbu script (legendary accounts state that he found and revived the script). He is widely perceived as a martyr for the Kiranti cause, because he was murdered by the Sikkimese Bhutia rulers, allegedly because they perceived his activities as a threat. He is usually depicted tied to a tree and bristling with arrows, for instance in a statue in Dharan (Tinkune), but also in icon-like prints and posters that can be found in people's homes.

---

[12] Cf. Gaenszle (in prep.) on the changes that Kiranti culture and religion are currently undergoing now that more and more people live outside the rural homeland.

[13] see, e.g., Schlemmer (2003/2004) for a critical assessment of the re-invention of the Kiranti past that came along with the ethnic revival in contemporary Nepal, in particular the widespread booklets and online publications that construct an ancient and glorious Kiranti past that is not grounded in historical evidence. Schlemmer notes that such a re-invention of history often originates from a mostly urban middle class that is disconnected from its rural homeland. According to my own observations, with the number of educated people rising in the villages, with roads being built and more people regularly commuting between cities and their villages, ethnic self-awareness is increasing also in the rural areas.

Figure 2.4: The statue of the mythical Kiranti king Yalambar in Mudhe Sanischare

2.2.2 The Yakkha

2.2.2.1 Ethnic affiliation

Within Kiranti, the largest subgroups are the Rai and the Limbu. While the Limbu speak a few very closely related languages, the term Rai is a broad category that subsumes at least 20 linguistically and ethnically distinct communities.

The Yakkha perceive themselves as closest to the Limbu both culturally and linguistically (see also Russell (1992: 90)). Marriages between Yakkha and Limbu are more common than between members of other Kiranti groups. The closest linguistic relative of Yakkha, however, is not Limbu, but the Belhare language, since Yakkha and Belhare share some innovations and unique features that are not found in any other Kiranti language (cf. §2.3 below). The most likely historical scenario is that the Yakkha have adapted culturally to the Limbu because the latter have been the economically and socially most powerful group in the region.

Formerly, the Yakkha were also known as Rai (Russell 1992: 90).[14] The Yakkha, however, stress that they neither belong to Rai nor to Limbu. In line with this, it

---

[14] Russell suggests that the name Rai was used when communicating with outsiders to benefit from the reputation of those Rai in the British Gurkha regiments. In present times, too, when talking about my research outside the Yakkha area, I was frequently confronted with the assumption that the Yakkha are a Rai group.

is now popular to use *Yakkha* or one's clan name as surnames instead of the formerly used exonymic surnames *Dewan* and *Jimi* that originate in Nepali administrative titles given to local tax collectors by the Gorkha kings.[15] Furthermore, origin myths that are known from many Rai groups, such as the story about Sumnima and Paruhang or the legends about the orphan hero Khocilipa/Khakculukpa (Ebert 2003a; Gaenszle 2000) are not perceived as native to Yakkha and are not widely known.

The nature of the historical link to Belhare, which is spoken near Dhankuta, 50 kilometers to the south of the core Yakkha area, is not known with certainty, but it is worth noting that Dahal (1985: 13, 47)[16] mentions that a group of Yakkha families had been integrated into the Athpahariya (Athpare) society. Bickel (1996: 21) notes that the people who speak Belhare are also known as Athpare, and that the two linguistic groups Athpare and Belhare are one group by cultural criteria: their languages are mutually unintelligible, which could be explained by such a migration scenario. This hypothesis is supported by the fact that other Yakkha groups have also out-migrated from the Yakkha homeland (cf. §2.1), most probably in search for arable land.

2.2.2.2 Language names

The term *Yakkha* is simultaneously used as a linguistic and as an ethnic name. Alternative names for the language are *Yakkha Ceʔya* (*ceʔya* meaning 'matter, talk, language') and *Jimi Bhasa*, the exonym used by Nepali speakers. As an ethnonym, the non-indigenous name *Jimi* is sometimes used synonymously with Yakkha. It is also a common surname for Yakkha people, introduced during the Gorkha rule. Titles such as *Dewan* and *Jimdar* (from Persian *jamindār*) were given to individuals and village headmen in the Yakkha area, in order to implement the Gorkha tax system, and they were adopted as surnames because of the power and high social status associated with them. Among the Limbu, the Mughal (Arabic) title *Subba* became a common surname, and among the Khambu, this happened with the title *Rai* (Whelpton 2005: 51). Apart from these non-indigenous surnames, however, ancestral clan names play a vital role in social life and in the ritual sphere (see §2.2.2.5 below).

The first syllable of *Yakkha* is traceable to the Proto-Kiranti root **rok*, which is the Kiranti autonym and has no cognates outside Kiranti. Cognates are found, e.g., in the Puma autonym *rakoŋ* (Bickel et al. 2009), in the Dumi autonym *roʔdi*

---

[15] Cf. Doornenbal (2009: 8) for the same observation in Bantawa.
[16] Cited in Russell (1992: 1).

(van Driem 1993a: 413) and in the Limbu autonym *yakthumba* (van Driem 1987: xix). The historical sound change from /r/ to /y/ is typical for Eastern Kiranti, to which Yakkha and Limbu belong. The neighbouring groups Lohorung, Yamphe and Yamphu also call their languages *Yakkhaba* (van Driem 1994: 347),[17] but their languages are clearly distinct from Yakkha.[18] The second syllable *kha* might be traced back to the Proto-Tibeto-Burman root **ka* for 'word, speech' (Matisoff 2003: 174).

2.2.2.3 Subsistence and economy

The Yakkha are primarily agriculturalists. The main crops are maize (*caloŋ*), rice (*cabhak*), millet (*paŋge*) and buckwheat (*khoriʔmaŋ*). They also grow soybeans (*cembek/chacek*), lentils (*tuya*), tea (Nepali *ciya*), cucumbers (*wabik*), tomatoes (*wariŋba*), onions (*chepi*), garlic (*maŋkhu*), yams (*khi*), potatoes (*sambakhi*), bananas (*camokla*), Indian leaf mustard (*yaro*), mushrooms (*muŋ*), and various kinds of greens, pumpkins and gourds. A typical household also has pigs, buffalos, oxen, chickens and goats. Pigs and chickens also feature prominently in the ritual design, as a sacrifice to the ancestors. Other means of subsistence are fishing, hunting and beekeeping.

The Yakkha press mustard oil (*kiwa*), they brew beer (*cuwa*), mostly from millet, and they distill liquor (*chemha*), also from millet. Alcohol is not just a refreshment, but also a medium of social exchange (e.g., in marriages and funerals) and a sacrifice in the ancestral rituals (see also Russell (1992: 124)). A main source of income is the cultivation and trade of cardamom (mostly called *alenchi*, from Nepali, though the Yakkha term is *cokceru*). Furthermore, various fermented, durable dishes are prepared, most famously *kinama* (fermented soybeans). Traditional agricultural instruments are still used today, because it is impossible to cultivate the terraced fields with machines. Some villages have electric mills to grind the grains, but mostly this is done with grinding stones. According to my observations in Tumok, educated people who have an income as teachers or in other village-level government posts do not necessarily abandon agriculture, but try to maintain both means of subsistence.

Recruitment in the British Gorkha army has long been a source of income in the Kiranti groups in general. In recent decades, labour migrations to Arab countries, to Hong Kong, Singapore and Malaysia has increased. Most households

---

[17] The marker *-ba* has the function of a nominalizer.

[18] A folk etymology relates the language name to the lexeme *yaksa* 'hut, resting place' (Kongren 2007a: 87). This word is a Tibetan loan (*rgyags-sa*) that is also known in Nepali (Turner 1931).

Figure 2.5: A Yakkha house in Tumok village

I got to know in Tumok received some sort of support from family members working abroad.

2.2.2.4 Material culture

A typical Yakkha house (*paŋ*) is shown in Figure 2.5. Yakkha houses (at least in Tumok) are white, with the lower part of the walls covered in red (a mixture of clay and cowdung). They are typically renovated once a year, before Dasain (the most important Hindu festival in Nepal), although the festival itself is not celebrated in Yakkha society anymore.[19] The houses have blue and red wooden railings and window frames, some of them beautifully carved. Every house has a terrace (*omphu*), in which guests are usually received. The roofs are thatched with straw or covered with tiles (or, as a recent development, tin).

The Yakkha have a rich tradition of processing bamboo (*phabu*). Bamboo products are abundant in all aspects of material culture, from house construction to manufacturing various kinds of sieves, baskets and the most delicate and tiny purses, combs and needles, as shown in Figure 2.6.

---

[19] The festival had been celebrated until recently, albeit, as argued by Russell (2004), with Yakkha-specific modifications. The recent abandonment of the Dasain festival can be understood as part of a broader process of de-Hinduization among the non-Hindu groups in Nepal. Other Hindu customs prevail, such as the question who may eat together, and who may serve food to whom.

Figure 2.6: Bamboo products: *sigikma* 'comb', *kaŋyoŋ* 'chicken basket', *phepi* 'purse'

Figure 2.7: Yakkha *phopma* (shawl)

Another craft is weaving mats from straw and maize leaves. Furthermore, fabrics and shawls are produced on looms. The pattern found on traditional Yakkha shawls (*phopma*) is shown in Figure 2.7.

2.2.2.5 Social organization and religion

The Yakkha religious sphere and social organization are shaped by the pan-Kiranti tradition that is called *munthum* in Yakkha, in which the ancestors play a major role. The term *munthum* also refers to a body of orally transmitted texts in which the deeds and journeys of the ancestors come alive. Gaenszle (in prep.) notes that, despite differences in ritual systems and practices, this ancestral tradition is shared by all Kiranti groups. The *munthum*

[...] comprises histories of the origin of the ancestors, beginning with the primal creation of the universe and the emergence of natural and cultural orders and continuing to the settlement of the ancestral territory. It also concerns the proper means of communicating with ancestors and ritually maintaining the order they have established. The term, then, has an additional meaning: it evokes a way of life predefined by the ancestors, a self-enclosed world rooted in the past. (Gaenszle 2000: 224)

The social order, but also the physical and mental health of individuals, is ultimately related to the ancestors. This is also illustrated by rituals such as *saya pokma* (literal translation: 'raising the head soul'), which is known in Yakkha and in other Kiranti groups. It is undertaken to re-unite individuals, whose well-being is endangered, with the primaeval ancestral order. In her anthropological-psychological study on Lohorung culture, for example, Hardman (2000) notes that the main frame of reference in that culture is one in which

... the 'natural' ancestral order [...], as recorded in their myths, has to be constantly recreated and the unity between nature, the superhuman, and the human reaffirmed. Failure to do this would lead to depression, increased sickness, possibly death, and ensuing chaos. In contrast, repetition of ancestral worlds and adherence to ancestral order acts like recharging the cosmos. It brings vitality. (Hardman 2000: 12–3)

For Yakkha people, the ancestral order is equally important. A key feature of this order is the division of the Yakkha society into clans (called *choŋ*), which is critical not only in marriage restrictions but also in the ritual sphere. Russell (1992: 201) notes the following clan names in Yakkha (square brackets indicate his transcriptions where deviating from the orthography used in this work): *Linkha, Chala* [challa], *Koyoŋwa* [koyoŋa], *Khamyahaŋ* [kammieŋ], *Limbukhim* [limbuhim], *Hoŋhoŋba, Koŋgren, Choŋgren, Maʔkruk, Yaʔyukhim, Taʔyum, Pubaŋgu, Oktubaŋ, Somyeŋ, Khayakhim* [khayakim], *Heŋwa, Ilumbaŋ, Tiksalaŋ, Thampara, Ibahaŋ, Yuwahaŋ.* I further recorded the clan names *Elaba, Hangsewa* and *Huture* in mythical narratives.

Apart from these clans, there are is another concept called *sametliŋ* 'spiritual clan'. There are different *sametliŋs* for the women and for the men of each clan. Women of one clan may, however, share their spiritual clan with men of another clan. In contrast to clan (*choŋ*) affinity, the *sametliŋ* of a woman does not change after marriage. The *sametliŋs* outside one's family are not widely known, in contrast to a person's *choŋ*. They are only significant in dealing with spirits (*cyaŋ*) (Russell 1992: 166).

Personal names (mostly Indo-Aryan nowadays), are not widely used. It is rather common to adress a person by the respective kinship term, or by a teknonym 'X's father' or 'X's mother'.

The ritual specialists responsible for holding the ancestral rituals are called *Maŋgaŋba* in Yakkha. They undertake rituals for each household on occasions like births, marriages and deaths. The task of the *Maŋgaŋbas* is to maintain the ancestral order and good relations with the spirit world (there are several potentially dangerous spirits such as *soghek* - ghosts of people who have died an unnatural death). Other religious practitioners are *chamwas*, *bijuwas* (a Rai term), *phedaŋbas* (a Limbu term), *dhamis* (a Nepali term), but I cannot offer a typology of their features and their tasks. Jointly celebrated festivals (above the clan level or even above the village level) are *casowa* (Nepali: *udhauli*) in late autumn and *yuchyaŋ* (Nepali *ubhauli*) in spring (Kongren 2007a: 102).[20] On these occasions and also on marriages, people gather in a circle and dance a complicated choreography slowly to the sound of huge drums beaten by some men in the circle (*keilakma* 'dancing the drum dance').

The Yakkha society is patrilineal and patrilocal. With regard to marriages, it is important to note that there are two distinct steps taken to incorporate the bride into the clan of her husband. The actual marriage is only the first step, called *mandata*. The second step is called *bagdata*, and is undertaken years, sometimes decades, after the marriage. In the *bagdata*, the husband has to ask his in-laws for their daughter again, and only after this ritual does she become a member of his clan. If the wife dies before the *bagdata* has been asked for, her natal home will undertake the death rites for her.

2.3 Genealogical affiliation

Yakkha is a Sino-Tibetan language, belonging to the Greater Eastern branch of Kiranti, a group of Tibeto-Burman languages spoken in Eastern Nepal.[21] Beyond this basic classification, the question of how to group Kiranti languages with other Sino-Tibetan languages is still a controversial issue, as in general, subgrouping in the large and incredibly diverse Sino-Tibetan language family has proven to be rather difficult (see, e.g., Hyslop 2011: Chapter 3 for an overview of the different models of reconstruction that have been proposed).

Shafer (1974) identified Kiranti (which he called East Himalayish) as a subbranch of Bodic, together with three further branches: Bodish (including Tibetan

---

[20] In his ethnological study, Russell (1992) does not mention these festivals, so their names as well as celebrating them this way might be a relatively new development.

[21] Although not undisputed, it is assumed by many scholars that Sino-Tibetan can be divided into a Sinitic and a Tibeto-Burman branch, the latter containing at least 300 languages (Bradley 1997; Matisoff 2003).

and Tamangic languages), West Himalayish and West Central Himalayish (including Magar and Chepang). Similarly, Bradley (1997) suggested that the Kiranti languages, together with Magaric and Newaric languages, form the sub-branch Himalayish.

A different view is entertained by LaPolla (2003), who includes Kiranti in a group he calls Rung (including, most importantly, the rGyalrongic languages, the Dulong languages, the Kiranti languages, Kham, and the West Himalayan languages Kinauri and Almora), on the basis of shared person marking morphology and a reflexive/middle suffix *-si (except for rGyalrong). What makes any classification even harder is that not even the question of the antiquity of person marking in Tibeto-Burman has been settled yet (see e.g DeLancey (2010); Jacques (2012a) who argue that such a system can be reconstructed, and LaPolla (2001; 2012), who argues that agreement marking systems in Tibeto-Burman languages are independent innovations).

Kiranti languages can be grouped into a Western and a Central-Eastern branch (with a Central and a Greater Eastern sub-branch), as shown in Figure 2.8 (Bickel & Gaenszle 2015). Central-Eastern Kiranti is characterized by a loss of voiced initials by merging voiceless and voiced initials (Michailovsky 1994). Voiced stops with phonemic value rarely occur, though voiced allophones are possible, as a result of post-nasal and intervocalic voicing, for instance in Yakkha and in Athpare (Ebert 2003c: 505).

Yakkha undoubtedly belongs to the Greater Eastern branch. A distinctive feature of Greater Eastern Kiranti languages is the change of pre-glottalized stops into aspirated stops (or zero, in the case of /*ʔt/, see further below): */ʔts/ > /tsʰ/, */ʔp/ > /pʰ/, */ʔk/ > /kʰ/ (see Table 2.1 for comparative data).[22] The Greater Eastern branch splits into Upper Arun (Lohorung, Yamphu and Mewahang) and Eastern Kiranti, to which Yakkha belongs. Eastern Kiranti is characterized by the change of initial */r/ and */R/ into /y/ (van Driem 1990).

Within Eastern Kiranti there are two groups, which are the various Limbu dialects on the one hand and the so-called Greater Yakkha group, with Chintang, Belhare, Athpare, Chiling and Yakkha, on the other hand. Some languages of the Greater Yakkha branch are characterized by the loss of the aspirated coronal stop, compare, e.g., Limbu *thuŋ* 'drink' with Yakkha (and Belhare) *uŋ* (Bickel 1997a). Furthermore, the aspirated affricate /tsʰ/ (see above) has undergone a further change to /s/ in Limbu, compare, e.g., Limbu *sarumma* with Yakkha *chalumma* 'second-born girl' (for further examples see Table 2.1).

---

[22] The table is based on data from van Driem (1993a; 1987); Bickel et al. (2009); Kongren (2007b) and my own data.

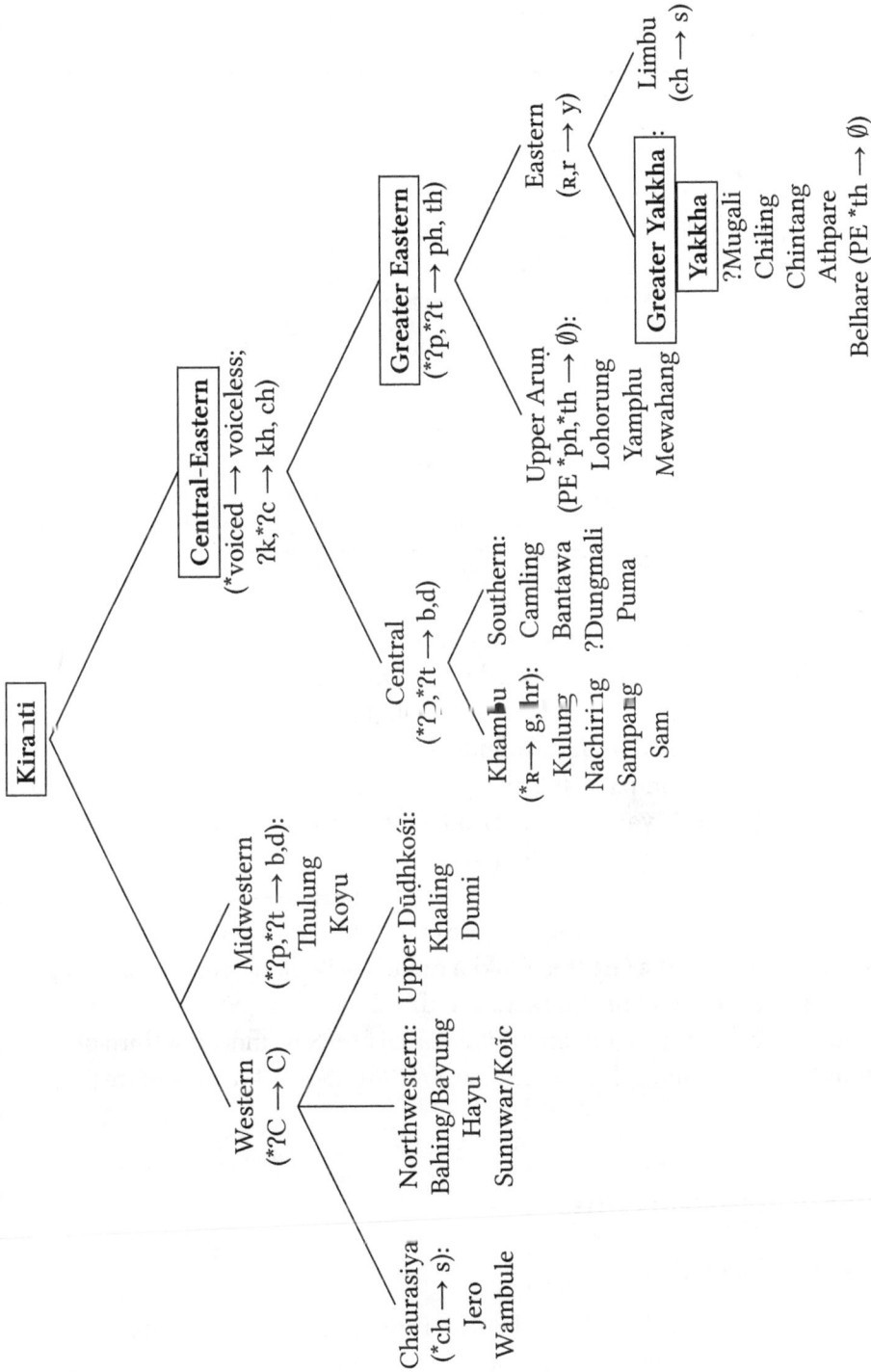

Figure 2.8: Kiranti subgrouping, according to Bickel (2008)

Table 2.1: Examples of Kiranti sound correspondences

Proto-Kiranti	Dumi (WESTERN)	Puma (CENTRAL)	Yakkha (EASTERN)	Limbu (EASTERN)	GLOSS
*/d/	de:n	ten	ten	tɛn	'village'
*/j/	ju	ca	ca	ca	'eat'
*/b/	bhiʔi	pooŋ	pik	pit	'cow'
*/r/	rep	rep	ep	yep	'stand'
*/r/	roʔdi	roduŋ	yakthuŋ	yak	'Kiranti' (autonym)
*/R/	rɨm	rum	yum	yum	'salt'
*/ch/		chapd-	chep	sap	'write'
*/ʔc/		chakd	chekt	sak	'close'
*/ʔp/	puŋ	buŋ	phuŋ	phuŋ	'flower'
*/ʔt/	tiŋ	duŋ	uŋ	thuŋ	'drink'
*/ʔt/		dok	ak	thak	'loom'

Rhotic consonants, although they do not occur word-initially in Yakkha, are found word-internally. The claim made by van Driem (1990) that [l] and [r] have a complementary distribution and are thus allophones in Eastern Kiranti cannot be confirmed for Yakkha: both sounds occur in similar environments word-internally (cf. Table 3.6 on page 49), and no environment was found in which [l] and [r] show allophonic variation in Yakkha (see also §3.1.3.4). Thus, although finding "proper" minimal pairs for /l/ and /r/ is difficult, /r/ is a phoneme in Yakkha.

Based on a comparison of the verbal person marking paradigm, the closest relative of Yakkha within the Greater Yakkha branch is Belhare. The two languages exclusively share the following markers: a suffix *-ka* ~ *-ga* indexing second person arguments (any role), and an underspecified nasal prefix *N-* indexing third person plural S and A (3>2.SG and 3pl>3) in Yakkha, and 3nsg.S and 3>2 in Belhare (Bickel 2003: 551).

2.4 Sociolinguistic context

2.4.1 Dialectal variation

The variety documented here is spoken in Tumok village and surrounding areas, e.g., in Salle. No detailed dialectal study has been undertaken for Yakkha yet. Based on phonological differences and distinct exclamative words, I tentatively propose three further dialects: one spoken in the area around Ankhinbhuin (Angbura, Hombong, Phakling), one spoken in the area around Dandagaun and one spoken towards the north, in Kingring and Kharang villages.

Table 2.2 illustrates dialectal differences. The Kharang dialect is different from the other dialects, for instance, in having a second person possessive marker *i-* instead of the unspecified nasal prefix that is found elsewhere, and in having a clause-final exclamative particle *ikhok*. Apart from this, I do not have data on this dialect.

Yakkha has a general phonological rule of voicing consonants in post-nasal and intervocalic position. The rule has different domains of application across the dialects: in Tumok and in Dandagaun it does not apply to aspirated consonants, while in Ankhinbhuin it applies to both aspirated and unaspirated consonants. Furthermore, I noticed that in Dandagaun, /o/ gets raised to /u/, at least in some lexemes. In the Tumok dialect, the person marker for first person acting on second is *-nen*, while in the Ankhinbhuin dialect it is *-nan* (cf. also the data from Omruwa (Angbura) in van Driem 1994). In Dandagaun and Ankhinbhuin honorific imperative forms calqued upon Nepali are used, while in this is not common in Tumok. I have no data on the varieties spoken in the south of the Dhankuta district, in the village of Namsaling in Ilam district and in India.

Table 2.2: Dialectal variation within the Yakkha region

TUMOK	DANDAGAUN	ANKHINBHUIN	KHARANG	GLOSS
mma	*mma*	*mma*	*ima*	'your mother'
nniŋga	*nniŋga*	*nniŋga*	*iniŋga*	'your'
i ~ ina ~ iha	*i ~ ina ~ iha*	*i ~ ina ~ iha*	*iruk*	'what'
cokma	*cukma*	*cokma*	(n.d.)	'do, make'
ŋkhya(ci)	*ŋkhya(ci)*	*ŋghya(ci)*	(n.d.)	'they went'
mphopma	*mphopma*	*mbhopma*	(n.d.)	'your shawl'
piʔnenna	*piʔnenna*	*piʔnanna*	(n.d.)	'I gave it to you'
coeba	*cama leŋniba*	*cama leŋniba*	(n.d.)	'please eat'
haʔlo	(no data)	*khoʔo ~ kho*	*ikhok*	(excl. ptcl.)
=pa	*=pa*	*=aŋ*	(n.d.)	(emph. ptcl.)

In Marek VDC in Dhankuta (Marek, Ghorlikharka, Jitpur, Andrung, Magwa, Saldang villages), a variety is spoken that is so different from the other Yakkha varieties (as perceived by the speakers of Yakkha, too) that it cannot be called a dialect of Yakkha any more. The linguistic differences notwithstanding, the speakers are perceived as belonging to the Yakkha group on ethnic grounds. The language is called Lumba-Yakkha in the Ethnologue (ISO 639-3: luu).[23] I have not heard this designation in Tumok, the language was usually referred to as *māreki bhāsā* (Nepali; 'the language from Marek'). The Marek variety has, for instance, undergone the sound change from /ch/ to /s/ that is also known from Limbu. Crucially, the pronominal paradigm and the verbal inflection are different from Yakkha, for instance the second person prefix *a-* (otherwise known from Athpare and Chintang, see Ebert 1997a; Bickel et al. 2007a) instead of the Yakkha suffix -*ka*. Table 2.3 provides some exemplary data collected in 2010 with a speaker from Marek, but no detailed study has been undertaken yet.

Table 2.3: Marek data in comparison with Tumok data

MAREK	TUMOK	GLOSS
hoʔli	*imin*	'how'
pisa	*picha*	'child'
seŋma	*chimma*	'to ask'
hima	*i ~ ina ~ iha*	'what'
mahuma	*maghyam*	'old woman'
pahuba	*paghyam*	'old man'
nhandi	*khaʔla*	'like this'
aŋga	*ka*	'I'
aŋciŋ	*kanciŋ*	'we' (du)
aŋniŋ	*kaniŋ*	'we' (pl)
ŋkhan	*nda*	'you' (sg)
habe	*heʔne*	'where'
hannalam	*heʔnhaŋ*	'where from'
akhaʔneʔna	*khemekana*	'you go'
=na	*=na*	(nominalizer)
-ma	*-ma*	(infinitive marker)

---

[23] Lewis, Simons & Fennig (2015), http://www.ethnologue.com, accessed on Dec. 20 2013.

2.4.2 Endangerment

According to the Nepali census of 2001 (Central Bureau of Statistics, Nepal 2001) and the UNESCO Working Paper No. 7 (Toba, Toba & Rai 2005) there are 14,648 native speakers out of about 17,000 ethnic Yakkha. The number of native speakers makes up 0.06 per cent of the Nepalese population. This census, however, seems highly optimistic to me, since Yakkha is barely spoken in half of the Yakkha area, and even where it is spoken the youngest generation (below 20 years of age) does not commonly use Yakkha, even though they might have a passive command of the language. Specific domains such as ritual, mythological and traditional ecological knowledge are known only by a few (usually) elderly people. I did not find any monolingual Yakkha speakers; all speakers are at least bilingual with Nepali,[24] and proficiency in other neighbouring languages such as Bantawa and Limbu is also common.

One reason why Yakkha speakers shift to Nepali is the already mentioned migration outward for economic and educational reasons, but there are also whole villages inside the homeland that have switched to Nepali. For instance, while Yakkha is still vividly spoken in Tumok, it is difficult to find speakers in the neighbouring villages Mamling, Waleng and in the old garrison town Chainpur (a former center for trade in the region). Most speakers of Yakkha are found in the south of the Yakkha region.

A well-known reason for this development is the low prestige that indigenous languages have long had compared to Nepali. Since the creation of the Nepali nation state in the eighteenth century under the rule of King Pṛthvī Nārāyaṇ Śāha (1723–1775), Nepali has been propagated as the national language, and people have not been encouraged to speak other languages. Much damage was also done under the Panchayat System (1961–1990), where the use of indigenous languages was actively discouraged under the policy of "One Nation, One Language" (Toba, Toba & Rai 2005: 20).

Language shift is complex and can be understood on both macro and interactional levels of analysis. In the Yakkha region, education beyond the primary

---

[24] The official language in Nepal is the Indo-Aryan language Nepali. It is used in official communication, in commerce and in education. Since the constitution of 1990 which followed the first *Jana Andolan* (People's uprising), all languages spoken as mother tongues in Nepal are considered national languages, which grants the speakers the right to be educated in their mother tongue (Turin 2007). This is, however, hard to implement, given that more than 100 languages are spoken in the country.

school level is available exclusively in Nepali or English.[25] At the primary level, Yakkha language classes have been introduced in a number of schools recently (starting in 2009), but Yakkha is not the medium of instruction in other subjects. Yakkha people are not represented in the government beyond village level (Central Bureau of Statistics, Nepal 2001). Even in the villages, official posts in education and administration are still overwhelmingly held by people from non-indigenous backgrounds, simply because there are not enough Yakkha people who could work in these positions. This social and economic bias exerts additional pressure on the speakers of Yakkha, and these dynamics are one of the reasons why Yakkha-speaking parents use Nepali with their kids.

Another factor destabilizing the language situation are marriages with people outside one's own linguistic community, for instance Yakkha-Limbu marriages. Generally, bilingual or multilingual families are of course not problematic, to the contrary, multilingualism is rather the norm world-wide (see Turin 2007). But with the additional pressure that comes from Nepali, children from multilingual families nowadays often grow up with Nepali as the only language they speak fluently.

These developments cannot simply be related to a lack of interest in the parents to pass on their language. According to my own observations, the tendency not to speak Yakkha is even present in the children of those people who have a high ethnic awareness and who are engaged in a number of activities towards preserving their language and culture. The tension between preserving one's ethnic and linguistic heritage and participating in modern society is well-known in theoretical approaches to language loss, but it is nevertheless hard to resolve for the affected individuals.

In the past decades, with multi-party democracy having started in 1990, and even more so in the post-monarchy era that has followed the civil war (1996–2006) and the second *Jana Andolan* (People's Uprising) in 2006, activities aiming at the preservation of the indigenous languages and cultures have increased. In the case of Yakkha, for instance, the Kirant Yakkha Chumma (Indigenous Peoples Yakkha Organization) have implemented Yakkha lessons in a few primary schools in the Yakkha region. School books have been completed up to class five already, with the plan to reach class eight. Dictionaries, literary works and even songs and music videos have been created lately by members of the com-

---

[25] This is also reflected in the negative correlation between the educational level and the number of Yakkha students. According to the 2001 census, the number of Yakkha students beyond the primary level was 6915, the number of those who have passed s.l.c was 878 and the number of those with a degree was 89 in 2001 (Central Bureau of Statistics, Nepal 2001).

munity who feel the urge to do something before it is too late (cf. §1.4). The long-term impact of this welcome development remains to be seen. To properly assess the endangerment of a language, an in-depth study in its own right would be necessary. The loss of Yakkha in a wide geographic area and in the youngest generation are, however, very clear and alarming signs.

3 Phonology

This chapter deals with the phoneme inventory and the phonological and the morphophonological rules and processes that are relevant in Yakkha. The ortho-graphy used here is explained in §1.2.2. The examples in this chapter, unlike in the other chapters, have two lines representing the Yakkha data: the upper line shows the data after the application of all phonological and morphophonologi-cal rules, and the lower line shows the underlying phonemic material with mor-pheme breaks. The orthography is used in both representations, and IPA is only used when necessary in the explanations in prose. §3.1 presents the phoneme inventory of Yakkha, §3.2 deals with the syllable structure and §3.3 discusses the treatment of loanwords, as they nicely illustrate the phonological features of Yakkha. §3.4 lays out the conditions by which stress is assigned. The abundant morphophonological processes and their connections to syllable structure, stress and diachronic processes are the concern of §3.5.

3.1 Phoneme inventory and allophonic rules

3.1.1 Vowel phonemes

Yakkha has only five basic vowels; it has two close vowels, the front /i/ and the back /u/, two close-mid vowels, the front /e/ and the back /o/, and an open vowel

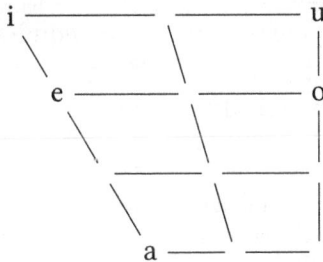

Figure 3.1: Yakkha vowel phonemes

/a/. In contrast to other Kiranti languages, there are no central vowels like /i/, /ʌ/ or /ə/. A chart with the vowel inventory is provided in Figure 3.1. In addition to these vowels, a front vowel [ɛ] may occur, but only as the contracted form of the diphthong /ai/ (see §3.1.2), not in any other environments. Minimal pairs are provided in Table 3.1. Tone, length or nasal articulation do not constitute phonemic contrasts in Yakkha.

Table 3.1: Minimal pairs for vowel phonemes

PHONEMES	EXAMPLES			
/e/ vs. /i/	nema	'lay, sow seed'	nima	'know, see'
	tema	'lean on an angle'	tima	'put down, invest'
/e/ vs. /a/	tema	'lean on an angle'	tama	'come'
	yepma	'stand'	yapma	'be rough'
/o/ vs. /u/	okma	'shriek'	ukma	'bring down'
	ho?ma	'prick, pierce'	hu?ma	'push, stuff'
/o/ vs. /a/	thokma	'spit'	thakma	'weigh, hand/send up'
	ho?ma	'prick, pierce'	ha?ma	'scrape off/out'
/u/ vs. /i/	ukma	'bring down'	ikma	'chase'
	umma	'pull'	imma	'sleep'

3.1.2 Diphthongs

Given that adjacent vowels are generally avoided in Yakkha, it does not come as a surprise that diphthongs, i.e., adjacent vowels in the same syllable, are rare. The four diphthongs /ai/, /ui/, /oi/ and /au/ were found, occuring marginally, as in ŋhai (a dish made from fish stomach), hoi! 'enough!', uimalaŋ 'steeply downhill', (h)au (a sentence-final exclamative particle) and ambau! (an exclamative expression indicating that the speaker is impressed by huge or dangerous things). Some speakers pronounce underlying sequences like /ŋond-si?-ma/ and /thend-si?-ma/ with nasalized diphthongs, [ŋoĩsi?ma] and [theĩsi?ma], respectively (instead of the more common pronunciations [ŋonsi?ma] and [thensi?ma]).[1]

---

[1] The nasalization is exceptional in these cases. Usually, the prosody of Yakkha supports the opposite process, namely the change of nasal vowels to nasal consonants, e.g., in borrowed Nepali lexemes (see §3.3). Nasals may, however, regularly change to nasalization of the preceding vowel in intervocalic environment and before glides and liquids, as in mẽ.u.le (/meN-us-le/) 'without entering' and mẽ.yok.le (/meN-yok-le/) 'without searching', see §3.5.5.2.

Most diphthongs have their origin in a multimorphemic or in a multisyllabic environment. The adverb *uimalaŋ*, for instance, like many other spatial adverbs in Yakkha, is composed of a stem (diachronically, most probably a noun) and the possessive prefix *u-*. The marginal nature of the diphthongs is confirmed also by the fact that they are found more in names and discourse particles than in lexemes with semantic content, and never in verbal roots. Occasionally, diphthongs are just one stage in a larger process of contraction. Consider the inflected form *waiʔ.na* '(he/she/it) exists', which is also found as [wɛʔ.na]. Its nonpast semantics and synchronically available contracted forms of verbs suggest that [waiʔ.na] used to be *[wa.me.na] historically. Table 3.2 provides an exhaustive list of lexemes containing diphthongs from the more than 2400 lexemes in the lexical database that builds the basis of the current analysis.

Table 3.2: Lexemes containing diphthongs

/au/	/oi/	/ui/	/ai/
(h)au	*coilikha*	*uimalaŋ*	*ŋhai*
(EXCLA)	(a village)	'steeply downhill'	'fish stomach'
ambau!	*hoi!*	*phakkui*	*Yaiten*
'holy smoke!'	'enough!'	'pig droppings'	(a village)
		waghui	*lai*
		'chicken droppings'	(EXCLA)

3.1.3 Consonant phonemes

Table 3.3 below shows the central and the marginal consonant phonemes of Yakkha. The phones that are not in parentheses clearly have phonemic status; they occur in basic, uninflected stems. The phonemic status of the phones in parentheses is not always straightforward (see discussion below). Where my orthography deviates from IPA, this is indicated by angle brackets.

3.1.3.1 The main phonemic distinctions in the consonants

Yakkha distinguishes six places of articulation: bilabial, alveolar, retroflex (or post-alveolar), palatal, velar and glottal. Retroflex plosives most probably made their way into Yakkha via Nepali loanwords. They are found only in a few Yakkha

Table 3.3: Yakkha consonant phonemes

	BILABIAL	ALVEOLAR	RETROFLEX	PALATAL	VELAR	GLOTTAL
PLOSIVES	p	t	(ʈ)		k	ʔ
ASP.	ph	th	(ʈh)		kh	
VOICED	(b)	(d)	(ɖ)		(g)	
VOICED-ASP.	(bh)	(dh)	(ɖh)		(gh)	
AFFRICATES		ts <c>				
ASP.		tsʰ <ch>				
VOICED		(dz) <j>				
VOICED-ASP.		(dzʰ) <jh>				
FRICATIVES		s				h
NASALS	m	n			ŋ	
NAS. ASP.	(mh)	(nh)			(ŋh)	
RHOTICS		r				
LATERALS		l				
GLIDES	w			j <y>		
GLIDES ASP.	wh					

lexemes, and no proper minimal pairs could be established. The retroflex series lacks a nasal, too. However, in the few words that are found with retroflex stops, they are robust, and pronouncing these words with an alveolar stop is not an option.

Yakkha fits well into the Eastern branch of Kiranti, for instance in the loss of phonemic contrast between voiced and unvoiced plosives. Generally, plosives, unless they are found in an environment that triggers voicing, are pronounced as voiceless. As always, a few exceptions occur that cannot be explained by some rule. The exact parameters of the voicing rule are laid out in §3.5.1. A robust phonemic contrast exists between aspirated and unaspirated consonants, as it is found in the plosives (except for the glottal stop), the affricate and the bilabial glide /w/. Aspiration of a stem-initial consonant, historically a morphological means to increase the transitivity in Tibeto-Burman (Michailovsky 1994; Jacques 2012b; Hill 2014), has become purely phonemic in Yakkha. The aspirated plosives have a strong fricative component. Three nasals are distinguished by their place of articulation: bilabial /m/, alveolar /n/ and velar /ŋ/. Yakkha has two fricatives /s/ and /h/, and two liquids, /l/ and /r/. The rhotic does not occur word-initially. In this position, */r/ has changed to the palatal glide /y/[2] (see also Table 2.1 in

---

[2] I use the grapheme <y> to represent IPA [j]; see §1.2.2 for the notes on the orthography used in this book.

Table 3.4: Minimal pairs for consonants

PHONEMES	EXAMPLES			
/k/ vs. /kh/	*ke?ma*	'come up'	*khe?ma*	'go'
	kapma	'carry along, have'	*khapma*	'thatch, cover'
/p/ vs. /ph/	*pakna*	'young guy'	*phak*	'pig'
	pekma	'fold'	*phekma*	'slap, sweep'
/t/ vs. /th/	*tumma*	'understand'	*thumma*	'tie'
	tokma	'get'	*thokma*	'hit with horns'
/c/ vs. /ch/	*cikma*	'age, ripen'	*chikma*	'measure, pluck'
	cimma	'teach'	*chimma*	'ask'
/k/ vs. /?/	*okma*	'shriek'	*o?ma*	'be visible'
/t/ vs. /?/	*-met*	(CAUS)	*-me?*	(NPST)
/p/ vs. /?/	*opma*	'consume slowly'	*o?ma*	'be visible'
/t/ vs. /r/	*ot*	'be visible' (stem)	*or*	'peel off'
/l/ vs. /r/	*khelek*	'ant'	*kherek*	'hither'
/y/ vs. /w/	*yapma*	'be uncomfortable'	*wapma*	'paw, scrabble'
	yamma	'disturb'	*wamma*	'attack, pounce'
/y/ vs. /l/	*yapma*	'be uncomfortable'	*lapma*	'accuse, blame'
/w/ vs. /wh/	*wapma*	'paw, scrabble'	*whapma*	'wash clothes'
	waŋma	'curve, bend'	*whaŋma*	'boil'
/s/ vs. /h/	*sima*	'die'	*hima*	'spread'
	somma	'stroke gently'	*homma*	'fit into'
/k/ vs. /ŋ/	*pekma*	'break'	*peŋma*	'peel'
	okma	'shriek'	*oŋma*	'attack'
/ŋ/ vs. /m/	*toŋma*	'agree'	*tomma*	'place vertically'
	tuŋma	'pour'	*tumma*	'understand'
/ŋ/ vs. /n/	*=ŋa*	(ERG)	*=na*	(NMLZ.SG)
/m/ vs. /n/	*makma*	'burn'	*nakma*	'beg, ask'
	mi?ma	'think, remember'	*ni?ma*	'count, consider'

Chapter 2 and the references therein).[3] The distribution of the rhotic consonant deserves a closer look, also in the perspective of other Eastern Kiranti languages (see §3.1.3.4 below). Table 3.4 provides minimal pairs for the basic consonant phonemes, mostly from verbal stems or citation forms.

---

[3] Furthermore, /y/ may be omitted before /e/ in some lexemes, but this process is subject to considerable individual variation.

3.1.3.2 Marginal consonant phonemes

Several of the phonemes occur only marginally, either in Nepali loanwords, or in just a handful of Yakkha lexemes. This basically applies to the already mentioned retroflex plosives and to all voiced obstruents, as voicing is generally not distinctive in Yakkha.[4] Some sounds are never found in uninflected lexemes, so that they only emerge as the result of some morphophonological processes that are triggered by the concatenation of morphemes with certain phonological features. Voiced-aspirated consonants and the aspirated nasals [mʰ], [nʰ] and [ŋʰ] belong to this group. The marginal sounds are included in parentheses in Table 3.3. The reader is referred to §3.5 for the details of the various morphophonological processes that lead to marginal phonemes.

3.1.3.3 The phonemic status of the glottal stop

The glottal stop is contrastive, as several minimal pairs in Table 3.4 demonstrate. The glottal stop surfaces only before nasals and laterals, so that one can find minimal pairs like *meŋ.khuʔ.le* 'without carrying' and *meŋ.khu.le* 'without stealing', or *men.daʔ.le* 'without bringing' and *men.da.le* 'without coming'. However, the glottal stop can also be the result of a phonological operation. Unaspirated stops, especially /t/, tend to get neutralized to [ʔ] syllable-finally (aspirated stops do not occur in this position). The glottal stop is also prothesized to vowel-initial words to maximize the onset. In certain grammatical markers, the glottal stop may also be epenthesized at the end of the syllable when it is followed by nasal consonants or glides (see (1)). This may happen only when the syllable is stressed, but the conditions for this epenthesis are not fully understood yet. It never occurs at the end of a word (if the word is defined by the domain to which stress is assigned).

(1)　　a.　*tu.mok.peʔ.na*　　　*ma.mu*
　　　　　/tumok=pe=na　　　mamu/
　　　　　Tumok=LOC=NMLZ.SG　girl
　　　　　'the girl from Tumok'

　　　　b.　*men*　　*baʔ.lo!*
　　　　　/men　　pa=lo/
　　　　　COP.NEG　EMPH=EXCLA
　　　　　'Of course not!'

---

[4] There are quasi minimal pairs such as *apaŋ* 'my house' and *abaŋ* 'I came', but both are inflected words and the difference is that *a-* in *apaŋ* is a prefix, and the rule that is responsible for the voicing of plosives excludes prefixes.

The glottal stop is less consonant-like than the other plosives. In certain environments, stems that end in a glottal stop may behave identically to stems consisting of open syllables (CV). For instance, if the stem vowel /e/ or /i/ (of a CV stem or a CVʔ stem) is followed by a vocalic suffix like -*a* (marking past or imperative), it changes into a glide /y/ and becomes part of the onset. This process is illustrated by the behavior of *kheʔma* 'go' and *piʔma* 'give', cf. Table 3.5. If the stem vowel (of a CV stem or a CVʔ stem) is a back vowel, a glide /y/ is inserted between stem and suffixes. If open or /ʔ/-final stems are followed by the suffix sequence -*a-u*, this sequence of suffixes is not overtly realized. Examples of these processes are provided in Table 3.5, contrasted with the behavior of stems with open syllables and stems that end in /p/, /t/ or /k/. The first column shows the underlying stem, the second column provides the citation form and the gloss, the third column shows the behavior before /l/, by means of the forms of the negative converb. The fourth and the fifth columns show the behavior before vowels, by means of intransitive 3.sg past forms (in -*a*),[5] and transitive 3sg.A>3sg.P past forms (in -*a-u*).[6]

To wrap up, the intervocalic environment distinguishes /ʔ/-final stems from stems that end in /p/, /t/ or /k/, while the infinitive and the environment before /l/ distinguishes /ʔ/-final stems from open stems.

The glottal stop at the end of verbal stems can be reconstructed to */t/, in comparison with other Eastern Kiranti languages (cf. §8.1 on the structure of the verbal stems).

3.1.3.4 The status of /r/ in Yakkha and in an Eastern Kiranti perspective

The rhotic /r/ does not occur word-initially in genuine Yakkha lexemes, due to the typical Eastern Kiranti sound change from */r/ to /y/ in word-initial position (see §2.3 and Bickel & Gaenszle 2015). There are words like *lok* 'anger' and *yok* 'place', but no words starting with /r/.[7] It can, however, occasionally be found in complex onsets, and syllable-initially in intervocalic environment. Table 3.6 shows that /r/ and /l/ can be found in very similar environments, even though

---

[5] Or detransitivized, depending on the original valency of the stem.

[6] The verb *cama* 'eat' is the only transitive verb that has an open stem in /a/. It is exceptional in having an ablaut. Open stems are rare, and not all of them are found among both transitive and intransitive verbs, so that some fields of the table cannot be filled.

[7] There are a few exceptions, such as the binomial (a bipartite noun) *raji-raŋma* which means 'wealth of land'. It might be a word that preserved an archaic phonological structure, or a loan (*rājya* means 'kingdom' in Nepali). Both options are possible and attested for the ritual register (the *Munthum*) of other Kiranti languages (Gaenszle et al. 2011).

Table 3.5: The glottal stop stem-finally, compared to vowels and other plosives

STEM	CITATION FORM	/_-l (NEG.CVB)	/_-a (3SG.PST)	/_-a-u (3SG>3SG.PST)
/ʔ/-final stems				
/khuʔ/	khuʔma 'carry'	meŋ.khuʔ.le	khu.ya.na	khu.na
/waʔ/	waʔma 'wear, put on'	mẽ.waʔ.le	wa.ya.na	wa.na
/soʔ/	soʔma 'look'	men.soʔ.le	so.ya.na	so.na
/kheʔ/	kheʔma 'go'	meŋ.kheʔ.le	khya.na	-
/piʔ/	piʔma 'give'	mem.biʔ.le	pya.na	pi.na
V-final stems				
/ca/	cama 'eat'	men.ja.le	ca.ya.na	co.na
/a/	ama 'descend'	mẽ.a.le	a.ya.na	-
/u/	uma 'enter'	mẽ.u.le	u.ya.na	-
/si/	sima 'die'	men.si.le	sya.na	-
/p/-, /t/-, /k/-final stems				
/lap/	lapma 'seize, catch'	mẽ.lap.le	la.ba.na	la.bu.na
/yok/	yokma 'search'	mẽ.yok.le	yo.ga.na	yo.gu.na
/phat/	phaʔma 'help'	mem.phat.le ~ mem.phaʔ.le	pha.ta.na	pha.tu.na

proper minimal pairs are rare. In some instances, intervocalic /r/ can be traced back to historical */t/, as in the complex predicates in (2).

(2) a. *pe.sa.ra.ya.na*
        fly[3SG]-PST-V2.COME-PST=NMLZ.SG
        'It came flying to me.'
     b. *phuŋ   chik.tu.ra=na*
        flower   pluck-3.P-V2.BRING-PST-3.P=NMLZ.SG
        'She plucked and brought a flower.'

According to van Driem (1990), [l] and [r] have a complementary distribution in Eastern Kiranti: [l] occurs word-initially and syllable-initially after stops, and [r] occurs between vowels and as the second component of complex onsets. The complementary distribution of [l] and [r] is a consequence of the general Eas-

Table 3.6: The phonemes /r/ and /l/ in similar environments

/r/	/l/
khorek 'bowl'	*ulippa* 'old'
phiʔwaru a kind of bird	*chalumma* 'second-born daughter'
(Nep.: *koṭerā*)	
tarokma 'start'	*caloŋ* 'maize'
kherek 'this side, hither'	*khelek* 'ant'
caram 'yard'	*sala* 'talk'
khiriri 'spinning round very fast'	*philili* 'jittering'
phimphruwa 'soap berry'	*aphlum* 'hearth stones'
(Nep.: *riṭṭhā*)	
hobrek 'rotten'	*phoplek* '[pouring] at once'
ṭoprak 'leaf plate'	*khesapla* 'a kind of fig tree'

tern Kiranti sound change from */r/ to /y/ in word-initial position, which left /r/ only in word-internal position.[8] It is plausible that [l] and [r], now partly in complementary distribution, were reanalyzed as an allophones as a consequence of this sound change. Van Driem's claim, however, could only partly be confirmed for Yakkha. In contrast to (Phedappe) Limbu (van Driem 1987, Schiering, Hildebrandt & Bickel 2010: 688) and other languages from the Greater Eastern branch of Kiranti such as Lohorung (van Driem 1990: 85), the rhotic is not found as an allophone of /l/ in intervocalic environment in Yakkha (compare the term for 'second-born daughter', *chalumma* (Yakkha) and *sarumma* (Limbu), Limbu data from van Driem & Davids (1985: 131)). Allophonic variation between /l/ and /r/ was not found for any environment in Yakkha. For instance, the negative converb *me(n)...le* does not have an allomorph [me(n)...re] after CV-stems in Yakkha, in contrast to the same converb in Limbu. Furthermore, the question whether C + /r/ are syllabified as .Cr and C + /l/ as C.l could not be answered satisfactorily for Yakkha, based on auditory and phonological evidence. For instance, /r/ as well as /l/ may trigger voicing in a preceding consonant, without any rule becoming

---

[8] The sound change is evident from correspondences such as Yakkha and Limbu *yum* 'salt' and its non-Eastern cognates, e.g., *rum* in Puma (Central Kiranti, Bickel et al. 2009: 393) or *rim* in Dumi (Western Kiranti, van Driem 1993a: 412).

apparent from the current data set (see Table 3.6). To sum up, there is more than sufficient evidence for the phonemic status of /r/ in Yakkha.[9]

It is possibly a rather new development that the rhotic may also appear in syllable-final position. As shown in (3), it may occur at the end of verbal stems that historically used to have a stem-final /t/-augment (cf. §8.1). This syllabification is only licensed when the following syllable starts with /w/. When the stem is followed by vowel sounds, /r/ will be syllabified as onset. Another process leading to syllable-final rhotics is metathesis, which is found in free allophonic variation, as in *tepruki ~ tepurki* 'flea' or *makhruna ~ makhurna* 'black'.

(3) a. *thur-wa-ŋ=na.*
         sew-NPST[3.P]-1SG.A=NMLZ.SG
         'I will sew it.'

     b. *nir-wa-ŋ-ci-ŋ=ha.*
         count-NPST-1SG.A-3NSG.P-1SG.A=NMLZ.SG
         'I will count them.'

3.1.3.5 Aspirated voiced consonants

Aspirated voiced plosives can result from the voicing rule (cf. §3.5), or from sequences of morphemes with consonants followed by /h/, as in (4a). In this way, aspirated consonants that are not found in simple lexemes can be created; they always involve a morpheme boundary, at least diachronically.[10] Another process leading to aspirated voiced consonants is vowel elision. If there is an underlying multimorphemic sequence of the shape /C-V-h-V/, the first vowel gets elided and /h/ surfaces as aspiration of the first consonant (see (4b)).

(4) a. *khe.i.ŋha*
         /kheʔ-i-ŋ=ha/
         go[PST]-1PL-EXCL=NMLZ.NSG
         'We went.'

---

[9] The postulation of a phoneme /r/ has implications for a possible orthography for future Yakkha materials. One of the current local orthographies, used, e.g., in Kongren (2007b) and in several school books (Jimi, Kongren & Jimi 2009), conflated /r/ and /l/ under the grapheme <ल>, the Devanagari letter for <l>. This turned out to be very impractical for the readers. It is not only too much abstracted away from the actual pronunciation, but also not justified by the phonological facts. It is my recommendation to change this in future publications, i.e., to write <र> (r) when a sound is pronounced as a rhotic and <ल> (l) when a sound is pronounced as a lateral.

[10] An exception is the word *ŋhai* 'fish stomach (dish)', for which no transparent multimorphemic etymology is available.

b. *ca.mha.ci*
/ca-ma=ha=ci/
eat-INF[DEONT]=NMLZ.NSG=NSG
'They have to be eaten.'

The environment that is required for the vowel elision is also provided by other forms of the verbal inflectional paradigm. In example (5), the underlying sequence /-ka=ha/ ([-gaha] due to intervocalic voicing) licenses the elision of the preceding vowel, which results in the realization of /h/ as aspiration of [g].

(5) a. *tun.di.wa.gha*
/tund-i-wa-ka=ha/
understand[3A]-2.P-NPST-2=NMLZ.NSG
'He/she/they understand(s) you.'

b. *tum.me.cu.ci.gha*
/tund-meʔ-ci-u-ci-ka=ha/
understand-NPST-DU.A-3.P-3NSG.P-2=NMLZ.NSG
'You (dual) understand them.'

3.2 Syllable structure

This section describes the parameters for the possible syllables in Yakkha. The structure of the syllable is maximally CCVC, i.e., VC, CV, CCV and CVC are possible as well. If a word-initial syllable starts with a vowel, a glottal stop is prothesized to yield a minimal onset. Syllables with CVV structure occur only in the form of diphthongs (see §3.1.2 above). They are exceedingly rare, and they can generally be traced back to bisyllabic or bimorphemic contexts. Syllables containing diphthongs are always open.

In a simple onset, any consonant can occur, with the exception of /r/, which got replaced by /y/ diachronically in Eastern Kiranti. Among the complex onsets, two sets have to be distinguished. The first set has the general shape CL, where L stands for liquids and glides. In this type of syllable, the first consonant can be a plosive, a fricative, an affricate or a nasal, while the second consonant can only be a liquid (/l/ or /r/) or a glide (/y/ or /w/). The onsets containing /y/ or /w/ result from contracted CVCV sequences diachronically. Some alternations between a monosyllabic and a bisyllabic structure, like *cwa ~ cu.wa* 'beer', *chwa ~ chu.wa* 'sugarcane', *nwak ~ nu.wak* 'bird' and *yaŋcuklik ~ yaŋcugulik* 'ant' suggest this. Comparison with related languages like Belhare and Chintang provides further evidence for a former bisyllabic structure: Chintang and Belhare have *cuwa* and *cua*, respectively, for 'water', and Belhare furthermore has *nua* for 'bird' (Bickel 1997a; Rai et al. 2011). For Athpare, both bisyllabic and monosyllabic forms are attested (Ebert 1997a).

On the other hand, complex onsets are not particularly uncommon in Tibeto-Burman. Word-initially, the status of CL sequences as complex onsets is robust, but word-internally, alternative syllabifications would be theoretically possible. This possibility can be ruled out at least for the clusters involving aspirated plosives, because aspirated plosives may never occur syllable-finally. A segmentation like [kith.rik.pa] or [aph.lum] would violate the restriction on a well-formed syllable coda in Yakkha, so that it has to be [ki.thrik.pa] and [a.phlum] ('policeman' and 'hearth', respectively). For unaspirated plosives, it is hard to tell how they are syllabified. Not all logically possible onsets occur, and some are only possible in morphologically complex (both inflected and derived) words. Some examples of complex onsets are provided in Table 3.7 and Table 3.8. Onset types not shown in the tables do not occur.

Table 3.7: Complex onsets with liquids

	/l/	/r/
/p/	*i.plik* 'twisted'	*ca.pra* 'spade'
/ph/	*a.phlum* 'trad. hearth'	*phim.phru.wa* 'soap berry'
/k/	*saklum* 'frustration'	*thaŋ.kra* 'store for grains'
/kh/	(-)	*ʈu.khruk* 'head'
/s/	(-)	*mik.srumba* 'blind person'
/n/	*nlu.ya.ha* 'they said'	(-)

The second set of onsets has the shape NC, where N stands for an unspecified nasal and C for any stem-initial consonant. This type of onset is found only when one of the nasal prefixes is attached to a stem, never in monomorphemic syllables, and never in syllables inside a word. The value of the nasal is conditioned by the place of articulation of the following consonant. Based on auditory evidence, I conclude that the nasal is not syllabified. However, as the processes related to prosody or to morphophonology either exclude prefixes from their domain or they apply across syllable boundaries as well, I could not find independent evidence for this claim. The nasal prefixes may have the following morphological content: 3PL.S/A and negation in verbs (see (6a) and (6b)), a second person possessive in nouns (see (6c)), and a distal relation in spatial adverbs and demonstratives (see (6d) and (6e)).

Table 3.8: Complex onsets with glides

	/w/	/y/
/p/	(-)	*pyaŋ.na* 'He/she gave it to me.'
/ph/	*tam.phwak* 'hair'	*ci.sa.bhya* 'It cooled down.'
/t/	*twa* 'forehead'	(-)
/ʈh/	*ʈhwaŋ* 'smelly' (IDEOPH)	(-)
/c/	*cwa* 'heart'	*cya* 'child'
/ch/	*chwa* 'sugarcane'	*op.chyaŋ.me* 'firefly'
/k/	(-)	*kya* 'Come up!'
/kh/	*o.sen.khwak* 'bone'	*khya* 'Go!'
/s/	*swak* 'secretly'	*sya.na* 'He/she died.'
/n/	*nwak* 'bird'	*(ayupma) nyu.sa.ha* 'I am tired.'

(6) a.   *mbya.gha*
          /N-pi?-a-ka=ha/
          3PL.A-give-PST-2.P=NMLZ.NSG
          'They gave it to you.'

     b.   *ŋkhyan.na*
          /N-khe?-a-n=na/
          NEG-go[3SG]-PST-NEG=NMLZ.SG
          'He did not go.'

     c.   *mbaŋ*
          /N-paŋ/
          2SG.POSS-house
          'your house'

     d.   *ŋkha?.la*
          /N-kha?.la/
          DIST-like_this
          'like that'

     e.   *nnhe*
          /N-nhe/
          DIST-here
          'there'

The coda is restricted to nasals, unaspirated plosives and, rarely, /r/ (cf. §3.1.3.4 above). The plosives are often unreleased or neutralized to [?] in the coda, unless

they are at the end of a word. While the glottal stop frequently occurs in syllable
codas, it is never found at the end of a phonological word (as defined by the stress
domain).

Figure 3.2 summarizes the possible syllable in Yakkha. If the form of a morpheme does not agree with the syllable structure, several strategies may apply.
If, for instance, a verbal stem ends in two consonants (C-s, C-t), as *chimd* 'ask'
or *yuks* 'put', and a vowel follows the stem in an inflected form, the stem-final
consonant becomes the onset of the next syllable (see (7)). If a consonant follows
the stem, the final consonant of the stem is deleted (see (8)).

ONSET		NUCLEUS	CODA
any consonant (except /r/)			unasp. plosive,
obstruent + liquid, glide		any vowel	nasal,
nasal + any consonant (except /r/)			/r/
any consonant (except /r/)		diphthong	

Figure 3.2: The syllable

(7)   a.   *chim.duŋ.na*
            /chimd-u-ŋ=na/
            ask-3.P[PST]-1SG.A=NMLZ.SG
            'I asked him.'

      b.   *chim.daŋ*
            /chimd-a-ŋ/
            ask-IMP-1SG.P
            'Ask me!'

(8)   a.   *chim.nen.na*
            /chimd-nen=na/
            ask-1>2[PST]=NMLZ.SG
            'I asked you.'

      b.   *men.chim.le*
            /men-chimd-le/
            NEG-ask-CVB
            'without asking'

In certain morphological environments and in fast speech, more complex onsets are possible, with the form NCL (nasal-consonant-liquid/glide), but this is restricted to particular inflected verb forms, namely third person plural or negated nonpast forms of verbs with open stems (or with CV? stems) (see (9)). Each part of the onset belongs to another morpheme. The complex cluster is a consequence of the deletion of the stem vowel. This process is further restricted to stems with back vowels (/a/, /u/ and /o/).

(9) a.   *nlwa.na*
          /N-lu?-wa=na/
          3PL.A-tell-NPST[3.P]=NMLZ.SG
          'They will tell him.'

     b.   *njwa.ŋan.na*
          /N-ca-wa-ŋa-n=na/
          NEG-eat-NPST-1SG.A[3.P]-NEG=NMLZ.SG
          'I will not eat it.'

3.3 The phonological treatment of Nepali and English loans

The phonological features of Yakkha are also reflected by the treatment of Nepali and English loans, as shown in Tables 3.9 and 3.10. Several processes may apply to adjust non-native lexemes to Yakkha phonology. Apart from the regular processes discussed below, many changes in the vowel qualities can be encountered, but they cannot be ascribed to any regular sound change.

As adjacent vowels are a marked structure in Yakkha, sequences of vowels, as well as vowels which are separated only by /h/, are typically changed to one vowel. The intervocalic /h/ is, however, not completely lost, but preserved as aspiration of the preceding consonant, as shown by the last three examples of Table 3.9. This process happens irrespective of how the words are stressed in Nepali.

Another typical process is the change of nasal vowels to nasal consonants:[11] hortative verb forms like *jum* 'Let's go!' or *herum* 'Let's have a look!' seem to have been built in analogy to the shape of Yakkha hortative verb forms, which also end in -*um*, at least in the transitive verbs. The words *ʈhoŋ*, *alenci* and *gumthali* illustrate the same process (and also the change of diphthongs to simple vowels).

---

[11] Marginally, nasal vowels may occur in Yakkha, but the environments are highly restricted, and a nasal realization of a vowel is always motivated by an underlying nasal consonant (cf. §3.5).

Table 3.9: Nepali loans in Yakkha

YAKKHA	NEPALI	GLOSS
jum	*jā.aũ*	'Let us go.'
herum	*'he.raũ*	'Let us have a look.'
ṭhoŋ	*ṭhāũ*	'place'
gumthali	*gaũthali*	'swallow'
alenci	*alaĩci*	'cardamom'
tuk.khi	*dukha*	'sorrow, pain'
du.ru	*dudh*	'(animals') milk'
chen	*ca.'hĩ*	(topic particle)
bhenik	*bi.'hā.na*	'morning'
bhya	*'bi.hā*	'wedding'

Table 3.10: English loans in Yakkha

YAKKHA	GLOSS
'roṭ	'road'
'phlim	'film'
'phren	'friend'
is.'ṭep	'step'
is.'kul	'school'

Some loans show the neutralization of voiced and voiceless consonants that is typical for Eastern Kiranti, e.g., *tukkhi* (from Nepali *dukha* 'sorrow, pain'). Probably, such words entered the Yakkha language in an earlier stage of the Nepali-Yakkha contact, when people were not yet bilingual. Nowadays there are many Nepali loans in Yakkha that are pronounced as in Nepali.

The word *duru* (from Nepali *dudh* 'milk') shows a strategy to satisfy the constraint against aspirated plosives at the end of the syllable or word (and against aspirated voiced plosives in general).[12]

---

[12] The use of goat and cow's milk and other milk products is very rare in Yakkha culture (noted also by Russell 1992: 128–30), and, thus, the borrowing of this word is not surprising.

Another typical process encountered was closing word-final open syllables by /k/. For example, *belā* 'time' becomes [belak], *bihāna* 'morning' becomes [bhenik] and *duno ~ duna* 'leaf bowl' becomes [donak] in Yakkha. Words that end with consonants other than /k/ may also be modified to end in /k/, e.g., *chu-ruk* 'cigarette', from Nepali *churoṭ*.

Some English loanwords, shown in Table 3.10, illustrate that complex codas and voiced codas are not acceptable in Yakkha. Word-initial clusters of fricative and plosive are also marked, and a vowel is prothesized to yield a syllable that corresponds at least to some of the prosodic constraints of Yakkha (but this also happens in the pronunciation of Nepali native speakers). Finally, as Yakkha has no distinctions of length or tenseness for vowels, the difference between, e.g., English *sheep* and *ship* is usually not noticed or produced if such words are borrowed. Both words are pronouned with a short [i], that is however slightly more tense than in English *ship*.[13]

The words selected here illustrate how some of the principles of the Yakkha sound system and the phonological rules are applied to non-native material. The Yakkha phonology in borrowed lexemes is not equally prominent among speakers. It depends on many factors, most obviously the proficiency in the donor languages and the time-depth of the borrowing.

3.4 Stress assignment

This section deals with the rules for stress assignment and the domain to which these rules apply. The rules for stress assignment can be laid out as follows: by default, the first syllable carries main stress. Closed syllables, however, attract stress. If there are closed syllables, the main stress moves to the last closed syllable, as long as it is not the final syllable of a word, demonstrated by the examples in Table 3.11 for nouns,[14] and in (10) for inflected verbal forms. The forms in these examples differ with regard to the position of the last closed syllable in the word, and thus, by the condition that makes the stress move from the first syllable towards the end (but only up to the penultimate syllable). Predicates that consist of more than one verbal stem behave like simple verbs in this respect (see (11)).

---

[13] The words displayed in the tables occurred regularly in at least some speakers' idiolects. Nevertheless, I do not want to make any strong claims about what is borrowed and what results from code-switching, as this is not the purpose of my study.

[14] Both simple and complex nouns (at least historically) can be found in this table. Their etymology does not affect stress assignment, though.

Table 3.11: Default stress

YAKKHA	GLOSS
ʹom.phu	'verandah'
ʹkho.rek	'bowl'
ʹca.ram	'yard'
ʹko.ko.mek	'butterfly'
ʹol.lo.bak	'fast'
ʹtok.ca.li	'buttocks'
ʹyok.yo.rok	'beyond, a bit further'
ʹkam.ni.bak	'friend'
wa.ʹriŋ.ba	'tomato'
cuʔ.ʹlum.phi	'stele, pillar, stick'
nep.ʹnep.na	'short one'
op.ʹchyaŋ.me	'firefly'
cik.ci.ʹgeŋ.ba	'Bilaune tree'

(10) a. ʹtum.me.cu.na
          /tund-meʔ-ci-u=na/
          understand-NPST-DU.A-3.P=NMLZ.SG
          'They (dual) understand him.'

      b. ˌndum.men.ʹcun.na
          /n-tund-meʔ-n-ci-u-n=na/
          NEG-understand-NPST-NEG-DU.A-3.P-NEG=NMLZ.SG
          'They (dual) do not understand him.'

      c. ˌtum.meʔ.ʹnen.na
          /tund-meʔ-nen=na/
          understand-NPST-1>2=NMLZ.SG
          'I understand you.'

(11) a. ʹluk.ta.khya.na
          /lukt-a-kheʔ-a=na/
          run-PST-V2.GO-PST[3SG]=NMLZ.SG
          'He ran away.'

b.   *luk.ta.ˈkhyaŋ.na*
       /lukt-a-kheʔ-a-ŋ=na/
       run-PST-V2.GO-PST-1SG=NMLZ.SG
       'I ran away.'

Examples like *ˈkam.ni.bak* 'friend' show that the stress never moves to the final syllable, even when the syllable is heavy. Patterns where the final syllable is stressed are possible though, because prefixes are not part of the stress domain. In monosyllabic nouns that host a possessive prefix, the stress generally remains on the stem, as in (12).

(12)   a.   *a.ˈpaŋ*
          /a-paŋ/
          1SG.POSS-house
          'my house'
    b.   *u.ˈphuŋ*
          /u-phuŋ/
          3SG.POSS-flower
          'his/her flower'

Yakkha has a category of obligatorily possessed nouns, and some of them, mostly kin terms, have undergone lexicalization. They are all monosyllabic. With regard to stress, the prefix is no longer distinguished from the stem, as shown by examples like *ˈa.mum* 'grandmother', *ˈa.pum* 'grandfather', *ˈa.na* 'elder sister', *ˈa.phu* 'elder brother'.[15] The words are, however, not morphologically opaque, as the first person possessive prefix *a-* can still be replaced by other prefixes in a given context, and then, the stress pattern changes to the expected one, e.g., *u.ˈmum* 'his grandmother'. An example for lexicalized obligatory possession beyond the domain of kinship is the word *ˈu.wa* 'liquid, nectar, water'.

The shift of stress described above occurs only in monosyllabic kin terms. In bisyllabic words, the stress is again on the first syllable of the stem or on the syllable that is closed. Terms like *a.ˈnun.cha* 'younger sibling' (both sexes) or *a.ŋo.ˈţeŋ.ma* 'sister-in-law' illustrate this.

As Yakkha is a predominantly suffixing language, there are not many prefixes that could illustrate the fact that the domain of stress does not include prefixes. Apart from the possessive prefixes, evidence is provided by reduplicated adjec-

---

[15] In the domain of kinship, forms with first person singular inflection are also used in default contexts, when no particular possessor is specified. The default possessive prefix for nouns denoting part-whole relations is the third person singular *u-*.

tives and adverbs like *pha.ʼphap* 'entangled, messy' or *son.ʼson* 'slanted, on an angle'. The base for these words are verbal stems, in this case *phaps* 'entangle, mess up' and *sos* 'lie slanted'. Their stress pattern allows the conclusion that this kind of reduplication is a prefixation (for the other morphophonological processes involved cf. §3.5).

Clitics generally do not affect stress assignment, since they are attached to the phrase and thus to a unit that is built of words to which stress has already been assigned.[16] Examples are provided in (13) for case clitics and in (14) for discourse-structural clitics.

(13)   a.   *ʼkho.rek.ci*
                /khorek=ci/
                bowl=NSG
                'the bowls'
    b.   *ʼtaŋ.khyaŋ.bhaŋ*
                /taŋkhyaŋ=phaŋ/
                sky=ABL
                'from the sky'
    c.   *ʼkam.ni.bak.ci.nuŋ*
                /kamnibak=ci=nuŋ/
                friend=NSG=COM
                'with the friends'

(14)   a.   *a.ʼyu.bak.se*
                /a-yubak=se/
                1SG.POSS-goods=RESTR
                'only my goods'
    b.   *u.ʼkam.ni.bak.ko*
                /u-kamnibak=ko/
                3SG.POSS-friend=TOP
                'his friend(, though)'

An exception to this rule is the nominalization in *=na* and *=ha*. These nominalizers may attach to the verbal inflection, in relative clauses, complement clauses or in main clauses (see §13.3). They are categorically unrestricted (i.e., taking not only verbal hosts), and not an obligatory part of the verbal inflection. However,

---

[16] The term 'clitic' may have two readings: (i) affixes that are categorically unrestricted (represented by the equals sign '=' instead of a hyphen '-'), or (ii) phonologically bound words, like demonstratives. The latter are written separately in the orthography used in this work, as they may also appear independently and they have the ability to head phrases.

if they attach to the verb, they are part of the stress domain. If this was not the case, stress assignment as in *luk.ta.'khyaŋ.na* 'I ran away.' would be unexpected, because then the stress would be on the final syllable of the stress domain, which violates the prosodic constraints of Yakkha. The anomalous behavior of the nominalizers is not unexpected in light of the fact that they are being reanalyzed from discourse markers to part of the inflectional morphology.[17]

It is hard to tell whether there is secondary stress. Even in words with five syllables, like in (14b), no secondary stress could be detected. Secondary stress was clearly audible in compounds such as those shown in Table 3.12. It is found on the first syllable of the second part of the compound, while the main stress remains on the first syllable of the whole compound. Such compounds may override the general restriction against stress on word-final syllables. In inflected verb forms, secondary stress can be found on the verbal stem, e.g., in ˌndum.men.cu.'ŋan.na 'We (dual) do not understand him.'; cf. also examples (10b) and (10c) above.

Table 3.12: Stress in compounds

YAKKHA	GLOSS
'ko.len.ˌluŋ	'marble stone' ('smooth stone')
'pi.pi.ˌsiŋ	'straw, pipe' ('([redup]suck-wood')
'yo.niŋ.ˌkhe.niŋ	'hither and thither' ('while thither-while hither')
'mo.niŋ.ˌto.niŋ	'up and down' ('while down-while up')
'sa.meʔ.ˌchoŋ	'protoclan' ('clan-top')
'lim.bu.ˌkhim	a clan name, composed of the term for the Limbu ethnic group and a word for 'house' in many Kiranti languages

Finally, one exception to the stress rules has to be mentioned. Yakkha has several triplicated ideophonic adverbs, where the first syllable is the base and the second and third syllable rhyme on the vowel, but replace the initial consonant with a liquid, a glide or a coronal stop, e.g., [se.re.'reː] 'drizzling', or [hi.wi.'wiː] 'pleasantly breezy' (cf. §6.4). In addition to the triplication, the vowel of the last syllable is lengthened, and the stress is always on the last syllable in these adverbs.

---

[17] For instance, they also show number agreement with verbal arguments, with =na indicating singular and =ha indicating nonsingular or non-countable reference.

3.5 Morphophonological processes

This section discusses the various morphophonological processes in Yakkha. The domains to which certain rules and processes apply are not always congruent. The existence of more than one phonological domain and the problems for theoretical approaches that assume a prosodic hierarchy have already been discussed for Limbu, another Eastern Kiranti language (Hildebrandt 2007; Schiering, Hildebrandt & Bickel 2010). Yakkha adds further support to challenges for the assumption that domains of prosodic rules are necessarily hierarchically ordered.

The following phonological domains could be identified in Yakkha morphophonology: the rules for stress assignment disregard prefixes and phrasal affixes. In contrast, the vowel harmony establishes a relation between the prefix and the stem only, ignoring the suffixes. The voicing rule has the broadest domain (cf. §3.5.1 below). Furthermore, some rules differentiate between morphologically simple and complex words (compounds). The voicing rule and also various repair operations of marked structures like adjacent obstruents are sensitive to morpheme boundaries, the latter, more precisely, to stem boundaries.

	prefix	stem(s)	suffixes	clitics
(1)		stress assignment		
(2-a)		voicing/N_		
(2-b)			voicing/V_V	
(3)	vowel harmony			

Figure 3.3: Summary of phonological domains

Figure 3.3 provides an overview of the different domains to which the morphophonological processes apply.[18] §3.5.1 deals with the voicing rule. The prefixation of underspecified nasals is treated in §3.5.2. A case of vowel harmony is described in §3.5.3. Adjacent vowels are not preferred in Yakkha, and strategies to avoid such undesirable sequences are treated in §3.5.4. §3.5.5 deals with consonants in intervocalic environments. §3.5.6 describes assimilations. The employment of nasals to repair marked sequences of adjacent obstruents as well as adjacent

---

[18] The morphological structure of the word is slightly simplified in the table, disregarding complex predicates that consist of more than one verbal stem. Complex predicates are treated identically to simple words by the stress rule and the voicing rule (except for the behavior of /c/).

$$\begin{array}{l}\text{C.UNVOICED} \rightarrow \text{C.VOICED/N\_} \\ \text{C.UNVOICED} \rightarrow \text{C.VOICED/V\_V} \\ \text{C.UNVOICED} \rightarrow \text{C.VOICED/\_L} \end{array}$$

Figure 3.4: Voicing rules

vowels in complex predicates is discussed in §3.5.7. Finally, §3.5.8 is concerned with a process of nasal copying which is found in the verbal inflection of many Kiranti languages.

3.5.1 Voicing

In Yakkha, unaspirated plosives and the affricate are voiced in intervocalic and postnasal environments and before liquids and glides, as schematized in Figure 3.4, where C stands for unaspirated plosives and the affricate, N for nasals and L for liquids and glides. Voicing predominantly applies at morpheme boundaries, but also inside words that, at least synchronically, cannot be split up further into separate morphemes. The rule is illustrated by example (15), with the stem-final /k/ of the verb *yokma* 'search', and by (16), with the stem-initial /t/ of the verb *tama* 'come'.

(15)   a.   *yoknenna.*
           /yok-nen=na/
           search-1>2[PST]=NMLZ.SG
           'I looked for you.'

       b.   *yogu*
           /yok-u/
           search-3.P[IMP]
           'Look for it!'

(16)   a.   *tameʔna.*
           /ta-meʔ=na/
           come[3SG]-NPST=NMLZ.SG
           'He will come.'

       b.   *ndamenna*
           /N-ta-meʔ-n=na/
           NEG-come[3SG]-NPST-NEG=NMLZ.SG
           'He will not come.'

Some environments containing liquids and glides that trigger voicing are given in Table 3.13, with both monomorphemic and multimorphemic words. Some words are found with either pronunciation, and the current conclusion is that allegro speech leads to voicing, and that this became the norm for some words, but not for others.

Table 3.13: Voicing before liquids and glides

	YAKKHA	GLOSS
/pl/	taplik ~ tablik	'story'
	hoblek	[manner of throwing or pouring] 'the whole/ at once'
/pr/	hobrek	'completely [rotten]'
	khibrum.ba	'fog' (also derogative for people of Caucasian phenotype)
/tr/	hoŋdrup	'pig as present for in-laws'
/kw/	cogwana	'he does it'
/pw/	ubwaha	'he earns [money]'
/khy/	maghyam	'old woman'
/tr/	phetrak ~ phedrak	'petal'
/pr/	capra ~ cabra	'spade with long handle'
/pl/	lupliba ~ lubliba	'earthquake'

As shown above, the voicing rule applies to lexical stems, but it also applies to inflectional morphemes and phrasal affixes (see (17)). Thus, the domain for voicing is bigger than the domain that is relevant for stress, as phrasal affixes undergo voicing, and as prefixes may trigger voicing as well.

(17) a. *hoŋmacibego.*
          /hoŋma=ci=pe=ko/
          river=NSG=LOC=TOP
          'in the rivers(, though)'
      b. *tummecuganabu.*
          /tum-meʔ-c-u-ka=na=pu/
          understand-NPST-DU-3.P.-2.A=NMLZ.SG=REP
          '(People say that) you (dual) understand him/her.'

After this outline of the basic properties of voicing in Yakkha, let us now turn to its details. The voicing rule needs further specification for prefixes. While nasal prefixes trigger voicing, vocalic prefixes are excluded from the voicing domain, irrespective of other factors such as stress. I have shown in §3.4 above that voicing is triggered neither in *a.'paŋ* 'my house' nor in *'a.pum* '(my) grandfather'. Only prefixes that consist of a nasal trigger voicing, as shown in (18).

(18)   a.   *mbaŋ*
            /N-paŋ/
            2sg.poss-house
            'your house'

       b.   *ŋ-gamnibak*
            /N-kamnibak/
            2sg.poss-friend
            'your friend'

In §3.4 on stress assignment, I mentioned reduplicated adjectives and adverbs. They also provide further evidence for the restriction of the voicing rule to nasal prefixes. I will exemplify this with the two adjectives *bumbum* 'compact and heavy' and *tutu* 'far up' (cf. §6.4 for more examples). The base of the adjective *bumbum* has the corresponding verbal stem *pups ~ pum* 'fold, press, tuck up', while the base of *tutu* is the adverbial root *tu* 'uphill'. In analogy to the stress behavior, my default assumption is that the reduplication is a prefixation, although the voicing facts would support either option. The stem allomorph *pum* is reduplicated to /pum-pum/ (the stem *pups* surfaces only before vowels) and, subsequently, the stem undergoes voicing, which is then spread to the first syllable to preserve the identity between the base and the reduplicated morpheme. In contrast to this, in *tutu* 'far up', the intervocalic environment that results from the reduplication does not trigger voicing.

As stated in the beginning of this section, voicing does not apply to aspirated plosives, at least not in the Tumok dialect (see (19)). Exceptions are found only in a handful of lexemes, mostly in ideophonic adverbs (see §6.4.4). However, aspirated plosives (and the affricate) get voiced when they occur in function verbs,[19] i.e., in word-medial position (see (20)). These complex predicates also constitute one domain for stress assignment, in contrast, for instance, to the southern neighbour language Chintang, where each verbal stem in a complex predicate constitutes a stress domain on its own (Bickel et al. 2007a: 57).

---

[19] Function verbs are grammaticalized verbs, glossed as 'V2' (see Chapter 10.)

(19) a. *ŋkhyanna.*
        /N-khy-a-n=na/
        NEG-go[3SG]-PST-NEG=NMLZ.SG
        'He did not go.'

     b. *mempha?le.*
        /meN-phat-le/
        NEG-help-CVB
        'without helping'

(20) a. *kam   cog-a-ghond-a-ga=i.*
        /kam   cok-a-khond-a-ka=i/
        work   do-IMP-V2.ROAM-IMP-2=EMPH
        'Go on working.'

     b. *hab-a-bhoks-a=na.*
        /hap-a-phoks-a=na/
        cry-PST-V2.SPLIT[3SG]-PST=NMLZ.SG
        'She broke out in tears.'

Yakkha has a class of composite predicates that consist of a noun and a verb. They show varying degrees of morphosyntactic freedom, but they are generally not as tightly fused as the verb-verb predicates. This is also reflected by stress: noun and verb each have their own stress, even if this results in adjacent stress. Voicing, too, treats both components as separate items (see (21)).[20]

(21) a. *'sa.ya   'pok.ma*
        /saya   pok-ma/
        head.soul raise-INF
        'to raise the head soul' (a ritual)

     b. *'luŋ.ma 'tuk.ma*
        /luŋma   tuk-ma/
        liver   pour-INF
        'to love'

     c. *'sak   'tu.ga.nai?*
        /sak   tug-a=na=i/
        hunger ache[3SG]-PST=NMLZ.SG=Q
        'Are you hungry?/ Is he hungry?/ Are they hungry?'

---

[20] These predicates form a lexical unit though, and the nouns do not enjoy the syntactic freedom that is expected of full-fledged arguments. These predicates are best understood as idiomatic phrases (cf. Chapter 9).

Between vowels, voiced stops may further assimilate to their surrounding material and become continuants, as several alternations between intervocalic [b] and [w] show. Thus, *kamnibak* 'friend' may also be pronounced [kamniwak], or the imperative of *apma* 'to come (from a visible distance on the same level)' can alternate between [aba] and [awa]. Like in Belhare (Bickel 1998), intervocalic /t/ may also become a continuant /r/, as some historical stem changes (e.g., **thut* → *thur*) and in function verbs show, e.g., the function verb *ris* that originates in the lexical stem *tis* 'apply, invest', or *raʔ* originating in the lexical stem *taʔ* 'bring (from further away)'.

The suffix *-ci* does not get voiced, neither in verbal nor in nominal inflection, as example (17) has already shown. This exceptional behavior might point towards a more complex historical form of this suffix. The only instance of a voiced marker *-ci* is in the second person dual pronoun *njiŋda* (you), which is complex at least from a historical perspective.

The affricate /tsʰ/ (written <c>) behaves exceptionally in other contexts, too. In the function verb *ca* 'eat' it does not undergo voicing (see (22a)),[21] for which there is no neat explanation yet. Example (22b) shows that voicing does apply to plosives in function verbs, and as example (23) shows, stem-initial /c/ does get voiced in other environments. In some morphemes, the affricate shows free variation, as in the additive focus clitic *=ca*. It is found both voiced and unvoiced, neither related to individual nor to dialectal differences.

(22) a. *incama*
          /in-ca-ma/
          trade-V2.EAT-INF
          'to sell'

      b. *hambiʔma*
          /ham-piʔ-ma/
          distribute-V2.GIVE-INF
          'to distribute (among people)'

(23) a. *njogwana.*
          /n-cok-wa=na/
          3PL.A-do-NPST=NMLZ.SG
          'They will do it.'

      b. *men-ja-le*
          /men-ca-le/
          NEG-eat-CVB
          'without eating'

---

[21] This function verb is the only one with initial /c/.

Another exception to the voicing rule has to be mentioned, as shown in (24a) and (24b). Stem-final /t/ remains voiceless between vowels. If the stem ends with a nasal and /t/, voicing applies, as in (24c), and stem-initial /t/ undergoes voicing as well. The absence of voicing at the end of stems can be explained with the history of the /-t/ final stems. Comparison with Chintang and Belhare (Bickel 2003; Bickel et al. 2007a) shows that there must have been geminated /tt/, resulting from a CVt stem to which the augment -t was added (discussed in §8.1). Voicing does not apply when there is more than one underlying consonant between the vowels.

(24) a. *mituna.*
          /mit-u=na/
          remember[PST]-3.P=NMLZ.SG
          'He remembered it.'

      b. *phatuci!*
          /phat-u-ci/
          help-3.P[IMP]-NSG.P
          'Help them!'

      c. *chem   endugana?*
          /chem   ent-a-u-ka=na/
          song   apply-PST-3.P-2.A=NMLZ.SG
          'Did you put on music?'

3.5.2 The prefixation of underspecified nasals

Yakkha has several nasal prefixes that do not constitute syllables of their own, but result in onsets that consist of prenasalized consonants. The prefixes are under-specified for the place of articulation, and thus they always assimilate to the place of articulation of the following consonant. The nasal prefixes also trigger voic-ing stem-initially, as could already be seen in §3.5.1 above. These nasal prefixes have several morphemic values, already mentioned in §3.2, and repeated here for convenience: they index third person plural S and A arguments on verbs (25a) and verbal negation (25b). The nasal prefixes also encode second person singu-lar possessors on nouns (25c), and in adverbs, they encode a distal relation (see (25d)). If the nasal prefix is attached to a nasal-initial stem, it yields an initial nasal geminate (see (26)).

(25) a. *m-by-a-ga-n=ha.*
          3PL.A-give-PST-2.P-NEG=NMLZ.NSG
          'They gave it to you.'

b. *ŋ-khy-a-n=na.*
NEG-go[3SG]-PST-NEG=NMLZ.SG
'He did not go.'

c. *m-baŋ*
2SG.POSS-house
'your house'

d. *ŋ-khaʔla*
DIST-like_this
'like that'

(26) a. *m-ma*
2SG.POSS-mother
'your mother'

b. *n-nhe*
DIST-here
'there'

If the stem begins with a vowel or /w/, the nasal is realized as a velar nasal (see (27)). This might lead us to the conclusion that actually /ŋ/ is the underlying form and gets assimilated. This would, however, be the only instance of a morphophonological change from a velar nasal to [m] or [n] in Yakkha, and, thus, this option seems unlikely to me.

(27) a. *ŋ-og-wa-ci=ha.*
3PL.A-peck-NPST-3NSG.P=NMLZ.NSG
'They (the roosters) peck them (the chicks).'

b. *ŋ-ikt-haks-u-ci.*
3PL.A-chase-V2.SEND-3.P[PST]-3NSG.P
'They chased them away.'

c. *kham ŋ-wapt-u=ha.*
soil   3PL.A-scratch-3.P[PST]=NMLZ.NSG
'They (the chicken) scratched the ground (they scrabbled about on the ground).'

A syllable with a nasal before the consonant is marked in terms of the sonority hierarchy (Jespersen 1904; Selkirk 1984; Hall 2000). Therefore, the following process can be noticed: if the preceding word (in the same clause) ends with a vowel, the nasal will resyllabify as the coda of the preceding word (see (28)), just as in Belhare (Bickel 2003: 547). I have shown above that the domains for stress and for voicing are not identical. This process adds a third domain of phonological rules to the picture, encompassing two words in terms of stress assignment, as each of the words carries its own stress. Even though the nasal belongs to the preceding word in terms of syllable structure, the choice of the nasal is determined by the following consonant, which also undergoes voicing due to the nasal. This suggests a sequence of morphophonological processes, of which this resyllabification is the last to apply.

(28)   a.   *liŋkhaci   namnuŋ   bagarin   jog-a.*
           /liŋkha=ci   nam=nuŋ   bagari   N-cok-a/
           Linkha=NSG   sun=COM   bet   3PL-do-PST
           'The Linkha clan had a bet with the sun.'   [11_nrr_01.003]

      b.   *chuʔmaŋ   gaksanoŋ,*   ...
           /chuʔ-ma   N-kaks-a-n=hoŋ/
           tie-INF   NEG-agree[3SG]-PST-NEG=SEQ
           'It (the cow) was not okay with being tied, ...'   [11_nrr_01.011]

      c.   *nnam   borakhyamanna.*
           /nna   N-por-a-khy-a-ma-n=na/
           that   NEG-fall-PST-V2.GO[3SG]-PST-NEG=NMLZ.SG
           'That (stele) did not topple over.'   [18_nrr_03.026]

      d.   *ka   heʔniŋcam   mandiʔŋanna.*
           /ka   heʔniŋ=ca   N-mandiʔ-ŋa-n=na/
           1SG   when=ADD   NEG-get_lost-1SG-NEG=NMLZ.SG
           'I would never get lost.'   [18_nrr_03.015]

3.5.3 Vowel harmony

Vowel harmony in Yakkha applies only to one prefix, namely to the possessive prefix *u-* for third person. It has an allomorph *o-* that is triggered when the stressed syllable of the stem contains the mid vowels /e/ or /o/, as illustrated by Table 3.14. Suffixes do not undergo vowel harmony in Yakkha, and neither do other prefixes.

One exceptional case has to be mentioned, the inflected form *khohetu* 'he/she carried it off'. This is a complex verb that consists of the two verbal stems *khuʔ* 'carry (on back)' and *het* (a V2, indicating caused motion away from a reference point). Apparently, the V2 makes the vowel in the first stem change to [o]. However, this is the only instance of vowel harmony that has been encountered beyond the domain defined above.

Table 3.14: Vowel harmony

BEFORE /e/ AND /o/		BEFORE /u/, /i/, /a/	
o-heksaŋbe	'behind her/him'	u-paŋ	'her/his house'
o-hop	'her/his nest'	u-hiŋgilik	'alive'
o-tokhumak	'alone'	u-ţukhruk	'her/his body'
o-senkhwak	'her/his bone'	u-mik	'her/his eye'
o-yok	'her/his place/spot'	u-tiŋgibhak	'its thorn'
o-poŋgalik	'(its) bud'	u-ţaŋ	'its horn'
o-phok	'her/his belly'	u-muk	'her/his hand'
o-ţesraŋ	'reverse'	u-nabhuk	'her/his nose'

3.5.4 Operations to avoid adjacent vowels

The processes that avoid vowel hiatus apply to adjacent vowels as well as to vowels that are separated by a glottal stop.[22] They are found in the verbal domain, since there are no suffixes or clitics beginning with a vowel in the nominal domain.

3.5.4.1 Vowel deletion

The suffixes -a and -u can get deleted when they are adjacent to another vowel. In sequences of /-a-u/, for instance, /a/ gets deleted (see (29a)). This rule, however, also interacts with the morphology. While the past (and imperative) suffix -a is deleted when it is followed by the third person patient marker -u, the same sequence, when it results from the nonpast marker -wa, results in the deletion of -u (see (29b)).

(29)   a.   *tunduŋna.*
       /tund-a-u-ŋ=na/
       understand-PST-3.P-1SG.A=NMLZ.SG
       'I understood her/him.'

       b.   *tundwaŋna.*
       /tund-wa-u-ŋ=na/
       understand-NPST-3.P-1SG.A=NMLZ.SG
       'I understand her/him.'

---

[22] Diachronically, stems ending in a glottal stop used to be CVt stems, and the /t/ got reduced to a glottal stop. Synchronically, stems ending in glottal stop often behave identical to stems that end in a vowel, in terms of morphophonological rules.

Suffix sequences of the underlying form /-a-i/ also result in the deletion of the suffix *-a* (see (30)). When /a/ is part of the stem, however, nothing gets deleted (see (30c)). Note also that intervocalic /h/ may become /y/, as in (30a).

(30) a. *kheiya.*
          /kheʔ-a-i=ha/
          go-PST-1PL=NMLZ.NSG
          'We went.'
      b. *tundigha.*
          /tund-a-i-ka=ha/
          understand[3.A]-PST-2PL-2=NMLZ.NSG
          'They understood you (plural).'
      c. *hakokŋa   caiwa.*
          /hakok=ŋa   ca-i-wa/
          later=INS   eat-1PL-NPST
          'We will eat later.'

Underlying sequences of three vowels are possible with open (CV and CVʔ) stems, in past and imperative forms with a third person patient. In these verb forms, both suffixes are deleted.

(31) a. *piŋ.na*
          /piʔ-a-u-ŋ=na/
          give-PST-3.P-1SG.A=NMLZ.SG
          'I gave it to him.'
      b. *soŋ.na*
          /soʔ-a-u-ŋ=na/
          look-PST-3.P-1SG.A=NMLZ.SG
          'I looked at it.'
      c. *ha!*
          /haʔ-a-u/
          bite-IMP-3.P
          'Bite (into) it!'
      d. *cam.na*
          /ca-a-u-m=na/
          eat-PST-3.P-1PL.A=NMLZ.SG
          'We ate it.'

3.5.4.2 Ablaut

Ablaut is found only in one verb, in *cama* 'eat'. Ablaut in some verbs is not unusual in Kiranti. The stem *ca* has an allomorph *co* that is not predictable from the phonological environment. It occurs when followed by other vowels, but not in all environments that would predict such a change if this was the condition. Its distribution over the paradigm is shown in Chapter 8, on page 248.

3.5.4.3 Insertion of glides

If the back vowels (/a/, /o/ and /u/) belong to a verbal stem and are followed by the suffix -a, the glide /y/ is inserted to avoid vowel hiatus. The morphological environment for these vowel sequences is provided by intransitive verbs, as well as in in transitive verb forms with first or second person patients (see (32)). A similar process can be encountered with stems that end in /ʔ/, with /ʔ/ being replaced by /y/, as in (32d).

(32) a. *mima uhoŋbe   uyana.*
          /mima u-hoŋ=pe   u-a=na/
          mouse 3SG.POSS-hole=LOC enter[3SG]-PST=NMLZ.SG
          'The mouse entered her mousehole.'

  b. *nam ayana.*
      /nam a-a=na/
      sun descend[3SG]-PST=NMLZ.SG
      'The sun went down.'

  c. *tayana.*
      /ta-a=na/
      come[3SG]-PST=NMLZ.SG
      'He came.'

  d. *soyaŋgana.*
      /soʔ-a-ŋ-ka=na/
      look-PST-1SG.P-2.A=NMLZ.SG
      'You looked at me.'

3.5.4.4 Gliding

Front vowels of verbal stems may also be reduced to glides when they are adjacent to /a/. The syllable nucleus of the stem becomes part of the onset, and the word is again reduced by one syllable, which is obvious because of the stress pattern. Examples (33a) and (33b) illustrate this for stems ending in glottal stops and (33c) shows the same process with an open stem.

(33) a. *'khyaŋ.na*
          /kheʔ-a-ŋ=na/
          go-PST-1SG=NMLZ.SG
          'I went.'
      b. *'pyaŋ.na*
          /piʔ-a-ŋ=na/
          go[3SG.A]-PST-1SG.P=NMLZ.SG
          'He gave it to me.'
      c. *'sya.na*
          /si-a=na/
          die[3SG]-PST=NMLZ.SG
          'He/she died.'

This may also happen when the stem has a back vowel. So far, this was only encountered for the verb *luʔma* (see (34)). Other verbs, e.g., *chuʔma* 'tie' appear in the expected form, e.g., *chuyaŋna* 'he tied me (to something)'.

(34) a. *'lyaŋ.na*
          /luʔ-a-ŋ=na/
          tell[3SG.A]-PST-1SG.P=NMLZ.SG
          'He told me.'
      b. *'lya.ha*
          /luʔ-a=ha/
          tell[3SG.A;1.P]-PST=NMLZ.NSG
          'He told us.'

3.5.5 Consonants in sonorous environment

3.5.5.1 Intervocalic /h/ and /w/

Intervocalic /h/ and /w/ also trigger vowel deletion. If the two vowels surrounding /w/ or /h/ have the same quality, the preceding vowel is deleted, even if this is the stem vowel. The deletion leads to new consonant clusters, i.e., to consonants followed by /w/ (see (35a)), or to aspirated voiced plosives (see (35b)).

(35) a. *njwan.na*
          /n-ca-wa-n=na/
          NEG-eat[3SG.A]-NPST-NEG=NMLZ.SG
          'He/she does not eat it.'

b.   *tun.di.wa.gha*
/tund-i-wa-ka=ha/
understand[3.A]-2PL.P-NPST-2=NMLZ.NSG
'He/they understand you (pl).'

If the vowels do not have the same quality and there is a transition from a close to an open vowel, intervocalic /h/ may also change to /y/ (see (36)).

(36)   a.   *tun.dwa.ci.ya*
/tund-wa-ci=ha/
understand[3SG.A]-NPST-3NSG.P=NMLZ.NSG
'He/she understands them.'

        b.   *ci.ya*   *maŋ.cwa*
             /ci=ha   maŋcwa/
             get_cold=NMLZ.NSG   water
             'cold water'

The change of vowels to glides and the realization of underlying /h/ as aspiration can even cross stem boundaries, as the following complex predicate, consisting of three verbal stems, shows (37). The underlying stems /piʔ/ and /heks/ fuse into [bhyeks].[23]

(37)   *a.cya*   *tu.ga.bhyek.sana*
       /a-cya   tuk-a-piʔ-heks-a=na/
       1SG.POSS-child   get_ill[3SG]-PST-V2.GIVE-V2.CUT-PST=NMLZ.SG
       'My child is about to get ill.'

3.5.5.2 Nasals in sonorous environment

Nasals in sonorous environments are prone to phonological alternations. Nasal vowels are not part of the phoneme set of Yakkha. They may be generated, however, in intervocalic environments at morpheme boundaries, or when a nasal occurs between a vowel and a liquid or a glide. This happens when the negative converb (marked by prefix and suffix: *meN-Σ-le*) attaches to an open stem, or to a stem with initial /w/, /y/ or /l/. The nasal in *meN-Σ-le* is not specified. If it attaches to stems that have initial consonants, it assimilates to their place of articulation. Examples are provided in Table 3.15.

---

[23] The V2 *-piʔ* indicates that a participant (the speaker, the subject or even someone else) is affected by the event, and the V2 *-heks* specifies the temporal reference of the event as immediate prospective. In pronunciation, they get fused to [bhyeks].

Another process producing nasal vowels was noticed in allegro forms of complex predicates such as *ŋonsipma* 'feel shy' and *thensipma* 'fit, suit', which were pronounced *ŋoĩsipma* and *theĩsipma* in fast speech.

Table 3.15: Nasals in sonorous environment

STEM	CITATION FORM	NEGATIVE CONVERB
/waʔ/	*waʔma* 'wear, put on'	*mẽ.waʔ.le* 'without wearing'
/a/	*ama* 'descend'	*mẽ.a.le* 'without descending'
/u/	*uma* 'enter'	*mẽ.u.le* 'without entering'
/lap/	*lapma* 'seize, catch'	*mẽ.lap.le* 'without catching'
/yok/	*yokma* 'search'	*mẽ.yok.le* 'without searching'

3.5.6 Assimilations

Syllable-final coronals assimilate to coronal fricatives, yielding a geminated fricative [sː] (written <ss>) (see (38)). This assimilation is connected to stress. In unstressed syllabes, no assimilation occurs, and the stem-final /t/ is simply deleted before fricatives (see (38c)). Occasionally, stem-final glottal stops can also undergo this assimilation, but this is subject to free variation.

(38) a. *es.se*
       /et-se/
       apply-SUP
       'in order to apply'

   b. *mis.saŋ*
       /mit-saŋ/
       remember-SIM
       'remembering'

   c. *ki.si.saŋ*
       /kisit-saŋ/
       be_afraid-SIM
       'being afraid'

The following examples show that this process does not apply to the other plosives /k/ and /p/. Stems ending in a glottal stop are treated like open stems, illustrated by (39c). Stems that have a coronal augment yield an underlying sequence

of three consonants when followed by /s/. In this case, nothing gets assimilated.
The general rule for augmented stems followed by consonants applies, i.e., the
augment is simply omitted, as illustrated in (40).

(39) a. *ap.se*
          /ap-se/
          shoot-SUP
          'in order to shoot'

      b. *cok.se*
          /cok-se/
          do-SUP
          'in order to do'

      c. *so.se*
          /soʔ-se/
          look-SUP
          'in order to look'

(40) a. *un.se*
          /und-se/
          pull-SUP
          'in order to pull'

      b. *chep.se*
          /chept-se/
          write-SUP
          'in order to write'

Furthermore, stems ending in a coronal stop, and occasionally also stems ending in a glottal stop, show regressive assimilation to a velar place of articulation,
as shown in (41).

(41) a. *phak.khuba*
          /phat-khuba/
          help-NMLZ
          'helper'

      b. *khek.khuba*
          /khet-khuba/
          carry_off-NMLZ
          'the one who carries it off'

    c.   *sok.khuba*
        /soʔ-khuba/
        look-NMLZ
        'the one who looks'

An optional regressive assimilation, conditioned by fast speech, can be found in underlying sequences of nasals followed by a palatal glide or a lateral approximant (/y/ or /l/), both stem-initially and stem-finally. In such environments, the nasal assimilates further, giving up its feature of nasality (see (42)).

(42)   a.   *lleŋmenna.*
          /N-leks-meʔ-n=na/
          NEG-become[3SG]-NPST-NEG=NMLZ.SG
          'It will not happen./It is not alright.'

       b.   *mẽyelle.*
          /meN-yen-le/
          NEG-obey-CVB
          'without listening/obeying'

       c.   *yyupmaci.*
          /N-yupma=ci/
          2SG.POSS-tiredness=NSG
          'your tiredness'[24]

3.5.7 Operations involving nasals

3.5.7.1 Nasality assimilation

The nasal consonants themselves also trigger several regressive assimilation processes. The affected consonants may change in nasality or in place of articulation. Coronals and the glottal stop are particularly prone to assimilations, while the velar and the bilabial stop are less inclined to assimilate. Stem-final /t/ and /ʔ/ will assimilate completely if they are followed by stressed syllables starting in /m/ (see (43a)). Under the same condition, stems ending in velar stops (both plain and augmented) undergo nasal assimilation, with the place of articulation being retained (see (43b) and (43c)).

(43)   a.   *pham.ˈmeŋ.na*
          /phat-me-ŋ=na/
          help[3SG.A]-NPST-1SG.P=NMLZ.SG
          'He/she helps me.'

---

[24] Some nouns are obligatorily marked for nonsingular, especially in experiential expressions.

b.   *peŋ.ˈmeʔ.na*
      /pek-meʔ=na/
      break[3SG]-NPST=NMLZ.SG
      'It breaks.'

c.   *naŋ.ˈmeʔ.na*
      /nakt-meʔ=na/
      ask[3SG]-NPST=NMLZ.SG
      'He asks.'

In stems that end in /n/ or /nd/ (with augmented /t/), the coda completely assimilates to [m]. In contrast to the assimilation discussed above, this assimilation is not sensitive to stress. For instance, stems like *tund* 'understand' and *yen* 'obey' have the infinitival forms *tumma* and *yemma*, respectively, with the stress falling on the first syllable. Stems ending in a velar stop or in a bilabial stop never assimilate completely; their place of articulation is retained. Compare, e.g., *pekma* 'break' (stem: *pek*) with (43b) above. Following a general rule in Yakkha, augmented stems (ending in two consonants) block assimilation and also other morphophonological processes, e.g., *chepma* 'write' (stem: *chept*). Furthermore, velar and bilabial nasals never assimilate to other nasals, in contrast to languages like Athpare and Belhare (Ebert 1997a; Bickel 2003).

3.5.7.2 Nasalization of codas

Nasalization of obstruents does not only happen as assimilation to nasal material. When obstruents are adjacent in complex predicates, the first obstruent, i.e., the stem-final consonant of the first stem, becomes a nasal in order to avoid a marked structure. Examples are provided in Table 3.16.[25] Within complex predicates this process is most frequently found in infinitival forms. In the inflected forms, morphological material (suffixes with vowel quality) gets inserted between the verbal stems, thus resolving the marked sequences of adjacent obstruents.

The nasal often retains the place of articulation of the underlying obstruent, but some assimilations are possible too, e.g., /sos-kheʔ-ma/ becoming *soŋkheʔma* 'slide off' (slide-go). If the underlying obstruent is a glottal stop, the place of articulation of the nasal is always conditioned by the following consonant, e.g., *han-cama* /haʔ-cama/ 'devour' (bite-eat).

As Table 3.16 shows, both simple (CVC) and augmented stems (CVC-s and CVC-t) are subject to this change from obstruent to nasal. The same change

---

[25] The V2 *-piʔ* has a suppletive form *-diʔ*, which cannot be explained by phonological operations. It occurs only in intransitive uses of *-piʔ* ~ *-diʔ* 'give' as a function verb. The inflected forms show that the underlying stem is *-piʔ*.

can be observed in reduplicated adverbs and adjectives, e.g., in *sonson* 'slanted' (derived from the verbal stem /sos/) or *simsim* 'squinting, blinking' (derived from the verbal stem /sips/).

This process is also sensitive to stress. The last item of Table 3.16, *um.'khe?.ma*, with the stress on the second syllable, can be contrasted with the nominalized *'up.khu.ba* 'something that collapses', with the stress on the first syllable. Here, the stem appears in the general form of *t*-augmented stems that are followed by consonants: the augment is simply omitted.

Table 3.16: Nasalization of obstruents stem-finally

CITATION FORMS		STEMS
yuncama	'laugh, smile'	/yut/ + /ca/
suncama	'itch'	/sus/ + /ca/
incama	'play'	/is/ + /ca/
hancama	'devour'	/ha?/ + /ca/
sendi?ma	'get stale'	/ses/ + /pi?/
mandi?ma	'get lost'	/mas/ + /pi?/
pendi?ma	'get wet'	/pet/ + /pi?/
phomdi?ma	'spill'	/phopt/ + /pi?/
sonsi?ma	'slide, slip'	/sos/ + /si?/
tomsi?ma	'get confused'	/tops/ + /si?/
yaŋsi?ma	'get exhausted'	/yak/ + /si?/
homkhe?ma	'get damaged'	/hop/ + /khe?/
soŋkhe?ma	'slide off'	/sos/ + /khe?/
umkhe?ma	'collapse'	/upt/ + /khe?/

3.5.7.3 Insertion of nasals

In addition to the nasalization of obstruents, nasals can be inserted in complex predication, if the following condition is met: if the V2 in a complex predicate starts with a vowel or in /h/, either the preceding consonants (the complete coda or only the augment of the first verbal stem) will become nasals, or, when the first stem has CV or CV? shape, the default nasal /n/ will be inserted between the two stems. Table 3.17 provides examples of citation forms of complex predicates with inserted nasals, and their underlying stems.

The process is not a blind insertion of phonetic material, i.e., it is not simply epenthesis. Remarkably, it is triggered by the phonological quality of non-
adjacent morphological material: the change of stops to nasals or the insertion
of nasals is conditioned by the availability of nasals in the morphology that attaches to the stem. The suffixes containing nasals have to attach directly to the
complex stem in order to trigger the insertion of nasals. Compare the examples
in (44). In (44a) and (44b), the sequence /pt/ becomes [mn], and the following /h/
is realized as the aspiration of [n]. In (44c), the inflection does not immediately
contain a nasal, and thus the phonological material of the stem remains as it is. It
gets resyllabified, however, and the /h/ is realized as aspiration of the preceding
consonant. Example (45), with the verb *le?nemma* 'let go, drop' illustrates the insertion of /n/ when a CV-stem (or CV?) and a vowel-initial stem are adjacent in
complex predication. The same condition as in (44) can be observed. Only nasal
material in the suffix string licenses the insertion of /n/ between the two verbal
stems.

(44) a. *lem.nhaŋ.ma*
          /lept-haks-ma/
          throw-V2.SEND-INF
          'to throw away/out'

      b. *lem.nhaŋ.nen?*
          /lept-haks-nen/
          throw-V2.SEND-1>2
          'Shall I throw you out?'

      c. *lep.thak.suŋ.na*
          /lept-haks-u-ŋ=na/
          throw-V2.SEND-3.P[PST]-1SG.A=NMLZ.SG
          'I threw her/him out.'

(45) a. *le?.nen.saŋ*
          /le?-end-saŋ/
          drop-V2.INSERT-SIM
          'stretching down'

      b. *u.laŋ*   *le.?en.du.ci.ya*
          /u-laŋ   le?-end-a-u-ci=ha/
          3SG.POSS-leg   drop-V2.INSERT-PST-3.P-NSG.P=NMLZ.NSG
          'It (the aeroplane) lowered its landing gear.'

The insertion of /n/ can affect the coda of the first stem, too. Stems ending
in /s/ may change to CV-? when followed by a vowel-initial stem, as in *ti?nama*

Table 3.17: The insertion of nasals in complex predication

CITATION FORMS	STEMS
hu.nhaŋ.ma 'burn down'	/huʔ/ + /haks/
lem.nhaŋ.ma 'throw away/out'	/lept/ + /haks/
khu.nhaŋ.ma 'rescue'	/khus/ + /haks/
iŋ.nhaŋ.ma 'chase off'	/ikt/ + /haks/
pheʔ.na.ma 'drop, leave at some place'	/phes/ + /a/
et.na.ma 'enroll, install somewhere (and come back)'	/et/ + /a/
tik.na.ma 'take along'	/tikt/ + /a/
tiʔ.na.ma 'deliver (and come back), bring'	/tis/ + /a/
yuk.na.ma 'put for s.b. and leave'	/yuks/ + /a/
leʔ.nem.ma 'drop'	/leʔ/ + /end/
hak.nem.ma 'send down'	/hakt/ + /end/
aʔ.nem.ma 'wrestle down'	/a/ + /end/
ak.nem.ma 'kick down'	/ak/ + /end/
leʔ.nem.ma 'drop'	/leʔ/ + /end/
lep.nem.ma 'throw down'	/lept/ + /end/

'deliver' (/tis + a/). This again suggests a sequence of processes, i.e., the insertion of /n/, followed by the change of /s/ to [ʔ]. It is not clear, however, why these citation forms do not simply resyllabify, e.g., to [tisama] instead of [tiʔnama], because this resyllabification is exactly what happens in the corresponding inflected forms. Apparently, speakers prefer to keep morpheme boundaries and syllable boundaries congruent in citation forms. Note that V2s starting in /h/ behave differently from V2s starting in a vowel, because a complex predicate consisting of /khus/ + /haks/ does not become [khuʔ.nhaŋ.ma] but *khu.nhaŋ.ma*.

Table 3.18 summarizes the processes of the preceding two sections, with examples for each process. To sum up, the insertion of nasals and the transformation of obstruents to nasals are employed to avoid marked structures such as adjacent vowels, adjacent obstruents, and impossible syllable codas, while also maintaining the identity of morpheme boundaries and syllable boundaries. This stands in contrast to inflected forms, where resyllabification is unproblematic.

Table 3.18: Repair operations in complex predicates involving nasals

OPERATION	CITATION FORM	V.LEX + V2
/C[1]+C/ → N[1].C	*hom.khe?.ma* 'get damaged'	/hop/ + /khe?/
/C[1]C[2]+V/ → C[1].nV	*mak.ni.ma* 'surprise'	/maks/ + /i/
/C[1]C[2]+hV/ → N[1].nhV	*lem.nhaŋ.ma* 'throw away/out'	/lept/ + /haks/
/s+hV/ → .nhV	*khu.nhaŋ.ma* 'rescue'	/khus/ + /haks/
/s+V/ → ?.nV	*ma?.ni.ma* 'lose'	/mas/ + /i/
/V+V/ → V?.nV	*a?.nem.ma* 'wrestle down'	/a/ + /end/

3.5.8 Nasal copying

In the verbal inflection of Kiranti languages, nasal morphemes can be realized up to three times in the suffix string, a process that was termed 'affix copying' or 'nasal copying', e.g., in van Driem (1987); Doornenbal (2009); Ebert (2003c); Bickel (2003). Alternative analyses have been proposed to explain this process: recursive inflection in Bickel et al. (2007a) and radically underspecified segments in Zimmermann (2012).

Yakkha nasal copying is illustrated by (46). Suffixes that consist of nasals or that contain nasals occur more than once under certain conditions, and without any semantic consequences. There are no contrasting forms that lack the copied suffixes. It is morphologically most economical to assume regressive copying, with the last nasal suffix serving as base. A comparison of the inflected forms in (46) below supports this reasoning, because the slots after the suffixes -*me?* and -*u* are filled with varying material.[26] What is remarkable about the nasal copying is that the value of the underspecified nasal is determined by non-adjacent segments.

(46) a. *piŋ.ciŋ.ha*
/pi?-a-u-N-ci-ŋ=ha/
give-PST-3.P-[N]-3NSG.P-1SG.A=NMLZ.NSG
'I gave it to them.'

---

[26] Note that the glosses '1sg.A' and 'EXCL' refer to the same morpheme, if the structure of the whole paradigm is taken into account. It is defined by the property [non-inclusive]. This collapse of markers is also found in the intransitive forms of the Belhare verbal inflection (Bickel 1995). For the sake of the readability of the glosses, the morphological analysis as well as the alignment patterns of particular morphemes are kept out of the glosses as far as possible.

    b.   *tun.dum.cim.ŋha*
       /tund-a-u-N-ci-m-ŋ=ha/
       understand-PST-3.P-[N]-3NSG.P-1PL.A-EXCL=NMLZ.NSG
       'We understand them.'

    c.   *ndum.men.cun.ci.ga.nha*
       /n-tund-meʔ-N-ci-u-N-ci-ga-n=ha/
       NEG-Σ-NPST-[N]-DU.A-3.P-[N]-3NSG.P-2.A-NEG=NMLZ.NSG
       'You (dual) do not understand them.'

The motivation for this copying process might be a phonological repair operation to yield closed syllables.[27] Repair operations involving nasals would not be uncommon for Yakkha, as I have pointed out in §3.5.7. An obvious shortcoming of this explanation is that nasals are not copied to all syllables that one would expect in light of a purely phonological condition (compare (47a) and (47b)).

(47) a. *ŋ-khy-a-ma-ga-n=na*   (*ŋkhyanmanganna).
       NEG-go-PST-PRF-2-NEG=NMLZ.SG
       'You have not come.'

    b. *ŋ-khy-a-ma-n-ci-ga-n=ha.*
       NEG-go-PST-PRF-[N]-DU-2-NEG=NMLZ.NSG
       'You (dual) have not come.'

An alternative analysis has been proposed by Zimmermann (2012), resulting from a comparison of several Kiranti languages. In her approach, the copying is a morpheme-specific process, happening only in the vicinity of certain suffixes. In line with her observations, all instances of copied nasals in Yakkha directly precede the suffix *-ci* (with the two morphological values 'dual' and '3NSG.P', see the paradigm tables in §8.4.6). Hence, it is the suffix *-ci* that licenses the nasal copying in Yakkha. The process as such and the phonological content of the copies are morphologically informed; they are based upon the presence of certain morphological markers. In the absence of *-ci* nothing gets copied, and the same holds for inflectional forms in which no nasals are available to serve as base. Hence, nasal copying is not just the blind fulfillment of a phonological constraint, as epenthesizing any nasal material would be. On the other hand, since no semantic content is added by the nasal copies, the operation is not purely morphological either, but located at the boundary between phonology and morphology.

---

[27] Cf. Schikowski (2012: 22) for the same explanation on Chintang suffix copying, although on p. 25 he points out that this explanation is not watertight, since some copying processes may even create open syllables.

Another observation made is that the nasal suffixes compete with regard to which suffix will serve as base for the copying. If we compare (48a) and (48b), we can see that here, the preferred choice is /n/, instantiated by the negation marker, although the closest available base in (48b) would be the velar nasal from the suffix -ŋ. This shows that the choice is not determined by the linear succession of the available nasals. The negation is the only morphological contrast between the two verb forms, and the nasal that is copied changes from /ŋ/ to /n/, compared to (48a). In (48c), there is a competition between /n/ and /m/ as bases, which is won by /m/. This selection principle holds throughout the inflectional paradigm, so that the hierarchy for the choice of the base must be /m/ > /n/ > /ŋ/.

(48)   a.   *tum.meŋ.cuŋ.ci.ŋha*
            /tund-meʔ-N-ci-u-N-ci-ŋ=ha/
            Σ-NPST-[N]-DU.A-3.P-[N]-3NSG.P-EXCL=NMLZ.NSG
            'We (dual, excl.) understand them.'

        b.   *ndum.men.cun.ci.ŋa.nha*
            /n-tund-meʔ-N-ci-u-N-ci-ŋ(a)-n=ha/
            NEG-Σ-NPST-[N]-DU.A-3.P-[N]-3NSG.P-EXCL-NEG=NMLZ.NSG
            'We (dual, excl.) do not understand them.'

        c.   *ndun.dwam.cim.ŋa.nha*
            /n-tund-wa-u-N-ci-m-ŋ(a)-n=ha/
            NEG-Σ-NPST-3.P-[N]-3NSG.P-1PL.A-EXCL-NEG=NMLZ.NSG
            'We (plural) do not understand them.'

4 Pronouns, demonstratives, quantifiers, numerals, interrogatives

This chapter describes the elements that can be found in the noun phrase, modifying or replacing a head noun. It is structured as follows: §4.1 deals with the personal pronouns, §4.2 discusses the possessive pronouns, and §4.3 is concerned with the demonstratives. §4.4 shows how indefinite reference is expressed, §4.5 deals with numerals and other quantifying elements. §4.6 then focuses on interrogative forms, including non-nominal interrogatives.

4.1 Personal pronouns

Yakkha personal pronouns are used to refer to persons, typically those participants to whom reference has already been made in discourse. Personal pronouns can take the structural position of a noun phrase (of any participant role) or they can function as heads of noun phrases, although the possibilities to be modified are restricted: relative clauses and demonstratives are not possible, for instance. Possible modifiers are quantifiers and numerals, but they follow the pronominal head, in contrast to noun phrases with nominal heads, which are mostly head-final. Pronouns, like noun phrases in general, are not obligatory, and they are frequently dropped in Yakkha.

The pronouns distinguish person and number. Clusivity, which is found in possessive pronouns, possessive prefixes and in the verbal inflection, does not play a role in the personal pronouns (compare (1a) and (1b)). An overview of the personal pronouns is provided together with the possessive pronouns in Table 4.1 below. The first and second person pronouns distinguish singular, dual and plural number. The morpheme *-ci* indicates dual number in the first and second person pronouns, while *-ni* indicates the plural. In the third person, *-ci* simply has a nonsingular meaning.[1]

---

[1] Note that in contrast to the pronominal paradigm, the verbal inflection distinguishes dual number also in the third person (cf. §8.2).

(1) a. *kaniŋ khe-i-ŋ=a.*
        1PL   go[PST]-1PL-EXCL=NMLZ.NSG
        'We (without you) went.'
    b. *kaniŋ khe-i=ha.*
        1PL   go[PST]-1PL=NMLZ.NSG
        'We (all) went.'

4.2 Possessive pronouns and nominal possessive inflection

4.2.1 Possessive pronouns

The possessive pronouns modify a head noun, indicating the possessor of the thing that is referred to by the noun (see (2a)). Since the head noun can be omitted when its reference has been established already, the possessive pronoun can also be the sole element in a phrase (see (2b)).

The possessive pronouns resemble the personal pronouns to some degree, but they are sufficiently different and irregular so that they establish a separate paradigm. Except for the third person nonsingular form, the roots all look slightly different from the corresponding personal pronouns. They all host the genitive enclitic *=ga*, though. The possessive pronouns distinguish number and person, including clusivity, a category that is absent from the personal pronoun paradigm. The inclusive forms have no parallel in the personal pronouns. Table 4.1 provides an overview of personal and possessive pronouns and possessive prefixes. The capital /N/ stands for an unspecified nasal that assimilates to the following consonant in place of articulation.

(2) a. *ak=ka*   *kucuma* *sy-a-ma=na.*
        1SG.POSS=GEN dog   die[3SG]-PST-PRF=NMLZ.SG
        'My dog has died.'
    b. *ak=ka=ca*   *sy-a-ma=na.*
        1SG.POSS=GEN=ADD die[3SG]-PST-PRF=NMLZ.SG
        'Mine has died, too.'

4.2.2 Possessive prefixes

Relationships of possession can also be expressed by attaching a possessive prefix to the head noun, which refers to the possessee. The prefixes index the number and person of the possessor. Their form is similar to that of the possessive pro-

Table 4.1: Personal and possessive pronouns, possessive inflection

	PERSONAL PRONOUN	POSSESSIVE PRONOUN	POSSESSIVE PREFIX
1SG	*ka*	*akka*	*a-*
1DU.EXCL	*kanciŋ*	*anciŋga*	*anciŋ-*
1PL.EXCL	*kaniŋ*	*aniŋga*	*aniŋ-*
1DU.INCL	*kanciŋ*	*enciŋga*	*enciŋ-*
1PL.INCL	*kaniŋ*	*eŋga*	*eN-*
2SG	*nda*	*ŋga*	*N-*
2DU	*njiŋda*	*njiŋga*	*njiŋ-*
2PL	*nniŋda*	*nniŋga*	*nniŋ-*
3SG	*uŋ*	*ukka*	*u- ~ o-*
3NSG	*uŋci*	*uŋciga*	*uŋci-*

nouns, which suggests that they have developed out of them. The nasals in the 1PL.INCL prefix *eN-* and in the 2SG prefix *N-* assimilate in place of articulation to the first consonant of their nominal host (see (3)). The third person singular prefix *u-* has the allomorph *o-* before stems containing /e/ or /o/. The possessees can also be nouns referring to sensations, as in (3a).

It is information structure that determines whether a pronoun or a prefix is used. If the possessive relationship is focused on, the pronoun has to be used.

(3)   a.   *n-yupma*
         2SG.POSS-sleepiness
         'your sleepiness'

       b.   *m-ba*
         2SG.POSS-father
         'your father'

       c.   *eŋ-gamnibak*
         1PL.INCL.POSS-friend
         'our friend'

Possessive prefixes only attach to nouns, and thus, they are affixes, not clitics. In co-compounds (see (4a)), and in cases where two nouns are conjoined in a noun phrase (see (4b)), both nouns host the possessive prefix.[2]

---

[2] Admittedly, all examples of co-compounds or coordinated nouns with possessive marking in the current data set are from the domain of kinship terms.

(4) a. *u-ppa*   *u-ma=ci=ca*
        3SG.POSS-father   3SG.POSS-mother=NSG=ADD
        'her parents, too'   [01_leg_07.152]

     b. *a-ma=nuŋ*   *a-na=ŋa*
        1SG.POSS-mother=COM   1SG.POSS-sister=ERG

        y-yog-a-n-niŋ=bi,   ...
        NEG-search-SBJV[1.P]-NEG-NEG.PL=IRR
        'If my mother and sister had not searched for me, ...' [42_leg_10.052]

4.2.3 Obligatory possession

Certain nouns nearly always appear with possessive prefixes, even when no clear possessor has been mentioned in the preceding discourse. The semantic domains which are relevant for obligatory possession are consanguineal kinship, spatial relations (relational nouns), body parts and other part-whole relations that are not body parts in the strict sense, such as *otheklup* 'half' or *ochon* 'splinter'. So far, 118 obligatorily possessed nouns could be found, which makes up roughly 9% of the nominal lexicon.[3] Some of the obligatorily possessed nouns are listed in Tables 4.2 and 4.3. Since obligatory possession is also found in the expression of spatial relations, several adverbs and relational nouns originate in obligatorily possessed nouns (cf. §6.3).

   With kinship terms, the first person singular possessive prefix is the default option, e.g., in the citation forms in elicitations, in general statements and in vocatives (as using names to address people is considered impolite). There are some lexicalized terms like *a-mum* 'grandmother', *a-pum* 'grandfather', *a-na* 'elder sister', characterized by a shift of stress to the first syllable. Recall that prefixes generally do not belong to the domain to which stress is assigned. In words like *a.'paŋ* 'my house', the domain of stress excludes the prefix, but several monosyllabic kin terms clearly have the stress on the first syllable: *'a.mum, 'a.pum, 'a.na, 'a.ni*. Even though the stress does not treat the prefixes like prefixes any more, the words are still transparent, as 'his grandmother' is *u.'mum*, not **u.'a.mum*.

   Terms for non-consanguineal family relations like *namba* 'father-in-law' or *taŋme* 'daughter-in-law' do not fall within the domain of obligatory possession

---

[3] In Bickel & Nichols (2005: 242) on obligatorily possessed nouns, this phenomenon is defined as "words for which an inflectional category of possession is obligatorily present". In the current Yakkha data at least some exceptions can be found, so that I conclude that obligatory possession is a rather gradual phenomenon in Yakkha. More data would be necessary in order to explain apparent exceptions and thus to paint a clearer picture of obligatorily possessed nouns in Yakkha.

Table 4.2: Obligatorily possessed nouns: kinship, spatial and temporal relations, body parts

CONSANGUINEAL KINSHIP	
acya	'child'
aphu	'elder brother'
ana	'elder sister'
aphaŋ	'father's younger brother'
akoŋma	'mother's younger sister'

SPATIAL AND TEMPORAL RELATIONS	
ucumphak	'day after tomorrow'
ulum	'middle, center' (relational noun)
oţemma	'plains'
uyum	'side' (relational noun)
okomphak	'third day after today'

BODY PARTS	
unabhak	'ear'
umik	'eye'
unamcyaŋ	'cheek'
unacik	'face'
utamphwak	'hair'
umuk	'hand'
uţaŋ	'horn'
ulaŋ	'leg'
uya	'mouth, opening'
ophok	'stomach'
osenkhwak	'bone'
uţiŋ	'thorn, fishbone'

Table 4.3: Obligatorily possessed nouns: Part-whole relations

PART-WHOLE RELATIONS	
opoŋgalik	'bud'
uchuk	'corner'
upusum	'crust'
uyin	'egg'
otheklup	'half'
okhop	'husk of rice'
uhup	'knot'
ukhuppa	'lid, cover'
ophetrak	'petal'
ochon	'thorn, splinter'
oyok	'place'
uwha	'wound'

(see example (5a)).[4] This does not mean that possessive prefixes are prohibited, they are just less frequent. The difference is nicely illustrated in (5b), from a wedding description that contains many kinship terms.

(5) a. *tabhaŋ   heʔne   tas-wa-ga=na?*
         male_in-law   where   arrive-NPST-2=NMLZ.SG
         'Where will (your) husband arrive?'

     b. *nhaŋa   jammai jammai jammai lokondi,*
         and_then   all   all   all   companion_of_bride
         [...] u-chim   u-phaŋ=ci   ...
         [...] 3SG.POSS-FyBW   3SG.POSS-FyB=NSG
         'And then, they all, the bride's companions, her paternal aunts and
         uncles ...'   [25_tra_01.091]

While the default option for kin terms is the first person prefix, for the other obligatorily possessed nouns it is the third person singular, as for instance in *u-ʈiŋ* 'thorn'. We find some lexicalized instances here as well, for instance *usa* 'fruit', stressed on the first syllable and lexicalized from the more general noun *sa*, translating as 'flesh, meat' and 'fruit flesh'. Another instance is *uwa* 'nectar, honey, (any) liquid', also stressed on the first syllable, with the original meaning 'water' or, more generally, 'liquid'.

---

[4] I thank Ram Kumar Linkha for pointing this out to me.

Other Kiranti languages also have obligatory possessive marking. Camling also has obligatory possessive marking on inherently relational nouns (Ebert 1997b: 41). Similarly, Doornenbal (2009: 98–100) lists classes of nouns that necessarily occur with possessive marking. In her grammar of Thulung, Lahaussois (2002: 72) mentions that an otherwise rare combination of possessive prefix and genitive marking is frequently found with inalienably possessed nouns such as nouns from the domains of kinship and body parts.

4.3 Demonstratives

The functional core of demonstratives is deixis. Demonstratives (just like pronouns and temporal adverbs such as 'tomorrow') are deictic; their reference depends on a center that is established in the particular utterance context and that may thus change with that particular utterance context (Bühler 1934; Fillmore 1971 (1997)). The point of reference is typically, but not necessarily, the speaker.

There are two sets of demonstratives in Yakkha, one set based on proximity and distance to the deictic center (spatial as well as anaphoric, see §4.3.1) and one set based on the inclination of the landscape, called *geomorphic* in Bickel (1997b). The latter are treated separately in §7.2 on the topography-based orientation system. The roots of the former set are pronominal, but they can become adverbial via derivations (see §4.3.2).

4.3.1 Proximal, distal and anaphoric deixis

Table 4.4 shows the forms expressing the three-fold distinction between proximal, distal and anaphoric demonstratives. The proximal forms are used to refer to objects or people that are close to the speaker and can be touched or pointed at, while the distal forms are used for objects or people further away as well as for referents that are not present in the speech situation. Narratives mostly use the distal forms, except in direct quotations. The anaphoric demonstratives are used to take up reference to some participant that had already been activated at a previous time in discourse; it is best translated as 'that very (person/thing/event)'. The members of this set of demonstratives are also found in correlative clauses (see §13.4). Demonstratives can be used adnominally (i.e., modifying a head noun) and pronominally (i.e., replacing a noun phrase) in Yakkha. Furthermore, demonstratives may replace personal pronouns in the third person, as the use of personal pronouns is considered somewhat rude.

Let us first take a look at the proximal-distal distinction. In example (6), the demonstratives are used in attributive function. The number distinction is en-

Table 4.4: Proximal, distal and anaphoric demonstratives

	PROXIMAL	DISTAL	ANAPHORIC
SG	*na*	*nna*	*honna*
NSG/	*kha*	*ŋkha(ci)* ~	*hoŋkha(ci)*
NON-COUNT		*nnakha(ci)*	

coded by the base forms for proximal deixis *na* (singular) and *kha* (nonsingular and non-countable reference).[5] Distal deixis is expressed by adding either a prefix *nna* or just a homorganic nasal to these roots (not segmented in the glosses).[6] No semantic difference between *nnakha* and *ŋkha* could be determined, and the latter seems like a contracted form of the former. In terms of stress assignment, these demonstratives may cliticize phonologically when they are used attributively, but they are generally able to carry their own stress. They naturally carry stress when they occur on their own, e.g., *khaci* 'these'.

(6) a. *na   babu*
          this boy
          'this boy'

     b. *nna   babu*
          that boy
          'that boy'

     c. *kha   babu=ci*
          these boy=NSG
          'these boys'

     d. *ŋkha babu=ci*
          those boy=NSG
          'those boys'

     e. *kha   kham*
          this mud
          'this mud/soil'

---

[5] The distinction between singular on the one hand and nonsingular/non-countable on the other hand is fundamental and robust in Yakkha, found not only in the demonstratives but also in nominalizations and in verbal agreement.

[6] In Belhare (Bickel 2003: 548), the lexeme corresponding to *nna* is *ina*. The same sound correspondence (between nasal prefix and prefix *i-*) is found between the Tumok and the Kharang dialects of Yakkha.

f. *ŋkha   kham*
    that   mud
    'that mud/soil'

As example (6) shows, all demonstratives can appear as nominal modifiers (see also (7)). The non-countable reference of *kha* can be illustrated by the difference between *toŋba* 'beer served in a small barrel and drunk with a pipe' and *cuwa* 'beer'. While the first has countable reference, the second is treated as a substance and hence has non-countable reference. The demonstrative *kha* may thus refer to nonsingular instances of count nouns (see (7b)) or to mass nouns (see (7c)). This distinction of number and countability is also reflected in the sentence-final nominalizers in these examples, which are etymologically related to the demonstratives (discussed at length in §13.3).

(7) a. *na   toŋba   imin   et-u-ga=na?*
         this   beer_in_barrel   how   like-3.P[PST]-2=NMLZ.SG
         'How do you like this tongba?'

     b. *kha   toŋba=ci   khumdu=ha=ci.*
         these   beer_in_barrel=NSG   tasty=NMLZ.NSG=NSG
         'These tongbas are tasty.'

     c. *kha   cuwa(*=ci)   khumdu=ha.*
         these   beer(*=NSG)   tasty=NMLZ.NC
         'This beer (beer of this house/area) is tasty.'

The demonstratives may also head noun phrases, hosting the phrasal morphology and triggering agreement (see (8)). They are more restricted than nominal heads of noun phrases, as they cannot take adnominal modifiers.

(8) a. *kha=ci   ucun=ha=c=em,   ŋkha=ci*
         these=NSG   nice=NMLZ.NSG=NSG=ALT   those=NSG

         ucun=ha=c=em?
         nice=NMLZ.NSG=NSG=ALT
         'Are these better, or those?'

     b. *na=go   ucun=na.*
         this=TOP   nice=NMLZ.SG
         'This one is nice.'

The anaphoric demonstratives identify referents that have already been activated in discourse, and are taken up again, as in (9). The speaker introduces her narrative with the fact that she has seen a film. Then, the listener makes a joke, distracting away from the film (not included in the example). The speaker re-introduces the topic with *honna*.

(9) a.   *ha,   imin   ka-ma=ha?*   *ka   khem   eko*
yes,   how   say-INF[DEONT]=NMLZ.NSG   1SG   before   one
philm   so-ŋ,   *men=na=i?*
film   watch[3.P;PST]-1SG.A   NEG.COP=NMLZ.SG=Q
'Yes, how to start? I saw a film before, right?'   [34_pea_04.005]

b.   *honna=be=jhen,*   *eko   jaŋgal=we   eko   yapmi*
that_very=LOC=TOP   one   jungle=LOC   one   person
khy-a-masa,   *men=na=i?*   *paghyam.*
go[3SG]-PST-PST.PRF   NEG.COP=NMLZ.SG=Q   old_man
'In that (film), a man had gone into a jungle, right? An old man.'
[34_pea_04.011]

In (10), a written narrative, the protagonist goes fishing to surprise his sick father but he loses the net in the strong current of the river. After losing the net, he says:

(10)   *honna   eko=se   jal   wa-ya-masa=na.*
that_very   one=RESTR   net   exist[3SG]-PST-PST.PRF=NMLZ.SG
'There had been only that very net.'   [01_leg_07.214]

Human reference is possible with *honna* as well, exemplified by (11).

(11)   *nnakhaʔla   cok-saŋ   honna   yapmi   bhirik=phaŋ*
like_that   do-SIM   that_very   person   cliff=ABL
lond-uks-u.
take_out-PRF-3.P[PST]
'In this way, he rescued that (afore-mentioned) man from the cliff.'
[01_leg_07.330]

In (12), also a written narrative, the referent taken up from the previous clause is a cradle.

(12) a.   *uŋ=ŋa   hoŋma=ŋa   eko   mina   yoŋ*
3SG=ERG   river=INS   one   small   cradle
yaŋ-kheʔ-ma-si-meʔ=na
flush-V2.CARRY.OFF-INF-AUX.PROG-NPST=NMLZ.SG
nis-uks-u.
see-PRF-3.P[PST]
'She saw a little cradle being carried off by the river. ' [01_leg_07.288]

b.   *nhaŋ*   *uŋ=ŋa*   *hattapatta* *honna*   *yoŋ*
     and_then   3SG=ERG   hastily   that_very cradle
     lab-uks-u.
     grab-PRF-3.P[PST]
     'And hastily she grabbed that cradle.'   [01_leg_07.289]

The singular form *na* could be etymologically related to a topic particle of the same form, as it is still found in Belhare or Puma, for instance (Bickel 2003; Bickel et al. 2009: 559). Furthermore, the demonstratives *na* and *kha* have developed into the nominalizers *=na* and *=ha* which show exactly the same distribution with regard to number and the count/mass distinction as the demonstratives (cf. §13.3). On a final note, clause-initial coordinators like *nhaŋ, nnhaŋ, khoŋ* and *ŋkhoŋ* (all paraphrasable with 'and then' or 'afterwards') are demonstratives with ablative marking historically.

4.3.2 Demonstrative adverbs and quantifiers

The proximal-distal-anaphoric distinction is also present in a set of demonstrative adverbs and quantifiers, as given in Table 4.5. Example (13) some more instances of anaphoric demonstrative adverbs based on the root *hon*. The sentence in (13a) is uttered at the end of a narrative, and the adverbs refer to the content and number of the events just related.[7] In (13b), *hoŋkha?niŋ* refers to the time at which the events took place (specified in a previous sentence), and in (13c), *honnhe* refers to the place just mentioned in the conversation.

(13)   a.   *liŋkha=ci=ga*   *lagi,* *hoŋkha?la=oŋ,*
        Linkha_clan_member=NSG=GEN   for   like_that=SEQ
        hoŋkhiŋ=se.
        that_much=RESTR
        'For the Linkhas, like that, that much only.'   [11_nrr_01.042]

    b.   *hoŋkha?niŋ*   *ten=be?=na*   *yalumma*
        that_very_time   village=LOC=NMLZ.SG talkative_granny
        a-mum=ŋa   *so-saŋ*   *ka-ya:*
        1SG.POSS-grandmother=ERG look-SIM say[3SG]-PST
        'At that time, a talkative old lady watching it said: ...' [41_leg_09.041]

    c.   *honnhe=maŋ*   *khe-me-ŋ=na.*
        right_there=EMPH   go-NPST-1SG=NMLZ.SG
        'I will go right there.' (in a talk about Mamling village, a new person shows up and states that she will go right to that village)

---

[7] Quantifying expressions (both for amount and size) are the topic of §4.5 below.

Table 4.5: Demonstrative adverbs and quantifiers

	PROXIMAL	DISTAL	ANAPHORIC
LOCATION	*nhe* 'here'	*nnhe* 'there'	*honnhe* 'where mentioned before'
TIME	*kha?niŋ* 'this time, now'	*ŋkha?niŋ ~ nnakha?niŋ* 'that time, then'	*honkha?niŋ* 'right at that time'
MANNER	*kha?la* 'like this'	*ŋkha?la ~ nnakha?la* 'like that'	*honkha?la* 'like mentioned before'
AMOUNT/ SIZE/ DEGREE	*khiŋ* 'this much' 'this big'	*ŋkhiŋ ~ nnakhiŋ* 'that much' 'that big'	*honkhiŋ* 'as much as mentioned before' 'as big as mentioned before'

4.4 Indefinite reference

Yakkha does not have a morphologically distinct class of indefinite pronouns; all pronouns and demonstratives are definite. There are, however, several strategies to convey indefinite reference, including the use of simple nouns. Occasionally, the numeral *eko* 'one' is also used for this purpose. In example (14a), *eko* refers to an object in a future and hence irrealis statement; in (14b), *eko* refers to a specific (known to the speakers), but still indefinite person (not determined in a way that the hearer can identify the referent).

(14) a. *uŋ   mit-a: haku eko paŋ   cok-ma*
          3SG think[3SG]-PST: now   one house make-INF
          ta-ya=na.
          come[3SG]-PST=NMLZ.SG
          'He thought: Now the time has come to build a house.'

          [27_nrr_06.006]

      b. *aniŋ=ga   eko mamu*
          1PL.EXCL.POSS=GEN one girl
          mas-a-by-a-ma=na.
          get_lost[3SG]-PST-V2.GIVE-PST=NMLZ.SG
          'One of our girls got lost.'

          [22_nrr_05.076]

Interrogatives can also function as indefinite pronouns, particularly in contexts where the referent is unknown to the speaker, as in (15). Interrogatives as indefinite pronouns may head noun phrases and can be modified (see (15a)); they may also modify nouns themselves (see (15b)). Using interrogatives for indefinite reference is a very common strategy cross-linguistically, which can be explained by the functional similarity of the two. Both express an information gap and vagueness at the utterance level (Haspelmath 1997: 170).

(15) a. *uɲci yuncamakekek i ŋ-ga-ya-masa.*
          3NSG funny   what 3PL-say-PST-PST.PRF
          'They had said something funny.'   [41_leg_09.029]
      b. *nhaŋa desan-masan n-da-me i=ha.*
          and_then malicious_ghost 3PL-come-NPST what=NMLZ.NSG
          'And then, some scary ghosts will come.'   [28_cvs_04.266]

As (16) shows, information that is known to the speaker, but that she does not want to disclose, is also covered by the interrogative-indefinite polysemy.

(16) *khy-a-ŋ=na=le, pheri kha?la=maŋ=ba, sala*
      go-PST-1SG=NMLZ.SG=CTR again like_this=EMPH=EMPH talk
      i=ha i=ha ta-me.
      what=NMLZ.NC what=NMLZ.NC come[3SG]-NPST
      'I just went, again, just like this, one talks about a little bit of this, a little bit of that.' (the speaker explains why she had gone, i.e., to talk, without specifying what they talked about)   [28_cvs_04.319]

Exhaustive reference, i.e., including all imaginable referents in a given context, is expressed by attaching the additive focus particle =ca to an interrogative pronoun (see (17)). This works with affirmative and with negated statements; in the latter case, it has the effect of exhaustive negation (see (17c)).

(17) a. *i=ha camyoŋba=ca a-sap*
          what=NMLZ.NC food=ADD 1SG.POSS-[STEM]
          thakt-wa-ŋ=ha.
          like-NPST[3.P]-1SG.A=NMLZ.NSG
          'I like any (kind of) food.'
      b. *eŋ=ga niŋ=be uɲci i=ha*
          1PL.INCL.POSS=GEN name=LOC 3NSG what=NMLZ.NC
          cok-ma=ca tayar n-leŋ-me.
          do-INF=ADD ready 3PL-become-NPST
          'They will be ready to do anything in our name.'   [01_leg_07.084]
      c. *ŋkha?la bhoŋ lop ka i=ha=ca*
          like_that COND now 1SG what=NMLZ.NC=ADD

> n-nakt-a-ŋa-n.
> NEG-ask_for-IMP-1SG.P-NEG
> 'If it is like that, do not ask me for anything right now.'
>
> [27_nrr_06.025]

Occasionally, the interrogative pronoun can also be doubled, often in combination with markers of focus or emphasis (see (18)).

(18) a. *chippakekek=na*   *i=na=i*   *i=na*
         disgusting=NMLZ.SG   what=NMLZ.SG=EMPH what=NMLZ.SG
         loʔwa=na
         like=NMLZ.SG
         'like some disgusting, undefinable (thing)'   [40_leg_08.054]

     b. *eh, ikhiŋ*   *mam=ha*   *i=ya*
         oh, how_much   big=NMLZ.NC   what=NMLZ.NC
         i=ya=le   *naŋ-me-c-u=ha*   *baŋniŋgo*
         what=NMLZ.NC=CTR ask-NPST-DU-3.P=NMLZ.NC TOP
         haʔlo!
         EXCLA
         'Oh, (we had thought that) they would ask for something big!'
         (instead, they asked for a minor favor)   [22_nrr_05.129]

Another strategy to express indefinite reference is to use an interrogative pronoun and to reduplicate the fully inflected verb (see (19)). Additionally, the interrogative phrase may host a topic marker =ko, which is not possible in interrogative utterances, since the inherent focus of interrogative phrases rules out topic marking on them. Both strategies help to disambiguate indefinite statements and interrogative utterances.

(19) a. *a-yaŋ*   *heʔne*   *mas-a-by-a=ha*
         1SG.POSS-money   where   get_lost[3SG]-PST-V2.GIVE-PST=NMLZ.NC
         mas-a-by-a=ha.
         get_lost[3SG]-PST-V2.GIVE-PST=NMLZ.NC
         'My money got lost somewhere.'

     b. *surke=ŋa*   *isa=ge=ko*   *khus-u-co-ya*
         Surke=ERG   who=LOC=TOP   steal-3.P-V2.EAT-PST
         khus-u-co-ya.
         steal-3.P-V2.EAT-PST
         'Surke (a dog) stole (food) from someone's house.'

c.   *na*   *inimma=be*   *a-ppa*   *a-ma=ci*
     this   market=LOC   1SG.POSS-father   1SG.POSS-mother=NSG
     he?ne   *m-phaps-a-khy-a*   *m-phaps-a-khy-a.*
     where   3PL-entangle-PST-V2.GO-PST   3PL-entangle-PST-V2.GO-PST
     'My parents got lost somewhere in this market.'[8]   [01_leg_07.163]

In practice, indefinite reference is often just realized by the omission of overt arguments, since overt personal pronouns are not required for accessible referents, not even for mentioning them for the first time. In (20), the referent talked about is only introduced by the verbal agreement: people talk about someone they saw walking away, without recognizing who it was.

(20)   *churuk*   *uŋ-saŋ*   *khy-a-ma=na.*   *isa=?lo?*
       cigarette   drink-SIM   go[3SG]-PST-PRF=NMLZ.SG   who=EXCLA
       'He has gone, smoking a cigarette. But who was it??'

4.5 Quantifiers, numerals and numeral classifiers

4.5.1 Quantification, size and degree

Yakkha has several quantifiers to indicate the amount, size, degree or intensity of the concepts expressed by nouns, adjectives or verbs. They are listed in Table 4.6, with the word classes with which they combine. The form *maŋpha* 'much/very' is special insofar as it may also express the degree of another quantifier, such as in *maŋpha pyak* 'really much'. The table also includes deictic quantifiers and degree words.

The difference between *mimik* and *miyaŋ* (both: 'a little') is subtle. Both can be found with nouns (see (21)) or verbs (see (22)), but *miyaŋ* is the typical choice with nouns, while *mimik* is found more often with verbs. Both words may also appear as proforms heading noun phrases, as (21a) and (21c) show.

(21)   a.   *nda=ca*   *miyaŋ=se*   *uŋ-u!*
           2SG=ADD   a_little=RESTR   drink-3.P[IMP]
           'You too, drink, just a little!'
     b.   *ka*   *miyaŋ*   *cama*   *py-a-ŋ-eba.*
           1SG   a_little   rice   give-IMP-1SG.P-POL.IMP
           'Please give me a little rice.'

---

[8] The word *inimma* is a neologism not widely in use.

Table 4.6: Quantifiers

YAKKHA	GLOSS	DOMAIN
mi	'a little'	A
miyaŋ	'a little'	N, V, A
mimik	'a little'	N, V
ghak	'all/whole'	N
tuknuŋ	'completely'	V, A
pyak	'much/ many/ very'	N, V, A
maŋpha	'much/very'	A, QUANT
ibibi	'very much/many'	N
khiŋ	'this much/this big' (deictic)	N, V, A
ŋkhiŋ	'that much/that big' (deictic)	N, V, A
hoŋkhiŋ	'as much/big as stated before' (deictic)	N

   c.   *mimik,   ŋ-khot-a-n   bhoŋ=se   kaniŋ*
       a_little   NEG-be_enough-PST-NEG   COND=RESTR   1PL[ERG]
       mimik   in-u-ca-wa-m-ŋ=ha.
       a_little   buy-3.P-V2.EAT-NPST-1PL.A-EXCL=NMLZ.NC
       'A little, only if is not enough we buy a little.'   [28_cvs_04.038]

(22)   a.   *kam=ca   cok-ma   haʔlo,   mimik*   ...
       work=ADD   do-INF[DEONT]   EXCLA   a_little
       'One also has to work a little ...'   [28_cvs_04.326]

      b.   *miyaŋ   ucun   ŋ-get-u-ŋa-n=na*
       a_little   nice   NEG-bring_up-3.P[PST]-EXCL-NEG=NMLZ.SG
       loppi.
       perhaps
       'Maybe I did not recall it (a story) so well.' (lit. 'I slightly did not
       recall it nicely, perhaps.')   [11_nrr_01.038]

      c.   *miyaŋ   taŋkhyaŋ   mopmop   cok-t-a-by-a.*
       a_little   sky   covered   make-BEN-IMP-V2.GIVE-IMP
       'Please make the sky a little cloudy.'   [37_nrr_07.100]

Furthermore, *miyaŋ* is also found with adjectives and adverbs (see (23)).

(23)   *hoŋ=bhaŋ   miyaŋ   yoʔyorok*
      hole=ABL   a_little   across
      'a little further away from the hole'   [04_leg_03.011]

The quantifier *pyak* is used with count and mass nouns. It has an intensifying function when it is combined with verbs and adverbs or adjectives. It indicates a large amount or a high degree of whatever is expressed by the head that it modifies. Thus, it can be rendered with English 'much', 'many' and 'very'. Examples are provided below in (24) for the nominal domain and in (25) for verbal and adverbial/adjectival uses. In (25a), *pyak* is further emphasized by the deictic degree particle *khiŋ*, yielding the exclamative 'how much!'.

(24) a. *pyak   sakheʔwa=ci*
          many   pigeon=NSG
          'many pigeons'   [01_leg_07.013]

      b. *pyak   ŋ-geŋ-me-n.*
          much   NEG-bear_fruit[3SG]-NPST-NEG
          'Not much will ripen.'   [01_leg_07.122]

      c. *pyak   yaŋ   ub-wa-ŋ.*
          much   money   earn-NPST[3.P]-1SG.A
          'I will earn much money.'   [01_leg_07.190]

(25) a. *ka   khiŋ   pyak   a-ma=ŋa   u-luŋma*
          1SG   this_much   much   1SG.POSS-mother=ERG   3SG.POSS-liver
          tuŋ-me-ŋ=na!
          pour-NPST-1SG.P=NMLZ.SG
          'How much my mother loves me!'   [01_leg_07.079]

      b. *suku   pyak   cond-a-sy-a-ma.*
          Suku   much   be_happy[3SG]-PST-MDDL-PST-PRF
          'Suku was very happy.'   [01_leg_07.151]

      c. *eko   pyak   thuŋdu=na   yapmi*
          one   very   rich=NMLZ.SG   person
          'a very rich man'   [04_leg_03.014]

Examples with *ibibi* (referring to an unspecific high quantity) are few; one is shown below in (26).

(26) *wathaŋ=be   ibibi   yapmi=ci   ta-saŋ   wasi-saŋ*
      water_tap=LOC   many_many   person=NSG   come-SIM   wash-SIM
      khe-saŋ   n-jok-ma-sy-a.
      go-SIM   3PL-do-INF-AUX.PROG-PST
      'At the watertap, many, many people kept coming, bathing, going.'
                                                                    [40_leg_08.049]

103

The exhaustive quantifier *ghak* 'all, whole' can refer to an exhaustive number or amount, as in (27a), or to a complete unit, as in (27b) and (27c). The potential ambiguity is resolved by the verbal number agreement, which has to be plural in the exhaustive reading.

(27)   a.   *ghak   limbu   m-bog-a-ma-ci=hoŋ,*   ...

            all   Limbu_person   3PL-get_up-PST-PRF-NSG=SEQ

            'As all the Limbus woke up, ...'   [22_nrr_05.027]

       b.   *ghak   ceʔya*

            whole   matter

            'the whole matter'   [01_leg_07.024]

       c.   *ghak   ten   mag-a-khy-a.*

            whole   village   burn[3SG]-PST-V2.GO-PST

            'The whole village burned down.'   [22_nrr_05.026]

The deictic quantifier *khiŋ* has to be interpreted with respect to the utterance context; it can refer to amount or size. In most cases, its use is accompanied by gestures that indicate the size or the amount of some entity. Occasionally, the nominal comitative can be found attached to *khiŋ* (see (28c)).

(28)   a.   *khiŋ   tukkhi   ŋ-aŋd-u*   ...

            this_much pain   3PL.A-endure-3.P[PST]

            'They endured so many troubles ...'   [14_nrr_02.07]

       b.   *mi=na   chun-d-eʔ=na,*   *khiŋ*

            small=NMLZ.SG   shrink[3SG]-V2.GIVE-NPST=NMLZ.SG   this_big

            leŋ-d-eʔ=na,   ...

            become[3SG]-V2.GIVE-NPST=NMLZ.SG

            'It shrinks, it becomes so small, ... '   [36_cvs_06.228]

       c.   *khiŋ=nuŋ   em-ma=niŋa   lak=nuŋ*

            this_much=COM   insert-INF=CTMP   salty=COM

            leks-a=bi.

            become[3SG]-SBJV=IRR

            'If one inserted this much, it would become salty.'

Like the demonstratives described in §4.3, *ŋkhiŋ* may express distal reference, i.e., 'that much' (compare (29a) and (29b)). In (29b), instead of indicating the size with his own hands, the speaker points to a piece of wood lying nearby. The distal reference is also used in general statements, as in (29c).

(29)   a.   *puchak   khiŋ=na*   *sa=na!*
            snake   this_much=NMLZ.SG   COP.PST[3SG]=NMLZ.SG
            'The snake was this big!' (The speaker is showing with her own hands
            how big it was.)
       b.   *puchak   ŋkhiŋ=na*   *sa=na!*
            snake   this_much=NMLZ.SG   COP.PST[3SG]=NMLZ.SG
            'The snake was that big!' (The speaker is pointing to a piece of wood
            lying nearby.)
       c.   *cuŋ=be   ŋkhiŋ*   *ucun*
            cold=LOC   that_much   nice
            m-phem-me-n=ha.
            NEG-bloom[3SG]-NPST-NEG=NMLZ.NSG
            'In winter, it does not bloom so nicely.' (=*ha* being used because
            of mass reference: blossoms in general, not a countable plurality of
            blossoms)

Anaphoric deixis is possible as well, using *hoŋkhiŋ*. The sentence in (30) follows a long enumeration of particular things the protagonist had to do, and
hoŋkhiŋ refers back to them.

(30)   *nhaŋ   nam   wandik=ŋa   lom-meʔ=niŋa*
       and_then   sun   next_day=INS   come_out[3SG]-NPST=CTMP
       hoŋkhiŋ   cok-ni-ma   pʌrne   sa=bu.
       that_much   do-COMPL-INF[DEONT]   having_to   COP.PST[3SG]=REP
       'And then, at the dawn of the next day, all that work had to be finished,
       people say.'   [11_nrr_01.010]

4.5.2 Numerals and classifiers

4.5.2.1 Cardinal numerals

The inherited Tibeto-Burman numerals have largely been lost in Kiranti (Ebert
1994). In Yakkha only the numerals *i* 'one', *hiC* 'two'[9] and *sum* 'three' are known.
Another numeral for 'one' is found, which is the Nepali loan *eko*. It already re-
places the Yakkha numeral *i* in several contexts. In counting, for instance, *eko*
prevails in the majority of cases. Some fixed expressions, like *i len* 'one day',
however, contain the Yakkha form. It is quite likely that the numeral *i* and the
interrogative root *i* share a common origin.

---

[9] The capital /C/ stands for a plosive. As the numeral does not occur independently, and as it
always assimilates to the following consonant, its place of articulation could not be determined.

Unlike in some Newari varieties,[10] numeral classification does not play a prominent role in Kiranti languages. Yakkha has one numeral classifier *-paŋ* for human
reference (cognate, e.g., with Belhare *-baŋ*, Athpare *-paŋ*, Camling *-po*, Bantawa
-pok, Hayu *-pu*). It is used only with the Yakkha numerals 'two' and 'three' (see
(31)). Nonsingular marking of the head noun is frequent, but optional (discussed
in §5.2.1). For numerals above 'three', borrowed Nepali numerals, as well as the
Nepali classifiers *jana* for humans and *(w)oṭa* for things are used (see (32a)). Some
words for measuring units or currency may also function as classifiers (see (32b)).

(31) a. *eko yapmi*
          one person
          'one man/person'

      b. *hip-paŋ   babu(=ci)*
          two-CLF.HUM   boy(=NSG)
          'two boys'

      c. *sum-baŋ   mamu(=ci)*
          three-CLF.HUM girl(=NSG)
          'three girls'

(32) a. *bis   ora   khibak=ca*
          twenty   CLF   rope=ADD
          'twenty ropes'   [11_nrr_01.012]

      b. *ah, pãc, chʌsay   rupiya*
          yes five six_hundred   rupee
          'five, six hundred rupees'   [28_cvs_04.075]

Since there is no classifier for non-human reference in Yakkha, the nonsingular
marker *=ci* has undergone reanalysis in order to fill the position of the classifier
(see (33)). This is the only instance where nonsingular *=ci* may occur inside a
noun phrase.

(33) a. *hic=ci   yaŋ=ci*
          two=NSG   coin=NSG
          'two coins'   [26_tra_02.032]

      b. *sum=ci   ceʔya*
          three=NSG word
          'three words'   [36_cvs_06.345]

---

[10] For instance, in Dolakha Newari (Genetti 2007: 220) and the Newari spoken in Dulikhel (own
observations).

Numeral expressions may also occur without a head noun; i.e., they can fill the structural position of a noun phrase (see (34)).

(34)   a.   *hip-paŋ=se*
              two-CLF.HUM=RESTR
              'only two people'   [36_cvs_06.578]

        b.   *hip-paŋ=ŋa*   *ni-me-c-u=ha.*
              two-CLF.HUM=ERG   know-NPST-DU-3.P=NMLZ.NC
              'The two of them know it (how to divinate).'   [22_nrr_05.081]

4.5.2.2 Counting events

Yakkha has a marker *-ma* to individuate and count events, i.e., to express 'once', 'twice', 'three times'. It only occurs with the inherited (Tibeto-Burman) Yakkha numerals.

(35)   a.   *ka*   *i-ma*   *pukt-a-ŋ=na.*
              1SG   one-COUNT   jump-PST-1SG=NMLZ.SG
              'I jumped once.'

        b.   *minuma=ŋa* *hip-ma*   *sum-ma*   *u-muk*   *hoŋ=be*
              cat=ERG   two-COUNT   three-COUNT 3SG-hand   hole=LOC
              end-uks-u=ca   *mima*   *lap-ma*
              insert-PRF-3.P=ADD mouse   catch-INF
              n-yas-uks-u-n.
              NEG-be_able-PRF-3.P-NEG
              'Although the cat tried to put its paw into the hole two or three times, it could not catch the mouse.'   [04_leg_03.009]

4.6 Interrogative proforms

Yakkha interrogatives are based on the roots *i* and *heʔ*. Table 4.7 provides an overview. While *i* may also occur independently, with the meaning 'what' (referring to events, see (36)), *heʔ* always occurs with further morphological material. Some interrogatives are easily analyzable into a base plus case marker, nominalizer or clause linkage marker, but others are not transparent. Interrogatives may also function as indefinite pronouns (see §4.4 above).

(36)   *i*   *leks-a?*
        what   happen[3SG]-PST
        'What happened?'

Table 4.7: Interrogatives

YAKKHA	GLOSS
i ~ ina ~ iya	'what'
isa	'who'
imin	'how'
ikhiŋ	'how much', 'how many', 'how big'
ijaŋ	'why'
heʔna ~ hetna	'which' (INT=NMLZ)
heʔne ~ hetne	'where' (INT=LOC)
heʔnaŋ ~ heʔnhaŋ ~ hetnaŋ ~ hetnhaŋ	'where from' (INT=ABL)
heʔniŋ ~ hetniŋ	'when' (INT=CTMP)

When the requested bit of information has a nominal nature, the base *i* occurs with the nominalizers *=na* or *=ha ~ =ya* (see §13.3). For example, food is expected to consist of several different items, and will be requested with the nonsingular/non-countable form *=ha ~ =ya* (see (37a)). Interestingly, these nominalized forms can also occur inside a noun phrase (see (37b)). In this example, *ina* does not request the identification of one item out of a set, as *heʔna* 'which' would. It rather implies that nothing is presupposed. The sentence is from a dowry negotiation, and here the speakers imply that there is nothing more to give to the bride. Similarly, when the identity of a person is requested but the speaker has no set of possible answers in mind, *isa* can occur inside a noun phrase (see (37c)). The context of this example was that some people were talking about the newly arrived researcher, and some other people who did not know about this fact (and did not see the researcher sitting around the corner) requested to know whom they were talking about.

(37) a. *i=ya*   *ca-ma?*
what=NMLZ.NSG   eat-INF
'What to eat?'

     b. *nani,*   *i=na*   *yubak?*   *n-chimd-uks-u.*
child, what=NMLZ.SG property 3PL.A-ask-PRF-3.P
'"Child, what property?" they asked her.'   [37_nrr_07.006]

108

c. *isa   mamu?*
who   girl
'What girl (are you talking about)?'

The interrogatives *ina/iya* and *isa* may also head noun phrases (without modifiers), host nominal morphology and appear as predicates of interrogative copular clauses (see (38)). When a noun phrase is headed by an interrogative, modifying material is not allowed, except for clauses in which the interrogatives have
an indefinite interpretation (discussed above in §4.4). The quantifying/degree interrogative *ikhiŋ* (derived from the demonstrative base *khiŋ* discussed in §4.5)
may also occur in noun-modifying position (see (39)).

(38) a. *i=ga   lagi ta-ya-ga=na?*
what=GEN   for   come-PST-2=NMLZ.SG
'What did you come for?'

      b. *na   i=ŋa   ħab-a=na?*
this   what=INS   cry[3SG]-PST=NMLZ.SG
'What made her cry?/Why does she cry?'   [13_cvs_02.050]

      c. *piccha=be   isa=ŋa   ghak*
child(hood)=LOC   who=ERG   all
nis-wa=ha?
know[3A;3.P]-NPST=NMLZ.NSG
'Who knows everything in childhood?'   [40_leg_08.079]
(a rhetorical question)

      d. *kha   yapmi=ci   isa=ci?*
these   person=NSG   who=NSG
'Who are these people?'

(39) a. *a-koŋma=ga   biha   ikhiŋ   sal=be*
1SG.POSS-MyZ=GEN   marriage   how_much   year=LOC
leks-a=na?
happen[3SG]-PST=NMLZ.SG
'In which year was your (my aunt's) marriage?'   [06_cvs_01.031]

      b. *ikhiŋ   miʔwa   ħond-end-u-g=ha!*
how_much   tear   uncover-V2.INSERT-3.P[PST]-2.A=NMLZ.NSG
'How many tears you have shed!'[11]   [37_nrr_07.111]

---

[11] The V2 *-end* indicates transitive motion downwards here.

Naturally, the same applies to *he?na* 'which' (see (40)); it always requests the identity of some item from a presupposed set.

(40)   a.   *he?na   des   wei-ka=na?*
            which   country   live[NPST]-2=NMLZ.SG
            'In which country do you live?'   [28_cvs_04.080]

       b.   *he?na   nis-u-ga=na?*
            which   see-3.P[PST]-2.A=NMLZ.SG
            'Which one did you see?'

The interrogative *ikhiŋ* is furthermore often found in exclamations about size, amount or degree, lacking the interrogative function (see (41) and (39b)).

(41)   a.   *lambu ikhiŋ   mi=na,   ammai   ikhiŋ*
            road   how_much small=NMLZ.SG oh_my! how_much
            mi=na   lambu lai!
            small=NMLZ.SG   road   EXCLA
            'How narrow the road is, oh my, what a narrow road!'
                                     [36_cvs_06.223]

       b.   *nna   dewan-ḍhuŋga baŋna   luŋkhwak sahro   cancan*
            that   Dewan-stone   so-called stone   very   high
            sa-ma=na,   pyak cancan, ikhiŋ   cancan!
            COP.PST-PRF=NMLZ.SG very high,   how_much high
            'That rock called Dewan stone was really high, it was very high, how high it was!'   [37_nrr_07.042]

       c.   *ikhiŋ   khumdu nam-my=a!*
            how_much tasty   smell[3SG]-NPST=NMLZ.NC
            'How good it smells!'

Examples of the other interrogatives are shown in (42).

(42)   a.   *ḍaktar=ci=be   khe?-ma   pʌryo,   hetniŋ,   hetne*
            doctor=NSG=LOC go-INF[DEONT] having_to when,   where
            khe?-ma=na=lai?
            go-INF=NMLZ.SG=EXCLA
            'He has to go to the doctor; when, and where to go?' [36_cvs_06.179]

       b.   *sondu   kha?la=na   cuŋ=be   tek   me-wa?-le*
            sondu   like_this=NMLZ.SG cold=LOC clothes NEG-wear-CVB
            jal   kapt-uks-u-g=hoŋ   hetnaŋ
            net   carry-PRF-3.P[PST]-2.A=SEQ where_from

       tae-ka=na?
       come[NPST]-2=NMLZ.SG
       'Sondu, where do you come from, in this cold, without clothes, and
       carrying this net?'   [01_leg_07.232]

c.   *ka*   *ijaŋ*   *cem-me-ŋ-ga=na?*
      1SG   why   cut-NPST-1SG.P-2.A=NMLZ.SG
      'Why do you cut me?'   [27_nrr_06.013]

d.   *kisa*   *saŋ-khek-khuwa,*   *hetne*
      deer   lead_by_rope-V2.CARRY.OFF-NMLZ   where
      sa-het-u=na   *haʔlo?*
      lead_by_rope-V2.CARRY.OFF-3.P[PST]=NMLZ.SG   EXCLA
      'The one who led the deer away, where did he lead it, by the way?'
                                                  [19_pea_01.024]

e.   *aniŋ=ga*   *ten*   *imin*
      1PL.EXCL.POSS=GEN   village   how
      et-u-ga=na?
      perceive-3.P[PST]-2.A=NMLZ.SG
      'How do you like our village?'

5 The noun phrase

The class of nouns is defined by the following structural features in Yakkha: nouns may head noun phrases and function as arguments of verbs without prior morphological derivations. Morphological categories typically associated with nouns are number and case. But since in Yakkha these operate on the phrasal level, the only category identifying lexical nouns is possessive inflection, marked by prefixes. Nouns typically refer to time-stable concepts like living beings, places or things, but also to some abstract or less time-stable concepts like *sakmaŋ* 'famine' or *ceʔya* 'language, matter, word'.

The sections of this chapter deal with the formation of nouns and some properties of lexical nouns (see §5.1), nominal morphology (see §5.2), relational nouns (see §5.3), and with the structure of the noun phrase (see §5.4).

5.1 Noun formation and properties of lexical nouns

5.1.1 Lexical nominalizations

Yakkha has three basic nominalizing devices, which will be discussed in more detail in Chapter 13. The common Tibeto-Burman nominalizers *-pa* and *-ma* are employed in lexical nominalization, deriving nouns that typically refer to types of persons, food, plants, animals and objects of material culture, e.g., *khikpa* 'roasted feather dish' (literally: be bitter-NMLZ; see Table 13.1 in Chapter 13 for more examples).[1] These markers attach to verbal roots (as far as one can tell since many such nouns are opaque). Occasionally, the marker can also attach to nominal roots, deriving nouns that are semantically associated with the meaning of the root, such as *Yakkhaba* 'Yakkha man, Yakkha person'.

As is common among Tibeto-Burman languages, Yakkha does not have a gender system; the nouns are not grouped into classes receiving distinct marking or triggering agreement across the noun phrase or the clause. In lexical nouns referring to persons, *-pa* marks default and male reference, and *-ma* marks female reference. This is particularly prominent in occupational titles (e.g., *thukkhuba/thuk-*

---

[1] This dish consists of roasted chicken feathers that are mixed with cooked rice.

khuma referring to male and female tailors, respectively) and in kinship terms (e.g., *namba* and *namma* for male and female in-laws, respectively). The marker *-pa* is also the default choice when a group contains members of both sexes, although another frequent option is to use co-compounds in such cases, e.g., *yakkhaba-yakkhamaci* 'the Yakkha men and women (~ the Yakkha people)'. In the current nominal lexicon (with 930 entries) there are 47 nouns ending in *-pa* and 120 nouns ending in *-ma*, most of which are not etymologically transparent, though.

Various zoological and botanical terms have lexicalized the markers *-ma* and *-pa*, so that such nouns invariably take one or the other marker. The lexeme for mouse is *mima*, for instance, and the lexeme for 'tiger' is *kiba*, regardless of whether it is a tiger or a tigress.

There are also 73 nouns that end in *-wa*, a morpheme probably cognate with *-pa*. These nouns are largely opaque; their roots cannot be determined any more. Examples are *hiʔwa* 'wind', *chiʔwa* 'nettle', *lagwa* 'bat', *takwa* 'long needle', and *lupliwa* 'earthquake'. Many of them are, again, botanical and zoological terms.[2]

Some nouns in Yakkha are lexicalized instances of headless relative clauses, e.g., *khuncakhuba* 'thief' (steal-eat-NMLZ), *hiŋkhuma* 'wife' (support-NMLZ), and *chemha* 'liquor' (be transparent-NMLZ), *tumna* 'senior' (ripen-NMLZ), *pakna* 'junior' (be raw-NMLZ). The nominalizers employed in these examples usually result in syntactic nominalizations, since they derive noun phrases, not nouns. They may either link attributive material to a head noun, or construct headless relative clauses (see Chapter 13 for a detailed description and abundant examples).

5.1.2 Compounding

Some kinds of nouns, particularly toponyms and nouns referring to kinship relations, botanical items, and objects of material culture tend to be multimorphemic. The most common pattern found is nominal compounding. Verb-noun compounds are found marginally, but the verbal roots always show some additional morphological material which can be traced back to nominalizations or infinitives.

5.1.2.1 Co-compounds and sub-compounds

Both co-compounds (symmetric compounds, *dvandva* compounds) and sub-compounds (hierarchical compounds, *tatpurusha* compounds) can be found in Yak-

---

[2] Nouns ending in *wa* can also be related to the lexeme for water or liquid in general, as it is the case in *kiwa* 'oil'; see below.

kha.[3] In sub-compounds, the first noun modifies the second, e.g., *laŋ-sup* 'sock' (literally: foot-sheath). In co-compounds, two conceptually close nouns stand as representatives of a concept or group that is more general than these two nouns, e.g., *pa-pum* for 'male ancestor' (literally: father-grandfather). The co-compounds generally refer to kinship relations or other groups of people. Table 5.1 and 5.2 provide more examples of each type.[4] Nepali nouns may also participate in nominal compounding (marked by [NEP] in the table).[5] Only sub-compounds combine Nepali roots with Yakkha roots.[6]

Table 5.1: Co-compounds

YAKKHA	GLOSS	COMPONENTS
cottu-kektu	'ancestors'	great-grandfather great-great-grandfather
pa-pum	'male ancestor'	father-grandfather
ma-mum	'female ancestor'	mother-grandmother
na-nuncha	'sisters'	elder sister-younger sibling
yakkhaba-yakkhama	'Yakkha people'	Y. man-Y. woman

Co-compounds are common in the languages of the eastern regions of Eurasia. The structural difference between co-compounds and sub-compounds is also reflected in their prosody: while sub-compounds constitute one stress domain, in co-compounds each component carries its own stress.[7] The components of either type of compound are treated as one phrase morphologically; case and number, which are both phrasal affixes in Yakkha, attach only once. Example (1a) shows a co-compound, (1b) shows a sub-compound. In cases of obligatorily possessed nouns, the possessive prefix attaches to both components of a co-compound, as

---

[3] The terms *dvandva* and *tatpurusha* come from the Sanskrit grammatical tradition.

[4] In current activities of language promotion, many neologisms are coined by some engaged speakers, like *mitniŋwa* 'belief' (literally: think-mind). It cannot be said with certainty which of them will become established in the language. So far, they are only used in written materials. Nevertheless these neologisms show that nominal compounding is a productive strategy to create new lexemes in Yakkha as it is spoken today.

[5] The lexeme *macchi* most probably has a Maithili origin: *marchāi* 'chili plant'. But it has undergone a substantial semantic shift, meaning 'chili plant', 'chili powder', and 'hot sauce or pickles' in Yakkha. In Belhare, its form is *marci* (Bickel 1997a).

[6] The nouns *muk* and *laŋ* refer to arm/hand and leg/foot, respectively.

[7] Cf. also Wälchli (2005: 3) on the intermediate position of co-compounds between words and phrases: "There are very few languages where co-compounds are undoubtedly words."

Table 5.2: Sub-compounds

YAKKHA	GLOSS	COMPONENTS
yaŋchalumba-aphu	'third-born elder brother'	third-born-elder_brother
laŋ-sup	'socks'	foot-sheath
laŋ-yok	'step, footprint'	foot-place
maŋme-muŋ	(a kind of mushroom)	eagle-mushroom
lupme-muŋ	(a kind of mushroom)	needle-mushroom
macchi-luŋkhwak	'mortar, grinding stone'	chili-stone
maksa-khamboʔmaŋ	'blackberry'	bear-raspberry
laŋ-kheʔwa	'toe'	leg-finger
laŋ-hup	'knee'	leg-thickening
lupta-kham	'landslide'	disperse/bury.NMLZ-ground
hamma-tek	'blanket'	cover/spread.INF-cloth
laŋ-phila	'thigh'	leg-thigh[NEP]
laŋ-tapi	'sole'	leg-hoof (probably [NEP])
muk-tapi	'palm of hand'	arm-hoof (probably [NEP])
dude-chepi	'milky onion'	milk[NEP](-e)-onion

in (1c). Since most co-compounds are from the domain of kinship, no instances of non-obligatorily possessed nouns with possessive marking in co-compounds could be found.

(1)   a.   *tukkhuba*   *tukkhuma=ci=ga*   *sewa*
            sick_man   sick_woman=NSG=GEN   service
            'service for sick men and women (i.e., medical service)'

                                                     [01_leg_07.300]

        b.   *kaniŋ*   *loʔa*   *wempha-babu=ci*
            1PL   like   male_teenager-boy=NSG
            'lads like we (are)'

                                                       [41_leg_09.075]

        c.   *u-ppa*   *u-ma=ci=ca*
            3SG.POSS-father   3SG.POSS-mother=NSG=ADD
            'her parents, too'

                                                       [01_leg_07.152]

Some sub-compounds appear in a fossilized possessive construction, such as *phakkusa* 'pork' or *wagusa* 'chicken meat'.

In the rather complex kinship system with frequent instances of obligatory possession (cf. §4.2.3), the prefixes marking possession usually attach to the first noun, as in *a-cya-mamu* 'my daughter' (1SG.POSS-child-girl) and *a-yem-namma* 'father-in-law's elder brother's wife' (1SG.POSS-father's elder brother's wife + female in-law). Exceptions are found in the terminology for in-laws on the cousin level, e.g., *khoknima-a-ŋoteŋma* 'father-in-law's sister's daughter who is younger than EGO (father's sister's younger daughter + my-female-in-law)'.

5.1.2.2 Toponyms

Among the toponyms, oronyms usually end in *luŋ* (PTB **r-luŋ* for 'stone', Matisoff 2003: 50). Examples are *Taŋwaluŋ* (Mt. Makalu), *Comluŋ* (Mt. Everest), *Phakṭaŋluŋ* (shoulder-rock, Mt. Kumbhakarna) or *Namthaluŋma* (locally important rocks, connected to a mythical story).

Another syllable appearing in toponyms is *liŋ*. It is most probably related to PTB **b-liŋ* for 'forest/field' (Matisoff 2003: 280) and occurs in names of Yakkha villages, e.g., *phakliŋ* (pig-field) or *mamliŋ* (big field), as it does in toponyms of other Tibeto-Burman languages, too.

Tibeto-Burman languages often have locational nominalizers referring to a place connected to some noun, e.g., in Classical Tibetan (Beyer 1992: 300). In Kiranti languages, one finds e.g., *-khom ~ -khop* in Thulung (cognate to Yakkha *kham* 'ground'), and *-dɛn* in Limbu (cognate to Yakkha *ten* 'village', Ebert 1994: 89). Yakkha employs another noun for this strategy, namely *laŋ*, with the lexical meaning 'foot'. It is, however, not a nominalizer; *laŋ* cannot be used to nominalize propositions, as in 'the place where he cut the meat'. In compounds, *laŋ* designates the area surrounding an object or characterized by it, as, e.g., in *khibu-laŋ* 'area around walnut tree' or *tonalaŋ* 'uphill area'. One also finds lexicalized instances, such as in (2), or metaphorical extensions, as in *pheksaŋlaŋ* 'malicious wizard' (literally: 'left-foot' or 'left-side'). It does not come as surprise that toponyms contain this marker, e.g., *lokphalaŋ* 'grove of lokpha bamboo (a huge kind of bamboo)'. However, the number of examples in the existing data do not allow conclusions about the productivity of *laŋ*.

(2) *maŋcwalaŋ=be   khy-a-ŋ.*
     water_tap=LOC   go-PST-1SG
     'I went to the public water tap.'   [40_leg_08.048]

This compounding strategy has developed from a relational noun construction (see (3) and §5.2.3 below). The relational noun *laŋ* locates an object (the FIGURE) next to the lower part of another object (the GROUND).

(3) siŋ=ga   u-laŋ=be
     tree=GEN   3SG.POSS-foot=LOC
     'below the tree' (the area around the tree, not right below its roots, and
     not right next to the stem either)

5.1.2.3 Botanical terms and nouns referring to liquids

Many botanical terms end in *siŋ* for 'tree' or in *phuŋ* for 'flower', e.g., *likliŋphuŋ*
'mugwort' and *kekpusiŋ* 'bull oak'. Above, in §5.1.1, nouns in -*wa* were discussed
as fossilized nominalizations. A homophonous morpheme with the etymological
meaning of 'water' is found in 14 lexemes referring to liquids, such as *cuwa* 'beer',
casakwa 'water in which uncooked rice has been washed' (rice-water), *lithuʔwa*
'sperm' and *mikwa* 'tear' (eye-water).

5.1.2.4 Lexical diminutives

Diminutive markers have been reported for various Kiranti languages (see Doornenbal 2009: 67 on Bantawa; Ebert 1997a: 95 on Athpare; Rutgers 1998: 85 on
Yamphu). Yakkha, too, has a class of nouns ending in a morpheme -*lik* ~ -*lek*
(without any independent meaning) and referring to small things or animals,
e.g., *siblik* 'bedbug', *taŋcukulik* 'pigtail, tuft of hair', *yaŋlik* 'seed', *khelek* 'ant',
phokcukulik 'navel', *moŋgalik* 'garden lizard', *makchiŋgilek* 'charcoal' and *poŋ-
galik* 'bud'. This is not a productive derivation process: -*lik* cannot attach to any
noun to indicate small size. The bases to which the diminutive attaches do not
necessarily exist as independent nouns; *sib* or *yaŋ*, for instance, do not exist.

Another diminutive-like marker, occuring only with animate nouns, is *cya* ~
cyak 'child', and it is found in terms for young animals in a fossilized possessive
construction, e.g., *phakkucyak* 'piglet' (historically: *phak=ka u-cya*) or *wagucya*
'chick' (historically: *wa=ga u-cya*).

5.1.2.5 Rhyming in compounds

Yakkha has a few nominal compounds that are built with rhymes and so-called
echo words as they are known in Nepali, where this is quite a productive strategy
to express associative plurality (e.g., *biskuṭ-siskuṭ* 'cookies and the like'). In Yakkha, there is, for instance, the name of a mythological bird, *Selele-Phelele*.[8] Further examples are *kamnibak-chimnibak* 'friends' (no independent meaning for

---

[8] Cf. file 21_nrr_04 of the corpus.

chimnibak could be established), *yubak-thiŋgak* 'goods, property' (no independent meaning for *thiŋgak* either) or *sidhak-paŋdhak* 'traditional, herbal medicine' (*sidhak* refers to medicine in general, *paŋdhak* could have been derived from *paŋ* 'house'). Rhyme-based morphology with reduplication and even triplication is very productive in adjectives and adverbials in Yakkha (see §6.4).

5.1.3 Proper nouns and teknonymy

Proper nouns identify a unique person, a place or some other entity, such as *Missaŋ* (a female name), *Homboŋ* (the name of a village) or *Kirant Yakkha Chumma* (the name of a social association). They differ from other nouns in that they rarely form compounds, and when marked as nonsingular, they only allow associative interpretations (X and her/his folks, X and the like).

One subgroup of proper nouns are teknonyms, i.e., names of adults derived from the name of their child, usually their first child. Referring to someone as father or mother of their eldest child is the respectful way to address or refer to older people, instead of using their names. The more frequent choice is, apparently, the name of the eldest son, but exceptions in favor of the eldest daughter's name are possible. Etymologically, teknonyms are possessive phrases, with the genitive =*ga* and the third person singular possessive prefix *u-* merged into a single syllable [gu], and the head nouns *ma* 'mother' and *(p)pa* 'father' (with geminated /p/ because of the possessive prefix).[9] The resulting word constitutes a single stress domain, with the first syllable carrying main stress. If the child's name does not end in a vowel, an epenthetic element *-e* is inserted. Examples are provided in (4).

(4) a. *Ram-e-guppa*
         Ram-EPEN-TEK.GEN.M
         'Father of Ram'

     b. *Bal-e-guma*
         Bal-EPEN-TEK.GEN.F
         'Mother of Bal'

---

[9] The nasal in the noun *ma*, in contrast, does not undergo gemination. The geminated *umma* that was offered by me in an elicitation earned the comment that this sounded like Limbu, not Yakkha.

5.1.4 The count/mass distinction

Mass nouns in Yakkha usually allow both mass and count readings, either referring to a concept as such, or to a unit or bounded quantity of that concept. Hence, the same lexeme may occur in different syntactic contexts without any morphological change or the addition of some classifying element. The verbal person marking, however, distinguishes the feature 'mass' from both singular and nonsingular. Mass nouns trigger the marker *=ha* on the verb (which is also found with nonsingular number). But with regard to all other verbal markers, the mass nouns trigger singular morphology. Neither the nonsingular marker *-ci* nor the singular clitic *=na* are possible on the verb when the nouns have a mass interpretation.

Compare the two uses of the words *yaŋ* 'money, coin' and *chem* 'music, song' in (5) and (6). In the (a) examples, these nouns have countable reference, as is evident from the presence of numerals and from the fact that they trigger number agreement on the verb (nonsingular *-ci* in (5a) and singular *=na* in (6a)). In the (b) examples, the nouns have mass reference, and hence do not take the nonsingular marker *=ci*. In fact, adding *=ci* would change the interpretation to nonsingular. The quantifier *pyak* in (5b) is of no help in determining semantic or structural differences, as it may have both a mass reading 'much' and a nonsingular reading 'many'.

(5)   a.   *hic=ci*   *yaŋ=ci*   *n-yuks-wa-ci=hoŋ,*
           two=NSG   coin=NSG   3PL.A-put_down-NPST-NSG.P=SEQ
           'After they will put down two coins, ...'   [26_tra_02.032]
     b.   *pyak*   *yaŋ*   *ub-w=ha.*
           much   money   earn-NPST[3SG.A>3.P]=NMLZ.NC
           'She earns a lot of money.'

(6)   a.   *ka*   *chem*   *chept-wa-ŋ=na.*
           1SG[ERG]   song   write-NPST[3.P]-1SG.A=NMLZ.SG
           'I will write a song.'
     b.   *chem(*=ci)*   *end-u-g=ha=i?*
           music(*=NSG)   apply-3.P[PST]-2.A=NMLZ.NC=Q
           'Did you turn on the music?'
           (It is clear from the context that the speaker did not refer to a plurality of songs, but to the sound coming out of the radio.)

As stated above, Yakkha does not have to add classifiers to distinguish between mass and count reference. There are, however, two markers that may convey

Table 5.3: Nouns with both count and mass reference

YAKKHA	GLOSS
cama	'(portion of) cooked rice'
ce?ya	'matter, language, word'
chem	'music, song'
chemha	'(glass of) liquor'
cuwa	'(glass/bowl of) beer'
kham	'ground, mud, (plot of) farm land'
khyu	'(portion of) cooked meat or vegetables'
maŋcwa	'(container with) water'
sa	'(portion of) meat'
yaŋ	'money, coin'
siŋ	'wood, tree'
tamphwak	'hair'

this distinction, namely the nominalizers =*na* and =*ha* in attributivizing function (etymologically related to the verb-final markers shown in (6)). In (7), while =*na* implies a bounded quantity, =*ha* implies mass reference. This distinction is parallel to the distinction in the demonstratives discussed in §4.3.

(7) a. *to=na* *cuwa*
uphill=NMLZ.SG beer
'the (bowl of) beer standing uphill'
  b. *to=ha* *cuwa*
uphill=NMLZ.NSG beer
'the beer uphill (i.e., the beer of the uphill households)'

A non-exhaustive list of nouns that allow both count and mass reference is provided in Table 5.3.

5.1.5 Inherent duality

Nouns that typically denote pairs, like legs, eyes, buttocks (but not inner organs like lungs and kidneys), usually occur with the nonsingular marker =*ci*. With regard to verbal agreement, they trigger plural instead of the expected dual marking. Apparently there is no need to maintain the plural/dual distinction with referents typically occurring in sets of two (see (8)).

(8) *a-tokcali=ci*   *n-dug=ha=ci*   (*tugaciha*).
     1SG.POSS-buttock=NSG   3PL-hurt-NMLZ.NSG=NSG
     'My bottom hurts.'

5.2 Nominal inflectional morphology

Nominal inflectional categories in Yakkha are (i) number, (ii) case and (iii) possession.[10] Number and case are generally encoded by clitics (phrasal suffixes). They
do not trigger agreement across the noun phrase. The case markers may also
attach to nominalized phrases or to anything else in nominal function (see §13.3
for examples). The only case that may appear phrase-internally is the comitative case, coordinating two nominal heads to form a noun phrase. Since case and
number markers operate on the phrasal level, the third category, possessor agreement, is the only category that applies exclusively to lexical nouns. It is encoded
by prefixes attaching directly to nouns (discussed together with the pronouns in
§4.2).

Further markers (particles) are possible on noun phrases, but since they pertain
to information structure, the reader is referred to Chapter 17 for their discussion.

5.2.1 Number

Yakkha distinguishes singular, dual and plural in the verbal domain and in pronouns, but only singular and nonsingular in nouns. Singular number is unmarked. The nonsingular marker is the phrasal suffix =*ci*, denoting that there
are multiple instances of the item in question, or that the item/person in question is accompanied by similar items/person (associative plurality). It attaches to
the rightmost element of the noun phrase (usually the nominal head), and thus
has scope over the whole noun phrase. The marker does not appear inside the
noun phrase, with the exception of numerals (see §4.5.2). Case markers follow
the number marker (see (9)).

(9) a. *kucuma*
         dog
         'a/the dog'
     b. *ghak*   *kucuma=ci=be*
         all   dog=NSG=LOC
         'at/to all the dogs'

---

[10] Inflectional in the sense of 'regularly responsive to the grammatical environment' (Bickel &
Nichols 2007).

The status of =*ci* as a phrasal clitic is clearly confirmed when looking at headless noun phrases or noun phrases where the order of head and modifier is reversed for reasons of information structure. The nonsingular marker may follow a genitive marker (see (10a)) or (syntactic) nominalizers (see (10b)), devices that would link modifying material to a head noun if there was one. In (10c), attributive material follows the head noun, and since it is the rightmost element, the nonsingular marker attaches to it.

(10) a. *heko=na   paṭi=ga=ci*
           other=NMLZ.SG   side=GEN=NSG
           'those (children) from the other side (i.e., the other wife)'

                                          [06_cvs_01.054]

      b. *hau,   kha=go,   eŋ=ga   yapmi*
           EXCLA these=TOP 1PL.INCL.POSS=GEN person
           loʔa=ha=ci=ca.
           like=NMLZ.NSG=NSG=ADD
           'Oh, these guys, they are like our people, too.'   [22_nrr_05.044]

      c. *pahuna   ta-khuba=ci*
           guest   come-NMLZ=NSG
           'the guests who are coming'   [25_tra_01.063]

5.2.1.1 Omission of nonsingular =*ci*

Number marking on nouns is not obligatory. With non-human reference it is frequently omitted. In (11a), it is clear from the context, from the demonstrative *ŋkha* and from the verbal agreement that *luŋkhwak* refers to more than one stone. With human referents, number marking cannot be omitted so easily (see (11b)). Another factor interacts with animacy/humanness here, namely generic vs. specific reference. In (11c), there is nonsingular human reference, but in a generic sense, referring to abstract classifications of people (those with whom one is/is not allowed to eat, in accordance with Hindu social law).[11] Here, the number marking can be omitted, in contrast to (b) where the noun refers to a specific group of people, namely the speaker's friends. With specific human reference, nonsingular marking was omitted only in songs, a genre which is expected to show deviations from spoken language, due to other constraints like rhythm and rhyming.

---

[11] The Yakkha belong to the Kiranti cultural sphere, but the past centuries of Hindu dominance have left their mark on the social organization of many Tibeto-Burman groups in Nepal.

(11) a. *ŋkha   mamu=ci=ŋa   ŋkha   luŋkhwak*
          those   girl=NSG=ERG   those   stone
          n-leks-u-ci=ha=bu.
          3PL.A-turn_over-3.P[PST]-3NSG.P=NMLZ.NSG=REP
          'Those girls have turned around those rocks, it is said.'

                                                    [37_nrr_07.118]

      b. **a-kamnibak*   *chimd-u-ŋ-ci-ŋ=ha.*
          1SG.POSS-friend   ask-3.P[PST]-1SG.A-NSG.P-1SG.A=NMLZ.NSG
          Intended: 'I asked my friends.'

      c. *ca-m=ha*   *yapmi*
          eat-INF[DEONT]=NMLZ.NSG   people
          men-ja-m=ha   *yapmi,   kha*
          NEG-eat-INF[DEONT]=NMLZ.NSG   people   these
          imin=ha=ci?
          how=NMLZ.NSG=NSG
          '(Are they) people with whom we should eat, or with whom we
          should not eat, of what kind (are they)?'   [22_nrr_05.040]

Number marking can also be omitted when a numeral is present in the noun
phrase (see (12a) and (12b)). However, instances with overt nonsingular marking,
as in example (12c), are far more frequent.

(12) a. *hip-paŋ*   *babu*
          two-CLF.HUM   boy
          'two boys'

      b. *hip-paŋ*   *paghyam-maghyam*
          two-CLF.HUM   old_man-old_woman
          'an old couple'   [01_leg_07.280]

      c. *sum-baŋ*   *phak-khuba   yapmi=ci*
          three-CLF.HUM   help-NMLZ   person=NSG
          'three servants'   [04_leg_03.015]

5.2.1.2 Associative interpretations of nonsingular marking

Nonsingular marking can be interpreted associatively, referring to people who
can be associated to the respective noun (see (13a) and (13b)), a feature that is
also found in other languages spoken in this area, e.g., in Newari (Genetti 2007:
98) and in Nepali (own observations). Occasionally, objects with nonsingular
marking can also be found with an associative interpretation (see (13c)), but this

is rare, at least in the current corpus; one rather finds enumerations of various objects than associative plural marking if a plurality of items is given.

(13) a. *a-koŋma=ci=nuŋ=le*   *wɛʔ=na?*
       1SG.POSS-MyZ=NSG=COM=CTR   exist[3SG]=NMLZ.SG
       'Oh, she lives with my aunt and her people?'   [06_cvs_01.074]

   b. *Lila   didi=ci*
       Lila   elder_sister=NSG
       'Sister Lila and her family'   [13_cvs_02.059]

   c. *i=ha*   *i=ha*   *yuncamakekek*   *ceʔya*
       what=NMLZ.NC   what=NMLZ.NC   funny   matter
       chumma=ci   *n-leks-a.*
       assembly=NSG   3PL-happen-PST
       'Various funny incidents, meetings and the like occurred there.'
                                                          [41_leg_09.008]

5.2.2 Core case markers (Group I)

Case, in the classical sense, is understood as the morphological marking on a noun or a noun phrase that indicates its syntactic relatedness either to a predicate (arguments or circumstantial participants) or to another noun (in the case of the genitive and the comitative). Yakkha distinguishes case clitics that operate on the noun phrase level, marking verbal arguments (Group I, discussed in this section), and markers that are functionally more flexible, and also less dependent phonologically (Group II, discussed in §5.2.3).

Case marking (ergative, genitive, comitative, equative) may also appear on dependent clauses that are often, but not necessarily, nominalized, as will be shown below and in Chapter 14 on adverbial clause linkage as well as in Chapter 15 on complementation. The parallelism between case markers and clause linkage markers is well-known in Kiranti and Tibeto-Burman in general (Genetti 1986; DeLancey 1985; Ebert 1993).[12]

Group I distinguishes seven cases, as shown in Table 5.4. Case, like number, is marked by enclitics in Yakkha, except for the nominative, which is the functionally and morphologically unmarked case in Yakkha. Since the case suffixes operate on the phrasal level, they attach to the rightmost element of the noun phrase. The case markers that start in a plosive have voiced allomorphs intervocalically and after nasals.

---

[12] It is, however, not clear yet whether there was a historical development from nominal case markers to clause linkage markers, or whether this parallelism is original to the system.

Table 5.4: Case markers (Group I)

CASE	MARKER	FUNCTION
nominative	Ø	intransitive subject, transitive patient, ditransitive theme and goal, citation form, location (restricted use), copular topic and predicate
ergative	=ŋa	transitive subject
instrumental	=ŋa	instrument, ditransitive theme, temporal reference
genitive	=ka	possession, material
locative	=pe	location, ditransitive recipients and goals, temporal reference
ablative	=phaŋ	source arguments
comitative	=nuŋ	coordination, associated referents, source arguments of some verbs

We know from other Kiranti languages that case markers can be stacked to yield more specific functions (e.g., Ebert 1994: 81; Dirksmeyer 2008: 6; Schikowski 2013: 26). Generally, composite case markers are common in Tibeto-Burman languages (DeLancey 1985: 60). In Yakkha, the locative or the ablative case marker can be added to the genitive of a proper noun to yield the meaning 'at/from X's place'. The ablative is also historically complex; see §5.2.2.6 below.

Several Kiranti languages have a (generally optional) dative marker -*lai*, e.g., Bantawa, (Doornenbal 2009), Puma (Bickel et al. 2007b), Camling, Athpare and Thulung (Ebert 1994)), which is homonymous with the Nepali dative marker –*lāī* and is probably a loan. Yakkha, however, does not employ this marker. It uses other strategies to mark semantic roles typically associated with dative marking: recipients and goals are either in the nominative or in the locative, and experiencers appear in various frames of argument realization, most prominently the Experiencer-as-Possessor frame. In the following, the cases of Group I and their functions will be introduced. More detailed information on argument realization and transitivity is found in Chapter 11.

5.2.2.1 The nominative (unmarked)

The nominative is morphologically and functionally the unmarked case in Yak-kha.[13] Participants in the nominative appear in their citation form, without any further marking. Intransitive subjects (S), transitive patients (P), ditransitive theme (T) and goal arguments (G), topic and comment of copular clauses, and to a certain extent locations, too, can be in the nominative and thus unmarked in Yakkha.[14] Example (14) shows S, P, T and G arguments in the nominative.[15]

(14) a. *ka   maŋcwa=be   khe-me-ŋ=na.*
          1SG   water=LOC   go-NPST-1SG=NMLZ.SG
          'I go to fetch water.'

      b. *nasa=ci   ŋ-und-wa-ci.*
          fish=NSG   3PL.A-pull_out-NPST-3NSG.P
          '(They) pull out the fish.'

      c. *ka   nda   caklet   pi-meʔ-nen=na.*
          1SG[ERG]   2SG   sweet   give-NPST-1>2=NMLZ.SG
          'I will give you a sweet.'

Yakkha shows a typologically common nominative/ergative syncretism: transitive subjects that are represented by a first or second person pronoun always appear unmarked (cf. §5.2.2.2).

Furthermore, both topic and comment in identificational copular constructions (see (15)), and the figure in existential/locative copular constructions (see (15c)) are in the nominative.

---

[13] Functional unmarkedness does not imply morphological unmarkedness, as research on marked-S languages has shown (Handschuh 2011; Brown 2001). In the Yakkha case system, morphological and functional unmarkedness coincide.

[14] With the discovery of ergativity, the term 'absolutive' came into use relatively recently to refer to the case of intransitive subjects and transitive objects when these have the same case, see McGregor (2009) and Haspelmath (2009) for summaries of the historical gestation of the term 'ergative'). Since then, research on ergativity has revealed that the system is far from uniform, and optional in many languages, other factors such as reference and information structure playing a greater role than had been expected. Haspelmath mentions the problem that the terminology of nominative-accusative and ergative-absolutive refers to an ideal system which is rarely found (Haspelmath 2009: 513). Both nominative and absolutive refer to the functionally unmarked case in a system, and their application usually extends well beyond marking S and P arguments. Therefore, I do not see the need to maintain the distinction between the terms 'nominative' and 'absolutive', since the unmarked case in an ergative system and the unmarked case in an accusative system have probably more shared properties than properties distinguishing them. Since 'nominative' is the older term, it will be used in this work.

[15] To keep the glosses as short and straightforward as possible, the nominative is generally not glossed.

(15) a. *na   ak=ka   paŋ   (om).*
      this 1SG.POSS=GEN house (COP)
      'This is my house.'

    b. *ka=go   arsale   leʔlo!*
      1SG=TOP person_from_year_eight CTR.EXCLA
      'I was born in the year eight (B.S.), man!'   [06_cvs_01.027]

    c. *nnakha=e   maŋcwa=ca   m-ma-ya-n.*
      that=LOC   water=ADD   NEG-be-PST[3SG]-NEG
      'There was no water, too.'   [42_leg_10.009]

Nominative arguments are also found in motion verb constructions, where a locative would be expected on the goal of the movement (see (16)). This option exists only for typical and frequent goals of movement, such as villages, work places, a school, a weekly market, etc. The respective nouns are never modified (see (17a), which was elicited in analogy to a sentence from the corpus, and which is well-formed only with a locative). Complements of verbs stating existence or location ('be at X') can generally not occur unmarked, but exceptions in the colloquial register are possible (see (17b)). The nouns in the nominative thus share features with incorporated nouns, although on other grounds they are not incorporated. Since the nouns mostly refer to names of places or landmarks, they refer to highly individuated participants, while incorporated nouns are often rather generic.

(16) a. *Poklabuŋ   tas-a-ma-c-u=hoŋ,*   ...
      Poklabung[LOC]   arrive-PST-PRF-DU-3.P=SEQ
      'When they arrived in Poklabung, ...'   [22_nrr_05.017]

    b. *ka   thuŋkha   khy-a-ŋ=niŋ,*   ...
      1SG steep_slope[LOC] go-PST-1SG=CTMP
      'When I was heading to the steep slopes, ...'   [40_leg_08.036]

(17) a. *uŋci=ga   ten*(=be)   khy-a-ma-ci,*   ...
      3NSG=GEN village*(=LOC) go-PST-PRF-DU
      'They went to their village, ...'   [22_nrr_05.037]

    b. *tumok   waiʔ-ŋa=na.*
      Tumok[LOC]   be[NPST]-1SG=NMLZ.SG
      'I am in Tumok.' (said on the phone)

5.2.2.2 The ergative =*ŋa*

Transitive and ditransitive A arguments are marked by the ergative =*ŋa* (see (18)), except when they are first or second person pronouns, which display an ergative/nominative syncretism (see (19)).

(18) a. *na,   jaba,   na   mamu=ŋa   luŋkhwak   pok-ma*
this   when   this   girl=ERG   stone   raise-INF

n-yas-u-n,   ...
NEG-be_able-3.P[PST]-NEG
'This one, when this girl could not raise the stone, ...' [37_nrr_07.039]

  b. *ka   a-ma=ŋa   khaʔla   ly-a-ŋ:*   ...
1SG   1SG.POSS-mother=ERG   like_this   tell[3SG.A]-PST-1SG.P
'Mother told me the following: ...'   [42_leg_10.011]

(19) a. *jeppa   nna   len   ka   a-ma=nuŋ*
really   that   day   1SG[ERG]   1SG.POSS-mother=COM

a-na=ga   ceʔya
1SG.POSS-eZ=GEN   matter

y-yen-u-ŋa-n=na=ŋa,   ...
NEG-obey-3.P[PST]-1SG.A-NEG=NMLZ.SG=ERG.CL
'Really, that day, because I did not listen to my mother's and my elder sister's warnings, ...'   [42_leg_10.051]

  b. *iya   nniŋda,   eh,   njiŋda   yoŋ-me-c-u-ga,*   ...
what   2PL[ERG]   oh   2DU[ERG]   search-NPST-DU-3.P-2.A
'Whatever you (dual) look for, ...'[16]   [22_nrr_05.084]

In Yakkha, first or second person reference can also be instantiated by full nouns instead of pronouns, which is unusual from the perspective of Indo-European languages. One may have a sentence with first or second person verbal person marking, but the structural position of the pronoun is occupied by a noun, as shown in (20).[17] In such participant configurations, there is overt ergative marking on the noun, in contrast to the nominative on pronouns with first or second person reference. To make a long story short, the differential agent marking (ergative or nominative) is mainly determined by word class (pronoun vs. noun), but also by reference (speech-act participants vs. third person participants).

---

[16] The speaker is correcting himself from plural to dual pronoun.

[17] Flexible agreement is discussed in §12.4. On the principles behind agreement in Tibeto-Burman see Bickel (2000).

(20) a. *phu=na   mamu=ŋa   yakkha   ceʔya*
      white=NMLZ.SG   girl=ERG   Yakkha   language
      nis-wa-g=hoŋ   maŋ-di-me-ŋ=na!
      know-NPST-2=SEQ   be_surprised-V2.GIVE-NPST-1SG=NMLZ.SG
      'I am surprised since you, a white girl, know Yakkha!'

    b. *a-phaŋ=ŋa   men=na,*
      1SG.POSS-MyZH=ERG   NEG.COP[3]=NMLZ.SG
      a-koŋma=ŋa=le   ta-ga=na   raecha!
      1SG.POSS-MyZ=ERG=CTR   bring[PST;3.P]-2.A=NMLZ.SG   MIR
      'Not the uncle, but you, auntie, really brought her here (the second
      wife)!'   [06_cvs_01.042]

The examples in (21) show that the ergative marker attaches to the final element
of the phrase, whether two nouns are conjoined by a comitative (see (21a) and
(b)) or whether the final element is a participle, as in (21c).[18]

(21) a. *lalubaŋ=nuŋ   phalubaŋ=ŋa   mamliŋ*
      Lalubang=COM   Phalubang=ERG   Mamling
      tas-a-ma-c-u.
      arrive-PST-PRF-DU-3.P
      'Lalubang and Phalubang arrived in Mamling.'   [22_nrr_05.041]

    b. *a-ma=nuŋ   a-na=ŋa*
      1SG.POSS-mother=COM   1SG.POSS-sister=ERG
      y-yog-a-n=niŋ=bi,   ...
      NEG-search[3A;1.P]-SBJV-NEG=CTMP=IRR
      'If my mother and sister had not searched for me, ...' [42_leg_10.052]

    c. *beuli=ga=ca   u-nuncha   parne=ŋa*
      bride=GEN=ADD   3SG.POSS-younger_sibling   falling=ERG
      chata   ham-met-wa.
      umbrella   spread-CAUS-NPST[3A;3.P]
      'Someone who is a younger sister of the bride, too, spreads an um-
      brella over her.'

                                                             [25_tra_01.053]

---

[18] The comitative marker may function as a coordinator, much like English 'and'. The verbal
person marking is triggered by the collective number features of both nouns (dual in (a), and
nonsingular in (b)). The negated form *yyogan* is found in all scenarios with third person acting
on first, except for 3SG>1SG.

For several Tibeto-Burman languages, ergative marking has been described as 'optional' and depending on pragmatic factors; see, e.g., LaPolla (1995) for a comparative account; Tournadre (1991) on Lhasa Tibetan; Coupe (2007) on Mongsen Ao and Hyslop (2011) on Kurtöp. Yakkha, however, has a strictly grammaticalized system of ergative marking; the ergative is obligatory on A arguments (under the above-mentioned conditions), which is in line with the findings on other Kiranti languages. Doornenbal (2009: 74) notes the same for Bantawa. Bickel (2003: 549) mentions an alignment split in Belhare that leaves first person singular pronouns unmarked.[19] The differential marking found on first and second person pronouns in Yakkha is determined by reference and word class, not by pragmatics.

On a final note, the ergative marker is also employed in adverbial clause linkage (see Chapter 14).

5.2.2.3 The instrumental =ŋ(a)

Yakkha exhibits an ergative-instrumental syncretism, which is not unusual, especially not in Kiranti. By formal criteria, except for one exception discussed below, the two cases cannot be distinguished. Functionally, though, they are distinct: the ergative marks animate agent arguments, while the instrumental typically marks inanimate participants like instruments (22a), effectors, forces and causes (22b).

(22) a. *chom=na*   *phiswak=ŋa*   *hot-haks-u=na.*
          pointed=NMLZ.SG   knife=INS   pierce-V2.SEND-3.P[PST]=NMLZ.SG
          'He pierced it with a pointed knife.'

      b. *kisiʔma=ŋa*   *solop*   *miyaŋ*   *eg-haks-uks-u.*
          fear=INS   immediately   a_little   break-V2.SEND-PRF-3.P[PST]
          'Out of fear, he immediately broke off a little (from the stick).'
                                                        [04_leg_03.023]

The medium for communication is also marked by the instrumental (23). In this usage, an allomorph =ŋ is possible.[20] In other Eastern Kiranti languages like

---

[19] Also non-Kiranti languages like Newari, Chepang and Kham have 'stable' grammaticalized ergative marking (LaPolla 1995), while this is not as clear for Classical Tibetan (DeLancey 2011c).

[20] Note the employment of exclusive vs. inclusive morphology in example (a). The speaker narrates the event from the perspective of the person who made the deontic statement, thus choosing the exclusive pronoun, despite the fact that the person she addresses is included. This shows that clusivity in Yakkha is not necessarily determined by including or excluding the addressee, but also by other people present in the speech situation.

Belhare, Chintang or Limbu, this function is taken over by a mediative/perlative marker *-lam* (Bickel 2003: 549; Schikowski 2012: 83; van Driem 1987: 51). A perlative case is not attested in Yakkha, at least not in the variety spoken in Tumok.

(23) a.   *aniŋ=ga*   *ceʔya=ŋ=bu*   *chem*
           1PL.EXCL.POSS=GEN   language=INS=REP   song
           lum-biʔ-ma=na=lai.
           tell-V2.GIVE-INF[DEONT]=NMLZ.SG=EXCLA
           'She says we have to sing a song in our language.' (reporting on the
           deontic statement of a person not included in the group)
                                                            [06_cvs_01.102]

       b.   *eŋ=ga*   *ceʔya=ŋ*   *sarab*
            1PL.INCL.POSS=GEN   language=INS   curse
            pi-ci=ha   *leks-a.*
            give-3NSG.P[3A;PST]=NMLZ.NSG   become[3SG]-PST
            'It happened that it (the sun) cursed them (the Linkha clan members)
            in our language.'   [11_nrr_01.031]

The instrumental also indicates temporal reference (see (24)). On a side note, it is very likely that the adverbial clause linkage markers *-saŋ* and *=niŋ(a)* (both marking cotemporality) are etymologically based on the ergative/instrumental case.

(24) a.   *wandik=ŋa*   *ta-meʔ=na.*
           next_day=INS   come[3SG]-NPST=NMLZ.SG
           'He will come tomorrow.'
       b.   *khiŋbelaʔ=ŋa*
            this_time=INS
            'at this time'

5.2.2.4 The genitive *=ka*

The genitive case is marked by the suffix *=ka* (mostly realized as [ga] as result of the voicing rule, see §3.5.1). It is used for possessive constructions, linking a possessor to a head noun (see (25)). As mentioned in §4.1 on possessive pronouns, the possessee may be inflected by a possessive prefix, as in (25b) and (25c). The possessive inflection may occur in addition to a genitive-marked possessor, or may replace it, as in (25c).

(25) a. *limbukhim=ci=ga   taŋme*
          a_clan=NSG=GEN   daughter-in-law
          'a daughter-in-law of the Limbukhims'   [37_nrr_07.002]

      b. *isa=ga   u-chya?*
          who=GEN   3SG.POSS-child
          'Whose child (is it)?'

      c. *m-ba   m-ma=ci*
          2SG.POSS-father   2SG.POSS-mother=NSG
          'your parents'

The head noun can also be omitted. The structure shown in (26a) is similar to a headless relative clause. Genitive-marked attributes may also be linked recursively to a head noun (see (26b)).[21]

(26) a. *heko=na   patti=ga=ci*
          other=MMLZ.SG   side=GEN=NSG
          'those (children) from the other one (i.e., the other wife)'
                                                         [06_cvs_01.033]

      b. *aniŋ=ga   liŋkha=ga   uhile   utpati*
          1SG.EXCL.POSS=GEN   a_clan=GEN   long_ago   origin
          mamliŋ=be   leks-a=na=bu.
          Mamling=LOC   happen[3SG]-PST=NMLZ.SG=REP
          'Our Linkha clan originated long ago in Mamling, they say.'
                                                         [11_nrr_01.002]

Relational nouns functioning as spatial adpositions also require the genitive, illustrated by (27). They are used in a possessive construction to which a locative must be added (see (27b); cf. also §5.2.3).

(27) a. *ṭebul=ga   mopparik*
          table=GEN   under
          'under the table'

      b. *saptakosi=ga   u-lap=pe*
          a_river_confluence=GEN   3SG.POSS-wing=LOC
          'on the shores of the Saptakosi'   [37_nrr_07.044]

The genitive is also employed to mark nominal modifiers referring to the material which the head noun is made of, as shown in (28).

---

[21] The example also shows that, at least in spoken language, discontinuous phrases are possible, since the adverb *uhile* belongs to the verb, but occurs inside the noun phrase.

(28) a. *kolenluŋ=ga   cuʔlumphi*
         marble=GEN   stele
         'a/the stele made of marble'   [18_nrr_03.001]

      b. *siŋ=ga   saŋgoŋ*
         wood=GEN   stool
         'a/the wooden stool'

      c. *plasṭik=ka   jhola=be*
         plastic=GEN   bag=LOC
         'in a plastic bag'   [13_cvs_02.045]

      d. *chubuk=ka   caleppa*
         ashes=GEN   bread
         'bread of ashes'[22]   [40_leg_08.056]

5.2.2.5 The locative *=pe*

Yakkha has only one locative case marker *=pe* ([be] when voicing applies; it can
be further reduced to [we] or simple [e]). Kiranti languages typically exhibit a
four-fold distinction of deictic locative case markers that respond to the hilly topography of the environment.[23] Such a case system consists of (i) one generic
locative and three further markers to locate items (ii) above, (iii) below or (iv)
on the same level as the deictic origin.[24] While other Eastern Kiranti languages
such as Limbu and Athpare also lack those altitudinal cases (Ebert 1997a: 118,
van Driem 1987: 49), Belhare, seemingly the closest relative of Yakkha, displays
them (Bickel 2001: 226). The locative marks the spatial coincidence of an entity
defined as FIGURE with an environment or landmark defined as GROUND (Levinson & Wilkins 2006: 3). It has a very general meaning, covering relations of
containment, proximity and contact, translatable as 'in', 'at' and 'on'. Examples
are provided in (29).

(29) a. *khorek=pe   cuwa*
         bowl=LOC   beer
         'There is beer in the bowl.'

      b. *nwak=ka   o-hop=pe*
         bird=GEN   3SG.POSS-nest=LOC
         'in the nest of the bird'

---

[22] A punishment for children: smearing ashes on their cheeks and slapping them.
[23] E.g., Camling, Bantawa, Puma, Thulung, Khaling (Ebert 1994); Yamphu (Rutgers 1998: 72);
    Belhare (Bickel 2001: 226).
[24] Termed 'vertical case' in Ebert (1994: 94); 'altitudinal case' in Dirksmeyer (2008: 62).

c. *o-thok=pe*   *toŋ-meʔ=na*
    3SG.POSS-body=LOC   fit[3SG]-NPST=NMLZ.SG
    'It suits/fits on her body.'

The basic locative construction (Levinson & Wilkins 2006: 15), the answer to the question 'Where is F?' is a copular construction with *wama* (with the suppletive nonpast stems *waiʔ, wεʔ, wei*) 'be, exist' (see (30a)). The same construction (with a different information structure) is generally used to introduce topics at the beginning of narratives (see (30b) and (30c)).

(30) a. *wa=ci*   *kaŋyoŋ=be*   *ŋ-waiʔ=ya=ci.*
         chicken=NGS   chicken_basket=LOC   3PL-be[NPST]=NMLZ.NSG=NSG
         'The chickens are in the chicken basket.' (a basket with small opening,
         to transport chicks)

    b. *panckapan=ga   kerabari=be*   *eko   mǎḍa   luŋkhwak*
        a_region=GEN   banana_plantation=LOC   one   huge   stone
        wε?=na.
        exist[3SG;NPST]=NMLZ.SG
        'In the banana plantations of Pǎckapan, there is a huge rock.'
                                                                [39_nrr_08.01]

    c. *eko   ten=be*   *eko   maghyam*
        one   village=LOC   one   old_woman
        wei-sa=na.
        exist[3SG;NPST]-PST=NMLZ.SG
        'In a village, there was an old woman.'   [01_leg_07.060]

Destinations of motion verbs and verbs of caused motion are generally marked by the locative, illustrated by (31). As explained above in §5.2.2.1, in certain scenarios the locative marking on the destinations of motion verbs can be omitted.

(31) a. *khali   puŋda=we*   *kheʔ-m=ha.*
         only   jungle=LOC   go-INF[DEONT]=NMLZ.NSG
         'Their only option was to go to the forest.'   [22_nrr_05.045]

    b. *ŋkhiŋbelak=pe   phopciba=ca   ok-saŋ*   *hop=pe*
        that_time=LOC   owl=ADD   shriek-SIM   nest=LOC
        pes-a-khy-a-ma.
        fly[3SG]-PST-V2.GO-PST-PRF
        'That time, the owl flew back to its nest, shrieking.'   [42_leg_10.042]

c. *khokpu=ga   siŋ=be   thaŋ-ma=ga   cog-a-ŋ.*
fig=GEN   tree=LOC   climb-INF=GEN   do-PST-1SG
'I tried to climb the fig tree.'   [42_leg_10.020]

d. *beula=ga   paŋ=be   beuli   ŋ-ghet-u=hoŋ, ...*
groom=GEN   house=LOC   bride   3PL.A-take_along-3.P[SBJ]=SEQ
'They take the bride into the groom's house and ...'

Example (32) shows three-argument constructions with locative-marked G arguments. Both inanimate and animate G arguments (i.e., goals and recipients) can be in the locative. Depending on the frames of argument realization, the locative is obligatory for some verbs, but optional for others (cf. §11.2.2 for a discussion of three-argument frames, alternations and differential object marking).

(32) a. *ka   a-cya=ci   iskul=be*
1SG[ERG]   1SG.POSS-child=NSG   school=LOC
paks-wa-ŋ-ci-ŋ=ha.
send-NPST-1SG.A-NSG.P-1SG.A=NMLZ.NSG
'I send my children to school.'

b. *uŋ=ŋa   ka=be   mendhwak   haks-wa=na.*
3SG=ERG   1SG=LOC   goat   send[3SG.A;3.P]-NPST=NMLZ.SG
'He sends me a goat.'

Ownership can be expressed by a verb of existence and the possessor in the locative (see (33)). The existential verb has a suppletive form *ma* for negated forms (33b).

(33) a. *ŋga=be   yaŋ   waiʔ=ya?*
2SG.POSS=LOC   money   exist[3SG;NPST]=NMLZ.NSG
'Do you have money?'

b. *eŋ=ga=be   yaŋ*
1PL.INCL.POSS=GEN=LOC   money
m-ma-n=ha.
NEG-exist[3;NPST]-NEG=NMLZ.NSG
'We do not have money.' (said among own family or group)

It is not surprising to find the locative marking extended to temporal reference. However, the more frequent marker in this function is the instrumental =*ŋa*. The locative in (34) might well be a Nepali calque, since, except for *na*, all words in (34) are Nepali loans.

(34) a.   *na   tihar   din=be*
           this   a_Hindu_festival   day=LOC
           'on this Tihar day'   [14_nrr_02.026]

      b.   *uncas   sal=be*
           thirty-nine   year=LOC
           'in the year thirty-nine'   [06_cvs_01.013]

There are also some fixed expressions with the locative, shown in (35).

(35) a.   *maŋcwa=be   khe-me-ka=na=i?*
           water=LOC   go-NPST-2=NMLZ.SG=Q
           'Are you going to get water (from the well)?'   [13_cvs_02.066]

      b.   *daura=be   khe-me-ŋ=na.*
           fire_wood=LOC   go-NPST-1SG=NMLZ.SG
           'I am going to fetch fire wood.'

There is a secondary locative marker *=ge ~ =ghe*,[25] used only with human reference, to express the notion 'at X's place' (see (36)).[26] The morpheme *=ge* is a
contraction of the genitive *=ga* and the locative *=pe*, a structure calqued from
Nepali, where one finds, e.g., *tapāī-ko-mā* 'at your place' (you-GEN-LOC), *mero-
mā* 'at my place' (mine-LOC).

(36) a.   *isa=ge?*
           who=LOC
           'At whose place?'

      b.   *bagdata   nak-se   khe?-ma*
           marriage_finalization   ask_for-SUP   go-INF[DEONT]
           pʌryo,   mapaci=ghe,   maiti=ci=ghe
           have_to.3SG.PST,   parents=LOC   natal_home=NSG=LOC
           khe?-ma=hoŋ,   ...
           go-INF[DEONT]=SEQ
           'One has to go and ask for the Bagdata (ritual), one has to go to the
           parents, to the wife's family, and ...'   [26_tra_02.013]

5.2.2.6 The ablative *=phaŋ*

The ablative *=phaŋ* (or [bhaŋ] due to voicing) marks the source of movement or
transfer (see (37)). Etymologically, it could be the result of stacking an older ab-

---

[25] Both forms are equally acceptable, and semantic differences could not be detected.
[26] The word *maiti* in (b) is a Nepali loan and refers to the natal home of a married woman.

lative =*haŋ* upon the locative marker =*pe*. Various other Kiranti languages have such complex ablative markers based on the locative marker (Ebert 1994: 81). In this light, it might also be noteworthy that Grierson lists an ablative -*bohuŋ* for a Yakkha dialect spoken in the beginning of the 20th century in Darjeeling (Grierson 1909). A possible cognate to the older marker =*haŋ* is the Belhare ablative =*huŋ* ~ =*etnahuŋ* (Bickel 2003: 549).[27]

(37) a. *taŋkheŋ=bhaŋ*   *tuknuŋ*   *percoʔwa*
           sky=ABL   thoroughly lightning
           uks-a-ma.
           come_down[3SG]-PST-PRF
           'Strong lightning came down from the sky.'   [21_nrr_04.017]

      b. *nna=be*   *ŋ-hond-u-n-ci-n=oŋ*   *nna*   *lupluŋ=bhaŋ*
           that=LOC NEG-fit-3.P-NEG-3NSG.P=SEQ that   cave=ABL
           tumhaŋ   *lond-a-khy-a=na.*
           Tumhang   come_out-PST[3SG]-V2.GO-PST=NMLZ.SG
           'As they did not fit there anymore, Tumhang came out of that cave.'
                                                         [27_nrr_06.005]

The ablative is also used to signify the starting point for a measurement of distance, as in (38).

(38) *i*   *let*   *u-cya=ŋa*   *u-ma*   *paŋ=bhaŋ*
       one day   3SG.POSS-child=ERG   3SG.POSS-mother house=ABL
       maŋdu *ta-meʔ-ma*   *mit-uks-u.*
       far   arrive-CAUS-INF   think-PRF-3.P[PST]
       'One day, the son wanted to bring his mother far away from the house.'
                                                         [01_leg_07.067]

The medium of motion and the technical medium of communication can also be marked by the ablative, in parallel to the functions of the Nepali ablative *bāṭa*.

(39) a. *kaniŋ*   *nawa=bhaŋ* *hoŋma* *kakt-wa-m-ŋa=na.*
           1PL[ERG]   boat=ABL   river   cross-NPST-1PL.A-EXCL=NMLZ.SG
           'We will cross the river by boat.'

      b. *kithrikpa=ŋa*   *solop*   *maik=phaŋ*
           policeman=ERG   immediately   microphone=ABL

---

[27] The form =*etnahuŋ* is most probably also combined of a locative and an ablative marker.

lu-ks-u-ci.
call-PRF-3.P[PST]-3NSGP
'The policeman immediately called out their names with the microphone.'

[01_leg_07.166]

c. *thawa=bhaŋ   to   ŋ-khy-a-ma=niŋ=go   mamu   nnhe=maŋ*
   ladder=ABL   up   3PL-go-PRF=CTMP=TOP   girl   there=EMPH
   wɛʔ=na=bu.
   exist[3SG]=NMLZ.SG=REP
   'When he climbed up on the ladder, the girl was right there (they say)!'   [22_nrr_05.111]

It is not unusual for Tibeto-Burman languages to display syncretisms between locative, allative and ablative (DeLancey 1985). In the majority of the Yakkha data, the Yakkha ablative marks the source, but there are quite a few examples with an ablative form (or an adverb derived by an ablative) marking the goal of a movement. Thus, Yakkha shows a syncretism between ablative and allative, to the exclusion of the locative.

(40) a. *heʔnang   khe-ks-a-ga=na?*
      where[ABL]   go-V2.CUT-PST-2=NMLZ.SG
      'Where are you about to go?'
   b. *yondhaŋ   khy-a.*
      across[ABL]   go-IMP
      'Go there.'
      'Go from there.'

Just like the secondary locative *=ge ~ =ghe*, the ablative shows a secondary form *=ghaŋ* that is used only with human reference, illustrated by (41a). Furthermore, the sentences in example (41) show that the ablative is not sensitive to topographic information. There is just one marker, used irrespective of directions and elevation levels with respect to the deictic center.

(41) a. *lumba=ghaŋ   ukt-u-ŋ-ci-ŋ,*
      Lumba=ABL   bring_down-3.P[PST]-1SG.A-3NSG.P-1SG.A
      lumbapasal=bhaŋ.
      shop_of_Lumba=ABL
      'I brought them down from Lumba (a person), from the Lumba shop.'
                      [36_cvs_06.049]

b.   [...]   *yaŋliham=bhaŋ=jhen,*   *koi.*
    [...]   lowland=ABL=TOP   some
    '[...] from the lowlands (local lowlands, not the Tarai), some people.'

                                            [36_cvs_06.465]

In some interrogative words and adverbs one can still see that they were composed of some root and an older ablative marker, e.g., in *nhaŋ* 'from here/and then' and *heʔnaŋ ~ heʔnhaŋ* 'from where'.[28]

(42)   a.   *heʔnaŋ*   *tae-ka=na,*   *mamu?*
          where_from   come[NPST]-2=NMLZ.SG,   girl
          'Where do you come from, girl?'
    b.   *mondaŋ*   *ky-a-ŋ=na.*
          below[ABL]   come_up-PST-1SG=NMLZ.SG
          'I came up from below.'

The ablative is generally not used for temporal reference. There is a postposition *nhaŋto* that covers this function (cf. §5.2.3 below).

5.2.2.7 The comitative *=nuŋ*

The comitative marker *=nuŋ* is cognate to Limbu *-nu*, Thulung *-nuŋ* (Ebert 1994: 81), Wambule *-no* (Opgenort 2004: 157), Bantawa *-nin* (Doornenbal 2009: 91), Chintang *-niŋ* (Schikowski 2012: 80). It can be used as a nominal coordinator, functionally similar to English *and* (symmetrical, with nouns of the same status, as defined in Haspelmath 2004a: 3). An example is given in (43a), a story title of the commonly found pattern 'X and Y'. Thus, by its very nature, this case marker can be found inside noun phrases, coordinating two nominal heads. The other case markers attach to the coordinate structure as a whole (see (43b)). The marker is phonologically bound to the first component of the coordinate structure.

Examples (43c) and (43d) serve to show that both parts of the coordinate structure contribute features to the person and number marking on the verbs. In (43c) the verb is marked for dual number, determined by the proper noun *ḍiana* and by the omitted pronoun *ka* 'I'. In (43d) the first person inclusive verbal marking is triggered by both *nniŋda* and *kaniŋ*.

(43)   a.   *suku=nuŋ*   *kithrikpa*
          Suku=COM   policeman
          'Suku (a girl's name) and the policeman'   [01_leg_07.143]

---

[28] Both forms *heʔnaŋ* and *heʔnhaŋ* are equally acceptable to the speakers, and semantic differences could not be detected.

b. *a-ma=nuŋ*   *a-na=ga*   *ceʔya*
1SG.POSS-mother=COM 1SG.POSS-sister=GEN matter
'the warnings of my mother and sister' [42_leg_10.051]

c. *hakhok=ŋa am-me-ŋ-ci-ŋ=ba,*   *ḍiana=nuŋ*
later=INS   come_over-NPST-EXCL-DU-EXCL=EMPH Diana=COM

am-me-ŋ-ci-ŋ,   *asen=ca.*
come_overNPST-EXCL-DU-EXCL yesterday=ADD
'Later, we will come of course, Diana and I, we will come; yesterday
(we came), too.' [36_cvs_06.376]

d. *la,*   *nniŋda=nuŋ kaniŋ haku cuŋ-i!*
alright 2PL=COM   1PL   now   wrestle-1PL[INCL;SBJV]
'Well, now let us wrestle!' [39_nrr_08.12]

The comitative is also used to mark peripheral participants that somehow accompany the main participants or that are associated with them (see (44)).

(44) a. *tabek,*   *kacyak, mina kondarik, caprak nhaŋ*
khukuri_knife, sickle, small spade,   spade   and_then

chomlaki=nuŋ   *puŋda=be*
split_bamboo=COM jungle=LOC

lab-a-cog-a-ŋ-ci-ŋ.
hold-PST-V2.MAKE-PST-EXCL-DU-EXCL
'Carrying khukuri, sickle, spades and split bamboo, we went into the
jungle.' (literally: 'made into the jungle')[29] [40_leg_08.008]

b. *ka=nuŋ kheʔ-ma=na*   *kamnibak*
1SG=COM go-INF[DEONT]=NMLZ.SG friend
'a friend who has to walk with me'

Some frames of verbal argument realization (both intransitive and transitive) require the comitative on their arguments, such as *cekma* 'talk', *toŋma* 'fit/agree/belong to', *kisiʔma* 'be afraid', *nakma* 'ask' and *incama* 'buy (from)' (see (45)).

(45) a. *mimik, ka=nuŋ seppa,*   *u-ppa=nuŋ=go*
a_little 1SG=COM RESTR.EMPH 3SG.POSS-father=COM=TOP

banda, n-jeŋ-me-n=na.
closed NEG-talk[3SG]-NPST-NEG=NMLZ.SG
'A little, just with me – with her father, nothing, she does not talk to
him.' [36_cvs_06.278]

---

[29] This V2 is only found in this one example so far, and thus, it is not treated in Chapter 10 on
complex predicates.

b. *limbu=ci=ga=nuŋ*
    Limbu_ethnic.group=NSG=GEN=COM

    toŋ-di-me=ppa,   *eŋ=ga=go*   [...]
    agree-V2.GIVE-NPST[3SG]=EMPH   1PL.INCL.POSS=GEN=TOP   [...]

    aru=ga=nuŋ   *n-doŋ-men.*
    other=GEN=COM   NEG-agree[3SG]-NPST-NEG
    'It is like the language of the Limbus, our (language). [...] It does not
    fit to the others.'   [36_cvs_06.256–58]

The comitative also plays a role in the derivation of some adverbs, as shown
in (46) (cf. §6.3). Furthermore, it is also found in clause linkage (cf. §14.7).

(46)   *khumdu=nuŋ*   *nam-ma*
        tasty=COM   smell-INF
        'to smell tasty'

5.2.3 Further case markers (Group II)

The markers of Group II are quite heterogenous; they do not define a class as
such. They can appear bound to their host or independently, i.e., stressed like a
separate word. Their phonological weight is also greater than that of the markers

Table 5.5: Case markers (Group II)

MARKER	FUNCTION
khaʔla	directional, 'towards'; manner 'like'
nhaŋto	temporal ablative, 'since, from X on'
haksaŋ	comparative, 'compared to'
haʔniŋ	comparative, 'compared to'
loʔa	equative, similative, 'like'
hiŋ	equative (size) 'as big as'
maʔniŋ	caritive, 'without'
bahek [NEP]	exclusive, 'apart from'
samma [NEP]	terminative, 'until, towards'
anusar [NEP]	'according to'
lagi [NEP]	benefactive, 'for'

of Group I; all of them are at least disyllabic. The case markers of Group II have a greater flexibility with regard to hosts they can select. Not only nominals are possible, but also adverbials. Some markers of Group II are not attested with nominal complements at all, like *kha?la* 'towards'. Furthermore, a number of the markers of Group II have hybrid word class status; they can also be used as adverbs. Some markers were borrowed into the language from Nepali, like *samma* 'until' or *anusar* 'according to'. Table 5.5 provides a summary of all Group II markers and their functions, described in detail in the following sections.

5.2.3.1 The direction and manner marker *kha?la*

The directional/manner marker *kha?la* 'towards, in the way of' is not attested with nouns, it only attaches to deictic adverbs. The directional reading is found when *kha?la* attaches to demonstrative adverbs typically occurring with motion verbs (see (47)). Etymologically, it is a combination of a demonstrative *kha* with an older allative or directional case marker. Cognates of such a marker are attested in several Kiranti languages: *-tni* in Bantawa (Doornenbal 2009: 84) and Puma (Sharma (Gautam) 2005), *-bai?ni ~ -?ni* in Chintang (Schikowski 2012: 83).

(47) a. *to=kha?la   ky-a!*
          up=towards come_up-IMP
          'Come up!'   [01_leg_07.329]

      b. *ŋkha limbu=ci   yo=kha?la   ŋ-khy-a.*
          those Limbu_person=NSG across=towards 3PL-go-PST
          'Those Limbus went away (horizontally).'   [22_nrr_05.017]

      c. *nniŋga=go,   mo,   mo=kha?la=ca*
          2PL.POSS=TOP down down=towards=ADD
          nis-uks-u-ŋ=ha.
          see-PRF-3.P[PST]-1SG.A=NMLZ.NSG
          'Your (home), below, downwards, I have seen it, too.'[30]
                                    [28_cvs_04.334]

The manner reading is found when *kha?la* attaches to demonstratives (see (48)).

(48) a. *ijaŋ bhasa   n-jiŋ-ghom-me=ha?*
          why language 3PL-learn-V2.ROAM-NPST=NMLZ.NSG
          hoŋ=kha?la=maŋ   ba?lo!
          that_very=like=EMPH   EMPH.EXCLA
          'Why do they walk around learning languages? Just like that! '
                                      [28_cvs_04.324]

---

[30] 'Downwards' could be any location outside the Himalayas.

b.   *nna=kha?la,   mamu,   i   cok-ma=?lo,   hamro   des?*
       that=like   girl   what   do-INF=EXCLA our   country
       '(It is) like that, what to do, girl, with our country?' [28_cvs_04.163]

The marker *kha?la* also has a homonymous adverbial counterpart[31] with a purely manner reading: 'like this', e.g., *kha?la om* 'It is like this.'

5.2.3.2 The temporal ablative marker *nhaŋto*

The marker *nhaŋto* (occasionally also *bhaŋto*) usually attaches to nouns or adverbs with temporal reference and marks the beginning of time intervals, regardless of whether they extend from a point in the past, present or future, as the examples in (49) illustrate. Example (49d) shows that it may also attach to demonstratives. The etymology of this marker is still transparent. It is composed of a demonstrative *na* with an (older) ablative *-haŋ* and the deictic adverb *to* 'up', yielding a phrase 'up from here'. This points towards a conceptualization of time as beginning below and flowing upwards. So far, this is just an educated guess, supported by the uses of some complex predicates, such as a combination of 'see' and 'bring up', best translated as 'having remembered'.

(49)   a.   *asen=nhaŋto*
           yesterday=TEMP.ABL
           'since yesterday'
     b.   *mi   wandik=nhaŋto*
           a_little later=TEMP.ABL
           'from a bit later on'
     c.   *lop=nhaŋto=maŋ*
           now=TEMP.ABL=EMPH
           'from now on'   [01_leg_07.030]
     d.   *nna=nhaŋto   sumphak cilleŋ   n-leks-u.*
           that=TEMP.ABL   leaf   face_up   3PL.A-turn-3.P[PST]
           'From that (event) on, they turned around the leaf plate to the proper
           side.'   [22_nrr_05.132]

This marker is occasionally also found as clause-initial coordinator used similarly to (50), which reflects the historical stage prior to becoming a bound marker. The previous clause is referred to by a demonstrative (not in these, but in plenty of other examples), resulting in a structure *nna, nhaŋto* 'that, and then upwards',

---

[31] Adverbial in the sense that it occurs independently, without nominal complements, and in the function of modifying verbs.

and eventually the clause-initial coordinator got reanalyzed as requiring a complement of some kind.

(50) a. *nhaŋto,*   *garo*   *n-cheŋd-et-wa=na,*
      and_then   wall   3PL.A-mason-V2.CARRY.OFF-NPST=NMLZ.SG
      to=khaʔla.
      up=towards
      'And then they mason the wall, upwards.'   [31_mat_01.093]

     b. *nhaŋto*   *phuna=chen*   *seg-haks-u-ŋ=hoŋ,*   ...
      and_then   white=TOP   choose-V2.SEND-3.P[PST]-1SG.A=SEQ
      'And then, I sorted out the white (bread), and ...'   [40_leg_08.060]

Marginally (in one case, to be precise), a synonymous marker *nhaŋkhe*, paraphrasable as 'from then on hither', was found with the same function.

(51)   *nhaŋkhe*   *u-ma*   *heʔniŋ=ca*   *issisi*
      and_then   3SG.POSS-mother   when=ADD   bad
      n-jog-uks-u-n.
      NEG-do-PRF-3.P[PST]-NEG
      'And then, he never did his mother bad again.'   [01_leg_07.082]

5.2.3.3 The comparative marker *haksaŋ/haʔniŋ*

The two comparative markers *haksaŋ* and *haʔniŋ* mark the standard in comparative and in superlative constructions. They are used interchangeably without any functional difference. Since they are treated in detail in Chapter 6, three examples shall suffice here. Examples (52a) and (52b) show comparative constructions, (52c) shows a superlative construction. The comparative markers can attach to all kinds of hosts, even to verbs. Etymologically they must have been converbal forms, since Yakkha has the converbal and adverbial clause linkage markers *-saŋ* and *=niŋ*, both indicating cotemporality. The structure of the Yakkha comparative markers could be calqued upon the structure of the Nepali comparative marker *bhanda*, which is a converbal form of the verb *bhannu* 'to say'. The identity of a possible verbal stem *hak* in Yakkha, however, could not be determined. Synchronically, the meaning of 'compare' is expressed by a complex verb *them-nima*. A likely candidate could be the verbal stem *haks*, which basically means 'send/send up', but is also used with the meaning 'weigh'.

(52) a. *nda*   *haʔniŋ*   *pak=na?*
      2SG   COMPAR   be_unripe=NMLZ.SG
      'Is he younger than you?'

b. *heko=ha   nwak=ci   haksaŋ   miyaŋ   alag   (...)*
other=NMLZ.NSG   bird=NSG   COMPAR   a_little   different   (...)
sa=na=bu.
COP.PST=NMLZ.SG=REP
'He was a bit different from the other birds, they say.'

[21_nrr_04.002]

c. *ghak   haʔniŋ   mi=na   mima*
all   COMPAR   small=NMLZ.SG   mouse
'the smallest mouse (of them all)'   [01_leg_07.003]

5.2.3.4 The equative and similative marker *loʔa*

The equative/similative *loʔa* marks the standard of an equation. It can have adverbial (53a) and nominal complements (a numeral in (53b)), even clausal, when they are embedded to verbs of perception or cognition. Example (53c) shows that the resulting equative phrase can be "fed" into a nominalization itself and thus made a referential phrase. The equative/similative marker is cognate to the comitative and adverbial clause linkage marker *-lo ~ lok ~ loʔ* in Belhare (Bickel 1993). The same marker is known as 'manner suffix' in Bantawa (Doornenbal 2009). There is one lexicalized instance of *loʔa*, the adverb *pekloʔa ~ pyakloʔa* 'usual(ly)', still morphologically transparent: its literal meaning would be 'like much/like many'.

(53)   a.   *khem   loʔa*
            before   like
            'like before'
      b.   *kaniŋ   ka-i-wa=niŋa   eko   loʔa   kheps-wa-m!*
            1PL   say-1PL-NPST=CTMP   one   like   hear-NPST[3.P]-1PL.A
            'When we say it, it sounds the same!'   [36_cvs_06.478]
      c.   *khem   loʔa=na   mekan!*
            before   like=NMLZ.SG   NEG.COP.2SG
            'You are not like someone from just before!' (said to someone who was a little tipsy but claimed to come right from work)

In a manner typical for Tibeto-Burman languages, this marker extends its function to clauses.[32] In (54) it takes over the function of a complementizer.

---

[32] See also DeLancey (1985) and Genetti (1991).

(54)　*ka*　　　*luʔ-meʔ-nen-in=ha*　　　　　*loʔa　cog-a-ni.*
　　　1SG[ERG]　tell-NPST-1>2-2PL=NMLZ.NSG　like　do -IMP-PL.IMP
　　　'Do as I tell you.'　　　　　　　　　　　　　　　　[14_nrr_02.019]

5.2.3.5 The equative marker for size *hiŋ*

The equative marker for size is etymologically related to the deictic adverb *khiŋ* (which is etymologically composed of the demonstrative *kha* and *hiŋ*). Attached to a noun phrase that functions as standard of comparison, this case marker indicates that an object is as big as the object referred to by the noun to which *hiŋ* attaches, as shown in (55). In this example, the whole phrase is nominalized and functions as the nominal predicate of a copular clause.

(55)　*m-muk*　　　　*a-laŋ*　　　　*hiŋ=na*　　　　　　*(om).*
　　　2SG.POSS-hand　1SG.POSS-foot　as_big_as=NMLZ.SG　(COP)
　　　'Your hand is as big as my foot.'

5.2.3.6 The privative marker *maʔniŋ*

The privative *maʔniŋ* is historically complex, similar to *haʔniŋ* above. It is composed of the negative existential copular stem *ma* (in third person singular, zero-marked) and the cotemporal adverbial clause linkage marker *=niŋ* (see (56)). In the same way as we have seen above for *loʔa* already, the privative phrase can be nominalized to serve as a nominal modifier, as shown in (56b).

(56)　a.　*i=ŋa*　　　*cama　niʔ-m=ha,*　　　　　　　*maŋcwa*
　　　　　what=INS　rice　cook-INF[DEONT]=NMLZ.NSG　water
　　　　　maʔniŋ?
　　　　　without
　　　　　'How (in what) shall we cook rice, without water?'　[13_cvs_02.108]
　　　b.　*wariŋba　maʔniŋ=ha*　　　　*khyu*
　　　　　tomato　without=NMLZ.NSG　curry_sauce
　　　　　'curry sauce without tomatoes in it'

5.2.3.7 Postpositions from Nepali

The benefactive/purposive postposition *lagi* (from Nepali *lāgi*), like in its source language, requires the genitive case. It can attach to proper nouns or to nominalized clauses like the infinitive in (57b). The genitive is, however, also found on purposive infinitival clauses without the postposition (see §14.3); it might well precede the point in time when *lagi* entered the Yakkha language.

(57) a. *hoʔi!*   *ak=ka*   *lagi* *iya=ca*   *tuʔkhi*
        enough! 1SG.POSS=GEN for   what=ADD   trouble
        n-jog-a-n.
        NEG-do-IMP-NEG
        'No, thanks. Do not bother about me (at all).'   [01_leg_07.186]

     b. *heʔniŋ-heʔniŋ=go* *yuncama=le*   *cok-ma*   *haʔlo!*
        when-when=TOP   laughter=CTR do-INF[DEONT]   EXCLA
        'Sometimes one just has to joke around, man!'   [36_cvs_06.263]

Another postposition from Nepali is *anusar* 'according to' (from Nepali *anusār*). It is typically found with nominalized clauses (see (58)).

(58) a. *ka-ya=na*   *anusar*
        say[3SG]-PST=NMLZ.SG   according_to
        'according to what was said/promised'   [11_nrr_01.012]

     b. *ka*   *nis-u-ŋ=ha*   *anusar*
        1SG[ERG]   see-3.P[PST]-1SG.A=NMLZ.NC   according_to
        'according to what I know/saw'   [25_tra_01.169]

The terminative postposition *samma* is used to specify the endpoint of an event (see (59)). This postposition is also found in clause linkage, in combination with native adverbial subordinators.

(59) *aniŋ=ga*   *ceʔya*   *hen*   *samma* *man=ha=bu.*
     1PL.EXCL.POSS=GEN   language   now   until   NEG.COP=NMLZ.NC=REP
     'Our language has not been established until now (they say).'
                                                                        [07_sng_01.06]

The exclusive postposition *bahek* 'apart from' serves to single out a referent to which the predication made in the sentence does not apply (see (60)).

(60) *taŋcukulik* *bahek=chen,*   *heŋ-nhak-ni-ma,*
     pig-tail   apart_from=TOP   cut-V2.SEND-COMPL-INF[DEONT]
     jammai, *kha* *ya-muŋ=ca,*   *ghak* *heŋ-nhaŋ-ma.*
     all   this   mouth-hair=ADD   all   cut-V2.SEND-INF[DEONT]
     'Apart from the pig-tail one has to cut it off, all, this beard too, all has to be cut off.' (context: funeral description)   [29_cvs_05.058]

In all the postpositions from Nepali, the phonological contrast between open-mid /ʌ/ and open /a/, which is present in the source language, is neutralized to open and long /a/.

5.3 Relational nouns

Yakkha has a class of relational nouns, in which specific meanings like 'root' are metaphorically extended to indicate more general spatial relations like 'under'. Usually, they occur in a possessive construction with the complement noun in the genitive and a possessive prefix attaching to the relational noun, which also hosts a locative case marker, as in (61a) and (61b). Relational nouns expressing spatial relations are a common source for case markers and postpositions in Tibeto-Burman (DeLancey 1985: 62).

(61)   a.   *phakṭaŋluŋ=ga*   *u-sam=be*
            Mount_Kumbhakarna=GEN   3SG.POSS-root=LOC
            'at the foot of Mount Kumbhakarna'   [18_nrr_03.001]

       b.   *caram=ga   u-lap=pe*   *camokla=nuŋ   ambibu=ga*
            yard=GEN   3SG.POSS-wing=LOC   banana=COM   mango=GEN

            u-thap   *ŋ-we?-ha.*
            3SG.POSS-plant   3PL-exist[NPST]=NMLZ.NSG
            'At the edge of the yard there are some banana trees and mango trees.'
                                                                                              [01_leg_07.176]

Relational nouns can also be found without the inflectional morphology between complement and relational noun, in a compound-like structure, as in (62a).[33] It is not only the locative but also the ablative which may attach to a relational noun, as shown in (62b). In this particular example, the ablative marking indicates a movement along a trajectory above the table.

(62)   a.   *hakhok=ŋa   ka   cend-a-ky-a-ŋ=hoŋ*
            later=INS   1SG   wake_up-PST-V2.COME_UP-PST-1SG=SEQ

---

[33] The person marking for third person on the main verb here is exceptional, since it refers to a first person participant. The expected regular first person inflection (*ipsamasaŋna*) would be possible as well. We know that such impersonal inflection is an alternative and frequent way to express first person nonsingular patients in Yakkha. This example is, however, the only instance in the corpus where this strategy is used for first person singular subject of an intransitive verb.

so-ŋ=niŋa=go   ka   luŋkhwak-choŋ=be
look-1SG=CTMP=TOP   1SG   stone-top=LOC

ips-a-masa.
sleep[3SG]-PST-PST-PRF

'Later, when I woke up and looked around, (I realized that) I had been sleeping on a rock.'   [42_leg_10.043]

b. *chalumma=ŋa*   *phuaba*   *ţebul-choŋ=bhan*   *bol*
    second_born_girl=ERG   last_born_boy   table-top=ABL   ball

lept-u-bi=na.
throw-3.P[PST]-V2.GIVE=NMLZ.SG

'Chalumma threw the ball over the table to Phuaba.'

Table 5.6 provides a summary and the original lexical nouns that are the bases for each relational noun. In (63), the relational noun is reduplicated, since the relation described is not one of location at the riverside, but one of movement along the river.

Table 5.6: Relational nouns

RELATIONAL NOUN	GLOSS	LEXICAL MEANING
choŋ ~ chom	above, on, on top of	'top, summit'
sam	below	'root'
lum	in, between	'middle'
yum	next to	'side'
hoŋ	inside	'hole'
lap	next to (upper part)	'wing'
laŋ	next to (lower part)	'leg'
heksaŋ	behind, after	'backside'
ondaŋ	in front of, before	'frontside'
chuptaŋ	to the right of	'right side'
pheksaŋ	to the left of	'left side'

(63)   *hoŋma=ga*   *u-lap-ulap*   *lukt-a-ma.*
       river=GEN   3SG.POSS-wing-REDUP   run[3SG]-PST-PRF
       'He ran along the shore of the river.'   [01_leg_07.216]

The two relational nouns *heksaŋ* and *ondaŋ* can, additionally, occur as adverbs. In the current corpus, they are mainly used adverbially (see (64)). As these examples show, *heksaŋ* and *ondaŋ*, in contrast to the other relational nouns, can also be used with a temporal interpretation.

(64) a.   *n-heksaŋ=be*   *cuwa*   *ta=ya.*
          2SG.POSS-behind=LOC beer   come[3SG;PST]=NMLZ.NSG
          'Some beer has arrived behind you.'

      b.   *tabhaŋ*   *panc* *hapta* *heksaŋ* *ta-me?=na.*
          son-in-law five   week   behind   come[3SG]-NPST=NMLZ.SG
          'The son-in-law comes five weeks later.'

      c.   *heksaŋ*   *so-ŋ-ci-ŋ*   *uŋci*
          later   look[PST]-1SG.A-3NSG.P-1SG.A   3NSG

          n-nis-u-n-ci-ŋa-n.
          NEG-see-3.P[PST]-NEG-3NSG.P-1SG.A-NEG
          'Later, when I looked for them, I did not see them.'   [41_leg_09.050]

Furthermore, there are spatial adpositions, presenting an orientation system that is based on the uphill/downhill distinction. They are treated in §7.4, together with the other word classes that are based on this topography-based system.

    Yakkha does not have a perlative/mediative *lam* or *lamma* case or postposition which is found in many of the surrounding languages.[34] There is also no postposition for the relation 'around'. This can only be expressed adverbially with *ighurum* (65).[35]

(65) *mi*   *em-saŋ*   *huŋ-ca-saŋ*   *ighurum* *yuŋ-i-misi-ŋ.*
     fire get_warm-SIM bask-V2.EAT-SIM around   sit-1PL-PRF.PST-EXCL
     '[...], we had sat around the fire, getting warm.'   [40_leg_08.033]

5.4 The structure of the noun phrase

The basic function of noun phrases is to establish reference. They occur as arguments of verbs, as complements of postpositions and as predicates in copular constructions. They may host morphology such as case and number markers and various discourse particles. Noun phrases are potentially complex; both co-

---

[34] E.g., in Chintang (Schikowski 2012); Belhare (Bickel 2003); Limbu (van Driem 1987), Athpare, Yamphu, Camling, Thulung (Ebert 2003c).

[35] This adverb has its origin in a noun *ighurum* 'round', which still exists synchronically in Yakkha.

ordinate and embedded structures can be found inside the noun phrase. Noun phrases can be headed by a lexical noun or by a pronoun, a demonstrative, a numeral, a quantifier or an adjective. Noun phrases that are not headed by a lexical noun are more restricted in the kind of modifying material they may contain. Noun phrases can also be headless, consisting just of some non-nominal material and a nominalizing device. Hence, no element in a Yakkha noun phrase is obligatory.

The default structure for headed noun phrases is head-final. Deviations from this pattern reflect discourse requirements, as will be discussed below. In noun phrases that are headed by personal pronouns or demonstratives, modifiers follow the head. Noun phrases with more than two modfiying elements are exceedingly rare.

5.4.1 Possessive phrases

Possessive phrases minimally consist of a noun (referring to the possessee) which is marked by a possessive prefix (indexing the possessor, see (66a)). If there is an overt possessor, marked by the genitive, the possessive prefix is generally optional (see (66b)), except for inherently possessed nouns such as core family terms and some other nouns implying part-whole relations. The possessive prefix may, however, also co-occur with a possessive pronoun, but only when the possessor has singular reference (see unacceptable (66c)). Recursive embedding is possible as well, but not found beyond two levels of embedding in the currently available data (66e).

(66) a. *(ak=ka)*   *a-cya=ci*
          (1SG.POSS=GEN)   1SG.POSS-child=NSG
          'my children'   [21_nrr_04.027]

      b. *ghak=ka   ḍaŋgak=ci*
          all=GEN   stick=NSG
          'everyone's sticks'   [04_leg_03.024]

      c. *eŋ=ga*   *(*en-)na-nuncha=ci*
          1PL.INCL.POSS=GEN   (*1PL.INC.POSS-)eZ-yZ=NSG
          'our sisters'   [41_leg_09.015]

      d. *beuli=ga   u-kamnibak*
          bride=GEN   3SG.POSS-friend
          'a friend of the bride'   [25_tra_01.089]

      e. *eko   khokpu=ga   u-thap=ka*   *u-sam=be*
          one   fig=GEN   3SG.POSS-plant=GEN   3SG.POSS-root=LOC
          'below a fig tree'   [42_leg_10.015]

5.4.2 Other modifiers: adjectives, numerals, quantifiers, demonstratives

Below, examples with numerals (see (67a)), demonstratives (see (67b) and (67c)), adjectives (see (67d) and (67e)) are shown. The examples also illustrate nominal morphology such as case markers, attaching to the rightmost element of the phrase, and optionally followed by discourse particles like the additive focus marker =*ca* or the restrictive focus marker =*se*.

(67) a. *eko a-muk=phaŋ*
          one 1SG.POSS-hand=ABL
          'from one of my hands'   [40_leg_08.022]

      b. *na tumna=ŋa*
          this elder=ERG
          'this elder one'   [40_leg_08.055]

      c. *ŋkha u-hiruʔwa=ci*
          those 3SG.POSS-intestine=NSG
          'those intestines'   [40_leg_08.039]

      d. *onek=ha   ceʔya=ca*
          joking=NMLZ.NSG matter=ADD
          'jokes, too'   [40_leg_08.057]

      e. *heko=na   whak=pe*
          other=NMLZ.SG branch=LOC
          'on another branch'   [42_leg_10.032]

      f. *honna=ga=se   ḍaŋgak*
          that_very=GEN=RESTR stick
          'only that person's stick'   [04_leg_03.025]

When the head noun is a pronoun or a demonstrative, the modifier is usually a quantifier or a numeral, and it follows the head. Occasionally other material elaborating on the identity of the pronominal referent is found as well, as in (68d).

(68) a. *iya-iya   nis-u-ga=na,   ŋkha ghak*
          what-what see-3.P[PST]-2.A-NMLZ.SG that all
          yok-met-a-ŋ=eba.
          search-CAUS-IMP-1SG.P=POL.IMP
          'Please tell me everything you saw.'   [19_pea_01.005]

      b. *kaniŋ ghak chups-i-ŋ=hoŋ,*   ...
          1PL   all   gather-1PL-EXCL=SEQ
          'As we all had gathered, ...'   [41_leg_09.054]

    c.   *uŋci   hip-paŋ*
         3NSG   two-CLF.HUM
         'the two of them'

    d.   *kaniŋ   yakkhaba   yakkhama=ci*
         1PL   Yakkha_man   Yakkha_woman=NSG
         'we Yakkha people'

5.4.3 Relative clauses

In (69) and (70), examples of relative clauses are given, constructed with the nominalizers *-khuba* and *=na/=ha* (treated in Chapter 13). They can be of considerable length and internal complexity. In (69c), three coordinated relative clauses serve to modify the same head noun, *whaŋsa* 'steam'.[36] They are joined by apposition and a comitative between the latter two relative clauses. This pattern of coordination is common. In (69d), the relative clause is preceded by an adjective and contains a complement-taking verb with an embedded infinitive.

(69) a. *ka   haksaŋ   tum=na   yapmi*
         1SG COMPAR elder=NMLZ.SG person
         'a person senior to me'   [40_leg_08.078]

     b. *khaʔla   otesraŋ=ha   pachem=ci!*
         like_this reverse=NMLZ.NSG young_boy=NSG
         'Such naughty boys!'   [40_leg_08.075]

     c. *caleppa   leps-a=ha,   ni-ya=ha*
         bread   deep_fry[3SG]-PST=NMLZ.NC fry[3SG]-PST=NMLZ.NC
         macchi=nuŋ   khi   whaŋd=ha   whaŋsa
         chili_sauce=COM yam boil[3SG;PST]=NMLZ.NC steam
         'the steam of deep-fried bread, fried chili and boiled yams'[37]
                                                    [40_leg_08.046]

     d. *issisi, khem-ma=i   me-ya-m=ha   ceʔya*
         ugly   hear-INF=FOC   NEG-be_able-INF=NMLZ.NC talk
         'ugly talk that one cannot listen to'   [36_cvs_06.600]

---

[36] Enumerations of coordinated items, with the comitative marker functioning as a coordinator (between the last two items if there are more than two), are common in Yakkha. These relative clauses are not embedded into one another; there are three different smells (or 'steams'), not the smell of yams that are cooked together with fried bread and sauce, which also would not make sense semantically, since *whaŋma* can only refer to boiling something solid in water.

[37] The lexeme *macchi* is a loan from Maithili. In Yakkha, it refers to chili peppers, but also to hot pickles and sauces.

Headless noun phrases, identical to headless relative clauses, are presented in
(70).

(70)   a.   *khi   khoŋ-khuba=ci*
            yam   dig-NMLZ=NSG
            'people digging yam'   [40_leg_08.009]

        b.   *to=na*
            up=NMLZ.SG
            'the upper one'

Some nouns take clausal complements (see §15.2.3).

5.4.4 Coordination

If nouns are coordinated in a noun phrase, they can either be juxtaposed (see
(71a)), or, by means of the comitative case marker, be attached to the penultimate
noun (see (71b)). The comitative may also coordinate adjectives. Example (71c)
shows again that several levels of embedding are possible: the coordinated nouns
may themselves be modified and these modifers may also be coordinated by =nuŋ.
Apposition is used relatively often; instead of using some more general term, one
often finds long enumerations of things. This could be a stylistic device to create
suspense in narratives, as exemplified in (71d).

(71)   a.   *yarepmaŋ,   likliŋphuŋ   nam-ma=niŋ=ca   ibibi*
            fern,   mugwort   smell-INF=CTMP=ADD   very_much
            sokma   ta-ya=na.
            breath   come[3SG]-PST=NMLZ.SG
            'When we sniffed at fern and mugwort plants, we regained quite
            some energy.'   [40_leg_08.018]

        b.   *paŋkhi=nuŋ   puŋdakhi*
            cultivated_yam=COM   wild_yam
            'cultivated yam and wild yam'   [40_leg_08.025]

        c.   *paŋ=be   phu=ha=nuŋ   makhur=ha   caleppa,*
            house=LOC   white=NMLZ.NC=COM   black=NMLZ.NC   bread,
            macchi,   khicalek=nuŋ   cuwa   py-a.
            pickles,   rice_dish=COM   beer   give-PST[1.P]
            'At home, they gave us white and black bread, pickles, khichadi and
            beer.'   [40_leg_08.051]

        d.   *uŋci=ŋa   tabek,   siŋ,   phendik,   lom-ma*
            3NSG=ERG   khukuri   wood   axe   take_out-INF

n-darokt-u.
3PL.A-start-3.P[PST]
'They started to take out khukuri knives, wooden clubs and axes.'

[41_leg_09.038]

Modifying material, too, can be coordinated by juxtaposition. Interestingly, when two sub-compounds are in apposition, the head noun of the first compound can be omitted, as shown in (72c).

(72)   a.   *phu-nuncha*   *na-nuncha=be*
           elder_brother-younger_sibling   elder_sister-younger_sibling=LOC
           pak=na
           be_unripe=NMLZ.SG
           'the youngest among the brothers and sisters'   [40_leg_08.052]

       b.   *hoŋkhaʔla*   *khi-ma=ha*   *tu-ma=ha*
           like_that_very   fight-INF=NMLZ.NC   wrestle-INF=NMLZ.NC
           ceʔya
           matter
           'the issue of fighting and wrestling like just told'   [41_leg_09.072]

       c.   *tondigaŋma*   *liŋkhacama-puŋda=ci*
           a_forest_name   a_forest_name-forest=NSG
           'the Tondigangma and Linkhacama forests'   [40_leg_08.011]

5.4.5 Combinatory possibilities

Concerning the combinatory potential inside the noun phrase, there seem to be only few restrictions. The average noun phrase, however, shows maximally two modifying elements, as illustrated below: NUM-ADJ-N in (73a), DEM-NUM-N in (73b), DEM-ADJ-N in (73c), POSS-NUM-N in (73d), POSS-DEM-N in (73e), DEM-QUANT in (73f). Other possibilities found are POSS-ADJ-N, ADJ-RC-N, NUM-RC-N, DEM-RC-N, POSS-NUM-N. The only recognizable tendency found was that of putting demonstratives first, although this is not a categorical rule.

(73)   a.   *eko*   *maḍa*   *tiʔwa*
           one   big   pheasant
           'one big pheasant'   [40_leg_08.036]

       b.   *na*   *eko*   *luŋkhwak=chen*
           this   one   stone=TOP
           'as for this one stone'   [37_nrr_07.007]

c. *na   makhruk=na   caleppa*
   this   black=NMLZ.SG   bread
   'this black bread'   [40_leg_08.053]

d. *chubuk=ka   hic=ci   caleppa*
   ashes=GEN   two=NSG   bread
   'two breads of ashes'   [40_leg_08.071]

e. *paghyam=ga   ŋkha   sala*
   old_man=GEN   that   talk
   'that talk of the old man'   [40_leg_08.076]

f. *kha   ghak   casak*
   this   all   uncooked_rice
   'all this uncooked rice'   [01_leg_07.016]

When the noun phrase is headed by a pronoun, only quantifiers or numeral modifiers are possible, and they follow the head, as has been shown above in example (68).

From these possibilities, the following (idealized) schema for a maximal noun phrase can be inferred (see Figure 5.1). As it was said above, the noun phrase is rather unrestricted, so that it is highly conceivable that noun phrases with an internal structure deviating from this schema can be found.

					N	
DEM	POSS	NUM	ADJ	RC	**PRON/**	NUM/
					DEM	QUANT

Figure 5.1: The maximal noun phrase

5.4.6 Information structure inside the noun phrase

When the order of head and attribute is reversed in a noun phrase, one can notice an increase in assertiveness to the right end of the phrase. In (74a), for instance, an assertion is made about an old man who has the habit of making jokes, a fact which sets the scene for what is to come: the old man plays a prank on the protagonist of the story. In (74b), the asserted information is not so much the fact that a market takes place, because the narrative is temporally embedded in a season known for events such as markets and fun fairs, but rather the fact that it is a comparatively big market. Modifying material to the right of the head noun is restricted to one element (as in Belhare, see Bickel 2003: 562).

(74) a. *nna   ighurum=be   a-pum   laktaŋge=ca*
         that round=LOC   1SG.POSS-grandfather   humorous=ADD
         wa-ya=na.
         exist[3SG]-PST=NMLZ.SG
         'In that round, a humorous old man was there, too.'   [40_leg_08.034]

   b. *inimma   maŋpha   ma=na   pog-a-ma.*
       market   quite   big=NMLZ.SG   rise[3SG]-PST-PRF
       'Quite a big market took place.'[38]   [01_leg_07.145]

Elements inside the noun phrase can also be focussed on or topicalized, as the following examples show. In (75a) *akkago* is a contrastive topic, in a (hypothetical) argument where one person brags about how many friends he has in contrast to the other person. In (75b), there is a contrastive focus marker inside the noun phrase, added because the assertion is made in contrast to a presupposition claiming that the opposite be true.

(75) a. *ak=ka=go   ibebe=ha   ghak   kamnibak=ci*
         1SG.POSS=GEN=TOP   everywhere=NMLZ.NSG   all   friend=NSG
         khaʔla=hoŋ   ŋ-waiʔ=ya=ci.
         like_this=SEQ   3PL-exist[NPST]=NMLZ.NSG=NSG
         'As for mine, I have friends everywhere, like this.'   [36_cvs_06.355]

   b. *na=go   aniŋ=ga=le   kham,   nniŋda   nhe*
       this=TOP   1PL.EXCL.POSS=GEN=CTR   ground   2PL[ERG]   here
       wa-ma   n-dokt-wa-m-ga-n=ha.
       live-INF   NEG-get-NPST-2PL.A-2-NEG=NMLZ.NSG
       'This is our land, you will not get the chance to live here.'

                                                          [22_nrr_05.012]

---

[38] The noun *inimma* is a neologism and not widely in use.

6 Adjectives and adverbs

Adjectives are lexical items specifying some property of a referent, while adverbs specify characteristics of an event such as cause, degree and manner, and ground it in space and time. They are treated in one chapter because they are often derived from the same roots, mostly of verbal origin.

The number of lexical adjectives and adverbs, i.e., those that cannot be traced back to verbal stems, is rather small. Nevertheless, adjectives and adverbs show some characteristics that motivate a separate lexical class. Most prominently, these are ideophonic patterns and the morphological processes of reduplication and triplication, which are highly productive in this class, but only marginally found in other word classes. The derivational morphology attached to the mostly verbal bases determines which structural position in the clause they will occupy, and hence, whether they have adjectival or adverbial function.

This chapter is structured as follows: adjectives are treated in §6.1. Comparative and equative constructions and the expression of degree are treated in §6.2. The derivations leading to the various types of adverbs are the topic of in §6.3. Reduplication, triplication and ideophonic patterns are so rich that they deserve their own section (§6.4).

Adjectives and adverbs that are employed for spatial orientation, involving a topography-based orientation system, will be discussed in Chapter 7.

6.1 Adjectives

6.1.1 Kinds of adjectives

The function of adjectives is the modification of nouns, either inside the noun phrase or as predicates of copular clauses. Many adjectives are based on verbal stems historically, but not all of these stems behave like full-fledged verbs synchronically, for instance in not showing the full range of inflectional possibilities that are known from verbs.

The major strategy for the derivation of adjectives is attaching the nominalizers =na (when the head noun has singular number) and =ha ~ =ya (when the head noun has nonsingular number or non-countable reference) to verbal roots, which

results in a minimal relative clause (see (1a) and (1b), and Chapter 13). The bases
of adjectives are not necessarily verbs, however. These nominalizers can link any
modifying material to a noun, regardless of its word class (see (1c)). This example
also shows that adjectives may head noun phrases, like minimal headless relative
clauses. Such headless relative clauses are different from lexical nouns; case and
number marking are allowed on them, but possessive marking is restricted to
lexical nouns.

(1) a.   *ci=ha*   *maŋcwa*
       get_cold=NMLZ.NC   water
       'cold water' (verbal: *maŋcwa cisabhya* 'The water got cold.')
   b.   *haŋ=ha*   *macchi*
       be_spicy=NMLZ.NC   pickles
       'hot pickles'
   c.   *nna*   *cancan*(=na)=bhaŋ*
       that   tall*(=NMLZ.SG)=ABL
       'from that tall one' (referring to a rock)   [38_nrr_07.040]

Some adjectives look like lexicalized inflected transitive verbs, like *cattuna*, meaning 'fat/strong' (no verbal root of this form attested) or the adjective in (2).[1]

(2)   *cend-u=na*   *a-na*
       wake_up-3.P[PST]=NMLZ.NSG   1SG.POSS-eZ
       'my witty elder sister'   [40_leg_08.057]

     Not all adjectival bases are synchronically found as verbs, though they show
the typical augmented structure of a verbal stem. Some adjectives show hybrid
behavior, illustrating their verbal origin. For instance, *khumdu* 'tasty' does not
have a corresponding verb with the citation form *khumma*. Yet, the adjective can
be inflected for number and negation like a verb. Person and TAM marking are
not possible though.[2] The same behavior is found for *ŋgolemninna* 'not smooth',
llininna 'not heavy'.

(3) a.   *khumdu=ha*   *caleppa*
       tasty=NMLZ.NC   bread
       'tasty bread'

---

[1] The example also illustrates how the lexical meaning of 'be awake' has been extended
metaphorically to mean 'witty, sprightly'.
[2] The affirmative forms always display *-u*, while the negative forms always display *-i*.

b. *kha   cuwa   ŋ-khumdi-n=ha!*
    this   beer   NEG-tasty-NEG=NMLZ.NC
    'This beer is not tasty!'

Some bases with unclear origin are *heko* 'other', *ucun* 'good' and *mam* 'big'.

(4) a. *mi=na   khesup*
        small=NMLZ.SG   bag
        'a/the small bag'
    b. *mãɖa   luŋkhwak*
        huge[NMLZ.SG]   stone
        'a/the huge rock'³

There are only very few adjectives that do not take the nominalizers *=na* and *=ha*. Another nominalizer, *-pa*, is found lexicalized in *ulippa* 'old'. Other adjectives appearing without prior nominalization are *maŋdu* 'far' and *upuŋge* 'free'. Lexemes with initial *u-* are occasionally found among adjectives, but more frequently so in adverbs. They originate from obligatorily possessed nouns (see §6.3).

Many roots can serve as adjectival or as adverbial bases (see also §6.3). A common marker for adverbial derivation is the comitative *=nuŋ* (also functioning as nominal case marker). Compare the use of *cattu* in (5a) and (5b).

(5) a. *cattu=na   pik   apt-u!*
        strong=NMLZ.SG   cow   bring_across-3.P[IMP]
        'Bring a fat/strong cow!'
    b. *ka   tondaŋ   um-meʔ-nen,   nda   cattu=nuŋ*
        1SG[ERG]   from_above   pull-NPST-1>2   2SG   strong=COM
        lab-u-g=hoŋ   tokhaʔla   ky-a.
        hold-3.P[IMP]-2.A=SEQ   upwards   come_up-IMP
        'I will pull you up, grab it firmly and come up!'   [01_leg_07.329]

6.1.2 Color terms

The system of Yakkha color terms⁴ is worth mentioning because it only has four basic color terms, with a privative distinction of *phamna* 'red' and *phimna* 'non-

---

³ This adjective has undergone a sound change: the nonsingular form is *mamha*, but the singular form became *mãɖa*, as a result of former *mamna*.

⁴ The following discussion of color terms relies on the natural stimuli in the environment, and on my observations of natural speech.

red', in addition to the two terms at both ends of a monochrome lightness-scale, *makhurna* 'black' and *phuna* 'white'. Such an economical system is rather rare crosslinguistically, but the prominence of red conforms to the distributional restrictions discovered in the seminal study of Berlin & Kay (1969: 2–3):

- All languages contain terms for white and black.

- If a language contains three terms, then it contains a term for red.

- If a language contains four terms, then it contains a term for yellow or green, but not both.

Via several derivations and combinations of the terms for red and non-red with the terms for black and white, one arrives at eleven color terms, shown in Table 6.1 (in their singular forms with *=na*). The term *phamna* comprises red, brown red and orange, and the term *phimna* covers everything non-red, from yellow over green to blue. There is another word *phiriryaŋna* for 'yellow', but it is only used for food items, and could be derived from the same root as *phimna*. Nowadays, a Nepali loan has entered the language, replacing *phimna* in as a term for 'yellow': *besareʔna*, derived from Nepali *besār* 'turmeric', which is, however, not used as a color term in Nepali. The monochrome terms can be used to specify the color terms with regard to their brightness or darkness, e.g., *maklup-maklupna phimna* for 'dark blue, dark green', or *maklup-maklupna phamna* for 'dark red, bordeaux red'.

In order to distinguish the colors on the large scale of what is covered by *phimna*, further modifications or comparisons can be made (see (6)).

(6) a. *sumphak* *loʔa=na*   *phim=na*
         leaf   like=NMLZ.SG   non-red=NMLZ.SG
         'as green as a leaf'
     b. *besar*   *loʔa=na*   *phim=na*
         turmeric   like=NMLZ.SG   non-red=NMLZ.SG
         'as yellow as turmeric'
     c. *massi*   *loʔa=na*   *phim=na*
         ink   like=NMLZ.SG   non-red=NMLZ.SG
         'as blue as ink'

It is very likely that the bases of the color terms are also verbs historically. (Doornenbal 2009: 292) mentions a verb *makma* 'be dark' for Bantawa, which must be cognate to *makhurna* 'black' in Yakkha. Yakkha has a verbal stem *phut*

Table 6.1: Color terms

STEM	GLOSS
phamna	'red'
phimna	'(yellow), green, blue'
phuna	'white'
makhurna	'black'
phalik-phalikna	'reddish, pink, violet (dark and light shades)'
phiʔlik-phiʔliŋna	'greenish, blueish (sky blue, petrol, light green)'
phiriryaŋna	'yellow (food)'
besareʔna [NEP]	'yellow'
phutiŋgirik	'bright white'
phutlek-phutlekna	'light grey, light yellow, light pink, beige'
maklup-maklupna	'dark brown/grey/blue/green/red'

referring to the process of becoming white, which has only been found in connection with hair so far. The syllables *-lik* and *-lek* occuring in the derivations are also known as lexical diminutives and from the derivation of adverbs. In addition to color terms, there are the lexemes *om(na)* 'bright, light', *kuyum(na)* 'dark' and *chyaŋchyaŋ(na)* 'transparent'.

6.1.3 Adjectives in attributive and in predicative function

In attributive function, the adjectives always appear in their nominalized form (i.e., as relative clauses), apart from the few exceptions mentioned above.

(7) a. *su=ha*   *cuwa*
         be_sour=NMLZ.NC   beer
         'sour beer'
     b. *lag=ha*   *nasa=ci*
         be_salty=NMLZ.NSG   fish=NSG
         'the salty fish'

In predicative function in copular clauses, some adjectives may appear simply in non-nominalized form. Compare the adnominal and predicative functions of *cancan* 'high' and *ucun* 'good/nice' in (8).

(8) a. nna   cancan=na   luŋkhwak
    that   high=NMLZ.SG   rock
    'this high rock'   [38_nrr_07.044]

    b. nna   dewan-ḍhuŋga   baŋna   luŋkhwak   sahro   cancan
        that   Dewan-stone   called   rock   very   high
        sa-ma=na.
        COP.PST[3SG]-PRF=NMLZ.SG
        'That rock called Dewan stone was very high.'   [38_nrr_07.039]

    c. ucun=na   paŋ
        good=NMLZ.SG   house
        'a nice house'

    d. purba   patti   dailo   yuŋ-ma=niŋ   ucun
        east   side   door   put-INF=CTMP   good
        n-leŋ-me-n.
        NEG-become[3SG]-NPST-NEG
        'If they (the Linkha clan members) put the door to the east, it will not
        be good.'   [11_nrr_01.016]

Other adjectives have to appear in nominalized form in the copular predicate, too. The nominalizers cannot be omitted in (9). While the base *mi* from (9a) is attested independently as a degree particle 'a little', the base *heko* is not attested independently.

(9) a. nhaŋ=go   lambu=ca=le   mi=na
    and_then=TOP   road=ADD=CTR   small=NMLZ.SG
    leŋ-d-e?=na!
    become-V2.GIVE-NPST[3SG]=NMLZ.SG
    'And then, the road, too, becomes narrow (unexpectedly)!'
                                               [28_cvs_04.011]

    b. kaniŋ   haksaŋ   heko=na   om.
        1PL   COMPAR   other=NMLZ.SG   COP
        'He is different from us.'   [21_nrr_04.009]

    c. uŋci=be=ca   niŋwa   heko=na
        3NSG=LOC=ADD   mind   other=NMLZ.SG
        leks-a=ha.
        become[3SG]-PST=NMLZ.NC
        'They also changed their mind.'   [41_leg_09.068]

6.2 Comparison, equation and degree

6.2.1 Degree

Adjectives can be modified by degree adverbs like *tuknuŋ* 'completely', *pyak* 'a lot', *mi/mimik/miyaŋ* 'a little', a deictic series of *khiŋ*, *ŋkhiŋ* and *hoŋkhiŋ* ('this much', 'that much', 'as much as mentioned before'). Most of them are not restricted to adjectives, but may also be used with nouns or verbs (see §4.5 for an overview). Furthermore, there are some Nepali loans like *sahro* or *ekdam*, both best rendered as 'very'. In (10a), the interrogative *ikhiŋ* 'how much' is used in an exclamative utterance.

(10) a. *pyak   cancan,   ikhiŋ   cancan!*
          very   high,   how_much   high
          '(It was) very high, how high!'   [38_nrr_07.039]
      b. *uŋ=ci=go   miyaŋ   mam=ha   n-sa=ba.*
          3NSG=TOP   a_little   big=NMLZ.NSG   3PL-COP.PST=EMPH
          'They were a little older (than me).'   [13_cvs_02.051]

There is no grammatical means to mark the excessive in Yakkha, which means that there is no regular way of stating that some property is beyond a certain tolerable measure, as expressed by the English particle *too*. Excessiveness is expressed by the quantifiers *pyak* '(very) much' or *tuknuŋ* 'completely', *ibebe* '(very/too) much' and consequently it is not possible in Yakkha to contrast 'very much' and 'too much'. Some adjectives have lexicalized the notion of excessiveness, all from the domain of taste: *khikcok* 'quite bitter', *lakcok* 'quite salty', *limcok* 'quite sweet'. Although it is always the same morpheme *-cok* that is involved, it is restricted to a very small semantic domain (at least according to the current data set), and thus it lacks the productivity that would be expected of a grammatical marker.

6.2.2 The equative

Equation is expressed by attaching the equative case *loʔa* 'like' to the standard of comparison (see (11)). The marker *-lo ~ lok ~ loʔ* is also known from Belhare as a comitative and an adverbial clause linkage marker (Bickel 1993) and as 'manner suffix' (deriving manner adverbs) from Bantawa (Doornenbal 2009: 299). In Yakkha, these functions are covered by the comitative marker *=nuŋ*. The equative *loʔa* may also be employed in complement clauses and equative clauses ('seem like [proposition]', 'do as told/do as if [proposition]').

(11) a. *gumthali   lo?a*
          swallow   like
          'like a swallow'

    b. *anar   lo?a   et-u-ŋ=ha.*
          pomegranate   like   perceive-3.P.PST-1SG=NMLZ.NSG
          'It seemed like pomegranate to me.'   [19_pea_01.011]

If properties are compared, the same structure is employed (see (12) and §6.1.2 for examples). The comparee may additionally be marked by an additive focus marker.

(12) a. *na   lo?a   nna=ca   mãḍa.*
          this   like   that=ADD   big
          'That one is as big as this one.'

    b. *phuama   chalumma   lo?a   keŋge?=na.*
          last_born_girl   second_born_girl   like   tall=NMLZ.SG
          'Phuama is as tall as Chalumma.'[5]

The following example shows that the resulting postpositional phrase may also be nominalized, yielding a headed relative clause in (13a), and a headless relative clause in (13b).

(13) a. *lupluŋ   lo?a=na   luŋdhaŋ=be*
          den   like=NMLZ.SG   cave=LOC
          'in a cave like a den'   [22_nrr_05.095]

    b. *u-ma   lo?a=na   sa=na=i.*
          3SG.POSS-mother   like=NMLZ.SG   COP.PST[3SG]=NMLZ.SG=EMPH
          'It was like a female.'   [19_pea_01.079]

The comparee is often omitted in natural discourse. The following two examples, with the comparees expressed by demonstratives were found in a narrative (14). Since the comparees have a strong tendency to be topical, they precede the standard of comparison.

(14) a. *hau,   kha=go,   eŋ=ga   yapmi*
          EXCLA   these=TOP   1INCL.POSS=GEN   person
          lo?a=ha=ci=ca.
          like=NMLZ.NSG=NSG=ADD
          'Oh, these guys, they look like our people, too.' [22_nrr_05.044]

---

[5] Terms based on birth rank are commonly used to adress/refer to people, also outside the family context.

b.   *ŋkha=ci=go   kaniŋ=nuŋ sahro toŋ-khuba loʔa*
      those=NSG=TOP   1PL=COM   very   fit-NMLZ   like

      men=ha=ci.
      NEG.COP=NMLZ.NSG=NSG
      'As for those (guys), they do not seem particularly similar to us!'
                                           [22_nrr_07.046]

6.2.3 The comparative and the superlative

The comparative and the superlative are covered by a construction in which either *haʔniŋ* or *haksaŋ* have to be attached to the standard of comparison, which
is a noun or a pronoun in the majority of cases (see (15)). Both comparative markers can be used interchangeably. The parameter of comparison does not receive
any comparative marking; it appears in its basic form. Both markers have their
origin in a converbal form (see also §5.2.3).

(15) a.   *heko=ha=ci=ga   haʔniŋ   pharak*
           other=NMLZ.NSG=NSG=GEN   COMPAR   different
           'different from the others people's (language)'
     b.   *heko=ha   nwak=ci   haksaŋ   miyaŋ   alag*   *[...]*
           otherNMLZ.NSG   bird=NSG   COMPAR   a_little   different   [...]
           sa=na=bu.
           COP.PST[3SG]=NMLZ.SG=REP
           'He was a bit different from the other birds, they say.'
                                           [21_nrr_04.002]

Often, the parameter of comparison is not expressed by an adjective, but by an
inflected verb (see (16)). Not only stative or ingressive-stative verbs are possible,
as (16b) with an embedded clause clearly shows.

(16) a.   *ka   uŋ   haʔniŋ   tum-ŋa=na.*
           1SG   3SG   COMPAR   be_ripe-1SG=NMLZ.SG
           'I am older than he is.'
     b.   *ka   nda haʔniŋ   lam-ma   ya-me-ŋ=na.*
           1SG   2SG   COMPAR   walk-INF   be_able-NPST-1SG=NMLZ.SG
           'I can walk (better/more) than you.' (Lit.: 'Compared to you, I can
           walk.')

The standard of comparison may also be an adverb, as in (17).

(17) u-laŋ=ci   encho   haʔniŋ   n-sas-a-ma.
      3SG.POSS-leg=NSG   some_time_ago   COMPAR   3PL-COP.PST-PST-PRF
      'Her legs got stronger than last time.' (Lit.: 'They became (something),
      compared to the last time.')

In the superlative, the standard of comparison is always the exhaustive quantifier
ghak 'all' (18).

(18) a. ghak   haʔniŋ   mi=na   mima
          all   COMPAR   small=NMLZ.SG   mouse
          'the smallest mouse'   [01_leg_07.003]
      b. ghak   haksaŋ   tum=na   paŋ
          all   COMPAR   old=NMLZ.SG   house
          'the oldest house'   [27_nrr_06.039]

6.3 Adverbs

Adverbs cover a wide range of functions, from grounding an event in time and
space to specifying its manner, intensity, cause and other characteristics of an
event. Adverbs in Yakkha can be grouped as follows:

- manner adverbs derived by the comitative *=nuŋ*

- temporal adverbs, mostly derived by the clause linkage marker *=niŋ*

- adverbs originating from obligatorily possessed nouns

- adverbs derived by *-lik ~ -lek ~ -rik*

- marginal derivations by *-lleŋ* and *-ci(k)*

- non-derived adverbs

- adverbs based on reduplication, triplication and ideophones (§6.4)

- adverbs used in spatial orientation, most of them embedded in a system of
  topography-based orientation (see §7.3)

The most common base for these derivations are verbal roots (most of them
attested synchronically), but other bases, such as demonstratives, are possible as
well. Some bases do not exist as independent words, so that their word class and
independent semantics cannot be reliably established.

6.3.1 Manner adverbs derived by the comitative *=nuŋ*

The major strategy to derive manner adverbs is attaching the comitative case clitic *=nuŋ* to roots of verbs with stative or ingressive-stative semantics (commonly both, which is evident from their interaction with tense-aspect morphology). The functions of the comitative marker range from nominal case marking to marking subordinate clauses, so that this type of adverb is strictly speaking a minimal adverbial clause.

Table 6.2 provides some examples of this adverbial derivation. The same roots can be turned into adjectives via the nominalizers *=na* and *=ha* (see (19), further examples in §6.1.1).[6] One adverb that was derived by the comitative, namely *tuknuŋ* (hurt=COM) has further developed into a degree marker with the meaning 'completely'.

Table 6.2: Manner adverbs derived by *=nuŋ*

VERBAL ROOT	ADVERB
chak 'be/get hard/difficult'	*chaknuŋ* 'hard, difficult'
cis 'be/get cold'	*cinuŋ* 'feeling cold'
khikt 'be/get bitter'	*khiknuŋ* 'tasting bitter'
li 'be/get heavy'	*linuŋ* 'heavily'
limd 'be/get sweet'	*limnuŋ* 'tasting sweet'
lakt 'be/get salty'	*laknuŋ* 'tasting salty'
nek 'be/get soft'	*neknuŋ* 'softly, gently'
nu 'be/get well'	*nunuŋ* 'well, healthy'
tuk 'hurt'	*tuknuŋ* 'painfully' ~ 'completely'

(19) a. *khuŋ-kheʔ-ma=niŋa*   *li-nuŋ=ca*
          carry_on_back-V2.CARRY.OFF-INF=CTMP   be_heavy=COM=ADD
          n-leŋ-me-n.
          NEG-become[3SG]-NPST-NEG
          'It will not get heavy when we carry it, too.'   [01_leg_07.044]

---

[6] Other Kiranti languages, e.g., Bantawa, Athpare, Chamling and Belhare, use the manner suffix *-loʔ* for the derivation of manner adverbs, which is also known as comitative case marker in some of them, e.g., in Belhare (Bickel 2003: 549) and in Athpare (Ebert 1994: 81). The cognate form in Yakkha has developed into an equative postposition. The only adverb derived by *loʔa* in Yakkha is *pyakloʔa* 'usually', etymologically 'like many/like much'.

b. *li=na*   *babu*
   be_heavy=NMLZ.SG   boy
   'a/the heavy boy'

6.3.2 Temporal adverbs

Many of the temporal adverbs, including the interrogative *hetniŋ ~ heʔniŋ* 'when' involve the particle *=niŋ*, which is also found as a clause linkage marker for contemporal events. In contrast to the manner adverbs, the base for temporal adverbs is not verbal. Some roots are adverbs by themselves, some are demonstratives. The deictic roots *nam*, *chim* and *khop*, denoting distances counted in years (with the utterance context as zero point), do not occur independently. In these adverbs, *=niŋ* is employed for past reference, while for future, the same roots end in *-ma*, e.g., *namma* 'next year', *chimma* 'two years later'. Table 6.3 provides an overview of the temporal adverbs.

Table 6.3: Temporal adverbs derived by *=niŋ*

ADVERB	GLOSS
heʔniŋ	'when'
asenniŋ	'(during) yesterday'
enchoʔniŋ	'on the day before yesterday' 'recently'
onchoʔniŋ	'long time ago'
khaʔniŋ	'this time'
ŋkhaʔniŋ	'that time'
hoŋkhaʔniŋ	'right at that time'
heniŋ	'(during) this year'
namniŋ	'last year'
chimniŋ	'two years ago'
khopniŋ	'three years ago'
namniŋ-chimniŋ	'some years ago'

Other temporal adverbs count the days before(i.e., in the past) or ahead (i.e., in the future) of the point of speaking. They are listed in Table 6.4 below, together with further temporal adverbs. Note that not all of them necessarily have the time of speaking as their point of reference. For instance, *wandikŋa* can mean 'tomorrow' or 'next day'. Two temporal adverbs can be compounded, yielding terms with less specific reference.

Table 6.4: Further temporal adverbs

ADVERB	GLOSS
wandik-ucumphak	'some days/time ahead'
okomphak	'two days after tomorrow'
ucumphak	'the day after tomorrow'
wandikŋa	'tomorrow, next day'
hen-wandik	'these days'
hensen	'nowadays'
hen	'today'
wandik	'later'
lop	'now'
khem	'shortly before'
asen	'yesterday'
encho ~	'day before yesterday'
achupalen	
asenlek	'some days ago'
asen-encho	'some time ago'

6.3.3 Adverbs based on obligatorily possessed nouns

A completely different etymological source for adverbs (and a few adjectives) are obligatorily possessed nouns. The possessive prefix can show agreement with the subject of the verb that is modified by the adverb, as in (20), but mostly, the third person form is used. The shift from a noun to an adverb is evident from the fact that these words do not have any nominal properties other than taking the possessive prefix. Further nominal modification or case and number marking, for instance, are not possible, and they are not arguments of the verbs; one would expect agreement morphology if this was the case. Table 6.5 shows some examples. To my knowledge, similar lexicalizations have not been described for other Kiranti languages, except for a few examples from Belhare mentioned by Bickel (2003: 563), who, e.g., provides a cognate to *ochoŋna* 'new'. In *uhiŋgilik* 'alive', not a noun, but the verb *hiŋma* 'survive' was the base for the derivation process, and the possessive prefix was probably added later, in analogy to the other adverbs.

(20) a. *a-tokhumak*   *yep-ma*   *n-ya-me-ŋa-n=na.*
          1SG.POSS-alone   stand-INF   NEG-be_able-NPST-1SG-NEG=NMLZ.SG

Table 6.5: Adverbs and adjectives originating in obligatorily possessed nouns

ADVERB/ADJECTIVE	GLOSS
uhiŋgilik	'alive'
ollobak	'almost'
otokhumak	'alone'
ohoppalik	'empty'
ochoŋ	'new'
ulippa	'old'
oleʔwa	'raw, unripe'
otesraŋ	'reversed'
uimalaŋ	'steeply down'
uthamalaŋ	'steeply up'

'I cannot stand alone.'   [27_nrr_06.017]

b. *o-tokhumak   nin-ca-meʔ=na.*
3SG.POSS-alone   cook-V2.EAT-NPST[3SG]=NMLZ.SG
'He cooks and eats alone.'

c. *eh,   na   nniŋ=ga   piccha=go   u-hiŋgilik*
oh   this   2PL=GEN   child=TOP   3SG.POSS-alive

wet=na,   haku=ca   tups-wa-m-ga=na.
exist[3SG]=NMLZ.SG   now=ADD   meet-NPST-2PL.A-2=NMLZ.SG
'Oh, your child is alive, you will meet her again.'   [22_nrr_05.087]

d. *lambu   o-tesraŋ   ikt-wa-m=na.*
road   3SG.POSS-opposite   chase-NPST-1PL.A=NMLZ.SG
'We follow the road in the opposite direction (i.e., we run in the wrong direction).'   [28_cvs_04.024]

6.3.4 Adverbs derived by *-lik ~ -lek*

Another marker that is frequently found in adverbs (and in some adjectives) is the lexical diminutive *-lik ~ lek* (occasionally also *-rik ~ -rek*), as shown in Table 6.6. It is also used in the derivation of lexical nouns that are characterized by their small size (see §5.1.2). Cognates of this marker exist in other Kiranti languages, e.g., *-let* in Athpare Ebert (1997a) and *-cilet* in Belhare (Bickel 2003). All of these adverbs have verbal stems as their base, and often the resulting adverbs occur

Table 6.6: Adverbs derived by *-lik* (and allomorphs)

ADVERB	GLOSS	VERBAL ROOT
cicaŋgalik-REDUP	'tumbling, overturning'	*caks* 'overturn'
hiklik	'turned around, upside down'	*hiks* 'turn'
iplik-REDUP	'properly [twisted]'	*ipt* 'twist, wring'
kakkulik-REDUP	'tumbling or rolling down'	*kaks* 'fall'
pektuŋgulik	'[folded] properly, many times'	*pekt* 'fold'
phoplek	'[pouring out] at once'	*phopt* 'spill, pour'
siklik	'[dying] at once'	*si* 'die'
sontrik	'[manner of] sliding, falling'	*sos* 'lie slanted'
wakurik	'bent, crooked'	*wakt* 'bend forcefully'
hobrek	'[rotten] completely'	*hop* 'rot'

with just these verbs, thus merely adding emphasis to the result of the verbal action, such as *iplik* '(properly) twisted'. Some forms in the table may also occur reduplicated. One ideophonic adverb ending in *-lek* was found, too: *piciŋgelek*, imitating a high-pitched voice, like the calls of eagles or owls. Some examples can be found below in (21).

(21) a. *maŋcwa   phoplek   lept-haks-u.*
          water   at_once   throw-V2.SEND-3.P[IMP]
          'Pour out the water at once.'

  b. *pektuŋgulik   pekt-u=hoŋ   u-lum=be*
      properly_folded   fold-3.P[PST]=SEQ   3SG.POSS-middle=LOC
      kaici=ŋa   yub-haks-u=na.
      scissors=INS   cut-V2.SEND-3.P[PST]=NMLZ.SG
      'He folded it properly and cut it through in the middle with scissors.'
          [Cut and Break Clips (Bohnemeyer, Bowerman & Brown 2010)]

6.3.5 Marginal derivations

Two further derivations were found, but each only with a handful of lexemes. One derivation creates adverbs based on verbal roots and a suffix *-ci(k)*,[7] and a reduplication of this complex of root and suffix. Three such adverbs were found, all from the semantic domain of experience: *hapcik-hapcik* 'whinily, weepily',

---

[7] Closing open syllables by /k/ is common in Yakkha and also known from the treatment of Nepali loans see §3.3.

chemci-chemci 'jokingly, teasingly', *yunci-yunci* 'smilingly'.

Another morpheme that is occasionally found in adverbs is *-lleŋ*. The currently known forms are: *cilleŋ* 'lying on back', *walleŋ* 'lying on the front', and *cilleŋ-kholleŋ* 'rocking, swaying' (like a bus on a bad road or a boat in a storm). There is a directional case marker *-leŋ* in Belhare (Bickel 2003; the notion expressed by *khaʔla* in Yakkha), and thus it is very likely that this derivation has the same source, although such a marker does not exist in Yakkha synchronically.

6.3.6 Non-derived adverbs

Finally, there are also a few adverbs that have no transparent etymology, such as *hani* 'fast', *swak* 'secretly', *tamba* 'slowly',[8] *pakha* 'outside' and *sori* 'together'. Interestingly, these adverbs cannot be turned into adjectives by nominalizing them; one could, for instance, not say *soriha yapmici 'the people who are together'.

6.4 Reduplication, triplication and ideophones

Rhyming patterns as well as ideophones are very common in Yakkha adverbs and adjectives, and often both are combined. Since they are exceedingly rare in the other word classes, they can be taken as an indicator (albeit rather statistic than categorical) for adverb-hood or adjective-hood. The bases for reduplication can be of verbal, adverbial or ideophonic nature. As always, there are some bases with obscure origin, too. The bases for triplication are always monosyllabic and lack independent meaning. Ideophonic adverbs are based on a similarity relation between their phonetic form and the concept they express. This is not necessarily a relation based on acoustic similarities (as in onomatopoeia); other senses such as sight, taste or smell can as well be involved in ideophonic expressions. Hence, the relation between signifier and signified is more iconic than in "core" lexemes, where the semantics and the phonological form are in an arbitrary relationship.

The phonological behavior of reduplicated/triplicated forms and that of ideophones often shows deviations from the core lexicon, such as peculiar stress patterns or unusual segments that do not occur in nouns or verbs of the language (such as /gh/ or /bh/ in Yakkha). This has already been noted for Bantawa by Rai & Winter (1997), who label them paralexemes, relating the exceptional behavior of such forms to their emphatic or expressive function (expressing feelings or the attitude of the speaker).

---

[8] The final syllable *-ba* is a nominalizer, but the origin of the stem *tam* is not known.

Reduplicated adjectives and adverbs are always stressed on the second syllable (*can.'can*). This suggests an analysis of reduplication as a prefixation. Bisyllabic words are generally stressed on the first syllable in Yakkha (cf. Chapter 3), but since prefixes are not part of the stress domain in Yakkha, words consisting of a prefix and a monosyllabic stem are stressed on the second syllable. Triplicated forms are always stressed on the last syllable, which is exceptional for Yakkha stress assignment.

6.4.1 Reduplication in adjectives

The reduplicated adjectives mostly relate to physical features like size, form or texture. Another group are adjectives based on experiencer verbs. The above-mentioned pattern of nominalization to indicate attributive or nominal usage (cf. §6.1.1) also holds for adjectives derived by reduplication (see (22)).

(22)   a.   *u-yabulu?a*   *ikhiŋ*   *jonjon=na!*
            3SG.POSS-lips   how_much   elevated=NMLZ.SG
            'How bulging his lips are!'

      b.   *chainpur*   *cancan=na=be*   *wai?=na.*
            Chainpur   high=NMLZ.SG=LOC   exist[3SG]=NMLZ.SG
            'Chainpur is in a high (place).'

      c.   *a-phok*   *gaŋgaŋ*   *leks-a=na.*
            1SG.POSS-stomach   burstingly_full   become[3SG]-PST=NMLZ.SG
            'My stomach is now full as a tick.'

Table 6.7 shows the verbal roots serving as bases (as far as they can be reconstructed) and the corresponding reduplicated adjectival forms. Generally, post-nasal voicing of unaspirated consonants applies, and is copied to the first syllable to yield maximal identity between base and reduplicated syllable. Thus, forms like *bumbum* or *jonjon* emerge, which are unusual from the perspective of Yakkha phonological rules, because they display voiced initial obstruents in a language that has largely lost the contrast between voiced and unvoiced obstruents. The only exception is *cancan*, which retains its unvoiced obstruents, but the affricate behaves exceptional also in other lexemes with respect to the voicing rule. With regard to the verbal bases, augmented stems (i.e., with a CVC-t structure) omit the augment /-t/ before reduplicating. Stems alternating between a CVC-s and a CVN structure (such as *caks ~ caŋ*), generally choose the CVN stem form as base for the reduplication (see §8.1 for stem formation). If the base has CVC structure and the consonants have the same place of articulation, this does not result in gemination in the reduplicated form. Rather, the coda consonant is omitted in

Table 6.7: Adjectives derived by reduplication

VERBAL BASE	ADJECTIVE	GLOSS
cand 'rise up'	*cancan*	'tall, high'
chekt 'close'	*chekchek*	'deep, low, narrow'
–	*chenchen*	'lying', 'sidesleeping'
chiks ~ chiŋ 'tighten, tie off'	*chiŋchiŋ*	'tight'
chuks ~ chuŋ 'be wrinkled'	*chuŋchuŋ*	'wrinkled'
cos 'push'	*jonjon*	'sticking out, bulging'
–	*gaŋgaŋ*	'[belly] full as a tick'
hupt 'tighten, unite'	*hubhub*	'buxom, compact'
kept 'stick, glue'	*kepkep*	'concave, sticking to'
–	*lenlen*	'horizontally huge, lying'
mopt 'cover, close'	*mopmop*	'covered'
–	*nepnep*	'short in height'
–	*pakpak*	'hollow, bowl-shaped'
pekt 'fold'	*pekpek*	'flat, thin, folded'
phaps ~ pham 'entangle'	*phaphap*	'[hair] entangled, scraggy'
phopt 'spill, turn over'	*phophop*	'face-down, overturned'
pok 'get up, rise'	*pokpok*	'in heaps, sticking out'
poks ~ poŋ 'explode'	*boŋboŋ*	'elevated, convex'
pups ~ pum 'tuck up, roll in fist'	*bumbum*	'[plastering a house] thickly'/ '[body parts] swollen'/ '[teeth] sticky'
pur 'cut off, break off'	*pupup*	'chubby, short and fat'
sos 'lie slanted'	*sonson*	'[sliding] horizontally'
yok 'search, look for'	*yokyok*	'carefully, balancing'

the first syllable (e.g., *pha.ˈphap*). Some of these adjectives can be combined to yield further meanings, e.g., *chekchek-boŋboŋ* (low-elevated) 'zig-zag, uneven'.

Some adjectives derived from experiential verbs are shown in Table 6.8. They always have causative semantics, as shown in (23). Their bases are from those experiential verbs that code the experiencer as possessor (cf. §11.1.10). These verbs consist of a noun (denoting a sensation or a body part) and a verb, often a motion verb. The reduplication only involves the verbal stem of these compounds. In attributive position, they host the usual nominalizers *=na* or *=ha*. Since the stem *keʔ* 'come up', that is involved in many of these compounds, ends in a glottal stop, which never occurs word-finally in Yakkha, it is replaced by /k/ at the end of the word.

Table 6.8: Adjectives derived from experiential verbs

VERBAL BASE	ADJECTIVE	GLOSS
lok-khot 'get furious'	*lok-khokhok*	'causing fury'
chik-ek 'get angry/hateful'	*chik-ekek*	'causing anger/hate'
hakamba-keʔ 'yawn'	*hakamba-kekek*	'causing to yawn'
luŋma-tukt 'love'	*luŋma-tuktuk*	'loveable, pitiable'
pomma-keʔ 'get lazy'	*pomma-kekek*	'making lazy'
yuncama-keʔ 'have to laugh'	*yuncama-kekek*	'funny, ridiculous'
chippa-keʔ 'be disgusted'	*chippa-kekek*	'disgusting'

(23) a. *batti   chik-ʔekek   leks-a=na!*
          electricity   causing_hate   become[3SG]-PST=NMLZ.SG
          'The power cuts drive me mad already!'

  b. *hakamba-kekeʔ=na   ceʔya*
          making_yawn=NMLZ.SG   matter
          'talk that makes me sleepy'

6.4.2 Reduplication in adverbs

Table 6.9 shows adverbs derived by reduplication. Their number is far lower than that of reduplicated adjectives. The verbs that provide the base for the adverbs may occur together with the adverbs that are derived out of them, see, e.g., (24a). In such cases, it is hard to say what the semantic contribution made by the adverbs is, apart from emphasis. In the same example the adverb also serves as base for a rhyme *miŋmiŋ*, which adds further emphasis. For *lumlum* 'loudly', it is not quite clear whether it may also have an onomatopoeic component.

(24) a. *maŋmaŋ-miŋmiŋ   m-maks-a-by-a-ma.*
          wondering-RHYME   3PL-be_surprised-PST-V2.GIVE-PST-PRF
          'They were utterly surprised.'   [22_nrr_05.028]

  b. *lumlum   mokt-u-ga=i!*
          loudly   beat-IMP[3.P]-2.A=FOC
          'Beat (the drum) loudly!'

Table 6.9: Adverbs derived by reduplication of verbal roots

VERBAL BASE	ADVERB	GLOSS
cend 'wake up'	*cencen*	'[sleeping] lightly'
chups 'gather'	*chumchum*	'gathered, economically, sparing'
chuŋ 'wrap, pack'	*chuŋchuŋ*	'sadly, sunken'
lus 'roar, deafen'	*lumlum*	'loudly, powerfully'
maks 'wonder'	*maŋmaŋ*	'wondering'
sips 'twinkle, squint'	*simsim*	'squinting, blinking'

Table 6.10: Reduplication of adverbs

VERBAL BASE	ADVERB
ipt 'twist, wring'	*iblik-iblik* 'twisted'
sips 'close [eyes]'	*simik-simik* 'blinking'
khik 'be bitter'	*ekhik-ekhik* 'tasting bitter'
khumdu 'tasty'	*ekhumdu-ekhumdu* 'tasting good'
maŋdu 'far'	*emaŋdu-emaŋdu* 'far away'
–	*esap-esap* 'swiftly'
–	*elok-elok* 'from far away'

Reduplication of independent adverbs (and adjectives) is also possible, expressing intensity or iterativity (see (25)).[9]

(25)   a.   *sakhi*   *iblik-iblik*   *ipt-a=na.*
            thread   twisted-REDUP   twist-PST[3SG]=NMLZ.SG
            'The thread is properly twisted.'
    b.   *batti*   *simik-simik*   *hand-u=na.*
            light   blinking-REDUP   burn-3.P[PST]=NMLZ.SG
            'The (electric) torch is blinking.'

Some of the reduplicated adverbs add /e-/ to each component, without further change of meaning (see Table 6.10). This is attested for Belhare, too, analyzed as marking extension (Bickel 1997a).

---

[9] See Doornenbal (2009: 304) for a similar point on Bantawa triplicated adverbs.

6.4.3 Triplication

Triplication patterns, similar to those found in Bantawa and Chintang (cf. Rai 1984; Rai & Winter 1997; Rai et al. 2005) were also found in Yakkha (see Table 6.11). Triplicated forms in Yakkha differ from those in the two languages mentioned above in three ways:

- they are not derived from stems that have an arbitrary, lexical, non-iconic meaning; most of them have an ideophonic component (i.e., an iconic relationship between the concept expressed and the phonological form)

- they never host the suffix -wa (which is a property of Chintang and Bantawa triplicated adverbs)[10]

- they always change the initial consonant in the syllables of the rhyme, i.e., only the vowel of the base is retained

The triplication pattern in Yakkha involves a syllable CV (occasionally CV-ŋ) functioning as the base, and two suffixed syllables building a rhyme, changing the initial consonant to /r/, /l/, or (rarely) to /t/, /c/, /k/ or /b/. Occasionally, the syllables building the rhyme are closed by a velar stop or nasal, as in *seleŋleŋ* or *siliklik*. The vowel remains the same in all three syllables. This process has to be analyzed as triplication and not simply as recursive reduplication, because bisyllabic words such as *huru* or *phili* do not exist.[11] Triplicated adverbs show a divergent stress pattern; it is always the last syllable that is stressed.

Some examples of triplicated adverbs are provided in (26). As (26b) illustrates, adjectives may be derived from these adverbs via the nominalizers =na and =ha.

(26) a. *o-heli*   *tururu*   *lond=ha.*
          3SG.POSS-blood   flowing   come_out[PST]=NMLZ.NSG
          'He was bleeding profusely.'
      b. *hiwiwi=na*   *hiʔwa*
          blowing_gently=NMLZ.SG   wind
          'a gentle wind'
      c. *ka*   *caram=be*   *khiriri*   *is-a-ŋ=na.*
          1SG   yard=LOC   spinning   revolve-PST-1SG–NMLZ.SG
          'I was spinning around in the yard.'

---

[10] The suffix is an adverbializer in these languages.

[11] The same was found in Chintang (Rai et al. 2005), while in Bantawa, some forms may also appear with just one repeated syllable, suggesting an analysis of triplication as recursive reduplication with the function of emphasis in Bantawa (Doornenbal 2009: 304).

d. *heko=na whak=pe a-tek*
other=NMLZ.SG twig=LOC 1SG.POSS-clothes
het-u=hoŋ ka haŋcaŋcaŋ chu-ya-ŋ.
get_stuck-3.P[PST]=SEQ 1SG dangling hang-PST-1SG
'My clothes got caught on another branch, and then I was dangling
there.' [42_leg_10.032]

Table 6.11: Adverbs involving triplication

ADVERB	GLOSS
bhututu	'farting sound'
gururu	'[coming] in flocks, continuously (e.g., at festivals)'
haŋcaŋcaŋ	'dangling'
hibibi	'[wind] blowing gently'
hururu	'[wind] blowing strongly' (also in NEP)
khiriri	'spinning, revolving'
lututu	'[dough, soup] being too thin'
pelele	(i) 'pulling something heavy or blocked'
	(ii) '[shawl, clothes] come undone'
phelele	'[bird flying] up high'
philili	'[butterfly] jittering'
phururu	'[manner of] strewing, dispersing'
pololo	'[bamboo, construction materials] being too long to handle'
pururu	'[flowing] in streams'
seleŋleŋ	'[wind] blowing strongly such that leaves start to rustle'
siliŋliŋ	'shaking'
siliklik	'fuming with anger'
serere	'[drizzling] thinly, [morning sunbeams] thinly'
sototo	'[walking, moving] one after the other'
thokokok	'shaking heavily [from fever, earthquake]'
tholoklok	'[boiling] vigorously'
tururu	'[blood, tears] flowing, dripping'
walaŋlaŋ	'bursting out in laughter'
yororo	'[fire wood heap, rice terrace] falling and tearing along'

6.4.4 Ideophonic adverbs

Several adverbs have ideophonic quality, i.e., there exists an iconic relationship between their form and some aspect of their meaning. The similarity relation may be based on sound as in onomatopoeia, but it may also be based on the visual, olfactory or haptic senses (Caughley 1997). Table 6.12 provides an overview; some examples from natural language are shown in (27). The adverbs that modify processes or activities have a reduplicated structure; only those that modify punctual events do not occur in reduplicated form. The bases for the reduplication can consist of up to three syllables. Ideophones often show some deviating behavior with regard to the general phonological outlook of a language. The same can be said about Yakkha ideophones. Initials such as /gʰ/ or /jʰ/ are not found beyond ideophones, and voiced initials like /b/ are rare, too.

(27)   a.   *na   picha   khoʔluk-khoʔluk*
          this   child   coughing-REDUP
          hot-a-s-heks-a=na.
          cough-PST-V2.DIE-V2.CUT-PST[3SG]=NMLZ.SG
          'This child is about to die, having a coughing fit.'

      b.   *u-laŋ   men-da-le=na   picha   khobak-khobak*
          3SG.POSS-leg   NEG-come-NEG=NMLZ.SG   child   crawling-REDUP
          lam-meʔ=na.
          walk-NPST[3SG]=NMLZ.SG
          'The child that cannot walk (yet) moves crawling.'

      c.   *boʔle-boʔle   ceŋ-meʔ=na.*
          stammering   talk-NPST[3SG]=NMLZ.SG
          'He is stammering.'

      d.   *sukluk   ips-a-khy-a=na.*
          dozing_off   sleep[3SG]-PST-V2.GO-PST=NMLZ.SG
          'She dozed off.'

      e.   *ka   ebbebe   kisit-a-ŋ   khoŋ   ghwa-ghwa*
          1SG   trembling   be_afraid-PST-1SG   so_that   bawling
          hab-a-ŋ.
          cry-PST-1SG
          'I was scared, so that I bawled out loudly.'   [42_leg_10.047]

      f.   *uŋci=ga   sokma   ʈhwaŋ   nam-ma.*
          3NSG=GEN   breath   smelling_awfully   smell[3]-PRF
          'Their breath smelled awfully.'   [41_leg_09.045]

Table 6.12: Ideophonic adverbs

ADVERB	GLOSS
boʔle-boʔle	'[manner of] stuttering, stammering'
chok	'suddenly [piercing]'
ebbebe	'trembling'
ghok-ghok	'pig grunts'
ghwa-ghwa	'bawling'
hesok-hesok	'[manner of] breathing with difficulty'
hobrok	'[falling, dropping] at once'
hoŋhak-hoŋhak	'[walking] with sudden steps (like drunken people)'
jhellek	'flashing'
kai-kai	'[sound of] weeping'
kerek-kerek	'chewing hard things (like bones)'
khobak-khobak	'[manner of] crawling'
khoblek	'[manner of] finishing the plate'
khoʔluk-khoʔluk	'[sound of] coughing'
kurum-kurum	'chewing hard, crunchy things (like chocolate)'
kyaŋ-kyaŋ	'barking lightly'
lak	'being dropped'
oenk-oenk	'buffalo grunts'
phorop-phorop	'[sound of] slurping (e.g., tea, soup)'
phutruk-phutruk	'[manner of] jumping around'
syaŋ	'[flying] like a rocket, by being thrown or shot'
sukluk	'dozing off for a short moment (like in a boring meeting)'
taŋpharaŋ-taŋpharaŋ	'staggering'
thaʔyaŋ-thaʔyaŋ	'[manner of] walking with difficulty'
thulum-thulum	'wobbling (like fat or breasts)'
ṭhek	'[manner of] hitting lightly'
ṭhwaŋ	'sudden bad smell'
ṭuk-ṭuk	'[sitting] squatted, crouching'
whaŋ-whaŋ	'[barking] loudly'
wop	'[manner of] slapping with full hand'
	'(producing a deep, loud sound)'
yakcik-yakcik	'[sound of] squeezing, chewing (e.g., chewing gum)'
yakpuruk-yakpuruk	'[sound of] squeezing (e.g., millet mash for beer)'
yaŋgaŋ-yaŋgaŋ	'[manner of] toppling over (humans and objects)'

7 The geomorphic orientation system

7.1 Introduction

Geomorphic[1] spatial expressions present an absolute system, relying on the features of the landscape. The anchor of this system is the inclination of the steep hills that shape so many aspects of life in the Kiranti area (see also Figure 7.1). The system is absolute, as the directions of uphill and downhill are grounded in the environment and do not depend upon the orientation of the speaker or any other object. It can also be deictic, however, because these directions are in many cases defined from the perspective of the utterance context.

As a distinctive feature of Kiranti languages, geomorphic systems have been the subject of a number of studies, for example by Allen (1972) for Thulung, Bickel (1994; 1999a; 1997b; 2001) for Belhare, Gaenszle (1999) for Mewahang, Dirksmeyer (2008) for Chintang.[2] What makes Kiranti languages special is that this topography-based deixis is also used for micro-location, for instance for distinguishing two glasses on a table or two branches on a tree.

There are two mapping systems, large-scale, defined by the global inclination of the Himalayas (roughly, 'uphill' can be equated with 'north' in this mapping system), and small-scale, defined by the cline of individual hills. As also pointed out for Belhare by Bickel (1997b: 55), the large-scale abstraction ignores the cline of individual hills, and the small-scale abstraction ignores horizontal planes on a hill. Large-scale abstractions can be exemplified by cases in which speakers refer to any location outside the Himalayas (even as far away as Europe or America) as 'downhill'. Small-scale abstractions can be exemplified by the division of the house: rooms on the same level of the house are divided into 'uphill' and 'downhill' rooms, depending on which side of the house faces the hill on which it is located. The latter can be extended to refer to 'up' and 'down', too (as in 'up into the sky').

---

[1] Terminology following Bickel (1997b).

[2] Geomorphic orientation systems are, however, not unique to Kiranti languages. Another famous example is the Mayan language Tzeltal (Brown & Levinson 1993).

Geomorphic deixis permeates Yakkha grammar; it features in a number of word classes and grammatical subsystems: in demonstratives, adverbs, postpositions, verbs and even interjections.[3] This shows how deeply rooted the geomorphic system is in the grammar of Yakkha, and how strongly environmental factors may shape a language.[4] Bickel & Gaenszle (1999) also point out the salience of the 'hill' conception in cultural domains such as architecture, rituals and mythology in the Kiranti cultural sphere. For Yakkha, this connection remains to be studied.

Figure 7.1: A typical trail in Tumok

In the following, I will briefly lay out the system, before illustrating its application in each word class. Geomorphic forms in Yakkha are based on two sets of roots, called /u/-forms and /o/-forms in the following discussion. They indicate a threefold distinction: words based on *tu* and *to* for 'uphill', on *mu* and *mo* for 'downhill' and on *yu* and *yo* for 'across (at the same altitude)'. The distinction

---

[3] Other Kiranti languages like Belhare, Bantawa or Khaling furthermore distinguish altitude in their locative case systems (Ebert 1994; Bickel 1997b).

[4] The Yakkha system (and Kiranti languages in general) also shows that spatial orientation is by no means universally egocentric (based on the body of the speaker), as had been claimed before the discovery of geomorphic deixis.

between the /u/-forms and the /o/-forms is one of deictic transposition, as in Belhare (see Bickel 1997b; 2001).

The schematic diagrams in Figure 7.2 and Figure 7.3 provide a bird's eye view on the deictic field, and the black dots indicate the speaker. In both sets, the deictic field is partitioned into four quadrants. In the /u/-forms, the point of reference for projecting the four quadrants (indicated by 'ø') is located within the speech situation. Objects located uphill from the interlocutors are indicated by forms based on *tu*, objects located downhill from the interlocutors are indicated by forms based on *mu*, and objects on the same level (to either side of them) are indicated by forms based on *yu* (see Figure 7.2). Contrasts like left/right or front/back do exist in Yakkha, but they are rarely used in the expression of spatial orientation. The speakers are able to provide the lexemes when they are asked, but I have no instance of recorded natural speech using *pheksaŋ* 'left' and *chuptaŋ* 'right'. From the available lexical information, the left side is connoted negatively; it is used metaphorically in a term for a malicious wizard, for instance. This also fits with the widespread perception of the left hand as impure in South Asian societies. The terms *ondaŋ* 'front' and *heksaŋ* 'back' are used more frequently than 'left' and 'right'.

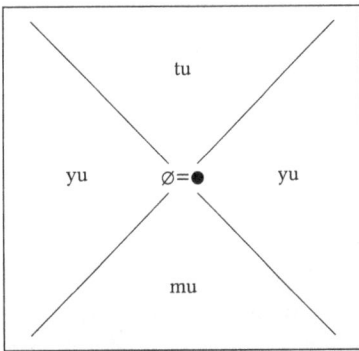

Figure 7.2: The deictic mapping system of the /u/-forms

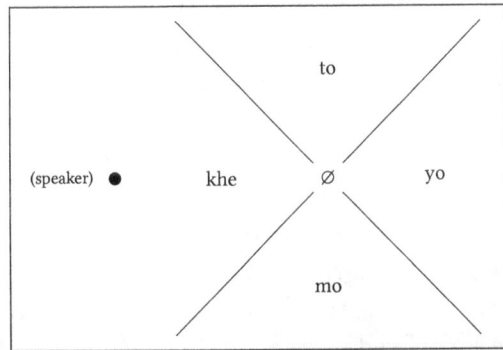

Figure 7.3: The transposed mapping system of *khe* and the /o/-forms

In the /o/-forms, the point of reference for projecting the four quadrants is transposed to a location that is not identical to the speech situation. The distinctions between 'uphill', 'downhill' and 'across' are now determined from the perspective of this transposed point of reference (see Figure 7.3; positioning the speaker on the left side of the diagram was an arbitrary choice, he could as well have been posited on the right side; of course with a consequent reversal of *yo*

```
┌─────────────────────────────────────┐
│                  to                   │
│                                       │
│                                       │
│   ─────────────── ∅ ───────────────   │
│                                       │
│                                       │
│                  mo                   │
└─────────────────────────────────────┘
```

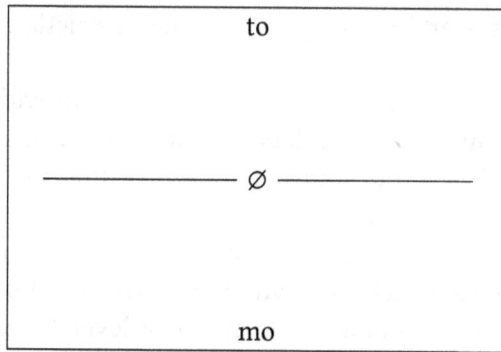

Figure 7.4: Object-centered usage of *mo* and *to*

and *khe*). Furthermore, if the transposed zero point is on the same elevation level as the interlocutors, a fourth root *khe* comes into play, indicating the field between this new zero point and the speech situation. This field opens up only in the transposed system. The transposed zero point is important for generic statements and when the speaker talks about events he saw in movies, for instance. Given the transposed zero-point, it is only natural that there are more adverbs derived from the /o/-forms than from the /u/-forms. The /o/-forms also serve as bases for spatial postpositions. Postpositions derived from the /u-/forms would only have the potential to locate objects with respect to the speech situation, not with respect to other objects.

The /o/-forms are also used to locate objects, or parts of objects, in relation to one another, for instance in order to determine the upper and the lower floor of a house, or in statements like 'I climbed up the tree', where one abstracts away from the topography. In this object-centered system of spatial orientation, the location of the speech situation is irrelevant. This is outlined in Figure 7.4. There are some fixed expressions like *mokhaʔla-tokhaʔla* 'up and down' (lit.: 'down and up'). Similarly, *yo* and *khe* are used to convey contrasting directions on the same level (regardless of where the speaker is located), for instance in expressions like *yokhaʔla-khekhaʔla* 'to and fro, back and forth'.

After this rather abstract characterization of the geomorphic orientation system of Yakkha, the remaining sections will illustrate how it is applied in each grammatical subsystem. Demonstratives (together with the interjections), are discussed in §7.2, adverbs in §7.3, postpositions in §7.4 and verbs in §7.5.

7.2 Demonstratives

There are two sets of demonstratives, one featuring the the deictic /u/-forms and one featuring the transposed /o/-forms, as summarized in Tables 7.1 and 7.2. Structurally, these subsets are different from each other, too. The /o/-forms are inherently adverbial and become nominal through nominalization with *=na* (SG) or *=ha ~ =ya* (NSG/NC). This is illustrated for *to* in example (1). These demonstratives can be used adnominally or pronominally. The /u/-forms are essentially adverbs, too, but they can also be used as interjections, i.e., as proforms for clauses (see example (2)). In this function they have a characteristic intonation. Uttered to attract the hearer's attention and to make him look in a particular direction, they are often accompanied by pointing gestures. The /u/-forms always locate an object with respect to the speech situation, i.e., the zero point is identical to the utterance context. This explains why the /u/-forms can combine with the proximal demonstratives, *na* and *kha* (cf. §4.3), to yield the topography-specific demonstratives shown in Table 7.1.

Table 7.1: Geomorphic demonstratives, /u/-forms

DIRECTION	ROOT (ADV/INTERJ)	DEMONSTRATIVE (SG/NSG, NC)
UP	*tu*	*tunna/tukha*
ACROSS	*yu*	*yunna/yukha*
DOWN	*mu*	*munna/mukha*

Table 7.2: Geomorphic demonstratives, /o/-forms and *khe*

DIRECTION	ROOT (adv.)	DEMONSTRATIVE (SG/NSG, NC)
UP	*to*	*tona/toha*
ACROSS (BEYOND)	*yo*	*yona/yoha*
ACROSS	*khe*	*khena/kheha*
DOWN	*mo*	*mona/moha*

(1)   a.   *to*   *khy-a!*
                 uphill   go-IMP
                 'Go up!'

      b.   *to=na*   *paŋ*
                 uphill=NMLZ.SG   house
                 'the upper house'

(2)   a.   *mu! puchak!*
                 INT   snake
                 'Look, down there! A snake!'

      b.   *tu! maŋme!*
                 INT   eagle
                 'Look, up there! An eagle!'

Examples of /u/-demonstratives are shown in (3). In (3a), the home of the person referred to by *buddhini* is located on the same level as the speaker's home, where she is sitting at the time of speaking. Example (3b) is from a mythical story that takes place in the environment and the array of villages as they are today, and the place called Manglabare is uphill from the speech situation (in Tumok village). The /u/-forms are also used for microlocation, such as pointing out a spider to the downhill side of the speaker, even if it is located on the same elevation level (see Figure 7.5).

(3)   a.   *nhaŋ*   *yunna*   *buddhini=ca*   *eko*
                 and_then   this_across   buddhist_woman=ADD   one
                 pi-ŋ.
                 give[PST]-1SG.A
                 'And I gave one to the buddhist woman (living) over there.'
                                                        [36_cvs_06.387]

      b.   *ŋ-ikt-uks-u-ci=hoŋ*   *tunna*   *maŋlabare*
                 3PL.A-chase-PRF-3.P[PST]-3NSG.P=SEQ   this_uphill   Manglabare
                 n-da-ya-by-a-ma..
                 3PL-come-PST-V2.GIVE-PST-PRF
                 'As they (the Limbus) chased them (Lalubang and Phalubang), they (the Limbus) already came up to Manglabare.' (lit. 'to Manglabare uphill')
                                                           [22_nrr_05.029]

In contrast, the /o/-forms are found in generic statements (see (4a)), and in procedural descriptions, that are detached from the here and now of the speech situation (see (4c)). They are also found in contexts that open up a secondary deictic field, such as in movies (see example (4b) from a pear story).

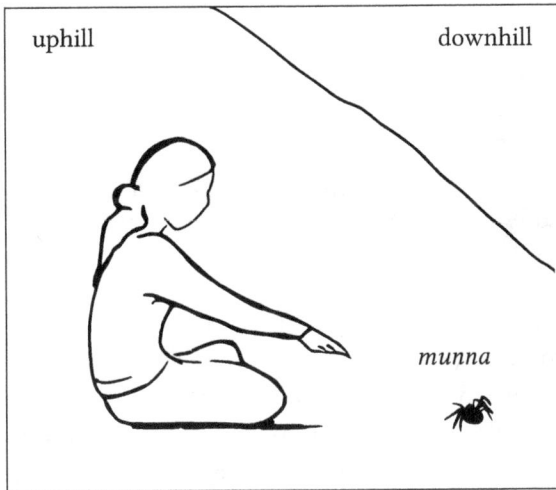

Figure 7.5: The /u/-forms in practice

(4) a. *nhaŋ*   *eko=bu,*   *mo=na*   *tala=ca*
         and_then   one=REP   downhill=NMLZ.SG   floor=ADD
         me-wa-m=ha=bu.
         NEG-live-INF[DEONT]=NMLZ.NSG=REP
         'And one more thing: the Linkhas shall not live on the ground floor,
         too, it is said.'   [11_nrr_01.040]

     b. *nhaŋŋa*   *hon=na*   *mamu=nuŋ,*   *saikal=be*
         and_then   that_very=NMLZ.SG   girl=COM   bicycle=LOC
         ta-yatasa=na   *yo=na*   *mamu=ca,*
         come[3SG]-PST.PROG=NMLZ.SG   across=NMLZ.SG   girl=ADD
         nhaŋŋa   *khaʔla*   *lukt-a-sy-a-ci,*
         and_then   like_this   bump_into-PST-MDDL-PST-DU
         men=na=i?
         COP.NEG=NMLZ.SG=Q
         'And that earlier girl and the girl that was coming on the bike, they
         collided like this, right?'[5]   [34_pea_04.025]

     c. *to=na*   *paŋ=be*   *ku-nuŋ-ma,*
         up=NMLZ.SG   house=LOC   guard-V2.SIT-INF[DEONT]
         sin-di-me,   *mo=na*   *paŋ=be*
         die-V2.GIVE[3SG]-NPST   downhill=NMLZ.SG   house=LOC

---

[5] The verb form *tayatasa* could not be analyzed, as no corresponding paradigm could be elicited.
According to the Nepali translations, I tentatively labelled it 'past progressive'.

> tha   n-leŋ-me-n,   ka-ma
> knowledge NEG-happen[3SG]-NPST-NEG, say-INF[DEONT]
> pʌryo ai?
> have_to TAG
> 'In the upper house, people keep sitting at the sickbed, someone dies
> eventually – in the lower house, they have no idea, one has to tell
> them, right?'[6]   [29_cvs_05.028]

As pointed out in the introduction, the /o/-forms are also used when two objects are located with respect to each other, as in such cases the zero point is also not identical to the speech situation, but located between the related objects, such as in (5). In this example, two people look downhill, seeing two swallows sitting on a parallel wires (as illustrated in Figure 7.6). Interlocutor A points out something about one of the swallows and interlocutor B wants to reconfirm whether he got the reference right. The zero point for the projection is located between the two birds. The demonstrative *tona* refers to the bird closer to the hill on which the interlocutors are located and that serves as the anchor of the relation, and *mona* refers to the bird on the wire further away from that hill. If the swallows had been located uphill from the interlocutors, the question would have been exactly the same as the one uttered in (5); the speech situation is irrelevant for the interpretation of this utterance.

(5) *to=na=em*   *mo=na=em?*
    uphill=NMLZ.SG=ALT downhill=NMLZ.SG=ALT
    '(Do you mean) the upper one or the lower one?'

The uphill-downhill distinction can also be mapped onto the human body, as in (6). These designations are used regardless of the orientation of a person, thus instantiating an exception to the topography-based system.

(6) a. *mo=ha*   *keŋ=ci*
       downhill=NMLZ.NSG tooth=NSG
       'lower teeth'
   b. *to=ha*   *keŋ=ci*
       uphill=NMLZ.NSG tooth=NSG
       'upper teeth'

---

[6] This example refers to another Yakkha custom: firing rifles for announcements, in pairs to announce marriages, and in single shots to announce the death of a member of the household. The choice of *tona* and *mona* in this example is arbitrary, it could as well be the other way round, as this is just an example made by the speaker to illustrate the custom; the sentence does not refer to any particular constellation of houses.

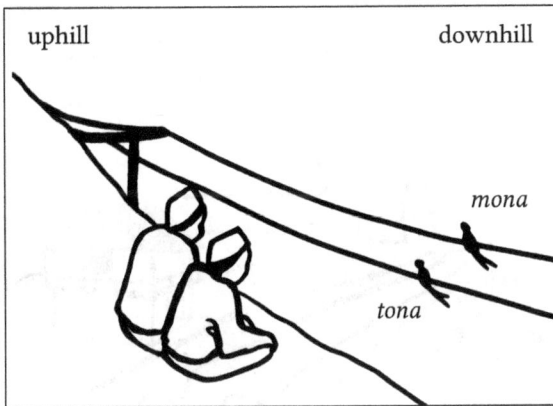

Figure 7.6: Illustration for example (5)

Things look slightly different on the horizontal plane: in example (7a), two houses are identified that are both on the same altitude level as the interlocutors. The house further away is referred to as *yona*, the closer one is *khena*, a distinction most closely rendered by 'there, thither' and 'here, hither' in the English translation (see also Figure 7.7, which features *mo* and *to* as well). In Figure 7.7, the couple in the foreground represents the speech situation.

(7)   a.   *eh,*   *khe=na*   *paŋ*   *menna,*
           oh   across_here=NMLZ.SG   house   NEG.COP=NMLZ.SG
           yo=na=le!
           across_there=NMLZ.SG=CTR
           'Oh, not the closer house, the next one!'
   b.   *mela=be*   *yo*   *khe*   *son-ca-saŋ*
           market=LOC   across_there   across_here   look-V2.EAT-SIM
           'looking around in the market'   [01_leg_07.152]

The quadrant indicated by *yo* is always beyond some (real or imagined) boundary on the horizontal level, i.e., it is projected from a zero point that must be distinct from the speech situation. The space between that boundary and the speech situation is the field indicated by *khe*.[7] In example (7a), the utterance context is relevant for the interpretation of *yo* and *khe*,[8] while this is not the case for the *mo/to* distinction in (6b), for instance. As mentioned above, the *yo/khe*

---

[7] In this light, it also makes sense that *khe* is never used in opposition to *yu*. A *khe*-quadrant opens up only when the zero point for the projection is transposed, while the field indicated by *yu* projects directly from the speech situation.

[8] Note that it is not the case that *yona* always refers to the object between an upper and a lower object (the same is true for Belhare, see Bickel 2001). If the speakers were standing on the level of the lower house, the demonstrative referring to it would change from *mona* to *yona*.

Figure 7.7: The transposed system in practice

contrast can also be used generically, independent of any particular utterance context, as in example (7b).

As the /u/-forms always rely on information that is retrievable from the utterance context, they are not compatible with the reportative marker =*bu*. Thus, while (8a) is perfectly fine, (8b) is pragmatically awkward.[9] Another example for /o/-forms combining with =*bu* is (4a) above.

(8)   a.   *to=na*   *minuma*   *lukt-a-khy-a=na=bu?*
            uphill=NMLZ.SG   cat   run[3SG]-PST-V2.GO-PST=NMLZ.SG=REP
            'It was said that the upper cat ran away?'

       b.   ?*tu-nna*   *minuma*   *lukt-a-khy-a=na=bu?*
            this_uphill   cat   run[3SG]-PST-V2.GO-PST=NMLZ.SG=REP
            Intended: 'It was said that the cat up there ran away?'

The examples in (9) show that the proximal/distal demonstratives (see §4.3.1) and the 'uphill'/'downhill' demonstratives are not mutually exclusive; they can be used together in one syntagm. The former indicate proximity or distance to the speaker, while the latter locate the objects with respect to each other and the cline of the hill. In (9a), the zero point is located between the upper and the lower

---

[9] The reportative marker can also be found on embedded speech, both direct and indirect; see also §15.2.2 and §17.3.1.

rocks of a group of rocks, and in (9b), the zero point is located in the middle of the road.[10]

(9) a. *na   mo=na   luŋkhwak*
         this   downhill=NMLZ.SG   stone
         'this lower rock (of a group of rocks)'   [37_nrr_07.031]

     b. *mo=na   u-lap,   to=na*
         downhill=NMLZ.SG   3SG.POSS-wing   uphill=NMLZ.SG

         u-lap,   na   lambu ghak   ak=ka=i!
         3SG.POSS-wing   this   road   all   1SG.POSS=GEN=EMPH
         'The uphill side, the downhill side, this road is all mine!'
                                                              [36_cvs_06.206]

The examples in (10) illustrate abstractions away from the closest hill as the achoring element. In (10a), *mu* refers to a place outside the hills and far away (Germany). In (10b), via reduplication of the initial CV-cluster, the root intensifies its meaning, i.e., *tutunna* refers to an object further away than *tunna*. These reduplications are also found in the corresponding adverbs (see §7.3 below).

(10) a. *mu,   [...]   nniŋ=ghe   i=ha*
         downhill   [...]   2PL.POSS=LOC   what=NMLZ.NSG

         cog-wa-m-g=ha?
         do-NPST-2PL.A-2=NMLZ.NSG
         'Downhill, where you live, what do you do (when someone dies)?'
                                                              [29_cvs_05.008]

     b. *tunna   cokcoki=nuŋ   tu-tunna   cokcoki*
         that_uphill   star=COM   REDUP-that_uphill   star
         'the star up there and the star even further up'

7.3 Adverbs

This section discusses the adverbs that belong to the geomorphic orientation system. In §4.3 a set of adverbs has been introduced that is based on a proximal/distal/anaphoric distinction. The adverbs discussed in the following are based on the same distinctions between /o/-forms and /u/-forms as the demonstratives discussed in §7.2 above. Tables 7.3 and 7.4 provide an overview of all geomorphic adverbial expressions in Yakkha.

---

[10] As the proximal/distal demonstratives *na/nna* show a functional overlap with *khena* and *yona*, these two sets are not expected to occur together.

Table 7.3: Geomorphic adverbs, the /u/-forms

	UP	ACROSS	DOWN
LOC/INTERJ	tu	yu	mu
LOC-PROX	tunhe	yunhe	munhe
LOC-DIST	tunnhe	yunnhe	munnhe
LOC-DIST-EMPH	tutunnhe	yuyunnhe	mumunnhe

Table 7.4: Geomorphic adverbs, /o/-forms and *khe*

| | UP | ACROSS | | DOWN |
	UP	PROX	DIST	DOWN
LOC/DIR	to	khe	yo	mo
DIR	tokhaʔla	khekhaʔla	yokhaʔla	mokhaʔla
ABL/DIR	tondaŋ	khendaŋ	yondaŋ	mondaŋ
LEVEL	topparik	khepparik	yopparik	mopparik
LEVEL-ABL	topparindaŋ	khepparindaŋ	yopparindaŋ	mopparindaŋ
QUANT	torok	kherek	yorok	morok
QUANT-EMPH	toʔtorok	kheʔkherek	yoʔyorok	moʔmorok
LOC-PROX	naʔto	naʔkhe	naʔyo	naʔmo
LOC-DIST	nnaʔto	nnaʔkhe	nnaʔyo	nnaʔmo
LOC-PROX-QUANT	naʔtorok	naʔkherek	naʔyorok	naʔmorok

The adverbs based on the proximal/distal distinction are *nhe* 'here' (see (11a)) and *nnhe* 'there' (with initial gemination of the nasal). The adverb *nnhe* is used to refer to distant locations and to locations in another deictic field, as it is opened up by a movie, for instance (see (11b) from a pear story) or by talking on the phone. The anaphoric form is *honnhe* 'just there, at a location mentioned earlier' (see also §4.3.2).

(11)   a.   *imin=na,   haku nhe,   hen=se;   haku*
            how=NMLZ.SG now   here   today=RESTR now
            soʔ-ma=na=lai!
            look-INF[DEONT]=NMLZ.SG=EXCLA
            'How is he; now he (the prospective groom) is here, only today; now we have to look at him!'   [36_cvs_06.374]

b. *dhakani=be   s-wa,*   *nnhe   eko   man=na.*
   basket=LOC   look-NPST[3SG.P]   there   one   COP.NEG=NMLZ.SG
   'He looks into the basket, and there is not even one.'

[34_pea_04.040]

These proximal and distal adverbs can be specified further by combining them with the /u/-forms of the geomorphic set, in the same way as it has been shown above for the demonstratives. Both sets rely on the utterance context, and are, therefore, compatible. Altogether, one arrives at three more forms for each 'here' and 'there': *tunhe/tunnhe* 'up here/there', *munhe/munnhe* 'down here/there' and *yunhe/yunnhe* 'across here/there'. The resulting complex forms are illustrated by the examples in (12).

(12) a. *ŋkha=nuŋ   nhe   gobar,   pik=ka   u-hi,*
         that=COM   here   cow_dung   cow=GEN   3SG.POSS-shit

         bachi=ga,   goru=ga   men=na,   munhe   khaʔla
         COW=GEN   OX=GEN   NEG.COP=NMLZ.SG   down_here   like_this

         yuŋ-ma=hoŋ   ʈika   waʔ-meʔ-ma.
         put-INF=SEQ   blessing   wear-CAUS-INF[DEONT]

         'With this (*dubo* grass), here, cow dung, from a female cow, not from an ox, one has to place it down here like this and apply a blessing (at the main door of the house).'   [31_mat_01.089]

      b. *munnhe   sombare   daju=ge   ŋ-waʔ=ya=ci=bu,*
         down_there   Sombare   eB=LOC   3PL-exist=NMLZ.NSG=NSG=REP

         hau   jeppa!
         EXCLA   really

         'Oh! Sombare brother down below has some (mushrooms), they say, really!'   [13_cvs_02.079]

      c. *ka=go   tunnhe   bhitta=be*
         1SG=TOP   up_there   wall=LOC

         heʔ-ma-sy-a-ŋ=na=le,   a-na=ŋa,
         cut-INF-AUX.PROG-PST-1SG=NMLZ.SG=CTR   1SG.POSS-eZ=ERG

         uks-a-ga=i,   uks-a   ly-a-ŋ=hoŋ,   ...
         come_down-IMP-2-EMPH   come_down-IMP   tell-PST-1SG=SEQ

         'I was cutting (grass) up there at the wall, but my elder sister said: please come down, come down, and ...'   [28_cvs_04.315]

As example (13) shows, the /u/-forms can also be used independently, in adverbial function.

(13)   *mu   jeṭha=ŋa   biha   cog-a   bhoŋ, mu*
         down   first_born_male=ERG   marriage do[3SG]-SBJV COND down
         jeṭha=ŋa   hiŋ-ma=na.
         first_born_male=ERG   support-INF[DEONT]=NMLZ.SG
         'If Jetha down here marries a girl, he has to care for her.' (pointing to someone sitting in the same room as the speaker, but in the corner pointing downhill)

                                                    [28_cvs_04.127]

A natural example of a reduplicated form is shown in (14). Typically, the reduplicated forms contrast an object further away with a closer object. In this example, however, the emphasis usually connected to this reduplication is not very strong; in the afterthought at the end of the sentence, the simple form *tunnhe* is used.[11] For instance, if the speaker points downhill towards two houses, the closer location is indicated by *munnhe* 'down there' and the one further down is indicated by *mumunnhe* 'further down there'.

(14)   *ka   ŋkhaʔla   bhoŋ   tu-tunnhe   bhauju=ghe*
         1SG   like_that COND REDUP-there_uphill   sister-in-law=LOC
         wa-ya-masa-ŋ=na   raecha,   tunnhe=ba.
         be-PST-PST.PRF-1SG=NMLZ.SG   MIR   there_uphill=EMPH
         'If it is like that, I had been uphill at my sister-in-law's house, just up there.'
                                                   [36_cvs_06.399]

The /o/-forms are used when the zero point is not located within the speech situation. Thus, they cannot combine in one word with the deictic forms *nhe* and *nnhe*. They can combine with other morphology, e.g., with case markers, to convey a variety of spatial notions, such as ablative and directive, shown in (15). The roots *mo*, *to* and *yo* are inherently locative, so that they cannot combine with the locative =*pe* (for instance, *mobe is ungrammatical). Forms as in (15a) can be used both with an ablative and a directive reading.

(15)   a.   *mondaŋ   ky-a=na.*
             from_below come_up[3SG]-PST=NMLZ.SG
             'He came up from below.'
   b.   *yondaŋ   eko   mamu   a-cya*
             from_over_there one   girl   1SG-child

---

[11] The mirative (see §17.3) is used here because the speaker finally remembers where she had been at a particular day some weeks prior to this conversation.

> *we=ppa=ʔlo!*
> exist[3SG;NPST]=EMPH=EXCLA
> '(But) I have a daughter from (my ex-husband) over there!'
>
> [06_cvs_01.018]

c. *tokhaʔla   khy-a!*
    upwards   go-IMP
    'Go upwards!'

The contrast between *yo* and *khe* (see also Figure 7.3 above) can be illustrated by the following context: the two villages Madi Rambeni and Madi Mulkharka are both located on a hill next to the hill on which Tumok is situated (see also the Map in Figure 2.2 in §2.1). These two hills are separated by a river (the Maya Khola), and thus both Madi Rambeni and Madi Mulkharka qualify as *yo* 'across' from Tumok. Both villages are roughly on the same altitude level as Tumok, but while Madi Mulkharka is right across (one can see its houses), Madi Rambeni is further away and out of sight. Thus, in a conversation (in Tumok) contrasting the two villages, Madi Mulkharka would be indicated by *khe*, while Madi Rambeni would be referred to by *yo*, since it is further away from Tumok than Madi Mulkharka.

Another set of adverbs is instantiated by adverbs such as *mopparik* 'right below' in (16). It refers to a place that is right below the point of reference, like a lower floor or a lower step on a ladder (*-parik* comes from the Nepali noun *paṭī* 'side').[12] This set of adverbs, like the forms in (15), can also be used as postpositions (see §7.4 below).

(16) *honna   sem-khuba   babu, pheri, i=ʔlo   mopparik*
      that_very pluck-NMLZ boy   again   what=EXCLA   right_below
      jhar-a   cok-ma-sy-a=na.
      descend-NATIV   do-INF-AUX.PROG-PST[3SG]=NMLZ.SG
      'That guy who was plucking, he was climbing down (the ladder).'

      [34_pea_04.036]

Furthermore, there are forms ending in the syllable *-rok* ~ *-rek*, i.e., *morok*, *torok*, *yorok* and *kherek*. They convey that something is located (or moving) a bit more in the respective direction than had been presupposed, thus quantifying the distance (see (17)). Example (18) illustrates the same with ablative forms.

---

[12] The change of coronal plosives to rhotics in intervocalic position is also attested elsewhere in the language, and closing a word-final CV syllable with /k/ is a common process in the 'Yakkhafication' of lexical material from Nepali, see §3.3.

(17) a. *hoŋkhaʔniŋŋa   naʔmasek   khi-khuwa   yapmi=ci*
           that_very_time   night   fight-NMLZ   person=NSG
           yorok   torok   ŋ-wa-ya-masa.
           a_bit_further   a_bit_up   3PL-be-PST-PST.PRF
           'At that time, those fighting people had been (scattered) a bit further away and a bit further uphill.'   [41_leg_09.057]

     b. *nna   ten=be=jhen,   mo,   yondaŋ   morok=ŋa*
           that   village=LOC=TOP   down   from_across   a_bit_down=INS
           limbu=ci=ca   ŋ-wa-ya-ma.
           Limbu_person=NSG=ADD   3PL-be-PST-PRF
           'In that village below, across and then a bit below from there, Limbu people were living, too.'   [22_nrr_05.009]

(18) a. *mondaŋ   kham   ket-u-eba.*
           from_below   ground   bring_up-3.P[IMP]-POL.IMP
           'Bring up mud from below.'

     b. *miyaŋ   morondaŋ   ket-u-eba.*
           a_little   from_further_below   bring_up-3.P[IMP]-POL.IMP
           'Bring it up from a bit further below.' (Context: the mud is better further downhill.)

The adverbs ending in *-rok~ -rek* can also be partly reduplicated, yielding forms like *moʔmorok* or *toʔtorok*. Tentatively, in analogy to the reduplications discussed above, I conclude that this amplifies the distance, too, but there are not enough examples in my data for any strong claims. The reduplicated forms are also used when nothing has been presupposed (cf. also §7.4 on postpositions).

(19) *beuli   siŋgara   cok-se   miyaŋ   yoʔyorok*
       bride   a_wedding_custom   do-SUP   a_little   a_bit_further
       ŋ-ghet-wa.
       3PL.A-take-NPST[3.P]
       'To dress the bride with the sari that the groom got her, they take her a bit further away.'   [25_tra_01.043]

    The last set of adverbs introduced here has the forms *naʔmo, nnaʔmo, naʔyo*, and so on. They are composed of the singular forms of the proximal/distal demonstratives and the /o/-forms, conveying 'down here', 'down there', 'across here' and so on (see Table 7.4). The cognate forms in Belhare are demonstratives that are marked for environmental case (see Bickel 2001: 226–27). The environmental case system was probably present in earlier stages of Yakkha, too, but apart from these adverbial forms, there is no trace of such a system synchronically. The forms have characteristic stress, i.e., on the first syllable. They locate the utterance context from the perspective of another location. In (20a), the zero point is Manglabare, a place above Tumok (the place of speaking, referred to by *naʔmo* 'down here'). In (20b), the point of reference is the sky, mentioned in the adverbial clause. The sentence in (20c) was uttered by someone who confused two roads, and the point of reference is the point of departure of the speaker's movement, before she confused the roads.

(20)   a.   *haku   nnakha   lalubaŋ=nuŋ   phalubaŋ=ga   ten=go*
            now   those   Lalubang=COM   Phalubang=GEN   village=TOP

            naʔmo=maŋ   sa,   eŋ=ga=e.
            down_here=EMPH   COP.PST[3SG]   1PL.INCL.POSS=GEN=LOC

            'Now, that village of Lalubang and Phalubang, though, was down here, in our area.'   [22_nrr_05.034]

     b.   *na   taŋkheŋ=be   pes-a-khy-a-ma=niŋa*
            this   sky=LOC   fly-PST-V2.GO-PST-PRF[3SG]=CTMP

            naʔmo   heko=ha   nwak=ci=ŋa   haku   nda   nhe
            down_here   other=NMLZ.NSG   bird=NSG=ERG   now   2SG   here

            uŋ-ma   n-dokt-wa-ga-n=na
            come_down-INF   NEG-get_to_do-NPST-2.A[3.P]-NEG=NMLZ.SG

            n-lu-ks-u.
            3PL.A-tell-PRF-3.P[PST]

            'When he flew up into the sky, down here the other birds told him: Now you will not get the chance to come down here any more.'
                                      [21_nrr_04.034–35]

     c.   *naʔyo=le   sa-ŋ=na,   nnaʔyo=le*
            over_here=CTR   COP.PST-1SG=NMLZ.SG   over_there=CTR

            khy-a-ŋ=na?
            go-PST-1SG=NMLZ.SG

            'But I was over here, did I go over there?'   [28_nrr_04.030]

With the introduction of these forms, one arrives at two sets that are translatable as 'down/up/across here' and 'down/up/across there', for instance *naʔmo* and forms like *munhe* for 'down here'. The contrast between forms like *naʔmo* and *munhe* is, of course, the zero point. While *naʔmo* implies a perspective from a location outside the speech situation (see (20) and (21)), *munhe* refers to a location in the downhill quadrant, as projected from the perspective of the speaker (see, e.g., examples (12a)—(c) above). The speaker can choose whether he wants to locate objects from his own perspective or from someone else's perspective, and sometimes this is fixed by sociolinguistic conventions. In imperatives, for instance, it would be inappropriate to use one's own perspective, they are always expressed with /o/-forms, as in (21).

(21) a. *naʔyo   ab-a.*
          over_here   come_across-IMP
          'Come over here (from where you are).'
      b. *naʔmo   uks-a.*
          down_here   come_down-IMP
          'Come down here (from where you are).'

The 'quantifying' or 'degree' derivation via *-rok* that was introduced above is also possible with *naʔto* (and the related forms), yielding forms like *naʔtorok* 'a bit closer up here'.

7.4 Postpositions

The geomorphic postpositions are formally identical to the adverbs described in §7.3. They take nominal complements that are marked by the genitive case (see §5.2.2.4). The possessive prefix is, however, not possible on these postpositions, which distinguishes them from relational nouns (cf. §5.3). Table 7.5 provides an overview on the postpositions.

The postpositions *mopparik* and *topparik* indicate a relation of parallel planes located above/below each other, such as stacked books or floors of a house (see (22a)). Example (22b) shows a corresponding adverbial in a (semi-transparent) ablative form.[13] The same is possible with *yopparik* and *khepparik* on the horizontal level.

If the speaker wants to express that an object is oriented towards a particular direction, the directional forms *tokhaʔla, mokhaʔla, yokhaʔla* and *khekhaʔla* are used; orientation away from another object is indicatd by the ablative forms *tondaŋ, mondaŋ, yondaŋ* and *khendaŋ* (see (23)).

(22) a. *ʈebul=ga   mopparik*
          table=GEN   right_below
          'below the table (on a lower level, e.g., on the ground)'

---

[13] In analogy to these examples, one could assume that there is also a directional *topparikhaʔla/mopparikhaʔla* to indicate directedness towards an upper/lower level, but such forms do not exist. Probably, *topparik* (and related forms) also have a directional meaning.

Table 7.5: Geomorphic postpositions

POSTPOSITION	GLOSS	INTERNAL STRUCTURE
mopparik	right below	'downhill-side[Nep.]'
topparik	right above	'uphill-side[Nep.]'
yopparik	right across	'across-side[Nep.]'
mokhaʔla	below, downwards	'uphill-DIR'
tokhaʔla	above, upwards	'uphill-DIR'
yokhaʔla	across, away	'across-DIR'
mondaŋ	from below	'downhill-ABL'
tondaŋ	from above	'uphill-ABL'
yondaŋ	from the same level	'across-ABL'
moʔmorok	a bit below	
toʔtorok	a bit above	
yoʔyorok	a bit further away	
kheʔkherek	a bit closer	

    b.   *kanciŋ   mopparindaŋ   ky-a-ci=ha.*
           1DU   from_right_below   come_up-PST-DU=NMLZ.NSG
           'We came up from the lower floor.'

(23)   a.   *ʈebul=ga   tokhaʔla*
            table=GEN   upwards
            'above the table (e.g., a lamp installed on the wall)'
    b.   *ʈebul=ga   mondaŋ   chwigam   kept-u=na.*
            table=GEN   from_below   chewing_gum   glue-3.P[PST]=NMLZ.SG
            'Someone stuck chewing gum below the table.'

The partly reduplicated forms *moʔmorok*, *toʔtorok* and *yoʔyorok* convey that an object is located a bit in the respective direction, from the perspective of the object referred to by the complement noun (see (24)).

(24)   a.   *uŋci-paŋ=ga   moʔmorok   eko   hoŋma*
            3NSG.POSS-house=GEN   bit_downhill   one   river
            wei-sa=na.
            exist-PST[3SG]=NMLZ.SG
            'A bit downhill from their house there was a river.'   [01_leg_07.283]

b. *hon=na*   *yuktham=ga*   *yoʔyorok*   *kheʔkherek*
   that_very=NMLZ.SG   place=GEN   bit_further   bit_closer
   'around that place/the surroundings of that place'   [01_leg_07.269]

7.5 Motion verbs

Several motion verbs have also lexicalized the uphill/downhill distinction, as shown in example (25) and in Table 7.6. Event specification with regard to the topography is highly frequent. Even though neutral forms are available (also included in the table), the pragmatically expected forms are those specifying the event for the *mo/to/yo* distinction. This specificity reaches well beyond 'classical' motion events. Small-scale motions, too, like putting, repairing, stacking, looking, turning or calling are often precisely specified with respect to their spatial orientation. This is achieved by means of complex predicates with different function verbs (see (25b) and Table 10.1 in Chapter 10). Motion away from a point of reference is not specified with respect to the topography, there are only the neutral verbs 'go' and 'carry off'. This is unexpected pragmatically: in motion events towards a point of reference, the speaker and the hearer are usually identifiable, and with them, the direction of the movement. In motion events away from a point of reference, as in 'go' and 'carry off', the direction of the movement is less predictable, and therefore, it would be more important pragmatically to specify events of going with regard to the topography-based distinctions.

Table 7.6: Geomorphic distinctions in motion verbs

	COME	BRING
NEUTRAL	*ta* 'come' (from a greater distance)	*taʔ* 'bring'
NEUTRAL	*kheʔ* 'go'	*khet* 'carry off'
UP	*keʔ* 'come up'	*ket* 'bring up'
ACROSS	*ap* 'come' (same level, small distance)	*apt* 'bring'
DOWN	*uks ~ uŋ* 'come down'	*ukt* 'bring down'

(25)   a.   *kanciŋ*   *to*   *tub-i=hoŋ*   *uks-a-ŋ-ci-ŋ=hoŋ*
            1PL   up   meet-1PL=SEQ   come_down-PST-EXCL-DU-EXCL=SEQ
            yo   *tas-a-ŋ-c-u-ŋ=ba.*
            across   arrive-PST-EXCL-DU-3.P-EXCL=EMPH

'Having met uphill (many people), we (two) came down (home) and arrived across (at a neighbour's house on the same level as the speaker's home).'

[36_cvs_06.395]

b. *na   eko=ŋa=go   thend-u-get-uks-a=ba,*
   this one=ERG=TOP   lift-3.P-V2.BRING_UP-3.P-PRF-PST=EMPH
   nna,   om   leks-a=niŋa.
   that   bright   become-PST[3SG]=CTMP
   'One of them lifted it (the rock) and carried it up (holding in his hands, not carrying on his back), while the sun came out.'   [37_nrr_07.086]

These topography-specific verbs are only compatible with suitable adverbial expressions. For instance, *apma* 'come over' can only be used with *yondaŋ* 'from a location on the same altitude level'. Interestingly, this verb is also used when 'coming over' implies climbing down 800 meters, crossing a river and then climbing up on the other side again.

8 Verbal inflection

This chapter deals with the inflectional morphology of the Yakkha verb. Word formation on the verb level is treated in Chapter 10 on complex predicates, and in §11.3 on transitivity operations.

The verbs can be grouped according to their stem forms and alternations (both treated in §8.1). Most verbal roots have a pre-vocalic and one or more pre-consonantal forms. There are lexical alternations and those that can be explained with morphophonological processes such as elision, voicing and assimilation.

Yakkha verbal inflection is highly polysynthetic and overwhelmingly suffixing; the verb can carry up to seven suffixes, while there is only one prefix slot. The finite verb is inflected for person and number of subject and object (treated in §8.2), polarity (§8.3), tense/aspect (§8.4) and mood (§8.5). Politeness or honorific distinctions are not grammaticalized in the Tumok dialect, except for the imperative, which has an additional politeness register. In the Dandagaun dialect, there is an honorific construction which is calqued upon the Nepali honorific verbal inflection (§8.6). The inflection of the copular verbs slightly deviates from the regular verbal inflection; it is treated in §8.7. Two further verbal markers that do not fit elsewhere (the nativizer -a and the knowledge marker -les) are treated in §8.8. The finite verb stands in opposition to infinitives, converbs and nominalizations that are restricted to polarity and, occasionally, number inflection (see §8.9).

Table 8.1 shows an overview of the most important verbal affixes in the regular verbal paradigm, and Table 8.2 shows schematically how all markers are distributed over the inflectional slots. Except for some idiosyncrasies in the inflection of copulas, there are no inflectional classes; all differences in inflectional behavior can be explained by morphophonology.

8.1 Stem formation

Yakkha verbal roots either have the simple shape (C)V(C), or a complex shape (C)V(C)-s or (C)V(C)-t, carrying one of the coronal augments -s and -t (~ -d ~ -r ~ -ʔ), which can be traced back to valency-increasing suffixes. Such augments

Table 8.1: Overview of the major verbal inflectional markers

	PERSON-NUMBER
-ŋ	1
-ka	2
-u	3.P
-nen	1>2
-i	1/2 plural
-ci	dual or 3 nonsingular P
N-	3 plural S/A
=na	singular
=ha	nonsingular or non-countable

	TENSE-ASPECT
-meʔ/-wa	nonpast
-a	past
-ma/-uks	perfect
-masa/-uksa	past perfect
-siʔ	progressive

	NEGATION
N-...-n	
-nin	plural negation

	MOOD
-a	imperative/subjunctive
-ni	optative

	INFINITIVE
-ma	infinitive

Table 8.2: Templatic representation of the verbal inflection

	PF	Σ	SF 1	2	3	4	5	6	7
PERSON MARKING	N- 3PL			-nen 1>2		-N (copy)	-ci ~ -cin DUAL -i ~ -in 1/2PL -ni 2PL.IMP		-u 3.P
NEGATION	N- NEG					-N (copy)			
TAM			-a PST/ IMP/ PST.SBJV -me? NPST -uks ~ -nuŋ PRF	-ma ~ -mi PRF	-sa ~ -si PST.PRF			-wa NPST	

	8	9	10	11	12	13	14	(15)	(16)
PERSON MARKING	-N (copy)	-ci 3NSG.P	-m 1/2PL>3	-ka 2	-ŋ(a) EXCL			(=na) NMLZ.SG (=ha) NMLZ.NSG	(=ci) NSG
NEGATION	-N (copy)					-n ~ -nin NEG			
TAM							-ni OPT		

can be found throughout Kiranti, but they also have cognates in Jinghpo, Written Tibetan, Magar, Chepang, some West Himalayaish languages and Qiangic languages (Matisoff 2003: 457–59).[1]

From a synchronic perspective, except for a handful of stems,[2] the distribution of the augments is not relatable to valency change, and hence they cannot be analyzed as synchronic grammatical suffixes. The augment -s surfaces only in inflected verb forms, and only before vowels and /w/ (see (1a)). The augment -t is also found before vowels and /w/ (see (1b)). When the pre-augmented root has CV structure, this augment may surface before other consonants as well,

---

[1] The term *(stem) augment* is well established in the Kiranti descriptive tradition, so I decided to keep with it in this work.
[2] See §11.3.8.

apparently having been re-analyzed as part of the stem (always as [ʔ] before C, compare (1c) with its citation form). Yakkha verbal stems never start with consonant clusters, which supports the analysis of complex onsets as originating in bisyllabic structures.

(1) a. *khem-ma   yas-u=na.*
         hear-INF   be_able-3.P[PST]=NMLZ.SG
         'He could hear it.' (citation form: *yama*)
     b. *chimd-u=na.*
         ask-3.P[PST]=NMLZ.SG
         'He asked her.' (citation form: *chimma*)
     c. *thur-u=na.*
         sew-3.P[PST]=NMLZ.SG
         'He sewed it.' (citation form: *thuʔma*)

Yakkha verbs can formally be grouped into intransitively and transitively inflected verbs. Several verb pairs are homophonous, but they have different valencies, e.g., *hot* 'cough'/'pierce', or *ap* 'come'/'shoot'. In §8.1.1, the different root types will be presented; §8.1.2 deals with the morphophonological behavior of the stems (for a detailed account of the morphophonology see §3.5).

A few stems in Yakkha are not monosyllabic. Historically they were bimorphemic (with both noun-verb and verb-verb combinations), but their etymology is at most partially transparent. Examples are *ta-rokt* 'start' and *ya-rokt* 'get to know, get informed', both containing the stem *tokt* 'get' (its word-internal allomorph [rokt]). Other examples are *na-hend* 'be jealous', where *na* could be 'nose' (but *hend* is not attested as independent verb), *themd-(n)i* 'compare' and *hes-ca* 'defeat'.[3] The structure of the morphemes clearly reveals that they are verbal stems historically, but an independent meaning could not be established.[4]

8.1.1 Stem types

8.1.1.1 Unaugmented roots

Unaugmented roots can have open ((C)V) or closed ((C)VC) structure, with CVʔ roots behaving exceptionally. Table 8.3 lists some verbs with unaugmented roots. Note that in most cases the stem surfaces as it is in the citation form (except for

---

[3] The stems are written with dashes to indicate the former morpheme boundary, which is still transparent since in all verbs one component is still relatable to an existing morpheme.

[4] For transparent noun-verb predicates and verb-verb predicates see Chapters 9 and 10, respectively.

CVn stems, which change to CVm). This is not the case with augmented stems, as will be discussed in the following section.

Table 8.3: Unaugmented roots (CV, CVʔ, CVC)

ROOT	CITATION FORM	GLOSS
ca	*cama*	'eat'
khi	*khima*	'quarrel'
u	*uma*	'enter'
a	*ama*	'descend'
soʔ	*soʔma*	'look'
hap	*hapma*	'cry'
cok	*cokma*	'do'
uŋ	*uŋma*	'drink'
um	*umma*	'suck'
cen	*cemma*	'chop, cut'

The consonants in the underlying forms of the roots may undergo voicing and regular assimilations when inflectional morphology attaches to them (discussed in §8.1.2). Verbs of the underlying structure /CVʔ/ behave exceptionally, since the root-final /ʔ/ gets deleted in the inflection, and the root vowels are less resistant to deletion, too. They may change into glides (/kheʔ-a/ becomes [khya], /piʔ-a/ becomes [pya]) or be deleted (/soʔ-wa/ becomes [swa]). Comparison with the closely related Chintang and Belhare languages shows that the Yakkha /CVʔ/ roots originate in *CVt historically. In Belhare, cognates to Yakkha /CVʔ/ roots have the form /CVr/ (Bickel 1997a); in Chintang, they have the form /CVd/ (CVḍ in Rai et al. 2011).

When open roots are followed by a vowel in the verbal inflection, either a glide [y] is inserted or the vowel of the suffix gets deleted (for details see §3.5). The verb *cama* behaves exceptionally in showing ablaut (with the suppletive root [co]).

8.1.1.2 Augmented roots

The two coronal augments *-s* and *-t* (~ *-d* ~ *-r* ~ *-ʔ* in Yakkha) are typical of Kiranti stem structure. Historically, they had a transitivizing function (Sprigg 1985; Michailovsky 1985; van Driem 1989; Matisoff 2003; Bickel 2003; Bickel et al. 2007a), but synchronically, they are not productive anymore, except for *-t*, which plays a role in the benefactive derivation.[5] Synchronically, only a handful of verbs still show correspondences between augmentation and increased valency (cf. Table 11.2 in §11.3.8).[6]

Four groups of augmented roots have to be distinguished:

- (i) open roots with augment -*s*

- (ii) closed roots with augment -*s*, alternating between CVCs and CVN

- (iii) open roots with augment -*r* ~ -*ʔ* (**-t*)

- (iv) closed roots with augment -*t* ~ -*d*

The roots of group (i) have the structure /CV-s/ (see Table 8.4). The augment surfaces only before vowels and /w/, e.g., *nisuna* 'he saw it' and *niswana* 'he will see it'.

Table 8.4: Augmented roots (CV-s)

ROOT	CITATION FORM	GLOSS
nis	*nima*	'see, know'
yas	*yama*	'be able (to do)'
cis	*cima*	'cool down'
us	*uma*	'boil, be cooked'
es	*(hi) ema*	'defecate'
chus	*chuma*	'shrink'

Roots of group (ii) have the underlying structure /CVC-s/, and before consonants they have an alternant CVN, the nasal having the same place of articulation as the underlying consonant (see (2) and Table 8.5). While the deletion of the augment in group (i) above can be explained by phonology alone (no syllable boundaries of the shape [s.C] are allowed in Yakkha), the alternation in group (ii) between CVC and corresponding CVN is lexical, although it is triggered phonologically, too.

---

[5] The benefactive is formed by a complex predicate, with the augment -*t* attached to the lexical root, followed by the V2 -*piʔ* 'give', see §11.3.3.

[6] In van Driem (1994) and Gvozdanović (1987), the stem-final -*t* was analyzed as part of a past suffix (such a suffix indeed exists in some Western Kiranti languages). This was not confirmed by my data, and not even by the data in these sources (collected by Gvozdanović), since -*t* also appears in the nonpast paradigms there.

This group contains only two types of roots: those ending in /ks/ and those ending in /ps/. Stems ending in a nasal and the augment -s, as they are, e.g., known in Chintang and Belhare (Schikowski 2012; Bickel 1997a), do not occur in Yakkha.[7]

(2) a. *a-cya*   *ips-a-khy-a=na.*
         1SG.POSS-child   sleep-PST-V2.GO-PST[3]=NMLZ.SG
         'My child fell asleep.'
     b. *im-khuba*
         sleep-NMLZ
         'sleeper'

Table 8.5: Augmented roots (CVC-s ~ CVN)

ROOT	CITATION FORM	GLOSS
ips ~ im	*imma*	'sleep'
tups ~ tum	*tumma*	'meet, find, get'
ceps ~ cem	*cemma*	'recover, get well'
sops ~ som	*somma*	'stroke'
uks ~ uŋ	*uŋma*	'come down'
paks ~ paŋ	*paŋma*	'send (people)'
kaks ~ kaŋ	*kaŋma*	'accept, fall down'
keks ~ keŋ	*keŋma*	'bear fruit, ripen'
hiks ~ hiŋ	*hiŋma*	'turn around'

The roots of group (iii) have the structure /CV-r/, originating in *CV-t roots (cf. Table 8.6). In this group, the augments have been reanalyzed as part of the root. They surface (as [ʔ]) before nasal and lateral consonants, the verb *hema* 'dry up' being an unmotivated exception (see (3a) and Table 8.6).[8] Before obstruents, the augment /r/ does not surface, which is the expected behavior. The augment -r surfaces before vowels and /w/, in the first case resyllabified as onset of the first syllable of the suffix string (see (3b)). This group shows that roots

---

[7] I could not detect regular correspondences between the CVNs stems found in Belhare, for instance, and any particular stem type in Yakkha: *haŋs* 'send (things)' corresponds to Yakkha *haks*, *homs* 'swell' corresponds to *homd*, and *hums* 'bury' corresponds to *hum* in Yakkha.

[8] This behavior stands in contrast to the other groups of roots, where augments never surface before consonants.

with augmented -*t* and root-internal -*t* (cf. above) have undergone different developments historically, the first having become /CV-r/, and the second having become /CV-ʔ/ in present-day Yakkha. Thus, an infinitive of the shape CVʔ-ma can have the underlying roots /CVt/, /CVʔ/ or /CV-r/.

(3)   a.   *men-niʔ-le*
          NEG-count-CVB
          'without counting'
   b.   *ikhiŋ*   *ucun=ha*   *tephen*   *thur-uks-u=ha!*
          how_much   nice=NMLZ.NC   clothing   sew-PRF-3.P[PST]=NMLZ.NC
          'He made such nice clothing!'

Table 8.6: Augmented roots (CV-r)

ROOT	CITATION FORM	GLOSS
her ~ he	*hema*	'dry up'
hor ~ hoʔ	*hoʔma*	'crumble, fall apart'
nir ~ niʔ	*niʔma*	'count'
por ~ poʔ	*poʔma*	'topple, fall, fell'
pher ~ pheʔ	*pheʔma*	'open widely'
thur ~ thuʔ	*thuʔma*	'sew'

The roots of group (iv) have the structure CVC-t ~ CVC-d, with either a plosive or a nasal preceding the augment (see Table 8.7). The augment, as expected, surfaces only before vowels and /w/, being resyllabified as onset of the first syllable of the suffix string (see (4)). Roots ending in /-nd/ are more prone to assimilation processes than the other roots. They assimilate in place of articulation to the following material, as the infinitives and (4c) show.

(4)   a.   *chim-nen?*
          ask-1>2
          'May I ask you?'
   b.   *chimd-a-ŋ!*
          ask-IMP-1SG.P
          'Ask me!'
   c.   *uŋ-khuba*   *yapmi*
          pull-NMLZ   person
          'the pulling man' (root: /und/)

Table 8.7: Augmented roots (CVC-t)

ROOT	CITATION FORM	GLOSS
ukt	*ukma*	'bring down'
tupt	*tupma*	'light up'
hokt	*hokma*	'bark'
cheŋd	*cheŋma*	'stack, raise'
und	*umma*	'pull'
hond	*homma*	'fit into'
chumd	*chumma*	'shrink (clothes)'
chimd	*chimma*	'ask'
homd	*homma*	'swell'

There is one exception among the CVC-t roots, and these are roots of the form /CVt/, originating in *CVt-t roots historically. The final /t/ of unaugmented /CVt/ roots got reduced to a glottal stop (see §8.1.1.1), and the augment got reanalyzed as part of the root, yielding a root of the shape CVʔ-t, which became CVt. In closely related languages like Chintang and Belhare, these roots show a geminate /tː/ (Bickel 1997a; Bickel et al. 2007a; 2010).[9] Although synchronically there is only one consonant /t/ in Yakkha, the roots still show reflexes of their historical complexity. For instance, they do not undergo voicing between vowels (see (5)). In the citation forms, these roots surface as CVʔ, like the CVʔ roots (*CVt) and the CVr roots (*CV-t). Table 8.8 shows Yakkha /CVt/ roots and their cognates in Chintang and Belhare.

(5) a. *ka*   *phat-a-ŋ!*   (not: *phadaŋ*)
        1SG   help-PST-1SG
        'Help me!'
     b. *ka*   *mit-a-ŋ!*   (not: *midaŋ*)
        1SG   remember-PST-1SG
        'Remember me!'

The root types and their basic alternation patterns are schematically summarized in Table 8.9. In this table, "CV" should read "(C)V" in all instances. For assimilations see Table 8.10.

---

[9] In Rai et al. (2011) these roots are listed as ending in /ʈː/ (<ट्ट>).

Table 8.8: Chintang and Belhare cognates of Yakkha CVt roots

YAKKHA	GLOSS	CHINTANG	BELHARE
khut	'bring to'	*khutt*	*khutt*
khet	'carry off'	*khatt*	*khatt*
ket	'bring up'	*katt*	n.d.
met	'CAUS'	*mett*	*mett*
mit	'think of, remember'	*mitt*	*mitt*
lit	'plant'	*lett*	n.d.
phat	'help'	*phatt*	*phatt* ('exchange')

Table 8.9: Representation of the basic root allomorphy

	UNDERLYING FORM	BEFORE V/-wa	BEFORE C
	UNAUGMENTED ROOTS		
(a)	CV(C)	CV(C)	CV(C)
	CV? (<*CVt)	CV	CV(C)
	AUGMENTED ROOTS		
(b)	CV-s	CV-s	CV
(c)	CVC-s ~ (C)VN	CVC-s	CVN
(d)	CV-r	CV-r	CV (before obstr.) ~
			CV? (before nas./liq.)
(e)	CVC-t	CVC-t	CVC
	CVt (<*(C)Vt-t)	CVt	CV? (before liq.) ~
			CVC (elsewhere)

8.1.2 Morphophonological behavior of stems

The previous section has introduced the root alternations in their basic forms, grouped according to pre-vocalic and pre-consonantal behavior. Depending on which consonant or vowel follows the root, further processes such as assimilation, gliding and voicing may apply (see Table 8.10). Except for the alternation between CVC-s and CVN, and the somewhat exceptional behavior of CV? roots, all alternations can be ascribed to phonological processes.

The following processes can be attested (cf. also §3.5): assimilation of root-final /n/, /p/ and /pt/ to a bilabial nasal (triggered by a bilabial nasal), assimilation of root-final /k/ and /kt/ to a velar nasal (also triggered by a bilabial nasal), intervocalic and postnasal voicing (e.g., in /cok/ and /ap/). CV roots with an augment (e.g., /pes/, /her/ and /thur/) show that the augment almost never surfaces before consonants. Root-final /t/ and /?/ easily assimilate to the following consonant.

Stress, in addition to the quality of the subsequent sound, plays a role in determining the allomorphs. A comparison of roots followed by either -*khuba* (a nominalizer, not stressed) or -*khe?* (a function verb, stressed in the citation forms), reveals that the stressed -*khe?ma* has greater phonological impact on the preceding verbal root, since all root-final consonants become nasals before -*khe?ma*. The forms in brackets represent unconditioned variations.

Table 8.10: Examples of stem allomorphs, mostly phonologically conditioned

Σ	Σ-*khuba*	Σ-*khe?*	Σ-*me?*	Σ-*san*	*meN*-Σ-*le*	Σ-*ci/-cu*	Σ-*wa*	Σ-V
khe?	khe(k)	-	khe(m)	khe	khe?	khe	-	khy (/_a) khe (/_i)
so?	so(k)	soŋ	so(m)	so(s)	so?	so	s	so
cok	cok	coŋ	coŋ	cok	jok	cok	cog	cog
in	in	iŋ	im	in	in	in	in	in
ap	ap	am	am	ap	ap	ap	ab	ab
pes	pe	peŋ	pe	pe	be	pe	pes	pes
thur	thu	thuŋ	thu	thu	thu?	thu	thur	thur
her	he	heŋ	he	he	he	he	her	her
haks	haŋ	haŋ	haŋ	haŋ	haŋ	haŋ	haks	haks
hops	hom	hom	hom	hom	hom	hom	hops	hops
hakt	hak	haŋ	haŋ	hak	hak	hak	hakt	hakt
chimd	chim	chim	chim	chim	chim	chim	chimd	chimd
chept	chep	chem	chem	chep	chep	chep	chept	chept
mit	mik	miŋ	mim	mis	mi?	mi?	mit	mit

8.2 Person, number and syntactic role marking

An outstanding characteristic of Kiranti languages is the intricate person marking. Yakkha is a "well-behaved" Kiranti language: the verb exhibits a complex
indexing system, where person (1, 2, 3 and clusivity for first person), number (singular, dual and plural, sometimes neutralized to nonsingular) and syntactic role
marking interact. The system is simply referred to as *person marking* in the following for the sake of readability. The person marking is overwhelmingly suffixing: there is only one prefix slot, which is filled by a homorganic and non-syllabic
nasal (see (6)). In transitive scenarios, generally both arguments are marked on
the verb, and hence the verbal inflection provides a clue about the transitivity of
the verb.[10] Due to morphophonological processes such as vowel elision to avoid
hiatus, some morphemes undergo changes or are rarely overtly realized. Example (6) also illustrates a further morphophonological process in Yakkha and many
other Kiranti languages, known as *suffix copying* or *nasal copying* (Bickel 2003;
Doornenbal 2009; Ebert 2003c; Schikowski 2012). Nasal suffixes in Yakkha can
be copied regressively and thus may appear up to three times in one suffix string
(see §3.5.7.2).

(6)   *m-bi-me-n-c-u-n-ci-ŋa-n=na.*
        NEG-give-NPST-[N]-DU-3.P-[N]-NSG.P-EXCL-NEG=NMLZ.SG
        'We (dual, exclusive) will not give it to them.'

The verbal inflection is the most complicated part of Yakkha morphology, not
just because of the number of affixes, but also because there is no one-to-one
mapping of form and function.[11] This asymmetry holds for both directions: one
functional slot (i.e., the reference to one participant or one scenario) can be marked by a combination of affixes. The first person plural exclusive, for instance,
is expressed by *-i*, *-ŋ* and (optionally) *=ha*. At the same time, many markers encode more than one category. The aforementioned *-i* contains the information
that the co-nominal of the marker is a first or second person plural subject of an
intransitive verb or a second person plural object of a transitive verb. Some markers encode only one category, like *-ka* for 'second person' or *-ŋ* for 'exclusive'.
Other markers are homophonous, like *-ci*, encoding either dual (any syntactic
role) or nonsingular (only third person patients). These are two different markers, since they occupy separate slots in the suffix string. In a few other Kiranti

---

[10] Although there are mismatches between semantic and morphological valency, see Chapter 11.
[11] From a comparative Kiranti perspective, however, the Yakkha verbal inflection looks fairly
     simple and regular.

languages, they have different shapes.[12] Ambiguities of affixes can usually be resolved via the morphological context in which the markers appear. Furthermore, a few person-number-role configurations have different markers depending on whether they are in the indicative, imperative or subjunctive mood.

Table 8.11 gives an overview of the person marking affixes in intransitive and transitive (indicative) inflection. Most affixes are restricted to certain syntactic roles. Some markers do not just encode the referential properties of one argument, but stand for whole scenarios, such as the portmanteau morphemes *-nen* marking first person acting on second, and *-m* marking first or second person plural acting on third person. A reference factor that shapes the person paradigm is the dominance of second person in scenarios with third person acting on second (3>2). Two examples for the influence of role must be mentioned here, too: firstly, the dual is not distinguished as consistently in the object marking as it is in the subject marking (both transitive and intransitive) and secondly, the loss of first person nonsingular object marking (from a historical perspective, discussed below).

Thus, the paradigm of person marking does not exhibit one particular alignment type but combinations of role-based (ergative, accusative, neutral) and reference-based or even scenario-based alignment, to be determined for each marker separately.[13] In one scenario, there are two possible inflections, namely 1PL.EXCL>2DU, where the suffix string *-nen-cin=ha* was regarded equally acceptable as *-nen-in=ha* by all speakers consulted.

Furthermore, the person inflection interacts with polarity, mood and tense/aspect markers, discussed further below. The cliticized markers *=na* and *=ha ~ =ya*, *~ =a* are nominalizers. In a manner that is common in Sino-Tibetan languages, they are frequently attached to the inflected verb, lending authority to assertions, or emphasis to questions (see Chapter 13 for a detailed analysis). Since they also encode number and role information, they are included in the discussion of person marking.

The verbal morphology is templatic, with one prefix slot and eleven suffix slots for person and number, established according to the sequences in which the affixes occur relative to each other (see Figure 8.1). The longest suffix string found

---

[12] Limbu, for instance, has *-si/-chi* for dual and *-si* for nonsingular patient (van Driem 1987: 75).

[13] An alternative view would be to say that languages like Yakkha lack alignment altogether, following a definition of alignment as a property of a whole language instead of as a property of one construction or even one marker. However, the person forms do not appear randomly in the paradigm; one can discern certain groupings and patterns that are pretty consistent across the whole language family, and these would not be acknowledged by dubbing the language as 'lacking alignment' or 'lacking grammatical relations'.

Table 8.11: Indicative person/number marking (intransitive and transitive)

A>P	TRANSITIVE							INTRANSITIVE
	1SG	1NSG	2SG	2DU	2PL	3SG	3NSG	
1SG			-nen(=na)			-u-ŋ(=na)	-u-ŋ-ci-ŋ(=ha)	-ŋ(=na)
1DU.EXCL			-nen-cin(=ha)			-ŋ-c-u-ŋ(=na)	-ŋ-c-u-ŋ-ci-ŋ(=ha)	-ŋ-ci-ŋ(=ha)
1PL.EXCL			-nen-in(=ha)			-u-m-ŋa(=na)	-u-m-ci-m-ŋ(=ha)	-i-ŋ(=ha)
1DU.INCL						-c-u(=na)	-c-u-ci(=ha)	-ci(=ha)
1PL.INCL						-u-m(=na)	-u-m-ci-m(=ha)	-i(=ha)
2SG	-ŋ-ka(=na)					-u-ka(=na)	-u-ci-ka(=ha)	-ka(=na)
2DU		-ka(=ha)				-c-u-ci-ka(=na)	-c-u-ci-ka(=ha)	-ci-ka(=ha)
2PL						-u-m-ka(=na)	-u-m-ci-m-ka(=ha)	-i-ka(=ha)
3SG	-ŋ(=na)		-ka(=na)			-u(=na)	-u-ci(=ha)	(=na)
3DU				-ci-ka(=ha)	-i-ka(=ha)	-c-u-ci(=ha)	-c-u-ci(=ha)	-ci(=ha)
3PL		(=ha)	N-...-ka(=na)			N-...-u(=na)	N-...-u-ci(=ha)	N-...(=ha=ci)

in the person inflection refers to the scenario 1DU.EXCL>3NSG and contains seven affixes, counting only the person suffixes (see (7a)); the shortest is third person singular (intransitive), which has only one optional slot, since third person singular subject indexing (both transitive and intransitive) does not have a dedicated marker (see (7b)).[14]

The schematic representation includes the slots for the nasal copying (-N). Slots no. 1, 3, 6, 13 and 14 are reserved for negation and TAM-marking; Slot 2 may contain either a person marker or a TAM marker.

(7) a. *tund-a-ŋ-c-u-ŋ-ci-ŋ(=ha).*
         understand-PST-N-DU-3.P-N-3NSG.P-EXCL=NMLZ.NSG
         'We (dual, excl.) understood them.'
     b. *khy-a(=na).*
         go-PST(=SG)
         'He went.'

2	4	5	7	8	9
-nen	*-N*	*-ci ~ -cin*	*-u*	*-N*	*-ci*
1>2	(copy)	DUAL	3.P	(copy)	3NSG.P
		-i ~ -in			
		1/2PL			

10	11	12	(15)	(16)
-m	*-ŋ(a)*	*-ka*	*(=na)*	*(=ci)*
1/2PL>3	EXCL	2	NMLZ.SG	NSG
			(=ha)	
			NMLZ.NSG/	
			NMLZ.NC/	

Figure 8.1: Templatic representation of indicative person/number suffixes

In the following, proceeding from left to right, the individual affixes will be discussed. In general, the labels for the morphemes stand for a maximal exten-

---

[14] The parentheses signalling the optionality of these markers will not be written in the following, except for where their optionality is explicitly discussed. They are optional from a morphological perspective, but not from an information-structural perspective, since under certain conditions they have to occur.

sion, since it is often the case that a morpheme is not found in all the expected slots.

The prefix slot can only be occupied by an unspecified nasal, which either marks third person plural (in S and A roles) or negation (see §8.3). As it is unspecified with regard to the place of articulation, it assimilates to the place of the initial consonant of the verb stem (see (8)). Before vowels and the glide /w/, it is realized as a velar nasal.

(8) a. *ŋ-khy-a=ha=ci.*
         3PL-go-PST=NMLZ.NSG=NSG
         'They went.'

     b. *m-bi-a-ga=na.*
         3PL.A-give-PST-2=NMLZ.SG
         'They gave it to you.'

     c. *n-chimd-a-ga=na.*
         3PL.A-ask-PST-2=NMLZ.SG
         'They asked you.'

     d. *n-yog-a-ga=na.*
         3PL.A-search-PST-2=NMLZ.SG
         'They searched for you.'

In the transitive paradigm, the prefix is not found in all expected scenarios; more precisely, it marks 3PL.A>2SG.P and 3PL.A>3.P. The only Kiranti language with a similar marker is Belhare, but there, the marker partly has NSG and 3>2 distribution (Bickel 2003: 551).[15] The prefix domain is surprisingly compact in Yakkha, compared to most of the surrounding languages: Limbu has four prefixes (van Driem 1997), Belhare has five prefixes (Bickel 2003), Chintang has eight prefixes (Schikowski 2012) and Bantawa has six (Doornenbal 2009). In this respect, Yakkha resembles its northern neighbors Yamphu and Kulung (Rutgers 1998; Tolsma 1999) and many Western Kiranti languages (Jacques 2012a: 93).

Among the suffixes, the first person marking slot (Slot 2) is occupied by the marker *-nen*, coding all and only those scenarios where the first person acts on the second person (see (9)). A speaker from Hombong village consistently pronounced this marker as *-nan*, and also the Omruwa (Angbura) materials in van

---

[15] Functionally similar markers in other Kiranti languages have been analyzed as inverse markers by Ebert (1991). In Yakkha, the distribution of this marker does not support such an analysis. According to this reasoning, inverse scenarios would be those with 3PL>2SG and 3PL>3, which would imply that 2DU and 2PL are lower-ranking arguments than 3SG. This is not confirmed by the alignment found in other constructions, where speech-act partipants generally outrank third person participants in Yakkha.

Driem (1994) and Gvozdanović (1987) show -*nan*, so that there may be some dialectal variation towards the western fringes of the Yakkha speaking area (the villages closer to the Arun river). This morpheme is unexpected from a comparative Kiranti perspective, since the cognate of this marker is generally -*na*, at least in Central and Eastern Kiranti. The most plausible explanation for the addition of /n/ is a preference for syllables being closed by nasals, as it is found elsewhere in the verbal inflection and in complex predication. This reasoning also explains why -*ci* and -*i* have the allomorphs -*cin* and -*in* in the 1>2 forms. Unfortunately, I have no explanation for why such a process is restricted to 1>2 scenarios, since open syllables are not completely ruled out in other inflectional forms.

(9)   a.   *pi?-nen=na.*
           give[PST]-1>2=NMLZ.SG
           'I gave it to you.'
      b.   *pi?-nen-in=ha.*
           give[PST]-PL=NMLZ.NSG
           'I gave it to you (plural).' OR
           'We (dual) gave it to you (plural).' OR
           'We (plural) gave it to you (singular/dual/plural).'

The functional distribution for scenarios of 1>2 is pan-Kiranti, although in some languages, -*na* can be found as a second person marker, for instance in Thulung (Lahaussois 2002: 148). The change from /a/ to /e/ seems to be a Yakkha innovation; it is also found in other Yakkha lexemes and affixes. Compare for instance the Belhare negation marker *man*- with Yakkha *men*-, or Belhare/Chintang *khatt* ('carry off') with Yakkha *khet*.

   Slot 4 is reserved for a nasal copy (glossed as [N] in this section), coming after the past marker -*a* or the nonpast marker -*me?* in Slot 3 (discussed below). This nasal copy is licensed by the dual marker -*ci*; it only appears when -*ci* is there, too. In the affirmative paradigm this slot is only filled in the forms for 1DU.EXCL>3.P (see (10)). Although this marker never co-occurs with -*nen*, it is clear from its interaction with the tense marking that it does not occupy the same slot as -*nen*: the past marker -*a* occupies the same slot as -*nen*, and -*a* precedes the nasal copy.

(10) a.   *tund-a-ŋ-c-u-ŋ=na.*
           understand-PST-[N]-DU-3.P-EXCL=NMLZ.SG
           'We (dual, excl.) understood him.'
      b.   *tum-me-ŋ-c-u-ŋ=na.*
           understand-NPST-[N]-DU-3.P-EXCL=NMLZ.SG
           'We (dual, excl.) understand him.'

Slot 5 is occupied either by -i ~ -in (coding 1/2PL.S and 2.P) or by -ci ~ -cin ~ -c (coding dual) in the indicative, or by a second person plural suffix -ni in the imperative (see §8.5). The suffix -i ~ -in will be examined first. Intransitive examples can be found in (11). The ambiguity of the marker is resolved by the addition of further morphological material: -ŋ(a) for exclusive and -ka for second person. If no further material is added, the forms have an inclusive reading (see (11c)).

(11)   a.   *khe-i-g=ha.*
                go[PST]-2PL-2=NMLZ.NSG
                'You went.'

        b.   *khe-i-ŋ=ha.*
                go[PST]-1PL-EXCL=NMLZ.NSG
                'We (excl) went.'

        c.   *khe-i=ha.*
                go[PST]-1PL=NMLZ.NSG
                'We (incl) went.'

In transitive verbs, the distribution of this marker is conditioned by the respective participant scenarios, i.e., by the referential properties of both argument and co-argument. In scenarios with third person acting on second, the alignment is role-based: -i clearly marks second person plural patients. In scenarios with first person agents, though, the marker (its allomorph -in) appears as soon as one participant has plural number (cf. Table 8.11 and example (9b)). Thus, its alignment in 1>2 scenarios is reference-based (number-based, to be precise), since the marker occurs regardless of which participant has plural number.

The dual marker -ci ~ -cin also has a very peculiar distribution. It marks dual subjects of intransitive verbs, and in transitive verbs its distribution depends on the person of the patient. It does not occur with first person patients, as this category got neutralized to zero marking (evidence for the former presence of first person patient marking is presented below). In the 1>2 paradigm cells it behaves analogously to -in: as soon as one argument has dual number (and no argument has plural number), -cin occurs (see (12)). In the 3>2 paradigm cells, -ci is aligned with the patient. In all cells with third person patients, it is aligned with the agent, since the dual distinction is not made for third person patients.

To sum up, this marker indexes all intransitive dual arguments, second person dual patients and agents, and transitive dual agents of all persons when the patient is a third person. Thus, one arrives at a combination of accusative (third person), neutral (second person) and reference-based (number-based, in 1>2 scenarios) alignment for the dual marker. When -ci is followed by the suffix -u, its vowel is omitted, yielding the fused form [cu].

(12)   *chim-meʔ-nen-cin=ha.*
        ask-NPST-1>2-DU=NMLZ.NSG
        'I will ask you (dual).' OR
        'We (dual) will ask you (sing., dual).'

Historically, the two suffixes *-i* and *-ci* used to mark first person patients, too, but the forms for first person nonsingular patients got lost, probably due to a face-preserving strategy equating first person patients with vague/indefinite reference (cf. §11.3.1.3). Luckily, the old forms are preserved in Gvozdanović (1987) (re-arranged and provided with an alternative analysis in van Driem 1994). Table 8.12 contrasts the contemporary forms from the Tumok dialect with those recorded by Gvozdanović in 1984 with a male speaker of 51 years from Omruwa (Angbura) village. The orthography used in this source was slightly adjusted here; <ng> was replaced by <ŋ>. In the original sources, the data contain tense markers, which are omitted here for better comparison.

Table 8.12: Comparison of old and new first person patient forms

OMRUWA DATA (1984)					
A>P	1SG.P	1DU.EXCL.P	1PL.EXCL.P	1DU.INCL.P	1PL.INCL.P
2SG.A	-ŋgana	-gaha	-gaha	–	–
2DU.A	-ŋciŋaha	-ŋciŋaha	-gaha	–	-
2PL.A	-ŋiŋana	-gaha	-gaha	–	–
3SG.A	-ŋna	-ŋciŋaha	-ŋciŋaha	-ciha	-ha
3DU.A	-ŋna	-ciha	-ha	-ciha	-ha
3PL.A	N- -ŋna	-ciha	-ha	-ciha	-ha

TUMOK DATA (2012)					
A>P	1SG.P	1DU.EXCL.P	1PL.EXCL.P	1DU.INCL.P	1PL.INCL.P
2SG.A	-ŋgana	-gaha	-gaha	–	–
2DU.A	-gaha	-gaha	-gaha	–	–
2PL.A	-gaha	-gaha	-gaha	–	–
3SG.A	-ŋna	-ha	-ha	-ha	-ha
3DU.A	-ha	-ha	-ha	-ha	-ha
3PL.A	-ha	-ha	-ha	-ha	-ha

The 1984 data are puzzling, which can partly be ascribed to inconsistent orthography. In the forms with second person agents for instance, one would expect the second person marker -*ga*. This can probably be attributed to a writing inconsistency (writing <ng> instead of <ngg>) or a hearing mistake. The form -*ŋ̥ciŋaha* in 3SG acting on 1PL.EXCL is unexpected, too, and cannot be explained. The nasal prefix coding 3PL.A had a greater distribution than nowadays, since it is found in the paradigm cell for 3PL acting on 1SG, too. Even though the 1984 data are rather sketchy and apparently not completely reliable, they show that first person patients were once marked more elaborately on the verb once than they are now. The dual number marker -*ci*, for instance, is found in almost all cells with first person dual patients.

Slot 7 is filled by -*u*, marking third person patients. When it follows the dual marker, both suffixes fuse into [cu], due to a strategy to avoid vowel hiatus. The suffix -*u* does not only cause vowel elision, it may itself be deleted, e.g., in the underlying sequence /-*wa-u-m*/, which is realized [wam] (see (13a)).

Slot 8 is filled by another nasal copy, which can be filled by -*ŋ* (see (13b)), -*m* (see (13c)) or -*n* (a negation marker).

(13)   a.   *pi-wa-m=na.*
              give-NPST[3.P]-1PL.A=NMLZ.SG
              'We (pl., incl.) give it to him.'
       b.   *tund-a-ŋ-c-u-ŋ-ci-ŋ=ha.*
              understand-PST-[N]-DU-3.P-[N]-3NSG.P-EXCL=NMLZ.NSG
              'We (dual, excl.) understood them.'
       c.   *tund-u-m-ci-m=ha.*
              understand[PST]-3.P-[N]-3NSG.P-1PL.A=NMLZ.NSG
              'We (pl., incl.) understood them.'

Slot 9 is filled by the marker -*ci* for third person nonsingular patients (see examples (13b) and (13c)). As mentioned above, third person patient marking does not distinguish dual and plural number. This marker is optional: it is omitted when the patient is low on the referential hierarchy, e.g., when it is inanimate (see (14a)) or when it has a rather vague reference (see (14b)).

(14)   a.   *kho-het-u,*   [...] *saikal=be*
              steal-V2.CARRY.OFF-3.P[PST] [...] bicycle=LOC
              thend-het-u,   [...], *phopt-haks-u.*
              lift-V2.CARRY.OFF-3.P[PST] [...] spill-V2.SEND-3P[PST]
              'He stole them (the pears) [...] he lifted them onto the bike, [...] he spilled them.'   [23_pea_03.019–028]

b. *yakpuca*   *yog-a-ma-c-u,*   *phusa*
porcupine   search-PST-PRF-DU.A-3.P,   pangolin

yog-a-ma-c-u.
search-PST-PRF-DU.A-3.P

'They (dual) looked for porcupines, they looked for pangolins.' (context: They did not hunt any.)

[22_nrr_05.015]

Slot 10 is filled by *-m*, coding first and second person plural agents acting on third person (also illustrated by (13a) and (13c)). Like the suffix *-nen*, it marks a whole scenario, not just the features of one participant. The suffix *-m* can be copied regressively, but maximally once, since the suffix combinations preceding *-m* never open up two copy slots.

The exclusive *-ŋ ~ -ŋa* in Slot 11 codes the non-inclusive, strictly speaking, because the first person singular is marked by this suffix, too. Although it is morphologically the marked form, it is the semantically unmarked form, defined by the exclusion of the adressee or some other person saliently present in the utterance context.[16] The morpheme is glossed '1SG' in singular and 'EXCL' in non-singular forms (see (15)). The allomorph *-ŋa* is found in the first person singular subjunctive, e.g., *kheʔŋa* 'I would go', *apŋa* 'I would come'. It is also found when the exclusive marker is followed by the negation marker *-n*. As for its distribition across the paradigm, it is found marking intransitive and transitive subjects. In the first person patient forms it got lost, except for scenarios with 1SG.P and an agent that has singular number (see also Table 8.12). As we have already seen, the exclusive suffix can be copied regressively (maximally twice). The inclusive/exclusive distinction present in the verbal inflection got lost in the personal pronouns, but it is maintained in the possessive pronouns and in the possessive inflection (see §4.2).

(15)   a.   *chimd-wa-ŋ=na.*
ask-NPST-1SG=NMLZ.SG
'I will ask him.'

b.   *chim-me-ŋ-c-u-ŋ-ci-ŋ=ha.*
ask-NPST-[N]-DU-3.P-[N]-3NSG.P-EXCL=NMLZ.NSG
'We (dual, excl.) will ask them.'

---

[16] In other Kiranti languages, the inclusive forms are the functionally unmarked choice, since they are also used with generic reference. In Yakkha, first person forms are rarely used in this way; rather, the opposite development took place: a strategy to express generic reference (syntactically a detransitivization) became the standard way to indicate first person nonsingular patients, and the same is optionally possible with agents, too, see §11.3.1.

The marker *-ka* ([ga] before vowels and [g(a)] before *=ha*) for second person fills Slot 12, illustrated by (16). It is unrestricted with regard to syntactic role: it appears in all paradigm cells with second person, except for 1>2, since there, the portmanteau suffix *-nen* applies. Example (16b) shows that it is not in the same slot as *-ŋ(a)*.

(16) a. *chim-me-c-u-ci-g=ha.*
ask-NPST-DU-3.P-3NSG.P-2=NMLZ.NSG
'You (dual) will ask them.'
  b. *chim-me-ŋ-ga=na.*
ask-NPST-1SG-2.A=NMLZ.SG
'You will ask me.'

Slots 13 and 14 are reserved for mood and negation suffixes. Finally, in slots 15 and 16 we find two clitics, but since they encode person as well, they are included in the discussion here. Both are optional morphologically, but certain discourse contexts require them (discussed in §13.3.3 for *=na* and *=ha*, and in §11.3.1.2 for *=ci*). The clitics *=na* and *=ha* originate in a nominalization of independent main clauses, but they also code number, partly ergatively (matching with the number of S and P), partly following reference-based alignment, with nonsingular outranking singular (see Table 8.11 on page 218 for their exact distribution).

The marker *=ci* is found occasionally on intransitive verbs with 3PL subjects. Its occurrence depends on the occurrence of *=ha*, and since this is a nominalized structure, *=ci* can be identified as the nominal nonsingular marker. It is optional, and only found when its co-nominal is salient in discourse or referentially high. The exact conditions have yet to be determined, though. The main, non-optional marker for 3PL subjects is the nasal prefix discussed in the beginning of this section. Example (17) contrasts forms with and without *=ci*.

(17) a. *pheri   sum-baŋ   n-leks-a=ha=ci.*
again   three-CLF.HUM   3PL-become-PST=NMLZ.NSG=NSG
'They became three again.'   [19_pea_01.048]
  b. *limbu=ci   nhaŋ   n-las-a-khy-a-ma.*
Limbu_person=NSG   and_then   3PL-return-PST-V2.GO-PST-PRF
'The Limbus went back afterwards.' (The story is not about the Limbus; they are referred to as a group; no particular individual is singled out.)

[22_nrr_05.040]

In the person marking of Yakkha, both reference and role condition the distributions and functions of the markers. Speech act participant arguments are treated differently from third person arguments. For instance, several markers refer to the category speech-act participant as a whole, e.g., *-nen*, *-m* and *-i*. Number is another referential factor; as we have seen for *-i* and *-ci*, number is more salient than role in several scenarios. Role, in particular the patient role, is important as a condition for alignment splits. Reference-based systems and/or inverse marking are not unknown in Kiranti and other Tibeto-Burman languages (see, e.g., Ebert (1991) for Belhare and Athpare, LaPolla (2007) for Rawang). Although reference is an important factor in Yakkha too, any attempt to generate one referential hierarchy from these intertwined conditions must fail, and none of the Yakkha person markers should be analyzed as an inverse marker. Figure 8.2 summarizes the alignment of the single markers. The single tables are organized like paradigms, with all possible participant scenarios. To take an example, the cell combined of 1A and 3P stands for scenarios where a first person agent acts on a third person patient. The shaded cells show which scenarios are marked by a particular marker. The last column (labelled S) stands for intransitive person marking. The crossed-out cells represent reflexive or partly reflexive scenarios, which cannot be expressed by the verbal person marking alone.

Two final notes are in order. Firstly, the third person singular (S and A arguments) marking is zero, in parallel to other Kiranti languages, and also in line with universal expectations (Siewierska 2011). Secondly, partial coreferentiality, e.g., propositions like 'you saved us (incl)' or 'I saw us (in the mirror)' cannot be expressed by the Yakkha person inflection.[17] Complete coreferentiality can be expressed by the reflexive construction (see §11.3.4).

8.3 Polarity

There are two sets of negation markers, one for nonfinite forms like converbs, participant nominalizations and infinitives, and one for finite inflected verbs. The first set is instantiated by the prefix *men-*.

In finite verbs, negation is marked by an underspecified nasal prefix and a suffix (*N-...-n*). In forms with 3PL.A and with 1PL.INCL.A, *-n* has the allomorph *-nin*.[18] By means of nasal copying *-n* can occur up to three times in one inflected form (see (18a)). Comparing this form to (18b), one can see that *-n* has replaced *-ŋ* in the copy slots; now it is the negation suffix that is copied. There is a hierarchy for the

---

[17] Jacques (2012a) notes the same for Rgyalrongic languages.
[18] This allomorph has a slightly larger distribution in the inflection of the copulas, see §8.7.

	1P	2P	3P	S
1A				
2A				
3A				

-*ka* '2' (neutral, except 1>2)

	1P	2P	3P	S
1A				
2A				
3A				

-*ŋ(a)* 'excl, 1sg' (neutral, except 1>2)

	1P	2P	3P	S
1A				
2A				
3A				

-*i* '1/2pl.S' & '2P' (ergative for 2, except 1>2)

	1P	2P	3P	S
1A				
2A				
3A				

Historical forms (recent loss of 1nsg.P forms): -*i* '1/2pl.S/P' (ergative)

	1P	2P	3P	S
1A				
2A				
3A				

-*u* '3P', -*ci* '3nsg.P' (accusative)

	1P	2P	3P	S
1A				
2A				
3A				

N- '3pl.S/A', zero '3sg.S/A' (accusative)

	1P	2P	3P	S
1A				
2A				
3A				

-*m* '1/2pl>3' (scenario-portmanteau)

	1P	2P	3P	S
1A				
2A				
3A				

-*nen* '1>2' (scenario-portmanteau)

	1P	2P	3P	S
1A				
2A				
3A				

-*ci* 'dual' (mixed: acc./neutral/ref.-based)

	1P	2P	3P	S
1A				
2A				
3A				

=*na* 'sg'; =*ha* 'nsg' (mixed: erg./ref.-based)

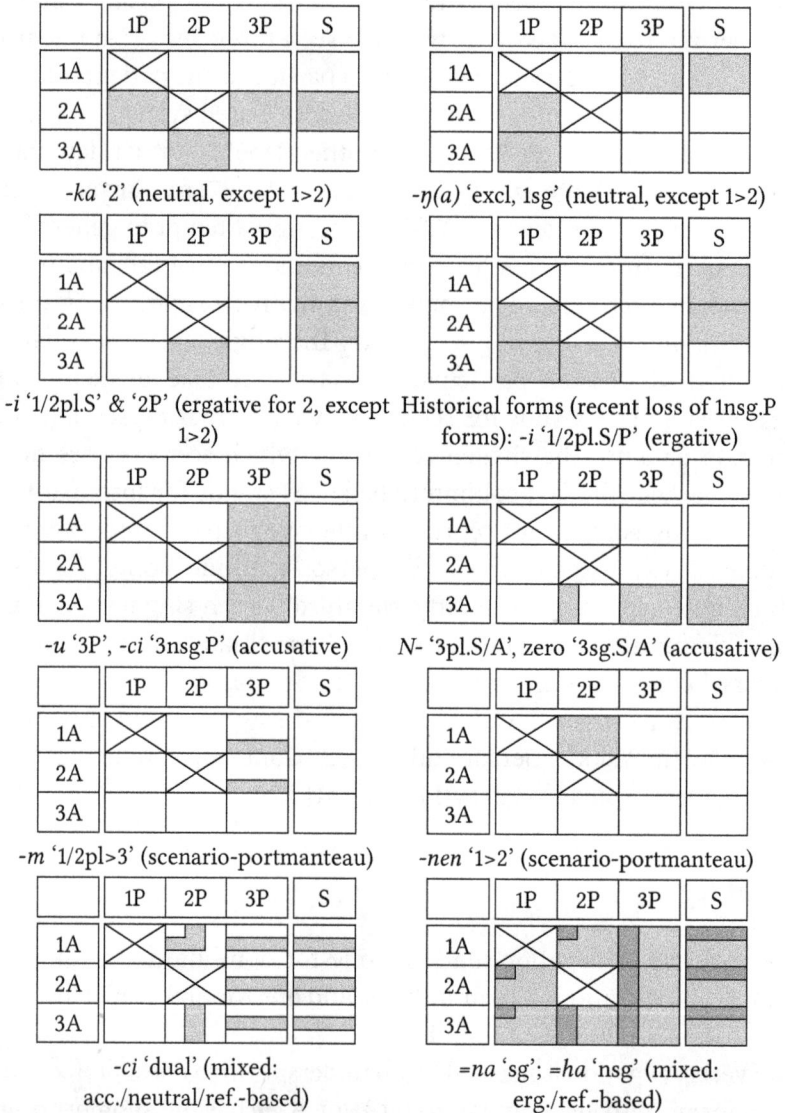

Figure 8.2: The alignment of individual person/number markers

choice of which suffix to copy, consistently followed throughout the paradigms: *-m > -n > -ŋ* (see also §3.5.8).

(18)   a.   *n-chimd-a-n-c-u-n-ci-ŋa-n=ha.*
           NEG-ask-PST-[N]-DU-3.P-[N]-3NSG.P-EXCL-NEG=NMLZ.NSG
           'We (dual, excl.) will not ask them.'
   b.   *chim-me-ŋ-c-u-ŋ-ci-ŋ=ha.*
           ask-NPST-[N]-DU-3.P-N-3NSG.P-EXCL=NMLZ.NSG
           'We (dual, excl.) will ask them.'

The unspecified nasal prefix assimilates in place to the first consonant of the verbal stem, as has been shown above for the nasal prefix coding third person plural subjects. For some forms, especially in the forms for first person acting on the second person, it is the only negation marking device (see (19)). Among related languages, only Belhare has this unspecified nasal prefix, too (Bickel 2003: 554).

(19)   a.   *chim-meʔ-nen=na.*
           ask-NPST-1>2=NMLZ.SG
           'I will ask you.'
   b.   *n-chim-meʔ-nen=na.*
           NEG-ask-NPST-1>2=NMLZ.SG
           'I will not ask you.'

Examples of the suffix *-nin* are provided in (20). As a comparison between (20a) and (20b) shows, it may trigger the nasal copying too, if no higher ranking nasal suffix is available. In forms with third person plural agents, the homophony between *N-* marking person and *N-* marking negation makes this prefix ambiguous in these particular forms. Functionally, it would make sense to say that the task of *-nin* is to disambiguate between affirmative and negative in those forms. But for the forms coding 1PL>3 this explanation does not make sense.

(20)   a.   *n-chimd-wa-m-ci-m-nin=ha.*
           NEG-ask-NPST-[N]-3NSG.P-1PL.A-NEG=NMLZ.NSG
           'We (incl.) will not ask them.'
   b.   *n-chimd-wa-n-ci-nin=ha.*
           NEG/3PL.A-ask-NPST-[N]-3NSG.P-NEG=NMLZ.NSG
           'They will not ask them.'

Paradigm tables can be found in §8.4.6, with the upper forms showing the affirmative and the lower forms showing the negative inflections.

8.4 Tense and aspect marking

The inflected verb is marked for tense in both the indicative and the subjunctive mood. Tensed forms stand in opposition to the non-tensed imperative mood. This section only treats tense and aspect in the indicative mood, where tense also shows more elaborate distinctions. The subjunctive is treated below in §8.5.

The basic distinction in tense marking is between nonpast and past tense, partly cross-cut by aspectual distinctions (progressive and continuative aspect, both expressed periphrastically). As predicates with inceptive semantics are quite widespread in Yakkha (as in Belhare, cf. Bickel 1996), past inflections often have a 'present' interpretation, referring to the inception of a state or event, e.g., *tugama* (hurt.PRF[3SG]) 'it started to hurt/it hurts'). Another consequence of this is that nonpast marking often gets a future or a general interpretation (i.e., not referring to a particular event, as in the nonpast *tuŋmeʔna* 'it will hurt/it generally hurts').

An overview of the tense/aspect distinctions and their markers is provided in Table 8.13. The relative simplicity of this overview is misleading, though, since further aspectual/Aktionsart distinctions, such as specifications for telicity and irreversibility, are indicated by complex predication (see Chapter 10). The tense/aspect analysis and labels presented here have to be understood as tentative, since no in-depth analysis of the lexical semantics of the verbs has been undertaken yet.

8.4.1 The nonpast

Yakkha overtly marks the nonpast in the indicative but not in the subjunctive. The nonpast is indicated by the two suppletive markers *-meʔ* and *-wa*, occurring in different slots of the verbal inflection. While *-meʔ* comes immediately after the stem and before the person marking (Slot 1), *-wa* follows the suffix *-i* '1/2pl' (Slot 6).

Historically, both markers are function verbs that got further grammaticalized to tense markers. They are different from function verbs in not triggering the double inflection that is found in complex predication, and also in not showing up in the citation forms, as function verbs generally do. The lexical verb *wama* 'sit, stay, live' still exists in Yakkha, but *meʔma* only exists with the stem *met* and the meaning 'put around the waist'. In Belhare and Bantawa, though, cognates with the meaning 'make, do, apply, cause' can be found (Bickel 1997a; Doornenbal 2009). The Yakkha causative marker *-met* is also cognate to the nonpast marker, and in analogy to the stems and augments treated in §8.1 above, *meʔ* originates in

Table 8.13: Tense and aspect inflection

NONPAST	PAST
NONPAST *-me?/* *-wa*	SIMPLE PAST *-a*
	PERFECT *-ama ~ -imi* *-uks*
	PAST PERFECT *-amasa ~ -imisi* *-uksa*
PROGRESSIVE INF + AUX.*si?*.NPST	PROGRESSIVE INF + AUX.*si?*.PST
CONTINUATIVE SIM.CVB + AUX.*khe?*.NPST	CONTINUATIVE SIM.CVB + AUX.*khe?*.PST

an unaugmented stem and *met* is the corresponding augmented stem. The final /?/ is often omitted (the omission being triggered by the following material), but it still has an impact on the following material: if *-ka* follows *-me?*, it does not get voiced, for instance. The sequence becomes [meka], not [mega], because more than one consonant stands between the vowels in the underlying structure.

The distribution of these two allomorphs is not random, but grammatically conditioned (see Table 8.14). In the intransitive paradigm, mostly *-me?* is found, except for first and second person plural, which take *-wa*. The picture is slightly more complex in the transitive paradigm. Again, the more common allomorph is *-me?*, but *-wa* occurs in the forms of third person acting on second person plural ('3>2pl'), and in the forms with a non-dual agent and a third person patient. Thus, the distribution of the markers can be seen as a secondary device to mark different scenario classes, albeit not according to a particular referential hierarchy. Example paradigms can be found in §8.4.6.

As for the development of this system I can only speculate but it is worth mentioning that in Yakkha complex predication, some function verbs (V2s) are employed to specify the transitivity features of a verb. It is possible that the historical V2 stems *-me?* and *-wa* have also been distributed according to transitivity features, and that via this stage their distribution was re-arranged so that they became markers of participant scenarios.

Table 8.14: Distribution of nonpast allomorphs

	INTRANSITIVE	TRANSITIVE			
		1	2	2PL	3
1SG	-me?		-me?		-wa
1DU	-me?		-me?		-me?
1PL	-wa		-me?		-wa
2SG	-me?	-me?			-wa
2DU	-me?	-me?			-me?
2PL	-wa	-me?			-wa
3SG	-me?	-me?	-me?	-wa	-wa
3DU	-me?	-me?	-me?	-wa	-me?
3PL	-me?	-me?	-me?	-wa	-wa

Let us now turn to the functional distribution of the category nonpast. As mentioned above, verbs marked by the nonpast often acquire a future reading (see (21)). Furthermore, the nonpast is found in general statements and in procedural texts, i.e., when the speaker does not have a particular temporal reference in mind (see (22)).

(21) a. *sombar=ŋa   ta-me?=na.*
          Monday=INS   come[3SG]-NPST=NMLZ.SG
          'He will come on Monday.'

     b. *wandik=ŋa   nam   phem-me?=na.*
          next_day=INS   sun   shine[3SG]-NPST=NMLZ.SG
          'Tomorrow the sun will shine.'

(22) a. *nhaŋto,   garo   n-cheŋd-et-wa=na,*
          afterwards   terrace   3PL.A-build-V2.CARRY.OFF-NPST=NMLZ.SG
          tokha?la.
          upwards
          'And then they build the terrace, upwards.'[19]   [31_mat_01.093]

     b. *panca=ci,   bhaladmi=ci*
          an_official_rank=NSG   respected_elder=NSG

---

[19] The example is from a description of the construction of houses, referring to the stabilization of terraced fields around the house by means of field stones.

n-yuks-wa-ci=hoŋ ceʔya n-jekt-wa.
3PL.A-put-NPST-3NSG.P=SEQ matter 3PL.A-talk-NPST
'They summon the officials and respected men, and they discuss the matter.' (a marriage description) [25_tra_01.008]

The nonpast is also possible in adverbial clauses, such as sequential (22b), cotemporal or conditional clauses, if the proposition is true or likely to become true (cf. Chapter 14).

8.4.2 The past tenses

The past tenses stand in complementary distribution to each other (and to the nonpast). Yakkha has the simple past, the perfect, and the past perfect. Morphologically, the perfect is a specification of the simple past, and the past perfect is a specification of the perfect, since in each form, some morphological material is added (see Table 8.13).

8.4.2.1 The simple past

The simple past is marked by -a, in the same slot as -meʔ. The two markers behave alike in preceding the second person marker -ka and they never co-occur (see (23)). The suffix is homophonous with the imperative and the Past Subjunctive (see §8.5), but ambiguities are resolved by context and partly by alternative person or negation marking suffixes in the non-indicative moods.

(23) a. *py-a-ga=na.*
          give[3.A]-PST-2.P=NMLZ.SG
          'He gave it to you.'
      b. *pi-meʔ-ka=na.*
          give[3.A]-PST-2.P=NMLZ.SG
          'He gives it to you.'

As for the morphophonology of this marker, it may cause the insertion of glides after vowels, as in *uyana* /u-a=na/ 'he entered', or *tayana* /ta-a=na/ 'he came'. In CVʔ stems, it causes the elision of /ʔ/, and the stem vowels /i/ and /e/ become [y], resulting in forms like *khyana* /kheʔ-a=na/ 'he went' (see also (23a)). When -a precedes the third person patient marker -u, the former gets deleted (see (24a)). The same happens when -a precedes -i, as in (24b). If such sequences occur after an open stem or a CVʔ stem, both suffixes are deleted (see (24c) and (e)). Another pair illustrating these processes is shown in (25). In (a) both suffixes undergo elision; in (b), since only two vowels are adjacent, a glide is inserted.[20] Interestingly, the underlying sequence /iʔ-a-i-/ is realized [iʔi], a sequence that is not found elsewhere in the language (cf. paradigm of *piʔma* 'give' on page 246). For more on morphophonology see §3.5. Paradigms of past inflections are provided in §8.4.6.

(24) a. *chimd-u-ŋ=na.*
/chimd-a-u-ŋ=na/
ask-PST-3.P-1SG.A=NMLZ.SG
'I asked him.'

    b. *khe-i=ha.*
/kheʔ-a-i=ha/
go-PST-1PL=NMLZ.NSG
'We (incl.) went.'

    c. *ta-ŋ=na.*
/taʔ-a-u-ŋ=na/
bring-PST-3.P-1SG.A=NMLZ.SG
'I brought him.'

    d. *pi-ga=na.*
/piʔ-a-u-ga=na/
give-PST-3.P-2.A=NMLZ.SG
'You gave it to him.'

(25) a. *ca-m=na.*
/ca-a-u-m=na/
eat-PST-3.P-1PL.A=NMLZ.SG
'We (plural) ate it.'

    b. *ca-ya-c-u=na.*
/ca-a-c-u=na/
eat-PST-DU-3.P=NMLZ.SG
'We (dual) ate it.'

The simple past refers to past events that are not specified further, for instance in truth value questions, such as in inquiries about whether a certain event happened or not, illustrated by (26).

---

[20] In Puma, a Kiranti language of the Southern Central branch, a similar vowel elision in the suffix string results in vowel lengthening and low tone (Bickel et al. 2006). For Yakkha, this could not be detected.

(26) a. *cek-met-u-m-ci-m-ga=m,*
           speak-CAUS-3.P-N-3NSG.P-2PL.A-2=ALT
           n-jek-met-u-m-ci-m-ga-n=ha=m?
           NEG-speak-CAUS-3.P-N-3NSG.P-2PL.A-2-NEG=NMLZ.NSG=ALT
           'Did you make them speak or did you not?' (talking about prospec-
           tive bride and groom)

                                                                     [36_cvs_06.323]

      b. *khokt-a-ga=na?*
           chop_off-PST-2.P=NMLZ.SG
           'Does it taste pungent?'   [36_cvs_06.011]

As mentioned above, many verbs in Yakkha (and generally in Kiranti, Ebert 2003c: 512) have ingressive-phasal Aktionsart, emphasizing the inception of the event, so that past inflection refers to the ongoing state or activity, e.g., in (26b). A common expression is shown in (27a), also rendered as 'it's done' (Nep. *bhayo*), the past suffix being hardly audible in fast speech. Another example of the numerous verbs with such a temporal profile is shown in (27b).

(27) a. *leks-a=ha.*   *[leksha]*
           become[3SG]-PST=NMLZ.NC
           'That's it.'

      b. *o-pomma=ci*   *ŋ-gy-a=ha=ci.*   *[ŋghyaci]*
           3SG.POSS-laziness=NSG 3PL-come_up-PST=NMLZ.NSG=NSG
           'He feels lazy.'

Habitual past statements can also be made using the simple past (28). There is no dedicated marker or construction for habitual aspect in Yakkha.

(28) *encho,*   *a-ppa*   *wa-ya=niŋa*
      long_ago 1SG.POSS-father exist[3]-PST=CTMP
      lit-u-m-ŋa=ba.
      plant[PST]-3.P-1PL.A-EXCL=EMPH
      'Long ago, when my father was still alive, we used to plant it.'

                                                                         [36_cvs_06.086]

In (29), the simple past refers to iterative events of reaching various places, which is conveyed by the duplicated question word.

(29) *didi,*   *ŋkhoŋ*   *heʔne*   *heʔne*   *tas-u-ga=na*
      sister,   afterwards where where reach[PST]-3.P-2.A=NMLZ.SG

laʔlo?
CTR.EXCLA
'Sister, where have you been?/Sister, which places did you reach?'

[36_cvs_06.183]

The simple past indicative cannot be distinguished from the past subjunctive in most person configurations, and thus, it is often not clear whether adverbial clauses are in the indicative or in the subjunctive, as can well be perceived in (28). However, since other tenses like the present, the perfect and past perfect (discussed below) are also possible in certain adverbial clauses, I assume that the simple past is possible as well.

Based on the past forms, two more tenses can be constructed, namely the perfect and the past perfect (discussed in the following sections).

8.4.2.2 The perfect

Roughly, the perfect tense, with the allomorphs *-ma* and *-uks*, marks events for the past, but with continuing relevance for the time of the utterance, again with interpretations depending on the internal temporal structure of the verbs. In (30a) the verb has a telic structure, so that the perfect expresses the successful accomplishment, while in (30b) and (30c) the verbs have ingressive-phasal semantics, so that the perfect expresses a state. In (30c), the function verb 'give' adds a semantic shade of completeness, translatable as 'already', sometimes also as 'certainly, inevitably'.

(30)   a.   *nhaŋ*   *ca-ma,*   *i=ʔlo,*   *lop*
           and_then   eat-INF[DEONT]   what=EXCLA   now
           whaŋd-uks-u-ŋ-ci-ŋ.
           boil-PRF-3.P-N-3NSG.P-1SG.A
           'And we have to eat them, I have just boiled them.'   [36_cvs_06.037]

       b.   *lop*   *sak=ŋa*   *n-sy-ama-ŋa-n=na.*
           now   hunger=INS   NEG-die-PRF-1SG-NEG=NMLZ.SG
           'I am not hungry now.' ('I did not get hungry.')

       c.   *u-laŋ=be*   *yeb-a-by-ama=na.*
           3SG.POSS-foot=LOC   stand[3SG]-PST-V2.GIVE-PRF=NMLZ.SG
           'She became independent already.' ('She already stands on her own feet.')

A typical constraint on the perfect crosslinguistically is that this tense marking is not compatible with specifying events in the past (see Bickel (1996: 176) for the same point on Belhare). In (31), for instance, the adverb *asen* is part of the adverbial clause only. The main clause ('... bad things have happened') implies that the things that happened still bear a certain relevance for the present, which is true, because the speakers utter an excuse for their rude behavior in the previous night when they were drunk.

(31)   *kaniŋ*   *asen*   *men-ni=nuŋ*   *men-ni=nuŋ=ca*
       1PL[ERG]   yesterday   NEG-know=COM.CL   NEG-know=COM.CL=ADD
       isisi   *leks-a-ma=ha.*
       ugly   happen[3SG]-PST-PRF=NMLZ.NC
       'Even though we did not notice it yesterday, something bad has happened.'
                                                                  [41_leg_09.064]

While the perfect expresses events that still have a certain relevance for the present, this tense form also figures prominently in narratives. It seems that this is a strategy to connect the content of the story told to the here and now of the utterance context and thus to make it more 'real' and create suspense. More research is needed to reveal the exact application of the perfect.

   As for the conditions of the perfect allomorphy, in the intransitive inflection, the form marked by the simple past suffix *-a* serves as base to which the suffix *-ma* for the perfect is attached. In forms with the suffix *-i* (i.e., where *-a* surfaces as [i]), the marker has an allomorph *-mi*, i.e., the suffix *-i* for 1/2PL regressively influences the vowel quality of the two suffixes *-a* and *-ma* (see (32)).

(32)   a.   *khy-a-ma-ci-ŋ=ha.*
            go-PST-PRF-DU-EXCL=NMLZ.NSG
            'We (dual) have gone.'
       b.   *khe-i-mi-ŋ=ha.*
            go-1PL-PRF-EXCL=NMLZ.NSG
            'We (plural) have gone.'

In the transitive paradigm, a suppletive allomorph *-uks* ~ *-nuŋ* (pre-vocalic vs. pre-consonantal alternants) comes into play. This allomorph never co-occurs with *-a*. As has been shown above for the allomorphy of the nonpast markers, this allomorphy is conditioned by scenario classes, i.e., by participant configurations, albeit with a slightly different distribution than in the nonpast allomorphy. Again, it is not possible to find one particular principle or hierarchy triggering the allomorphy. The perfect allomorphy is less complex than the nonpast allomorphy: it partly indicates inverse vs. direct scenarios (with a 3>1, 3>2 and 2>1 scenarios being inverse and marked by *-ma*), but it also indicates number of the agent in all scenarios with a third person patient, since in those forms all dual agents trigger *-ma*, while singular and plural agents trigger *-uks*. In the suffix string, *-uks ~ -nuŋ* shares Slot 1 with NPST *-meʔ* and *-a*, and *-ma ~ -mi* follows *-a* (which surfaces as [i] in 1/2PL forms) in Slot 2.

Table 8.15 shows the distribution of the allomorphs across the intransitive and transitive inflectional paradigms, see page 245 for the intransitive inflection and page 249 for the transitive inflection.

Table 8.15: Distribution of perfect allomorphs

| | INTRANSITIVE | TRANSITIVE | | |
		1	2	3
1SG				-uks
1DU			-nuŋ	-ma
1PL				-uks
2SG				
2DU	-ma			-ma
2PL				-uks
3SG				
3DU		-ma	-ma	-ma
3PL				-uks

The etymological sources of these markers are also function verbs. At least *-uks* has the unmistakable structure of a verbal stem. Its lexical origin could either be the verb *uks* 'come down' or *yuks* 'put, keep'. The pre-consonantal variant *-nuŋ* of *-uks* is also reminiscent of morphophonological processes in complex predicates. The origin of *-ma* could not be traced. These markers differ from function verbs in not appearing in the infinitival forms (citation forms, for instance) and in not licensing the recursive inflection that is typical for complex predication (cf. Chapter 10).

8.4.2.3 The past perfect

The perfect marking, in turn, serves as base to which *-sa ~ -si* is attached (*-si* is triggered by suffix *-i*, in analogy to the perfect allomorphy of *-ma ~ -mi*). Thus, one arrives at the complex past perfect markers *-amasa ~ -imisi* and *-uksa*, with the same distribution across the participant scenarios as found in the perfect. The suffix *-sa* might be etymologically related to the past copular stem *sa*.

This tense form expresses events that happened prior to another event that has been activated in discourse, as shown in (33).

(33) a. *hakt-a-ŋ-ga-ni*   *bhoŋ* *mit-amasa-ŋ=na.*
   send-SBJV-1SG.P-2.A-OPT COMP think-PST.PRF-1SG=NMLZ.SG
   'I had hoped that you would send me something.' (said either after receiving a parcel or after realizing that nothing was sent)
  b. *heʔne* *khy-amasa-ga=na?*
   where go-PST.PRF-2=NMLZ.SG
   'Where had you gone?' (it was clear from the context that the person was on the way back to her village)
  c. *u-mik*   *encho=ba*   *homd-uksa=na,*
   3SG.POSS-eye long_ago=EMPH swell-PST.PRF=NMLZ.SG
   hensen=go   *nu-yama=na.*
   these_days=TOP get_well-PRF=NMLZ.SG
   'His eye had been swollen before, but these days it got well.'

8.4.3 The progressive

The progressive is constructed from an infinitival form of the lexical verb and the auxiliary *siʔ*, which can carry person markers and either Present or simple past inflection. This construction resembles infinitival complement constructions and has probably developed out of such a construction. But here, the two predicates are fused at a lower level. This is also reflected by the morphology and by stress assignment, which treat the whole complex as one unit. The auxiliary, unlike matrix verbs in complement constructions, does not carry main stress; it forms one domain for stress assignment with the lexical verb. The auxiliary does not have an infinitival form (in contrast to complement-taking verbs, which may appear in the infinitive and thus be embedded recursively into other complements). Inflectional prefixes, which attach to the matrix verb in complement constructions, attach to the infinitive of the lexical verb in the progressive (compare (34a) with (34b) and (c)). This leads to the unusual situation of an infinitive marker standing between the prefix and the suffixes of an inflected verb.[21]

---

[21] This construction is best characterized as a hybrid between synthetic and analytic (periphrastic) marking, since the auxiliary behaves like a verbal stem at least with regard to the suffixes it may host. Thus, it is not treated with regard to the slot analysis.

(34)   a.   *haku   nda   nhe   uŋ-ma*
              from.now.on   2SG   here   come_down-INF
              n-dokt-wa-ga-n=na.
              NEG-get_chance-NPST[3.P]-2SG.A-NEG=NMLZ.SG
              'Now you will not get the chance to come down here any more.'
                                                       [21_nrr_04.035]

        b.   *nna   seʔni=ŋa   caleppa   l-lem-ma-sy-a=ha.*
              that   night=INS   bread   3PL-fry-INF-AUX.PROG-PST=NMLZ.NC
              'That night they were frying bread.'   [40_leg_08.032]

        c.   *uŋ=ŋa   pyak   sakheʔwa=ci=ŋa   casak*
              3SG=ERG   many   pigeon=NSG=ERG   uncooked_rice
              ŋ-gom-ca-ma-sim-me=ha
              3PL-pick_up-V2.EAT-INF-AUX.PROG-NPST=NMLZ.NSG
              nis-uks-u-ci.
              see[3SG.A]-PRF-3.P-3NSG.P
              'He saw many pigeons who were picking up (pecking with their beaks) and eating the rice.'   [01_leg_07.013]

Semantically, the progressive generally marks events as ongoing at the point of speaking (present progressive) or at a point prior to the speech situation (past progressive). However, looking at (34c), it becomes clear that the speech situation is not the only possible temporal anchor for the present progressive, since in this example, the point of reference is the event denoted by the main verb 'see', and the progressive marking of the embedded clause has to be interpreted with respect to the main clause.

The progressive is also commonly found in adverbial clauses with *-niŋ*, the marker for the cotemporality of two linked clauses (see (35)).

(35)   *u-sa   sem-saŋ   u-sam=be*
          3SG.POSS-fruit   pluck-SIM.CVB   3SG.POSS-root=LOC
          ca-ma-sy-a-ŋ=niŋ,   ...
          eat-INF-AUX.PROG-PST-1SG=CTMP
          'As I was plucking and eating the fruits under the tree, ...'[22]
                                                 [42_leg_10.017]

Interestingly, the progressive auxiliary is sensitive to the speech-act-participant (SAP/non-SAP) distinction. It is inflected like an intransitive verb when third person P arguments are involved, also when the semantic head is a transitive verb

---

[22] The noun *sam* is a relational noun, with the metaphorical meaning 'under/at the bottom of'.

(see (36a)). The auxiliary verb shows agreement with the S or the A of the lexical verb. A transitive example as in (34c) also shows that despite the intransitive person marking the lexical verb is still able to assign the ergative case to the subject (*sakhe?waciŋa*). When the object is a speech act participant, it shows transitive person marking, as exemplified in (36b) and (c). This process is not surprising given the abundance of differential marking that is triggered by the referential properties of arguments in Yakkha.

(36) a.   *ka*   *kucuma*   *yok-ma-si-me-ŋ=na.*
          1SG[ERG]   dog   search-INF-AUX.PROG-NPST-1SG=NMLZ.SG
          'I am looking for the dog.' (**yokmasiwaŋna*)

  b.   *ka*   *nda*   *yok-ma-si-me?-nen=na.*
          1SG[ERG]   2SG   search-INF-AUX.PROG-NPST-1>2=NMLZ.SG
          'I am looking for you.'

  c.   *photo=ci*   *so?-me?-ma-sy-a-ŋ-ga=na.*
          photo=NSG   look-CAUS-INF-AUX.PROG-PST-1SG.P-2.A=NMLZ.SG
          'You were showing me the photos.'

8.4.4 The periphrastic continuative

This construction has developed out of a converb construction, in analogy to a similar construction in Nepali. The lexical head is marked by the converbal marker -*saŋ* and the main verb is invariably *khe?ma* 'go', but it has undergone grammaticalization to an auxiliary, from motion verb semantics to the expression of continuous events, similar to the English expression 'go on doing'. A formerly biclausal construction has become monoclausal.

The continuative expresses that an event goes on over a longer stretch of time. It applies regardless of whether the verb has active, volitional semantics (37a) or rather change-of-state semantics (see (37b)). Example (37a) also shows that the auxiliary is compatible with the perfect tense. Example (37b) shows that in contrast to the periphrastic progressive, prefixes attach to the auxiliary. In (37c), the construction is shown with a transitive lexical verb. The auxiliary is still inflected intransitively, showing agreement with the A argument of the lexical verb.

(37) a.   *nakha?la*   *luk-khusa*   *ca-saŋ*   *khy-ama-ci=niŋa,*   ...
          like_that   tell-RECIP   EAT.AUX-SIM.CVB   go-PRF-DU=CTMP
          'As the two went on arguing (lit: with each other) like that, ...'
          [01_leg_07.340]

b. *yapmi=ci   pu-saŋ   ŋ-khy-a.*
   person=NSG grow-SIM.CVB 3PL-go-PST
   'The number of the people grew continuously.'   [27_leg_06.003]

c. *iŋ-nhaŋ-saŋ   ik-saŋ   khy-a-ci=niŋa,*   ...
   chase-V2.SEND-SIM   chase-SIM   go-PST-DU=CTMP
   'As they (dual) went on chasing them away, ...'   [22_nrr_05.015]

8.4.5 The transitive completive

The marker *-i ~ -ni* for completive events is only found in transitive verbs. It
surfaces as [i] before vowels and as [ni] before consonants (see (38) and (39)).

(38)   a. *mend-i.*
           finish-COMPL[3A;3P]
           'It is finished.'
       b. *chimd-i-ŋ=na.*
           ask-COMPL[3P;PST]-1SG.A=NMLZ.SG
           'I finished asking him.'

The marker partly behaves like a function verb, and is thus not treated in the
slot analysis (see also §10.2.2): it precedes Slot 1 in the inflection, and it stands in
complementary distribution with the V2 *-pi?* 'give', which (among many other
functions) indicates completive notions in intransitive predicates. The marker *-i*
~ -ni also surfaces in the citation forms, like a function verb. There is, however, no
lexical verb (at least not synchronically) that it relates to. The two markers often
create lexicalized pairs of intransitive and causative verbs (see (39), repeated from
Chapter 10, where more examples can be found). Roots like *maks* never occur
independently; either *-i ~ -ni* or *-pi?* have to attach to them and specify their
valency.

(39)   a. *maŋmaŋ-miŋmiŋ   m-maks-a-by-a-ma.*
           surprised-REDUPL   3PL-surprise-PST-V2.GIVE-PST-PRF
           'They were utterly surprised.'   [22_nrr_05.026]
       b. *ka   nda   mak-ni-me?-nen=na.*
           1SG[ERG]   2SG[NOM]   surprise-COMPL-NPST-1>2=NMLZ.SG
           'I will surprise you.'

8.4.6 Tense/aspect paradigm tables

8.5 Mood

Apart form the indicative, Yakkha distinguishes subjunctive, optative and imperative mood. These mood inflections generally do not allow the nominalizing clitics =*na* and =*ha*, since they are functionally connected to assertions and questions (but see below for an exception).

Table 8.16: Nonpast paradigm of *khe?ma* 'go' and *apma* 'come' (affirmative and negative)

	khe?ma 'go'	*apma* 'come'
1SG	*khemeŋna*	*ammeŋna*
	ŋkheme?ŋanna	*ŋammeŋanna*
1DU.EXCL	*khemeŋciŋha*	*ammeŋciŋha*
	ŋkhemenciŋanha	*ŋammenciŋanha*
1PL.EXCL	*kheiwaŋha*	*abiwaŋha*
	ŋkheiwaŋanha	*ŋabiwaŋanha*
1DU.INCL	*khemeciya*	*ammeciya*
	ŋkhemencinha	*ŋammencinha*
1PL.INCL	*kheiwha*	*abiwha*
	ŋkheiwanha	*ŋabiwanha*
2SG	*khemekana*	*ammekana*
	ŋkhemekanna	*ŋammekanna*
2DU	*khemecigha*	*ammecigha*
	ŋkhemenciganha	*ŋamenciganha*
2PL	*kheiwagha*	*abiwagha*
	ŋkheiwaganha	*ŋabiwaganha*
3SG	*kheme?na*	*amme?na*
	ŋkhemenna	*ŋamenna*
3DU	*khemeciha*	*amme?ciya*
	ŋkhemencinha	*ŋamencinah*
3PL	*ŋkheme(haci)*	*ŋamme(haci)*
	ŋkhemen(haci)	*ŋamen(haci)*

Table 8.17: Nonpast paradigm of *tumma* 'understand' (affirmative and negative)

Each cell gives the affirmative form (first) and the negative form (second).

	1SG	1NSG	2SG	2DU	2PL	3SG	3NSG
1SG			tummeʔnenna / ndummeʔnenna	tummeʔnencina / ndummeʔnencinha	tummeʔneninha / ndummeʔneninha	tundwaɲna / ndundwaɲanna	tundwaɲciɲha / ndundwaɲciɲanha
1DU.EXCL			tummeʔnencina / ndummeʔnencinha	tummeʔnencina / ndummeʔnencinha	tummeʔneninha / ndummeʔneninha	tummeɲcuɲna / ndummencuɲanna	tummeɲcuɲciɲha / ndummencunciɲanha
1PL.EXCL			tummeʔnencina / ndummeʔnencinha	tummeʔnencina / ndummeʔnencinha	tummeʔneninha / ndummeʔneninha	tundwamɲana / ndundwamɲanna	tundwamcimɲha / ndundwamcimɲanha
1DU.INCL						tummecuna / ndummencunna	tummecuciha / ndummencuncinha
1PL.INCL						tundwamna / ndundwamninna	tundwamcimha / ndundwamcimninha
2SG	tummeɲgana / ndummeɲganna	tummeɲgana / ndummeɲganna				tundwagana / ndundwaganna	tundwacigha / ndundwanciganha
2DU	tummekaha / ndummekanha	tummekaha / ndummekanha				tummecugana / ndummencuganna	tummecucigha / ndummencunciganha
2PL	tummekaha / ndummekanha	tummekaha / ndummekanha				tundwamgana / ndundwamganna	tundwamcimgha / ndundwamcimganha
3SG	tummeɲna / ndummeɲanna	tummeɲna / ndummeɲanna	tummekana / ndummekanna	tummecigha / ndummenciganha	tundiwagha / ndundiwaganha	tundwana / ndundwanna	tundwaciya / ndundwancinha
3DU	tummeha / ndummenha	tummeha / ndummenha	tummekana / ndummekanna	tummecigha / ndummenciganha	tundiwagha / ndundiwaganha	tummecuna / ndummencunna	tummecuciha / ndummencuncinha
3PL	tummeha / ndummenha	tummeha / ndummenha	ndummekana / ndummekaninna	tummecigha / ndummenciganha	tundiwagha / ndundiwaganha	ndundwana / ndundwaninna	ndundwaciha / ndundwancininha

Table 8.18: Simple past, perfect and past perfect paradigm of *apma* 'come'

	PST	PST.NEG	PRF	PRF.NEG	PST.PRF	PST.PRF.NEG
1SG	abaŋna	ŋabaŋanna	abamaŋna	ŋabamaŋanna	abamasaŋna	ŋabamasaŋanna
1DU.EXCL	abaɲciŋha	ŋabanciŋanha	abamaɲciŋha	ŋabamanciŋanha	abamasaŋciŋha	ŋabamasanciɲanha
1PL.EXCL	abiŋha	ŋabiŋanha	abimiŋha	ŋabimiŋanha	abimisiŋha	ŋabimisiɲanha
1DU.INCL	abaciha	ŋabancinha	abamaciha	ŋabamancinha	abamasaciha	ŋabamasancinha
1PL.INCL	abiha	ŋabinha	abimiha	ŋabiminha	abimisiha	ŋabimisinha
2SG	abagana	ŋabaganna	abamagana	ŋabamaganna	abamasagana	ŋabamasaganna
2DU	abacigha	ŋabanciganha	abamacigha	ŋabamanciganha	abamasacigha	ŋabamasanciganha
2PL	abigha	ŋabiganha	abimigha	ŋabimiganha	abimisigha	ŋabimisiganha
3SG	abana	ŋabanna	abamana	ŋabamanna	abamasana	ŋabamasanna
3DU	abaciha	ŋabancinha	abamaciha	ŋabamancinha	abamasaciya	ŋabamasancinha
3PL	ŋabahaci	ŋabanhaci	ŋabamhaci	ŋabamanhaci	ŋabamashaci	ŋabamasanhaci

Table 8.19: Simple past paradigm of *piʔma* 'give' (affirmative and negative, with singular T argument)

	1SG	1NSG	2SG	2DU	2PL	3SG	3NSG
1SG			piʔnenna / mbiʔnenna	piʔnencina / mbiʔnencina	piʔnenina / mbiʔnenina	piɲa / mbiɲaɲa	piɲciɲa / mbiɲciɲanha
1DU.EXCL			piʔnenna / mbiʔnenna	piʔnencina / mbiʔnencina	piʔnenina / mbiʔnenina	pyaɲcuɲa / mbyancuɲanna	pyaɲcuɲciɲa / mbyancuɲciɲanha
1PL.EXCL			piʔnenna / mbiʔnenna	piʔnencina / mbiʔnencina	piʔnenina / mbiʔnenina	pimɲana / mbimɲanna	pimcimɲa / mbimcimɲanha
1DU.INCL						pyacuna / mbyancunnaha	pyacuciha / mbyancuncinha
1PL.INCL						pimna / mbimninna	pimcimha / mbimcimninha
2SG	pyaŋgana / mbyaŋganna	pyagha / mbyaganha				pigana / mbiganna	picigha / mbinciganha
2DU	pyaŋgana / mbyaŋganna	pyagha / mbyaganha				pyacugana / mbyancuganna	pyacuigha / mbyancuciganha
2PL	pyaŋgana / mbyaŋganna	pyagha / mbyaganha				pimɲgana / mbimɲanna	pimcimgha / mbimcimganha
3SG	pyaɲɲa / mbyaɲanna	piya / mbyanha	pyagana / mbyaganna	pyacigha / mbyanciganha	piigha / mbiiganha	pina / mbinna	piciya / mbincinha
3DU	pyaɲɲa / mbyaɲanna	piya / mbyanha	pyagana / mbyaganna	pyacigha / mbyanciganha	piigha / mbiiganha	pyacuna / mbyancunna	pyacuciya / mbyancuncinha
3PL	pyaɲɲa / mbyaɲanna	piya / mbyanha	mbyagaŋha / mbyaganinna	pyacigha / mbyanciganha	piigha / mbiiganha	mbina / mbininna	mbiciya / mbincininha

Table 8.20: Simple past paradigm of *chimma* 'ask' (affirmative and negative)

	1SG	1NSG	2SG	2DU	2PL	3SG	3NSG
1SG			*chimnenna* / *nchimnenna*	*chimnencinha* / *nchimnencinha*	*chimneninha* / *nchimneninha*	*chimduŋna* / *nchimduŋanna*	*chimduŋciŋha* / *nchimduŋciŋanha*
1DU.EXCL						*chimdaŋcuŋna* / *nchimdancuŋanna*	*chimdaŋcuŋciŋha* / *nchimdancuŋciŋanha*
1PL.EXCL						*chimdumŋana* / *nchimdumŋanna*	*chimdumciŋha* / *nchimdumcimŋanha*
1DU.INCL						*chimdacuna* / *nchimdancunna*	*chimdacuciha* / *nchimdancuncinha*
1PL.INCL						*chimdumna* / *nchimdumninna*	*chimdumcimha* / *nchimdumcimninha*
2SG	*chimdaŋgana* / *nchimdaŋganna*					*chimdugana* / *nchimduŋanna*	*chimduciŋha* / *nchimdunciŋanha*
2DU		*chimdagha* / *nchimdaganha*				*chimdacugana* / *nchimdancuŋanna*	*chimdacucigha* / *nchimdancuncigaŋanha*
2PL						*chimdumgana* / *nchimdumganna*	*chimdumcimgha* / *nchimdumcimganha*
3SG	*chimdaŋna* / *nchimdaŋanna*		*chimdagana* / *nchimdaganna*	*chimdacigha* / *nchimdanciganha*	*chimdigha* / *nchimdigaŋanha*	*chimduna* / *nchimdunna*	*chimduciya* / *nchimduncinha*
3DU		*chimdaha* / *nchimdanha*				*chimdacuna* / *nchimdancunna*	*chimdacuciha* / *nchimdancuncinha*
3PL			*nchimdagana* / *nchimdaganinna*			*nchimduna* / *nchimduninna*	*nchimduciha* / *nchimduncininha*

247

Table 8.21: Simple past paradigm of *cama* 'eat' (affirmative and negative)

	1SG	1NSG	2SG	2DU	2PL	3SG	3NSG
1SG			caʔnenna / njaʔnenna	caʔnencina / njaʔnencina	caʔnenina / njaʔnenina	caɲa / njaɲanna	caɲciɲha / njanciɲanha
1DU.EXCL						cayaɲcuɲa / njayancuɲanna	cayaɲcuɲciɲha / njayancuɲciɲanha
1PL.EXCL						camɲana / njamɲanna	camciɲha / njamciɲanha
1DU.INCL						cayacuna / njayancunna	cayaciha / njayancuncinha
1PL.INCL						camna / njamninna	camciɲha / njamcimninha
2SG	cayaɲgana / njayaɲgana					cogana / njogana	cociɲha / njonciɲanha
2DU		cayagha / njayaganha				cayacugana / njayancugana	cayacuciɲha / njayancunciɲanha
2PL		cayagha / njayaganha				camgana / njamganna	camciɲha / njamcimɲanha
3SG	coyaɲa ~ cayaɲa / njayaɲanna	coya ~ caya / njayanha	coyagana ~ cayagana / njayaganna	coʔyacigha ~ cayacigha / njayancigha	coigha ~ caigha / njaigha	cona / njonna	cociya / njoncinha
3DU			cayagana / njayaganna	cayacigha / njayanciganha	caigha / njaiganha	cayacuna / njayancunna	cayacuciya / njayancuncinha
3PL		caya / njayanha	njayagana / njayaganinna			njona / njoninha	njociya / njoncininha

Table 8.22: Perfect paradigm of *chimma* 'ask' (affirmative and negative)

	1SG	1NSG	2SG	2DU	2PL	3SG	3NSG
1SG			chimnupnenna nchimnupnenna	chimnupnencinha nchimnupnencinha	chimnupneninha nchimnupneninha	chimduksupna nchimduksupnganna	chimduksupciyha nchimduksupciyanha
1DU.EXCL			chimnupnencinha nchimnupnencinha	chimnupnencinha nchimnupnencinha	chimnupneninha nchimnupneninha	chimdamapcupna nchimdamancupnganna	chimdamapcupciyha nchimdamancunciyanha
1PL.EXCL			chimnupnencinha nchimnupnencinha	chimnupnencinha nchimnupnencinha	chimnupneninha nchimnupneninha	chimduksumpana nchimduksumpnganna	chimduksumcimpha nchimduksumcimyanha
1DU.INCL						chimdamacuna nchimdamancunna	chimdamacuciha nchimdamancuncinha
1PL.INCL						chimduksumna nchimduksumninna	chimduksumcimha nchimduksumcimninha
2SG	chimdamagana nchimdamaganna	chimdamagana nchimdamaganna				chimduksugana nchimduksuganna	chimduksucigha nchimduksunciganha
2DU	chimdamagha nchimdamaganha	chimdamagha nchimdamaganha				chimdamacugana nchimdamancuganna	chimdamacuigha nchimdamancunciganha
2PL	chimdamagha nchimdamaganha	chimdamagha nchimdamaganha				chimduksumgana nchimduksumganna	chimduksumcimgha nchimduksumcimganha
3SG	chimdamapna nchimdamapanna	chimdamagana nchimdamaganna	chimdamagana nchimdamaganna	chimdamacigha nchimdamanciganha	chimdimigha nchimdimiganha	chimduksuna nchimduksunna	chimduksuciya nchimduksuncinha
3DU	chimdamha nchimdamamanha	chimdamagana nchimdamaganinna	chimdamagana nchimdamaganinna	chimdamacigha nchimdamanciganha	chimdimigha nchimdimiganha	chimdamacuna nchimdamancunna	chimdamacuciha nchimdamancuncinha
3PL	chimdamha nchimdamamanha	chimdamagana nchimdamaganinna	chimdamagana nchimdamaganinna	chimdamacigha nchimdamanciganha	chimdimigha nchimdimiganha	chimduksuna nchimduksuninna	chimduksuciha nchimduksuncininha

8.5.1 The subjunctive

The subjunctive mood is crosscut by what is best described as a tense distinction (nonpast/past). The nonpast subjunctive does not have a dedicated marker, but is simply characterized by the absence of tense marking. It is used for hypothetical statements, hortatives, warnings, threats, and permissive questions ('May I ...?'). The past subjunctive is found in counterfactual statements, but also in adverbial clauses, especially in conditionals, when the speaker assesses the chances for the condition to come true as rather low (see §14.8 and §14.13). The past subjunctive is marked by -a, and hence, the forms of the past subjunctive paradigm are, in most cases, identical to the past indicative forms, without the clitics =na and =ha, however.[23] In third person plural forms of intransitive verbs, the negation in the past subjunctive looks different from the past indicative (e.g., ŋkhyanhaci 'they did not go' vs. ŋkhyanin 'they might not go').

The negated forms are built in analogy to the indicative negated forms, i.e., either with N-...-n or N-...-nin. Here, one can note a slight extension of the domain of -nin: the form chim, for third person acting on first, has the negative counterpart nchimnin, since monosyllabic *n-chim-n would not be a well-formed syllable in Yakkha. Surprisingly, some negated forms of the nonpast subjunctive are marked by =na in the intransitive paradigm, which is the only exception to the rule that the nominalizing clitics do not occur in the mood paradigms.[24] It is unusual, however, that the singular form =na occurs invariably, and never =ha. Alternatively, this marker =na could be analyzed as a dedicated marker for nonpast subjunctive negative forms.

Intransitive subjunctive paradigms are provided in Table 8.23, exemplified by kheʔma 'go', with a few forms not attested. Since the suffix -a is deleted in the presence of the suffix -i, the forms with first and second person plural are identical in the nonpast subjunctive and the past subjunctive. A transitive paradigm for the nonpast subjunctive is shown in Table 8.24. In the form for 2SG>1SG, chim-

---

[23] Alternatively, one could propose that Yakkha has no mood distinction in the past, but the clitics =na and =ha instead, which overtly mark the indicative. However, first of all, these clitics are optional also in the indicative, as they fulfill a discourse function. Secondly, a few forms in the inflectional paradigms of past indicative and past subjunctive indeed look different from each other (see right below in the text).

[24] An ad-hoc explanation is that negations are more assertive than affirmative forms and thus allow this marker. The question why only the present negated forms take =na can be answered similarly. The present forms are more 'real' and thus more assertive. They denote rather likely events, while the past subjunctive denotes events that are more detached from the speech situation, such as highly hypothetical and counterfactual events. The syncretism of past and irrealis forms is not unusual crosslinguistically and can be attributed to a semantic feature of 'dissociativeness' that they have in common (see, e.g., Bickel (1996: 88) for the same point on the Belhare system).

Table 8.23: Subjunctive paradigm of *kheʔma* 'go'

| | NONPAST SUBJUNCTIVE | | PAST SUBJUNCTIVE | |
	AFFIRMATIVE	NEGATIVE	AFFIRMATIVE	NEGATIVE
1SG	*kheʔŋa*	*ŋkheʔŋanna*	*khyaŋ*	*ŋkhyaŋan*
1DU.EXCL	*kheciŋ*	*ŋkheciŋanna*	*khyaŋciŋ*	*ŋkhyanciŋan*
1PL.EXCL	*kheiŋ*	*ŋkheiŋanna*	*kheiŋ*	*ŋkheiŋan*
1DU.INCL	*kheci*	*ŋkhecinna*	*khyaci*	*ŋkhyancin*
1PL.INCL	*khei*	*ŋkheinna*	*khei*	*ŋkhein*
2SG	*kheka*	*ŋkhekanna*	*khyaga*	*ŋkhyagan*
2DU	*kheciga*	*ŋkheciganna*	*khyaciga*	*ŋkhyancigan*
2PL	*kheiga*	*ŋkheiganna*	*kheiga*	*ŋkheigan*
3SG	*khe*	—	*khya*	*ŋkhyan*
3DU	*kheci*	—	*khyaci*	*ŋkhyancin*
3PL	*ŋkhe(ci)*	—	*ŋkhya(ci)*	*ŋkhyanin*

daŋga, an /a/ gets epenthesized to resolve the impossible sequence of consonants in the underlying form /chimd-ŋ-ga/, making this form identical to the past subjunctive form.

Some typical examples of the nonpast subjunctive are provided in (40): questions, hortatives, warnings, threats and permissive questions.

(40) a. *heʔne   khe-i?*
          where   go-1PL[SBJV]
          'Where should we go?'

      b. *imin   cog-u-m?*
          how   do-3.P-1PL.A[SBJV]
          'How should we do it?'

      c. *ciya   hops-u-m?*
          tea   sip-3.P-1PL.A[SBJV]
          'Shall we have tea?'

      d. *sori   khe-ci-ŋ?*
          together   go-1DU-EXCL[SBJV]
          'May we go together?' (asking someone who is not coming with the speaker)

251

    e.   *lem-nhaŋ-nen?*
        throw-V2.SEND-1>2[SBJV]
        'Shall I throw you out?'

    f.   *kaŋ-khe-ka!*
        fall-V2.GO-2[SBJV]
        'You might fall down!'

    g.   *uŋ-u-m!*
        drink-3.P-1PL.A[SBJV]
        'Let's drink!'

    h.   *haku   im-ci*
        now   sleep-DU[SBJV]
        'Let's sleep now (dual).'

Some examples of the Past Subjunctive are provided in (41). Mostly, they are found in counterfactual clauses (with the irrealis clitic *=pi ~ =bi*), but also in vague statements about the future, i.e., when the realis status cannot be confirmed yet. The overwhelming majority of conditional clauses are in the past subjunctive.

(41)   a.   *manuŋ=go   heco=bi.*
           otherwise=TOP   win[3SG;SBJV]=IRR
           'If not, he would have won!'

      b.   *casowa   n-jog-a-n   bhoŋ*
           Casowa_festival   NEG-do[3SG]-SBJV-NEG   COND
           puṇḍaraŋma=ga   o-lok   khom-me.
           forest_goddess=GEN   3SG.POSS-anger   scratch[3SG]-NPST
           'If Casowa is not celebrated, the forest goddess will get angry.'
                                                        [01_leg_07.119]

A very nice contrastive example of nonpast and past subjunctive is shown in (42). The speaker considers doing something and first is unsure, using the past subjunctive. Then, as she is more determined, she uses the nonpast subjunctive.

(42)   a.   *ki   nhe=le   ips-a-ŋ?*
           or   here=CTR   sleep-SBJV-1SG
           'Or should I sleep right here?'   [36_cvs_06.220]

      b.   *nhe   im-ŋa   haʔlo.*
           here   sleep-1SG[SBJV]   EXCLA
           'I could sleep here anyway.'   [36_cvs_06.221]

Table 8.24: Nonpast subjunctive paradigm of *chimma* 'ask' (affirmative and negative), becomes optative by addition of *-ni*

	1SG	1NSG	2SG	2DU	2PL	3SG	3NSG
1SG			chimnen / nchimnen	chimnencin / nchimnencin	chimnenin / nchimnenin	chimduŋ / nchimduŋan	chimduŋciŋ / nchimduŋciŋan
1DU.EXCL			chimnen / nchimnen	chimnencin / nchimnencin	chimnenin / nchimnenin	chimcuŋ / nchimcuŋan	chimcuŋciŋ / nchimcuŋciŋan
1PL.EXCL			chimnen / nchimnen	chimnencin / nchimnencin	chimnenin / nchimnenin	chimdumŋa / nchimdumŋan	chimdumcimŋa / nchimdumcimŋan
1DU.INCL						chimcu / nchimcun	chimcuci / nchimcuncin
1PL.INCL						chimdum / nchimdumnin	chimdumcim / nchimdumcimnin
2SG	chimdaŋga / nchimdaŋgan	chimdaŋga / nchimdaŋgan				chimduga / nchimdugan	chimduciga / nchimduncigan
2DU	chimga / nchimgan	chimga / nchimgan				chimcuga / nchimcugan	chimcuciga / nchimcuncigan
2PL	chimga / nchimgan	chimga / nchimgan				chimdumga / nchimdumgan	chimdumcimga / nchimdumcimgan
3SG	chimŋa / nchimŋan	chim / nchimnin	chimga / nchimgan	chimciga / nchimcigan	chimdiga / nchimdigan	chimdu / nchimdun	chimduci / nchimduncin
3DU	chim / nchimnin	chim / nchimnin	chimciga / nchimcigan	chimciga / nchimcigan	chimdiga / nchimdigan	chimcu / nchimcun	chimcuci / nchimcuncin
3PL	chim / nchimnin	chim / nchimnin	chimŋa / nchimŋanin	chimciga / nchimcigan	chimdiga / nchimdigan	chimdu / nchimdunin	chimduci / nchimduncinin

8.5.2 The Optative

The optative is morphologically marked by the suffix *-ni* , which is attached to the nonpast subjunctive forms described above. It expresses the speaker's wish for an event to be realized, while its realization is beyond the speaker's reach, as in the examples in (43). The expression *leŋni*, the third person singular optative of *leŋma* 'be, become' is also used to state agreement on the side of the speaker when he is asked or encouraged to do something.

(43)   a.   *o-chom=be   tas-u-ni.*
             3SG.POSS-summit=LOC   reach-3.P-OPT
             'May she reach the top./ May she be successful.'
      b.   *ucun   leŋ-ni.*
             good   become[3SG]-OPT
             'May it (your work) turn out nicely.'
      c.   *miʔ-ŋa-ni.*
             think-1SG.P-OPT
             'May he remember me.'
      d.   *mit-aŋ-ga-ni.*
             think-1SG.P-2.A-OPT
             'May you remember me.'

The optative is also found in purposive adverbial clauses with the purposive/conditional conjunction *bhoŋ*, discussed in §14.9 (see also (44)).

(44)   *ap-ŋa-ni   bhoŋ   ka-ya-ŋ=na.*
      come-1SG-OPT   COND   call-PST-1SG=SG
      'She called me, so that I would come.'

Negation is marked by *N-...-n*, and by *N-...-nin* when there is no vowel preceding the suffix. Table 8.25 illustrates this by means of the third person intransitive forms.

8.5.3 The Imperative

The Imperative expresses orders and requests. It is coded by the morpheme *-a*, like the simple past and the past subjunctive. The conflation of past and imperative morphology is also known from other Kiranti languages (Bickel 2003; Ebert 2003a) and apart from that it is crosslinguistically common, too. Thus, imperative forms are almost identical to the past forms, except for a new plural morpheme *-ni*.

Table 8.25: Optative, third person (intransitive)

	OPTATIVE	
3SG	*kheʔni*	*ŋkheʔninni*
3DU	*khecini*	*ŋkhecinni*
3PL	*ŋkheʔni*	*ŋkheʔninni*

The negated imperative expresses negative requests and negative orders (i.e., prohibitions). It is also used in implorations like, e.g., *nsisaŋan!* 'Do not kill me!'. Paradigms can be found in Table 8.26 for intransitive and in Table 8.27 for transitive verbs.

Imperatives directed at more than one person show dual or plural morphology (see (45)). Imperatives can be intensified by adding person inflection and the emphatic marker *=i* (see (45b) - (45d)).

(45)   a.   *ab-a.*
           come-IMP
           'Come.'

      b.   *ab-a-ga=i!*
           come-IMP-2=EMPH
           'Come!'

      c.   *ab-a-ci-ga=i!*
           come-IMP-DU-2=EMPH
           'Come!' (dual)

      d.   *ab-a-ni-ga=i,*   *nakhe*   *omphu=be*
           come-IMP-PL-2=EMPH,   hither   verandah=LOC
           yuŋ-a-ni-ga=i!
           sit-IMP-PL-2=EMPH
           'Come, and sit down here on the verandah!' (plural)

The imperatives show a second register, increasing the politeness of the order or request. The marker *=eba* (historically probably a combination of the two emphatic markers *=i* and *=pa*) can be added to the imperative forms to make them more polite, similar to the function of the particle *na* in Nepali (46). This politeness, however, can be countered ironically by adding *=ʔlo* to these polite imperatives, an exclamative particle which usually signals that the patience of the speaker is getting low (see (46c), *ca* has ablaut).[25]

(46)   a.   *ab-a=eba.*
           come-IMP=POL.IMP
           'Please come.'

   b.   *ŋ-ab-a-n=eba.*
           NEG-come-IMP-NEG=POL.IMP
           'Please do not come.'

   c.   *co=eba=ʔlo!*
           eat[IMP]=POL.IMP=EXCLA
           'Eat already!'

8.6 Periphrastic honorific inflection

Honorific inflection in indicatives is not found in the Tumok dialect, but during a short stay in Dandagaun village I noticed a honorific construction which is similar to the Nepali honorific construction in its form and function. The construction uses an infinitival form of the lexical verb and a copular auxiliary. The function of the auxiliary is carried out up by the verb *leŋma* 'be, become'. It is inflected intransitively and shows agreement with the subject (S or A) of the semantic head. The Nepali source construction is built by adding an inflected form of a copula (always third person, *huncha/hunna/bhayo/bhaena* 'is/is not/was/was not') to the infinitival form of the semantic head, which is used for both addressing people and talking about people. For instance, *garnuhuncha* is the honorific way of saying both 'he does' and 'you do' in Nepali. In Yakkha, it is not a fixed third person form of *leŋma* that is added to the infinitive, but the verb is inflected for second person, too, showing agreement with the S argument (see (47), I have no data for transitive forms). Naturally, the first person is impossible with honorifics.

(47)   a.   *heʔne*   *kheʔ-ma*   *leks-a-ga=na?*
           where   go-INF   be-PST-2SG=SG
           'Where did you go?'

---

[25] Combinations of emphatic particles and information-structural clitics with =*ʔlo* result in a word with regard to stress (e.g., ['co.e 'ba.ʔlo] in (46c)). According to the voicing rule, this complex of two stress domains is still one word, however. Other examples of this phonological fusion of particles are *'leʔ.lo, 'haʔ.lo, 'caʔ.lo* (see Chapter 17).

Table 8.26: Imperative paradigm, intransitive verbs

	IMPERATIVE	NEGATED	IMPERATIVE	NEGATED
	kheʔma 'go'		*apma* 'come'	
2SG	*khya*	*ŋkhyan*	*aba*	*ŋaban*
2DU	*khyaci*	*ŋkhyancin*	*abaci*	*ŋabancin*
2PL	*khyani*	*ŋkhyanin*	*abani*	*ŋabanin*

Table 8.27: Imperative paradigm, transitive verbs

	1SG	1NSG	3SG	3NSG	DETRANS
			piʔma 'give'		
2SG	*pyaŋ* *mbyaŋan*		*pi* *mbin*	*pici* *mbincin*	*pya* *mbyan*
2DU		*pya* *mbyan*	*pyacu* *mbyancun*	*pyacuci* *mbyancuncin*	*pyaci* *mbyancin*
2PL			*pyanum* *mbyanumnin*	*pyanumcim* *mbyanumcimnin*	*pyani* *mbyanin*
			chimma 'ask'		
2SG	*chimdaŋ* *nchimdaŋa*		*chimdu* *nchimdun*	*chimduci* *nchimduncin*	*chimda* *nchimdan*
2DU		*chimda* *nchimdan*	*chimdacu* *nchimdancun*	*chimdacuci* *nchimdancuncin*	*chimdaci* *nchimdancin*
2PL			*chimdanum* *nchimdanumnin*	*chimdanumcim* *nchimdanumcimnin*	*chimdani* *nchimdanin*

b. *he?naŋ   ta-ma   leks-a-ga=na?*
   where.from   come-INF   be-PST-2SG=NMLZ.SG
   'Where do you come from?'

This construction also has a corresponding imperative, again analogous to the Nepali construction, with the infinitive and the third person optative form of the auxiliary verb *leŋma*, which is *leŋni* in Yakkha (see (48)), and *hos* in Nepali.[26]

(48) a. *toŋba   pi?-ma   leŋ-ni=ba.*
          beer   suck-INF   be[3SG]-OPT=EMPH
          'Please drink the beer.'
      b. *kinama   ca-ma   leŋ-ni=ba.*
          fermented_soybean_dish   eat-INF   be[3SG]-OPT=EMPH
          'Please eat the *kinama*.'

The functional domain of the honorific inflection in Yakkha slightly differs from the source language. While in Nepali the honorific pronouns and verb forms are also used to address elders within the family and other respected, but very close people like the husband (not the wife), the Yakkha honorific inflection rather signals respectful behavior that is connected to social distance (as far as could be told after my short stay in Dandagaun).

8.7 The inflection of the copulas

In this section, the inflection of two copular verbs will be discussed. The inflectional categories are similar to those in the regular verbal inflection, i.e., person, polarity and TAM, but they show some formal and functional peculiarities. For instance, two prefix slots can be found in the copular inflection. Furthermore, some forms make a nonpast/future distinction, which is not found in the regular verbal inflection. As for the semantics of the inflectional forms presented here, I can only present tentative conclusions. Further examples of the use of the copulas are shown in §11.1.11.

8.7.1 The identificational copula (with a zero infinitive)

The identificational copula is used to express identification, equation and class inclusion (see (49)). It does not have an infinitival form. The stem of this copula

---

[26] *Toŋba* is millet beer that is served in a small wooden or nowadays aluminum barrel, with a lid and a pipe, hence the verb 'suck'.

is zero in the present tense and *sa* in the past tenses. In the affirmative present forms, the copula has overt forms only for speech-act participants, and even there it is optional. In the other tenses and in negated clauses, the copula is obligatory.

(49) a.   *ka, ka   kha?la   ŋan=na=ba!*
           1SG 1SG like_this COP.1SG.NPST=SG=EMPH
           'I, I am just like this!'   [21_nrr_04.006]

      b.   *nda   isa=ga   u-cya   gan?*
           2SG   who=GEN   3SG.POSS-child   COP.2SG.NPST
           'Whose child are you?'

      c.   *ka=ca   chalumma   ŋan.*
           1SG=ADD   second_born_daughter   COP.1SG.NPST
           'I am also a second-born daughter.'

An overview of the person and tense/aspect inflection of the identificational copula is provided in Table 8.28. In the present tense, the copular inflection consists of suppletive forms that resemble the person markers. Deviations from the verbal person marking are, however, the dual forms starting in *nci-* instead of *-ci*, the plural forms starting in *si-* instead of *-i* and of course the complete zero marking for the third person in the affirmative. No stem could be identified in these forms; it probably had little phonological weight and got lost.[27] A further idiosyncrasy of all present forms (affirmative and negative) is that they end in /n/, which does not seem to carry any semantic load. It is unlikely that this is a stem, because the person markers usually come as suffixes; at least one would have to explain why the order of stem and suffixes is reversed here. Note that, due to the absence of specific markers, the dual forms of the third person and the first person inclusive are identical.

Negation in the present forms is marked by the prefix *me(N)-*, which is also found as negation marker in nonfinite forms like infinitives and converbs. In the past, negation is marked as in the regular verbal inflection, by the combinations of prefix and suffix *N-...-n* or *N-...-nin*. The nasal copying known from the verbal inflection is found in the copular inflection too, with the same constraints applying as described in §3.5.8. The third person singular nonpast form *menna* also functions as interjection 'No'.

The person marking in the past tense forms is more regular than in the nonpast, since they have a stem to which the regular person markers can attach. The identificational copula distinguishes five inflectional series in the past tenses. There is the the simple past ('Past I'), expressed by the past stem *sa* and the regular per-

---

[27] The development of identificational or equational copulas out of inflectional material is not unknown in Tibeto-Burman; it is also found, e.g., in Northern Chin DeLancey (2011b: 9).

Table 8.28: Person and tense/aspect inflection of the identificational copula

	NPST.AFF	NPST.NEG	PST.I.AFF	PST.I.NEG	PST.II.AFF	PST.II.NEG
1SG	ŋan	meʔ-ŋan	sa-ŋ=na	n-sa-ŋa-n=na	sa-ya-ŋ=na	n-sa-ya-ŋa-n=na
1DU.EXCL	nciŋan	me-nciŋan	sa-ŋ-ci-ŋ=ha	n-sa-n-ci-ŋa-n=na	sa-ya-ŋ-ci-ŋ=ha	n-sa-ya-n-ci-ŋa-n=na
1PL.EXCL	siŋan	me-siŋan	s-i-ŋ=ha	n-s-i-ŋa-n=ha	sa-i-ŋa-n=ha	n-sa-i-ŋa-n=ha
1DU.INCL	ncin	me-ncin	sa-ci=ha	n-sa-n-ci-n=ha	sa-ya-ci=ha	n-sa-ya-n-cin=ha
1PL.INCL	sin	me-sin	s-i=ha	n-s-i-n=ha	sa-i=ha	n-sa-i-n=ha
2SG	kan	me-kan	sa-ga=na	n-sa-ga-n=na	sa-ya-ga=na	n-sa-ya-gan=na
2DU	ncigan	me-cigan	sa-cig=ha	n-sa-n-ci-ga-n=ha	sa-ya-ci-g=ha	n-sa-ya-n-ci-gan=ha
2PL	sigan	me-sigan	s-i-g=ha	n-s-i-ga-n=ha	sa-i-g=ha	n-sa-i-ga-n=ha
3SG	—	men	sa=na	n-sa-n=na	sa-ya=na	n-sa-ya-n=na
3DU	—	mencin	sa-ci=ha	n-sa-n-ci-n=ha	sa-ya-ci=ha	n-sa-ya-n-ci-n=ha
3PL	—	men(=ha=ci)	n-sa=ha=ci	n-sa-nin=ha	n-sa-ya=ha	n-sa-ya-nin=ha

son inflection (*sa* is reduced to *s* when followed by *-i* for 1/2PL). This past stem can also host the past marker *-a ~ -ya*, and it is not clear yet what the semantic effect of this is, hence this category is simply called 'Past II' here (see Table 8.28). Furthermore there is the perfect (not included in the table), which is marked regularly by the already familiar perfect marker *-ma ~ -mi* preceding the person inflection of the Past II forms (e.g., *sayamaŋna* for first person singular). What is different from the regular intransitive marking is the occurrence of the negation marker *-nin* in third person negated past forms, which is otherwise only found in the transitive paradigms. The fourth and fifth inflectional series are only attested in negated forms; they are discussed below.

The simple past forms are the most frequently used tense forms of the identificational copula in the current corpus. Unfortunately, the analysis of the past tenses cannot be corroborated by much natural data, so that the precise answer to the question of their application has to be left for a later stage (but see (50) for a few examples).

(50)   a.   *uŋci=go*   *miyaŋ*   *mam=ha*   *n-sa.*
            3NSG=TOP   a_little   big=NMLZ.NSG   3PL-COP.PST
            'They were a bit older.'

       b.   *uŋ*   *tuknuŋ*   *luŋmatuktuk=na*   *sa-ya-ma.*
            3SG   completely   loving=NMLZ.SG   COP.PST[3SG]-PST-PRF
            'She was a very loving person.'[28]   [01_leg_07.061]

       c.   *pyak*   *encho*   *ka*   *miya*   *sa-ya-ŋ=niŋa.*
            much   long_ago   1SG   small   COP.PST-PST-1SG=CTMP
            'Long ago, when I was a child, ...'   [42_leg_10.002]

A further negated inflectional paradigm can be found for the present tense (only 1/2PL forms are attested, see (51)) and for Past I and II (see Table 8.29). These forms are marked by attaching a prefix *ta- ~ ti-* to the copular stem, to the right of the negation prefix, which is *me-*, (not *N-* as in the past forms shown above). This is the only instance of a second prefixal slot in the entire verbal inflection.[29] Corresponding affirmative forms are not attested. Superficially, the semantics of these forms are equivalent to the forms shown in Table 8.28, see (51a); so the tentative conclusion is that this prefix only has an emphatic function.

---

[28] This example also shows the narrative function of the Perfect tense; it frequently occurs in stories (see §8.4.2.2).

[29] A further puzzle is that the attested nonpast forms are identical to the corresponding forms in Past I, but it can be explained by the absence of a dedicated nonpast marker and the deletion of PST *-a* due to 1/2PL *-i.*

(51)   a.   *kaniŋ   hironi*   *me-ti-siŋan?*
            1SG   bollywood_heroine   NEG-EMPH-COP.NPST.1PL
            'Aren't we Bollywood heroines?' (same: *mesiŋan*)
       b.   *elaba=ci=ŋa*   *n-lu-ks-u-ci:*   *nniŋda*
            a_clan=NSG=ERG   3PL.A-tell-PRF-3.P-3NSG.P   2PL
            yakkhaba   *me-ti-sigan=ha.*
            Yakkha_person   NEG-EMPH-COP.NPST.2PL=SG
            'The Elabas told them: you are not Yakkhas.'   [39_nrr_08.07]

Table 8.29: Alternative past and negation inflection of the copula

	NEG.PST.I.EMPH	NEG.PST.II.EMPH
1SG	*me-ta-sa-ŋa-n=na*	*me-ta-sa-ya-ŋa-n=na*
1DU.EXCL	*me-ta-sa-n-ci-ŋa-n=ha*	*me-ta-sa-ya-n-ci-ŋa-n=ha*
1PL.EXCL	*me-ti-s-i-ŋa-n=ha*	*me-ta-sa-i-ŋa-n=ha*
1DU.INCL	*me-ta-sa-n-ci=ha*	*me-ta-sa-ya-n-ci-n=ha*
1PL.INCL	*me-ti-s-i-n=ha*	*me-ta-sa-i-n=ha*
2SG	*me-ta-sa-ga-n=na*	*me-ta-sa-ya-ga-n=na*
2DU	*me-ta-sa-n-ci-ga-n=ha*	*me-ta-sa-ya-n-ci-ga-n=ha*
2PL	*me-ti-s-i-ga-n=ha*	*me-ta-sa-i-ga-n=ha*
3SG	*me-ta-sa-n=na*	*me-ta-sa-ya-n=na*
3DU	*me-ta-sa-n-ci-n=ha*	*me-ta-sa-ya-n-ci-n=ha*
3PL	*me-ta-sa-nin=ha*	*me-ta-sa-ya-nin=ha*

8.7.2 The existential verb *wama*

The existential verb *wama* is probably the only verb that has a purely static temporal profile, i.e., without containing the notion of the inception of the state (exactly as in Belhare, see Bickel 1996: 212). It may translate as 'be, exist, live, stay' and is found in copular frames expressing location, existence and also in clauses with adjectival predicates (see (52) for examples). In many other Kiranti languages, a cognate of the verb *yuŋma* 'sit, live, exist' has this function. In Yakkha, *yuŋma* is restricted to the meaning 'sit (down)'. A paradigm of various tense inflections of *wama* is provided in Table 8.30 on page 266.

(52) a. *uhiŋgilik*   *wɛʔ=na.*
    alive   be[NPST;3SG]=NMLZ.SG
    'She is alive.'

    b. *n-na*   *n-nuncha*
    2SG.POSS-elder_sister   2SG.POSS-younger_sibling
    ŋ-waiʔ=ya=ci?
    3PL-exist[NPST]=NMLZ.NSG=NSG
    'Do you have sisters?'

The stem *wa* of this verb has several allomorphs. There are the nonpast allomorphs *wai(ʔ) ~ wɛʔ*, which have resulted from a contraction of the stem and the nonpast marker (/wa-meʔ/), diachronically. Such processes are also found in other verbs; take, e.g., the underlying form /leŋdimeʔna/ which is also found as [leŋdeʔna] in fast speech. In the verb of existence, however, this contraction is lexicalized, since it may also host the nonpast marker. Marked by nonpast *-meʔ*, these forms have continuative or future semantics, extending the state beyond the time of the utterance context, as shown in (53). Furthermore, the verb has an allomorph *wai* (bisyllabic) in the past forms.

(53) *nna*   *tas-wa=na=be*   *yog-a-n-u-m,*   *nna=be,*
    that   reach-NPST=NMLZ.SG=LOC   search-IMP-PL-3.P-2PL.A   that=LOC
    nniŋ=ga   *mamu*   *wa-meʔ=na.*
    2PL.POSS=GEN   girl   be[3SG]-NPST=SG
    'Search there where it lands (a clew of thread), your girl will (still) be there.'   [22_nrr_05.095]

Since with the absence of *-meʔ* in the nonpast the 1/2.PL forms (marked by the suffix *-i*) became identical in the present and in the simple past, they have received further marking: instead of the expected *wa-i=ha* for 1PL.INCL.NPST or *wa-i-g=ha* for 2PL.NPST one finds *wa-i-niti-ha* and *wa-i-niti-gha*, respectively. The marker *-niti* is not attested elsewhere in the verbal morphology.[30]

In the negation paradigm, forms with a suppletive stem *ma* exist alternatively to forms with *wai*, throughout all tense forms (*mai* in the plupast, in analogy to affirmative *wai*). The most commonly heard form is the third person *manna/man-*

---

[30] There is a second person plural suffix *-ni* in the imperative paradigm, and we have seen above that there is a prefix *ta- ~ ti-* in some forms of the past inflection of the identificational copula. It is possible that there is an etymological link between *-niti* and these affixes, but any claims in this regard would be highly speculative.

haci, stating the absence of something (see (54a)).[31] As in the affirmative forms, attaching the nonpast marker results in a future reading (see (54c)). I have one contrastive example suggesting that *ma*-forms are not interchangeable with *wa* (and its allomorphs), and thus that *ma* is not simply an allomorph of *wa* (compare (54b) and (c)). Unfortunately, the current data set is not sufficient to determine the exact difference between these two negated stems. The *ma*-series is more frequent in my Yakkha corpus.

(54) a. *sambakhi=ci   ma-n=ha=ci.*
          potato=NSG   exist.NEG-NEG=NMLZ.NSG=NSG
          'There are no potatoes.'

      b. *ŋ-wa-meʔ-ŋa-n.*
          NEG-stay-NPST-1SG-NEG
          'I will not stay.'

      c. *nda   ta-me-ka=niŋ   ka   m-ma-me-ŋa-n.*
          2SG   come-NPST-2=CTMP   1SG   NEG-be-NPST-1SG-NEG
          'I will not be here when you come.'

In addition to the nonpast inflections, three past series were found, formed similarly to the regular verbal inflection: a simple past formed by *-a*, a perfect formed by adding *-ma* ~ *-mi* to the simple past, and another past tense ('Past II', yet unanalyzed) formed by adding *-sa* ~ *-si* to the simple past forms. This Past II has no parallel forms in the regular verbal inflectional paradigm. The simple past again seems to be the default choice (see (55a)), and the other two are more specific. The perfect is found in narratives, relating to events that have some relevance for the story, i.e., in sentences setting the stage for further information to come (see (55b) and (55c), from the beginning of a narrative and from childhood memories, respectively). The Past II forms refer to events that preceded another salient event in the past. In (55d), the speaker refers to the time when people came to propose a marriage to her daughter, but the conversation takes place already after the wedding, which was the main topic of the conversation.

(55) a. *ŋkhaʔniŋ   eko   paŋ=ca   m-ma-ya-n=niŋa*
          that_time   one   house=ADD NEG-exist[3SG]-PST-NEG=CTMP

---

[31] Since the other person forms show an initial geminate, I assume that the third person underwent formal reduction due to frequent use. The form *ma(n)* is also the base for postpositions and conjunctions. Combined with the adverbial clause linkage marker *=niŋ* it has developed into the privative case *maʔniŋ* 'without', and combined with the clause linkage marker *=hoŋ* it yields the clause-initial conjunction *manhoŋ* 'otherwise'.

> tumhaŋ=ŋa   paŋ   cog-uks-u.
> Tumhang=ERG   house   make-PRF-3.P
> 'Back then, when there was not a single house, Tumhang made a house.'   [27_nrr_06.038]

b. uŋci=nuŋ   pyak   yaŋ   m-ma-ya-ma-n.
   3NSG=COM   much   money   NEG-exist[3SG]-PST-PRF-NEG
   'They did not have much money.'   [01_leg_07.304]

c. buŋga-bic=pe   wa-i-mi-ŋ.
   Bunga-beach=LOC   live-1PL-PRF-EXCL
   'We lived at Bunga Beach (a place in Singapore).'   [13_cvs_02.062]

d. njiŋda   m-mai-sa-n-ci-ga-n=ha.
   2DU   NEG-exist-PST-NEG-DU-2-NEG=NSG
   'The two of you had not been here (when they came).'
                                                       [36_cvs_06.306]

Subjunctive forms can be found as well, both in the nonpast subjunctive (56a), e.g., for hortatives, and in the past subjunctive (56b), e.g., for irrealis clauses. The past subjunctive is identical to the simple past. Table 8.30 shows the inflections with a few forms marked by '(?)', which means that they have been reconstructed, but not attested.

(56) a. kaniŋ   wa-i.
         1PL   be-1PL[SBJV]
         'Let us live/stay (here).'

      b. a-ma=nuŋ   a-na=ŋa
         1SG.POSS-mother=COM   1SG.POSS-eZ=ERG

         y-yog-a-n=niŋ=bi   ka   hensen
         NEG-search-SBJV-NEG=CTMP=IRR   1SG   nowadays

         ŋ-wa-ya-ŋa-n=bi.
         NEG-exist-SBJV-1SG-NEG=IRR
         'If my mother and sister had not looked (for me), I would not be alive now.'   [42_leg_10.052]

8.8 Further markers

Two further markers that do not fit in the previous sections have to be mentioned. First, there is a suffix -a, attached to Nepali verbal roots when they occur as loans with Yakkha light verbs, as shown in (57).

Table 8.30: Person and tense/aspect inflection of *wama* 'be, exist, live'

	NPST.AFF	NPST.NEG	PST.AFF	PST.NEG	PST.II.AFF	PST.II.NEG
1SG	waiwaiʔ-ŋa=na	ŋ-waiʔ-ŋa-n=na m-ma-ŋa-n=na	wa-ya-ŋ=na	ŋ-wa-ya-ŋa-n=na m-ma-ya-ŋa-n=na	wai-sa-ŋ=na	ŋ-wai-sa-ŋa-n=na m-mai-sa-ŋa-nna
1DU.EXCL	wai-ŋ-ci-ŋ=ha	ŋ-wai-n-ci-ŋa-n=ha m-ma-n-ci-ŋa-n=ha	wa-ya-ŋ-ci-ŋ=ha	ŋ-wa-ya-n-ci-ŋa-n=ha m-ma-ya-n-ci-ŋa-n=ha	wai-sa-ŋ-ci-ŋ=ha	ŋ-wai-sa-n-ci-ŋa-n=ha m-mai-sa-n-ci-ŋa-n=ha
1PL.EXCL	wai-niti-ŋ=ha	ŋ-wai-niti-ŋa-n=ha (?) m-ma-i-ŋa-n=ha	wa-i-ŋha	ŋ-wa-i-ŋa-n=ha m-ma-i-ŋa-n=ha	wa-i-si-ŋ=ha	ŋ-wa-i-si-ŋa-n=ha m-ma-i-si-ŋa-n=ha
1DU.INCL	wai-ci=ha	ŋ-wai-n-ci-n=ha m-ma-n-ci-n=ha	wa-ya-ci=ha	ŋ-wa-ya-n-ci-n=ha m-ma-ya-n-ci-n=ha	wai-sa-ci=ha	ŋ-wai-sa-n-ci-n=ha m-mai-sa-n-ci-n=ha
1PL.INCL	wai-niti=ya	ŋ-wai-niti-n=ha (?) m-ma-i-n=ha	wa-i=ya	ŋ-wa-i-n=ha m-ma-i-n-n=ha (?)	wai-s-i=ha	ŋ-wa-i-si-n=ha m-mai-s-i-n=ha
2SG	wai-ka=na	ŋ-wai-ka-n=na m-ma-ga-n=na	wa-ya-ga=na	ŋ-wa-ya-ga-n=na m-ma-ya-ga-n=na	wai-sa-ga=na	ŋ-wai-sa-ga-n=na m-mai-sa-ga-n=na
2DU	wai-ci-g=ha	ŋ-wai-n-ci-ga-n=ha m-mai-n-ci-ga-n=ha	wa-ya-ci-g=ha	ŋ-wa-ya-n-ci-ga-n=ha m-ma-ya-n-ci-ga-n=ha	wai-sa-ci-g=ha	ŋ-wai-sa-n-ci-ga-n=ha m-mai-sa-n-ci-ga-n=ha
2PL	wai-niti-g=ha	ŋ-wai-niti-ga-n=ha (?) m-ma-i-ga-n=ha	wa-i-g=ha	ŋ-wa-i-ga-n=ha m-ma-i-ga-n=ha (?)	wai-s-i-g=ha	ŋ-wai-s-i-ga-n=ha m-mai-s-i-ga-n=ha
3SG	waiʔ=na	ŋ-wai-n=na m-ma-n=na	wa-ya=na	ŋ-wa-ya-n=na m-ma-ya-n=na	wai-sa=na	ŋ-wai-sa-n=na m-mai-sa-n=na
3DU	wai-ci=ha	ŋ-wai-n-ci-n=ha m-ma-n-ci-n=ha	wa-ya-ci=ha	ŋ-wa-ya-n-ci-n=ha m-ma-ya-n-ci-n=ha	wai-sa-ci=ha	ŋ-wai-sa-n-ci-n=ha m-mai-sa-n-ci-n=ha
3PL	ŋ-waiʔ=ha=ci	ŋ-wai-nin=ha m-ma-nin=ha	ŋ-wa-ya-ci	ŋ-wa-ya-n=ha=ci m-ma-ya-n=ha=ci	ŋ-wai-s=ha=ci	ŋ-wai-sa-n=ha=ci m-ma-sa-nin=ha

(57) a. *khic-a*   *cog-u!*
          press-NATIV   do-3.P[IMP]
          'Record it!'

      b. *i=ha=ca*   *im-ma*   *por-a*
          what=NMLZ.NC=ADD   buy-INF   have_to-NATIV

          n-joŋ-me-ŋa-n.
          NEG-do-NPST-1SG-NEG
          'I do not have to buy anything.'   [28_cvs_04.187]

Another marker functions like a complement verb, despite being a bound morpheme. The marker *-les* states that the subject has knowledge or skills and is able to perform the activity denoted by the lexical verb. As the suffix has the typical structure of a verbal stem, it has probably developed out of a verb. However, there is no verb with the stem *les* synchronically.

(58) a. *phuama=ŋa=ca*   *cek-les-wa,*   *hau!*
          last_born_girl=ERG=ADD   speak-know-NPST[3A;3.P]   EXCLA
          'Phuama also knows how to speak, ha!'   [36_cvs_06.503]

      b. *pheŋ-les-wa-m-ci-m-ŋa.*
          plough-know-NPST-1PL.A-3NSG.P-1PL.A-EXCL
          'We know how to plough (with oxen).'   [28_cvs_04.152]

8.9 Non-finite forms

Non-finite forms in Yakkha include the infinitive marked by *-ma* and occasionally *-sa* (attested only in negated complement constructions with *yama* 'be able to'), a nominalization in *-khuba* (which constructs nouns and participles with S or A role) and several converbal forms, all attached directly to the stem: the supine converb in *-se*, the simultaneous converb in *-saŋ* and the negative converb marked by *meN-...-le* (discussed in Chapter 14).

The infinitive occurs in infinitival complement constructions and in the deontic construction (all discussed in Chapter 15). The latter allows for some further marking such as negation by *men-*, the nominalizing clitics *=na* and *=ha*, and the nonsingular marker *=ci* to indicate nonsingular objects (cf. §15.1.7). From a functional perspective, the infinitive with a deontic reading is finite, as it can stand independently as an utterance and does not rely upon another syntactic unit.

Occasionally, the infinitive is also found in infinitival adverbial clauses and in adverbial clauses that usually contain inflected verbs, i.e., clauses marked in =niŋ(a) (cotemporal events), =hoŋ (sequential events) and bhoŋ (conditional clauses). This is the case when the reference of the arguments is not specified, i.e., in general statements, best rendered with 'when/ if one does X, ...' (see Chapter 14).

Note that there is a special negation marker me(N-) which is only found in nonfinite forms and in the inflection of the copula, i.e., in infinitives, the nominalization in -khuba and the negative converb. Except for this negation marker and the clitics on the deontic infinitives, no tense/aspect, mood or person marking is found on non-finite forms.

9 Noun-verb predicates

This chapter deals with idiomatic combinations of a noun and a verb. These predicates occupy a position somewhat between word and phrase. Lexically, a noun-verb predicate always constitutes one word, as its meaning is not directly predictable from its individual components (with varying degrees of metaphoricity and abstraction). But since the nouns enjoy considerable morphosyntactic freedom, speaking of noun incorporation here would be misleading. About 80 noun-verb predicates are attested so far, with rougly two thirds referring to experiential events.

There are two main morphologically defined patterns for noun-verb predicates. In the first pattern (Simple noun-verb predicates) the predicate consists of a noun and a verb that are juxtaposed in N-V order, such as *lam phakma* 'open way, give turn' or *tukkhuʔwa lamma* 'doze off' (discussed in §9.1).[1] The second pattern (the experiencer-as-possessor construction) is semantically more restricted and also different morphologically. It expresses experiential events, with the experiencer coded as possessor, as for instance *hakamba keʔma* 'yawn' (literally 'someone's yawn to come up'). This pattern is discussed in §9.2.

9.1 Simple noun-verb predicates

Most of the simple noun-verb predicates are relatively transparent but fixed collocations. They denote events from the semantic domains of natural phenomena, e.g., *nam phemma* 'shine [sun]', *taŋkhyaŋ kama* 'thunder' (literally 'the sky shouts'), some culturally significant actions like *kei lakma* 'dance the drum dance' and also verbs that refer to experiential events and bodily functions, such as *whaŋma tukma* 'feel hot' (literally 'the sweat (or heat) hurts'). Experiential concepts are, however, more frequently expressed by the experiencer-as-possessor construction.[2]

---

[1] The same pattern is also used as a strategy to incorporate Nepali nouns into the Yakkha morphology, with a very small class of light verbs, namely *cokma* 'make', *wama* 'exist, be' and *tokma* 'get', cf. §11.1.11.

[2] There is no clear explanation why some verbs expressing bodily functions, like *chipma chima* 'urinate' belong to the simple noun-verb predicates, while most of them belong to

Table 9.1 provides some examples of simple noun-verb predicates. Lexemes in square brackets were not found as independent words beyond their usage in these compounds. Some verbs, like weather verbs (e.g., *nam phemma* 'shine [sun]' and *wasik tama* 'rain') and some experiential predicates (e.g., *wepma sima* 'be thirsty' and *whaŋma tukma* 'feel hot'), for instance, do not allow the expression of additional arguments; their valency is zero (under the assumption that the nouns belonging to the predicates are different from full-fledged arguments). If overt arguments are possible, they behave like the arguments of standard intransitive or standard transitive verbs. They trigger agreement on the verb, and they take nominative or ergative case marking (see §11.1).

The predicates vary as to whether the noun or the verb carries the semantic weight of the predicate, or whether both parts play an equal role in establishing the meaning of the construction. In verbs like *wepma sima* 'be thirsty' (lit. 'thirst – die') or *wasik tama* 'rain' (lit. 'rain – come'), the noun carries the semantic weight,[3] while in verbs like *kei lakma* 'drum – dance', *cabhak lakma* 'paddy – dance', the nouns merely modify the verbal meaning. The nouns may stand in various thematic relations to the verb: in *wepma sima* 'be thirsty', the noun has the role of an effector, in predicates like *hiʔwa phemma* 'wind – blow' it is closer to an agent role. In *saya pokma* 'head-soul – raise',[4] it is a patient.

There are also a few constructions in which the noun is etymologically related to the verb, such as *chipma chima* 'urinate', *sokma soma* 'breathe' and *phiʔma phima* 'fart' (cognate object constructions). The nouns in these constructions do not contribute to the overall meaning of the predicate.[5]

Concerning stress assignment and the voicing rule (see §3.4 and §3.5), noun and verb do not constitute a unit. Both the noun and the verb carry equal stress, even if the noun is monosyllabic, resulting in adjacent stress, as in ˈsak.ˈtuk.ma. As for voicing, if the initial stop of the verbal stem is preceded by a nasal or a vowel, it remains voiceless. This stands in contrast to the verb-verb predicates (see Chapter 10), which are more tightly fused in other respects, too. Compare,

the experiencer-as-possessor frame. Some verbs show synonymy across these two classes, e.g., the two lexemes with the meaning 'sweat': *whaŋma lomma* (literally '(someone's) sweat comes out', an experiencer-as-possessor predicate, with the experiencer coded as possessor of *whaŋma*) and *whaŋmaŋa lupma* (literally 'the sweat disperses', a simple noun-verb predicate).
[3] This is the reason why noun-verb collocations have also become known as light verb constructions (after Jespersen (1965), who used this term for English collocations like *have a rest*).
[4] 'Raising the head soul' is a ritual activity undertaken by specialists to help individuals whose physical or psychological well-being is in danger.
[5] Semantically empty nouns are also attested in the experiencer-as-possessor construction (cf. below). They are called "eidemic" in Bickel (1995; 1997c); and "morphanic" (morpheme orphans) in Matisoff (1986).

Table 9.1: Simple noun-verb predicates

PREDICATE	GLOSS	LITERAL TRANSLATION
cabhak lakma	'do the paddy dance'	(paddy – dance)
chakma pokma	'troubled times to occur'	(hardship – strike)
chipma chima	'urinate'	(urine – urinate)
cuŋ tukma	'feel cold'	(cold – hurt)
himbulumma cama	'swing'	(swing – eat)
hiʔwa phemma	'wind blow'	(wind – be activated [weather])
hoŋga phaŋma	'crawl'	([STEM] – [STEM])
kei lakma	'do the drum dance'	(drum – dance)
laŋ phakma	'make steps'	(foot/leg – apply)
lam phakma	'open way, give turn'	(way – apply/build)
lambu lembiʔma	'let pass'	(way – let–give)
muk phakma	'help, serve'	(hand – apply)
nam ama	'sit around all day'	(sun – make set)
nam phemma .	'be sunny'	(sun – be activated [weather])
phiʔma phima	'fart'	(fart – fart)
sak tukma	'be hungry'	(hunger – hurt)
setni keʔma	'stay awake all night'	(night – bring up)
sokma soma	'breathe'	(breath – breathe)
susuwa lapma	'whistle'	([whistle] – call)
tukkhuʔwa lapma (~ lamma)	'doze off'	([STEM] – call)
taŋkhyaŋ kama	'thunder'	(sky – call)
uwa cama	'kiss'	(nectar/liquid – eat)
wa lekma	'rinse'	(water – turn)
wasik tama	'rain'	(rain – come)
wepma sima	'be thirsty'	(thirst – die)
wepma tukma	'by thirsty'	(thirst – hurt)
wha pokma	'septic wounds to occur'	(septic wound – infest)
whaŋma tukma	'feel hot'	(heat/sweat – hurt)
yak yakma	'stay over night'	([STEM] – stay over night)
yaŋchan chiʔma	'regret'	([STEM] – get conscious)
chemha=ŋa sima	'be intoxicated, be drunken'	(be killed by alcohol)
cuŋ=ŋa sima	'freeze'	(die of cold)
sak=ŋa sima	'be hungry'	(die of hunger)
whaŋma=ŋa lupma	'sweat'	(heat/sweat – disperse/strew)

for instance, *cuŋ tukma* 'be cold' (N+V, 'cold—hurt') with *ham-biʔma* 'distribute among people' (V+V, 'distribute—give').

There are different degrees of morphological fusion of noun and verb, and some nouns may undergo operations that are not expected if they were incorporated. They can be topicalized by means of the particle *=ko* (see (1a)), and two nouns selecting the same light verb may also be coordinated (see (1b)). Such examples are rare, though. Note that (1a) is from a collection of proverbs and sayings, in which rhythm and rhyming constraints could lead to the insertion of particles such as *=ko*. In most cases the noun and verb occur without any intervening material. The noun may also be modified independently, as the spontaneously uttered sentence in (1c) shows. Typically, the predicates are modified as a whole by adverbs, but here one can see that the noun may also be modified independently by adnominal modifiers. The modifying phrase is marked by a genitive, which is never found on adverbial modifiers.

(1)   a.   *makkai=ga   cama,   chiʔwa=ga   khyu,*
           maize=GEN   cooked_grains   nettle=GEN   curry_sauce
           cabhak=ko   lak-ma,   a-ŋoteŋma=jyu.
           paddy=TOP   dance-INF   1SG.POSS-female_in-law=HON
           'Corn mash, nettle sauce, let us dance the paddy dance, dear sister-in-law.'

                                                              [12_pvb_01.008]

      b.   *kei=nuŋ   cabhak   lak-saŋ   ucun   n-joŋ-me.*
           drum=COM   paddy   dance-SIM   nice   3PL-do-NPST
           'They have a good time, dancing the drum dance and the paddy dance.'[6]

                                                              [01_leg_07.142]

      c.   *a-phok   tuk=nuŋ=ga   sak*
           1SG.POSS-stomach   hurt=COM=GEN   hunger
           tug-a=na.
           hurt-PST[3SG]=NMLZ.SG
           'I am starving.' (literally 'A hunger struck (me) that makes my stomach ache.')

Some of the nouns may even trigger agreement on the verb, something which is also unexpected from the traditional definition of compounds, which entails that compounds are one unit lexically and thus morphologically opaque (see, e.g.,

---

[6] The interpretation of 'dancing the paddy dance with drums' can be ruled out here, because the drums are not played in the paddy dance.

Fabb 2001). Example (2a) and (2b) are different in this respect:[7] while predicates that contain the verb *tukma* 'hurt' are invariably inflected for third person singular (in other words, the noun *whaŋma* triggers agreement; overt arguments are not possible), predicates containing *sima* 'die' show agreement with the overtly expressed (experiencer) subject in the unmarked nominative (2b).[8] Some meanings can be expressed by either frame (compare (2b) and (2c)), but this is not a regular and productive alternation.

(2)   a.   *whaŋma   tug-a=na.*
            sweat   hurt[3SG]-PST=NMLZ.SG
            'I/you/he/she/it/we/they feel(s) hot.'

      b.   *ka   wepma   sy-a-ŋ=na.*
            1SG   thirst   die-PST-1SG=NMLZ.SG
            'I am thirsty.'

      c.   *wepma   tug-a=na.*
            thirst   hurt[3SG]-PST=NMLZ.SG
            'I/you/he/she/it/we/they is/are thirsty.'

Note that if *wepma* in (2b) were a regular verbal argument, an instrumental case would be expected, since it is an effector with respect to the verbal meaning. And indeed, some noun-verb predicates require an instrumental or an ergative case on the noun (see (3)).[9]

(3)   a.   *(chemha=ŋa)   sis-a-ga=na=i?*
            (liquor=ERG)   kill-PST-2.P=NMLZ.SG=Q
            'Are you drunk?'

      b.   *sak=ŋa   n-sy-a-ma-ŋa-n=na.*
            hunger=INS   NEG-die-PST-PRF-1SG-NEG=NMLZ.SG
            'I am not hungry.'

Some verbs participating in noun-verb predicates have undergone semantic changes. Note that in (3) the nouns *sak* and *chemha* do not have the same status with regard to establishing the semantics of the whole predicate. The verbal stem *sis* 'kill' in (a) has already acquired a metaphorical meaning of 'be drunk,

---

[7] Many Yakkha verbs have inchoative-stative Aktionsart so that the past inflection refers to a state that still holds true at the time of speaking.

[8] The same argument realization is found in the Belhare cognates of these two verbs (Bickel 1997c). For the details of argument realization in Yakkha see Chapter 11.

[9] Yakkha has an instrumental/ergative syncretism. Therefore, in intransitive predicates =ŋa is interpreted as instrumental; in transitive predicates it is interpreted as ergative.

be intoxicated' (with the experiencer coded like a standard object). The noun is frequently omitted in natural speech, and if all arguments are overt, the experiencer precedes the stimulus, just like in Experiencer-as-Object constructions (see (4) and Chapter 11.1.6).[10] In contrast to this, the stem *si* in (b) is not polysemous; the noun is required to establish the meaning of the construction.

(4)　　*ka*　　*macchi=ŋa*　　　　　*haŋd-a-ŋ=na.*
　　　　1SG　　pickles/chili=ERG　　taste_hot-PST-1SG.P=NMLZ.SG
　　　　'The pickles/chili tasted hot to me.'

Despite a certain degree of morphosyntactic freedom, the nouns are not full-fledged arguments. It is not possible to demote or promote the noun via transitivity operations such as the causative or the passive, or to extract it from the noun-verb complex via relativization (see ungrammatical (5)).

(5)　　a.　　**lakt-i=ha*　　　　　　　　　*cabhak*
　　　　　　　dance-1PL[PST]=NMLZ.NSG　　paddy
　　　　　　　Intended: 'the paddy (dance) that we danced'
　　　　b.　　**tug-a=ha*　　　　　　　　*sak*
　　　　　　　hurt[3SG]-PST=NMLZ.NSG　　hunger
　　　　　　　Intended: 'the hunger that was perceivable'

To sum up, simple noun-verb predicates behave like one word with respect to lexical semantics, adjacency (in the overwhelming majority of examples), extraction possibilities for the noun (i.e., the lack thereof). They behave like two words as far as clitic placement (including case), coordination, modifiability, stress and voicing are concerned. Thus, they are best understood as lexicalized phrases.

9.2 Experiencer-as-possessor constructions

Following a general tendency of languages of South and Southeast Asia, Yakkha has a dedicated construction for the expression of experiential concepts, including emotional and cognitive processes, bodily functions, but also human character traits and their moral evaluation. In Yakkha, such concepts are expressed by predicates that are built from a noun and a verb, whereby the noun is perceived as the location of this concept, i.e., the "arena" where a physiological or psychological experience unfolds (Matisoff 1986: 8). These nouns are henceforth referred to as psych-nouns, but apart from referring to emotions and sensations,

---

[10] The same development has taken place in Belhare (Bickel 1997c: 151).

they can also refer to body parts and excreted substances. Example (6) illustrates the basic pattern:

(6) *u-niŋwa*   *tug-a=na.*
     3SG.POSS-mind hurt[3SG]-PST=NMLZ.SG
     'He was/became sad.'

The verbs come from a rather small class; they denote the manner in which the experiencer is affected by the event, many of which refer to motion events. The experiencer is morphologically treated like the possessor of the psych-noun; it is indexed by possessive prefixes. The expression of experiential concepts by means of a possessive metaphor is a characteristic and robust feature of Kiranti languages (cf. the "possessive of experience" in Bickel (1997c), "emotive predicates" in Ebert (1994: 72), and "body part emotion verbs" in Doornenbal 2009: 219), but this is also found beyond Kiranti in South-East Asian languages, including Hmong-Mien, Mon-Khmer and Tai-Kadai languages (Matisoff 1986; Bickel 2004b). In other Tibeto-Burman languages, such as Newari, Balti and Tibetan, for instance, experiencers are marked by a dative (Beyer 1992; Genetti 2007; Read 1934), an option which is not available, at least not by native morphology, in most Kiranti languages.

Experiencer-as-possessor constructions are not the only option to express experiential events. The crosslinguistic variation that can be found within experiential predicates is also reflected in the language-internal variation of Yakkha. We have seen simple noun-verb predicates in §9.1 above. Other possibilities are simple verbal stems like *haŋma* 'taste hot/have a spicy sensation' (treating the experiencer like a standard P argument), *eʔma* 'perceive, like, have an impression, have opinion' (treating it like a standard A argument) and the historically complex verb *kisiʔma* 'be afraid' (treating it like a standard S argument). Verbs composed of several verbal stems may also encode experiential notions, such as *yoŋdiʔma* 'be scared' (a compound consisting of the roots for 'shake' and 'give'). It is the experiencer-as-possessor construction though that constitutes the biggest class of experiential predicates. About fifty verbs have been found so far (cf. Tables 9.2 through 9.5), but probably this list is far from exhaustive.

This section is organized as follows: the various possibilities of argument realization within the experiencer-as-possessor frame are introduced in §9.2.1 introduces, §9.2.2 looks at the principles behind the semantic composition of possessive experiential predicates, and §9.2.3 deals with the morphosyntax of these predicates and with the behavioral properties of experiencers as non-canonically marked S or A arguments.

9.2.1 Subframes of argument realization

A basic distinction can be drawn between predicates of intransitive valency and transitive or labile[11] valency. Within this basic distinction, the verbs can be further divided into various subframes of argument realization (see Tables 9.2 through 9.5 at the end of the section). In all classes, the experiencer is marked as possessor of the psych-noun, i.e., as possessor of a sensation or an affected body part.

In the class of intransitive verbs, the psych-noun triggers third person marking on the verb, as in (6) and (7). Intransitive verbs usually do not have an overt noun phrase referring to the experiencer; only the possessive prefix identifies the reference of the experiencer. When the experiencer has a special pragmatic status, and is thus marked by a discourse particle, it can be overtly expressed in either the nominative or in the genitive (compare example (16c) and (17d) below). As this is quite rare, the reasons for this alternation are not clear yet.

In some cases, the noun is conceptualized as nonsingular, triggering the according number markers on the verb as well (see (7a)). One verb in this group is special in consisting of two nouns and a verb (see (7b)). Both nouns take the possessive prefix. Their respective full forms would be *niŋwa* and *lawa*. It is not uncommon that the nouns get reduced to one syllable in noun-verb predicates.

(7) a. *a-pomma=ci*   *ŋ-gy-a=ha=ci.*
         1SG.POSS-laziness=NSG   3PL-come_up-PST=NMLZ.NSG=NSG
         'I feel lazy.'

     b. *a-niŋ*   *a-la*   *sy-a=na.*
         1SG.POSS-mind   1SG.POSS-spirit   die[3SG]-PST=NMLZ.SG
         'I am fed up/annoyed.'

The transitive group can be divided into five classes (cf. Tables 9.3, 9.4 and 9.5 on pages 282–283). In all classes, the experiencer is coded as the possessor of the psych-noun (via possessive prefixes), and hence this does not need to be explicitly stated in the schematic representation of argument realization in the table.

In class (a) the experiencer is realized like a standard transitive subject (in addition to being indexed by possessive prefixes): it triggers transitive subject agreement and has ergative case marking (only overtly marked if it has third person reference and is overt, which is rare). The stimulus is unmarked and triggers object agreement (see (8a)).

---

[11] See also §11.2.1.

Class (b) differs from class (a) in that the psych-noun triggers object agreement, invariably third person and in some cases, third person plural (see (8b)). No stimulus is expressed in class (b). This class has the highest number of members.

(8) a. *uŋ=ŋa*   *u-ppa*   *u-luŋma*   *tukt-uks-u=na.*
         3SG=ERG 3SG.POSS-father 3SG.POSS-liver pour-PRF-3.P=NMLZ.SG
         'He loved his father.' (literally 'He poured his father his liver.')

     b. *a-yupma=ci*
         1SG.POSS-sleepiness=NSG

         cips-u-ŋ-ci-ŋ=ha.
         complete-3.P[PST]-1SG.A-3NSG.P-1SG.A=NMLZ.NSG
         'I am well-rested.' (literally 'I completed my sleep(s).')

Predicates of class (c) show three possibilities of argument realization. One possibility is an unexpected pattern where the stimulus triggers object agreement, while the psych-noun triggers subject agreement, which leads, oddly enough, to a literal translation 'my disgust brings up bee larvae' in (9a). Despite the subject agreement on the verb, the psych-nouns in this class do not host an ergative case marker, an option that is available, however, for verbs of class (d). The experiencer is indexed only by the possessive prefix in this frame; overt experiencer arguments were not found. The stimulus can be in the nominative or in the ablative in class (c), but if it is in the ablative, the verb is blocked from showing object agreement with the stimulus, showing 3>3 agreement instead (see (9b)). The third option of argument realization in class (c) is identical to class (a) (cf. the comments in (9a) and (b)). Reasons or conditions for these alternations, for instance in different configurations of the referential properties of the arguments, could not be detected.

(9) a. *thaŋsu=ga*   *u-chya=ci*   *a-chippa*
         bee=GEN   3SG.POSS-child=NSG 1SG.POSS-disgust
         ket-wa-ci=ha.
         bring_up-NPST-3NSGP=NMLZ.NSG
         'I am disgusted by the bee larvae.'
         (same: *thaŋsuga ucyaci achippa ketwaŋciŋha* - (1SG>3PL, class (a)))

     b. *njiŋda-bhaŋ*   *a-sokma*   *hips wa-na!*
         2DU=ABL   1SG.POSS-breath   whip-NPST[3A>3.P]=NMLZ.SG
         'I get fed up by you.'
         (same: *njiŋda asokma himmeʔnencinha!* - 1SG>2DU, class (a))

In class (d), the psych-noun also triggers transitive subject agreement, and it exhibits ergative marking. The object agreement slot can be filled either by the stimulus or by the experiencer argument (see (10a)).[12]

Class (e) is exemplified by (10b). Here, the experiencer is the possessor of a body part which triggers object agreement on the verb. Some verbs may express an effector or stimulus overtly. Others, like *ya limma* 'taste sweet' cannot express an overt A argument, despite being inflected transitively (see (10c)). This pattern is reminiscent of the transimpersonal verbs (treated in §11.1.7).

(10) a. *a-lawa=ŋa*   *na?-ya-ŋ=na.*
          1SG.POSS-spirit=ERG   leave-V2.LEAVE-PST-1SG.P=NMLZ.SG
          'I was frozen in shock.' (literally 'My spirit left me.')

      b. *(cuŋ=ŋa)*   *a-muk=ci*   *khokt-u-ci=ha.*
          (cold=ERG)   1SG.POSS-hand=NSG   chop-3.P[PST]-3NSG.P=NMLZ.NSG
          'My hands are tingling/freezing (from the cold).' (literally 'The cold chopped off my hands.')

      c. *a-ya*   *limd-u=na.*
          1SG.POSS-mouth   taste_sweet-3.P[PST]=NMLZ.SG
          'It tastes sweet to me.'

Many of the transitive verbs are attested also with intransitive inflection without further morphological marker of decreased transitivity, i.e., they show a lability alternation (see (11)).

(11) a. *n-lok*   *khot-a-ŋ-ga=na=i?*
          2SG.POSS-anger   scratch-PST-1SG.P-2.A=NMLZ.SG=Q
          'Are you angry at me?'

---

[12] There are (at least) two concepts, *saya* and *lawa*, that are related to or similar to 'soul' in Yakkha and the Kiranti metaphysical world in general. Gaenszle (2000) writes about these two (and other) concepts in Mewahang (also Eastern Kiranti, Upper Arun branch):

> The concept of *saya* is understood to be a kind of "vital force" that must be continually renewed (literally "bought") by means of various sacrificial rites. [...] The vital force *saya* makes itself felt [...] not only in subjective physical or psychic states but also, and in particular, in the social, economic, religious and political spheres - that is, it finds expression in success, wealth, prestige and power. The third concept, *lawa* (cf. Hardman (1981: 165), Hardman 1990: 299) is rendered by the Nepali word *sāto* ('soul'). This is a small, potentially evanescent substance, which is compared to a mosquito, a butterfly or a bee, and which, if it leaves the body for a longer period, results in loss of consciousness and mental illness. The shaman must then undertake to summon it back or retrieve it. (Gaenszle 2000: 119)

b.   *o-lok*   *khot-a=na.*
  3SG.POSS-anger   scratch[3SG]-PST=NMLZ.SG
  'He/she got angry.'

For two verbs, namely *nabhuk-lemnhaŋma* 'dishonor (self/others)' (literally 'throw away one's nose') and *nabhuk-yuŋma* 'uphold moral' (literally 'keep one's nose'), there is one more constellation of participants, due to their particular semantics. The experiencer can either be identical to the agent or different from it, as the social consequences of morally transgressive behavior usually affect more people than just the agent (e.g., illegitimate sexual contacts, or an excessive use of swearwords).[13] The morphosyntactic consequences of this are that the verbal agreement and the possessive prefix on the noun may either have the same conominal or two different conominals. Taken literally, one may 'throw away one's own nose' or 'throw away somebody else's nose' (see (12)). Note that due to the possessive argument realization it is possible to have partial coreference, which is impossible in the standard transitive verbal inflection (cf. §8.2).

(12)   a.   *u-nabhuk*   *lept-haks-u=na.*
      3SG.POSS-nose   throw-V2.SEND-3.P[PST]=NMLZ.SG
      'She dishonored herself.'
    b.   *nda*   *eŋ=ga*   *nabhuk(=ci)*
      2SG[ERG]   1PL.INCL.POSS=GEN   nose(=NSG)
      lept-haks-u-ci-g=ha!
      throw-V2.SEND-3.P[PST]-3NSG.P-2.A=NMLZ.NSG
      'You dishonored us all (including yourself)!'

In §9.1 cognate object constructions like *chipma chima* 'urinate' were discussed. In these cases, the noun is cognate to the verb and does not actually make a semantic contribution to the predicate. Such developments are also found in the experiencer-as-possessor frame. Example (13a) and (13b) are two alternative ways to express the same propositional content. Note the change of person marking to third person in (b). The noun *phok* 'belly' is, of course, not etymologically related to the verb in this case, but it also does not make a semantic contribution. Further examples are *ya limma* 'taste sweet' (*ya* means 'mouth') and *hi ema* 'defecate' (*hi* means 'stool').

---

[13] This concept is particularly related to immoral behavior of women. It is rarely, if ever, heard that a man 'threw away his nose'.

(13)   a.   *ka   khas-a-ŋ=na.*
            1SG   be_full-PST-1SG=NMLZ.SG
            'I am full.'
   b.   *a-phok*   *khas-a=na.*
            1SG.POSS-belly   be_full[3SG]-PST=NMLZ.SG
            'I am full.'

All frames of argument realization with examples are provided in Tables 9.2 through 9.5.[14]

9.2.2 Semantic properties

The experiencer-as-possessor predicates are far less transparent and predictable than the simple noun-verb predicates. The nouns participating in this structure refer to abstract psychological or moral concepts like *lok* 'anger', *yupma* 'sleepiness' and *pomma* 'laziness', or they refer to body parts or inner organs which are exploited for experiential metaphors. The lexeme *luŋma* 'liver', for instance, is used in the expression of love and greed, and *nabhuk* 'nose' is connected to upholding (or eroding) moral standards. The human body is a very common source for psychological metaphors, or as Matisoff observed:

> [...] it is a universal of human metaphorical thinking to equate mental operations and states with bodily sensations and movements, as well as with physical qualities and events in the outside world. (Matisoff 1986: 9)

In Yakkha, too, psychological concepts are treated as concrete tangible entities that can be possessed, moved or otherwise manipulated. Many verbs employed in experiencer-as-possessor predicates are verbs of motion and caused motion, like *keʔma* (both 'come up' and 'bring up', distinguished by different stem behavior), *kaŋma* 'fall', *haŋma* 'send', *lemnhaŋma* 'throw', *pokma* 'raise' or *lomma* (both 'take out' and 'come out'). Other verbs refer to physical change (both spontaneous and caused), such as *khoŋdiʔma* 'break down', *himma* 'whip/flog' or *kipma* 'cover tightly'. Most of the predicates acquire their experiential semantics only in the particular idiomatic combinations. Only a few verbs have intrinsic experiential semantics, like *tukma* 'hurt/be ill'.

---

[14] Stems in square brackets in the tables were not found as independent words beyond their use in these collocations.

Table 9.2: Intransitive experiencer-as-possessor predicates

PREDICATE	GLOSS	LITERAL TRANSLATION
{(S[EXP]-NOM/GEN) V-s[3]}		
chipma lomma	'have to pee'	(urine – come out)
hakamba keʔma	'yawn'	(yawn – come up)
hakchiŋba keʔma	'sneeze'	(sneeze – come up)
heli lomma	'bleed'	(blood – come out)
hi lomma	'have to defecate'	(shit – come out)
laŋ miŋma	'twist/sprain leg'	(leg – sprain)
laŋ sima	'have paraesthetic leg'	(leg – die)
miʔwa uŋma	'cry, shed tears'	(tear – come down)
niŋ-la sima	'be fed up'	([mind] – [spirit] – die)
niŋwa kaŋma	'give in, surrender'	(mind – fall)
niŋwa khoŋdiʔma	a)'be mentally ill'	(mind – break down)
	b)'be disappointed/sad'	
niŋwa ima	'feel dizzy'	(mind – revolve)
niŋwa tama	'be satisfied, content'	(mind – come)
niŋwa tukma	'be sad, be offended'	(mind – be ill/hurt)
niŋwa wama	'hope'	(mind – exist)
phok kama	'be full'	(stomach – be full/saturated)
pomma keʔma	'feel lazy'	(laziness – come up)
saklum phemma	'be frustrated'	(frustration – be activated)
ṭaŋ pokma	'be arrogant, naughty'	(horn – rise)
yuncama keʔma	'have to laugh, chuckle'	(laugh – come up)
yupma yuma	'be tired'	(sleepiness – be full)

Table 9.3: Transitive experiencer-as-possessor predicates, Class (a)

PREDICATE	GLOSS	LITERAL TRANSLATION
Class (a): {A[EXP]-ERG P[STIM]-NOM V-a[A].p[P]}		
chik ekma	'hate'	(hate – make break)
lok khoʔma	'be angry at'	(anger – scratch)
luŋma kipma	'be greedy'	(liver – cover tightly)
luŋma tukma	'love, have compassion'	(liver – pour)
na hemma	'be jealous'	([jealousy] – [feel])

Table 9.4: Transitive experiencer-as-possessor predicates, Class (b)

PREDICATE	GLOSS	LITERAL TRANSLATION
Class (b): {A[EXP]-ERG P[NOUN]-NOM V-a[A].p[3]}		
hi ema	'defecate'	(stool-defecate)
iklam saŋma	'clear throat, harrumph'	(throat – brush)
khaep cimma	'be satisfied, lose interest'	([interest] – be completed)
miʔwa saŋma	'mourn (ritually)'	(tear – brush)
nabhuk lemnhaŋma	'dishonor self/others'	(nose – throw away)
nabhuk yuŋma	'uphold own/ others' moral'	(nose – keep)
niŋwa chiʔma	'see reason, get grown up'	(mind – [get conscious])
niŋwa cokma	'pay attention'	(mind – do)
niŋwa hupma	'unite minds, decide together'	(mind – tighten, unite)
niŋwa lapma	'pull oneself together'	(mind – hold)
niŋwa lomma	'have/apply an idea'	(mind – take out)
niŋwa piʔma	'trust deeply'	(mind – give)
niŋwa yuŋma	'be careful'	(mind – put)
saya pokma	'raise head soul (ritually)'	(head soul – raise)
semla saŋma	'clear throat, clear voice'	(voice – brush)
sokma soma	'breathe'	(breath – breathe)
yupma cimma	'be well-rested'	(sleepiness – be completed)

Table 9.5: Transitive experiencer-as-possessor predicates, Classes (c)–(e)

PREDICATE	GLOSS	LITERAL TRANSLATION
Class (c): {P[STIM]-NOM V-a[3].p[P]} ~ {P[STIM]-ABL V-a[3].p[3]} ~ {Class (a)}		
chippa ke?ma	'be disgusted'	(disgust – bring up)
niŋsaŋ puŋma	'lose interest, have enough'	([interest] – [lose])
sokma himma	'be annoyed, be bored'	(breath – whip/flog)
sap thakma	'like'	([STEM] – send up)
Class (d): {A[NOUN]-ERG P[STIM]-NOM V-a[3].p[A/P]}		
niŋwa=ŋa cama	'feel sympathetic'	(mind=ERG – eat)
niŋwa=ŋa mundi?ma	'forget'	(mind=ERG – forget)
hop=ŋa khamma	'trust'	([STEM]-ERG – chew)
niŋwa=ŋa apma	'be clever, be witty'	(mind=ERG – bring)
lawa=ŋa na?nama	'be frozen in shock, be scared stiff'	(spirit=ERG – leave)
Class (e): {P[STIM]-ERG V-a[3].p[3]}		
muk khokma	'freezing/stiff hands'	(hand-chop)
mi?wa saŋma	(part of the death ritual)	(tear - brush off)
ya limma (transimp.)	'taste good'	(mouth - taste sweet)

9.2.3 Morphosyntactic properties

9.2.3.1 Wordhood vs. phrasehood

Experiencer-as-possessor predicates host both nominal and verbal morphology. A possessive prefix (referring to the experiencer) attaches to the noun, and the verbal inflection attaches to the verb. The verbal inflection always attaches to the verbal stem, so that the verbal prefixes stand between the noun and the verb (see (14)). It has been shown above that some of the psych-nouns can be inflected for number as well as trigger plural morphology on the verb, and that others may show case marking (see (8b) and (10a)).

(14) *a-luŋma*   *n-duŋ-me?-nen=na.*
      1SG.POSS-liver   NEG-pour-NPST-1>2=NMLZ.SG
      'I do not love you./I do not have compassion for you.'

The experiencer argument, which is always indexed by the possessive prefix on the noun, is rarely expressed overtly. It may show the following properties: it is in the nominative or in the genitive when the light verb is intransitive, and in the ergative in predicates that show transitive subject agreement with the experiencer argument (class (a) and (b)).

Noun and verb have to be adjacent, as shown by the following examples. Constituents like degree adverbs and quantifiers (see (15a) and (15b)) or question words (see (15c)) may not intervene.

(15) a. *tuknuŋ*   *u-niŋwa*   (*tuknuŋ*)   *tug-a-ma,*   [...]
          completely   3SG.POSS-mind   (*completely)   hurt[3SG]-PST-PRF
          'She was so sad, ...'   [38_nrr_07.009]

      b. *ka   khiŋ   pyak   a-ma=ŋa*   *u-luŋma*
          1SG so_much   much   1SG.POSS-mother=ERG   3SG.POSS-liver
          (*khiŋ   pyak)   *tuŋ-me-ŋ=na!*
          (*so_much   much)   pour[3SG.A]-NPST-1SG.P=NMLZ.SG
          'How much my mother loves me!'   [01_leg_07.079]

      c. *ijaŋ   n-lok*   (*ijaŋ*)
          why   2SG.POSS-anger   (*why)
          khot-a-ŋ-ga=na=i?
          scratch-PST-1SG.P-2SG.A=NMLZ.SG=Q
          'Why are you angry at me?'

Information-structural clitics, usually attaching to the rightmost element of the phrase, may generally stand between noun and verb, but some combinations were judged better than others (compare (16a) with (16b)). Compare also the impossible additive focus particle *=ca* in (16a) with the restrictive focus particle *=se* and the contrastive particle *=le* in (17). Overtly expressed experiencer arguments may naturally also host topic and focus particles, just like any other constituent can. This is shown, e.g., by (16b), (17c) and (17d).

(16) a. *a-yupma=ci(*=ca)*
          1SG.POSS-sleepiness=NSG(*=ADD)
          n-yus-a=ha=ci.
          3PL.A-be_full-PST=NMLZ.NSG=NSG
          Intended: 'I am tired, too (in addition to being in a bad mood).'

      b. *u-ṭaŋ=ca*   *pog-a-by-a=na.*
          3SG.POSS-horn=ADD   rise[3SG]-PST-V2.GIVE-PST=NMLZ.SG
          'She is also naughty.'

c. *ka=ca*   *a-yupma=ci*
1SG=ADD   1SG.POSS-sleepiness=NSG

n-yus-a=ha=ci.
3PL.A-be_full-PST=NMLZ.NSG=NSG

Only: 'I am also tired (in addition to you being tired).' (not, e.g., 'I am tired in addition to being hungry.')

(17)   a. *a-saklum=ci=se*
1SG.POSS-need=NSG=RESTR

m-phen-a-sy-a=ha=ci.
3PL-be_activated-PST-MDDL-PST=NMLZ.NSG=NSG

'I am just pining for it.'

    b. *uŋ=ŋa*   *u-ma*   *u-chik=se*
3SG=ERG   3SG.POSS-mother   3SG.POSS-hate=RESTR

ekt-uks-u-sa.
make_break-PRF-3.P[PST]-PST.PRF

'He had nothing but hate for his mother.'   [01_leg_07.065]

    c. *ka=go*   *a-sap=le*
1SG=TOP   1SG.POSS-[stem]=CTR

thakt-wa-ŋ=na.
send_up-NPST[3.P]-1SG.A=NMLZ.SG

'But I like it.' (said in contrast to another speaker)

    d. *uk=ka=se*   *o-pomma=ci*
3SG=GEN=RESTR   3SG.POSS-laziness=NSG

ŋ-gy-a=ha=ci.
3PL.A-come_up-PST=NMLZ.NSG=NSG

'Only he was lazy (not the others).'

The noun can even be omitted, in case it was already active in discourse, such as in the question-answer pair in (18). It is, however, not possible to extract the noun from the predicate to relativize on it, neither with the nominalizer *-khuba* nor with the nominalizers *=na* and *=ha* as shown in (19) (cf. Chapter 13). Furthermore, in my corpus there is not a single example of a noun in a possessive experiential construction that is modified independently. The predicate is always modified as a whole, by adverbial modification. A certain degree of morphological freedom does not imply that the noun is a full-fledged argument.

(18)   a. *ŋkha*   *mamu=ci*   *n-sap*
those   girl=NSG   2SG.POSS-[STEM]

                thakt-u-ci-g=ha=i?
                send_up-3.P[PST]-3NSG.P-2.A=NMLZ.NSG=Q
                'Do you like those girls?'

    b.   *thakt-u-ŋ-ci-ŋ=ha!*
         send_up-3.P[PST]-1SG.A-3NSG.P-1SG.A=NMLZ.NSG
         'I do!'

(19) a. **kek-khuba*   *(o-)pomma*
        come_up-NMLZ[S/A] (3SG.POSS-)laziness
        Intended: 'the laziness that comes up'

    b. **ky-a=na*   *(o-)pomma*
        come_up-PST=NMLZ.SG (3SG.POSS-)laziness
        Intended: 'the laziness that came up'

The noun-verb complex as a whole may serve as input to derivational processes, such as the creation of adjectives by means of a reduplication and the nominalizer *=na* or *=ha*, shown in (20).

(20) a. *uŋ* *tuknuŋ*   *luŋma-tuk-tuk=na*   *sa-ya-ma.*
        3SG completely liver-REDUPL-pour=NMLZ.SG be[3]-PST-PRF
        'She was such a kind (loving, caring) person.'   [01_leg_07.061]

    b. *ikhiŋ*   *chippa-ke-keʔ=na*   *takabaŋ!*
        how_much disgust-REDUPL-come_up=NMLZ.SG spider
        'What a disgusting spider!'

    c. *nna* *chik-ʔek-ʔek=na*   *babu*
        that hate-REDUPL-make_break=NMLZ.SG boy
        'that outrageous boy'

Wrapping up, just as we have seen above for the simple noun-verb predicates, the noun and the verb build an inseparable unit for some processes, but not for others; the predicates show both word-like and phrasal properties. Semantically, of course, noun and verb build one unit, but they can be targeted by certain morphological and syntactic processes: the nonsingular marking on psych-nouns, psych-nouns triggering agreement, the possibility of hosting phrasal clitics, and the partial ellipsis. The ambiguous status of these predicates is also reflected in their phonology: noun and verb are two units with respect to stress and voicing.

    Another feature distinguishes the possessive experiencer predicates from compounds: nouns in compounds are typically generic (Fabb 2001: 66, Haspelmath 2002: 156). As the noun in the possessive experiential predicates hosts the possessive prefix, its reference is made specific. The contiguity of noun and verb, the derivation of adjectives and the restrictions on extraction and modification also clearly show that noun and verb are one unit. All these conflicting properties of Yakkha add further support to approaches that question the notion of the word as opaque to morphosyntactic processes (as, e.g., stated in the Lexical Integrity Principle). The possessive experiential predicates may best be understood as lexicalized phrases, such as the predicates discussed in §9.1 above.

9.2.3.2 Behavioral properties of the experiencer arguments

Experiencers as morphologically downgraded, non-canonically marked subjects do not necessarily have to be downgraded in other parts of the grammar. As observed by Bickel (2004b), Tibeto-Burman languages, in contrast to Indo-Aryan languages, show a strong tendency to treat experiencers as full-fledged arguments syntactically. Yakkha confirms this generalization. In syntactic constructions that select pivots, the experiencer argument is chosen, regardless of the fact that it is often blocked from triggering verbal agreement. The nominalizer -khuba (S/A arguments) selects the experiencer, because it is the most agent-like argument in the clause (see (21)). As the ungrammatical (21c) shows, the stimulus cannot be nominalized by -khuba.

(21) a. *takaban*   *u-chippa*   *kek-khuba*   *mamu*
          spider   3SG.POSS-disgust   come_up-NMLZ   girl
          'the girl who is disgusted by spiders'
      b. *o-pomma*   *kek-khuba*   *babu*
          3SG.POSS-laziness   come_up-NMLZ   boy
          'the lazy fellow'
      c. **chippa*   *kek-khuba*   *camyonba*
          disgust   come_up-NMLZ   food
          Intended: 'disgusting food' (only: *chippakeke?na*)

Another process that exclusively selects S and A arguments is the converbal clause linkage, which is marked by the suffix -*san*. It implies that two (or more) events happen simultaneously, and it requires the referential identity of the S and A arguments in both clauses. Example (22) illustrates that this also holds for experiencer arguments.

(22) a. *o-pomma*   *kes-san*   *kes-san*   *kam*
          3SG.POSS-laziness   come_up-SIM   come_up-SIM   work
          cog-wa.
          do-NPST[3.P]
          'He does the work lazily.'

b. *uŋ   lok   khos-saŋ   lukt-a-khy-a=na.*
3SG anger   scratch-SIM   run[3SG]-PST-V2.GO-PST=NMLZ.SG
'He ran away angrily.'

In causatives, the experiencer is the causee, as is evidenced by the verbal marking in (23). There is no overt marking for 1.P, but the reference is retrieved from
the opposition to the other forms in the paradigm — with third person object
agreement, the inflected form would have to be *himmetugha.*

(23)   *khem=nuŋ   manoj=ŋa   a-sokma*
Khem=COM   Manoj=ERG   1SG.POSS-breath
him-met-a-g=ha!
whip-CAUS-PST-2.A[1.P]=NMLZ.NSG
'Khem and Manoj (you) annoy me!'

The last syntactic property discussed here is the agreement in complement-
taking verbs that embed infinitives, as for instance *yama* 'be able' or *tarokma*
'begin', shown in (24). Basically, the complement-taking verb mirrors the agreement that is found in the embedded verb. Those predicates whose experiencer
arguments do not trigger agreement in the verb do not show agreement in the
complement-taking verb either. Other restrictions are semantic in nature, so
that, for instance, 'I want to get lazy' is not possible, because being lazy is not
conceptualized as something one can do on purpose. Thus, the agreement facts
neither confirm nor contradict the generalization made above. A more interesting case is the periphrastic progressive construction, with the lexical verb in the
infinitive and an intransitively inflected auxiliary *-si?* (infinitial form and auxiliary got fused into one word). The auxiliary selects the experiencer as agreement
triggering argument (see (24b)).

(24)   a.   *ka   nda a-luŋma   tuk-ma*
1SG[ERG]   2SG   1SG.POSS-liver   pour-INF
n-ya-me?-nen=na.
NEG-be_able-NPST-1>2=NMLZ.SG
'I cannot love you./I cannot have pity for you.'
b.   *nda   ka   ijaŋ   n-lok*
2SG[ERG]   1SG   why   2SG.POSS-anger
kho?-ma-si-me-ka=na?
scratch-INF-AUX.PROG-NPST-2=NMLZ.SG
'Why are you being angry at me?'

10 Complex predication

This chapter deals with complex predication, i.e., with predicates that consist of multiple verbal stems. Yakkha follows a common South Asian pattern of complex predication where the verbs do not combine freely, but where a class of function verbs (cf. Schultze-Berndt 2006) has undergone grammaticalizations and lexicalizations (since not all verb-verb combinations are transparent).[1]

They are employed in various semantic domains; they specify the temporal structure or the spatial directedness of an event, they change the argument structure of a predicate, and they may also pertain to other kinds of information, such as modality, intentionality or the referential properties of the arguments. Notably, there are semantic restrictions; the function verbs select lexically defined subsets of verbal hosts, a matter which leaves potential for a deeper investigation. The two simple examples below show the verb *pi?ma* 'give' functioning as a benefactive marker (see (1a)), and the verb *khe?ma* 'go' functioning as a marker of directedness away from a reference point (see (1b)).

(1) a. *ka   katha   lend-a-by-a-ŋ.*
         1SG   story   exchange-IMP-V2.GIVE-IMP-1SG.P
         'Tell me a story.'
     b. *kisa   lukt-a-khy-a=na.*
         deer   run-PST-V2.GO-PST[3SG]=NMLZ.SG
         'The deer ran away.'

Both lexicalized and grammaticalized instances can be found among the complex predicates in Yakkha, and the line between lexicalizations and grammaticalizations is not always easy to draw. Most of the function verbs (V2s) display multiple functions, which are in close interaction with the lexical semantics of the verbal base they combine with. The expressive potential of function verbs is vast, and the productivity and transparency of complex predicates show great

---

[1] The concatenation of verbs to specify the verbal semantics is a frequent pattern in South Asia and beyond; see for instance Butt (1995); Hook (1991); Masica (2001); Nespital (1997); Pokharel (1999) on Indo-Aryan languages, and Matisoff (1969); DeLancey (1991); Bickel (1996); Ebert (1997a); Doornenbal (2009); Kansakar (2005) on other Tibeto-Burman languages, and Peterson (2010) on a Munda language.

variability, a fact that supports the view that the boundary between grammati-calization and lexicalization cannot always be drawn sharply.

This chapter is organized as follows: §10.1 introduces the formal properties of the Yakkha CPs and §10.2 discusses the functional range of each V2.

10.1 Formal properties

Complex predicates (CPs) are defined as expressing one event in a monoclausal structure that contains a sequence of verbs (Givón 1991). This makes complex predication similar to the definition of serial verb constructions (Aikhenvald 2006; Durie 1997), and yet there are significant differences, as we shall see below.

In Yakkha, usually two (and maximally four) verbal roots may be combined to yield a more specific verbal meaning.[2] The basic structure of a CP in Yakkha is as follows: the first verbal stem carries the semantic weight, and the second stem (the function verb or 'V2') takes over the "fine-tuning" of the verbal semantics, as in (2),[3] where the function verb -*nes*, with the lexical meaning 'lay', contributes aspectual (continuative) information. The class of V2s in Yakkha is closed (syn-chronically) and relatively small; it comprises just twenty-five verbs.[4] Most of the V2s have a corresponding lexical verbal stem, but there are also three morphemes that behave like function verbs without having a transparent verbal etymology (treated here as well, because of their similarity to "proper" function verbs. Com-plex predicates (including transparent and non-transparent CPs) roughly make up one third of the verbal lexicon. In the recorded data of natural discourse, CPs make up only 17% (across genres), but the current size of the corpus does not allow any strong statistical claims.

(2) *ka*　　　*yog-u-nes-wa-ŋ=ha.*
　　　1SG[ERG]　search-3.P-V2.LAY-NPST[3.P]-1SG.A=NMLZ.NC
　　　'I (will) keep searching for it.'　　　　　　　　　　[18_nrr_03.008]

---

[2] I have no evidence for predicates consisting of more than four stems in my Yakkha corpus, but I do not have negative evidence either.

[3] As several stems have more than one function, depending on their lexical host, I have decided to gloss them with their lexical meaning.

[4] There are a few V2 that only occur once in my data, and that are not treated further here, as generalizations about their function in complex predication are not possible yet: *yukt* 'put down (for)', *cok* 'make' and *rokt* (*tokt*) 'get'.

As mentioned in the introduction, Yakkha has both grammaticalized and lexicalized CPs; one and the same V2 may have simultaneously developed a regular and productive function and an unpredictable, idiomatic meaning, which is not too surprising, as both developments have their origin in the metaphorical extension of verbal meanings. The distinction between lexicalized and grammaticalized forms is gradual, which has long been acknowledged in the typological literature (Lehmann 2002; Diewald 2010; Lichtenberk 1991; Himmelmann 2004) and in methodological approaches to grammar writing and lexicography (Schultze-Berndt 2006; Mosel 2006; Enfield 2006).[5] Structurally, there is no way to distinguish lexicalized and grammaticalized CPs; they show completely identical behavior. Thus, although it may hold on the level of individual tokens, the distinction between symmetrical and asymmetrical complex predicates that is made in Aikhenvald (2006), is not useful in determining the different types of CPs in Yakkha. There is, however, a tendency towards grammaticalization in the function verbs. All of the V2s have a grammaticalized function, and just some of them appear in idiosyncratic verb combinations as well. In order to capture the correspondences between the lexical semantics of the V2s on the one hand and their lexicalized and grammaticalized occurrences on the other hand, an excursus into the lexicon is inevitable in this chapter.

The CPs in Yakkha roughly match criteria (a)—(e) of the definition of serial verb constructions in Aikhenvald (2006: 1):

- (a) The verbs act together to refer to one single event.

- (b) No overt marker of coordination, subordination, or syntactic dependency may occur.

- (c) CPs are monoclausal (clause-final markers occur only after the last verb).

- (d) CPs share tense, aspect and polarity values (i.e., these values can only be specified once).[6]

- (e) CPs share core (and other) arguments.

- (f) Each component of the construction must be able to occur on its own.

---

[5] Cf. also the distinction between 'collocation' and 'construction' in Svensén (2009).

[6] However, tense and aspect interact with the meanings of the V2 independently of the lexical verbs, and some V2 block certain tense/aspect markers, e.g., the immediate prospective V2 *-heks* 'be about to' is not possible with imperfective aspect.

Criterion (a) and the question what constitutes one event is not trivial; most events one can think of are inherently complex and consist of several subevents. The criterion developed in Bohnemeyer et al. (2007) proved to be useful in answering this question. It refers to the tightness of packaging of subevents that constitute one complex event. Bohnemeyer et al. (2007) call this criterion the *Macro-Event-Property (MEP)*:

> A construction has the MEP if it packages event representations such that temporal operators necessarily have scope over all subevents. (Bohnemeyer et al. 2007: 504–5)

This criterion applies to all CPs in Yakkha, regardless of their individual functions.

Criterion (b) distinguishes Yakkha CPs from infinitive constructions with auxiliaries, from complement-taking verbs and from periphrastic tense forms involving converbal markers.

Criterion (c), monoclausality, usually correlates with eventhood.[7] As the CPs constitute one word (by the criteria of stress, morphophonological rules and clitic placement), the question of monoclausality is trivial in Yakkha. Further formal criteria are clause-final markers such as nominalizers, converbs; they are never found inside a CP.

Criterion (d) is restricted to modal and polarity markers in Yakkha, while the V2s interact with tense and aspect markers in their own ways.

Most definitions of serial verbs have the requirement that at least one argument should be shared. In nearly all of the Yakkha CPs in my data, all arguments are shared; the CPs are formed by nuclear juncture in the sense of Foley & Van Valin (1984: 190).

Yakkha CPs differ from serial verbs as defined above, and also from function verbs as they are defined by Schultze-Berndt (2006: 362) in criterion (f): not all function verbs can be found synchronically as independent lexical verbs. One morpheme (the middle marker *-si?*) looks and behaves like a verbal stem, but can be traced back to a Proto-Tibeto-Burman suffix.[8] The fact that suffixes even got reanalyzed as V2s show how salient complex predication is in the organization of the Yakkha verbal system. Another hybrid marker is *-i ~ -ni*, tentatively called *transitive completive* here. It occurs in paradigmatic opposition to another V2 *-pi? ~ -di?* 'give' which is found on intransitive verbs, yielding causative-inchoative

---

[7] But cf. Foley (2010) for a different view and counterexamples.
[8] The cognate Belhare reflexive marker *-chind* is a result of exactly the same development (Bickel 2003: 560).

correspondences like *ma?nima* 'lose' - *mandi?ma* 'get lost'. This marker (*-i* ~ -*ni*) has no corresponding lexical verb either, and it does not license the typical double inflection that is found on CPs (see the discussion of the morphological structure of the CPs that follows this paragraph). But its occurrence in infinitives and its opposition to another V2 make it look like a V2 itself. Note that these two markers *-si?* and *-i* ~ -*ni*, although discussed here along with V2s, are not labelled 'V2' in the glosses.

In what follows I will outline the morphological structure of the CPs. The Yakkha pattern (and generally the Kiranti pattern) of complex predication differs from what we know from its Indo-Aryan sister construction (mostly termed *(explicator) compound verbs* in the Indo-Aryan descriptive tradition). In Indo-Aryan CPs, the inflection typically applies only to the V2 (Montaut 2004; Butt 1997; Hook 1991). In Yakkha, both verbs take inflectional material, though their inflection is subject to certain rules. They are laid out below, similar to Doornenbal's analysis of Bantawa CPs (Doornenbal 2009: 251).

- Prefixes attach to the first verb (V.lex).

- The full suffix string attaches to the final, typically the second, verb (V2).

- The V.lex takes maximally one inflectional suffix, and only if it has purely vocalic quality (i.e., *-a* 'PST/IMP/SBJV', *-i* '1/2PL' or *-u* '3.P').

- There is no morphology on the first verb that is not underlyingly present in the complete suffix string, i.e., no morphologically empty 'dummy elements' are inserted.

- Only inflectional suffixes, but not phrasal clitics,[9] clause-level particles or clause linkage markers attach to the V.lex.

- Marked vowel or consonant sequences may block the inflection of the V.lex (for details see further below).

This pattern is henceforth called *recursive inflection* (following the terminology and analyis in Bickel et al. 2007a on Chintang). As these rules show, the recursive inflection is both phonologically and morphologically informed. A prosodic constraint requires a disyllabic host for the V2, but the fulfillment of this requirement is conditioned by the availability of inflectional material, i.e., no dummy

---

[9] Placing clitics between the verbal stems is indeed possible, for instance in Chintang (Bickel et al. 2007a).

material is inserted. Example (2) above and example (3) illustrate the recursive inflection: the first verb hosts the prefix and maximally one inflectional suffix, while the full suffix string and further material attach to the second verb. The V2 -*khe?* 'go' indicates the directedness of the movement away from a point of reference, and the V2 -*nes* 'lay' indicates continuative aspect in (2).

(3) *asen*   *lukt-i-khe-i-ŋ=ha.*
yesterday   run-1PL-V2.GO-1PL-EXCL=NMLZ.NSG
'Yesterday we ran away.'

Suffixes containing consonants cannot stand between lexical verb and V2. The infinitive marker -*ma*, for instance, only attaches to the second verb, hence the verb in (3b) has the citation form *khuŋkhe?ma*. In this respect, Yakkha is different from closely related languages such as Bantawa and Puma, where the infinitive marker attaches to both verbs in a CP (Doornenbal 2009; Bickel et al. 2006).[10] Yakkha CPs seem to be more tightly fused than the corresponding constructions in neighbouring languages, also with respect to other features such as stress and clitic placement (cf. §3.5.1).

Certain phonological conditions may block the inflection of the first verb, too, namely V2 stems that start in /h/ or in a vowel (or stems that consist merely of a vowel). This is exemplified for /h/-initial V2 in (4), and for vowel-initial V2 in (5).

(4) a. *so-haks-u-ci*   *se=ppa.*
look-V2.SEND-3.P[PST]-3NSG.P   RESTR=EMPH
'He just glanced at them (his eyes following them as they went).'
[34_pea_04.044]

    b. *yuŋ-heks-a!*
sit-V2.CUT-IMP
'Sit here (while I go somewhere else).'

(5) a. *u-laŋ=ci*   *le?-end-u-ci=ha.*
3SG.POSS-leg=NSG   drop-V2.INSERT-3.P[PST]-3NSG.P=NMLZ.NSG
'It (the plane) lowered its landing gear.'

    b. *jhyal*   *peg-end-u=na.*
window   shatter-V2.INSERT-3.P[PST]=NMLZ.SG
'He (accidentally, unfortunately) shattered the window.'

---

[10] Doornenbal (2009: 255), for instance, provides the infinitive of 'forget': *manmakhanma*.

Furthermore, when certain stem combinations result in phonologically marked sequences like CV-V(C) and CVʔ-V(C), [n] may be inserted (see (6) and §3.5.7 for the exact conditions, e.g., for the reason why this does not happen in cases like (5a)).

(6)   a.   *leʔ-nen-saŋ*
           /leʔ-end-saŋ/
           drop-V2.INSERT-CVB
           'dropping'

      b.   *pin-nhaŋ-saŋ*
           /piʔ-haks-saŋ/
           give-V2.SEND-CVB
           'marrying off (one's daughter)'

The first verb and the function verb do not necessarily have the same valency, as several of the previous examples and (7) show. In (7a), the sequence is transitive-intransitive, yielding an intransitive predicate; the sequence in (7b) is notably labile-ditransitive, yielding an intransitive predicate. Thus, either verb can be relevant for the argument structure of the whole predicate. However, the components of a CP are nearly always synchronized with respect to their valency; in general, the inflectional morphology attaching to the CP must be either from the transitive or from the intransitive paradigm.

The two predicates shown in (7) both have non-transparent, lexicalized semantics, but there is a difference in the relations between first verb and V2. In (7a), the verb *khus* with the independent meaning 'steal' acquires a new meaning in combination with a V2 with motion verb semantics. Apart from 'go', other V2s are possible as well, such as *-ra* 'come', that can indicate that someone came fleeing. The verb *maks* in (7b) does not occur independently, only in combination with various V2s. The V2 here mainly specifies the intransitive valency.[11]

(7)   a.   *khus-a-khy-a=na.*
           steal-PST-V2.GO[3SG]-PST=NMLZ.SG
           'He escaped.'

      b.   *maks-a-by-a=na.*
           be_surprised-PST-V2.GIVE[3SG]-PST=NMLZ.SG
           'He was surprised.'

---

[11] It might seem anti-intuitive, but the function of the V2 'give' is indeed detransitivization, similar to so-called 'give' passives (more below).

V2s can also be further grammaticalized to become suffixes and lose their verbal qualities. For instance, the etymological sources of the two nonpast allomorphs -me? and -wa are most certainly the two verbal stems me? ~ me 'do, apply'[12] and wa 'exist' (their choice depending on the participant scenario, see §8.4.1). These two morphemes occupy different slots in the verbal inflection, they do not occur in the infinitives, and they do not license the recursive inflection, which shows that they are not treated as V2s any more. In a similar way, the perfect tense markers -ma and -uks seem to have developed from verbal stems.[13]

10.2 The functions of the V2s

Table 10.1 provides an overview of the various V2 stems, their productive functions and their lexical origin, as far as it could be determined. As one can see, it is rather the norm that the V2s have more than one meaning or function; they are multi-faceted, which reflects the degree of their grammaticalization. Instances of lexicalizations will be discussed in the corresponding sections on each V2. The grammatical functions and the occurrence of a V2 in a lexicalized CP usually show some semantic parallels.

As the table shows, many V2s are motion verbs; they are used to specify events with respect to their relation to the surrounding landscape, along the two parameters of (i) the cline of the hill and (ii) the directedness towards or away from a point of reference, which is often, but not necessarily, the speech situation.

For the V2s whose functions are mostly related to argument structure (-pi?, -i, -ca, -si?) the reader is also referred to §11.3. Some V2s, especially those specifying the spatial orientation, can only attach to a host that matches in transitivity, while others are not constrained regarding transitivity. They inflect intransitively when their lexical host verb is intransitive, and transitively when the lexical verb

---

[12] At least diachronically, as evidence from neighbouring languages shows. In Yakkha, this verb only means 'put (waistband) around the waist'.

[13] Butt (2010: 66) makes a point that function verbs ('vector verbs' in Butt (2010) and most works from the Indo-Aryan descriptive tradition) are a class distinct from, e.g., auxiliaries. This is confirmed by the Yakkha data as well as data from neighbouring languages such as Chintang (Bickel et al. 2007a), as function verbs and auxiliaries can co-occur in one clause. However, her claim that vector verbs are not subject to historical change as much as auxiliaries are cannot be confirmed in light of the verbal origin of some verbal suffixes in Yakkha and other Kiranti languages. The grammaticalization path proposed in Hopper & Traugott (1993: 108), namely: lexical verb (>vector verb) > auxiliary > clitic > affix is unlikely, as the CPs are already one word phonologically, and the historical change towards an affix apparently took place without the intermediate stage of an auxiliary.

is transitive. The valency values in the table have to be understood as maximally possible values.

The functions of the V2s pertaining to the temporal structure of a predicate have to be understood as tentative labels; since in-depth analysis of the verbal semantics, tense and aspect in Yakkha goes beyond the scope of this work and deserves a study in its own right.

10.2.1 The V2 *-pi?* (benefactive, affected participants)

Verbs of giving are often found grammaticalized as benefactive markers crosslinguistically. In Yakkha, the verb *pi?ma* 'give' has acquired the following grammatical functions: benefactive/malefactive, indicating affected participants (without necessarily expressing a causer), and a completive notion, translatable as 'already', 'inevitably' or 'definitely'. Furthermore, it is found as a marker of intransitive valency in intransitive-causative pairs of lexicalized CPs.

In the benefactive function, the argument structure of the predicate changes, and a beneficiary participant is added as G argument to the verbal argument structure (note the agreement with the first person patient in (8b)). The morphosyntactic properties of the benefactive derivation are discussed in §11.3.3.

(8) a. *end-u-bi-ŋ=ha.*
         insert-3.P[PST]-V2.GIVE-1SG.A=NMLZ.NSG
         'I poured her (some sauce).'
     b. *ka   katha   lend-a-by-a-ŋ.*
         1SG   story   exchange-IMP-V2.GIVE-IMP-1SG.P
         'Tell me a story.'

The effect on the 'beneficiary' is not necessarily a desirable one; the V2 can also be employed to convey malefactive or at least undesirable events, as shown by (9). Beneficiaries and also negatively affected participants gain syntactic properties that are typical of arguments; they trigger agreement in the verb and they qualify as antecedents of reciprocal derivations (see §11.3.3).

(9) a. *yakkha ce?ya   cek-ma=niŋa   limbu   ce?ya*
         Yakkha language speak-INF=CTMP   Limbu   language
         ceŋ-bi-me=ha!
         speak-V2.GIVE-NPST[1.P]=NMLZ.NSG
         'While talking in Yakkha, they answer in Limbu!'
     b. *khus-het-i-bi.*
         steal-V2.CARRY.OFF-COMPL-V2.GIVE[3.P;PST]
         'He stole it (the basket) from him and carried it away.' [34_pea_04.024]

Table 10.1: Yakkha V2s, their functions and their lexical origins

V2	FUNCTION	LEX. MEANING	VALENCY
-pi?	(a) benefactive/malefactive (b) affected participants	'give'	3
(-pi? ~ -di?)	(c) telic, completive (intrans.)		1
-i ~ -ni	completive (trans.)	(only V2)	2
-ca	(a) reflexive, (b) autobenefactive, (c) middle (intentional)	'eat'	2 (but often detransitivized)
-si?	middle (unintentional)	(only V2)	1
-khe?	(a) motion away (b) telic (S/P arguments)	'go'	1
-ra (*ta)	motion towards	'come (from fur- ther away)'	1
-ra? (*ta?)	caused motion towards	'bring (from fur- ther away)'	3
-uks	motion down towards	'come down'	1
-ukt	caused motion down towards	'bring down'	3
-ap	motion towards	'come (from close nearby)'	1
-apt	caused motion towards	'bring (from close nearby)'	3
-ris (*tis)	caused motion to a distant goal	'invest, place'	3
-bhes	caused horizontal motion	'send, bring here'	3
-end ~ -neN	(a) caused motion downwards, (b) accidental actions, regret	'insert, apply'	3
-ket	caused motion up and towards	'bring up'	3
-haks ~ -nhaŋ	(a) caused motion up and away (b) irreversible caused change- of-state	'send'	3
-khet ~ -het	(a) caused motion away (b) telic, excessiveness (transi- tive)	'carry off'	3
-a ~ -na	do X and leave object behind	(only V2)	3
-nes	continuative	'lay'	3
-nuŋ	continuative	(probably yuŋ 'sit')	1
-bhoks	punctual, sudden events	'split'	2
-heks	(a) immediate prospective (b) do separately	'cut'	2
-ghond	spatially distributed events	'roam'	2
-si?	prevent, avoid	(probably sis 'kill')	2
-so?	find out, experience	'look'	2

c. *a-nuncha*   *a-namcyaŋ=be*
    1SG.POSS-younger_sibling 1SG.POSS-cheek=LOC
    thokt-a-by-a-ŋ=na!
    spit-PST-V2.GIVE-PST-1SG.P=NMLZ.SG
    'My little brother spat on my cheeks!'

The V2 *-piʔ* 'give' can also indicate that some participant is affected by the event in undesirable ways, a common function in East Asian languages, also known as *adversative passive* or *'give' passive* (Keenan & Dryer 2007; Yap & Shoichi 1998). This usage differs from the benefactive in semantic and in formal ways. In the benefactive derivation the lexical verb can be marked by a suffix *-t* under certain conditions (see §11.3.3). This is not possible in non-benefactive functions of *-piʔ*. Furthermore, the resulting CP is always intransitive. A volitional agent and an intentional action are not necessarily implied. The affected participant is often non-overt, and its reference is retrieved from the context or from possessive marking (see (10c)-(10d)). The affected-participant usage of *-piʔ* can be distinguished from the benefactives also by a special infinitival form of this V2, the suppletive stem *-diʔ*, which is only found in the intransitive usage of 'give'.

(10) a. *wasik   n-da-ya-n,*   *nnakha   ghak*
          rain   NEG-come[3SG]-PST-NEG   that   all
          her-a-by-a=hoŋ,   ...
          dry-PST-V2.GIVE[3SG]-PST=SEQ
          'It did not rain, (and) after all that (i.e., their crops) dried up, ...'
                                                              [14_kth_02.005]

      b. *ka   tug-a-by-a-ŋ=na.*
          1SG   get_ill-PST-V2.GIVE-PST-1SG=NMLZ.SG
          'I got ill.'

      c. *a-khon*   *thot-a-by-a=na.*
          1SG.POSS-neck   get_stiff-PST-V2.GIVE[3SG]-PST=NMLZ.SG
          'My neck got stiff.'

      d. *a-yaŋ*   *mas-a-by-a=ha.*
          1SG.POSS-money   lose-PST-V2.GIVE[3SG]-PST=NMLZ.NSG
          'My money got lost.' (note that the pronunciation is [masabhya])

The following semantic minimal pair also illustrates the semantic nuance added by *-piʔ* in contrast to *-kheʔ*. Example (11a) is a statement about food that has been rotten for some time past, while in (11b) this fact is a new discovery that forces people to change their plans for the meal.

(11) a.   *kind-a-khy-a=na.*
           decay-PST-V2.GO[3SG]-PST=NMLZ.SG
           'It is rotten (since long ago.)'

      b.   *kind-a-by-a=na.*
           decay-PST-V2.GO[3SG]-PST=NMLZ.SG
           'It is rotten (but we had the plan to eat it now).'

The V2 *-pi? ~ -di?* is also found in lexicalized CPs, contributing transitivity information. Certain lexical stems never occur independently; they have to be in a complex predicate construction. Their valency is not specified; different V2s may combine with them to specify their transitivity. There are two corresponding sets of predicates: one intransitive, built by adding the V2 *-pi? ~ -di?* 'give', and one transitive, built by adding the marker *-i ~ -ni* (see §10.2.2 below) to the lexical verb. This alternation is illustrated by (12) and (13). The alternations do not always have the same direction in terms of argument structure. In (12), the intransitive subject corresponds to the P argument in the corresponding transitive predicate, while in (13), it corresponds to the A argrument. Table 10.2 provides further examples of this symmetrical alternation.

(12) a.   *maŋmaŋ-miŋmiŋ   m-maks-a-by-a-ma.*
           surprised-REDUPL   3PL-wonder-PST-V2.GIVE-PST-PRF
           'They were utterly surprised.'   [22_nrr_05.026]

      b.   *ka   nda   mak-ni-me?-nen=na.*
           1SG[ERG]   2SG   wonder-COMPL-NPST-1>2=NMLZ.SG
           'I will surprise you.'

(13) a.   *ka   mund-a-by-a-ŋ=na.*
           1SG   forget-PST-V2.GIVE-PST-1SG=NMLZ.SG
           'I was forgetful.'

      b.   *mu?-ni-nen=na.*
           forget-COMPL-1>2=NMLZ.SG
           'I forgot you.'

A different kind of lexicalization is shown in (14). Here, the lexical verb has an independent meaning (see (14a)), but it changes in unpredictable ways in the CP. However, the notion of an affected participant remains valid in this example, too.

(14) a.   *khap yoŋ-ma   tarokt-uks-u.*
           roof   shake-INF   start-PRF-3.P[PST]
           'The roof started shaking.'   [27_nrr_06.031]

Table 10.2: Transitivity alternations indicated by *-pi?* ~ *-di?* and *-(n)i*

INTRANSITIVE		TRANSITIVE	
mundi?ma	'be forgetful'	*mu?nima*	'forget'
maŋdi?ma	'be surprised'	*maknima*	'surprise'
mandi?ma	'get lost'	*ma?nima*	'lose'
phomdi?ma	'spill, get spilled'	*phopnima*	'spill'
himdi?ma	'(be) spread'	*hipnima*	'spread'

b. *pik   yoŋ-a-by-a=na.*
    cow   shake-PST-V2.GIVE[3SG]-PST=NMLZ.SG
    'The cow got scared.'

Furthermore, the V2 *-pi?* may emphasize the orientation towards an end point or to the completion of an event, best translatable with the adverb *already* in English (see (15)).

(15) a. *mi=go   sy-a-by-a-ma*   [*sebyama*].
          fire=TOP   die-PST-V2.GIVE[3SG]-PST-PRF
          'But the fire has gone out already.' (said to indicate that there is no need to extinguish it)

      b. *makai   end-i-bi-g=ha?*
          corn   insert-2PL-V2.GIVE-2=NMLZ.NSG
          'Did you already plant the corn?'   [06_cvs_01.080]

      c. *ca-ya-by-a-ŋ=na.*
          eat-PST-V2.GIVE-PST-1SG=NMLZ.SG
          'I already finished eating (the whole procedure is done, including washing hands).'

Finally, *-pi?* ~ *-di?* can also express that something happens immediately, inevitably, without delay or with certainty. Such a function, again, is only found with intransitive verbs (see (16)).

(16) a. *duru   nam-ma=hoŋ   a-chippa*
          cow_milk   smell-INF=SEQ   1SG.POSS-disgust
          ŋ-gen-di-me.
          3PL-come_up-V2.GIVE-NPST
          'Smelling milk, I will certainly get disgusted.'

b. *am-di-me-ŋ=na.*
come-V2.GIVE-NPST-1SG=NMLZ.SG
'I will come without delay.'

To conclude, this V2 shows an immense variety of functions (the Nepali trans-lations need as much as three different verbs to cover the range of this marker: *dinu* 'give', *hālnu* 'insert' and *saknu* 'finish'), and a deeper understanding of the interactions of this V2 with the respective lexical hosts would require more re-search.

10.2.2 The quasi-V2 *-i ~ -ni* (completive)

The marker *-i ~ -ni* partly behaves like a V2,[14] although is does not correspond to a lexical verb. It marks completed transitive actions (see (17) and §8.4.5). As it codes transitivity information, it stands in complementary distribution with the intransitive completive use of the V2 *-pi?* 'give', as examples (12) and (13) and Table 10.2 in §10.2.1 above have illustrated. The alternation between *-i* and *-ni* is phonologically conditioned: the allomorph *-ni* surfaces before consonants (see §3.5). If *-i* is followed by a vowel, it may also become a glide, as in (17c).

(17)   a.   *uŋci-camyoŋba   ŋ-geks-a-n,   nam=ŋa   ghak*
3NSG.POSS-food   NEG-ripen[3SG]-PST-NEG   sun=ERG   all
her-i.
dry-COMPL[PST;3.P]
'Their food did not ripen, the sun dried up everything.'
[14_nrr_02.004]

b.   *nhaŋ   pik=ci=ca   chu?-ni-ma   pʌrne=bu,*
and_then   cow=NSG=ADD   tie-COMPL-INF[DEONT]   have_to=REP
luŋkhwak=ca   ho?-ni-ma   pʌrne.
stone=ADD   pierce-COMPL-INF[DEONT]   have_to
'And he both had to tie the cows, they say, and he had to hole out a (grinding) stone.'[15]
[11_nrr_01.005]

c.   *n-chimd-y-uks-u-n-ci-ŋa-n=ha.*
NEG-ask-COMPL-PRF-3.P[PST]-NEG-3NSG.P-1SG.A-NEG=NMLZ.NSG
'I have not finished asking them.'

---

[14] Like V2 stems, it appears in the infinitival form of a CP, in contrast to inflectional affixes that never occur in infinitives, even when they have V2 origin (cf. §10.1). It does not license the recursive inflection pattern, though.

[15] Context: the protagonist has to finish tasks within one night in order to win a bet.

There are also some lexicalized instances of this marker. In *toknima* 'touch', for instance, the interpretation is holistic and cannot be achieved by analytic decomposition of the predicate into its components. The verbal stem *tok(t)* means 'get' when it occurs independently. Another example is *themnima* 'compare', with a stem *themd* that is not attested independently.

10.2.3 The V2 *-ca* (reflexive, middle, autobenefactive)

The polysemous V2 *-ca* 'eat' covers both grammatical and lexical functions. It has grammaticalized into a reflexive marker, characterized by detransitivizing effects on the syntax. Related to these functions, but semantically distinct, is the employment in autobenefactive derivations and in lexical compounding. The lexicalized CPs are verbs of grooming and social interaction: what they all have in common is the typically intended and beneficial affectedness of the subject. In this function, *-ca* does not necessarily have a detransitivizing effect.

The reflexive is constructed by attaching *-ca* 'eat' to the lexical verb (see (18)). The resulting CP is always intransitively inflected. The A and P arguments have identical reference and thus they are expressed by a single noun phrase, which is in the nominative case and triggers agreement on the verb. See §11.3.4 for a detailed discussion of the reflexive function of *-ca*).

(18) *babu=ci   n-jond-a-ca-ya-ci.*
      boy=NSG   3PL-praise-3.P-V2.EAT-PST-NSG
      'The boys praised themselves.'

In the following, the autobenefactive effect of *-ca* will be described. Example (19a) shows the stem *pha?* 'knit, weave, plait', which is typically transitive, with the result of the activity as object. However, the addition of *-ca* changes the interpretation to 'knit something for oneself' shown in (19b). The verbal peson marking also changes to intransitive, but a P argument can still be expressed; semantically this is still a transitive verb.

(19) a. *tamphwak   pha?-uks-u-g=ha.*
          hair   weave-PRF-3.P[PST]-2.A=NMLZ.NC
          'Did you plait (your) hair?'
      b. *ka   phurluŋ   phan-ca-me-ŋ=na.*
          1SG little_box weave-V2.EAT-NPST-1SG=NMLZ.SG
          'I weave a *phurlung* (little box out of bamboo stripes) for myself.'

The verb *so?* 'look' in (20) is also transitive. It changes to intransitive inflection when -*ca* is attached, and the former P argument is now marked with a locative (20b). This is not a reflexive construction, the semantics do not entail that the A argument looks at photos of herself. Rather, the V2 alters the semantics to the effect that a specific P argument is not necessary. If it is overtly expressed, it hosts a locative case marker. Omitting overt arguments is fine in both clauses, as all arguments can be dropped easily in Yakkha, but in (a) a P argument is still implied, which is not the case for (b). The typical situation here is that someone is looking at nothing in particular, but enjoying a nice view, or someone who dreams with his eyes wide open.

As already mentioned, the valency of the lexical verb is not necessarily changed in the autobenefactive. In contrast to the reflexive and the reciprocal, intransitive verbs can serve as input to this derivation, as the verb *khe?ma* 'go' in (21). The V2 here indicates an action that is intended for one's own enjoyment, i.e., going to the police post without a particular reason, but just to have a chat with the policemen.

(20)   a.   *so-ks-u-ga=na=i?*
            look-PRF-3.P[PST]-2.A=NMLZ.SG=Q
            'Have you looked at it?'
    b.   *ka*   *(phoṭo=be)*   *son-ca-me-ŋ=na.*
            1SG   (phoṭo=LOC)   look-V2.EAT-NPST-1SG=NMLZ.SG
            'I look dreamily (at the photos).'

(21)   *a-ppa*   *pulis=be*   *khen-ca-me?=na.*
        1SG.POSS-father   police=LOC   go-V2.EAT[3SG]-NPST=NMLZ.SG
        'Father goes to the police (to have a chat).'

Another verb illustrating the use of the V2 -*ca* is *koncama* 'take a walk', derived from the transitive verb *kot* 'walk (around, from place to place)' in (22a), from a poem about a butterfly.[16] The underived verb *kot* is transitively inflected and takes the respective stations as objects, but never the goal of a movement. As (22b) shows, the V2 adds the notion of 'consuming' and enjoying a walk.

(22)   a.   *phuŋ*   *phuŋ*   *kos-saŋ*
            flower   flower   walk-SIM
            'walking from flower to flower'   [04_leg_03.038]
    b.   *kon-ca-se*   *khe-i?*
            walk-V2.EAT-SUP   go-1PL[SBJV]
            'Shall we go for a walk?'

---

[16] The stem is realized as [kos] due to assimilation to the following sibilant.

To wrap up, the self-benefactive use of the V2 *ca* may, but does not have to result in detransitivization. The P argument can still be expressed, but it is typically less central to the event.

The V2 *-ca* is also found in verb-verb sequences with holistic, unpredictable meanings, where the V2 interacts individually with the respective verbal meanings. Occasionally *-ca* refers to the literal eating in verb-verb sequences, as in *sincama* 'hunt, i.e., kill and eat', *ŋoncama* 'fry and eat', *komcama* 'pick up and eat' and *hamcama* 'devour, bite and eat'. This transparent usage is possibly the etymological source from which the various grammaticalized functions and metaphorical meanings have emerged. A few examples, such as those shown in (23), suggest that *-ca* may also convey adversative contexts, pretty much the opposite of the autobenefactive notion.

(23) a.   *moŋ-ca-khuba*   *babu*
            beat-V2.EAT-S/A.NMLZ   boy
            'the boy who gets beaten up (regularly)'

      b.   *cuŋ=ŋa*   *n-laŋ=ci*
            cold=ERG   2SG.POSS-leg=NSG
            khokt-u-co-ci=ha?
            chop-3.P[PST]-V2.EAT[3.P;PST]-NSG=NMLZ.NSG
            'Did your legs get stiff from the cold?' (Lit.: 'Did the cold chop off and eat your legs?')

The lexicalized predicates with *-ca* are presented in Table 10.3. Their semantics are non-compositional and non-transparent. They cover bodily functions and sensations, social interactions and actions performed for one's own benefit or enjoyment. Formally, they are not different from the reflexive and autobenefactive examples shown above, but transitive predicates are more frequent within the lexicalized predicates. Examples of the metaphorical predicates are provided in (24).

(24) a.   *haiko=ha=ci*
            other=NMLZ.NSG=NSG
            lem-u-ca-ŋ-ci-ŋ=ha.
            flatter-3.P[PST]-V2.EAT-1SG.A-NSG.P-1SG.A–NMLZ.NSG
            'I cheated the others.'

      b.   *ka*   *mi*   *huŋ-u-ca-ŋ=na.*
            1SG[ERG]   fire   bask-3.P[PST]-V2.EAT-1SG=NMLZ.SG
            'I basked in the heat of the fire.'

Table 10.3: Some lexicalizations with the V2 *-ca* 'eat'

VERB	GLOSS	LEX. STEM	GLOSS
chemcama	'tease'	*chemd*	'tease'
hencama	'defeat'	*hes*	–
lemcama	'cheat, deceive'	*lem*	'flatter, persuade'
luncama	'backbite'	*lu?*	'tell'
incama	'sell'	*in*	'buy'
	'buy and eat'	*in*	'buy'
oncama	'overtake, outstrip'	*ond*	'block'
huŋcama	'bask'	*huŋ*	–
incama	'play'	*is*	'rotate, revolve'
suncama	'itch'	*sus*	'get sour'
yuncama	'laugh, smile'	*yut*	'sharpen'

c. ka   uŋ   luk-ma=be
    1SG[ERG] 3SG   run-INF=LOC
    ond-u-ca-ŋ=na.
    block-3.P[PST]-V2.EAT-1SG.A=NMLZ.SG
    'I outstripped him in running.'

The most transparent use of *ca* is shown in (25): the V2 retains its lexical meaning. The same content could as well be expressed in two independent clauses. The verbs participating in the CP share all arguments, which motivates the choice of a CP instead of two clauses.

(25) ka   makkai   ŋo-c-wa-ŋ=ha.
      1SG[ERG]   corn   fry-V2.EAT-NPST[3.P]-1SG.A=NMLZ.NSG
      'I make popcorn and eat it.'

Having looked at the whole range of functions of the V2 *-ca* 'eat', it is obvious that perceiving this marker merely as a syntactic valency-decreasing device is not justified. Rather, the common core of all the uses of this V2 is the volitionally and beneficially affected agent (with the exception of a few adversative usages).

The affectedness of the agent is also a property of the literal meaning of the verb *eat*. As pointed out in Næss (2009: 37), it is central to the semantics of *eat* and *drink* verbs. Næss argues that this semantic property of the event also makes it less prototypically transitive, as the agent shares the property of affectedness with patient arguments. Thus, the A and the P are not maximally distinct in *eat* and *drink* verbs. Verbs of eating often exhibit properties typical of intransitive verbs crosslinguistically, which possibly also gave rise to the grammaticalization of *-ca* into detransitivizing markers of reflexivity, autobenefactive, adversative notions and reciprocality (see §11.3.5) in Yakkha.

The extreme polysemy of the V2 *-ca* is not at all surprising, as the activity of eating is universal to human existence, and is thus expected to be a rich source for metaphors (Newman 2009). The use of 'eat' in the expression of experiental events is a prominent pattern in Central and South Asia generally, that is thus found in other Tibeto-Burman languages, and in Indo-Aryan languages (Hook & Pardeshi 2009: 154, Pramodini 2010). While the grammaticalization to passive markers is also found elsewhere (Heine & Kuteva 2002: 122), the use of 'eat' as marker of reflexivity is, to my best knowledge, not yet reported for other languages, although such a development is, for the reasons laid out above, very plausible.

10.2.4 The quasi-V2 *-si?* (middle, unintentional)

The marker *-si?* is not a verb historically, but it behaves according to the V2 pattern, triggering the recursive inflection and being part of the infinitives, which is why it is mentioned here as well (see below for its historical development). The morpheme is found with detransitivizing function as a middle marker (see (26) and §11.3.6), but also in less transparent intransitive verb-verb combinations, that will be shown in this section. The grammatical and lexical functions of *-si?* all share the semantic feature of indicating unintentional or involuntary actions. All verbs derived by the middle involve animate or human subjects.

(26) a. *kamala=ŋa   sakhi   phaps-u=na.*
          Kamala=ERG   thread   entangle-3.P[PST]=NMLZ.SG
          'Kamala entangled the thread.'
      b. *mendhwak=ci   phaps-a-sy-a-ci.*
          goat=NSG   entangle-PST-MDDL-PST-[3]DU
          'The two goats lost their way.'

The component of unintentional actions is best illustrated in (27). The simple verb *tupma* 'meet' is intransitive and inherently reciprocal (see (27a)). The middle specifies that the event happened spontaneously and unintentionally (see (27b)). The examples in (28) show further middle verbs.

(27) a. *wandik   tub-i?*
          tomorrow   meet-1PL[SBJV]
          'Shall we meet tomorrow?'

     b. *tub-a-sy-a-ŋ-ci-ŋ=ha.*
          meet-PST-MDDL-PST-EXCL-[1]DU-EXCL=NMLZ.NSG
          'We (dual) ran into each other.'

(28) a. *cuwa=ŋa   hipt-a-sy-a-ga=na=i?*
          beer=INS   choke-PST-MDDL-PST-2=NMLZ.SG=Q
          'Did you choke on the beer?'

     b. *ka   kolem=na=be   sos-a-sy-a-ŋ=na.*
          1SG   slippery=NMLZ.SG=LOC   slide-PST-MDDL-PST-1SG=NMLZ.SG
          'I slipped on the slippery ground.'

     c. *chimd-a=nuŋ   chimd-a=nuŋ*
          ask-PST[3SG]=COM   ask-PST[3SG]=COM
          tops-a-sy-a-ŋ=na.
          confuse-PST-MDDL-PST-1SG=NMLZ.SG
          'As she asked and asked, I got confused.'

Example (29) shows lexicalized predicates containing *-siʔ*, all from the experiential domain. A look at the independent meanings of the lexical roots here shows that the semantics of these predicates are non-compositional, and non-transparent.

(29) a. *cond-a-sy-a=bi=ba.*
          praise[3SG]-PST-MDDL-PST=IRR=EMPH
          'She would have been happy.'   [13_cvs_02.056]

     b. *ŋond-a-sy-a-ga=na=i?*
          remain-PST-MDDL-PST-2=NMLZ.SG=Q
          'Do you feel shy?'

The middle marker is also used in imperatives, with the function of turning commands into implorations. By using the middle, the speaker acknowledges the affectedness of the addressee, or he implies that it is against the addressee's will (e.g., in (30b)). In this function, the volition of the subject is allowed and even required, as (30b) and (30c) show.

(30) a. *pog-a!*
          stand_up-IMP
          'Stand up!'

b.   *pog-a-sy-a.*

stand_up-IMP-MDDL-IMP

'Please, stand up.' (to a person who was not willing to stand up)

c.   *yok-t-a-by-a-sy-a,*

search-BEN-IMP-V2.GIVE-IMP-MDDL-IMP,

so-t-a-by-a-sy-a.

look-BEN-IMP-V2.GIVE-IMP-MDDL-IMP

'Please search her (the missing girl) for us, look for us.'

[22_nrr_05.084–5]

As for the etymology of the marker, it behaves like a V2 in the Kiranti languages, but it is a reconstructed suffix already in Proto-Tibeto-Burman. A sibilant suffix with middle semantics is well attested in many Tibeto-Burman languages, e.g., in Dulong-Rawang and Padam (LaPolla 1996: 1944) and in languages of the West Himalayish branch (Matisoff 2003: 471). The verbal behavior of the marker is a Kiranti innovation, resulting from reanalysis of a suffix to a verbal stem, under the pressure to have a structure that is analogous to the other verbal operations that are marked by V2s in Kiranti languages (see Bickel (2003: 560) for the same development in Belhare).[17] The middle marker in Yakkha does not have a stativizing effect on the temporal structure of the verb (reconstructed as a proto-function of this morpheme, Matisoff (2003: 471)). Most of the verbs have ingressive-stative Aktionsart, which is why they are usually marked for past while referring to present (stative) events.

10.2.5 The V2 -*kheʔ* (motion away, telicity)

The V2 *kheʔ* 'go' is found with intransitive telic verbs, emphasizing their orientation towards an end point, or the irreversibility of an event. Example (31a), for instance, was uttered to emphasize that the subject is already fast asleep, implying that it is useless to try and wake up that person. The other examples in (31) illustrate the application of this V2 to indicate irreversible intransitive events.

(31)   a.   *ips-a-khy-a=na.*

fall_asleep-PST-V2.GO[3SG]-PST=NMLZ.SG

'She has fallen asleep (better not wake her up).'

---

[17] In some Kiranti languages the marker has reflexive and reciprocal semantics, e.g., in Limbu (van Driem 1987: 86), in Kulung (Tolsma 1999: 61) and in Chintang (Bickel et al. 2010: 300). In Thulung and Wambule it is found as a detransitivizer or 'stativizer' (Lahaussois (2003: 209), Opgenort (2004: 351)).

b. *a-ma*   *sy-a-khy-a,*   *i*

       1SG.POSS-mother   die-PST-V2.GO[3SG]-PST=NMLZ.SG   what

       cok-ma=na?

       do-INF=NMLZ.SG

       'My mother has died, so what to do?'   [06_cvs_01.020]

c. *wa*   *bhale*   *ka-ya-khy-a.*

       cock   cock   call-PST-V2.GO[3SG]-PST

       'The cock crowed already.'[18]   [11_nrr_01.011]

d. *ulippa paŋ*   *hor-a-khy-a=na.*

       old   house   crumble-PST-V2.GO[3SG]-PST=NMLZ.SG

       'The old house crumbled down.'

The development of a motion verb into a marker of telicity is common; the motion semantics get extended to a movement in time and changes-of-state in general. Examples that involve literal motion events are, however, also fairly frequent with *-khe?*, as the verbs in (32) illustrate. In these examples, the lexical verb denotes the kind of motion, and the V2 specifies the direction away from a point of reference.

(32) a. *chemha*   *phom-khem-me=ha.*

       liquor   spill[3SG]-V2.GO-NPST=NMLZ.NC

       'The liquor will spill.'

b. *uimalaŋ=be*

       steep_slope_downwards=LOC

       sos-a-khy-a=na.

       lie_slanted[3SG]-PST-V2.GO-PST=NMLZ.SG

       'He slipped on the steep slope (landing on his back and sliding off).'

c. *kakkulik*   *kaks-a-khy-a=na.*

       rolling   fall[3SG]-PST-V2.GO-PST=NMLZ.SG

       'She tumbled down (in somersaults).'   [06_cvs_01.020]

d. *nhaŋ*   *pes-a-khy-a-ma.*

       and_then   fly[3SG]-PST-V2.GO-PST-PRF

       'And then he has flown away.'   [21_nrr_04.030]

e. *limbu=ci*   *nhaŋ*   *n-las-a-khy-a-ma.*

       Limbu_group=NSG   after_that   3PL-return-PST-V2.GO-PST-PRF

       'The Limbus went back afterwards.'   [22_nrr_05.035]

---

[18] Context: the time is over and the protagonist loses his bet.

Lexicalized complex predicates are possible as well. In (33), the combination of *khus* 'steal' and V2 -*khe?* 'go' has acquired the meaning *escape*, without an action of stealing being implied. As in the examples in (32), the V2 specifies also the direction away from a point of reference. The same is possible with the V2 -*ra* 'come' to indicate that someone comes fleeing from a location further away.

(33) *ŋ-khus-a-khy-a-n=na.*
       NEG-escape-PST-V2.GO[3SG]-PST-NEG=NMLZ.SG
       'He did not escape.'

In some instances, the V2 -*khe?* retains its original lexical meaning, and simply means 'go', as in the sequence of events shown in (34). The transitive verbs 'fry' and 'eat' have been detransitivized to synchronize the argument structure with the final verb 'go'. So far, this is the only instance where the participants do not bear equal relations to the verb, as the location where the frying and the eating take place is in a source relation to the action of going.

(34) *camraŋ=be   cama   i=ya*
       Camrang=LOC   food   what=NMLZ.NC
       n-ni-ca-ya-khy-a-ma=hoŋ,   ...
       3PL-fry-V2.EAT-PST-V2.GO-PST-PRF=SEQ
       'After they have fried and eaten some food in Camrang and gone away, ...'
       [22_nrr_05.034]

The whole range of -*khe?* in CPs, thus, represents a continuum from the lexical meaning of 'go', via unspecific motion away from a point of reference, to a grammaticalized and regular telic function, by metaphorically extending a movement in space to a movement in time.

10.2.6 The V2 -*ra* (motion towards)

The V2 -*ra* (*ta) 'come (from further away)' specifies an event in terms of a motion towards a point of reference, while being unspecified for the uphill/downhill distinction. The lexical source verb is *tama*, but initial /t/ becomes /r/ intervocalically in all V2 stems.

(35) a. *arap=phaŋ*   *khus-a-ra-ya=na.*
            Arab_countries=ABL   escape[3SG]-PST-V2.COME-PST=NMLZ.SG
            'He came escaping from (working in the) Arab countries.'

b. *cuncula   [...]   ten=be   las-a-ra-ya-ma.*
    Cuncula   [...]   village=LOC   return[3SG]-PST-V2.COME-PST-PRF
    'Cuncula has returned home.'   [01_leg_07.307]

c. *dharan   men-da-le*
    Dharan   NEG-reach-CVB
    hiks-a-ra-ya=na.
    turn_around[3SG]-PST-V2.COME-PST=NMLZ.SG
    'Without reaching Dharan, he turned around and came back.'

An actual movement in space is not implied here either, equal to *-khe?* discussed above. The function of *-ra* can also be metaphorically extended, just as in the English translation (see (36)).

(36)   *hiŋ-a-ra-ya=na.*
       survive[3SG]-PST-V2.COME-PST=NMLZ.SG
       'He came back to life.'

10.2.7 The V2 *-ra?* (caused motion towards)

The lexical source verb of *-ra?* (*ta?*) refers to bringing something from further away, and this meaning component is preserved in the CPs, too. It specifies transitive events for directedness towards a point of reference. As such, the V2 can either modify a motion verb (see (37a)) or express a sequence of events (see (37b)).

(37)   a.   *nhaŋ   ak=ka   kamnibak=ci hip-paŋ*
            and_then   1SG.POSS=GEN   friends=NSG   two-CLF.HUM
            tikt-u-ra-wa-ŋ-ci-ŋ.
            lead-3.P-V2.BRING-NPST-1SG.A-3NSG.P-1SG.A
            'And I will bring along two of my friends.'   [14_nrr_02.24]

       b.   *eko   phuŋ   chikt-u-ra=na.*
            one   flower   pluck[3SG.A;PST]-3.P-V2.BRING=NMLZ.SG
            'She plucked a flower and brought it.'

It is also possible to turn a transitive verb into a motion verb by adding *-ra?* (see (38)). Since the stem *momd* 'cover' is transitive, the V2 has to be transitive, too.

(38)   *eŋ=ga   ten   khibrumba=ŋa*
       1PL.INCL=GEN   village   fog=ERG

momd-u-ra=na.
cover[3SG.A;PST]-3.P-V2.BRING=NMLZ.SG
'The fog came (lit.: brought) covering our village.'

10.2.8 The V2 *-uks* (motion down towards)

If intransitive motion is directed downwards and towards a point of reference, the V2 *-uks* 'come down' is used to specify this path.

(39) *taŋkhyaŋ   ka-ya=na=hau.*   *ikhiŋ=na!*
      sky   speak[3SG]-PST=NMLZ.SG=EXCLA   such=NMLZ.SG
      hor-uks-heks-a=na.
      burst-V2.COME.DOWN-V2.CUT-PST=NMLZ.SG
      'It thundered, indeed. Such a loud one! It (the sky) is about to break down
      on us.'   [13_cvs_02.088–89]

10.2.9 The V2 *-ukt* (caused motion down towards)

The V2 *-ukt* 'bring down' denotes caused motion down and towards the deictic center, both with monotransitive and ditransitive verbs. The resulting CP has the argument realization of the indirective frame, showing agreement with the T argument (cf. Chapter 11). This verb is compatible with the adverb *mo* 'downhill' (versus *yo* and *to*), although this would be a somewhat redundant expression. Note that in combination with CV or CVʔ stems that also have /u/ as stem vowel, the stems fuse into one syllable, as shown in (40b).

(40) a. *ŋ-gamnibak   (mo)   tikt-ukt-u.*
         2SG.POSS-friend   (down)   guide-V2.BRING.DOWN-3.P[IMP]
         'Bring your friend down here.'
      b. *thuŋkha=bhaŋ   siŋ*
         steep_slope=ABL   wood
         khu-kt-u-m-ŋ=ha.
         carry-V2.BRING.DOWN-3.P[PST]-1PL.A-EXCL=NMLZ.NC
         'We brought down fire wood from the steep slopes.'

10.2.10 The V2 *-ap* (motion towards, from close nearby)

The V2 *-ap* 'come' denotes intransitive motion towards a point of reference, crucially from close nearby and from the same level with respect to the inclination of the hill, e.g., from a neighbouring house which is on the same elevation level.

Such predicates are compatible with the adverb *yondaŋ*, which refers to sources on the same level.

(41) yo=na   paŋ=bhaŋ   las-a-ab-a=na.
      across=NMLZ.SG   house=ABL   return-[3SG]-V2.COME-PST=NMLZ.SG
      'She came back from the house across.'

10.2.11 The V2 -*apt* (caused motion towards, from close nearby)

The V2 -*apt* 'bring' expresses caused motion towards a point of reference, from nearby and from the same elevation level with respect to the hill, in analogy to the intransitive -*ap* above. The resulting CP has the argument realization of the indirective frame (cf. §11.1.9). As example (42b) illustrates, this V2 is also used for small-scale movements.

(42) a. ŋ-gamnibak   tikt-apt-u.
          2SG.POSS-friend   guide-V2.BRING-3.P[IMP]
          'Bring your friend here.'
      b. jhola pe?le?le   und-apt-u-ga=i.
          bag   IDEOPH   pull-V2.BRING-3.P[IMP]-2=EMPH
          'Pull out the bag (from behind the heap of clothes, towards oneself).'

The transitivity of the two verbal stems has to match. In (43), no literal 'bringing' of the substance is involved, at least not if bringing is understood as carrying something in a container outside one's own body.

(43) nhaŋ   chemha=ca   uŋ-apt-a-ŋ-c-u-ŋ=ba.
      and_then   liquor=ADD   drink-V2.BRING-PST-EXCL-DU-3.P-EXCL=EMPH
      'We drank liquor and came (lit.: brought it) here.'   [36_cvs_06.398]

10.2.12 The V2 -*ris* (caused motion to a distant goal)

The V2 -*ris* (*tis), with the lexical meaning 'place, invest' (e.g., place a pot on the fire, invest money in some project), indicates caused motion towards a distant goal, implying that the object will remain there. The resulting predicate again exhibits the argument realization of the indirective frame (cf. Chapter 11). This V2 is not specified for the vertical dimension, and it is compatible with adverbial specifications for either *mo* 'down', *to* 'up' or *yo* 'across', but naturally not with adverbials expressing proximity to the deictic center.[19]

---

[19] In both examples, two V2 are involved. The V2 -*a* ~ -*na* 'leave' fuses with the inflectional material (/-u-a-u/) to result in [o].

(44) a. *ŋ-gamnibak*   *u-paŋ=be*
       2SG.POSS-friend   3SG.POSS-house=LOC

       tikt-u-ris-o.
       lead-3.P-V2.PLACE-V2.LEAVE[3.P;IMP]
       'Deliver your friend at his home.'

    b. *uŋci-ten=be*   *ikt-u-ris-o.*
       3NSG.POSS-village=LOC   chase-3.P-V2.PLACE-V2.LEAVE[3.P;IMP]
       'Chase them to their village.'

10.2.13 The V2 *-bhes* (caused horizontal motion towards)

The V2 *-bhes* has the lexical meaning 'send [towards]', 'bring [towards]'. It signifies that caused motion takes place on the same elevation level and towards the point of reference, for either small-scale or large-scale movements. Example (45a) shows transfer from a very short distance, the application of the blessing on the forehead (by sticking cooked rice on the forehead). Example (45b) shows the employment of this V2 for a large-scale movement. This V2 is only compatible with adverbs derived from the root *yo* 'across'.

(45) a. *ţika*   *ţal-a*
       blessing_on_forehead   stick-NATIV

       n-jog-u-bhes-u=hoŋ,   …
       3PL.A-make-3.P-V2.BRING-3.P[PST]=SEQ
       'After they applied the blessings, …' (as remembered by a bride who
       got blessed)   [25_tra_01.049]

    b. *nhaŋ,*   *nna,*   *laluban=nuŋ*   *phalubaŋ*
       and_then   that   Lalubang=COM   Phalubang

       ŋ-ikt-a-bhes-uks-u-ci.
       3PL.A-chase-PST-V2.BRING-V2.PRF-3.P-3NSG.P
       'And then, they chased Lalubang and Phalubang here.'
                                           [22_nrr_05.023]

10.2.14 The V2 *-end* (caused motion downwards)

The V2 *-end* (~ *-nen* before consonants)[20] has the lexical meaning 'apply, insert'. As a V2, it indicates caused motion downwards, as shown by the examples in (46). Here, the motion is not specified for the direction towards or away from a point of reference.

---

[20] Cf. the citation forms *leʔnemma, lepnemma* and *huʔnemma* for the examples in (46).

(46) a. *u-laŋ=ci*   *le?-end-u-ci=ha.*
          3SG.POSS-leg=NSG   drop-V2.INSERT-3.P[PST]-3NSG.P=NMLZ.NSG
          'It (the plane) lowered its landing gear.'

      b. *nhaŋ*   *pho?*   *n-lept-end-wa.*
          and_then   IDEOPH   3PL.A-throw-V2.INSERT-NPST[3.P]
          'They throw it down swiftly (the fishing net).'   [13_cvs_02.009]

      c. *hut-end-u-ŋ=na.*
          push-V2.INSERT-3.P[PST]-1SG.A=NMLZ.SG
          'I pushed him down.'

The V2 *-end* can also express caused motion downwards as a result of another action (see (47)). Furthermore, using this V2 may also convey regret. Saying *pegenduŋna* ('I shattered it') sounds more regrettingly than the underived *peguŋna*.

(47) a. *tabek=ŋa*   *siŋ=ga*   *u-whak*
          khukuri_knife=INS   tree=GEN   3SG.POSS-BRANCH
          cen-end-u=na.
          chop-V2.INSERT-3.P[PST]=NMLZ.SG
          'He cut down the branch with a Khukuri knife.' (Cut-and-break clips, Bohnemeyer, Bowerman & Brown 2010)

      b. *u-sa*   *seps-end-u.*
          3SG.POSS-fruit   pluck-V2.INSERT-3.P[IMP]
          'Get the fruits down (plucking).'

10.2.15 The V2 *-ket* (caused motion up and towards)

The V2 *-ket* 'bring up', signifies caused motion up and towards a reference point (see (48)). There is a corresponding intransitive stem *-ke?* 'come up', but it has not been found yet as V2.

(48) a. *na*   *eko=ŋa=go*   *thend-u-get-uks-u=ba.*
          this   one=ERG=TOP   lift-3.P-V2.BRING.UP-PRF-3.P[PST]=EMPH
          'Someone has lifted it up (carried it up in one's hands).'
                                                                    [37_nrr_07.082]

      b. *thithi*   *end-u-get-uks-u=na.*
          upright   insert-3.P-V2.BRING.UP-3.P[PST]-PRF=NMLZ.SG
          'He inserted it upright at an elevated place.'   [37_nrr_07.083]

The movement upwards may also happen on a very small scale. In (49), for instance, the speaker does not refer to someone plucking further downhill, but just one meter below herself.[21]

(49)   *maŋkhu   seps-u-get-u=ha.*
       garlic   pluck-3.P-V2.BRING.UP-3.P[PST]=NMLZ.NSG
       'She plucked and brought up the garlic.'

Furthermore, at least one example suggests that 'bring up' can also be understood metaphorically, as referring to a movement in time, where the past is equated with lower altitude.[22]

(50)   *nna   namda   ka   piccha   nhaŋto*
       that   festival   1SG[ERG]   child   since
       nis-u-get-u-ŋ=na.
       see-3.P-V2.BRING.UP-3.P[PST]-1SG.A=NMLZ.SG
       'I have been attending this festival since childhood.'   [41_leg_09.006]

10.2.16 The V2 *-haks* (caused motion away, irreversibility)

The V2 *-haks ~ -nhaŋ* 'send (things)' expresses caused motion away from a point of reference (see (51)), and away from the agent (in contrast to *-khet* 'carry off' described below). Although its lexical meaning is 'send (things)', as a V2 it is also used with animate T arguments, including human referents.

(51)   a.   *ka   mima   o-hoŋ=be*
            1G[ERG]   mouse   3SG.POSS-hole=LOC
            hut-haks-u-ŋ=na.
            push-V2.SEND-3.P[PST]-1SG.A=NMLZ.SG
            'I pushed the mouse (back) into her hole.'

---

[21] In Kiranti languages, the topography-based specification of events reaches a level of much greater distinction than speakers of European languages are generally used to (cf. Chapter 7, and Bickel 1999a; 2001; Ebert 1999b; Gaenszle 1999).

[22] The postposition *nhaŋto* 'since' in this example literally means 'and then up', providing support to this hypothesis. Further support for the hypothesis that the past is conceptualized as 'below' comes from an idiomatic Noun-Verb Predicate, *setni keʔma*, literally 'bring up the night', which refers to staying awake until the morning.

    b.   *ţebul=be   cuwa   tug-haks-u=ha.*
            table=LOC   beer   wipe-V2.SEND-3.P[PST]=NMLZ.NSG
            'She wiped the beer from the table.'[23]

    c.   *luŋkhwak   luŋkhwak   seg-haks-u.*
            stone   stone   chose-V2.SEND-3.P[IMP]
            'Sort out stone by stone (from the grains).'

    d.   *wasik   ta-ya=hoŋ   honma   uks-a,*
            rain   come[3SG]-PST=SEQ   river   come_down[3SG]-PST
            ŋkhoŋ   yokhaʔla   chekt-haks-a=na.
            and_then   across   block-V2.SEND-PST[3SG]=NMLZ.SG
            'After the rain, a river came down, and we redirected it.'[24]

Like the V2s *-kheʔ* 'go' and *-khet* 'carry off', *-haks* also conveys telicity and actions with irreversible consequences, as illustrated by the examples in (52). This V2 was particularly prominent in the data elicited with the cut-and-break clips (Bohnemeyer, Bowerman & Brown 2010).

(52)   a.   *solop   miyaŋ   eg-haks-u-su.*
            immediately   a_little   break-V2.SEND-3.P[PST]-PST.PRF
            'Immediately he broke off a little.'   [04_leg_03.079]

      b.   *a-yaŋ   cum-haks-u-ŋ=ha.*
            1SG.POSS-money   hide-V2.SEND-3.P[PST]-1SG.A=NMLZ.C
            'I mislaid my money.'

      c.   *hu-haks-u=na.*
            accuse-V2.SEND-3.P[PST]=NMLZ.SG
            'He accused her.'[25]

      d.   *a-phu=ŋa   cekt-haks-u=ha.*
            1SG.POSS-eB=ERG   talk-V2.SEND-3.P[PST]=NMLZ.NC
            'My elder brother did/finalized the talking.'[26]   [36_cvs_06.363]

      e.   *a-niŋwa=be=ha   ceʔya*
            1SG.POSS-mind=LOC=NMLZ.NC   matter
            lu-haks-u=ha.
            tell-V2.SEND-3.P[PST]=NMLZ.NC
            'She blabbered out my secret thoughts.'

---

[23] Despite the ablative semantics of the verbs, the locative is the standard case choice with this verb.

[24] The verb *chekthaksana* is detransitivized and passive-like structurally, but this structure can also express first person nonsingular agents (see §11.3.1.1).

[25] This is probably a metaphorical use of *huʔ* 'burn'.

[26] Context: wedding negotiations.

The V2 -*haks* may also attach to the lexical verb *haks*, an option that has not been found with other V2s so far. It implies that something was sent via an intermediate station, e.g., another house where the adressee has to go and get his things, or via a post office.

(53) *salen* *haks-haks-u=na.*
      message   send-V2.SEND-3.P=NMLZ.SG
      'He sent the message (via some institution).'

Furthermore, this V2 is frequently used when the P or T argument of a verb is human (discussed in detail in §11.3.7). This is surprising because the lexical verb *haks* 'send' implies inanimate T arguments. There is a strong tendency for referentially high objects (mostly P and T; as G arguments are expected to be referentially high anyway) to occur in a complex predicate construction, and one V2 choice for this is obviously -*haks*.

(54) a. *i=ca* *n-lu-n-ci-n=ha,*
          what=ADD   NEG-tell-NEG-3NSG.P-NEG=NMLZ.NSG
          so-haks-u-ci   *se=ppa.*
          look-V2.SEND-3.P[PST]-3NSG   RESTR=EMPH
          'He did not say anything to them, he just glanced at them.'
                                                    [34_pea_04.044]
      b. *kaniŋ*   *na=haŋ*   *iŋ-nhaŋ-ma=na.*
          1PL[ERG]   this=ABL   chase-V2.SEND-INF[DEONT]=NMLZ.SG
          'We have to chase him away from here (this place).'   [21_nrr_04.010]
      c. *kaniŋ*   *lon-nhaŋ-ma*   *sin.*
          1PL   take_out-V2.SEND-INF[DEONT]   COP.1PL.INCL
          'He has to expel us.'

10.2.17 The V2 -*khet* (caused motion along with A)

The V2 -*khet* ~ -*kheʔ* ~ -*(h)et* indicates that the object is carried off or is in some way separated from its original location, remaining with the A argument. The lexical source verb is *khet* 'carry off'. In the infinitives, the form is always -*kheʔ*, while in the inflected forms, the V2 surfaces as -*het* or even -*et*. These predicates either express a manner of caused motion away from a reference poin, as in (55a) and (55b), or a sequence of doing something and literally carrying off the object, as in (55c) and (55d).

(55)   *ghak   yaŋ-het-i=nuŋ=ga*   *wasik*
        all   flush-V2.CARRY.OFF-COMPL=COM=GEN   rain
        'a rain that flushed away everything'   [38_nrr_07.076]

(55)   *jaŋgal=be   sa-het-u=hoŋ,*   ...
        forest=LOC   lead_by_rope-V2.CARRY.OFF-3.P[PST]=SEQ
        'He led it (the goat) into the jungle, ...'   [20_pea_02.026]

(55)   *yubak   coŋ-kheʔ-ma.*
        goods   shift-V2.CARRY.OFF-INF[DEONT]
        'The goods have to be unloaded and carried off.'

(55)   *khus-het-uks-u=ha*   *hola.*
        steal-V2.CARRY.OFF-PRF-3.P[PST]=NMLZ.NSG   probably
        'He probably stole it and carried it off.'   [20_pea_02.014]

Like *-raʔ* 'bring' described above, *-khet* 'carry off' can also be used metaphorically, carrying various interpretations. In (56a), it is employed to satisfy the requirement of matching valency within a CP. The verb *-kheʔ* 'go' would be impossible here because it is intransitive, while *uŋ* 'drink' is transitive. The same holds for transimpersonal verbs (see (56b) and (c)).[27] With such verbs the V2 has to be transitive. In these examples, *-khet* has a telicizing effect, similar to the effect of *-kheʔ* 'go' in intransitives. The lexical stems *lokt* and *hand* have ingressive semantics, i.e., when they are inflected for past, they refer to ongoing events. After *-khet* has been added, they are oriented towards the end point, as these examples show.

(56)   a.   *khem   uŋ-het-u-ŋ=na.*
              before   drink-V2.CARRY.OFF-3.P[PST]-1SG.A=NMLZ.SG
              'I had drunken it before and left.'

        b.   *maŋcwa   lokt-het-u=ha.*
              water   boil-V2.CARRY.OFF-3.P[PST]=NMLZ.SG
              'The water boiled down.'

        c.   *micuʔwa   hand-het-u=na.*
              bamboo_torch   burn-V2.CARRY.OFF-3.P[PST]=NMLZ.SG
              'The bamboo torch burned down.'

Another interpretation of *-khet* was found, e.g., with cognition verbs such as *miʔma* 'think, hope, want, remember', but also with other verbs. In (57) the V2 functions as a marker of degree, intensity or excessiveness.

---

[27] Transimpersonal verbs always show transitive person marking, but an overt A argument cannot be expressed.

(57) a.   *nna   hoŋ=be   iha=le   we?=na   bhoŋ*
            that   hole=LOC what=CTR exist[3SG]=NMLZ.SG COMP

           so?-ma   mit-het-u-ŋ.
           look-INF   think-V2.CARRY.OFF-3.P[PST]-1SG.A
           'I badly wanted to see what was inside that hole.'   [42_leg_10.024]

      b.   *maŋpha   tas-het-u=ha.*
           very_much   arrive-V2.CARRY.OFF-3.P[PST]=NMLZ.NC
           'It became very/too much.'

10.2.18 The quasi-V2 *-a ~ -na* (do X and leave object)

The marker *-a ~ -na* expresses that the action was carried out at a location not identical to the point of reference and that the subject has returned, leaving the object there, like for instance in *phe?nama* 'drop someone at X' and *e?nama* 'enroll someone' (e.g., in a boarding school). There is no corresponding independent simple verb *ama* or *nama*, but there is the complex verb *na?nama* with the meaning 'to leave', which looks as if the first verb and the V2 are identical.

This marker, due to its limited phonological content, undergoes several morphophonological operations, like ablaut and the insertion of consonants, so that it is not always easy to distinguish *-a* from other morphological material in the verbal inflection. When the first suffix following the stem contains a consonant, the V2 surfaces as *-na*, e.g., in *na?nanenna* 'I left you'. If the stems are followed by the suffix *-u*, the sequence /-u-a-u-/ will be realized as /-u(?)o/, /-o(?)o/ or simply /o/ (see (58)). If there is the underlying sequence /-a-a/, it will either be realized as /aya/ or as /a?a/ (see (59)). Furthermore, the ablaut (/a/ to /o/) triggers a change of *-uŋha* in the suffix string to *-oŋha*.

(58) a.   *tisuona.*
           /tis-u-a-u=na/
           place-PST-V2.LEAVE-1SG.P-2.A=NMLZ.SG
           'You delivered him (and returned).'

      b.   *nyubak   kamalabe*
           /n-yubak   kamala=be/
           2SG.POSS-goods   Kamala=LOC

           hakto?oksoŋha.
           /hakt-u-a-uks-u-ŋ=ha/
           send-3.P-V2.LEAVE-PRF-3.P[PST]-1SG.A=NMLZ.NSG
           'I have sent your goods to Kamala (so you can get them there).'

    c.   *umaŋachen*   (...)   *lambu* *lambu* *yaksaŋnuŋ*
        /u-ma=ŋa=chen   (...)   lambu lambu yaksaŋ=nuŋ/
        3SG.POSS-mother=ERG=TOP (...) road   road   grass=COM

        seula   *eksaŋ*   *yukso?okso.*
        /seula   ek-saŋ   yuks-u-a-uks-u/
        green_stalk break-SIM put-3.P-V2.LEAVE-PRF-3.P[PST]
        'His mother (...) broke off some gras and stalks along the road and
        left them (to help the son orient himself back home).' [01_leg_07.072]

(59)   a.   *tisayaŋgana.*
        /tis-a-a-ŋ-ga=na/
        place-PST-V2.LEAVE-1SG.P-2.A=NMLZ.SG
        'You delivered me (and returned).'

    b.   *pasupatinathpe*   *phesa?aŋna.*
        /pasupatinath=pe   phes-a-a-ŋ=na/
        Pashupatinath=LOC   bring-PST-V2.LEAVE-PST-1SG.P=NMLZ.SG
        'He brought me to Pashupatinath (and returned without me).'

10.2.19 The V2 *-nes* (continuative)

The V2 *-nes* 'lay' marks continuative events, i.e., events that are ongoing for
longer than expected, and which are not oriented towards an end point. It is
found with both transitive and intransitive verbs (see (60).) Examples (a) to (c)
show the combination of *-nes* with activity verbs, and example (60d) shows that
in ingressive-stative verbs, the contintuative applies to the resulting state.

(60)   a.   *wasik* *n-da-me-n=niŋa*   *nam*
        rain   NEG-come-NPST-NEG=CTMP   sun
        phen-a=na   *phen-a=na,*
        shine[3SG]-PST=NMLZ.SG   shine[3SG]-PST=NMLZ.SG
        phen-a-nes-a=na.
        shine-PST-V2.LAY-[3SG]-PST=NMLZ.SG
        'While there is no rain, the sun was shining and shining, it kept shin-
        ing.'
                                                        [38_nrr_07.075]

    b.   *le?namcuk* *kei*   *m-mokt-u-nes-uks-u=ha.*
        whole_day   drum   3PL.A-beat-3.P-V2.LAY-PRF-3.P[PST]=NMLZ.NSG
        'They have kept playing the drums the whole day long.'

    c.   *whaŋma=ŋa* *lupt-u-nes-u=na.*
        sweat=ERG   disperse-3.P-V2.LAY-3.P[PST]=NMLZ.SG
        'She kept sweating (e.g., after a long run).'

d.   *ka=ca*   *hiŋ-a-nes-a-ŋ=na.*
1SG=ADD   survive-PST-V2.LAY-PST-1SG=NMLZ.SG
'I have survived, too.'

10.2.20 The V2 *-nuŋ* (continuative)

The V2 *-nuŋ* adds a continuative reading, similar to the function of *-nes* described above. I tentatively suggest the verb *yuŋ* 'sit' as the etymological source of this V2. Firstly, the grammaticalization of 'sit' into a continuative marker would be a very common development historically, and secondly, I have shown that the insertion of a nasal occurs in vowel-initial and /h/-initial V2s, so that replacing /y/ with [n] seems plausible, too. So far, all examples found with this V2 were intransitive or detransitivized (see (61)).

Punctual events, like in (61a), get an iterative reading when *-nuŋ* is added. States and activities can also be extended by means of *-nuŋ* (see (61b), (61c)). In several instances, the two V2s *-nuŋ* and *-nes* seem to be interchangeable without any change in meaning. However, while *-nes* is more frequently combined with past tense, *-nuŋ* is typically found in nonpast contexts. The exact difference between *-nuŋ* and *-nes* cannot be established with certainty yet.

(61)   a.   *a-laŋ=ci*   *ŋ-aŋ-khe-nuŋ-me=ha.*
1SG.POSS-leg=NSG   3PL-descend-V2.GO-V2.SIT-NPST=NMLZ.NSG
'My legs keep falling down (from the seat).'

   b.   *heʔniŋ=ca*   *ŋonsi-nuŋ-meʔ=na.*
when=ADD   feel_shy-V2.SIT[3SG]-NPST=NMLZ.SG
'She is always shy.'

   c.   *tek*   *leŋ-nuŋ-meʔ=na.*
clothes   exchange-V2.SIT[3SG]-NPST=NMLZ.SG
'She keeps changing her clothes.'

10.2.21 The V2 *-bhoks* (punctual, sudden events)

The function of the V2 *-bhoks* has developed from the lexical meaning 'split'. Adding this V2 to a lexical verb results in a punctual reading, or in the implication that an event happens suddenly and unexpectedly (see (62)).

(62)   *a-nabhak*   *yokt-u-bhoks-u-ŋ=na.*
1SG.POSS-ear   prick-3.P-V2.SPLIT-3.P[PST]-1SG.A=NMLZ.SG
'Suddenly I pierced through my ear (after trying some time and then applying too much pressure).'

With telic verbs, the event is distilled to an end point (see (63)), while with activities and ingressive-stative verbs, like in (64), the initial point of an event is emphasized by *-bhoks.*

(63)   a.   *luŋkhwak   thend-u-bhoks-u-ŋ=na.*
             stone   lift-3.P-V2.SPLIT-3.P[PST]-1SG.A=NMLZ.SG
             'I lifted the stone (with great difficulties, at once).'
      b.   *mi   mi=na   et-u-ŋ=na,*
             fire   small=NMLZ.SG   perceive-3.P[PST]-1SG.A=NMLZ.SG
             khatniŋgo   ma   leks-a-bhoks-a=na.
             but   big   become[3SG]-PST-V2.SPLIT-PST=NMLZ.SG
             'It seemed to me that the fire was small, but suddenly it flamed up.'

(64)   a.   *cumabya=ha   ceʔya   haku   khom-bhoŋ-ma.*
             hidden=NMLZ.SG   language   now   dig-V2.SPLIT-INF[DEONT]
             'We have to start digging out the (our) hidden language now.'
      b.   *okt-a-bhoks-a-ma-ŋ=ba,*
             shriek-PST-V2.SPLIT-PST-PRF-1SG=EMPH
             hab-a-bhoks-a-ma-ŋ=ba.
             cry-PST-V2.SPLIT-PST-PRF-1SG=EMPH
             'Suddenly I shrieked, I broke out in tears.'   [13_cvs_02.034]

10.2.22 The V2 *-heks* (immediate prospective, do separately)

The V2 *-heks* is used when the event denoted by the main verb is about to begin, as shown in (65). Its literal meaning is 'cut, saw'. Note, again, that because of the inceptive semantics of many verbs, it is usually the past form that is used. The V2 may attach to verbs of any temporal structure, and restrictions on the semantics of the arguments (e.g., animacy or volition) were not encountered. With activities and states, the V2 conveys that the activity or state is about to start. With telic verbs, the V2 conveys that the end point is approaching. Example (66b) shows a combination of a completive notion and the 'immediate prospective' notion.

(65)   a.   *o-theklup   leks-heks-a=na.*
             3SG.POSS-half   become-V2.CUT[3SG]-PST=NMLZ.SG
             'Almost half (of the book) is finished.'
      b.   *sabun   mend-heks-a=na.*
             soap   finish-V2.CUT[3SG]-PST=NMLZ.SG
             'The soap is about to be finished.'

    c.   *ucun=na   lambu(=be)*
           nice=NMLZ.SG way(=loc)
           tas-heks-u-m=na.
           arrive-V2.CUT-3.P[PST]-1SG.A=NMLZ.SG
           'We are about to get to the nice road.'

(66) a.   *la   toŋnuŋ   leks-heks-a=na.*
           moon   full   become-V2.CUT[3SG]-PST=NMLZ.SG
           'The moon is about to be full.'

    b.   *hops-i-heks-u-ŋ=ha.*
           sip-COMPL-V2.CUT-3.P[PST]-1SG.A=NMLZ.NC
           'I am about to finish (the soup).'

This V2 has a second meaning, translatable as 'do separately'. The corresponding construction in Nepali is [V.STEM]-*dai garnu*. This usage of -*heks* is often found in commands, for instance when the speaker encourages the hearer to start or go on with some activity while the speaker leaves the speech situation (see (67)).

(67) a.   *yuŋ-heks-a.*
           sit-V2.CUT-IMP
           'Sit down (while I leave for a moment).'

    b.   *co-heks-u.*
           eat-V2.CUT-3.P[IMP]
           'Keep eating (without me).'

    c.   *thukpa hops-heks-wa-ŋ=ha.*
           soup   sip-V2.CUT-NPST[3.P]-1SG.A=NMLZ.NSG
           'I am sipping soup (noone else does).'

10.2.23 The V2 -*ghond* (spatially distributed events)

The V2 -*ghond* has the literal meaning of 'roam, wander around'. This marker refers to actions and events that happen distributed over various locations, in the same manner as has been analyzed for the cognate Belhare marker -*kon ~ -gon* (Bickel 1996: 163). This V2 may attach to intransitive and transitive stems, and can be inflected either way, too (see (68)).

(68) a. *he?ne   maŋdu maŋdu kha luplum=ci=be*
     somewhere far   far   those den=NSG=LOC
     wa-ya-ghond-a
     exist-PST-V2.ROAM-PST
     i-ya-ghond-a=niŋ=ca,   …
     revolve-PST-V2.ROAM[3SG]-PST=CTMP=ADD
     'While he also used to live and walk around somewhere far, far away,
     in those caves, …'   [18_nrr_03.013]

   b. *na maghyam he?niŋ=ca sis-u-ghond-wa=na.*
     this old_woman when=ADD kill-3.P-V2.ROAM-NPST=NMLZ.SG
     'This old woman always walks around drunken.' (lit. she walks
     around being killed)

   c. *ijaŋ yoniŋ-kheniŋ n-jiŋ-ghom-me=ha?*
     why thither-hither 3PL-learn-V2.ROAM-NPST=NMLZ.NSG
     'Why do they walk around learning (languages)?'

Note that in (68b), the experiencer is treated like s standard P argument by case and the verbal person marking (indexed by the '3.P' suffix). This does not prevent the experiencer argument from taking part in complex predication, which usually synchronizes the argument structure of the single components of one CP. This again shows the importance of generalized semantic roles as parameter along which the syntax of Yakkha is organized.

Example (69) from a conversation clearly shows that the first verb is the semantic head, and that -*ghond* has lost its lexical meaning 'walk around'. It merely adds the notion of spatial distribution. In the answer (69b), the speaker refers to the event in question without using the V2.

(69) a. *ŋkha i=ya   het-u-ghond-wa-ga?*
     that what=NMLZ.NSG cut-3.P-V2.ROAM-NPST-2
     'What are you cutting (at various places)?' (said reproachfully)
                       [28_cvs_04.321]

   b. *are ha?lo, ijaŋ me-he?-ma?   abbui!*
     hey EXCLA why NEG-cut-INF[DEONT] EXCLA
     'Goodness, why not to cut? Holy crackers!'   [28_cvs_04.323]

10.2.24 The V2 *-si?* (avoid, prevent)

The V2 *-si?* is always inflected transitively. It is probably etymologically connected to *sis* 'kill'.[28] In a CP, *-si?* means 'avoid, prevent'. The lexical verb denotes an action that prevents something else from happening, like 'catch' in (70a) and (70b), and 'scold' in (70c). The event which shall be avoided is not necessarily expressed overtly; it is usually obvious from the utterance context.

(70) a. *picha kaŋ-khe?-ma   n-dokt-u-n=na,*
           child   fall-V2.GO-INF   NEG-get-3.P[PST]-NEG=NMLZ.SG,

           u-ma=ŋa
           3SG.POSS-mother=ERG

           lab-i-si=na.
           catch-COMPL-V2.PREVENT[3.P;PST]=NMLZ.SG
           'The child could not fall down because its mother held it.'

     b. *lukt-heks-a=na,*
           run-V2.CUT-PST[3SG]=NMLZ.SG

           lam-si?-ma=na.
           catch -V2.PREVENT-INF[DEONT]=NMLZ.SG
           'She is about to run away, we have to hold her.'

     c. *mokt-heks-uksa=na,*   *nhaŋ*
           beat-V2.CUT-PST.PRF[3.P]=NMLZ.SG and_then

           thind-i-si-ŋ=na.
           scold-COMPL-V2.PREVENT[3.P;PST]-1SG.A=NMLZ.SG
           'He was about to beat him, so I scolded and stopped him.'

10.2.25 The V2 *-so?* (experiential)

The V2 *-so?* means 'look', and it is used as experiential marker, translatable with 'try X and find out oneself' (see (71)). Note that this is not a complementation strategy, as one cannot express clauses like 'I found out that X did Y' or 'I tried to X' by means of this V2. Yakkha utilizes complement taking predicates to convey such meanings. The V2 is also not a means to express a conative, since it neither reduces the valency nor implies that the attempt fails (see Vincent (2013) for an overview of the different usages of the term 'conative'). The crucial meaning component of *-so?* is 'experiencing something by trying out oneself'. The grammaticalization of perception verbs to such a marker is common in South Asian and South East Asian languages.

---

[28] In the Nepali translations, the predicates were paraphrased using *mārnu* 'kill'.

(71)   a.   *liŋmi=ŋa   chapt-u-so!*
              straw=INS   thatch-3.P-V2.LOOK[3.P;IMP]
              'Try and thatch (the roof) with straw!' (said as advice against tin roofs)
      b.   *kheps-u-so!*
              listen-3.P-V2.LOOK[3.P;IMP]
              'Listen and find out!'
      c.   *chimd-u-ŋ-so-ŋ?*
              ask-3.P-1SG-V2.LOOK-1SG.A[3.P;SBJV]
              'May I ask and find out?'

This V2 behaves exceptional with regard to the material that can stand between the verbal stems. Usually the first verbal stem can be inflected only by one suffix, and only if the suffix consists of a vowel. However, as shown in (71c), the inflection on the first stem can include a nasal, if a nasal is available in the inflection.

11 Transitivity

This chapter deals with argument structure, valency alternations and transitivity operations in Yakkha. The term argument structure is understood here as "the configuration of arguments that are governed by a particular lexical item" (Haspelmath & Müller-Bardey 2004: 1130). In §11.1, the different verb frames of argument realization are identified by the number of possible arguments and their case and agreement properties. Several verbs occur in more than one frame; their alternations are treated in §11.2.[1] Apart from those alternations that result in straightforward classes, there are also transitivity operations that are more productive and not related to certain verb classes (see §11.3). One has to distinguish between operations that change the argument structure by adding or removing argument roles, and those that merely change the argument realization by changing the case or person marking properties for an argument.

Many markers of transitivity operations have been verbs historically. They are also found as parts of lexically complex predicates, and the grammatical functions are often related to the lexical meanings of these markers. This multiplicity of functions can be viewed as a result of simultaneous grammaticalization and lexicalization processes of certain verbs (see also Chapter 10).

11.1 Frames of argument realization

11.1.1 Theoretical preliminaries

Before starting with the description of the argument frames, some methodological and terminological remarks are in order. The argument frames are identified by three parameters: agreement, case and the question of how the verbal semantics interact with these two formal means. For this purpose, generalized semantic roles (GSRs) are identified for each predicate. Following Bickel (2011a), these roles are labelled as follows: A stands for the most agent-like argument of a transitive

---

[1] Only predicates with nominal arguments are discussed in this chapter. For predicates taking clausal complements see Chapter 15.

predicate,[2] P stands for the most patient-like argument of transitive predicates, S stands for the sole argument of intransitive predicates. For three-argument verbs, the most theme-like argument has the label T and the most goal-like argument has the label G. By relying on generalized semantic roles to identify the arguments of a predicate, one does not imply that these roles build coherent classes of arguments that are characterized by some common semantic or formal property. For example, locative-marked arguments can have the semantic role of a goal, a recipient, a location, a source or a stimulus. Crucially, GSRs make sense only in relation to the particular predicates or predicate classes. No further morphosyntactic consequences, e.g., pivots in some constructions, can be inferred from these terms, as different types of pivots may occur in Yakkha syntax (see Chapters 13, 14 and 15). The argument realization does not always match with the semantic transitivity, e.g., in transimpersonal verbs (see §11.1.7). Nevertheless, a "standard" intransitive and a "standard" transitive frame could be identified, which are the most common frames of argument realization. As arguments are frequently dropped in Yakkha, many examples in this chapter come from elicited data.

In the following, I will outline the two parameters of argument realization in Yakkha, which are person marking and case marking. As for person marking, Yakkha distinguishes intransitive and transitive inflectional paradigms (compare the marking of the verbs with regard to the role of the argument *kaniŋ* in example (1)). Thus, there are three possible values: arguments may trigger intransitive (subject) agreement, transitive subject agreement or object agreement (the latter two being indicated as A or P in the glosses).[3]

(1)   a.   *kaniŋ   khe-i=ha.*
             1PL   go-1PL[PST]=NMLZ.NSG
             'We went.' (S)

    b.   *kaniŋ   kei   kheps-u-m=na.*
             1PL[ERG] drum hear-3.P[PST]-1PL.A=NMLZ.SG
             'We heard the drum.' (A)

    c.   *uŋci=ŋa   kaniŋ kheps-a=ha.*
             3NSG=ERG 1PL   hear-PST[1.P]=NMLZ.NSG
             'They heard us.' (P)

---

[2] Yakkha does not exhibit differences between A arguments of two-argument and three-argument predicates, so that they do not have to be distinguished.

[3] For the function of the frequently occurring main clause nominalization see §13.3.3. For the conditions of the nominative-ergative syncretism see §5.2.2.2.

The agreement markers are not uniformly aligned, so that, for the purposes of this chapter, person marking is presented as tripartite, i.e., agreement with S is different from agreement with A and also different from agreement with P.[4] The reader should bear in mind that the indications in the glosses (A, P) refer only to the type of person marking, following a common labelling tradition for languages where the verbs show agreement with more than one argument. These labels facilitate reading the glosses, but they should not be conflated with the semantic roles of the verbal arguments, which can be S, A, P, T, G.[5]

Arguments can be marked with an ergative, a nominative, a genitive, a locative, an instrumental and, albeit less commonly, with a comitative or an ablative. Yakkha has an ergative/instrumental syncretism; the case marking does not distinguish between agent and instrument, but subsumes both roles under the umbrella category 'effector' (Van Valin & Wilkins 1996). In the following sections, schematic diagrams will illustrate the mapping of the semantic roles to the case and agreement properties for each argument frame. Altogether, 22 verb frames can be established. They can roughly be divided into intransitively inflected verbs, transitively inflected verbs, three-argument verbs, experiencer-as-possessor predicates, copular verbs and light verbs.

In the schematic diagrams of the frames of argument realization, capital letters stand for the respective GSRs of a predicate. Labels like 'ERG' indicate the case marking. The agreement is indicated with 's', 'a' and 'o' (standing for intransitive subject person marking, transitive subject person marking and transitive object person marking, respectively), with the corresponding GSR following in square brackets.[6]

11.1.2 The standard intransitive frame {S-NOM V-s[S]}

In the standard intransitive frame, the subject is in the unmarked nominative case (not written in the glosses) and triggers agreement on the verb. Verbs such as *imma* 'sleep', *posiʔma* 'vomit' and *numa* 'get well, recover' belong to this frame.

(2) a. *ka   posit-a-ŋ=na.*
         1SG   vomit-PST-1SG=NMLZ.SG
         'I vomited.'

---

[4] The person marking on the Yakkha verb combines accusative, ergative, neutral and hierarchical alignment, see Chapter 8.2 on the verbal morphology.

[5] To illustrate this with an example: the verb *cimma* 'learn' is semantically transitive; it has an A argument (the learner) and a P argument (the thing learned, the knowledge acquired). The verb is, however, inflected with intransitive morphology (triggered by the semantic A argument, the learner), thus behaving like the verb in (1a) with respect to person marking.

[6] The same notational convention is employed, e.g., in Schikowski, Bickel & Paudyal (2015).

b. *nda   nu-ga=na?*
    2SG   get_well[PST]-2=NMLZ.SG
    'Are you fine?'

c. *n-yag-a-sy-a-ga-n=na=i?*
    NEG-feel_exhausted-PST-MDDL-PST-2-NEG=NMLZ.SG=Q
    'Are you not exhausted?'

11.1.3 The intransitive experiencer frame {A-NOM P-LOC/INS/ABL/COM V-s[A]}

Some experiencer verbs allow the expression of overt stimulus arguments, despite being identical to the standard intransitive frame with respect to its person marking morphology. The stimulus can be marked by various peripheral cases like the ablative, the locative, the instrumental and the comitative, as illustrated by example (3a) and (3b). These experiencer verbs are typically etymologically complex (both Noun-Verb and Verb-Verb compounds), as they often have bisyllabic stems, and Kiranti languages, following a broader tendency in Southeast Asian languages, are typically characterized by monosyllabic morphemes (Matisoff 1990a). Some verbs of this frame have metaphorical meaning: 'to be hungry' is expressed as in (3c), without the intention to exaggerate or to be ironic.

(3) a. *ka   nda=bhaŋ/nda=nuŋ   kisit-a-ŋ=na.*
         1SG   2SG=ABL/2SG=COM   be_afraid-PST-1SG=NMLZ.SG
         'I was afraid of you.'

     b. *ka   coklet̪=pe   kam-di-me-ŋ=na.*
         1SG   sweets=LOC   pine_over-V2.GIVE-NPST-1SG=NMLZ.SG
         'I pine over sweets.'

     c. *sak=ŋa   n-sy-a-ma-ŋa-n=na.*
         hunger=INS   NEG-die-PST-PRF-1SG-NEG=NMLZ.SG
         'I am not hungry.'

11.1.4 The motion verb frame {A-NOM P-LOC V-s[A]}

Motion verbs are intransitively inflected, but they have two arguments, as they entail a mover (A) and the location or goal of the movement (P) in their conceptualization. This is also borne out by the natural language data: most of the motion verbs express the location overtly, marked by a locative. In a language that has generally more covert than overtly realized arguments, this can be counted as a strong indicator for the entailment of the locative argument in the verbal semantics. The location or goal can be expressed by an adverb, as in (4a), or by a noun phrase (see (4b) - (4d)).

(4)   a.   *kucuma*   *he?ne*   *khy-a=na?*
           dog   where   go[3SG]-PST=NMLZ.SG
           'Where did the dog go?'

     b.   *koŋgu=be*   *thaŋ-a=na.*
           hill=LOC   climb[3SG]-PST=NMLZ.SG
           'He climbed on the hill.'

     c.   *saŋgoŋ=be*   *yuŋ-a=na.*
           mat=LOC   sit_down[3SG]-PST=NMLZ.SG
           'He sat down on the mat.'

     d.   *taŋkheŋ=be*   *pes-a-khy-a=niŋ,*   ...
           sky=LOC   fly[3SG]-PST-V2.GO-PST=CTMP
           'When he (the bird) flew into the sky, ...'   [21_nrr_04.031]

Under certain circumstances the locative on the goal argument can be omitted, e.g., when the location is a specific place with a name, or if it is a place that one typically moves to, such as villages, countries, the school, the work place and the like (see (5) and Chapter 5.2.2.1).[7] Only unmodified nouns can appear without the locative, if the reference of the noun is narrowed down and made definite, e.g., by a possessive or demonstrative pronoun, it has to take the locative case (see (5c)).

(5)   a.   *liŋkha=ci=ga*   *te?ma*   *bagdata*
           a_clan=NSG=GEN   clan_sister   finalization_of_marriage
           nak-se   *mamliŋ*   *ta-ya-ma.*
           ask_for-SUP   Mamling   come[3SG]-PST-PRF
           'A Linkha clan sister came to Mamling to ask for her *bagdata* (ritual).'
                                                         [37_nrr_07.002]

     b.   *hi?wa*   *pes-a=na.*
           wind   fly[3SG]-PST=NMLZ.SG
           'He flew (up) into the air.'   [21_nrr_004.051]

     c.   *nna*(=be)=go*   *imin*   *thaŋ-ma?*
           that*(=LOC)=TOP   how   climb-INF
           'But how to climb to that (place)?'   [22_nrr_05.098]

---

[7] Example (a) refers to a marriage custom called *bagdata*, see Chapter 2.2.2.5.

11.1.5 The standard monotransitive frame {A-ERG P-NOM V-a[A].o[P]}

This frame characterizes the majority of the monotransitive verbs, such as *nima* 'see' and *mokma* 'beat'. The verb shows agreement with both A and P. The A argument is marked by an ergative case *=ŋa* (see (6a)), except for first and second person pronouns, which exhibit an ergative/nominative syncretism (see also Chapter 5.2.2.2).[8] The condition for the ergative/nominative syncretism is identical to this frame throughout all the transitively inflected frames. The P arguments are in the nominative case.

(6) a. *isa=ŋa*   *chemha*   *tuks-u=ha?*
      who=ERG   liquor   spill-3.P[PST]=NMLZ.NC
      'Who spilled the liquor?'

    b. *ka*   *iya=ca*
      1SG[ERG]   what=NMLZ.NC=ADD
      ŋ-kheps-u-ŋa-n=ha.
      NEG-hear-3.P[PST]-1SG.A-NEG=NMLZ.NC
      'I did not hear anything.'

11.1.6 The experiencer-as-object frame {A-NOM P-ERG V-a[P].o[A]}

Experiential events often show deviations from the standard marking patterns of argument encoding (see, e.g., Bhaskararao & Subbarao 2004 and Malchukov 2008). There is one frame in Yakkha that is identical to the standard monotransitive frame, but the marking of A and P is reversed; the experiencer triggers object agreement on the verb, while the stimulus triggers subject agreement (zero for third person singular) and hosts the ergative case clitic. Notwithstanding the non-canonical agreement and case properties, the preferred constituent order is A-P-verb, and constructions with an S/A pivot, for instance, select the experiencer. The majority of the verbs belonging to this frame are related to the ingestion of food or to the consumption of other supplies, illustrated in (7).

(7) a. *ka*   *macchi=ŋa*   *haŋd-a-ŋ=na.*
      1SG   pickles=ERG   taste_spicy-PST-1SG.P=NMLZ.SG
      'The pickles tasted hot to me.'[9]

---

[8] Note that nouns with first and second person reference are possible in Yakkha (as if saying 'An old woman AM tired'; see also §12.4). If they are A arguments of transitive verbs, they are marked by an ergative, other than the first and second person pronouns.

[9] The Maithili loanword *macchi* has developed several meanings in Yakkha, namely 'chili plant', 'chili powder' and 'hot pickle or sauce'.

b. *ka   haŋha=ŋa   khot-a-ŋ=na.*
1SG   hot_spices=ERG   have_enough-PST-1SG.P=NMLZ.SG
'I have enough spice (in my food).'

c. *nasa=ga   ŋai=ŋa   khikt-a-ŋ=na.*
fish=GEN   stomach=ERG   taste_bitter-PST-1SG.P=NMLZ.SG
'The fish stomach tasted bitter to me.'

Verbs that refer to being affected by natural or supernatural powers also follow the object-experiencer frame, e.g., *teʔnima* 'be possessed, suffer from evil spirit' in (8a). The verb 'be drunk' is expressed as shown in (8b). The stem *sis* literally also means 'kill' with an animate, intentional A argument, but as the example shows, metaphorical meanings are possible as well. Notably, in this predicate, the stimulus is often omitted; *sis* has undergone a metaphorical extension towards the meaning of 'being drunk'.

(8) a. *puŋdaraŋma=ŋa   teps-y-uks-u=na.*
forest_goddess=ERG   be_possessed-PRF-3.P[PST]=NMLZ.SG
'He is possessed by the forest goddess.'

b. *(raksi=ŋa)   sis-a-ga=na=i?*
liquor=ERG   kill-PST-2.P=NMLZ.SG=Q
'Are you drunk?'

11.1.7 The transimpersonal frame {S-NOM V-a[3].o[S]}

The transimpersonal frame is similar to the object-experiencer frame. The verbs inflect transitively, but there is no overt A argument, the verbs show default third person singular subject agreement (zero). The sole argument is in the nominative and triggers object agreement on the verb. Diachronically there probably was an overt A, but the only remnant found synchronically is the agreement; all attempts at producing an overt A were regarded as ungrammatical. Malchukov (2008) notes that such constructions tend to be experiencer constructions crosslinguistically. In Yakkha, however, transimpersonal verbs are not experiencer verbs, as the subjects of these verbs are not typically animate, sentient beings. Verbs belonging to this frame often have change-of-state semantics, e.g., *cikma* 'ripen', *lokma* 'boil', *homma* 'swell', *huʔma* 'be blocked', *ŋomma* 'remain', shown in (9).

(9) a. *a-nabhuk   hut-u=na.*
1SG.POSS-nose   be_blocked-3.P[PST]=NMLZ.SG
'I have a blocked nose.'

   b.   *a-laŋ=ci*   *homd-u-ci=ha.*
       1SG.POSS-leg=NSG   swell-3.P[PST]-NSG.P=NMLZ.NSG
       'My legs are swollen.'

   c.   *cama*   *ŋond-u=ha.*
       rice   remain-3.P[PST]=NMLZ.NC
       '(Some) rice remained.'

   d.   *cuwa*   *cikt-u=ha.*
       beer   ripen-3.P[PST]=NMLZ.NC
       'The beer is well-fermented.'

An agent or cause can only be expressed indirectly, via adverbial clauses such as in (10). A transitive structure, with an overt A argument can be achieved by a causative derivation, as shown in (11b) (see (10a) for the same verbal stem without a causative derivation).

(10)   *tumbuk* *poks-a=niŋa*   *ten*   *lus-u=na.*
       gun   explode[3SG]-PST=CTMP village deafen-3.P[PST]=NMLZ.SG
       'When the gun exploded, the village was deafened (by the noise).'

(11)   a.   *maŋcwa* *lokt-u=ha.*
          water   boil-3.P[PST]=NMLZ.NC
          'The water boiled.'

      b.   *kamala=ŋa*   *maŋcwa* *lok-met-wa=ha.*
          Kamala=ERG   water   boil-CAUS-NPST[3.P]=NMLZ.NC
          'Kamala boils water.'

Transimpersonal verbs are a solid class in Kiranti languages, found, e.g., in Limbu (van Driem 1987: 451), in Thulung (Allen 1975: 42) and in Bantawa (Doornenbal 2009: 222). In Yakkha, 29 transimpersonal verbs have been found so far.[10]

---

[10] The following transimpersonal verbs have been found so far in Yakkha: *chamma* 'spread, increase', *cemma* 'get well, recover', *choma* 'tingle', *cikma* 'ripen', *cipma* 'rise' (only for water), *hekma* 'get stuck, choke', *heʔma* 'be entangled, hang, snag', *homma* 'swell'(stem: *homd*), *homma* 'fit into' (stem: *hond*), *huʔma* 'be blocked', *keŋma* 'bear fruit', *khakma* 'freeze', *khekt* 'freeze, harden', *khopma* 'fit around something', *leʔma* 'flourish, be prosperous', *lokma* 'boil', *mopma* 'be clouded, be dull', *ŋomma* 'remain', *oʔma* 'hatch', *pheʔma* 'bloom', *phiŋma* 'get clear', *puʔma* 'spill, overboil', *sipma* 'evaporate', *suncama* 'itch', *tapma* 'last long', *wemma* 'get intoxicated, be insolent', *yeŋma* 'be strong, be tough'.

11.1.8 Marginally occurring frames

11.1.8.1 The locative object frame {A-ERG P-LOC V-a[A].o[3]}

One verb, *tama* 'arrive (at)', differs from the standard monotransitive frame in marking the P argument with the locative case. The object agreement slot is always filled by default third person object agreement: speech-act participants cannot be the objects of this verb. Rather, one would express such content as 'arrive at your place', with a third person object agreement.

(12) *laluban=nuŋ*   *phaluban=ŋa*   *mamliŋ=be*
      Lalubang=COM   Phalubang=ERG   Mamling=LOC
      tas-a-ma-c-u.
      arrive-PST-PRF-DU-3.P
      'Lalubang and Phalubang have arrived in Mamling.'   [22_nrr_05.041]

11.1.8.2 The semi-transitive frame {S-ERG V-a[S].o[3]}

In the semi-transitive frame, the verb is transitively inflected and the sole argument receives ergative marking, but overt objects are suppressed. The verb shows default third person singular object agreement, as in (13). The expression of the P (the excreted substance) is not just considered redundant, but unacceptable.[11] This frame is like the mirror-image of the trans-impersonal frame discussed above. So far, however, the verb *oma* 'vomit' in (13) is the only member of this frame.

(13) *tug-a-by-a=na*   *yapmi=ŋa*
      get_sick-PST-V2.GIVE-PST[3SG]=NMLZ.SG   person=ERG
      os-u=ha.
      vomit-3.P=NMLZ.NC
      'The sick person vomited.'

11.1.8.3 The double nominative frame {A-NOM P-NOM V-s[A]}

This frame was found only for one verb, but it is listed for the sake of completeness. The verb *cimma* 'learn' is inflected intransitively, although it takes two arguments. Both A and P are in the nominative, and A triggers the verbal person marking (see (14a)). With transitive agreement morphology the verb becomes

---

[11] See Li (2007: 1480) for a similar class of verbs in Nepali.

the ditransitive verb 'teach' (see (14b)). Except for the additional argument, this alternation is identical to the labile alternation discussed in §11.2.1.

(14) a. *hari   iŋlis   cind-a=na.*
         Hari   English   learn[3SG]-PST=NMLZ.SG
         'Hari learned English.'

      b. *kamala=ŋa   hari   iŋlis   cind-u=na.*
         Kamala=ERG   Hari   English   teach-3.P[PST]=NMLZ.SG
         'Kamala taught Hari English.'

11.1.9 Three-argument verbs

The case and agreement properties of the subjects of three-argument verbs are not different from those of monotransitive verbs. The argument realization of the T and G arguments, however, deserves a closer look. It is determined by both semantic roles and the referential properties of the arguments. The choice of the agreement triggering argument for the nominalizing clitics =na and =ha need not be the same as for the verbal agreement. The nominalizers are partly aligned according to the referential properties of the arguments and partly according to their role. This is discussed in detail in §8.2 and §13.3.3 and will not figure prominently in the following treatment of three-argument frames.

11.1.9.1 The double object frame {A-ERG G-NOM T-NOM V-a[A].o[G]}

In the double object frame, both T and G arguments are in the nominative case. The verb agrees with the A and usually with the G argument, except for some pragmatically marked scenarios where T becomes the agreement trigger (see §11.2.2). The choice of the nominalizer on the finite verb depends on T when T has third person reference: singular T triggers =na, and nonsingular or non-countable T triggers =ha (compare (15b) and (15c)). The verbs belonging to this frame are typically verbs of caused possession and benefactives (both derived and underived), and thus, the G arguments are typically animate in this frame.

(15) a. *ka   a-ni   mendhwak*
         1SG[ERG]   1SG.POSS-aunt   goat
         hakt-wa-ŋ=na.
         send-NPST[3.P]-1SG.A=NMLZ.SG
         'I send my aunt a goat.'

b. *ka*   *nda eko coklet̩ pi?-nen=na.*
1SG[ERG] 2SG one   sweet give[PST]-1>2=NMLZ.SG
'I gave you a sweet.'

c. *ka*   *nda pyak coklet̩ pi?-nen=ha.*
1SG[ERG] 2SG many sweet give[PST]-1>2=NMLZ.NSG
'I gave you many sweets.'

11.1.9.2 The indirective frame {A-ERG G-LOC/ABL/COM T-NOM V-a[A].o[T]}

The indirective frame is more frequent than the double object frame, i.e., there are more verbs that follow this frame. The G argument may have goal or source role and is marked by a locative (see (16)) or, occasionally, by an ablative or comitative case (see (17)), while the T argument is in the nominative and triggers object agreement on the verb (including the nominalizers). Mostly, caused motion is expressed by verbs of this frame.

(16) a. *ka*   *a-cya=ci*   *iskul=be*
1SG[ERG] 1SG.POSS-child=NSG   school=LOC
paks-wa-ŋ-ci-ŋ=ha.
send-NPST-1SG.A-NSG.P-1SG.A=NMLZ.NSG
'I send my children to school.'

b. *ak=ka*   *khorek cula=ga*   *u-yum=be*
1SG.POSS=GEN bowl   hearth=GEN   3SG.POSS-side=LOC
yuks-uks-u-ŋ=na.
put-PRF-3.P[PST]-1SG.A=NMLZ.SG
'I have put my bowl next to the hearth.'

c. *ama=ŋa*   *a-nuncha*   *netham=be*
mother=ERG   1SG.POSS-younger_sibling bed=LOC
nes-u=na.
lay-3.P[PST]=NMLZ.SG
'Mother laid my younger sister on the bed.'

(17) a. *kha?niŋgo tu?khi leŋ-me?=niŋa*
but   trouble happen[3SG]-NPST=CTMP
heko=ha=ci=nuŋ   *yaŋ*   *naŋ-ca-ma*   *ucun*
other=NMLZ.NSG=NSG=COM   money beg-V2.EAT-INF nice
men.
NEG.COP
'But in difficult times, it is not good to ask others for money.'
[01_leg_07.257]

b. *haku   nhaŋto   m-ba=nuŋ   nasa*
   now   TEMP.ABL   2SG.POSS-father=COM   fish
   ŋ-in-wa-n-ci-ŋa-n=ha.
   NEG-buy-NPST-NEG-3NSG.P-EXCL-NEG=NMLZ.NSG
   'From now on I will not buy fish from your father.'   [01_leg_07.208]

The locative can also mark adjuncts, yielding clauses that look superficially identical to the indirective frame. However, the adjuncts have to be distinguished from locative-marked arguments. In (18), for instance, it is straightforward that the locative-marked noun phrases refer to circumstances such as time, place, manner, quantity (Tesnière 1959: 108) and are thus adjuncts. However, the decision whether a participant is an argument or an adjunct is not that trivial for all the predicates.

(18) a. *a-ppa=ŋa   ka   omphu=be   nis-a-ŋ=na.*
          1SG.POSS-father=ERG   1SG   verandah=LOC   see-PST-1SG.P=NMLZ.SG
          'Father saw me on the verandah.'

      b. *a-ma=ŋa   tan=be   tek*
          1SG.POSS-mother=ERG   loom=LOC   fabric
          akt-u=na.
          weave-3.P[PST]=NMLZ.SG
          'Mother wove (a piece of) fabric on the loom.'

11.1.9.3 The secundative frame {A-ERG G-NOM T-INS V-a[A].o[G]}

The verbs of the secundative frame denote events of throwing, hitting, covering, applying, exchanging, events of creative or destructive impact. The T argument is marked by an instrumental case, but it is not always an instrument in the classical sense of "used by the agent to act on the patient" (Andrews 1985: 140), as (19a) shows. The G argument is in the unmarked nominative and triggers agreement on the verb (including the nominalizers). Some verbs of this frame may alternate with the indirective frame (the 'spray-load alternation', see §11.2.2).

(19) a. *ka   cabak=ŋa   paŋge   lend-u-ŋ=ha.*
          1sg   rice=INS   millet   exchange-3.P[PST]-1SG.A=NMLZ.NSG
          'I exchanged rice for millet.'

      b. *u-ppa=ŋa   hammana=ŋa   picha*
          3SG.POSS-father=ERG   blanket=INS   child
          ept-u=na.
          cover-3.P[PST]=NMLZ.SG
          'The father covered his child with a blanket.'

c. *eko phiswak=ŋa sum=ci ṭukra*
    one knife=INS three=NSG piece
    yub-u-ci=ha.
    cut-3.P[PST]-3NSG.P=NMLZ.NSG
    'He cut it into three pieces with a small knife.' (Cut-and-break clips,
    Bohnemeyer, Bowerman & Brown 2010)

11.1.10 The experiencer-as-possessor frame
{S-GEN/NOM POSS-N V-s[3]}
{A-GEN/ERG P-NOM POSS-N V-a[A].o[3]}

Experiential predicates are characterized by the core participant being emotionally or sensationally affected by the event. This makes the thematic role 'experiencer' less agent-like, which is often reflected in the treatment of experiencer arguments as non-prominent ("downgrading" in Bickel 2004b), e.g., by non-
canonical case marking or by deviating agreement patterns (Levin & Rappaport
Hovav 2005: 22, Næss 2007: 185). We have already seen a class of experiential
predicates in Yakkha that code their A arguments like standard objects. However, downgrading of an argument in one part of grammar, for instance, in case
marking, does not necessarily imply downgrading in other domains, for instance
access to pivothood or reflexivization (Bickel 2004b: 77).

Most experiential events in Yakkha, and generally in Kiranti languages, are
expressed by complex predicates consisting of a noun and a verb, and the experiencer (i.e., the A argument) is coded as the possessor of the noun (see §9.2).[12] The
nouns that belong to such predicates denote sensations, feelings, character traits,
moral qualities or affected body parts (hence, the term *psych-noun*). Noun-verb
compounds for the expression of experiential events are not unique to Yakkha
or Kiranti languages; they belong to a broader Southeast Asian pattern (Matisoff
1986).

Morphosyntactically, the psych-noun hosts a possessive prefix that refers to
the experiencer. The noun may also trigger agreement on the verb (see (20) for
examples). Some psych-nouns are conceptualized as nonsingular and thus trigger nonsingular verbal agreement. The predicates can be grouped into intransitively and transitively inflected verbs. Some verbs show alternations. The two
schematic diagrams above only show the most common frames of the experiencer-as-possessor predicates, corresponding to (20a) and (20b), respectively. In
(20c), the stimulus triggers object agreement. For a detailed description of the
subframes and alternations see §9.2.1.

---

[12] See Bickel (1997c) for Belhare.

(20) a. *ŋ=ga*   *yupma(=ci)*   *n-yus-a(=ci)?*
          2SG.POSS=GEN   sleepiness(=NSG)   3PL-be_full-PST(=NSG)
          'Are you tired?'
      b. *ŋ-khaep*   *cips-u-ga=na=i?*
          2SG.POSS-interest/wish   complete-3.P[PST]-2.A=NMLZ.NSG=Q
          'Are you satisfied?'
      c. *nda*   *ka   ijaŋ   n-lok*
          2SG[ERG]   1SG   why   2SG.POSS-anger
          khot-a-ŋ-ga=na?
          have_enough-PST-1SG.P-2SG.A=NMLZ.SG
          'Why are you mad at me?'

11.1.11 Copular and light verb frames

Copular clauses are different from the other clauses insofar as the predicate is
not a verb but a nominal, adjectival or locative constituent (Dryer 2007: 225).
The constituents in copular clauses do not have semantic roles. Yakkha has two
copular frames which can roughly be characterized as the identificational and
the existential frame.[13] While the equational frame is expressed by a copular verb
(that is lacking an infinitival form) or by a copular particle *om* that is not found
elsewhere in simple clauses, the existential frame is expressed by two standard
intransitive verbs: *wama* 'be, live, exist' and *leŋma* 'become, happen, come into
being'.

11.1.11.1 Frame (a): Identification, equation, class inclusion

Two different forms participate in Frame (a): a copular verb that shows the expectable inflectional categories of person, number, tense/aspect and polarity, and
a copular particle *om* that can also refer to any person, but is not inflected, apart
from the nonsingular marker *=ci* (see (21c)). They are used to equate or identify
two entities, and to state class inclusion (see (21)). The forms of the copular verb
are suppletive in the nonpast; in the past forms it has a stem *sa* (see §8.7 on the
morphology of the copulas). The copular verb and the particle are optional, and
thus they are often omitted. The particle is also used as affirmative interjection
om 'yes'. The domains of these two copular devices overlap, and in one instance

---

[13] Such a two-way distinction in the copular frames is common in languages of the Himalayan
region (see, e.g., Genetti 2007 on Newari, and Matthews 1984 on Nepali), but the exact distribution of the copular verbs probably differs from language to language.

they were found combined, too (see (21d), where this combination seems to yield emphasis).

(21) a. *ka   khasi   ŋan.*
          1SG   castrated_goat   COP.1SG
          'I am a castrated goat.'   [31_mat_01.074]

     b. *ka   isa   om?*
          1SG   who   COP
          'Who am I?'

     c. *susma=nuŋ   suman   na   nuncha   om=ci.*
          Susma=COM   Suman   eZ   yB   COP=NSG
          'Susma and Suman are (elder) sister and (younger) brother.'
                                                                [01_leg_07.035]

     d. *ka   na   puɳda=ga   khuncakhuwa   ŋan   om!*
          1SG   this   jungle=GEN   thief   COP.1SG   COP
          'I am the thief of this jungle!'   [01_leg_07.335]

11.1.11.2 Frame (b): Existence, attribution, location, possession

Two verbs occur in Frame (b): the verb *wama* 'be, live, exist' is a stative verb expressing existence. Its stem shows irregular behavior: the basic stem form is *waiʔ ~ waeʔ ~ weʔ*, and additionally *ma* can be found in some negated forms (see §8.7 for the inflection of the copulas). This verb can occur in the motion verb frame, expressing location or possession (see (22a)). It can also be used to express a property of the copular topic, with an adjective as the predicate (see (22b) and (22c)).

(22) a. *ibebe   pyak   encho   paŋ=ci*
          somewhere   much   long_time_ago   house=NSG
          m-ma-ya-nin=ha.
          NEG-exist-PST-PL.NEG=NMLZ.NSG
          'Once upon a time there were no houses.'[14]   [27_nrr_06.001]

     b. *bani   man=na.*
          habit   exist.NEG.NPST[3SG]=NMLZ.SG
          'There is no (such) habit.'

     c. *nna   cuʔlumphi   haku=ca   ceŋaceŋ*
          that   stele   now=ADD   straight_upright

---

[14] The adverbial phrase *ibebe* is a fixed expression that originates in *ibe-ibe* 'somewhere-somewhere'.

> wae?=na.
> be[3SG;NPST]=NMLZ.SG
> 'This stele stands straight upright even now.' [18_nrr_03.030]

d. piccha=go uhingilik we?=na.
child=TOP alive existNPST[3SG]=NMLZ.SG
'But the child is alive.' [22_nrr_05.087]

The second verb of frame (b) is the ingressive-phasal verb *lenma* (stem: *leks*) 'become, come into being, happen', shown in (23). Apart from this meaning it is also used to express non-permanent properties, as in (23c).[15]

(23) a. na=ga suru imin leks-a=na bannin.
this=GEN beginning how become[3SG]-PST=NMLZ.SG as.for
'As for how she came into being...' [14_nrr_02.002]

   b. honka?la leks-a=hon, ...
like_that become[3SG]-PST=SEQ
'As it became like that, ...' [11_nrr_01.019]

   c. limlim lim=nun len-me.
sweet sweet=COM become[3SG]-NPST
khun-khe?-ma=nina li=nun=ca
carry-V2.CARRY.OFF-INF=CTMP heavy=COM=ADD
n-len-me-n.
NEG-become[3SG]-NPST-NEG
'The sweet will be tasty. While carrying, it also will not be heavy.'
[01_leg_07.044]

Example (24) from a pear story shows a nice minimal pair between the identificational and the existential copula (*sana* and *waisa*). The identificational copula only takes nominal predicates. The question word *imin* 'how' is nominalized, and combined with the identificational copula. The existence of the snow is, however, expressed by the existential verb *wama*.

(24) i=na, la, thon=ca imin=na
what=NMLZ.SG, FILLER, place=ADD how=NMLZ.SG
sa=na, hiun=le wai-sa, i=ya?
COP.PST[3SG]=NMLZ.SG snow=CTR exist-PST[3SG] what=NMLZ.NC
'What, well, what kind of place was it, there was snow, what was it?'

---

[15] In (c), the property as such is of course permanent, but the subordinate clause puts the property in the perspective of a specific time.

(Context: the speaker is unsure, because she is trying to understand what happens in the pear story film. Her interpretation of the distorted quality of the footage is that it must be a snowy place.) [19_pea_01.002]

11.1.11.3 Light verbs

The light verb strategy is commonly used to introduce Nepali verbs or light verb constructions into Yakkha. The construction is parallel to the Nepali source construction, but the Nepali light verbs are replaced by the Yakkha lexemes *wama* 'exist, be' and *cokma* 'do'.

The resulting structure also gets formally adjusted to the Yakkha morphosyntax. In Nepali, some S/A arguments (e.g., of knowledge and experiential predicates) are marked by the dative *-lāī* (the Nepali translation of (25a) would be *ma-lāī ali-ali thāhā cha*), and the verb shows third person agreement with the noun in the nominative. But as there is no dative case in Yakkha, the result of the calquing is a nominative-marked subject and a light verb that triggers third person agreement. In light verb constructions which are not calques from experiential predicates, the verb agrees with the subject (S or A, see (25b)). Although overt P arguments are possible, as *nam* 'sun' in (25b), the light verbs found so far are always inflected intransitively, and A arguments in the ergative case were not found.

(25) a. *ka*   *mimik*   *thaha*   *wae?=na.*
          1SG   a_bit   knowledge   exist[3SG]=NMLZ.SG
          'I know a little bit.'   [13_cvs_02.022]
      b. *liŋkha=ci*   *nam=nuŋ*   *bʌgʌri*   *n-jog-a.*
          a_clan=NSG   sun=COM   bet   3PL-do-PST
          'The Linkhas had a bet with the sun.'   [11_nrr_01.003]

The same strategy is also used for borrowing Nepali verbal stems into Yakkha (see (26), with the Nepali verb *haraunu* 'lose'). The Nepali stems are integrated into Yakkha by means of the suffix *-a* (also found in related languages, e.g., *-ap* in Belhare, Bickel 2003: 559). The resulting lexeme *hara* is then treated like any other noun by the light verb.

(26) *ŋkhoŋ*   *liŋkha*   *baji=be*   *har-a*   *cog-a-khy-a.*
      and_then   a_clan   bet=LOC   lose-NATIV   do[3SG]-PST-V2.GO-PST
      'And then the Linkha man lost the bet.'   [11_nrr_01.012]

11.2 Valency alternations

The frames introduced in §11.1 show various alternations. Different types of alternations have to be distinguished: some just change the argument realization, e.g., differential case marking, which is triggered by pragmatic factors such as scenario classes. Other alternations, e.g., the inchoative-causative lability, change the argument structure.

The labile verbs will be discussed in §11.2.1, §11.2.2 deals with the alternations among the three-argument frames.[16]

11.2.1 Lability

Labile verbs are characterized by variable transitivity of the same verbal stem, which is not brought about by means of a morphological derivation. Letuchiy (2009: 224) classifies labile verbs into different types: the inchoative/causative alternation, the reflexive alternation, the reciprocal alternation, the passive (extremely rare) and the converse type. According to this classification, Yakkha has the inchoative/causative[17] and the reflexive.[18] The current lexical database contains 77 labile verbs. The inchoative/causative alternation is patient-preserving; the reflexive alternation is agent-preserving (see also Letuchiy 2009: 223).

As lability is defined by the absence of morphological marking, it is hard to tell which form of a labile pair is the basic form. The intransitive verb can be considered the basic form semantically and formally, as less participants are involved in the event, and as the verb hosts less inflectional morphology than the transitive verb.[19]

---

[16] For alternations found among the experiencer-as-possessor predicates see §9.2.

[17] The inchoative/causative type is equated with 'labile' in Haspelmath (1993), whose definition of labile verbs is more restrictive.

[18] Furthermore, Yakkha shows morphologically unmarked detransitivizations that can have both passive and antipassive interpretations, but they do not change the semantic roles of the arguments and hence they are not lexical alternations. They are treated below in §11.3 on transitivity operations. Letuchiy acknowledges the passive-type as labile, but considers unmarked antipassives *quasi-lability*, because his crucial defining feature for lability is a change of the semantic roles. But if semantic role change is required, his inclusion of the passive alternation is misleading. In passives, the semantic roles do not change; the undergoer of 'beat' does not have different semantic roles in the active vs. the passive voice.

[19] From a first impression, there are definitely also differences in frequency among the labile verbs. Some are rather used transitively and some intransitively, depending on which function of a verb is more plausible in natural discourse. The existing corpus is not big enough for significant statistic analyses.

11.2.1.1 Inchoative-causative lability

By far the majority of the labile verbs belong to the inchoative-causative class, a fact that goes along with the crosslinguistic findings in Letuchiy (2009). The intransitive verbs denote states or spontaneous changes of state. No agent or causer argument is entailed in the verbal semantics.[20] In the corresponding transitive verb, a causer argument that brings about the event is added, and the P argument corresponds to the S of the intransitive verb. Examples (27a), (27c) and (27e) show the inchoative verbs with S undergoing a spontaneous change of state, while (27b), (27d) and (27f) show the corresponding transitive verbs with an A argument bringing about that change of state. The verb *cimma*, meaning both 'learn' and 'teach', basically belongs to the same alternation, but it has one additional argument. The intransitively inflected verb has two arguments and the transitively inflected verb has three arguments (see §11.1.8.3).

(27) a. *dailo   hos-a=na.*
          door   open[3SG]-PST=NMLZ.SG
          'The door opened.'

      b. *a-ppa=ŋa   dailo   hos-uks-u=na.*
          1SG.POSS-father=ERG   door   open-PRF-3.P=NMLZ.SG
          'Father has opened the door.'

      c. *siŋ   eg-a=na.*
          wood   break[3SG]-PST=NMLZ.SG
          'The piece of wood broke.'

      d. *uŋ=ŋa   siŋ   eg-u=na.*
          3SG=ERG   wood   break-3.P[PST]=NMLZ.SG
          'He broke the piece of wood.'

      e. *phuama   yupma=ci=bhaŋ   cend-a=na.*
          last-born_girl sleepiness=NSG=ABL   wake_up[3SG]-PST=NMLZ.SG
          'Phuama woke from her sleep.'

      f. *ka   uŋ   cend-u-ŋ=na.*
          1SG[ERG]   3SG   wake_up-3SG.P[PST]-1SG.A=NMLZ.SG
          'I woke her up.'

---

[20] Notably, inchoative ('anticausative' in Creissels 2014) readings do not always express events that do not have an agent or a causer argument. Sometimes, the A is merely not relevant for a certain event, and thus it is not part of the underlying concept of the event, and has to be left unexpressed, as shown, e.g., for facilitative readings of anticausatives in Tswana by Creissels (2014).

There are border cases of lability. In Yakkha, many events are expressed by complex predicates. In these predicates, the first stem contains the lexical verb, such as the labile stem *khiks ~ khiŋ* 'stretch, grow' in (28). The second verbal stem is from the closed class of function verbs (V2s, see Chapter 10); they specify the verbal semantics, for instance with regard to the temporal structure. In (28a), the V2 *-kheʔ* 'go' emphasizes the telicity of the event. It is sensitive to transitivity, too. The V2 *-kheʔ* is only compatible with intransitive interpretations (see ungrammatical (28b)). Thus, complex predication can have the secondary function of indicating transitivity features.

(28) a. *ikhiŋ   khiks-a(-**khy**-a)=na!*
           how_much   stretch[3SG]-PST(-V2.GO-PST)=NMLZ.SG
           'How tall she became!'

      b. *a-laŋ=ci   khiŋ(*-**kheʔ**)-ma=ci.*
           1SG.POSS-leg=NSG   stretch(*-V2.GO)-INF[DEONT]=NSG
           Intended: 'I have to stretch my legs.'

11.2.1.2 Reflexive lability

The stems of this class alternate between a transitive reading and an intransitive reading with reflexive semantics. Strictly speaking, no argument is removed in reflexives, but the A and P have identical reference and collapse into one single intransitive subject role formally (Haspelmath & Müller-Bardey 2004: 1134). In the transitive reading, an external P argument is added. Typically, the verbs undergoing this alternation refer to actions involving the body. The examples in (29) illustrate the reflexive alternation with three verb pairs.

(29) a. *uŋci=ŋa   men-ni-ma=nuŋ   cum-a-ŋ=na.*
           3NSG=ERG   NEG-see-INF=COM.CL   hide-PST-1SG=NMLZ.SG
           'I hid, so that they cannot see (me).'

      b. *ripu=ŋa   khorek   cum-u=na.*
           Ripu=ERG   bowl   hide-3.P[PST]=NMLZ.SG
           'Ripu hid the bowl.'

      c. *ka=ca   mimiʔ   wasiʔ-a-ŋ=hoŋ,   ...*
           1SG=ADD   a_little   wash-PST-1SG=SEQ
           'After washing myself a little, ...'   [40_leg_08.050]

      d. *a-nuncha   wasiʔ-wa-ŋ=na.*
           1SG.POSS-younger_sibling   wash-NPST[3.P]-1SG.A=NMLZ.SG
           'I wash my little sister.'

e. *a-chya*   *(tek=ŋa)*   *ept-a=na.*
1SG.POSS-child   (cloth=INS)   cover[3SG]-PST=NMLZ.SG
'My child covered itself (with the blanket).'

f. *yenda*   *ept-a-n-u-m.*
millet_mash   cover-PST-PL-3.P[IMP]-2PL.A
'Cover the millet mash.'

11.2.2 Alternations in three-argument verbs

Alternations in three-argument verbs are mostly conditioned by pragmatic factors such as topicality or the referential properties of the arguments.[21] Typically, in events with three arguments, the G arguments (goals, recipients) are animate, definite and thus also more topic-worthy, whereas the T arguments have a strong tendency to be inanimate, indefinite and thus less topic-worthy. Events in which this expected scenario is reversed are more marked pragmatically, and this could be reflected in the morphosyntax of the clause (Dryer 1986; Siewierska 2003, Haspelmath 2004b; 2005; 2007, Malchukov, Haspelmath & Comrie 2010a). Some of the referential effects are found exclusively in three-argument verbs in Yakkha, for instance a case of hierarchical agreement, where the T and the G argument compete for an agreement slot. One has to distinguish between argument-based alternations, i.e., effects that are conditioned by the referential properties of only one argument, and scenario-based alternations, i.e., effects that are conditioned by the properties of both T and G in relation to each other.

11.2.2.1 The spray-load alternation

One class of verbs shows alternations between the indirective and the secundative frame, also known as *spray-load alternation* (Levin 1993; Malchukov, Haspelmath & Comrie 2010b; Malchukov & Comrie 2015). Either the T argument is in the instrumental case and the G triggers object agreement on the verb (for the secundative frame, see (30a)), or the G argument is in the locative and the T triggers object agreement (for the indirective frame, see (30b)).

(30) a. *ka*   *makai=ŋa*   *dalo*   *ipt-wa-ŋ=na.*
1SG[ERG]   corn=INS   sack   fill-NPST[3.P]-1SG=NMLZ.SG
'I filled the sack with corn.' (secundative)

---

[21] My investigation of referentiality effects in three-argument verbs (see also Schackow 2012b) has been inspired by the EUROBabel project Referential Hierarchies in Morphosyntax (RHIM) and a questionnaire on three-argument constructions, designed by Anna Siewierska and Eva van Lier (not published).

b. *gagri=be   maŋcwa   ipt-u.*
pot=LOC   water   fill-3.P[IMP]
'Fill the water into the pot.' (indirective)

The verb *ipma* 'fill' in (30) can only have inanimate G arguments. Verbs with a greater variability of possible arguments may show restrictions on this alternation. Some verbs, for instance, block the secundative frame when the G argument is inanimate, e.g., (31a), which renders the indirective frame the only possibility (see (31b)). In order to license the secundative frame, the G argument has to have the potential to be affected by the event (31c). The verb *lupma* 'scatter, disperse, strew' provides another example of this restriction. Again, the secundative frame is the preferred option for animate G arguments, while the indirective is used when inanimate G arguments are involved (32b) (context: the preparation of millet beer). In (32a), the G argument is non-overt, but it has human reference, which can be inferred from the context: a funeral.

(31) a. **ka   maŋcwa   luŋkhwak=ŋa*
1SG[ERG]   water   stone=INS
lept-u-ŋ=ha.
throw-3.P[PST]-1SG=NMLZ.NSG
Intended: 'I threw a stone into the water.' (*secundative)

b. *ka   lunkhwak   maŋcwa=be   lept-u-ŋ=na.*
1SG[ERG]   stone   water=LOC   throw-3.P[PST]-1SG=NMLZ.SG
'I threw a stone into the water.' (indirective)

c. *ka   nda   luŋkhwak=ŋa   lep-nen=na.*
1SG[ERG]   2SG   stone=INS   throw[PST]-1>2=NMLZ.SG
'I threw a stone at/to you.' (secundative)

(32) a. *kham=ŋa   lupt-u-ga=i.*
soil=INS   scatter-3.P[IMP]-2=EMPH
'Cover him with sand.'

b. *yenda=be   khawa   lupt-u-g=ha=i?*
millet_mash=LOC   yeast   disperse-3.P[PST]-2=NMLZ.NSG=Q
'Did you add the yeast to the millet mash?'

11.2.2.2 Alternations related to the animacy of G

One could see in the spray-load alternation that the unmarked nominative is preferred for animate, sentient G arguments. For some verbs, this results in alternations between the double object frame and the indirective frame. In (33a), the G argument is human, moreover it is a speech-act participant, and thus the highest on the referential hierarchy (Silverstein 1976). Hence, the double object frame is chosen, the verb agrees with G, and both T and G are in the nominative. In (33b), the G has third person inanimate reference, and the frame changes to indirective, with G in the locative, and T triggering the agreement.[22]

(33) a. *ka   nda sandhisa khuʔ-nen=na.*
       1SG[ERG] 2SG present   bring[PST]-1>2=NMLZ.SG
       'I brought you a present.'

    b. *uŋ=ŋa   kitab(=ci)   iskul=be*
       3SG=ERG book(=NSG) school=LOC
       khut-u-ci=ha.
       bring-3.P[PST]-3NSG.P=NMLZ.NSG
       'He brought the books to school.'

Some verbs only change the case marking of G without changing the agreement. The verb *hambiʔma* 'distribute' is a benefactive derivation of *hamma* 'distribute, divide, spread'. In the typical scenario, the G argument is referentially high, the T argument is low, and the argument realization follows the double object frame, as in (34a). When the G argument changes to inanimate reference, as in example (34b), it has to be in the locative case, but the verb does not change to the indirective frame; and thus the agreement remains with G. Furthermore, instead of using the nonsingular marker *=ci* on the G argument *ten* 'village', it is marked for nonsingular number by reduplication, which indicates a plurality of subevents. This kind of plural marking is not encountered when the G argument is human, as shown in example (34c).

(34) a. *ka   nniŋda phoṭo(=ci)*
       1SG[ERG] 2PL   photo(=NSG)
       ham-biʔ-meʔ-nen-in=ha.
       distribute-V2.GIVE-NPST-1>2-2PL=NMLZ.NSG
       'I distribute the photos among you.'

    b. *sarkar=ŋa   yaŋ   ten-ten=be*
       government=ERG money village-village=LOC
       ŋ-haps-u-bi-ci=ha.
       3PL.A-distribute-3.P[PST]-V2.GIVE-3NSG.P=NMLZ.NSG
       'The government distributed the money among the villages.'

---

[22] There is no number hierarchy at work in these alternations. The number of T is not the crucial factor, but nonsingular was chosen to illustrate the agreement.

c. *ka   piccha=ci   yaŋ*
1SG[ERG]   child=NSG   money
haps-u-bi-ŋ-ci-ŋ=ha.
distribute-3.P[PST]-V2.GIVE-1SG.A-NSG.P-1SG.A=NMLZ.NSG
'I distributed the money among the children.'

11.2.2.3 Scenario-based alternations

Not only case marking, but also the verbal person marking can be subject to reference-based alternations. The Yakkha verb agrees with only one object, so that there is the potential for competition between T and G arguments as to which argument will trigger the agreement. The universal tendency for agreement to be triggered by arguments that are speech act participants, animate or topical has already been mentioned by Givón (1976). This tendency can lead to hierarchical alignment of agreement, understood as agreement that is not determined by syntactic roles but by the referential properties of the arguments (Nichols 1992: 66). This is well-studied for monotransitive verbs, but not for three-argument verbs.[23]

There are two verbs of the double object class which allow animate/human T arguments, namely *soʔmeʔma* 'show' and *cameʔma* 'feed'. Etymologically, both verbs are causatives, but they show the same behavior as non-derived verbs. Usually, the verb shows object agreement with G in this frame (see (35a)), but when G has third person reference and T is a speech act participant (SAP), the verb agrees with T instead of G. The case marking of G also changes to locative, so that the verb now belongs to the indirective frame (see (35b)).

(35) a. *a-ni=ŋa*   *ka   u-phoṭo*
1SG.POSS-elder.sister=ERG   1SG   3SG.POSS-photo
soʔmet-a-ŋ=na.
show-PST-1SG.P=NMLZ.SG
'My elder sister showed me her photo.' (T[3]→G[SAP])

b. *ka   nda   appa-ama=be   soʔmeʔ-nen=na.*
1SG[ERG]   2SG   mother-father=LOC   show[PST]-1>2=NMLZ.SG
'I showed you to my parents.' (T[SAP]→G[3])

This alternation is scenario-based, as it only applies in the T[SAP]→G[3] constellation. In (36), both T and G are are speech-act participants, and the agreement

---

[23] The most prominent example for hierarchical alignment in ditransitives is the Yuman language Jamul Tiipay (Miller 2001: 162–163, discussed, e.g., in Siewierska 2003: 348).

remains with the G argument. This scenario is also pragmatically marked, which is why locative marking on G is possible (though not obligatory) here.

(36) uŋ=ŋa   ka   nniŋda(=be)   soʔmet-i-g=ha.
      3SG=ERG   1SG   2PL(=LOC)   show[3SG.A;PST]-2PL-2=NMLZ.NSG
      'He showed me to you (plural).' (T[SAP]→G[SAP])

In some contexts, this may yield more than one interpretation. As it is always the speech-act participant that triggers the agreement, a clause like in (37) is ambiguous. Note that the two verbs differ with respect to the acceptability of the locative on G. The effects of the T[SAP]→G[SAP] scenario are summarized in Figure 11.1.

	G[SAP]	G[3]
T[SAP]	V-o[G], G-LOC/NOM	V-o[T], G-LOC soʔmeʔma 'show' V-o[T], G-NOM cameʔma 'feed'
T[3]		V-o[G], G-NOM

Figure 11.1: The effects of the T[SAP]→G[3] scenario

(37) ka   nda   kiba(*=be)   cameʔ-meʔ-nen=na.
      1SG[ERG] 2SG   tiger(*=LOC) feed-NPST-1>2=NMLZ.SG
      'I will feed you to the tiger!' (T-agr) OR
      'I will feed the tiger to you!' (G-agr)

The T[SAP]→G[3] scenario may also restrict alternations. The verb nakma (stem: nakt) 'ask, beg' alternates (almost) freely between the double object frame (see (38)) and the indirective frame (see (39)). It is the only verb that shows this alternation. The argument encoding is conditioned by the question of which argument is central in a given discourse.

(38) a. ka   nda   chemha   nak-nen=na.
          1SG[ERG]   2SG   liquor   ask[PST]-1>2=NMLZ.SG
          'I asked you for liquor.'
      b. ka   i=ya=ca   n-nakt-a-ŋa-n!
          1SG   what=NMLZ.NSG=ADD   NEG-ask-IMP-1SG.P-NEG
          'Do not ask me for anything!'   [27_nrr_06:25]

(39) a. *uŋ=ŋa   ka=be   unipma   nakt-u=ha.*
           3SG=ERG 1SG=LOC   money   ask-3.P[PST]=NMLZ.NC
           'He asked me for his money.'

    b. *uŋ=ŋa   appa-ama=be   ka   nakt-a-ŋ=na.*
           3SG=ERG mother-father=LOC   1SG   ask-PST-1SG.P=NMLZ.SG
           'He asked my parents for me (i.e., to marry me).'

However, when the T is a speech act participant and the G is not, as in (39b), the indirective frame is the only option. Clauses like the one in (40) are ungrammatical. Thus, the particular scenario in which the T is a speech act participant and the G is a third person restricts the alternations in the argument realization of this verb.

(40) **uŋci   ka   n-nakt-u-n-ci-n.*
      3NSG   1SG   NEG-ask-3.P[IMP]-NEG-NSG.P-NEG
      Intended: 'Do not ask them for me.'

The preceding section has shown how the argument realization in three-argument verbs can be conditioned by referential factors. The scenario T[SAP]→G[3] leads to an obligatory change in person and case marking for the verbs *soʔmeʔma* 'show' and *cameʔma* 'feed', and to a restriction in the alternation possibilities for the verb *nakma* 'ask, beg'. Hierarchical alignment, partly combined with inverse marking, is also known from the verbal paradigms of other Tibeto-Burman languages, e.g., from rGyalrong (Nagano 1984), Rawang (LaPolla 2007), and to some extent from other Kiranti languages, too, like Hayu and Dumi (Michailovsky 2003; van Driem 1993a). In the Yakkha verbal person marking, however, hierarchical alignment as it is found in the three-argument verbs shown above is not found in the monotransitive paradigms.[24]

11.3 Transitivity operations

This section discusses operations that bring about some change in the transitivity of a verb. The transitivity operations distinguish between argument structure modifying and argument structure preserving operations, just as the valency alternations distinguish between argument-structure modifying and preserving

---

[24] Several morphemes in Yakkha verbal person marking are scenario-sensitive, see §8.2. However, the alignment of the verbal person marking in Yakkha is too heterogenous to be captured by one principle or one hierarchy. It also includes ergative, accusative, tripartite and neutral alignment (cf. also Witzlack-Makarevich et al. 2011 for a Kiranti-wide study).

alternations (see §11.2). Some of the operations change the semantics of a predicate by introducing or removing certain arguments, while other operations are related to requirements of information flow, thereby promoting or demoting certain participants syntactically. Not all of these operations are overtly marked, and detransitivizations have no dedicated marking at all.

This section is organized as follows: §11.3.1 discusses two unmarked detransitivations: the passive and the antipassive, §§11.3.2–§11.3.6 discuss the transitivity operations that are overtly marked on the verb: the causative, the benefactive, the reflexive, the reciprocal and the middle. Most of these operations involve the attachment of a function verb (V2) to the lexical verb (see also Chapter 10). §11.3.7 deals with a pattern of complex predication that is required by certain pragmatically marked scenarios (with referentially high P or T arguments). Finally, §11.3.8 introduces some stem alternations that must have been productive valency-increasing morphology in an earlier stage of Kiranti. As these stem alternations are marked, they do not fit into the previous section (on unmarked alternations); and since they are no longer productive, they do not fit into the section on productive transitivity operations either. But as they provide a glimpse into the history of transitivity operations in Yakkha, they are included in this section.

11.3.1 Unmarked detransitivizations

The detransitivizations, although morphologically unmarked and thus formally identical to lability (see §11.2.1), have to be carefully distinguished from lability, because the arguments are merely demoted with regard to some of their morphosyntactic properties; they are not removed semantically. The detransitivizations are syntactic operations; they are less restricted, whereas the labile verbs build a closed lexical class. The formal identity of detransitivization and lability may lead to overlaps and ambiguities (discussed below).

11.3.1.1 The passive detransitivization

Transitive verbs can be intransitively inflected, and thus receive a passive reading. In the passive, the P argument is the pragmatically salient argument and gets promoted to the intransitive subject syntactically, i.e., it becomes the sole agreement triggering argument. The A argument can still be expressed, but it does not trigger agreement and has to be in an oblique case (the ablative =*bhaŋ* ~ =*haŋ*). I cannot make strong claims about the naturalness of obliquely expressed A arguments in the passive, as there is not a single example of this use of the ablative in my recorded natural language data.[25] It is possible that the ablative is calqued upon the Nepali postposition *dvārā* 'by means of'.[26] In (41) and (42), the (a) examples illustrate the formal properties of the passive, with the corresponding transitive active clauses in the (b) examples.

(41)   a.   *na   wa   magman=bhaŋ   sis-a=na.*
             this   chicken   Magman=ABL   kill[3SG]-PST=NMLZ.SG
             'This chicken was killed by Magman.'

       b.   *magman=ŋa   na   wa   sis-u=na.*
             Magman=ERG   this   chicken   kill-3.P[PST]=NMLZ.SG
             'Magman killed this chicken.'

(42)   a.   *na   paŋ   a-phu=bhaŋ*
             this   house   1SG.POSS-elder_brother=ABL

             cog-a=na.
             make[3SG]-PST=NMLZ.SG
             'This house was built by my elder brother.'

       b.   *a-phu=ŋa   na   paŋ*
             1SG.POSS-elder_brother=ERG   this   house

             cog-u=na.
             make-3.P[PST]=NMLZ.SG
             'My elder brother built this house.'

As for three-argument verbs, in verbs of the double object frame, both T and G arguments can be promoted to subject status, illustrated in (43). Just as in the monotransitive verbs, the inflection changes to intransitive in the passive voice.

(43)   a.   *na   phuŋ   nda=bhaŋ   khut-a=na.*
             this   flower   2SG=ABL   bring[3SG]-PST=NMLZ.SG
             'This flower was brought by you.' (T → S)

       b.   *ka   phuŋ   (nda=bhaŋ)   khut-a-ŋ=na.*
             1SG   flower   2SG=ABL   bring-PST-1SG=NMLZ.SG
             'I was brought a flower by you.' (G → S)

The situation is different for three-argument verbs of the indirective frame (with G in the locative) and the secundative frame (with T in the instrumental). Here, only the argument in the unmarked nominative can be promoted to subject. The passive of the indirective frame is shown in (44).

---

[25] Remember that clauses with all arguments overtly expressed are exceedingly rare in Yakkha.
[26] Ebert (1997a: 123) provides examples of similar uses of the ablative in the closely related Athpare language, but it seems to be a marginal option in Athpare, too.

(44) a.   *on   siŋ=be   thund-a=na.*
           horse   tree=LOC   tie[3SG]-PST=NMLZ.SG
           'The horse was tied to the tree.'
    b.   *babu=ŋa on   siŋ=be   thund-u=na.*
           boy=ERG horse   tree=LOC   tie-3.P[PST]=NMLZ.SG
           'The boy tied the horse to the tree.'

The passive is typically employed when the transitive object is more salient than the subject in a particular section of discourse. In (45) from a narrative, the passive is not motivated by a topical patient, but by the unknown identity of the agent, as the whole sentence was uttered in surprise and all elements in it were equally new. The story is about a bride who wants to take some megaliths from her maternal home to her in-laws' village. In the course of the narration, the girl has to solve various tasks and is confronted with many difficulties, but finally she succeeds: one morning, the people from the in-laws' village find one of the rocks in their village, rocks that actually belong miles further downhill. As they have no clue about how this happened, the passive is used to avoid reference to the agent in the utterance in (45).

(45)   *namthaluŋ=beʔ=na   luŋkhwak   nhe*
       Namthalung_rock=LOC=NMLZ.SG   stone   here
       ket-a-ma,   eko!
       bring_up[3SG]-PST-PRF,   one
       'The rock of Namthalung was brought here, one (of them)!'
                                        [37_nrr_07.085]

The passive is also used when the speaker wants to be unspecific about the reference of the agent, comparable to using the indefinite pronoun *one* in English or *man* in German. In (46a), no overt A argument is possible. Distinct agreement and negation suffixes as well as the choice of the nonpast allomorph *-men* in (46a) (vs. *-wa*) show that the inflection is intransitive (compare with transitive (46b)). Note, however, that the form in (a) can also have a first person nonsingular A reading, discussed below in §11.3.1.3.

(46) a.   *i=ya=ca   cok-ma*
           what=NMLZ.NC=ADD   do-INF
           n-ya-me-n=na.
           NEG-be_able[3SG]-NPST-NEG=NMLZ.SG
           'One cannot do anything (about it).' or
           'We cannot do anything (about it).'

b.   *(kaniŋ)*   *i=ya=ca*   *cok-ma*
   1PL[ERG]   what=NMLZ.NC=ADD   do-INF
   n-yas-wa-m-nin=na.
   NEG-be_able-NPST[3.P]-1PL.A-NEG.PL=NMLZ.SG
   'We cannot do anything (about it).'

There are several verb stems that are ambiguous between inchoative and passive readings when they are detransitivized, i.e., between argument structure modifying and argument structure preserving detransitivizations. This ambiguity is found for all events that can be conceptualized either with or without external causation, for instance *kept* 'stick, glue', *ek* 'break', *pek* 'shatter', *hos* 'open', *her* 'dry', *lond* 'come/take out'. The context provides clues about whether an agent is implied or not. In (47), the ambiguity can be resolved by including an oblique-marked A argument to distinguish the passive in (47a) from the ambiguous reading in (47b).

(47)   a.   *na*   *jhyal*   *phuaba=bhaŋ*   *peg-a=na.*
          this   window   last_born_male=ABL   shatter[3SG]-PST=NMLZ.SG
          'This window was shattered by Phuaba (the youngest of the brothers).'

    b.   *na*   *jhyal*   *imin*   *peg-a=na?*
          this   window   how   shatter[3SG]-PST=NMLZ.SG
          'How did this window break?' or
          'How was this window broken?'

Another way to distinguish inchoative from passive readings is the specification of the predicate by a second verbal stem (V2). In §11.2.1, it was mentioned that certain V2 in complex predicates are sensitive to transitivity. Some V2 occur only in inchoative readings, and thus they rule out a passive reading. Consider (48), and how the meaning changes from the caused motion of a liquid in (48a) and (48b) to spontaneous motion in (48c).

(48)   a.   *chemha*   *tuks-a=ha.*
          liquor   pour[3SG]-PST=NMLZ.NC
          'The liquor was poured.'

    b.   *uŋ=ŋa*   *khorek=pe*   *maŋcwa*   *tuks-u=ha.*
          3SG=ERG   bowl=LOC   water   pour-3.P[PST]=NMLZ.NC
          'He poured the water into the bowl.'

    c.   *chemha*   *tuks-a-khy-a=ha.*
          liquor   pour[3SG]-PST-V2.GO-PST=NMLZ.NC
          'The liqour spilled/ran over.' not: *'The liquor was poured.'

11.3.1.2 The antipassive detransitivization

The antipassive detransitivization, just like the passive, is expressed simply by intransitive inflection. Potential ambiguities are resolved by the context. Antipassives are found in many Kiranti languages, e.g., in Puma, in Chintang, in Belhare (Bickel 2011b; Schikowski 2013), in Bantawa (Doornenbal 2009: 221), and in Athpare (Ebert 1997a: 122). In Yakkha, as in most Kiranti languages, the P argument may still be expressed overtly in the antipassive detransitivization. The P is in the nominative, just as it would be in transitive clauses, but the verb is inflected intransitively and agrees only with the agent, whose case marking changes from ergative to nominative.

The choice of this construction is related to the referential status of the P argument. If it is non-referential, indefinite or non-specific, the odds for the use of the antipassive are higher. General statements, for instance, tend to be in the antipassive. If one uses a detransitivized verb in a question as in (49), it will be understood as inquiring about the habit of a person, not as a question about a specific situation. This is why it is not possible to anchor this clause temporally (except for purposes of irony).

(49) (*hen=go)   chemha uŋ-meʔ=n=em
      (*today=TOP) liquor   drink[3SG]-NPST=NMLZ.SG=ALT
      ŋ-uŋ-meʔ=n=em?
      NEG-drink[3SG]-NPST=NMLZ.SG=ALT
      'Does she drink raksi (liquor) or not (*today)?'

If the statement is made rather about the manner of the event than about the result, the antipassive is likely to be used as well. Compare detransitivized *cokma* 'do, make' and *cekt* 'talk, speak' in (50a) and (51a) with the transitive uses in (50b) and (51b).[27]

(50) a. khatniŋ=go liŋkha ekdam cog-a=nuŋ
          but=TOP   a_clan very   do[3SG]-PST=COM
          cog-a=nuŋ
          do[3SG]-PST=COM
          'as the Linkha man worked and worked'   [11_nrr_01.008]
      b. uŋ=ŋa   na   paŋ   cog-uks-u=na.
          3SG=ERG this   house do-PRF-3.P[PST]=NMLZ.SG
          'He has made this house.'

---

[27] The stem alternations in (b) are phonologically triggered; they do not encode transitivity.

(51) a. *menuka=le   ucun=nuŋ   ceŋ-meʔ=na!*
       Menuka=CTR   nice=COM   speak[3SG]-NPST=NMLZ.SG
       'Menuka talks nicely!'

   b. *nnakha   nak-se   ŋ-gheʔ-me=hoŋ   ceʔya*
      those   ask-SUP   3PL-go-NPST=SEQ   matter
      n-jekt-wa.
      3PL.A-speak-NPST[3.P]
      'After they go there to ask (for the girl), they discuss the matter.'
                                                              [25_tra_01.007]

The antipassive is also found in procedural descriptions, as the speaker refers to general facts rather than to specific situations. Example (52a) provides a description of the long and highly formalized wedding procedure. It may also play a role whether an event has already been introduced in a text. In (51b), which was uttered shortly before (52a) in the same recording session, the verb *cekma* 'talk' is introduced with the transitive inflection and with an overt P argument *ceʔya* 'matter', but when it is taken up again, the detransitivized form is used and the object is omitted (see (52a)). Similarly, the stem *lend ~ lem* 'exchange' had been introduced in the transitive inflection and taken up in the intransitive form in (52a). In (52b), though, the object *sala* cannot be omitted for lexical reasons; the verb *sala lend* 'discuss' (lit. 'exchange matters') is a fixed expression.

(52) a. *kuʈuni=ci   panca   bhaladmi=ci*
       matchmaker=NSG   an_official_rank   respected_elder=NSG
       jammai   sala   n-lem-me,   n-jeŋ-me.
       all   matter   3PL-exchange-NPST,   3PL-talk-NPST
       'The matchmakers, the officials, the respected elders, all discuss, they talk.'   [25_tra_01.017]

   b. *ŋ-khaep   cim=nuŋ   sala*
      2SG.POSS-interest   be_satisfied=COM   matter
      lend-u-ga-i!
      exchange-3.P[IMP]-2=EMPH
      'Talk until you are satisfied!'

As for three-argument verbs, in the double object class either T or G can be demoted. Example (53a) shows a clause where the G argument is demoted, and (53b) shows a clause where the T argument is demoted.

(53) a. *nhe   maŋcwa   m-bi-me-n=ha.*
       here   water   NEG-give[3SG]-NPST-NEG=NMLZ.NC
       'They do not serve water here.' (T → P)

b. *nhe ghak m-bi-me-n=ha,*   *yaŋ*
    here all   NEG-give[3SG]-NPST-NEG=NMLZ.NSG, money
    kap-khuba se=ppa
    own-NMLZ   RESTR=EMPH
    'They do not serve everyone here, only the rich people.' (G → P)

As already mentioned, there is the option to retain the demoted argument in a detransitivized clause (see example (49) above). In (54), the noun phrase *kulpitrici* has a generic reading, similar to incorporated nouns, but the noun can still be inflected for nonsingular.

(54) *ochoŋ=ha*   *cayoŋwa pahile kulpitri=ci*   *m-bim-me.*
      new=NMLZ.NC   food   at_first ancestor=NSG 3PL-give-NPST
      'They give the new food to the ancestors at first.'   [01_leg_07.137]

Actually, this clause is ambiguous between passive and antipassive reading. This example could as well mean 'The ancestors are given the new food at first'. The interpretation has to be inferred from the context. In this particular example, *kulpitrici* was not yet active in discourse. The word order, too, speaks against the topicality of this constituent and the passive interpretation. The plural agreement on the verb is triggered by the (non-overt) A argument that does not change throughout the text: *yakkhaci* 'the Yakkha people'. Ambiguities between passivized and antipassivized clauses in Yakkha are always encountered when both A and P have third person, the same number features and are both equally low in referential salience. Consider the verb *kheps ~ khem* 'hear, listen' in (55), for example. Both verb forms are inflected intransitively, but (55a) is a passive, while (55b) is an antipassive.

Another regularity noticed is that, since antipassives often express generic statements about the world as such, they are more likely to be in the nonpast, while passives more often occur with past morphology.

(55) a. *ceʔya kheps-a-m=ha.*
          matter   hear[3SG]-PST-PRF=NMLZ.NC
          'The matter has been heard.'   [18_nrr_03.004]
      b. *Dilu reɖio khem-meʔ=na?*
          Dilu   radio   hear[3SG]-NPST=NMLZ.SG
          'Does Dilu listen to the radio (generally)?'

A phenomenon that is related to the antipassive detransitivization is the frequent omission of nonsingular marking on nouns generally, and the omission of a verbal plural marker for S and P arguments (see §5.2.1.1). The nouns in (56a) are not marked for plural, which does not generally prevent them from triggering plural agreement on the verb in Yakkha.[28] The verb shows object agreement with the nouns, but the suffix *-ci* referring to the plural number is missing. The full form would be *yogamacuci.* The agreement is not missing because the reference is singular, but because the nouns are non-referential. The predicate refers to the general activity of porcupine hunting and pangolin hunting, and it is not even clear yet if the hunt will be successful in this particular case. The same effect is found for agreement with S arguments in intransitive verbs, shown in (56b). The fully inflected verb form would be *ŋgammehaci,* but the verb here functions as a marker of evidentiality, woven into a narration in order to release the speaker from being fully responsible for the content of the utterance, and thus the A of the verb has no clear reference.

(56) a. *yakpuca*   *yog-a-ma-c-u,*   *phusa*
          porcupine   look_for-PST-PRF-DU.A-3.P,   pangolin
          yog-a-ma-c-u.
          look_for-PST-PRF-DU.A-3.P
          'They (dual) looked for porcupines, they looked for pangolins (but
          did not hunt any.)'   [22_nrr_05.015]

      b. *maŋmaŋ-miŋmiŋ*   *m-maks-a-by-a-ma*
          amazed-ECHO   3PL-be_surprised-PST-V2.GIVE-PST-PRF
          ŋ-gam-me=pa
          3PL-say-NPST=EMPH
          'They (plural) were utterly surprised, people say.'   [22_nrr_05.031]

11.3.1.3 Syncretisms of detransitivization and 1NSG reference

Both the passive and the antipassive may have a second reading, with the omitted argument having first person nonsingular reference. Thus, the passive construction may also refer to 1NSG A arguments, while the antipassive construction may refer to 1NSG P arguments. This system is slowly replacing the older, more complex verbal person marking for first person nonsingular arguments. When speakers are confronted with the detransitivized forms out of the blue, usually the first interpretation that is offered is the one with first person nonsingular arguments, and not with generic arguments.

---

[28] If a noun is not marked for plural, it may still trigger plural agreement on the verb. The only constraint found for the relatively freely organized agreement in Yakkha is that when the noun has plural marking, it has to trigger plural marking in the verb, too.

As for the antipassive forms, the detransitivized verbal inflection is in many cases already identical to the forms with 1NSG P reading; it has replaced various formerly present markers for 1NSG P argument (see Table 11.1 and Table 8.12 in §8.2). Given that the nominalizing clitics =na and =ha are optional markers, the intransitive forms with 2sg and 3sg S arguments are identical to most of the transitive forms with first person P argument (the shaded cells in Table 11.1). The same syncretism is found in the imperative forms (also shown in Table 11.1).

The only way to formally differentiate between the antipassive and first person P arguments is the presence of an ergative-marked A argument in transitive active clauses, as shown in (57). As overtly realized arguments are rare, the only element that could distinguish the two constructions is often missing.

(57) a. *cyaŋkuluŋ=ci=ŋa*   *tuʔkhi   m-bi-me-n.*
          ancestral_god=NSG=ERG   pain   NEG-give[3A;1.P]-NPST-NEG
          'The ancestors will not make us suffer.'   [01_leg_07.117]

      b. *uŋci=ŋa   phophop=na*   *sumphak=pe=se   camyoŋba*
          3NSG=ERG   upside_down=NMLZ.SG   leaf=LOC=RESTR   food
          pim-me=ha   *mit-a-ma-ci.*
          give[3A;1.P]-NPST=NMLZ.NSG   think-PST-PRF-DU
          'They (dual) thought: They only give us the food in an upside-down leaf plate.'   [22_nrr_05.053]

(58) a. *cyaŋkuluŋ=ci=ŋa*   *tuʔkhi   m-bi-me-n.*
          ancestral_god=NSG=ERG   pain   NEG-give[3A;1.P]-NPST-NEG
          'The ancestors will not make us suffer.'   [01_leg_07.117]

      b. *uŋci=ŋa   phophop=na*   *sumphak=pe=se   camyoŋba*
          3NSG=ERG   upside_down=NMLZ.SG   leaf=LOC=RESTR   food
          pim-me=ha   *mit-a-ma-ci.*
          give[3A;1.P]-NPST=NMLZ.NSG   think-PST-PRF-DU
          'They (dual) thought: They only give us the food in an upside-down leaf plate.'   [22_nrr_05.053]

The lack of agreement marking for certain participants in a language with otherwise abundant agreement morphology is suspicious and calls for an explanation. Considering the broader Kiranti perspective, the equation of generic or indefinite reference with first person undergoers developed independently in many Eastern Kiranti languages, with different morphological realizations. In Puma, a

Table 11.1: Antipassive-1NSG.P syncretisms

INDICATIVE			
A>P	1SG	1NSG	INTRANSITIVE
1SG			-ŋ(=na)
1DU.EXCL			-ci-ŋ(=ha)
1PL.EXCL	(reflexive)		-i-ŋ(=ha)
1DU.INCL			-ci(=ha)
1PL.INCL			-i(=ha)
2SG	-ŋ-ka(=na)	-ka(=na)	
2DU			-ci-ka(=ha)
2PL	-ka(=ha)		-i-ka(=ha)
3SG	-ŋ(=na)		(=na/=ha)
3DU			-ci(=ha)
3PL		(=ha)	n-...(=ha=ci)
IMPERATIVE			
A>P	1SG	1NSG	INTRANSITIVE
2SG	-aŋ		-a
2DU			-a-ci
2PL		-a	-a-ni

Southern-Central Kiranti language, the antipassive is marked by the prefix *kha-*, and this marker is also found as regular 1NSG.P agreement prefix. Bickel & Gaenszle (2005: 6) note further that indefinite pronouns and generic nouns with the meaning 'people' have developed into first person patient markers in Limbu and Belhare.

Bickel and Gaenszle suggest a functional motivation. The speaker, in the patient role, downplays or minimizes the reference to himself as a politeness strategy. Bickel and Gaenszle, for the (geographically) Southern Kiranti languages, relate this to contact with the Maithili (Indo-Aryan) speaking Sena principalities in the 17th-18th centuries.[29] In the course of this contact, Hindu religion

---

[29] The alliances of Kirat (Kiranti) kings and Sena kings began in Makwanpur, and were later extended eastward to Vijayapur. Kiranti military power probably helped the Sena rulers to

and custom had a strong impact on Kiranti traditions and languages (see also Gaenszle et al. 2005 on Chintang). The intense contact with spoken and written Maithili probably introduced formal registers with grammaticalized honorific distinctions, which the Kiranti languages were lacking. Thus, the speakers resorted to the strategy of identifying first person with an indefinite reference. Particularly striking is the exclusive choice of the patient role for this equation, throughout the Central and Eastern Kiranti languages (except for Yakkha, where this strategy got extended to A arguments, too). Bickel and Gaenszle explain this with the sensitive role of patients, especially recipients, in Kiranti societies.[30] As the Yakkha territory is located to the north of the core contact zone, this pattern must have spread from the south into the Yakkha speaking areas.

The equation of a passive interpretation with a first person agent is, to my knowledge, not a Kiranti-wide pattern, although one can easily imagine that it has developed in analogy to the antipassive equation. In (59), the detransitivized clause can have two interpretations.

(59) *kisa   sis-a=na.*
      deer   kill[3SG]-PST=NMLZ.SG
      'The deer was killed./We killed the deer.'

The passive interpretation is generally less accessible, the default interpretation in such cases implies a first person nonsingular A argument. The passive was even completely rejected in (60a). Instead, speakers offered (60b), with a first person nonsingular A argument. Note that the ablative marking on A is optional.[31] Just as in the antipassive, the downgraded argument can still be overt, but it does not trigger verbal agreement. The motivation for downgrading the first person participant is probably the same politeness strategy as in the antipassive: omission of explicit reference to first person nonsingular by agreement markers, without changing anything else in the structure. Another example is provided in (60c).

(60) a. **Numa   u-ppa=bhaŋ   tablik*
          Numa   3SG.POSS-father=ABL   story

---

defend their rule against others, e.g., the Mughals. Kiranti chiefs also acted as judicial officers in Vijayapur (Pradhan 1991: 76).

[30] Exchanging gifts, money and alcoholic beverages is formalized in weddings and funerals, and has a social function.

[31] The verb is *lumbiʔma* 'tell', a benefactive of 'tell'. Derived transitives do not behave differently from non-derived transitives, at least not with regard to the passive construction.

      lut-a-by-a=na.
      tell[3SG]-PST-V2.GIVE-PST=NMLZ.SG
      Intended: 'Numa was told a story by her father.'

b. *Numa   kaniŋ(=bhaŋ)   tablik   lut-a-by-a=na.*
     Numa   1PL(=ABL)   story   tell[3SG]-PST-V2.GIVE-PST=NMLZ.SG
     'Numa was told a story by us.' OR 'We told Diana a story.'

c. *hoŋma   yokhaʔla   chekt-haks-a=na.*
     river   across   block[3SG]-V2.SEND-PST=NMLZ.SG
     'We redirected the river.'

The passive politeness construction is definitely younger than the antipassive politeness construction, as the antipassive forms have become the standard verbal inflection for first person patients (see §8.4.6 for paradigm tables). Marginally, one can find different, more complex forms in these paradigm cells, with overt agreement markers for all participants, especially in the generation of older speakers. But speakers always pointed out that the less complex forms are more common, and this is also borne out by the corpus data. In a paper by Gvozdanović (1987: 425), who made the first agreement paradigm of Yakkha available, the first person patient forms still distinguish singular, dual and plural number of both A and P (cf. §8.2 for the details). Apparently, these forms got replaced by the less explicit politeness forms, as they were semantically bleached due to overuse. The antipassive became the default form to indicate first person P arguments. One could speculate whether the same is going to happen with the passive forms, as the passive already seems to be the less salient interpretation for these forms.

11.3.2 The causative construction

Causatives are constructed morphologically, by attaching the suffix *met ~ meʔ* to the stem of the lexical verb. The marker has developed from a lexical verb *met* 'make, do, apply', in the same way as in other Kiranti languages (Limbu, Puma, Bantawa, Chintang, see van Driem 1987; Bickel et al. 2006; Doornenbal 2009); in Yakkha its lexical meaning got narrowed down to 'tie cloth around the waist'.

    Both direct and indirect causation can be expressed by the causative. The causative marker is only used to introduce an animate causer to the verb frame, never inanimate causes such as weather phenomena, illnesses and other circumstances. The intentionality of the causer, however, is not relevant in the Yakkha causative formation. With some verbs, the causative marker is found to have an applicative function, where instead of a causer, a P argument is added to the argument structure (discussed further below).

UNDERIVED	CAUSATIVE
	A
S/A →	P/G
P →	T

Figure 11.2: Mapping of roles in the causative derivation

The causative derivation applies to both intransitive and transitive verbs, deriving minimally a monotransitive predicate. The S/A argument of the underived predicate becomes the P argument of the causative predicate, while a causer is added and becomes the A argument in the causative construction. The causer triggers subject agreement accordingly, and is marked by the ergative case. In (61), the case marking changes from oblique in (61a) to ergative in (61b), as the role of the tiger changes from stimulus to causer.

(61) a. *hari   kiba=nuŋ   kisit-a=na.*
          Hari   tiger=COM   be_afraid-PST[3SG]=NMLZ.SG
          'Hari was afraid of the tiger.'
      b. *kiba=ŋa   hari   kisi-met-u=na.*
          tiger=ERG   Hari   be_afraid-CAUS-3.P[PST]=NMLZ.SG
          'The tiger frightened Hari.'

Arguments (other than the causer) retain their respective cases (nominative, instrumental, locative), so that the causative derivation yields different three-argument frames. The standard monotransitive frame (with the P argument in the nominative) results in the double object frame in the causative, with the former A becoming the G argument and the P becoming the T (outlined in Figure 11.2 and illustrated by (62)).

(62) a. *ka   photo   soʔ-wa-ŋ=na.*
          1SG[ERG]   photo   look-NPST[3.P]-1SG.A=NMLZ.SG
          'I will look at the photo.'
      b. *ku   nda   photo   soʔ-meʔ mc ncn=na.*
          1SG[ERG]   2SG   photo   look-CAUS-NPST-1>2=NMLZ.SG
          'I will show you the photo./ I will make you look at the photo.'

More examples of causatives resulting in double object constructions are provided in (63). All of them illustrate that the causer triggers subject agreement and the causee triggers object agreement on the verb.

(63) a. *uŋ=ŋa   ka   chem   luʔ-met-a-ŋ=na.*
       3SG=ERG   1SG   song   tell-CAUS-PST-1SG.P=NMLZ.SG
       'He made me sing a song.'

    b. *ka   mim-meʔ-me-nen=na.*
       1SG[ERG]   remember-CAUS-NPST-1>2=NMLZ.SG
       'I will remind you.'

    c. *ŋkha   yapmi=ci   koi   namphak*
       those   person=NSG   some   wild_boar
       si-met-uks-u-ci,   ...
       kill-CAUS-PRF-3.P[PST]-3NSG.P
       'Those people, (he) made some of them hunt wild boar, ...'

                                              [27_nrr_06.033]

If the underived verb is a motion verb, the causative results in a three-argument construction of the indirective frame, with the G in the locative case.

(64) a. *a-kamnibak   ten=be   tas-u=na.*
       1SG.POSS-friend   village=LOC   arrive-3.P[PST]=NMLZ.SG
       'My friend arrived in the village.'

    b. *m-baŋ=be   ta-met-i.*
       2SG.POSS-house=LOC   arrive-CAUS-COMPL[3.P;IMP]
       'Deliver it (the rock) at your home.'   [37_nrr_07.011]

If the causative is applied to non-canonically marked constructions such as they are found in the expression of experiential events, the experiencer becomes the causee. Experiencers can be coded as standard objects (shown in (65a)). Despite this non-canonical marking, the experiencer becomes the causee and triggers object agreement in the causative construction (see (65b)). The stimulus, formally identical to A arguments in the non-causative predicate, is in the instrumental case and does not trigger agreement in the causative.[32] Thus, in causatives of the object experiencer construction, nothing changes for the experiencer; it remains the argument that is coded as object.[33]

(65) a. *siŋ=ŋa   ŋ-khot-a-ŋa-n=na.*
       fire_wood=ERG   NEG-have_enough-PST-1SG.P-NEG=NMLZ.SG
       'I do not have enough fire wood.'

---

[32] The instrumental is homophonous with the ergative but it is clearly not an ergative here, in the classical definition of marking an A as opposed to S and P.

[33] Marginally, the right context provided, interpretations with the stimulus as the causee are also possible, e.g., *ṭailorŋa tek khopmetuha* 'The tailor made the fabric be enough' (i.e., he cut the pieces carefully).

b. *ka   uŋci   cama=ŋa*
1SG[ERG]   3NSG   food=INS
kho?-met-wa-ŋ-ci-ŋ=ha.
have_enough-CAUS-NPST[3.P]-1SG.A-NSG.P-1SG.A=NMLZ.NSG
'I serve them food.' (lit. 'I make them have enough food.')

In the possessive experiencer construction, the experiencer does not even trigger agreement in the underived verb (see (66a)), but is still treated as object by the verbal agreement of the causative verb in (66b). Thus, the causative shows that the morphosyntax of Yakkha is not sensitive to case marking or agreement but to generalized semantic roles. As the experiencer is the A in (65) and the S in (66), it becomes the causee in the respective causative constructions.

(66) a. *a-sokma   hips-a-by-a=na.*
1SG.POSS-breath   thrash[3SG]-PST-V2.GIVE-PST=NMLZ.SG
'I am annoyed.'
b. *khem=nuŋ   rajiv=ŋa   a-sokma*
Khem=COM   Rajiv=ERG   1SG.POSS-breath
him-met-a-g=ha!
whip-CAUS-PST-2.A[1.P]=NMLZ.NSG
'Khem and Rajiv(, you) annoy me!'

Some causatives have idiomatic, lexicalized meanings, such as the verb *yok-me?ma* 'tell about something, make someone curious'. The lexical meaning of *yokma* is 'search'. Another instance is *incame?ma* 'play with someting'. Literally, it translates as 'make something revolve for fun' (see (67)).

(67) a. *muŋri   caram=be   i-ca-ya=na.*
Mungri   yard=LOC   revolve-V2.EAT-PST[3SG]=NMLZ.SG
'Mungri played in the yard.'
b. *kha?la   (nasa)   in-ca-met-uks-u-ŋ=niŋ*
like_this (fish)   revolve-V2.EAT-CAUS-PRF-3.P[PST]-1SG.A=CTMP
'while I played (with the fish) like this'   [13_cvs_02.026]

Some instances of causative morphology have applicative interpretations. The argument added is not a causer, but an object. Consider (68), where no specific causee argument can be identified, as the interpretation of (68b) is not 'she makes her spread the umbrella'. The causative here is used to distinguish whether an action is performed on oneself or on another participant. The underived verb *hamma* 'spread over' always refers to covering oneself, and not to spreading something at another location. A second factor might be the pragmatic saliency and frequency of the causative-marked event. Covering a person with a blanket or umbrella is performed more often than encouraging the person to cover oneself.[34] Another verb following this pattern is *wa?mepma* 'dress someone/ help to put on clothes' (see (68c)). The causative construction, in such cases, indicates the causation of a state (being dressed, being covered).

(68) a. *ka*   *phopma*   *haps-wa-ŋ=na.*
          1SG[ERG]   blanket   spread-NPST[3.P]-1SG.A=NMLZ.SG
          'I cover myself with a blanket.'

      b. *beuli=ga=ca*   *u-nuncha*   *pʌrne=ŋa*
          bride=GEN=ADD   3SG.POSS-younger_sibling   falling=ERG
          chata   *ham-met-wa.*
          umbrella   spread-CAUS-NPST[3.P]
          'Equally, a younger sister of the bride spreads an umbrella (over the
          bride).'   [25_tra_01.053]

      c. *ka*   *a-nuncha*   *tek*
          1SG[ERG]   1SG.POSS-younger_sibling   cloth
          wa?-met-u-ŋ=na.
          put_on-CAUS-3.P[PST]-1SG.A=NMLZ.SG
          'I helped my younger sister to get dressed./ I dressed my younger
          sister.'

The causative of the transitive verb *ko?ma* 'walk (from place to place)' also deviates from the classic causative function. The meaning of *ko?me?ma* is 'walk someone around', i.e., not just making someone walk but actually walking with them and guiding them (see (69)).

(69) *ka*   *a-kamniwak=ci*
      1SG[ERG]   1SG.POSS-friend=NSG
      ko?-met-wa-ŋ-ci-ŋ=ha.
      walk-CAUS-NPST-1SG.A-NSG.P-1SG.A=NMLZ.NSG
      'I walked my friends around.'

The verbs derived by the causative behave identically to simple stems in most respects. The A argument can be a privileged syntactic argument in constructions that select S/A pivots. It can, for instance, undergo a participant nominalization

---

[34] Spreading an umbrella over the bride and groom is an integral component of the wedding ceremony.

with the nominalizer -*khuba* that derives nouns or noun phrases with the role of
S or A (70).

(70) a. *cok-khuba*
          do-NMLZ
          'doer, someone who does (something)'
      b. *hiʔwa=be*   *camyoŋba*   *ca-mek-khuba*
          wind=LOC   food   eat-CAUS-NMLZ
          'someone (a bird) who feeds (his children) in the air' [21_nrr_04.003]

11.3.3 The benefactive construction

The benefactive is marked by the suffix -*t*[35] attached to the lexical root and by the
V2 -*piʔ* 'give', resulting in a complex predicate that has a beneficiary argument
in addition to the arguments of the lexical verb. The suffix -*t* is usually added
to yet unaugmented stems such as *cok* 'do' or *soʔ* 'look' (becoming *cokt* and *sot*,
respectively). Stems with an augmented -*s*, however, do not provide a coherent
picture. The stems with the bilabial stop in the coda, like *haps* 'spread, distribute'
and *tups* 'meet, find', do not host the suffix -*t* in the benefactive derivation, but
stems with the velar stop in the coda, like *leks* 'overturn' and *haks* 'send', for
instance, change to *lekt* and *hakt*. More examples are necessary to find out if
this is a phonological regularity. Hence, the use of this suffix is both functionally
and phonologically conditioned. Adding -*t* to the lexical stem in the benefactive
could be a strategy to distinguish the benefactive from the other uses of the V2
piʔ (discussed in §10.2.1).

The addition of a beneficiary argument changes the marking and behavioral
properties of a verb. The beneficiary is promoted to an argument; it is in the unmarked nominative case and triggers object agreement, illustrated by (71). Both
intransitive and transitive verbs can undergo the benefactive derivation (see (71)).
The latter result in double object constructions.

(71) a. *ceŋ*   *pok-t-a-by-a-ŋ*   *lu-ks-u.*
          upright   stand_up-BEN-IMP-V2.GIVE-IMP-1SG.P   tell-PRF-3.P[PST]
          'Stand upright for me, he told him.'   [27_nrr_06.18]
      b. *ka*   *chem*   *lu-t-a-by-a-ŋ.*
          1SG   song   tell-BEN-IMP-V2.GIVE-IMP-1SG.P
          'Sing me a song.'

---

[35] This marker is a remnant of a formerly productive Proto-Tibeto-Burman transitivizing suffix.
Apart from its employment in the benefactive function, this marker is not productive in Yakkha;
it has been re-analyzed as part of the stem in Kiranti languages in general, see §8.1.

If the beneficiary has nonsingular number, it also triggers the third person non-singular agreement with object arguments that is typically found on infinitives with a deontic reading (see §15.1.7).

(72)   *yenda*   *taŋ-biʔ-ma=ci.*
       millet_mash   take_out-V2.GIVE-INF[DEONT]=NSG
       'The millet mash (for brewing beer) has to be taken out for them.'

Example (73) is a nice semantic minimal pair illustrating that the benefactive is inappropriate in non-benefactive contexts. While in (73a) the benefactive deriva-tion of the stem *haps* 'spread, distribute' is possible and necessary, in (73b) the verb has to be used without the benefactive derivation. The G argument *ten-ten* 'villages' in (73a) gains something from the event of distributing, which is not the case for the G argument *klas-ci* 'classes' in (73b). Furthermore, this example shows that the benefactive derivation does not necessarily change the argument realization of a verb that already has three arguments.

(73)   a.   *sarkar=ŋa*   *yaŋ*   *ten-ten=be*
             government=ERG money village-REDUP=LOC
             ŋ-haps-u-bi-ci=ha.
             3PL.A-distribute-3.P[PST]-V2.GIVE-NSG.P=NMLZ.NSG
             'The government (plural) distributed the money among the villages.'
      b.   *uŋci=ŋa*   *picha=ci*   *klas=ci=be*
             3NSG=ERG   child=NSG   class=NSG=LOC
             ŋ-haps-u-ci=ha.
             3PL.A-distribute-3.P[PST]-NSG.P=NMLZ.NSG
             'They distributed the children among the classes.'

The events denoted by the benefactive derivation do not necessarily happen to the advantage of the 'beneficiary', as (74) shows. The crucial semantic com-ponent of the benefactive is a volitional, intentional agent, acting in order to bring about an event that affects the 'beneficiary', either in desirable or in unde-sirable ways. Example (74) also offers insight into the morphological structure of complex predicates. The benefactive applies to an already complex predicate, consisting of the lexical stem *pek* 'shatter' and the V2 *-haks* 'send' (which adds a notion of irreversibility to the meaning of the lexical verb). However, the ex-isting complex structure is not opaque to the derivational morphology, as the benefactive suffix *-t* attaches to both stems.

(74) a. *ak=ka*
            1SG.POSS=GEN

            pek-t-hak-t-a-by-a-ŋ=na   *loʔwa,*
            shatter-BEN-V2.SEND-BEN-PST-V2.GIVE-PST-1SG.P=NMLZ.SG   as,

            nna=ga=ca
            that=GEN=ADD

            pek-t-hak-t-u-bi-wa-ŋ=ha.
            shatter-BEN-V2.SEND-BEN-3.P-V2.GIVE-NPST-1SG.A=NMLZ.NSG
            'As he destroyed mine, I will also destroy his (house, family etc.).'
                                                      [21_nrr_04.029]

    b. *eko yapmi=ga   o-keŋ*
            one person=GEN   3SG.POSS-tooth

            en-d-hak-t-u-bi=na.
            uproot-BEN-V2.SEND-BEN-3.P-V2.GIVE[3.P;PST]=NMLZ.SG
            'He pulled out some man's tooth.'

Two examples from a narrative are provided in (75). The beneficiary here has first person nonsingular reference, and is thus not indexed on the verb by overt markers (cf. §8.2 on person marking).

(75) a. *aniŋ=ga*   *khaʔla=na*   *piccha=ca*
            1PL.EXCL.POSS=GEN in_this_way=NMLZ.SG child=ADD

            tups-a-by-a-ga.
            find-PST-V2.GIVE-PST-2[1.P]
            'You also found (this) our daughter for us.'   [22_nrr_05.115]

    b. *kanciŋ nakt-a-ŋ-c-u-ŋ=na=cen*   *ina*
            1DU   ask_for-PST-EXCL-DU.A-3.P.PST-EXCL=NMLZ.SG=TOP what

            baŋniŋ, na   phophop=na   *sumphak cilleŋ*
            TOP,   this upside_down=NMLZ.SG leaf   facing_up

            lek-t-a-by-a.
            overturn-BEN-IMP-V2.GIVE-IMP[1.P]
            'As for what we asked you for: this overturned leaf plate, turn it on
            the right side for us.'   [22_nrr_05.126–7]

The beneficiary does not only trigger agreement on the verb. Plenty of examples show that the benefactive verb can undergo the reciprocal derivation[36] when an

---

[36] The reciprocal is constructed by the suffix *-khusa* attached to the (last) stem of a verb and the verb *cama* 'eat' as auxiliary. Although the reciprocal derivation of a benefactive predicate still has two arguments, the person inflection in the reciprocal construction always shows the intransitive morphology.

action is performed bidirectionally, and the (minimally) two participants have each the role of agent and beneficiary/maleficiary, as shown in (76).

(76) a. *piccha=ci   caram   pheŋ-bi-khusa*
          child=NSG   yard   sweep-V2.GIVE-RECIP
          ca-me-ci=ha.
          eat.AUX-NPST-[3]DU=NMLZ.NSG
          'The children sweep the yards for one another.'[37]

      b. *kanciŋ   moja   pham-bi-khusa*
          1DU   sock   knit-V2.GIVE-RECIP
          ca-me-ci=ha.
          eat.AUX-NPST-[1]DU=NMLZ.NSG
          'We knit socks for each other.'

      c. *anciŋ-cuwa=ci*   *uk-nim-bi-khusa*
          1DU.EXCL.POSS-beer=NSG   drink-COMPL-V2.GIVE-RECIP
          ca-ya-ŋ-ci-ŋ=ha!
          eat.AUX-PST-EXCL-DU-EXCL=NMLZ.NSG
          'We (dual, exclusive) accidentally drank up each other's beer!'

An operation that is not available for verbs derived by the benefactive is reflexivization. Expressing propositional content such as in (77) by the form *thum-bi-ca-me-ŋ=na* is ungrammatical. The semantics of the Yakkha benefactive entail that the benefactor and the beneficiary must not have the same reference. The expression of actions for oneself can be achieved simply by attaching the reflexive morphology (the V2 *-ca*) to the verb stem, without prior benefactive derivation (cf. also §11.3.4).

(77) *kurta*   *thun-ca-me-ŋ=na.*
      long_shirt   sew-V2.EAT-NPST-1SG=NMLZ.SG
      'I sew a *kurta* for myself.'

11.3.4 The reflexive construction

Yakkha does not have reflexive pronouns. The reflexive is constructed by a complex predicate with the V2 *-ca* 'eat'. It indicates that the A and P argument of the predicate have identical reference. The resulting verb gets detransitivized with regard to case and person marking, as shown in (78). This construction can only express complete coreferentiality, so that propositions like 'I saved us' can

---

[37] First person dual inclusive and third person dual are identical in intransitively inflected verbs.

neither be expressed by the verbal morphology nor by the reflexive derivation in Yakkha. The various other functions of this V2 are treated in §10.2.3. Apart from reflexive constructions, it also occurs in many lexicalized predicates with classical middle semantics, such as grooming and social interactions. Some of the labile verbs that are discussed in §11.2.1 also show reflexive semantics when they are inflected intransitively, without attaching the reflexive marker.

(78) *nda (aphai) moŋ-ca-me-ka=na.*
      2SG (self)   beat-V2.EAT-NPST-2=NMLZ.SG
      'You beat yourself.'

The examples below show that the reflexive can also apply to a quantified noun phrase (79a), to a question pronoun (79b), and to negated propositions (79c). There are no dedicated negative pronouns in Yakkha; negation is constructed by a question pronoun with the additive focus clitic *=ca* and verbal negation markers. In irrealis (question and negation) contexts, both singular and nonsingular inflection is possible, depending on the potential referents that the speaker has in mind (or what the speaker assumes the addressee has in mind).

(79) a. *ghak sar   n-so-ca-ya.*
          all   teacher 3PL-look-V2.EAT-PST
          'All teachers looked at themselves.'
      b. *isa   u-chik   ekt-a-ca-ya=na.*
          who 3SG.POSS-hate make_break[3SG]-PST-V2.EAT-PST=NMLZ.SG
          'Who is angry at himself?'
      c. *isa=ca   n-so-ca-ya-n=ha=ci.*
          who=ADD NEG-look-V2.EAT-PST-NEG=NMLZ.NSG=NSG
          'No one looked at themselves.'

In three-argument verbs, there are two potential candidates for coreference with A. Whether A controls G or T is a matter of the original frame of the verb. For double object verbs, coreference with T is ungrammatical (see (80a)), while coreference with G is fine (see (80b)).[38] It is not possible for T and G to be coreferential in the reflexive derivation, i.e., to express propositions like 'I showed him to himself (in the mirror)'.

---

[38] It seems crosslinguistically unexpected that the coreference of A and G is accepted, while the coreference of A and T is ungrammtical. Kazenin states the implicational universal that '[...] if a language allows verbal marking of indirect reflexives, it allows verbal marking of direct reflexives as well.' (Kazenin 2001: 918).

(80) a. *ka   ama   (aphai   photo=be)
         1SG[ERG]   mother   (self   photo=LOC)
         so?men-ca-me-ŋ=na.
         show-V2.EAT-NPST-1SG=NMLZ.SG
         Intended: 'I show myself to mother (on the photo).'

      b. ka   (aphai)   coklet   pin-ca-me-ŋ=na.
         1SG[ERG]   (self)   sweet   give-V2.EAT-NPST-1SG=NMLZ.SG
         'I give myself a sweet.'

As for three-argument verbs of the indirective frame, A can be coreferential with the argument in the nominative. This is illustrated by the verb *thumma* 'tie to'. In (81a) the frame is shown for comparison. Example (81b) shows the reflexive, where the locative G argument is retained and the nominative T argument is coreferential with A, and thus unexpressed. The A argument changes its case marking from ergative to nominative.

(81) a. a-ppa=ŋa   on   siŋ=be   thund-u=na.
         1SG.POSS-father=ERG   horse   tree=LOC   tie-3.P[PST]=NMLZ.NSG
         'My father tied the horse to the tree.'

      b. a-nuncha   siŋ=be
         1SG.POSS-younger_sibling   tree=LOC
         thun-ca-me?=na.
         tie-V2.EAT[3SG]-NPST=NMLZ.SG
         'My brother ties himself to a tree.'

Reflexivization is possible with verbs of the experiencer-as-possessor frame (cf. §11.1.10 and §9.2), too, as shown above in example (79b).

In complex sentences, e.g., in embedded complement clauses, the reflexive V2 can mark the main verb, although the reflexive semantics actually apply to the predicate in the embedded clause (see (82)).[39] This is, however, only possible in the type of complement construction that embeds infinitives, where the embedded and the main clause S/A argument are necessarily coreferential.[40]

(82) uŋ=ŋa   photo   cok-ma   min-ca-me?=na.
     3SG=ERG   photo   make-INF   want-V2.EAT[3SG]-NPST=NMLZ.SG
     'She wants to take a photo of herself.'

---

[39] The complement-taking predicate *mi?ma* means 'want' when it takes infinitival complements; its meaning in other constructions is 'hope, like, think' (see also Chapter 15).

[40] Note that the ergative on A is retained in this construction, which suggests that the A argument belongs to the embedded transitive clause (a case of backward control).

11.3.5 The reciprocal construction

The reciprocal is constructed by attaching the suffix -*khusa* to the stem of the lexical verb and employing the verb *cama* 'eat' as auxiliary (see (83a)). The lexical verb and the auxiliary have to be adjacent, but the degree of morphological fusion is lower than in the reflexive construction and complex predication in general. Inflectional prefixes attach to the auxiliary, not to the lexical verb. As the reciprocal expresses mutual actions, it is characterized by at least two participants that both simultaneously have the role of actor and undergoer. The reciprocal participants are fused into one noun phrase. The construction only applies to transitive verbs, and it always formally detransitivizes the predicate, by assigning the nominative case to the A arguments and by inflecting the auxiliary intransitively, even when the lexical verb is a three-argument verb, as in (83b): here, the G argument is coreferential with A and hence it is omitted, while the T remains on the surface, retaining the case marking of its frame of argument realization (unmarked nominative in the double object frame). Contexts where reciprocals of double object verbs have coreferential A and T arguments are hard to imagine, and those proposed were rejected (see ungrammatical (83c)).

Inherently reciprocal verbs such as *tupma* 'meet', *tuma* 'fight', *khima* 'quarrel' and *cuŋma* 'wrestle' are intransitive in Yakkha; they do not permit the reciprocal operation.

(83) a. *kanciŋ [...] sok-khusa=se   ca-ya-ŋ-ci-ŋ.*
          1DU   [...] look-RECIP=RESTR   eat.AUX-PST-EXCL-DU-EXCL
          'We (dual, excl) just looked at each other.' (A=P)   [40_leg_08.070]

      b. *kanciŋ phuŋ   pi-khusa   ca-me-ci=ha.*
          1DU   flower   give-RECIP   eat.AUX-NPST-1DU=NMLZ.NSG
          'We (dual, incl) give flowers to each other.' (A=G)

      c. **kanciŋ ama(=be)   soʔmek-khusa*
          1DU   mother(=LOC)   show-RECIP

          ca-me-ci=ha.
          eat.AUX-NPST-[1]DU=NMLZ.NSG
          Intended: 'We showed each other to mother (e.g., on a photo).' (*A=T)

The antecedent of the coreferential argument always has to be the agent, as with the reciprocal of *nis* 'see, know', yielding 'introduce, get to see/know each other' in (84a). Coreferential T and G are possible, however, when the causative marker -*met* is attached to the auxiliary, so that the reciprocal construction serves as input to a causative construction (see (84b)). The arguments that are fused into one noun phrase are the A and P arguments of the reciprocal construction, and simultaneously they are T and G arguments of the causative construction *nikhusa came?ma* 'introduce to each other', which shows transitive person marking and ergative case marking on A. The causative verb *nime?ma*, without the reciprocal, also exists; it is a three-argument verb with the meaning 'introduce (X to Y)'.

(84) a. *kaciŋ   ni-khusa   ca-me-ci=ha.*
          1DU   see/know-RECIP   eat.AUX-NPST-[1]DU=NMLZ.NS
          'We will get to see/know each other.' (A=P)

      b. *uŋ=ŋa   uŋci   ni-khusa*
          3SG=ERG   3NSG   see/know-RECIP

          ca-met-u-ci=ha.
          eat.AUX-CAUS-3.P[PST]-NSG.P=NMLZ.NSG
          'He introduced them (to each other).' ([[A=P.RECIP], G=T.CAUS])

In the indirective frame (characterized by locative or ablative marking on the G argument, see §11.1.9), the reciprocal construction can express coreference of A and T or A and G, regardless of the case and agreement properties of the arguments in the corresponding non-reciprocal predicate. The possibilities are restricted only by the verbal semantics, i.e., whether the T or the G argument is animate/human and thus eligible for being coreferential with A. In (85a), the A argument is coreferential with T, while in (85b), A is coreferential with G.

(85) a. *uŋci   hoŋma=be   luŋ-khusa   ca-ya-ci=ha.*
          3NSG   river=LOC   drown-RECIP   eat.AUX-PST-[3]DU=NMLZ.NSG
          'They (dual) drowned each other in the river.' (A=T)

      b. *uŋci   yaŋ   khu-khusa   ca-me-ci=ha.*
          3NSG   money   steal-RECIP   eat.AUX-NPST-[3]DU=NMLZ.NSG
          'They steal money from each other.' (A=G)

In the secundative frame (characterized by instrumental marking on the T argument, see §11.1.9), animate or human T arguments are hardly conceivable, and thus, only instances with coreferential A and G could be attested, as shown in (86).

(86) *ibebe   n-juŋ-a-ma,   ikhiŋ=ga   tabek=ŋa*
      anywhere   3PL-fight-PST-PRF   so_big=GEN   khukuri_knife=INS

      ce-ŋkhusa   n-ja-ya=em,   barcha=ŋa   hok-khusa
      cut-RECIP   3PL-eat.AUX-PST=ALT   spear=INS   pierce-RECIP

n-ja-ya=em,   *luŋkhwak=ŋa*   *lep-khusa*   *n-ja-ya,*
3PL-eat.AUX-PST=ALT   stone=INS   throw-RECIP   3PL-eat.AUX-PST

ikhiŋ=ga   *bhuiṭar=ŋa*   *ap-khusa*   *n-ja-ya.*
so_big=GEN   catapult=INS   shoot-RECIP   3PL-eat.AUX-PST

'They fought so much, with knives so big, whether they cut each other with knives, whether they stabbed each other with lances, they threw stones at each other, they shot each other with a really big catapult.'

[39_nrr_08.21–2]

Derived verbs can also serve as input to the reciprocal construction, as shown for the benefactive in (87a) and for the causative in (87b).

(87)   a.   *kanciŋ*   *ṭopi*   *pham-bi-khusa*   *ca-me-ci=ha.*
          1DU   cap   knit-V2.GIVE-RECIP   eat.AUX-NPST-[1]DU=NMLZ.NSG
          'We knit caps for each other.'

    b.   *kaniŋ*   *cuwa=ŋa*   *kho?-me?-khusa*   *ca-i-wa.*
          1PL   beer=INS   have_enough-CAUS-RECIP   eat.AUX-1PL-NPST
          'We serve each other beer.' (Lit. 'We make each other have enough beer.')

11.3.6 The middle construction

Middle verbs are characterized by denoting an event that"affects the subject of the verb or his interests", to take up the definition by Lyons (1969: 373). Characteristic for a middle situation is the low elaboration of participants in an event (Kemmer 1993: 3). Agent and patient have the same reference, just as in the reflexive. In the middle, however, agent and patient are less distinct conceptually, because many of the events do not presuppose a volitional agent. Volitionality is a crucial feature of a prototypical agent (Hopper & Thompson 1980; Foley & Van Valin 1984). Hence, the middle is semantically less transitive than a reflexive, but still more transitive than an intransitive verb (Kemmer 1993: 73).

The Yakkha middle is marked by *-si?* , which behaves like a function verb, despite originating in a suffix, as comparison with other Tibeto-Burman languages shows (see §10.2.4). The distinctive semantic criterion of the middle marker *-si?* in Yakkha is the low intentionality and volitionality on part of the subject. The middle derivation detransitivizes the verbs (compare (88a) and (88b)). With a few verbs, *-si?* may indicate a reciprocal reading, but, crucially, only when the action was performed unintentionally (see (89)).

(88) a. *ka   bhitta=be   kila   likt-u-ŋ=na.*
          1SG[ERG]   wall=LOC   nail   drive_in-3.P[PST]-1SG.A =NMLZ.SG
          'I drove a nail into the wall.'

      b. *ka   likt-a-sy-a-ŋ=na.*
          1SG   drive_in-PST-MDDL-PST-1SG=NMLZ.SG
          'I got stuck (in the mud, head first).'

(89) a. *ka   hen=ca   a-ṭukhruk   dailo=be*
          1SG[ERG]   today=ADD   1SG.POSS-head   door=LOC
          lukt-i-ŋ=na.
          knock-COMPL[3.P;PST]-1SG.A=NMLZ.SG
          'I knocked my head at the door even today.'

      b. *lukt-a-sy-a-ŋ-ci-ŋ=ha.*
          knock-PST-MDDL-PST-EXCL-[1]DU-EXCL=NMLZ.NSG
          'We (dual) bumped into each other.'

The semantics of verbs that take the middle marker cover the situation types commonly associated with the category of middle crosslinguistically: grooming and body care, motion, change in body posture, reciprocal events, emotion, cognition and spontaneous events. The middle marker -*siʔ* encodes grammatical functions as well as lexicalized meanings, just as the reflexive/autobenefactive V2 -*ca* (see §10.2.3). For more on -*siʔ* see §10.2.4.

11.3.7 V2 stems signalling animate T arguments

Certain scenarios in three-argument verbs require additional marking in Yakkha. As the T argument of three-argument verbs is typically less topic-worthy, salient or lower on a referential hierarchy than the G argument, one could expect an increase in morphological complexity in the verb when the T argument is higher on the referential hierarchy or when the G argument is lower than expected, i.e., 'the construction which is more marked in terms of the direction of information flow should also be more marked formally' (Comrie 1989: 128). Such a marking is comparable to inverse marking for agent and patient, as found, e.g., in Algonquian languages (Zúñiga 2007). According to Haspelmath (2007: 90), such verbal marking has not been found for the relation of T and G in three-argument verbs yet.

Yakkha, too, does not have one dedicated marker for 'inverse' scenarios of T and G. But there is a tendency for animate or human T (and P) arguments to require a serial verb construction, and thus more complexity in the verb. Several V2 stems can be found in this function, most prominently -*khet* ~ -*het* 'carry off', -*end* 'insert', -*raʔ* 'bring' and -*haks* 'send'. As there are several V2s with different semantics, it is not their only function to indicate referentially high T arguments. They can even be found with inanimate T arguments. The crucial point is that certain scenarios cannot be expressed without using them, as for instance in example (90). The stealing of things is expressed by a simple verb stem (see (90a)), while stealing a person cannot be expressed with a simple verb. Instead, the complex construction with the V2 -het 'carry off' is used, implying caused motion away from a point of reference (see (90b)). If, instead, the V2 -haks 'send' is applied to the lexical stem khus 'steal', the meaning changes to 'rescue' (see (90c)). The simple stem khus, however, cannot express events with human T arguments.

(90) a. *pasal=bhaŋ   yaŋ   khus-uks-u=ha.*
          shop=ABL   money   steal-PRF-3.P[PST]=NMLZ.NC
          '(He) has stolen money from the shop.'

      b. *ka   ijaŋ   a-paŋ=bhaŋ*
          1SG   why   1SG.POSS-house=ABL
          khus-het-a-ŋ-ga=na?
          steal-V2.CARRY.OFF-PST-1.P-2.A=NMLZ.SG
          'Why did you steal me from my home?'

      c. *kiba=bhaŋ   khus-haks-a-ŋ-ga=na.*
          tiger=ABL   steal-V2.SEND-PST-1.P-2.A=NMLZ.SG
          'You saved me from the tiger.'

Some examples from natural texts are provided in (91).

(91) a. *nhaŋa   nnakha   yapmi   ta-khuwa=ci*
          and_then   those   person   come-NMLZ=NSG
          ikt-haks-u=ci.
          chase-V2.SEND-3.P[PST]-NSG.P
          'And then she chased away those people who were coming.'
                                                          [14_nrr_02.034]

      b. *ak=ka   kamniwak=ci   hip-paŋ*
          1SG.POSS=GEN   friend=NSG   two-CLF.HUM
          tikt-u-ra-wa-ŋ-ci-ŋ.
          guide-3.P-V2.BRING-NPST-1SG.A-3NSG.P-1SG.A
          'I will bring along two of my friends.'   [14_nrr_02.023]

A very typical example is also the verb *pinnhaŋma* 'send off' shown in (92), which has already acquired a fixed meaning 'marry off (one's daughter)'.

(92) *m-ba=ŋa*   *nda* *ka=be*
2SG.POSS-father=ERG   2SG   1SG=LOC
pin-nhaŋ-me-ŋ=na=bu=i?
give-V2.SEND-NPST-1SG.P=NMLZ.SG=REP=Q
'(Did they say that) your father will give you to me (in marriage)?'

It can be concluded that the higher complexity and greater semantic specification of an event via serialization is necessary in, but not restricted to events with
referentially high T (and occasionally also P) arguments.

11.3.8 Historical excursus: Stem augments

Yakkha verbal stems can be divided into unaugmented and augmented roots (see
also §8.1). Both open ((C)V) and closed ((C)VC) stems can be extended by the
coronal augments -*s* and -*t*. These augments can be related to transitivizing suffixes in Proto-Tibeto-Burman, often with -*s* coding a causative and -*t* coding a
directive or a benefactive derivation (see Matisoff 2003: 457, van Driem 1989: 160).
Synchronically, however, the augmentation does not constitute a productive pattern.

Some reflexes of this old system can, however, still be found in correspondences such as in Table 11.2, albeit only for a small fraction of the verbal lexicon.
Complete stem triads (consisting of an unaugmented, an -*s*-augmented and a -
t-augmented root) are exceedingly rare, and synchronically, many intransitive
verbs with augmented stems exist as well, which clearly shows that a regular correspondence between augmentation and transitivization is not given synchronically.[41] The stem alternations do not necessarily entail an increase in the number
of arguments; sometimes just the properties of the arguments change, along with
the case and person marking. For instance, *haks* and *hakt* both mean 'send', but
the goal of *haks* is in the locative case and referentially unrestricted, while *hakt*
takes a human goal in the nominative, which also points to the former use of the
augment /-t / as a benefactive marker. We have seen above in §11.3.3 that there
is also a suffix -*t* in the benefactive derivation, which is probably also related to
these old suffixes. It is only employed as a secondary marker, accompanying the
primary benefactive marker, the V2 -*piʔ*.

The stem *tup* 'meet' also undergoes the stem alternation. While the unaug-

---

[41] Comparing the stems in Yakkha with other Kiranti languages, the form and meaning of the
augmented stems do not correspond across individual languages. Unaugmented stems in one
Kiranti language may have augments in another language, and augments may differ for cognate roots, which adds support to the reconstruction of these augments as non-integral part
of the verbal stem, i.e., as suffixes.

Table 11.2: Stem augmentation and transitivity correspondences

(C)V(C)	(C)V(C)-s	(C)V(C)-t
ap 'come' (same level, close)		apt 'bring'
	haks 'send somewhere'	hakt 'send to someone'
keʔ 'come up'		ket 'bring up'
kheʔ 'go'		khet 'carry off'
khuʔ 'carry'	khus 'steal'	khut 'bring'
luʔ 'tell, say'	lus 'deafen, roar'	lut 'tell for someone'
	maks 'wonder, look around'	makt 'see in dream'
si 'die'	sis 'kill'	
ta 'come' (general)	tas 'arrive at'	taʔ 'bring to'
	uks 'come down'	ukt 'bring down'
yuŋ 'sit'	yuks 'put'	yukt 'put for s.o.'

mented stem is inherently reciprocal and is thus inflected intransitively (and thus, necessarily, takes nonsingular arguments), the stem *tups* is transitively inflected and takes two arguments that cannot have identical reference.

(93) a. *kanciŋ   tub-a-ŋ-ci-ŋ=ha.*
          1DU   meet-PST-EXCL-DU-EXCL=NMLZ.NSG
          'We met.'

      b. *ka   ŋ-gamnibak*
          1SG[ERG]   2SG.POSS-friend
          n-dups-u-ŋa-n=na.
          NEG-meet-3.P[PST]-1SG.A-NEG=NMLZ.SG
          'I did not meet/find your friend.'

12 Simple clauses

As pointed out in Dryer (2007: 224), at least four perspectives come to mind when talking about clause types: (i) the distinction between declarative, interrogative, and imperative speech acts, (ii) the distinction between main and subordinate clauses, (iii) the properties of clauses and their constituents as building blocks of discourse, and (iv) types of clauses based on different kinds of predicates and their argument structure. The purpose of this chapter is to provide a bird's eye view from all four perspectives. An in-depth treatment of the argument structure can be found in Chapter 11, some aspects of information structure are dealt with in Chapter 17 and subordinate clauses are the topic of Chapters 13, 14 and 15.

The chapter is structured as follows: §12.1 discusses general structural properties of simple independent clauses, §12.2 lays out constituent structure. Different types of illocutionary acts and how they affect the shape of a clause are discussed in §12.3. Finally, §12.4 introduces the regularities of agreement in Yakkha. In line with what is known about agreement in Tibeto-Burman languages in general, the agreement in Yakkha is less restricted than in Indo-European languages and does not require a complete matching between the referential features of the agreement markers and their controllers.

12.1 Basic clausal properties

Independent clauses present propositional content independently of other syntactic units. They are the unit in which any grammatical category of a language can be expressed, other than in dependent clauses (relative clauses, complement clauses or adverbial clauses), which are often restricted in some way. Some operators generally function on the level of an independent clause, like the mirative *rahecha* (a Nepali loan) or exclamative particles like *baʔlo* and *haʔlo* (see (1a)). The reportative marker *=bu* is also found clause-finally (see (1b)), but occasionally it is also found on embedded clauses containing indirect speech and on constituents inside the clause (see §17.3.1).

Most markers, for instance information-structural particles and case markers, are found both on clausal constituents and on clauses, which is not unusual in

Tibeto-Burman. There are, however, tendencies for certain markers to appear on noun phrases (e.g., the topic marker =*ko*, the contrastive focus marker =*le*, the emphatic marker =*maŋ*) or rather on clauses or both (case markers, several postpositions, the restrictive focus marker =*se*, the additive focus marker =*ca*, the reportative marker =*bu*).

Another feature which distinguishes independent clauses is the clause-final afterthought position which is accompanied by an intonation break as a means to provide additional information about one of the (overt or omitted) referents (see (2)). All kinds of arguments are possible in the afterthought position.

Yakkha has verbal clauses, copular clauses and verbless clauses, the latter reflecting a copular structure without a copula, usually with identificational or ascriptive semantics.

(1) a. *n-so-ks-u=na*   *rahecha*   *baʔlo!*
      NEG-look-PRF-3.P[PST]=NMLZ.SG   MIR   EXCLA
      'Oh, he did not look into it!'   [34_pea_04.039]

    b. *yondaŋ=ca*   *khendaŋ=ca*   *pik=ci=le*
      from_thither=ADD   from_hither=ADD   cow=NSG=CTR
      n-du-ma-sim-me=ha=bu,   *ibebe=ga.*
      3PL-step_on-INF-AUX.PROG-NPST=NMLZ.NSG=REP   everywhere=GEN
      'Here and there, cows are trampling everywhere, it is said, everywhere.'

                                              [39_nrr_08.25]

(2) a. *liŋkha=ci*   *nam=nuŋ*   *bʌgʌri*   *n-jog-a,*   *bʌgʌri.*
      a_clan=NSG   sun=COM   bet   3PL-do-PST   bet
      'The Linkhas had a bet with the sun, a bet.'   [11_nrr_01.003]

    b. *ŋkhaʔla*   *lu-saŋ*   *uŋ=ŋa*   *nna,*   *luŋkhwak,*   *cuʔlumphi*
      like_that   tell-SIM   3SG=ERG   that   stone   stele
      thukt-uks-u,   *nna*   *kolenluŋ=ga.*
      erect-PRF-3.P[PST]   that   marble=GEN
      'Telling them like that, he erected that stone, the stele, out of marble.'

                                              [18_nrr_03.021]

    c. *heksaŋ*   *nna*   *miyaŋ*   *n-thog-haks-uks-u=na*
      later   that   a_little   3PL.A-hit-V2.SEND-PRF-3.P=NMLZ.SG
      raecha,   *pik=ci=ŋa,*   *goru=ci=ŋa.*
      MIR   cow=NSG=ERG   OX=NSG=ERG
      'Later, they hit off some of it (the stone), the cows, the oxen.'

                                              [39_nrr_08.03]

12.2 Constituent order

Yakkha has a flat clause structure; there is no evidence for a unit like the verb phrase (verb and arguments). The unmarked constituent order is head-final in phrases and sov in clauses, with increasingly rhematic status towards the end of the clause. Focal information is often put in pre-verbal position (see (3)). Noun phrases are optional (see (4a)), and clauses where all arguments are represented by noun phrases are rather rare. In complex clauses, the main clause is mostly in final position (see (4b)). Yakkha is both head- and dependent-marking on the clausal level, since it has both case marking of arguments and verbal person indexing.

(3) a.   *ilen*   *paŋdaŋba=ga*   *u-ni?ma*
         one_day   landlord=GEN   3SG.POSS-money

         mas-a-by-a-masa.
         lose-PST-V2.GIVE-PST-PST.PRF[3]
         'One day, the landlord's money got lost.'

     b.   *aniŋ=ga*   *liŋkha=ga*   *uhile*   *utpatti*   *mamliŋ=be*
         1PL.EXCL=GEN   a_clan=GEN   long_ago   origin   Mamling=LOC

         leks-a=na=bu.
         happen-PST=NMLZ.SG=REP
         'Our Linkha clan's origin, long ago, was in Mamling, they say.'
                                                                                       [11_nrr_01.002]

     c.   *tabaŋ*   *hetne*   *tas-wa-ga=na.*
         male_in-law   where   arrive-NPST-2=NMLZ.SG
         'Where will (your) husband arrive?'

(4) a.   *mund-y-uks-u-ga=na=i?*
         forget-COMPL-PRF-3.P-2=NMLZ.SG=Q
         'Did you forget it?'

     b.   *tek*   *whap-se*   *khe-me-ŋ=na.*
         clothes   wash-SUP   go-NPST-1SG=NMLZ.SG
         'I go to wash clothes.'

sov is the default constituent order, but a fronted P argument is possible when it is more topical than the A argument, as in (5a). Such examples are best rendered by English passive constructions. When the object position is filled by embedded direct speech, the preferred order is the one with the object preceding the A argument, as shown in (5b).

(5) a. *hoṭʌl=beʔ=ya   camenwa   cica=ci=ŋa*
      hotel=LOC=NMLZ.NSG   food   fly=NSG=ERG
      m-bupt-wa=ha.
      3PL.A-surround-NPST[3.P]=NMLZ.NSG
      'The food in the hotel is surrounded by flies.'   [01_leg_07.053]

    b. *ka,   ka   khaʔla   ŋana=ba   uŋ=ŋa   lu-ks-u-ci.*
      1SG   1SG like_this   COP.1SG=EMPH   3SG=ERG   tell-PRF-3.P-3NSGP
      'I, I am just like this; it (the bird) told them (the other birds).'
      [21_nrr_04.006]

Initial constituents often carry topic markers like *=chen* (a loan, from Nepali *cāhĩ*) or *=ko*. In (6), these particles mark contrastive topics.

(6) a. *eŋ=ga=chen   nna   man=na.*
      1PL.INCL=GEN=TOP   that   COP.NEG=NMLZ.SG
      'We do not have that (custom).'   [29_cvs_05.165]

    b. *kham=go   m-bi-me=ha.*
      soil=TOP   3PL.A-give-NPST=NMLZ.NSG
      'As for soil, they offer it (throwing it into the grave).'[1] [29_cvs_05.159]

In copular clauses the topic (referential or locational) naturally precedes the complement, which can be adjectival, nominal or locative (see (7)). Copulas in affirmative clauses are not obligatory. There are different copulas for equational/ascriptive and existential/locative complements. The details are discussed in §11.1.11.

(7) a. *nhaŋ,   henca-khuba=chen   yakkha   om.*
      and_then   win-NMLZ=TOP   of_Yakkha_affiliation   COP
      'The winner is/will be Yakkha.' (from a story where two groups fight about whether they are Yakkha or not)   [39_nrr_08.17]

    b. *haku   camyoŋba   nak-ma=na   ṭhaun   ma-n.*
      now   food   ask-INF=NMLZ.SG   place   COP.NEG-NEG
      'Now there is nowhere to ask for food.'   [14_nrr_02.10]

    c. *u-yum=be   waiʔ=na.*
      3SG.POSS-side=LOC   exist[3]=NMLZ.SG
      'It is next to it.'

---

[1] In contrast to water, as one interlocutor had claimed before.

12.3 Illocutionary functions

12.3.1 Declarative clauses

Yakkha distinguishes declarative, imperative, hortative, and various types of interrogative and exclamative clauses. Independent declarative clauses either have a verbal or a copular predicate, as many examples in §12.1 and §12.2 have shown. Among the clauses with a verbal predicate, the declarative and interrogative clauses have to be specified for tense. There is one emphatic particle =*pa* (originating in a nominalizer) which is found in declarative, hortative and imperative clauses, but never in questions (see (8)). The exclamative force can be amplified by attaching the exclamative particle =*ʔlo* to =*pa*. The resulting unit expressing both emphasis and exclamative force is an independent word as far as stress is concerned, but the voicing rule still applies (see (8c)).

(8)   a.   *ɖuŋga=go   ka-i-wa=ba,   kaniŋ=go.*
          boat=TOP   say-1PL-NPST=EMPH   1PL=TOP
          'We just say 'ɖuŋga', we.' (speaker puzzled about not finding a Yakkha word for 'boat' and having to use the Nepali word instead)

                                                  [13_cvs_02.006]

  b.   *men=ba!*
          COP.NEG[3]=EMPH
          'Of course not!'

  c.   *yo,   nhe   pi-haks-a-masa   baʔlo!*
          across   here   give-V2.SEND-PST-PST.PRF[1.P]   EMPH.EXCLA
          '(My father) over there had sent me here (in marriage), man!'

                                                  [06_cvs_01.016]

Much more frequent on declarative as well as on interrogative clauses are the clitics =*na* and =*ha*, originating from clausal nominalizations, a common development in Tibeto-Burman languages (and beyond). They are never found on hortatives, optatives or imperatives. Their function is hard to pin down by one neat term, but "assertive force" may give the reader an idea of their function. They occur more frequently than the emphatic =*ba*. They are discussed at length in Chapter 13.

Declaratives (and imperatives) can also be emphasized by another marker =*i*, as shown in (9).

(9)   a.   *ca-i-ŋ=na=i.*
          eat-COMPL-1SG=NMLZ.SG=EMPH
          'I finished eating.'   [36_cvs_06.241]

     b.   *ab-a-ga=i!*
          come-IMP-2=EMPH
          'Come!'

Other clause-final markers that have already been mentioned are the mirative and the reportative marker, the latter is frequently found in reported speech and in passed-down narratives, and in all other contexts where the speaker wants to free himself of the responsibility for the content of the utterance.

12.3.2 Hortative and optative clauses

Hortative clauses are uttered when the speaker wants to urge or encourage someone to do something together. There is no dedicated hortative marker, the verb just appears in the main clause subjunctive[2] first person dual or plural inflection and without any tense/aspect specification. (10a) shows an intransitive example, (10b) shows a transitive example with an additional particle *au*. It may occur in hortatives and imperatives, lending force to the request or order. The constituent order is like in declarative clauses, presuming overt arguments are there at all.

In general, the subjunctive just expresses vagueness about some future event. If it is used with first person singular or with exclusive inflection, it becomes a permissive question, with the typical intonation contour of high pitch at the end of the clause (see (11a)). With second or third person, the subjunctive can be rendered with 'you might [...]' or 'he might [...]', and can express warnings (see (11b)), threats (11c) and statements about possibilities in general.

(10) a. *cuŋ-i,*   *kaks-i.*
        wrestle-1PL[SBJV] make_fall-1PL[SBJV]
        'Let us wrestle, let us fight!'   [39_nrr_08.15]

    b. *a-na,*   *a-ma=ŋa*   *py-a=ha*
        1SG.POSS-sister 1SG.POSS-mother=ERG give-PST[1.P]=NMLZ.NSG
        yaŋ=ŋa   *limlim* *inca-c-u,*   *au?*
        money=INS sweets buy-DU-3.P[SBJV] INSIST
        'Sister, let us buy sweets with the money that mother gave us, shall we?'   [01_leg_07.042]

---

[2] There are two subjunctives in Yakkha: the main clause subjunctive and the dependent clause subjunctive, the latter being identical to the past inflection in most person configurations, cf. Chapter 8.

(11) a. *ka   khe?-ŋa,   au?*
            1SG go-1SG[SBJV] INSIST
            'I am off, allright?'

      b. *kaks-i-khe-i-ga!*
            fall-PL-V2.GO-PL-2[SBJV]
            'You (plural) might fall down!'

      c. *lem-nhaŋ-nen?*
            throw-V2.SEND-1>2[SBJV]
            'Shall I throw you out?'

The above-mentioned emphatic particle *=pa* in combination with hortatives is shown in (12).

(12) a. *lamdhaŋ=ca khond-u-m=ba,   aniŋ=ga   ya=ca*
            field=ADD   dig-3.P-1PL.A=EMPH 1PL.EXCL=GEN mouth=ADD
            hond-u-m=ba
            open-3.P-1PL.A=EMPH
            'Let us dig our fields and also open our mouths.'[3]   [07_sng_01.14]

      b. *haku   khe-ci=ba*
            now   go-DU=EMPH
            'Now let us (dual) go!'

The optative expresses the wish of the speaker for something to happen that is beyond his immediate control. It is constructed with subjunctive forms to which the marker *-ni* is added (13). Optative forms can also be found in purposive adverbial clauses (rendered by 'in order to [...]'). Verbal negation is possible in these forms as well. Full paradigms can be found in §8.5.

(13) a. *siŋ   pu-ni.*
            tree   grow[3SG]-OPT
            'May the tree grow.'

      b. *mi?-ŋa-ni.*
            think-1SG.P-OPT
            'May he remember me.'

---

[3] The exclusive is used here because the researcher was present during the song (a spontaneous song about the endangerment of the Yakkha language, and an encouragement for the hearers to speak the language), even though the people addressed are of the singer's group. It might also be due to the unnatural recording situation that the singer was not sure whom to address with her song. In later recordings, speakers vary as to whether they use the inclusive or the exclusive forms when the fieldworker is present, which can partly be attributed to including her and partly to ignoring her or forgetting about her presence.

12.3.3 Imperative and prohibitive clauses

Imperatives are uttered to make the addressee do something. Prohibitives are used to prevent the addressee from doing something. The imperative marker is -*a*,[4] identical to the past marker, but the person inflection at least partly differs from declaratives, so that most forms are distinct from their past counterparts. Imperatives have a colloquial register (14a) and a polite register (14b). The polite forms have an additional marker -*eba*, which has probably developed from the emphatic particles =*i* and =*pa*. They are used for elders, guests and other respected people. This is the only instance of grammaticalized politeness forms in the Tumok dialect of Yakkha.[5]

(14)   a.   *hani*   *ket-u!*
           quickly   bring_up-3.P[IMP]
           'Bring it up quickly!'

       b.   *naʔtorok*   *naʔtorok*   *ket-u-eba!*
           a_bit_further_up   a_bit_further_up   bring_up-3.P[IMP]-POL.IMP
           'Bring it a bit further up, please!'

Formally, prohibitives are negated imperatives (see §8.5 for the morphology). The examples in (15) contrast imperatives with prohibitives in the colloquial register.

(15)   a.   *khy-a!*
           go-IMP
           'Go!'

       b.   *ŋ-khy-a-n!*
           NEG-go-IMP-NEG
           'Do not go!'

       c.   *kisa*   *ab-a-n-u-m!*
           deer   shoot-IMP-PL-3.P-2PL.A
           'Shoot (plural) the deer!'

       d.   *maksa*   *ŋ-ab-a-n-u-m-nin!*
           bear   NEG-shoot-IMP-PL-3.P-2PL.A-NEG
           'Do not (plural) shoot the bear!'

---

[4] Often deleted as a strategy to avoid vowel hiatus.

[5] In Dandagaun village, people make politeness distinctions also in declaratives and questions. They use a calqued form from Nepali, which is discussed in §8.6.

Arguments can be expressed overtly in imperatives, including S and A arguments. They are not calls or vocatives, since they are not set apart by an intonational break, and since vocatives may precede them, as in (16a). If the person addressed by the imperative of a transitive verb is referred to by a noun and not by a pronoun, it will be marked by the ergative.

(16)   a.   *lu,*   *lu,*   *mamu,*   *nda=ca*   *phat-a-ŋ.*
           INIT   INIT   girl   2SG=ADD   help-IMP-1SG.P
           'Come on, come on girl, help me too!'   [07_sng_01.01]

       b.   *ka*   *um-me-ŋ,*   *nninda* *lakt-a-ni,*   *nhaŋ*   *kaniŋ*
           1SG   enter-NPST-1SG   2PL   dance-IMP-PL and_then 1PL
           ikhiŋ   *lakt-iʔ-wa.*
           how_much dance-1PL-NPST
           'I will enter (the basket), you (plural) dance. And how much we will dance!'   [14_nrr_02.29]

Occasionally, one finds the second person marker combined with the emphatic marker *=i* attached to the imperative, which increases the insistence of the request or command. This marker is also found on declarative clauses.

(17)   a.   *mendhwak* *ghororo*   *sa-ga=i!*
           goat   forcefully   pull_with_rope[IMP]-2=EMPH
           'Pull the goat forcefully!'

       b.   *ab-a-ga=i!*
           come_across-IMP-2=EMPH
           'Come here!'

12.3.4 Interrogative clauses

12.3.4.1 Polar questions

Polar questions obligatorily host the clause-final clitics *=na* and *=ha* if they contain a verb,[6] and a particle *i* that is found both phonologically bound and unbound. When it occurs unbound, it carries its own stress and has an initial glottal stop prothesized (not written in the orthography), as all vowel-initial words have (see (18)). The conditions for the alternation between bound and unbound are not clear yet. The word order is the same as in declaratives. Polar questions are typically answered by repeating the (verbal or nonverbal) predicate (see (19)), or by

---

[6] It is misleading, however, to perceive these clitics as markers of polar questions, because they occur in other clause types as well.

one of the interjections *om* 'yes', and *menna* or *manna* for 'no' (identificational and existential/locational, respectively).[7]

(18) a. *nda   yakkhama   mekan=na=i?*
          2SG   Yakkha_woman   COP.2SG.NEG=NMLZ.SG=Q
          'Aren't you a Yakkha woman?'   [36_cvs_06.547]

      b. *nda   lak-ma   mi?-me-ka=na=i?*
          2SG   dance-INF   think-NPST-2=NMLZ.SG=Q
          'Do you want to dance?'

      c. *ka   i?*
          1SG   Q
          'You mean me?'

      d. *men=na=i,   kha?la   so-nhaŋ-se   i?*
          NEG.COP=NMLZ.SG=EMPH   like_this   watch-V2.SEND-SUP   Q
          'In order to watch them (as they leave)?'   [36_cvs_06.489]

(19) a. *yakthu=i?*
          enough=Q
          'Did you have enough?'

      b. *yakthu.*
          enough.
          'I had enough.'

In conversations, one often hears tag questions like *mennai?* 'isn't it?'. They request a confirmation from the interlocutor that the propositional content of the preceding utterance is true (see examples in (20)). Sometimes they may just convey uncertainty on behalf of the speaker, since in (20c), from a pear story, the interlocutor is not supposed to know about the content.

(20) a. *to   thaŋ-a-ŋ-ci-ŋ,   men=na=i?*
          up   climb-PST-EXCL-DU-EXCL   COP.NEG=NMLZ.SG=Q
          'We climbed up, didn't we?'   [36_cvs_06.267]

      b. *pi-uks-u,   men=na=i?*
          give-PRF-3.P[PST]   COP.NEG=NMLZ.SG=Q
          'She gave it to her, didn't she?'   [36_cvs_06.381]

      c. *nhaŋ=na   kha?la   lukt-a-sy-a-ci,*
          and_then=INS   like_this   collide-PST-MDDL-PST-DU

---

[7] On a sociolinguistic side note, when meeting someone familiar (or calling on the phone, nowadays), one often asks whether the interlocutor has already eaten rice or drunken tea, depending on the time of day.

men=na=i?
COP.NEG=NMLZ.SG=Q
'And then they collided like this, didn't they?'   [34_pea_04.025]

12.3.4.2 Disjunctive questions

Disjunctive questions consist of two juxtapposed alternative scenarios, both marked by the alternation marker =*em* (21). If it attaches to a word that ends in /a/ or /e/, the first vowel gets deleted, e.g., /nhaŋ=le=em/ 'or afterwards' is pronounced [nhaŋlem]. This marker is not only found in interrogative clauses. Occasionally, it also attaches to hypothetical clauses, not following the template of two juxtaposed alternatives, but rather expressing uncertainty (see (21c)). Although the verb in this clause is marked for nonpast, and hence is in realis mood, the marker =*em* weakens the realis interpretation of this utterance, and thus it is best rendered with a subjunctive in the English translation.

(21) a. *nniŋda   yakkha*   *om=em,   men=em?*
          2PL   of_Yakkha_affiliation COP=ALT   COP.NEG=ALT
          'Are you (plural) Yakkha or not?'   [39_nrr_08.10]

     b. *khumdu=em   ŋ-khumd-in=em?*
          tasty=ALT   NEG-tasty-NEG=ALT
          'Is it tasty or not?'

     c. *nda   i=ya=ca*   *men-gap-khuba*
          2SG   what=NMLZ.NSG=ADD   NEG-carry-NMLZ
          luʔ-ni-me-ŋ=n=em.
          tell-COMPL-NPST-1SG.P=NMLZ.SG=ALT
          'He might tell me: You have nothing.'   [36_cvs_06.349]

12.3.4.3 Content questions

Content questions contain one of the interrogative pro-forms introduced in §4.6. Question words remain in situ (see (22a)), even in adverbial clauses such as (22b) and embedded clauses such as (22c). The embedded clause in (22c) reflects direct speech (see the imperative and the person marking). Question words or phrases are often marked by the focus marker –*le*. In declaratives, it marks contrastive information, and it is also often found in mirative contexts. In questions, it implies that the speaker is particularly clueless and very eager to get the answer.

(22) a. ŋ=ga   paŋ   heʔne   om?
         2SG.POSS=GEN   house   where   COP
         'Where do you live?'   [01_leg_07.160]

     b. heʔna   ceʔya   yok-se   ta-ya=na.
        which   matter   search-SUP   come[3SG]-PST=NMLZ.SG
        'Which language did she come to search for?'

     c. ka   ina=le   khut-a-ŋ   ly-a-ŋ-ga=na?
        1SG   what.SG=CTR   bring-IMP-1SG.P   tell-PST-1SG.P-2.A=NMLZ.SG
        'What did you tell me to bring (you)?'[8]

There is an interjection *issaŋ* that can be provided as an answer when the person asked does not know the answer either. It has a rising intonation contour just like questions, and means as much as 'I do not know' or 'no idea', but often contains the subtext 'How am I supposed to know?', and is thus very similar in usage to the Nepali interjection *khoi*. It can be used as an answer to any question type.

More information on the discourse-structural particles touched upon in this chapter can be found in Chapter 17.

12.3.5 Exclamative clauses

Strictly speaking, exclamative clauses are not a distinct clause type because their formal structure is identical to interrogative clauses. They always contain the interrogative quantifier *ikhiŋ* (or its nominalized forms *ikhiŋna/ikhiŋha*) which is used to inquire about the size, amount or degree of nominal, verbal and adjectival concepts. Functionally, exclamations can be defined as declaratives with high expressive value, containing some extreme and especially remarkable information (König & Siemund 2007: 316). Although they are questions syntactically, their falling intonation differs from that of questions, which have a rising intonation towards the end of the clause.

(23) a. ikhiŋ   ucun,   hen=na   din=be
        how_much   nice   today=NMLZ.SG day=LOC
        tub-i=ha!
        meet-1PL=NMLZ.NSG
        'How nice (that) we met today!'   [10_sng_03.003]

---

[8] The somewhat unusual verb form *khutaŋ* 'bring me!' is found here because structurally, this is embedded direct speech.

b. *ka   ikhiŋ   pe-me-ŋ=na!*
    1SG   how_much   fly-NPST-1SG=NMLZ.SG
    'How much (how high) I will fly!'   [21_nrr_04.032]

c. *ikhiŋ   chippakeke?=na   takabaŋ!*
    how_much   disgusting=NMLZ.SG   spider
    'What a disgusting spider!'

12.4 Flexible agreement

The syntax of the agreement in Yakkha and Tibeto-Burman in general is much more flexible than in Indo-European languages. As noted earlier by Bickel (2000), the purely identificational agreement that is known from Indo-Aryan is accompanied by associative (appositional and partitive) agreement types.

In appositional agreement, the noun phrase that corresponds to the agreement marker is semantically an apposition to the antecedent of that marker, but syntactically it is the argument. In the clauses in (24) the person value of the arguments is only revealed by the verbal person marking. The corresponding nouns provide additional information about the referent, while they are the arguments syntactically. We know that the ergative case is not overtly marked on arguments that are represented by first and second person pronouns. It is overtly marked on nouns with first or second person reference (see (24c)), which shows that the differential agent marking is determined by a combination of person features and word class.

(24) a. *mamu   he?ne   khe-i-g=ha.*
          girl   where   go[PST]-2PL-2=NMLZ.NSG
          'Where did you girls go?'

      b. *kamnibak   sori   yuŋ-i=hoŋ   uŋ-u-m.*
          friend   together sit-1PL[PST]=SEQ drink-3.P-1PL.A[SBJV]
          'Having sat down together, let us friends drink.'

      c. *a-koŋma=ŋa=le   ta-ga=na   raecha.*
          1SG.POSS-aunt=ERG=CTR   bring[PST]-2.A[3.P]=NMLZ.SG   MIR
          'You, auntie, really brought her (the second wife)!'   [06_cvs_01.042]

      d. *phu-na   yapmi   pham=na   yapmi*
          white=NMLZ.SG person red=NMLZ.SG person
          leks-a-ŋ=na.
          become-PST-1SG=NMLZ.SG
          'I, the white person, turned red.'

The second type is partitive agreement, shown in (25). Here, the verbal person marking refers to a group of potential referents, while the noun phrase refers to the subset of actual referents. The verb here shows nonsingular number marking, although the referent of the A argument has singular number.[9] In (25b) this referential mismatch extends from an embedded clause into the main clause, as it is found on both the matrix verb *kama* 'say' and the verb in the embedded speech *khuma* 'steal'. The sentence is paraphrasable with 'But none of them said: **we** stole the money', although it is clear from the question pronoun (and from how the story proceeds) *isa* 'who' that the purpose of the clause is to single out one referent.

(25) a. *nniŋda   sum-baŋ=be   isa=ŋa   yaŋ*
          2PL   three-CLF.HUM=LOC who=ERG   money
          khus-uks-u-m-ga?
          steal[PST]-PRF-3.P-2PL.A-2
          'Who of you three stole the money?'

      b. *khaʔniŋgo   isa=ŋa=ca   khus-u-m-ŋa=ha*
          but   who=ERG=ADD   steal[PST]-3.P-1PL.A-EXCL=NMLZ.NC
          ŋ-ga-ya-ma-nin.
          3PL.A-say-PST-PRF-PL.NEG
          'But none of them said: I stole the money.'   [04_leg_03.018]

      c. *isa=ja   n-nis-u-nin=na.*
          who=ADD   NEG-see-3.P[PST]-NEG.PL=NMLZ.SG
          'None of them had seen her.'   [22_nrr_05.071]

---

[9] With pronouns like 'who' and 'none' it is not always easy to determine the semantic number. In Yakkha, however, if one inquires about the identity of more than one person, one generally uses the nonsingular marker *isa=ci*.

13 Nominalization and relativization

In Sino-Tibetan languages one commonly finds a pattern of syntactic nominalizations that participate in various constructions, creating noun phrases, nominal modifiers and relative clauses, but also nominalized embedded clauses, and independent main clauses. This convergence of functions has been referred to as the 'Standard Sino-Tibetan Nominalization' (SSTN) pattern (Bickel 1999c: 271) and has been widely studied (Matisoff 1972; DeLancey 1989a; Genetti 1992; Genetti et al. 2008; Saxena 1992; Ebert 1994; DeLancey 1999; Bickel 1999c; Watters 2002; Noonan & Fanego 2008; Doornenbal 2008). DeLancey (2011a) has even proposed nominalization as the major driving force for syntactic change in Tibeto-Burman.

The nominalization processes found in Yakkha fit well into the broader Sino-Tibetan pattern, extending far beyond the derivation of lexical nouns. Their functions cover (a) the derivation of nouns, (b) the construction of relative clauses, adjectives and other adnominal modifiers, and (c) a function beyond reference: they may occur on finite embedded complement clauses, in auxiliary constructions, and in independent main clauses. The nominalization of main clauses serves discourse-structural purposes, as will be shown in §13.3.3 below.

Yakkha has three sets of nominalizers, one set for lexical nominalizations (marked by -pa and -ma, treated in §13.1), and two for mainly syntactic nominalizations, namely the subject nominalizers -khuba and -khuma (treated in §13.2) and the universal nominalizers =na and =ha (see §13.3). §13.4 briefly deals with correlative clause constructions.

13.1 Lexical nominalization: *-pa* and *-ma*

The first set contains the suffixes -pa ~ -ba ~ -wa and -ma, of which -pa (and its allomorphs) can be traced back at least to Proto-Bodic; it is found with nominalizing and related functions in Tibetan, Sherpa, Tamangic languages and other Kiranti languages (DeLancey 2002; 2011a; Genetti 1992). In Yakkha, this set is used solely for lexical nominalizations, with -pa and its allomorphs for generic and male reference, while -ma is generally reserved for female reference (related to an old system of gender marking). Some exceptions where both -pa and -ma have generic reference were found, too.

These nominalizers are mostly found in occupational titles, in names of mythical beings and gods, in zoological terms, in names for kinds of food and in kinship terminology (cf. appendix). Some examples are provided in Table 13.1. As this table shows, many of the forms are not transparent; their base or part of it does not occur independently. A few adjectives and adverbs were found with -pa, too, such as *ulippa* 'old' and *tamba* 'slowly', but this is not the typical derivational pattern for adjectives or adverbs in Yakkha; the suffixes -pa and -ma are not productive in Yakkha.

Table 13.1: Lexical nominalizations with -*pa* and -*ma*

LEXEME	GLOSS	BASES
kucuma	'dog'	–
kiba	'tiger'	–
hibumba	'dung beetle'	dung-roll-NMLZ
cikciŋwa	'wasp'	–
caleppa	'bread'	eat-fry-NMLZ
miksrumba	'blind person'	eye-[STEM]-NMLZ
cagaŋba	'grain dish' (Nep. *ḍheḍo*)	eat–[STEM]-NMLZ
maŋgaŋba	'ritual specialist'	god-[STEM]-NMLZ
camyoŋba	'food'	eat-[STEM]-NMLZ
wariŋba	'tomato'	–
khibrumba	'fog, cloud'	–

13.2 Participant nominalization (S/A arguments): -*khuba*

13.2.1 Formal properties

The default form of this nominalizer is -*khuba*, but -*khuma* is found occasionally with female reference. This marker derives nominals that may either modify a head noun (see (1a)) or function as noun phrases themselves (see (1b) and (c)). Morphologically, it is an affix; it always attaches directly to the verbal stem. Syntactically, it has the whole phrase in its scope.

(1) a. *heko=ha=ci   mok-khuba babu*
    other=NMLZ.NSG=NSG beat-NMLZ boy
    'the boy who beats the others'

    b. *heko=ha=ci   mok-khuba*
    other=NMLZ.NSG=NSG beat-NMLZ
    'someone who beats others'

    c. *mok-khuba*
    beat-NMLZ
    'beater'

These nominals may be long and internally complex, as shown by the examples in (2). This makes *-khuba* different, for instance, from the English nomina agentis in *-er*.

(2) a. *eŋ=ga   yakkhaba=ga   kha ceʔya*
    1PL.INCL.POSS=GEN Yakkha_person=GEN this language
    yok-khuba   Helihaŋ
    search-NMLZ Helihang
    'Helihang, who searches for this language of us Yakkha'
    [18_nrr_03.032]

    b. *samundra=ga u-yum=be   inca-khuba*
    ocean=GEN   3SG.POSS-side=LOC play-NMLZ
    'someone (who is) playing on the shores of the ocean' [13_cvs_02.057]

In a relative clause structure, the constituent order is usually head-final, but postposed relative clauses are possible as well. Impressionistically, restrictive relative clauses (those that narrow down the reference of a head noun out of a set of possible referents) tend to occur preposed, while appositional relative clauses (those that add descriptive information about a noun) tend to occur postposed.

(3) a. *eko yapmi kisa si-khuba*
    one person deer kill-NMLZ
    'a man killing/having killed a deer'

    b. *babu sem-khuba*
    boy pluck-NMLZ
    'the boy who is plucking'

If the nominalization results in a noun, it may head NPs and host all nominal morphology: case, number and possessive prefixes. The examples in (4) serve to illustrate that the resulting nominals can be modified or quantified just as simple nouns can.

(4) a. *kha   cyabruŋ-lak-khuba=ci*
         these   drum-dance-NMLZ=NSG
         'these drum-dancers'   [25_tra_01.071]

     b. *jammai   kam   cok-khuba=ci*
         all   work   do-NMLZ=NSG
         'all the workers'   [25_tra_01.098]

As the nominalizer attaches directly to the verbal stem, there is no TAM marking on the verb, and the TAM interpretation is retrieved from the context. The verb may host the negation marker *men-*, which is also found on other nonfinite verbal forms such as converbs and infinitives (see (5a)). Another verbal property is illustrated in (5): the noun in *-khuba* may still be modified by adverbs. However, it is not clear yet whether nominal and verbal properties could occur simultaneously, e.g., in a phrase like *jammai ṭhwaŋ namkhubaci* 'all the awfully stinking ones'.

(5) a. *kaniŋ=nuŋ   men-doŋ-khuba   nwak*
         1PL=COM   NEG-agree-NMLZ bird
         'the bird that does not belong to us/that is different from us'
                                                                 [21_nrr_04.004]

     b. *makhurna   waghui   loʔa   ṭhwaŋ*
         black   chicken_droppings like   [smelling]awfully
         nam-khuba
         smell-NMLZ
         'something black, smelling awfully, like chicken droppings'
                                                                 [42_leg_10.017]

Complement-taking verbs with embedded infinitives can be in the scope of the nominalizer as well, as (6) shows. The infinitive *hiŋma* 'support' is embedded into *yama* 'be able to X'.

(6) *hiŋ-ma   ya-khuba   babu=be   kheʔ-ma.*
     support-INF   be_able-NMLZ   boy=LOC   go-INF[DEONT]
     'You have to marry a man who can support you.'   [28_cvs_04.112]

The constituents of the relativized clause can also be focussed on by means of the additive focus marker (see (7a)), and they can be emphasized, as in (7b), with *ŋkhiŋ* 'that much'.

(7)   a.   *sa=maʔniŋ=ca   leŋ-khuba*
             meat=without=ADD be_alright-NMLZ
             'someone who is fine even without (eating) meat'

       b.   *yapmi=ci=nuŋ=ca   ŋkhiŋ   sala*
             people=NSG=COM=ADD that_much matter
             me-leŋ-khuba=ci.
             NEG-exchange-NMLZ=NSG
             'They were of the kind that does not talk that much with people, too.'
                                      [22_nrr_05.046]

A few lexicalized nominalizations with *-khuba* and *-khuma* can be found, too: *khuncakhuba* 'thief' (steal-eat-NMLZ), *thukkhuba* 'tailor' (sew-NMLZ), *hiŋkhuba* 'husband', *hiŋkhuma* 'wife' (support-NMLZ), *yaben-pekkhuba* 'diviner' (sign-divine-NMLZ). Note the parallelism of *-khuba* referring to generic/male nouns and *-khuma* referring to female nouns, as in the lexical nominalizations discussed in §13.1. This suggests that *-khuba* and *-khuma* are historically complex.[1]

13.2.2 Grammatical relations

Descriptions of other Kiranti languages call equivalent constructions 'nomen agentis' or 'active/agentive participle' (Tolsma 1999; Rutgers 1998; Ebert 1997a; 1999a; Doornenbal 2009). One should note, however, that the nominalization may apply to verbs of any semantics, and the resulting nouns do not just refer to typical agents (see Bickel (2004a: 180) for the same point on closely related Belhare). Subjects of stative verbs like *namma* 'smell, emit odour', *haŋma* 'have spicy sensation' or *tukma* 'be ill' can also be the targets of this nominalization.

The resulting nominal always refers to the S in intransitive verbs, and to the A for all transitive verbs (two-argument and three-argument), but never to any lower argument. This is illustrated by (8): S and A arguments are possible results of the nominalization, while P arguments are not (see (8c)). Nominalizing morphology that indicates a grammatical relation is common in Kiranti languages, and it is also known, e.g., from Dolakha Newari and from Kham (see Genetti (1992: 409), Ebert 1999a: 376).

---

[1] The syllable *khu* is also found in the reciprocal marker *-khusa*.

(8) a. *paip pek-khuba   babu*
           pipe break-NMLZ boy
           'the boy who broke/breaks the water pipe' (A)
    b. *leŋ-khuba   tabhaŋ*
          become-NMLZ son-in-law
          'the prospective son-in-law' (S)
    c. **babu=ŋa pek-khuba   paip*
          boy=ERG break-NMLZ pipe
          Intended: 'the pipe that was/will be broken by the boy' (*P)

Non-canonically marked S and A arguments, e.g., possessive experiencers or locative marked possessors undergoing the nominalization have the same status as standard S and A arguments (i.e., in the ergative or nominative case and being indexed on the verb). In (9a), the experiencer S argument is coded as possessor of the sensation, literally translatable as 'someone whose laziness comes up'. In (9b), the semantic relation expressed is possession, but it is coded with an existential construction and a combination of genitive and locative marking on the A argument.

(9) a. *o-pomma   kek-khuba   yapmi*
          3SG.POSS-lazyness come_up-NMLZ person
          'a lazy guy'
    b. *kai=ga=be   wa-ya,   wa-khuba=ŋa*
          some=GEN=LOC exist[3SG]-PST exist-NMLZ=ERG
          me-wa-khuba   m-bi-n-ci-nin
          NEG-exist-NMLZ 3PL.A-give[PST]-C-3NSG.P-NEG
          'Some (people) had (food), and those who had (food) did not give it to those who did not have it.'   [14_nrr_02.012]

13.2.3 Predicative use of the nominalized forms

Some examples even point towards a predicative use of the nominalized forms, as opposed to the expected referential use shown in the examples above. As we will see in §13.3 below, this function of -*khuba* is similar to what is found for the nominalizers =*na* and =*ha*.

Shown below is a prime example to illustrate the function of nominalization as a discourse-structural device in Yakkha (see (10)). It is from a written narrative. The narrator remembers a fight with his brother. Both boys want to let out the chicks from the cage, and in the course of the fight, they accidentally kill them by squeezing them with the cage door. The nominalization is employed to yield a vivid narrative style, at a point where the event line approaches its climax, i.e., the accidental killing of the chicks. The verb of saying has to be set back against the content of the embedded direct speech, which contains the crucial information for what happens next. The fact that the nominalized form *kakhuba* 'the one who says' occurs before the embedded direct speech supports this explanation. In the typical structure, the finite verb of saying would be the last element in the sentence. But as focal elements tend to come sentence-finally, and as the embedded speech here contains the focal information, the constituent structure is reversed. On a further note, the embedded speech itself contains a nominalizer *=ha*. This nominalizer has quite the opposite function here: it serves to put emphasis on the claim uttered by the boys (cf. §13.3.3 below). The example nicely illustrates how nominalizers are employed to carve out a text by means of backgrounding and foregrounding chunks of information.

(10) ka   ka-khuba   ka   hon-wa-ŋ-ci-ŋ=ha!,
      1SG   say-NMLZ   1SG   open-NPST-C-3NSG.P-1SG.A=NMLZ.NSG,

      a-phu   ka-khuba   ka   hon-wa-ŋ-ci-ŋ=ha!
      1SG.POSS-eB   say-NMLZ   1SG   open-NPST-C-3NSG.P-1SG.A=NMLZ.NSG
      'I said: "I will let them out!", and my elder brother said: "I will let them
      out!"'   [40_leg_08.065]

Example (11) is from a narrative account of what happened at a festival. The sentence describes some young men who feel ashamed of what they had done the night before when they were drunk. As such, the sentence which is nominalized by *-khuba* is rather like a comment, set apart from the main event line.

(11) nhaŋ   koi-koi   sulemwalem   leŋ-khe-khuba.
      and_then   some-some   with_hanging_heads   become-V2.GO-NMLZ
      'And some of them hung their heads.'   [37_nrr_07.074]

13.3 The nominalizers =*na* and =*ha* ~ =*ya*

The nominalizers =*na* and =*ha* ~ =*ya* have a wide range of functions. They are clitics, attaching to the rightmost element of a phrase, whether this is an inflected verb, a stem (of any word class), a case-marked phrase or a clause. The resulting nominal may fill the structural position of a nominal head, an adnominal modifier (adjectives, participles, relative clauses), a complement clause, or a finite, independent main clause. Nominalized main clauses have several and, at first sight, contradictory discourse functions.

§13.3.1 is concerned with uses of this nominalization in adnominal modification, while §13.3.2 deals with complementation. §13.3.3 discusses main clause nominalization.

The markers =*na* and =*ha* ~ =*ya* indicate singular and nonsingular number, respectively, shown in (12). The marker =*ha* also refers to non-countables, substances and more abstract concepts (see (12c)). Example (13) illustrates the same point with the interrogative root *i*.[2] The nominalizers turn the interrogative root into a pronoun, in order to inquire about a particular referent. This number distinction in nominalization is also found in Athpare and in Belhare, both also from the 'Greater Yakkha' branch of Eastern Kiranti (Ebert 1997a: 130, Bickel 1999c: 278).

(12)   a.   *pham=na*   *wariŋba*
              red=NMLZ.SG   tomato
              'red tomato'

        b.   *pham=ha*   *wariŋba=ci*
              red=NMLZ.NSG   tomato=NSG
              'red tomatoes'

        c.   *onek=ha*   *ceʔya*
              joking=NMLZ.NC   matter
              'jokes'

(13)   a.   *i=na*
              what=NMLZ.SG
              'what' (presupposing one item)

        b.   *i=ha*
              what=NMLZ.NSG/NC
              'what' (presupposing many items or mass reference)

It should be emphasized for the following discussion that the traditional sense of the term *nominalizer* is too narrow with regard to Yakkha and in Sino-Tibetan nominalization in general (hence Bickel's (1999) term *Standard Sino-Tibetan Nominalization*). The markers =*na* and =*ha* do not regularly derive nouns, although one occasionally finds lexicalized expressions, such as *chemha* 'liquor' (be transparent-NMLZ), *tumna* 'senior' (ripen-NMLZ), *pakna* 'junior' (be raw-NMLZ), *haŋha* 'hot spice' (taste hot-NMLZ), *bhenikna* 'morning ritual' (morning-NMLZ). Rather, they turn any material into referential expressions, behaving identically or very much like noun phrases, either with or without a head noun.

---

[2] The interrogative root *i* is the base for many interrogative words. In isolation, it may be used to ask about states-of-affairs, as in *i leksa?* 'What happened?'.

Etymologically, the nominalizers are related to a set of demonstratives: *na* 'this', *kha* 'these' (see §4.3). These demonstratives have exactly the same distribution with regard to number and mass/abstract reference as the nominalizers (compare examples (12) and (13) with (14)).

(14)   a.   *na   sambakhi*
            this   potato
            'this potato'

       b.   *kha   sambakhi=ci*
            these   potatoes=NSG
            'these potatoes'

       c.   *kha   kham*
            this   soil
            'this soil'

       d.   *kha   ce?ya*
            this   matter
            'this matter/language'

So far, not many restrictions on the inflectional properties of the nominalized or relativized verb phrases could be detected. The only restriction is that certain clausal moods which are expressed by verbal inflection (optative, imperative) cannot be fed into the nominalization process. As far as person and tense/aspect marking is concerned, anything is possible. Example (15a) shows a verb inflected for the progressive. The nominalization may also apply recursively (see (15b)).

(15)   a.   *lop   pok-ma-si-me=ha*   *yaŋli*
            now   rise-INF-AUX.PROG-NPST[3SG]=NMLZ.NSG   sprout
            'the sprouts that are shooting now'

       b.   *he?=na=be?=ya=ci?*
            which=NMLZ.SG=LOC=NMLZ.NSG=NSG
            '[The people] from which place?'

13.3.1 Relativization

13.3.1.1 Adnominal modification and relativization

The nominalizers are frequently found as relativizers. In contrast to the nominalizer -*khuba*, =*na* and =*ha* are almost unresticted with respect to grammatical relations. Core participants as well as non-core participants can serve as a relativization site for =*na* and =*ha*. The only thematic relation that has not been found is A, as A arguments get nominalized by *-khuba*.[3] In this respect, Yakkha is radically different from its neighbors, where the corresponding markers are unconstrained with respect to grammatical relations (Ebert 1997a; Bickel 1999c). Relativizations on S arguments do occur, but they are much rarer than relativizations on objects or other kinds of participants, since this grammatical relation is also covered by the marker *-khuba*. The examples in (16) show relativizations on core arguments.

(16) a.   *ci=ha*   *maŋcwa*
          be_cold=NMLZ.NSG   water
          'cold water' (S)

     b.   *nda*   *nis-u-ga=na*   *chem*
          2SG[ERG]   know-3.P[PST]-2=NMLZ.SG   song
          'a song that you know' (P)

     c.   *chemha*   *yukt-u=na*   *mamu*
          liquor   put_for-3.P[PST]=NMLZ.SG girl
          'the girl that was served liquor' (G)

     d.   *beula=ŋa*   *khut-u=ha*   *tephen*
          groom=ERG   bring-3.P[PST]=NMLZ.NSG clothes
          'the clothes brought by the groom' (T)   [25_tra_01.054]

Some relativizations of objects have lexicalized into adjectives. Example (17a) is from the canonical transitive class. Example (17b) is originally from the class of transimpersonal verbs (cf. Chapter 11). In this class, the sole argument is expressed as the object of a morphologically transitive verb, and the verb shows default third person A marking, i.e., zero. An A cannot be expressed with transimpersonal predicates.

(17) a.   *a-na*   *mi*   *cend-u=na*
          1SG.POSS-eZ a_little wake_up-3.P=NMLZ.SG
          sa-ya=na.
          COP.PST-PST[3SG]=NMLZ.SG
          'My elder sister was rather witty.'   [40_leg_08.057]

     b.   *ikhiŋ*   *yeŋd-u=na*   *yapmi*   *lai!*
          how_much be_tough-3.P=NMLZ.SG person EXCLA
          'What a tough person!'

---

[3] There is no direct negative evidence, unfortunately, but in the whole corpus of recorded language data (roughly 13.000 words), not a single instance of A arguments nominalized by *=na* or *=ha* was detected, neither did I hear it in conversations or elicitations. Thus, even if nominalization or relativization over A was possible, it would be a rather marked structure.

The relativization of non-core participants such as locations, temporal expressions or comitatives is illustrated by (18).[4]

(18) a. *nna o-hop   wa-ya=na   siŋ,   nna=ca*

         that 3SG.POSS-nest exist-PST[3SG]=NMLZ.SG tree, that=ADD

         et-haks-u!

         strike-V2.SEND-3.P[IMP]

         'That tree **where he has his nest**, destroy that too!' [21_nrr_04.020]

    b. *la   mem-phem-meʔ=na   seʔni=ŋa*

         moon NEG-shine-NPST=NMLZ.SG night=INS

         'in a **moonless** night'   [14_nrr_02.21]

    c. *ca-m=ha   yapmi*

         eat-INF[DEONT]=NMLZ.NSG people

         men-ja-m=ha   yapmi,   kha

         NEG-eat-INF[DEONT]=NMLZ.NSG people   these

         imin=ha=ci?

         how=NMLZ.NSG=NSG

         'What kind (of people) are they? (Are they) people **with whom we should eat**, or **with whom we should not eat**, of what kind (are they)?'

                                            [22_nrr_05.040]

Not only inflected verbs but also case-marked phrases (19) and simple nouns (20a) can be turned into adnominal modifiers by means of the nominalizers. Example (20b) shows that even converbs can undergo this nominalization, though it has to be mentioned that this possibility was only found for the negation converb *men-...-le.*

(19) a. *jarman=beʔ=na   mamu*

         germany=LOC=NMLZ.SG girl

         'the girl from Germany'

    b. *nasa=ci,   u-ṭiŋ=nuŋ=ha=ci*

         fish=NSG 3SG.POSS-spike=COM=NMLZ.NSG=NSG

         'the fish, those with spikes'   [13_cvs_02.046]

(20) a. *bhenik=na   cama*

         morning=NMLZ.SG rice

         'the (portion of) rice from the morning'

---

[4] Regarding (c), the question with whom one may eat is fundamental in the highly stratified Hindu society. This example from a narrative thus also illustrates the impact that Hindu rule has had on Kiranti society in the past centuries.

b. *u-laŋ*   *men-da-le=na*   *picha*
    3SG.POSS-leg   NEG-come-CVB=NMLZ.SG   child
    'the child that cannot walk yet'

Many roots in Yakkha may be used either as adverbs or as adjectives. Adjectives in adnominal use are again derived by means of the nominalizers. Compare the adverbs and predicative adjectives in (21a, c, e, g) with the adnominal adjectives in (21b, d, f, h).

(21) a. *haku imin coŋ-me-ci-g=ha?*
          now   how   do-NPST-DU-2=NMLZ.NSG
          'Now how will you do it?'   [22_nrr_05.109]

      b. *na   imin=na,   kaniŋ=nuŋ   men-doŋ-khuba   nwak.*
          this how=NMLZ.SG   1PL=COM   NEG-agree-NMLZ   bird
          'What kind of bird is this, not belonging to us.'   [21_nrr_04.004]

      c. *ka   to   taŋkhyaŋ=be   pe-nem-me-ŋ=na.*
          1SG   up   sky=LOC   fly-V2.LAY-NPST-1SG=NMLZ.SG
          'I will keep flying up into the sky.'   [21_nrr_04.033]

      d. *to=na   paŋ*
          up=NMLZ.SG   house
          'the upper house'

      e. *khem   nis-u-ŋ=na.*
          before   see-3.P[PST]-1SG=NMLZ.SG
          'I saw it before.'

      f. *khem=na   kamniwak*
          before=NMLZ.SG   friend
          'the friend from before'

      g. *luŋkhwak sahro cancan sa-ma=na.*
          stone   very   high   COP.PST-PRF=NMLZ.SG
          'The rock was really high.'   [38_nrr_07.039]

      h. *cancan=na   luŋkhwak*
          high=NMLZ.SG   stone
          'a high rock'

Adjectives may also be derived from verbal roots with (ingressive-)stative semantics (22) (cf. also Chapter 6).

(22) a. *chem=ha   maŋcwa*
          be_clear=NMLZ.NSG   water
          'clear water'

b. *haŋ=ha*   *macchi*
    be_spicy=NMLZ.NSG   pickles
    'spicy pickles'

13.3.1.2 Headless and internally headed relative clauses

Besides adnominal modification, one often encounters headless relative clauses, i.e., noun phrases that lack a head noun (see (23)). The relative clause takes the structural position that would otherwise be filled by the head noun.

(23) *nhaŋ*   *sapthakt-wa-c-u=na*   *ibilag-ibilag*
      and_then   like-NPST-DU-3.P=NMLZ.SG   secretly-REDUP
      khus-het-i-ya-ma-c-u=na.
      steal-V2.CARRY.OFF-COMPL-PST-PRF-DU-3.P=NMLZ.SG
      'And they (dual) secretly stole one (girl) whom they liked.'
                                                      [22_nrr_05.064]

The reference of the head noun is retrieved from the context, but there is a syntactic constraint, too. As A arguments may not undergo this kind of relativization, headless relative clauses are always interpreted as referring to the object of a transitive verb (see (24a)) or as the sole argument of an intransitive verb (see (24b)). As the S and the P arguments are treated identically, this is a case of ergative alignment in syntax.

(24) a. *nna   tas-wa=na=be*
          that   reach[3SG.A]-NPST[3.P]=NMLZ.SG=LOC
          yog-a-ca-n-u-m,   *nna=be.*
          search-IMP-DU.A[IMP]-3PL.P-3.P-2PL.A   that=LOC
          'Look for it **where it lands**, in that (place).'   [22_nrr_05.090]
      b. *nda*   *cekt-a-ga=na*
          2SG[NOM]   speak-PST-2=NMLZ.SG
          ŋ-kheps-u-ŋa-n=na.
          NEG-hear-3.P[PST]-1SG.A-NEG=NMLZ.SG
          'I did not hear **what you said**.' (presupposing one word was said)

In contrast to the almost unconstrained adnominal modification, headless relative clauses referring to non-core participants were not found. The absence of the head noun would make their interpretation rather difficult. For instance, leaving out *din* 'day' from a clause like in (25) is not possible.

(25) na   mamu=ŋa   nna   luŋkhwak   khet-u=na
      this   girl=ERG   that stone   carry_off-3.P[PST]=NMLZ.SG
      *(din)   i   leks-a-ma=na   baŋniŋ,   ...
      *(day)   what   happen-PST[3SG]-PRF=NMLZ.SG   about   ...
      'As for what happened on the day when the girl carried off that stone, ...'
                                                          [38_nrr_07.042]

While headless relative clauses show properties of noun phrases, such as number and case marking and the possibility of being referred to anaphorically by demonstratives (see *nna* in (24a)), they do not have noun properties: there is no evidence for possessive prefixes attaching to the headless relative clause. Furthermore, the argument marking inside the headless relative clause remains as in simple clauses. There are, for instance, no genitives on core arguments, as, e.g., in the English clause *His talking annoyed me*.

A marginally occurring type of relative clause are internally headed relative clauses (called "circumnominal" in Lehmann 1984). Internally headed relative clauses are relative clauses whose head noun is not extracted but remains in the same structural position as it would be in a main clause. This type has been reported for other Tibeto-Burman languages, too; see, e.g., Bickel (2005: 3) and Bickel (1999c) for closely related Belhare, DeLancey (1999: 245) for Tibetan, and Coupe (2007: 255) for Mongsen Ao. In Yakkha, this type is rather marginal. All examples are elicited, and natural data would be necessary for a better understanding of this structure. An example is shown in (26). The main verb *tumma* 'find' can only take nominal, but not clausal complements. Thus one cannot, for instance, add the complementizer *bhoŋ* to the embedded verb, or interpret it as 'I found out that a man was killed by a tiger'. The object can only be the noun *yapmi* 'person', so that the surrounding material must be a relative clause.

(26) kiba=ŋa   eko   **yapmi**   sis-u=na
      tiger=ERG   one   person   kill-3.P[PST]=NMLZ.SG
      tups-u-ŋ=na.
      find-3.P[PST]-1SG.A=NMLZ.SG
      'I found a man who was killed by a tiger.'

The ergative alignment found for headless relative clauses is also found for internally headed relative clauses. Relativizing over an A argument is ungrammatical and instead, a relative clause marked by *-khuba* was offered in the elicitation (see (27a)). Example (27b) also resulted from the attempt to elicit a transitive clause relativizing over an A argument. The transitive verb was changed to an imperfective structure which, by means of an intransitively inflected auxiliary, is also (morphologically) intransitive. This suggests that the ergativity is the result of a morphosyntactic, not a semantic constraint. An A, at least in the third person, would carry an ergative marker, which would clash with the object properties that the noun has with respect to the main clause. On the other hand, the ergativity is not surprising anyway, as relativization by =na and =ha generally does not allow A arguments as head nouns. The difference to the more common head-final structure lies only in the exclusion of non-core participants such as locations or comitatives.

(27) a. *eko   yapmi   kiba   si-khuba   tups-u-ŋ=na.*
          one   person tiger kill-NMLZ   find-3.P[PST]-1SG.A=NMLZ.SG
          'I found a man who killed a tiger.' (A: -*khuba*)
      b. *eko   yapmi   syau   sem-ma-sy-a=na*
          one   person apple   pluck-INF-AUX.PROG-PST[3SG]=NMLZ.SG
          tups-u-o-ŋ=na.
          find-3.P[PST]-V2.LEAVE-1SG.A=NMLZ.SG
          'I found (and passed) a man who was plucking apples.' (S)

An ambiguity with finite complement clauses further complicates the analysis of headless relative clauses. All of the potential instances of internally headed relativization found in my corpus could also be complements of verbs of perception or cognition. As nothing is extracted in internally headed relativization, the constituent structure of the relative clause is identical to simple clauses, and one cannot distinguish structurally between 'I heard the one who was talking' and 'I heard that someone talked'. Both clauses refer to identical situations in the real world; one cannot hear that someone talks without actually hearing the person talking. One structural criterion to find out whether the embedded clause is a complement or a relative clause could be agreement. Example (28a) is from a narrative, while (28b) is made up in analogy, but with different number features. As the argument *tori* ('mustard', a mass noun) triggers =*ha* on the main verb *oʔma* 'be visible' and *eko phuŋ* 'one flower' triggers =*na*, one could infer that they are arguments of the main verb, rather than taking the whole clause to be the argument. However, one could as well interpret this behavior as long distance agreement out of a finite complement clause, which would not be surprising in Yakkha complementation (see Chapter 15). Hence, the question of how to distinguish internally headed relative clauses and complement clauses cannot be answered satisfactorily, at least not with perception verbs that allow both clausal and nominal complements.

(28) a.   *saptakosi=ga*   *u-lap=pe*   *tori*
              a_river_confluence=GEN 3SG.POSS-side=LOC mustard
              phet-a=ha=ca
              bloom[3SG]-PST=NMLZ.NSG=ADD
              ot-a=ha=bu,   *nna=bhaŋ.*
              be_visible[3SG]-PST=NMLZ.NSG=REP that=ABL
              'Even the mustard blooming at the shores of Saptakosi was visible, from that (rock).'   [38_nrr_07.041]

      b.   *saptakosi=ga*   *u-lap=pe*   *eko* *phuŋ*
              a_river_confluence=GEN 3SG.POSS-side=LOC one   flower
              phet-a=na=ca   *ot-a=na=bu,*
              bloom[3SG]-PST=NMLZ.SG=ADD be_visible[3SG]-PST=NMLZ.SG=REP
              nna=bhaŋ.
              that=ABL
              'Even a flower blooming at the shores of Saptakosi was visible, from that (rock).'

Ambiguities between relative clauses and complement clauses are common (see, e.g., Bickel (1999c: 272), Noonan (2007: 120, 143). In Yakkha, the complemental structure probably gave rise to internally headed relative clauses. All instances displaying this ambiguity in the Yakkha corpus involve verbs of perception or cognition (e.g., 'see', 'hear', 'remember', 'forget'), which leads to the conclusion that the complemental structure must have been the original structure. It must have been gradually expanded to other types of main verbs, namely those which rule out a complemental reading, as the elicited example in (27) above.

13.3.2 Complementation

Complementation is the topic of Chapter 15. For now it suffices to say here that the finite clausal complements of verbs of saying, perception or cognition are always marked by one of the nominalizers, except for quoted direct speech. Optionally, a complementizer *bhoŋ* can be added to the nominalized complement clause (see (29b)). It is worth noting that all complement-taking verbs of this class also take nominal objects. The verb *miʔma* has very unspecific semantics; it translates as 'think, remember', and as a complement-taking verb, it translates as 'hope, think, want', depending on whether the embedded clause is finite or infinitival.

    Finite complementation in Yakkha exhibits double agreement. The embedded subject (S or A) simultaneously triggers agreement in the matrix verb and in the embedded verb, shown by both clauses in (29) (also known as 'copy-raising'). Rather than seeking for a purely structural explanation, a semantic motivation seems more likely to me. Perceiving or thinking about an event always involves perceiving or thinking about the participants, and the agreement marking on the matrix verb reflects this semantic property.

(29) a. *nda   cama   ca-ya-ga=na   mi-nuŋ-nen=na.*
          2SG   rice   eat-PST-2=NMLZ.SG   think-PRF-1>2=NMLZ.SG
          'I have thought you ate the (portion of) rice.'

      b. *yag-a-sy-a-ŋ=na*   *bhoŋ*
          be_exhausted-PST-MIDDLE-PST-1SG=NMLZ.SG comp
          n-nis-a-ma-ŋ-ga-n=na?
          NEG-see-PST-PRF-1SG.P-2.A-NEG=NMLZ.SG
          'Don't you see that I am exhausted?'

The nominalized clause can also be the complement of postpositions that are otherwise found to embed nouns (see (30)). The postposition *anusar* is borrowed from Nepali.

(30) a. *ka-ya=na*   *anusar*
          say-PST[3SG]=NMLZ.SG   according_to
          'according to what he promised'   [11_nrr_01.008]

      b. *ka   luʔ-meʔ-nen-in=ha*   *loʔa   cog-a-ni.*
          1SG[ERG]   tell-NPST-1>2-PL=NMLZ.NSG   like   do-IMP-PL.IMP
          'Do as I tell you.'   [14_nrr_02.19]

13.3.3 Stand-alone nominalizations

13.3.3.1 A versatile discourse strategy

The extension of nominalizations to main clauses is a common feature of Sino-Tibetan languages. Finite nominalizations, or 'stand-alone nominalizations' were first noted by Matisoff (1972) for Lahu (Loloish). Despite the wealth of syntactic studies on nominalization in Tibeto-Burman (see, e.g., Matisoff 1972; Noonan 1997; Noonan & Fanego 2008; DeLancey 1999; 2002; Genetti 1992; Doornenbal 2008; Genetti et al. 2008; Watters 2008; DeLancey 2011a), the main clause function was said to be poorly understood until recently (Genetti et al. 2008: 101). Ebert (1994: 110) mentions nominalized sentences in several Kiranti languages and associates them with lively speech and with focus, as they frequently occur in questions and in negated sentences.

The most detailed discussions of this phenomenon can be found for Belhare and some other Kiranti languages (Bickel 1999c) and for Kham (Watters 2002). Bickel (1999c) identifies focus marking as the functional core of main clause nominalizations, i.e., highlighting controversial information in discourse and (re-)instantiating information with strong assertive force and authoritative power. For Kham, Watters (2002: 369) concludes that main clause nominalization serves to mark thematic discontinuity with the surrounding context, which is employed for narrative stage-setting and for highlighting pivotal events in narratives. In Chantyal, nominalized main clauses may also have a mirative reading (Noonan & Fanego 2008). Doornenbal (2008: 89) made similar findings for Bantawa. Main clause nominalization is not restricted to Sino-Tibetan languages, though. Yap & Grunow-Hårsta (2010) discuss the non-referential uses of nominalization with respect to languages spoken in Asia in general. This phenomenon is not restricted to Asia either, as studies by Woodbury (1985) and by Wegener (2012) show (the list is not meant to be exhaustive).

The crosslinguistic occurrence of finite nominalizations suggests a deeper functional-pragmatic motivation for this process. As Matisoff (1972: 246) has already observed in his study of Lahu, nominalizations "objectify and reify a proposition". By applying a linguistic strategy, namely turning a proposition into a noun-like entity, inherently ephemeral events are identified with inherently time-stable objects, for the purpose of giving them more "reality".

As I will show, this effect gave rise to various functions in Yakkha, which seem to be contradictory at first sight. The functions are very similar to what has been found for Belhare and Kham. Main clauses are nominalized to set them apart from the surrounding discourse, which may result both in backgrounding and in foregrounding information, depending on the genre and the given discourse context.

Plenty of the examples above have already shown that the clitics =na and =ha may attach to finite, independent clauses. They may also attach to nonverbal predicates in copula constructions, as (31) shows. The use of the copula *om* is possible, but not obligatory here.

(31) *m-muk*   *a-laŋ*   *hiŋ=na*   *(om)*.
      2SG.POSS-hand   1SG.POSS-foot   as_big_as=NMLZ.SG   (COP)
      'Your hand is as big as my foot.'

As already noted by Matisoff (1972), nominalized clauses are often paraphrasable with "It is the case that [proposition]". By nominalizing a clause, the speaker emphasizes some state-of-affairs as an independent fact. This is often necessary when some controversial or contrastive information is involved, for instance in negotiations, as in (32) and (33) from narratives (cf. Bickel (1999c) for the same point). In (32), there are two parties, namely a bride against her natal home, arguing about a megalith that she wants to take to her new home as dowry.

(32) a. ŋkhatniŋgo na mamu=ŋa ka, eko=chen ka
 but this girl=ERG 1SG, one=TOP 1SG[ERG]
 mit-u-ŋ=na.
 want-3.P[PST]-1SG.A=NMLZ.SG
 'But this girl (said): I, I want one thing.'
 b. *saman py-haks-a=na,*
 property give-V2.send-PST[3SG]=NMLZ.SG
 n-lu-ks-u-ci.
 3PL.A-tell-PRF-3.P.PST-NSG
 'The property was already transferred, they told them.'
 [38_nrr_07.004]

In (33), the speakers, inhabitants of a village, assure the protagonists of the narrative that they can have anything they ask for. They say this out of gratitude and possibly fear, because the protagonists are believed to be sourcerers, and they had just miraculously 'found' a girl (whom they had in fact kidnapped themselves some days earlier).

(33) *i=ya njiŋda yoŋ-me-c-u-ga,* ŋkha kaniŋ
 what=NMLZ.NSG 2.DUAL search-NPST-DU.A-3.P-2 that 1PL[ERG]
 pi-meʔ-nen-in=ha.
 give-NPST-1>2-PL=NMLZ.NC
 'Whatever you look for, we will give it to you.' [22_nrr_05.079]

Example (34) is another instance of a nominalized clause, which is uttered in order to convince the hearer about the truth of the propositional content (cf. Ebert (1997a) for the same point on Athpare).

(34) *nda n-si-me-ka-n=na,* ka ucun=na thoŋ=be
 2SG NEG-die-NPST-2-NEG=NMLZ.SG 1SG nice=NMLZ.SG place=LOC
 khem-meʔ-nen=na.
 carry_off-NPST-1>2=NMLZ.SG
 'You will not die, I will take you to a nice place.' [27_nrr_06.010]

The nominalized clauses are very frequent in assertions (both affirmative and negated, in fact, negated clauses without nominalizers are very rare), and also in questions, particularly in polar questions (see (35a)). Nominalization is absent from mood paradigms (imperative, subjunctive and optative), from irrealis and counterfactual clauses, and from adverbial subordination (exemplified by a sequential clause in (35b)), i.e., from any non-assertive clause type, except for interrogatives. Given this distribution, the main clause nominalization could best be characterized as assertive force marker. The proposition in question is not part of the background that is shared by all discourse participants, which is why it needs to be reinstantiated, a process which is in line with the focus analysis found in Bickel (1999c).

(35) a. *ta-ya=na=i?*
          come[3SG]-PST=NMLZ.SG=Q
          'Did she come?'

      b. *khus-het-a-ma-c-u-(*=na)=hoŋ,*   ...
          steal-V2.CARRY.OFF-PST-PRF-DU.A-3.P(*=NMLZ.SG)=SEQ   ...
          'After they have stolen her, ...'   [22_nrr_05.060]

The use of main clause nominalization differs greatly across text genres. In narratives, nominalized main clauses are rarer than in conversational data. For Kham, a Tibeto-Burman language spoken in western Nepal, Watters (2002) observed three uses of nominalization, which are (i) stage-setting, (ii) marking pivotal events or turning points in a story, and (iii) marking comments or some information that is set apart from the main event line.

The situation in Yakkha is similar to Watters's observations on Kham. Example (36a) shows a nominalized clause used in stage-setting, as it is often found in the beginning of narratives. Example (36b) is the first nominalized sentence after a long stretch of non-nominalized sentences in a narrative containing the autobiographical story of a girl who was attacked by an owl. It is self-explaining that the sentence in (36b) is pivotal for the story. The example also illustrates the use of nominalization in mirative contexts. The sentences in (36c) and (36d) illustrate the third function of main clause nominalization: both represent comments that are set apart from the main event line. They are from the same owl story, uttered as comments, after the whole event has been told. The pragmatic function of nominalization – establishing facts by reifying propositions – also has an effect on the interpretation of non-nominalized clauses. As they are in complementary distribution to the nominalized clauses, the hearer knows that more information is to come after a non-nominalized clause and that the speaker has not finished unfolding the main event line yet.

(36) a.   *eko   Selele-Phelele   baŋna   nwak*
           one   Selele-Phelele   so-called   bird

           wa-ya=na=bu.
           exist-PST[3SG]=NMLZ.SG=REP
           '(Once) there was a bird called Selele-Phelele.'   [21_nrr_04.01]

      b.   *siŋ-choŋ=be   so-ŋ=niŋa=go   phopciba=le*
           tree-top=LOC   look-1SG.A[PST]=CTMP=TOP   owl=MIR

           we?=na!
           exist[3SG.NPST]=NMLZ.SG
           'When I looked up into the tree, there is an owl!'   [42_leg_10.018]

      c.   *jeppa   nna   len   ka   ...   ollobak   paro=be*
           really   that   day   1SG   ...   almost   heaven=LOC

           tas-u-ŋ=na.
           arrive-3.P[PST]-1SG.A=NMLZ.SG
           'Really, that day, ... I had almost gone to heaven. '   [42_leg_10.051]

      d.   *a-ʈukhuruk=pe   og-a-ŋ=na   lo?wa*
           1SG.POSS-head=LOC   peck-PST-1SG.P=NMLZ.SG   like

           en-si-me-ŋ=na.
           perceive-MIDDLE-NPST-1SG=NMLZ.SG
           'It feels as if it was still pecking me on my head.'   [42_leg_10.056]

The already mentioned mirative use is exemplified by example (37). Yakkha has
a contrastive focus particle *=le* which is found in mirative contexts (for examples
see (36b) and (38b), cf. Chapter 17). Yakkha has also borrowed the Nepali mirative
marker *rahecha ~ raicha*, and the majority of sentences marked by *rahecha* occur
in the nominalized form (37).

(37) *khus-het-u=ha   raicha!*
      steal-V2.CARRY.OFF-3.P[PST]=NMLZ.NSG   MIR
      'He stole it!'   [20_pea_02.016]

In conversations, nominalized main clauses tend to be the norm, and non-nominalized clauses are the exception, since conversations can be perceived as con-
stant negotiations about the status of some propositional content. Speakers express their opinions, try to convince the hearers about something, or they ask
about facts. In (38a), one can see a deontic clause, containing an assessment
of the speaker about the necessity of the propositional content. Example (38b),
as mentioned above, shows another instance of a mirative clause. The speaker,
having lost her way in the dark, talks to herself, first asking herself and then
correcting her own assumptions on which way leads to her home.

(38) a. *u-milak*   *meŋ-khok-ma=na=bu,*   *kucuma=ga,*
         3SG.POSS-tail NEG-cut-INF[DEONT]=NMLZ.SG=REP dog=GEN
         kahile=ca.
         when=ADD
         'Their tail should not be cut off, the dog's, never.'   [28_cvs_04.225]

    b. *are,* *heʔne* *khy-a-ŋ=na*   *lai,*   *ka?* *lambu=go*
         oh!? where go-PST-1SG=NMLZ.SG EXCLA 1SG way=TOP
         naʔmo=le   *sa=na.*
         down_here=CTR COP.PST[3SG]=NMLZ.SG
         'Holy crackers, where did I go? The way was down here!'
                                              [28_cvs_04.027]

Nominalized main clauses could also be perceived as instances of insubordination – the recruitment of formally subordinate clauses to provide material for new main-clause types (Evans 2007). The semantic range of insubordination is typically associated with interpersonal control, modals (such as hortative and deontic meanings), and presupposed material, contrastive focus, or reiteration. Nominalized main clauses in Yakkha fit the characterization of "formally subordinate", as they are are formally identical to embedded clauses (complement clauses and relative clauses). Historically, =na and =ha can be related to a set of demonstratives, which renders both their development to relativizers, complementizers, and also their use in non-embedded clauses plausible (assuming embedding to a zero copula). This reasoning is supported by the fact that the copular structure can also be found synchronically, especially in negated forms as in (39).[5]

(39) *kanciŋ*   *mokt-a-ŋ-c-u-ŋ=na*   *men=na.*
     1DU[ERG]   beat-PST-EXCL-DU.A-3.P-EXCL=NMLZ.SG NEG.COP=NMLZ.SG
     'It is not the case that the two of us have beaten him.'   [36_cvs_06.154]

However, the high frequency of nominalized main clauses makes it unlikely that there is synchronically an underlying embedded structure in each instance with a zero verb meaning 'be the case that'.[6] Rather, the main clause function is the result of reanalyzing a subordinate structure. The same path is described in DeLancey (2011a), who proposed nominalization as the major driving force for syntactic change in Tibeto-Burman:

---

[5] Generally, Kiranti languages do not need a copula for the expression of equation or identification (Bickel (1999c: 276), Ebert 1994: 105).

[6] Matisoff (1972) made the same conclusion for Lahu.

[...] in many Tibeto-Burman languages the finite construction of the verb reflects an earlier construction in which the sentence or verb phrase is nominalized. The construction often includes a copula, of which the nominalized sentence is then an argument, but the copula may be dropped over time [...]. Frequently such constructions lose their marked status and become the ordinary finite construction, resulting in the creation of new verbal categories and systems. (DeLancey 2011a: 343)

The "drift from referent identification to event predication and the expression of speaker's stance" in Tibeto-Burman languages apparently even belongs to a broader Asian typological picture, as suggested in Yap & Grunow-Hårsta (2010). The Yakkha main clause nominalization might be on its way to lose its marked status and to become an integral part of the verbal person marking, moving on from the domain of pragmatics to syntax. In one finite verb form, this has already happened: in the third person plural intransitive forms, =ha is optionally followed by the nominal nonsingular clitic =ci, which is not found in any other inflected verbal forms. Other Kiranti languages, e.g., Limbu and Bantawa, employ nominalized forms in tense and aspect marking (van Driem 1993b; Doornenbal 2008).

13.3.3.2 The alignment of =na and =ha in main clauses

In relative clauses, the choice of =na and =ha is naturally determined by the number features of the head noun, i.e., =na when the head noun has singular number, and =ha when it has nonsingular or non-countable reference. In the nominalization of main clauses, since the nominalizers have become part of the predicate, there must be a different strategy. What we find is a combination of role-based and reference-based alignment (see Table 13.2). The examples in (40) illustrate this for intransitive sentences. Here, the sole argument of the clause determines the choice of either =na or =ha. In transitive verbs, in scenarios with third person objects (3.P) and with third person acting on second person (3→2), one finds ergative alignment. The choice of the markers is determined by the number of the P argument, shown in (41).

(40) a. *khy-a=na.*
          go-PST[3SG]=NMLZ.SG
          'He/she went.'

      b. *khy-a-ci=ha.*
          go-PST-DU=NMLZ.NSG
          'They (dual) went.'

(41) a.   *na   toŋba   imin   et-u-ga=na?*
           this   beer   how   like-3.P-2=NMLZ.SG
           'How do you like this *tongba*?'[7]

      b.   *kha=ci   imin   et-u-g=ha?*
           these=NSG   how   like-3.P-2=NMLZ.NSG
           'How do you like these?'

Reference-based alignment can be found in scenarios with speech-act participant objects, except for 3→2. Nonsingular number outranks singular, which means that as soon as one participant has nonsingular number, the marker *=ha* has to be used, regardless of the syntactic roles. The marker *=na* is only found when both A and P have singular number. The combination of role-based and reference-based alignment can also be found for other person markers (see §8.2).

Table 13.2: Alignment of the nominalizers *=na* and *=ha*

	INTRANSITIVE	TRANSITIVE					
		1SG.P	1NSG.P	2SG.P	2NSG.P	3SG.P	3NSG.P
1SG.A	*=na*			*=na*			
1NSG.A	*=ha*				*=ha*		
2SG.A	*=na*	*=na*				*=na*	*=ha*
2NSG.A	*=ha*		*=ha*				
3SG.A	*=na*	*=na*					
3NSG.A	*=ha*		*=ha*	*=na*	*=ha*		

Participants that have non-countable reference trigger *=ha* (see (42)). When mass nouns, e.g., *maŋcwa* 'water' or *cabhak* 'uncooked rice' trigger the singular marker *=na*, this means that they have a bounded quantity, like water in a cup or one portion of rice. Thus, the nominalizers have also acquired a classificatory function.

(42) a.   *n-jek-les-wa-ŋa-n=na.*
           NEG-speak-know-NPST-1SG-NEG=NMLZ.SG
           'I do not know how to speak it (one particular word).'

      b.   *yakkha   ceʔya   n-jek-les-wa-ŋa-n=ha.*
           Yakkha   matter   NEG-speak-know-NPST-1SG.A-NEG=NMLZ.NSG
           'I do not know how to speak Yakkha.'

---

[7] *Tongba* is beer served in a small barrel, to be drunken through a pipe.

If the object is a proposition, =*ha* is found as well, except for complements of verbs of perception and cognition, which show agreement with arguments of the embedded proposition.

(43)   *cilleŋ=be*   *haku* *nhaŋto* *camyoŋba* *py-a;*   *kanciŋ*
       overturn=LOC now   since   food   give-IMP[1.P]   1DU[ERG]
       khiŋ=se   *naŋ-me-ŋ-c-u-ŋ=ha.*
       this_much=RESTR   ask-NPST-EXCL-DU-3.P-EXCL=NMLZ.NC
       'From now on, give us the food in a leaf that is turned around (to the right side); we only ask for this much.'   [22_nrr_05.123]

In ditransitive verbs of the double object frame (see §11.1.9), the choice of =*na* or =*ha* is determined by the T argument (i.e., indirective alignment), at least if it has third person reference, which is mostly the case. As the regular person marking is determined by the G argument (i.e., secundative alignment), a double object verb ends up indexing all three arguments (A, G and T). The marking may undergo alternations under certain conditions (see §11.2.2).

(44)   a.   *ka*   *nda* *eko* *coklet* *pi?-nen=na.*
            1SG[ERG] 2SG   one   sweet   give[PST]-1>2=NMLZ.SG
            'I gave you a sweet.'
       b.   *ka*   *nda* *pyak* *coklet(=ci)*   *pi?-nen=ha.*
            1SG[ERG] 2SG   many   sweet(=NSG)   give[PST]-1>2=NMLZ.NSG
            'I gave you many sweets.'

13.4 Correlative clauses

The correlative construction consists of a relative clause and a main clause. The first clause contains a deictic element that narrows down the possible reference, and the second clause contains the statement about that referent. This parallelism of question and answer was also called "correlative diptych" by Lehmann (1988), because both clauses contain a reference to the participant about whom a statement is made. As Yakkha does not have relative pronouns, it utilizes interrogative pronouns in the relative clause. The main clause contains a noun or a demonstrative.

Bickel (1999d: 25) suggests that the correlative construction has developed from a commonly found strategy of structuring discourse, which he calls "informational diptych", in parallel to Lehmann's terminology. Here, too, the first part is used to announce the kind of information one would supply, often followed by a topic marker, before conveying the information in the second part of the diptych. This strategy is common in Yakkha, too, especially in narratives (see Chapter 17).

All kinds of participants and relations can be expressed with correlative clauses: quantities, locations, points in time, manner. The relation in (45a) expresses the amount of an object, (45b) shows relativization over a possessor, while (45c) relativizes over a temporal reference.

(45) a. *ka   ikhiŋ   nis-uks-u-ŋ,   khiŋ*
          1SG[ERG]   how_much   know-PRF-3.P[PST]-1SG   as_much
          ka-me-ŋ=na.
          say-NPST-1SG=NMLZ.SG
          'I will say as much as I (got to) know.'

      b. *isa=ga   u-cya=ci   mokt-u-ci=ha*
          who=GEN   3SG.POSS-child=NSG   beat-3.P[PST]-3NSG.P=NMLZ.NSG
          uŋ   bappura=ci!
          3SG   pitiful_person=NSG
          'The poor people whose children got beaten!' (Lit.: 'Those whose children got beaten are pitiful.')   [41_leg_09.042]

      c. *heʔniŋ   hoŋ-khe-me   ŋkhatniŋ=ŋa   ka=ca*
          when   crumble-V2.GO-NPST[3SG] then=INS   1SG=ADD
          sy-a=na   mit-a.
          die-PST[3SG]=NMLZ.SG   think-IMP[1.P]
          'When it (the stele) crumbles down, consider me dead, too.'
          [18_nrr_03.017–018]

Usually, the question pronoun in the relative clause and the demonstrative in the main clause come from the same paradigm, but the next example shows that this is not a rigorous constraint. While the question pronoun in the relative clause refers to a location, the corresponding noun phrase in the main clause refers to the food found in this location.

(46) *nhaŋ   heʔne   camyoŋba   wa=ya   nakha   camyoŋba*
      and_then   where   food   exist[3SG]-SBJV   that   food
      nak-se   khe-i.
      ask-SUP   go-1PL[SBJV]
      'Let us go where the food is, to ask for that food, they said.'
      [14_nrr_02.009]

Correlative clauses are rather known as a typical Indo-Aryan feature. They are not very common in Tibeto-Burman languages further north, which suggests that correlative clauses in Yakkha have developed as calques on Nepali correlative clauses.

14 Adverbial clause linkage

14.1 Introduction

This chapter deals with the types of adverbial clause linkage in Yakkha. Adverbial clause linkage is defined here in a broad sense, i.e., as any type of clause linkage that does not result from verbal subcategorization (i.e., complement clauses) and nominal modification (i.e., relative clauses). Adverbial clauses are always marked by clause-final morphemes, and generally display the same constituent order as in independent clauses. Despite being quite diverse formally, what they all have in common is one functional property: they modify the propositional content of a clause adverbially. Adverbial clauses lack an autonomous profile; the event they refer to has to be interpreted in the perspective of another event.[1]

The majority of clause linkage variables analyzed here suggest that adverbial clause linkage in Yakkha falls into two basic types: (i) converbal clauses,[2] non-finite, with overall operator scope and (ii) finite[3] adverbial clauses (containing an inflected verb), allowing not only overall operator scope, but also main clause operator scope. Table 14.1 roughly summarizes their characteristics (see also Bierkandt & Schackow submitted).[4] However, the individual clause linkage types show varying degrees of semantic integration and dependency on the main clause, and the morphosyntactic properties of these adverbial clauses do not always correlate in expected ways. Distinctions made by one variable, e.g., coreference of certain arguments, may be crosscut by other variables, e.g., finiteness

---

[1] The lack of an autonomous profile is, of course, also true for complement clauses and relative clause, see, e.g., the definition of subordination in Cristofaro (2003).

[2] see, e.g., Haspelmath (1995), who defines converbs as non-finite adverbial forms that modify verbs or clauses.

[3] "Finiteness" is understood here as a property of the verb. Used in this sense, finiteness does not entail all the properties typically associated with main clauses. Although the verb carries inflectional markers (for person, TAM and negation) and can thus be regarded as finite in some types of adverbial clauses, these clauses cannot, for instance, have a right-detached position. Likewise, they cannot contain certain clause-level operators such as the mirative *rahecha* (see also Lehmann (1988: 220) for a scale of desentialization in clause linkage typology).

[4] The percentages given in this chapter rely on the corpus described in §1.3.2, containing 3012 clauses and roughly 13.000 annotated words.

Table 14.1: Some characteristics of converbal and finite clause linkage

VARIABLES	CONVERBAL	FINITE
finiteness	stem	inflected verb
shared S/A arguments	mostly	constraint-free
operator scope (polarity, illoc.)	overall	overall or main clause only only
center-embedding	between 15 and 33%	maximally 2%

or operator scope, adding support to notions of clause linkage as an essentially multidimensional phenomenon (which are at least as old as Haiman & Thompson 1984). Some variables, like center-embedding (not embedding in the structural sense, only positional, see below), have to be assessed statistically, not categorically. Furthermore, a comparison of illocutionary operators and negation reveals that operator scope does not always behave in a uniform way. Thus, a definition of types of adverbial clause linkage (and also any other subordination type) necessitates a fine-grained analysis of a considerable number of variables, in order to see how the properties cluster in particular languages (cf. Bickel (2010) for a general approach and Schackow et al. (2012) for a case study on Puma (also Kiranti)).

Table 14.2 shows an overview of the individual Yakkha clause linkage types and their markers, classified according to their semantics. Apart from the two major types just mentioned, other types such as infinitival adverbial clauses are possible. Some of the clause linkage markers participate in more than one clause linkage construction, e.g., =hoŋ (sequential clauses, narrative clause-chaining) and =nuŋ (circumstantial clauses and temporal clauses with the meaning 'as long as'). Some markers may combine with information-structural particles to yield further types, such as concessive and counterfactual clauses. The forms also demonstrate another common Tibeto-Burman characteristic: the use of case markers for clause linkage (cf. case markers for genitive =ga, ergative =ŋa and comitative =nuŋ).

In the remainder of this chapter, the clause linkage constructions will be discussed with regard to their morphosyntactic and semantic properties. Important parameters are operator scope, focussing possibilities and the ability to occur center-embedded (a statistical rather than a categorical variable in Yakkha). An adverbial clause is center-embedded if it occurs inside the main clause, i.e., if it

Table 14.2: Adverbial clause linkage types in Yakkha

TYPE	SEMANTICS	MARKER
converbal	supine, purpose of movement	*-se*
infinitival	purpose	*-ma=ga*
infinitival	causal	*-ma=ŋa*
converbal	simultaneous, manner	*-saŋ*
converbal	negation	*meN-...-le*
infinitival	manner ('...ly/in a way that', 'as much as')	*=nuŋ*
finite (SBJV)	temporal ('as long as')	*=nuŋ*
finite/infinitival	conditional, temporal	*bhoŋ*
finite (OPT)	purpose	*bhoŋ*
finite/infinitival	sequential	*=hoŋ*
finite	narrative clause chaining	*=hoŋ*
finite	concessive	*=hoŋ=ca*
finite	cotemporal	*=niŋ(a)*
finite	counterfactual	*=niŋ(=go)=bi* *=hoŋ(=go)bi*
finite	interruptive	*=lo*

is both preceded and succeeded by material of the main clause (examples will be shown in the individual sections).

Among the scope properties, the main distinction is that between overall scope and main clause scope (as proposed in Bierkandt & Schackow submitted). Overall scope implies that the operator has scope over the whole sentence, including the link between the two events, as in (1): the negation has scope over the whole event, allowing for different interpretations, depending on the question where the focus is (e.g., on 'he', on 'play', on 'after', on 'ate' and so on). This scope type indicates a rather close semantic link between the two clauses, and may lead to a phenomenon such as *negative transport*, as we will see below (cf. Horn 1989: Ch. 5, and Bickel 1993 for Belhare).

(1)   *He did not play after he ate.*

In the case of main clause scope, in contrast, the operator does not reach beyond the main clause, as exemplified by (2). The value of the scope parameter is straightforward to establish for negation, but it is potentially problematic for illocutionary force (cf. below).

(2) *After reaching his home, he did not feel like eating any more.*

14.2 The supine converb *-se*

The supine converb is marked by the suffix *-se* attaching directly to the stem of the verb in the dependent clause. The converbal clause expresses the purpose of a motion event or caused motion event, i.e., the verb in the main clause always has to have motion semantics. The moving participant of the main clause has to be coreferential with the S or A of the supine clause: if the main verb is intransitive, the subjects of both clauses have to be coreferential (see (3a)); if the main verb is transitive, the subject of the converbal clause is coreferential with the P of the main clause (see (3b)).

(3) a. *yakkha ce?ya   cin-se   ta-ya-ŋ=na.*
         Yakkha language learn-SUP come-PST-1SG=NMLZ.SG
         'I came to learn the Yakkha language.'
     b. *a-ppa=ŋa   yaŋ   nak-se paks-a-ŋ=na.*
         1SG.POSS-father=ERG money ask-SUP send-PST-1SG.P=NMLZ.SG
         'Father sent me to ask for money.'   [01_leg_07.202]

For one speaker, who has lived in Kathmandu for many years, the constraint on coreference appeared to be less strict. The subject of *uŋma* 'drink' in (4) is coreferential with the G argument of the main verb, not with the argument that is caused to move.[5]

(4) *raksi uŋ-se   ŋgha=ci=ha   jammai jammai*
     liquor drink-SUP those=NSG=NMLZ.NSG all   all
     ŋ-haps-u-bi-wa-ci=ha.
     3PL.A-distribute-3.P-V2.GIVE-NPST-3NSG.P=NMLZ.NSG
     'They distribute the liquor among all the people, in order to drink it.'
                                                          [25_tra_01.130]

---

[5] This might be due to influence from parallel constructions in Nepali that are less constrained with regard to coreference.

The subordinate clause can be center-embedded, exemplified here by (5a):[6] the verb *whapma* would license an ergative, but an ergative is ungrammatical here, because the overt argument belongs to the intransitive main clause. Center-embedding can also be determined by semantic factors, as in (5b). The deictic adverb *to* belongs to the main clause, as such adverbs generally come with motion verbs. It was found that 33.8% of the sentences with supine converbs gave positive evidence for the converbal clause to be center-embedded, which is the highest number among the adverbial clauses.[7] Examples (4) and (5) also show that dependent and main verb do not have to be adjacent, but in most cases they are.

(5) a. *maghyam(*=ŋa)*   *tek=ci*   *whap-se*   *hoŋma=be*
old_woman(*=erg)   fabric=NSG   wash-SUP   river=LOC
khy-a-ma.
go[3SG]-PST-PRF
'The old woman went to the river to wash clothes.'   [01_leg_07.286]

   b. *ka*   *to*   *cin-se=ca*   *kheʔ-ma*   *ŋan.*
1SG   up   teach-SUP=ADD   go-INF[DEONT]   COP.1SG
'I have to go up to teach, too.'   [36_cvs_06.102]

Occasionally, the supine converbal marker -se is found in combination with the conjunction *bhoŋ*, which is used for conditional, complement and purpose clauses (see §14.9), and which is less restricted semantically and in terms of coreference. In (6a), the reason for adding this conjunction is probably that the requirement of coreference between the A of the converbal clause and the P of the transitive motion verb is not met. The reason why the conjunction is used in (6b) is not clear, however.

(6) a. *ŋkha*   *u-in=ci*   *taŋ-se*   *bhoŋ*   *a-muk*
those   3SG.POSS-egg=NSG   take_out-SUP   PURP   1SG.POSS-hand
end-u-ŋ=niŋa=go,   ...
insert-3.P[PST]-1SG.A=CTMP=TOP
'When I put my hand inside (the hole in the tree) to take out its eggs, ...'
   [42_leg_10.028]

---

[6] See also example (3b).
[7] All percentages are from (Bierkandt & Schackow submitted), who used the same corpus that serves as database for this grammar, containing 3012 clauses. The positive evidence established does not tell us anything about the percentage of clauses that are not center-embedded, because this information can only be established in clauses with a sufficient number of overt arguments.

b. *maŋdu   ten=bhaŋ   nniŋda tup-se   bhoŋ*
    distant   village=ABL   2PL   meet-SUP   PURP
    ta-i-mi-ŋ=ha   *i,   aŋoteŋba=ci.*
    come-1PL[PST]-PRF-EXCL=NMLZ.NSG   FOC   brother_in-law=NSG
    'We came from far away from (our) villages to meet you, brothers-in-
    law.'

[41_leg_09.028]

A supine clause is tightly linked to the main clause; any operator which can be
attached to the main verb, whether of negation or of illocutionary force, will have
scope over the whole complex event of movement with a purpose, illustrated for
deontic modality in (5b) above and for imperative, hortative and interrogative
mood in (7) below.

(7) a. *ah,   so-se   ab-a-ci,   au?*
         yes   look-SUP   come_over-IMP-DU   INSIST
         'Yes, please come over to look (at the newlyweds), will you?'

[36_cvs_06.416]

     b. *khi   khon-se   puŋda=be   khe-ci.*
         yam   dig-SUP   forest=LOC go-DU[HORT]
         'Let us go into the forest to dig yams.'   [40_leg_08.006]

     c. *wa=ci   ijaŋ   ca   ca-se*
         chicken=NSG   why   food   eat-SUP
         n-da-me-n=ha=ci?
         NEG-come-NPST-NEG=NMLZ.NSG=NSG
         'Why do the chicken not come to eat?'   [40_leg_08.069]

It is, however, possible to focus on the event denoted by the supine clause, as
the next example illustrates by means of negation. The motion verb in the main
clause contains the presupposed information and the supine clause contains the
asserted information. In fact, this is the case for the majority of supine converbal
constructions.[8] In (8a), the speaker corrects another speaker's claim that the researcher came to do sightseeing. Hence, the purpose of coming is the controversial information, not the fact that she came. The purpose clause which contains
the previous claim hosts the topic marker =*go*, while the new, corrected purpose
clause receives the contrastive focus marker =*le*, which is also frequently found
in mirative contexts. Both operators are otherwise found on constituents, not at

---

[8] As also noted by Haspelmath (1995: 12–7), a subordinate clause (which converbal clauses are)
narrows down the reference of the main clause.

the end of clauses, which indicates that the converbal clause is not clause-like, but occupies the structural position of an adverbial in the sentence. The negated copula in (8a) emphasizes the contrast between purpose 1 and purpose 2. The same clause could also be paraphrased by (8b), with the negation marked on the main verb, and the converbal clause attracting focus.[9]

(8) a. *so-se=go*   *men=na,*   *por-a*   *cok-se=le*
         look-SUP=TOP   NEG.COP.3SG=NMLZ.SG   study-NATIV   do-SUP=CTR
         ta-ya-ma=na.
         come[3SG]-PST-PRF=NMLZ.SG
         'Not to look (at our village), she came to study!'   [28_cvs_04.165]

     b. *so-se*   *n-da-ya-ma-n=na.*
         look-SUP   NEG-come[3SG]-PST-PRF-NEG=NMLZ.SG
         'She did not come to look.'

Example (9) illustrates the same point for the scope and focus of questions. While the scope is over the whole event, i.e., over the connection between dependent and main clause, the focus of the question targets the converbal clause. This sentence was uttered when two people met at a water tap, and hence, the main verb 'come' must be part of the presupposition.[10]

(9) *tek*   *whap-se*   *ta-ya-ga=na?*
     clothes   wash-SUP   come-PST-2=NMLZ.SG
     'Did you come to wash clothes?'

Example (10) and (11) illustrate that the focus inherent in the negation (and the illocutionary force in (10)) may either be on the supine clause or on the whole event, but not on the main clause alone. Regardless of the focus options, both (10a) and (10b) can be circumscribed with 'It is not the case that you should go to watch the bride',[11] and (8a) can be circumscribed with 'It is not the case that she came to study'. Thus, negating the supine clause necessarily results in the negation of the whole event, just as negating the main event necessarily entails the negation of the purposive event, because it is always interpreted in the perspective of the main clause.

---

[9] In such a clause, the defautl reading is the one where the converbal clause attracts focus, but it could also entail that the whole event of 'coming in order to look' did not take place at all.

[10] Questions relating to what one is doing or where one is going are a common way of greeting someone in the colloquial register.

[11] Two interpretations are possible: the absence of obligation, or a prohibition.

Negating the main event without negating the purposive event is not possible with *-se* (see unacceptable (11a)). In order to achieve such an interpretation, a different strategy has to be used, namely the less restrictive purpose construction with the infinitive and *bhoŋ* (11b).

(10) a. *beuli   so-se   ŋ-khy-a-n,   cama   ca-se   seppa!*
          bride   look-SUP   NEG-go-IMP-NEG   food   eat-SUP   RESTR
          'Do not go to look at the bride, only to eat the food.'

    b. *beuli   so-se   ŋ-khy-a-n,   ka=nuŋ   wa-ya!*
          bride   look-SUP   NEG-go-IMP-NEG   1SG=COM   stay-IMP
          'Do not go to look at the bride, stay with me!'

(11) a. **im-se   bhya=be   ŋ-khy-a-ŋa-n=na.*
          sleep-SUP   wedding=LOC   NEG-go-PST-1SG-NEG=NMLZ.SG
          Intended: 'In order to sleep, I skipped the wedding.'
          (possible, but implausible reading: 'I did not go to the wedding to sleep.')

    b. *im-ma   bhoŋ   bhya=be   ŋ-khy-a-ŋa-n=na.*
          sleep-INF   PURP   wedding=LOC   NEG-go-PST-1SG-NEG=NMLZ.SG
          'In order to sleep, I skipped the wedding.'

It has been mentioned above that discourse particles targeting constituents, such as the topic marker *=go* and the focus marker *=le*, can be attached to supine clauses. Other constituent focus markers found on supine clauses are the additive focus particle *=ca* (see (12a)) and the restrictive focus particle *=se* (see (12b)). In (12a), the additive focus marker has scope over the whole event; the event of going is not presupposed here. However, as main clauses cannot host constituent focus markers, *=ca* has to be attached to the converbal clause. The situation is different in (12b), where the restrictive focus marker *=se* targets only the event denoted by the converbal clause.

(12) a. *kaniŋ   piknik   ca-se=ca   khe-i-mi-ŋ=ha.*
          1PL   picnic   eat-SUP=ADD   go-1PL[PST]-PRF-EXCL=NMLZ.NSG
          'We also went for a picnic.'   [01_leg_07.268]

    b. *chemha   uŋ-se=se   ta-ya=na,*
          liquor   drink-SUP=RESTR   come[3SG]-PST=NMLZ.SG
          eŋ=ga   ce?ya   cin-se
          1PL.INCL=GEN   language   learn-SUP
          n-da-ya-n=na!
          NEG-come[3SG]-PST-NEG=NMLZ.SG
          'He just came to drink liquor, not to study our language.'

As I have shown above, the converbal clause and the main clause may have intervening constituents between them, although the corpus does not contain many instances of this. In (13), the question word constitutes the focussed information and is thus found in the preverbal position, the preferred position for focussed constituents.

(13)   *tukkhi   ca-se   i   khe?-ma=lai?*
       pain   eat-SUP   what   go-INF[DEONT]=EXCLA
       'Why should I go (and marry) to earn troubles?'   [06_cvs_01.052]

14.3 Infinitival purpose clauses in *-ma=ga*

Another way of expressing purpose involves an infinitive which is marked by the genitive marker (cf. §5.2.2.4). The purposive use of the genitive seems to be interchangeable with purpose clauses in *bhoŋ* (discussed below), but *bhoŋ* is not restricted to infinitives and thus more frequent. This construction is not only found with motion events; any event happening for the sake of another event can be expressed like in (14). The clause linkage is less tight here. There is no constraint on the coreferentiality of the arguments. In (14a), one could argue that the constituent marked by the genitive is actually modifying the noun (*kuʈunı*), but one also finds plenty of examples like (14b) and (c), where there is no noun. Argument marking remains as in simple clauses, as is evidenced by (c). This example also shows that the infinitive of purpose can be negated independently.

(14)   a.   *khoŋ   nak-se   khe?-ma=ga   eko   kuʈuni*
            afterwards   ask-SUP   go-INF=GEN   one   matchmaker
            n-yog-wa.
            3PL.A-search-NPST[3.P]
            'In order to go and ask (for the bride), they look for a matchmaker.'
                                                                    [25_tra_01.04]
       b.   *kaîci   kob-u=hoŋ   hek-ma=ga*
            scissors   pick_up-3.P=SEQ   cut-INF=GEN
            thag-u=na.
            open-3.P[PST]=NMLZ.SG
            'He picked up and opened the scissors in order to cut (something).'
                                      [Cut-and-break clips, Bohnemeyer, Bowerman & Brown (2010)]
       c.   *uŋci=ŋa   men-ni-ma=ga   cum-i.*
            3NSG=ERG   NEG-see-INF=GEN   hide-1PL[PST]
            'We hid, so that they would not see us.'

435

14.4 Infinitival causal clauses in *-ma=ŋa*

Infinitives carrying an ergative marker are interpreted as finite causal adverbial clauses, as in (15). Causal interpretations may, however, also obtain in temporal clauses marked by *=niŋ* and *=hoŋ*. The causal infinitives require coreference between the dependent and main clause S and A arguments, while the finite clause linkage types show no constraints in this respect.

(15)   a.   *cuŋ=chen pyak tuŋ-me=hoŋ=ca   yoniŋ-kheniŋ*
             cold=TOP   very   hurt-NPST=SEQ=ADD   thither-hither
             koʔ-ma=ŋa,   cameŋwa ca-saŋ   lak-ma
             walk-INF=ERG.CL food   eat-SIM dance-INF
             puk-ma=ŋa   ina=ca   thaha
             jump-INF=ERG.CL what=ADD knowledge
             l-leks-a-n=na.
             NEG-become-PST-NEG=NMLZ.SG
             'Even though it was very cold, because of walking around, eating, dancing and jumping, we did not notice anything.'   [01_leg_07.270]

      b.   *leʔnamcuk   puŋda   koʔ-ma=ŋa   sak*
             whole_day jungle   walk-INF=ERG hunger
             tug-a-by-a.
             hurt[3SG]-PST-V2.GIVE-PST
             'Having wandered around in the jungle the whole day, we got hungry.'

                                         [40_leg_08.016]

14.5 The simultaneous converb *-saŋ*

The simultaneous converb, marked by the suffix *-saŋ* attaching directly to the verbal stem, connects two events that happen at the same time or during the same period (see (16a)). The verb in the converbal clause cannot host any inflectional morphology; the converbal clause is dependent on the main clause regarding its TAM interpretation and the reference of its arguments. The converbal clause may also express the manner of how the main activity is done (see (16b), (c) and (17)). The S and A arguments of both clauses have to be coreferential. The construction cannot be used to refer to events that start during another event, i.e., for propositions like 'While walking, I slipped and fell'. Both events have to be ongoing at the point of reference. Punctual verbs like 'cough' and 'jump' receive an iterative reading in a converbal clause in *-saŋ* ((16b) illustrates this effect).

(16) a.   *yapmi   paŋ-paŋ=be   nak-saŋ   kheʔ-ma.*
          people   house-house=LOC   ask-SIM   go-INF[DEONT]
          'The people have to go from house to house, asking (for food).'
                                                                    [14_nrr_02.30]

      b.   *khi=ga   u-thap   yok-saŋ   maŋcusiŋcu*
          yam=GEN   3SG.POSS-plant   poke-SIM   so-and-so

          khond-a-ŋ-c-u-ŋ.
          dig_out-PST-EXCL-DU-3.P-EXCL
          'Poking the yam plants, we somehow dug around (without satisfying
          results).'   [40_leg_08.012]

      c.   *sondu=ŋa   kisi-saŋ   luks-u: ...*
          Sondu=ERG   be_afraid-SIM   tell-3.P[PST]
          'Frightened, Sondu told him: ...'   [01_leg_07.200]

The case marking of the subjects in example (16a) and (16c) provides evidence for
the converbal clause occurring center-embedded, which could be affirmed for
15% of the simultaneous converb clauses in the present corpus. The nominative
case in (16a) and the ergative case in (16c) undoubtedly belong to the respective
main verbs, as the verbs in the converbal clauses would license different case
marking (see §11.1). The opposite scenario can also be found, where the overt
argument belongs to the converbal clause, as in (17), where the main verb would
have licensed an ergative case marker.

(17) *sondu   consi-saŋ   inca-ma=ga   khet-uks-u-ci.*
      Sondu   be_happy-SIM   sell-INF=GEN   carry_off-PRF-3.P[PST]-3NSG.P
      'Happily, Sondu carried them (the fish) off to sell them.'   [01_leg_07.229]

The above mentioned coreference constraint is strictly semantic, applying irrespective of the question of argument realization. In (18), the subject is a non-
canonically marked experiencer, realized as the possessor of the laziness (cf.
§11.1.10). As long as the argument is highest-ranking in terms of semantic roles,
i.e., the most agent-like argument, it qualifies for the coreference constraint of
the simultaneous converb.[12]

(18) *o-pomma   ke-saŋ   ke-saŋ   kam*
      3SG.POSS-laziness   come_up-SIM   come_up-SIM   work

---

[12] The reduplication of the converb, as in this particular example, signifies either ongoing or
   iterative events.

cog-wa.
do-NPST[3SG.A;3.P]
'He does the work lazily.'

The constraint on coreference can be weakened under certain conditions: in constructions with unspecific or generic reference, it is not always observed (see (19a)). The sentence in (19b) is interesting because the subjects of two converbal clauses have to be combined to yield the reference of the main clause subject.

(19) a. *sala   len-saŋ   len-saŋ   len   khe-meʔ=na.*
          matter exchange-SIM exchange-SIM day   go-NPST[3SG]=NMLZ
          'Chatting and chatting the day goes by.'
      b. *lok   kho-saŋ   yunca-saŋ ghak   pog-i-ŋ.*
          anger   scratch-SIM laugh-SIM all   stand_up-1PL-EXCL
          'Partly angry, partly laughing, we all got up.'   [40_leg_08.042]

Despite the close bonds between converbal clause and main clause, the converbal clause may have considerable length and internal complexity, as shown in example (20a), which features embedded direct thought in its converbal clause. One also finds sequences of several converbal clauses linked to one main verb, as in (20b) from a procedural text (cf. also (19b)).

(20) a. *ka=go   yapmi   isiʔ   ŋan=na   rahecha   mis-saŋ*
          1SG=TOP   person   ugly   COP.1SG=NMLZ.SG   MIR   think-SIM
          u-ma   las-apt-uks-u.
          3SG.POSS-mother   return-V2.BRING-PRF-3.P[PST]
          'Thinking: "I am a bad person!", he brought his mother home.'
                                                             [01_leg_07.081]
      b. *maŋgaŋba=ŋa   hon=na   yoŋ-saŋ*
          ritual_specialist=ERG that_very=NMLZ.SG   shake-SIM
          munthum   thak-saŋ   haks-wa=na.
          ritual_knowledge   recite-SIM   send-NPST[3.P]=NMLZ.SG
          'Shaking that (gourd) and reciting the Munthum, the Manggangba
          does the worship.'   [01_leg_07.135]

It should also be mentioned that this converbal structure is used for a periphrastic continuative aspect construction that is probably calqued upon a similar structure in Nepali, too (see (21), and §8.4).

(21) uŋ   tamba   pu-saŋ   pu-saŋ   khy-a-ma=hoŋ,   ...
      3SG   slowly grow-SIM   grow-SIM   go[3SG]-PST-PRF=SEQ
      'Having grown slowly, ...'   [01_leg_07.005]

The simultaneous converb is interesting with regard to scope and focus properties, because it shows that negation and illocutionary force operators may show distinct behavior.

Let us first consider negation. Always marked on the main verb, the negation scopes over the whole event, ([A while B]NEG). The focus of the negation, however, is attracted by the converbal clause, also known as 'negative transport' (Horn 1989). As pointed out by Bickel (1993) on the corresponding converbal construction in Belhare, the converbal clause conveys rhematic information, elaborating on the main predication, and as such qualifies for being focussed on. A sentence like (22a) cannot be interpreted with only the main predicate being negated, as the whole sentence is under the scope of the negation. To convey an interpretation with negation focussing on the main clause, another construction, for instance the causal construction in (22b), has to be used (cf. also Bierkandt & Schackow submitted). A reading with the main clause negated is not possible under any circumstances.

(22) a. sala   len-saŋ   kam
          matter   exchange-SIM   work
          n-jog-u-m-nin=ha.
          NEG-do-3.P[PST]-1PL.A-PL.NEG=NMLZ.NSG
          *'Chatting, we didn't work.'
          'We didn't work chatting (but quietly).'
      b. sala   lem-ma=ŋa   kam
          matter   exchange-INF=ERG work
          n-jog-u-m-nin=ha.
          NEG-do-3.P[PST]-1PL.A-PL.NEG=NMLZ.NSG
          'As/Because we chatted, we didn't work.'

Negating both subevents at the same time is impossible as well. One sub-clause has to be foregrounded, similar to the effect of dissociating *figure* and *ground* that is known from Gestalt psychology (see, e.g., Jackendoff (1983), called "Rubin effect" in Bickel 1991: 48). In other types of clause linkage, the choice may fall on either of the clauses, but the simultaneous converb allows only one reading with regard to negation. It is thus different from the supine converb, where negation could as well have a coordinative reading, i.e., with both subevents negated.

(23)   *chem   lu-saŋ   n-lakt-i-ŋa-n=ha.*
       song   sing-SIM   NEG-dance-1PL-EXCL-NEG=NMLZ.NSG
       *'We didn't sing and didn't dance.'
       'We didn't dance singing.'

Looking at the behavior of illocutionary operators, the picture is different, though. Illocutionary operators have scope over the whole event, too ([A while B]ILLOC), but this may result either in focus on the converbal clause (with the main clause presupposed, see the question in (24a)), or in focus on both clauses (with nothing presupposed, see the question in (24b) and the imperatives in (24c) and (24d)). Thus, illocutionary operators behave differently from polarity operators in the simultaneous converb construction.

(24)   a.   *kos-saŋ   tai-ka=na,   a-na=u?*
            walk_around-SIM   come[NPST]-2SG=NMLZ.SG   1SG.POSS-eZ=VOC
            'Do you come walking, sister? (Did you come to us on a walk?)'
                                                          [36_cvs_06.564]

       b.   *chem   lus-saŋ   lakt-i-g=ha=i?*
            song   sing-SIM   dance-2PL[PST]-2-NMLZ.NSG=Q
            'Did you sing and dance?'

       c.   *chem   lu-saŋ   lakt-a-ni!*
            song   sing-SIM   dance-IMP-PL
            'Sing and dance!'

       d.   *hoŋkha   so-saŋ   so-saŋ   paŋ=be*
            those_very   look-SIM   look-SIM   house=LOC
            las-a-khy-a   yu   a-cya.
            return-IMP-V2.GO-IMP   EXCLA   1SG.POSS-child
            'Look at those (sticks marking the way) and go home, my son.'
                                                          [01_leg_07.078]

14.6 The negative converb *meN...le*

The negative converb is marked by the prefix *meN-* and the suffix *-le* being attached to the uninflected verb stem. The reason not to analyze these markers as a circumfix is that the prefix *meN-* occurs as negation marker in other syntactic contexts as well, for instance with infinitives and nominalizations, and occasionally in comitative clause linkage. The negative converb is used to express that the event in the main clause will take place without another event, as shown in example (25). Apart from the negation, its semantics are rather unspecified, e.g., with regard to the temporal relation obtaining between the clauses. In (25), the events are in a sequential relationship; in (26) they happen at the same time. Roughly 14% of negative converbal clauses were found center-embedded.

(25) a. *ka cama men-ja-le ŋ-im-meʔ-ŋa-n=na.*
1SG food NEG-eat-CVB NEG-sleep-NPST-1SG-NEG=NMLZ.SG
'I will not go to sleep without eating.'

b. *yo=na paŋ=be men-da-le*
across=NMLZ.SG house=LOC NEG-arrive-CVB

hiks-a-ab-a-ŋ=na.
return-PST-V2.COME-PST-1SG=NMLZ.SG
'I came back without reaching the house across.'

Although the verb in the converbal clause does not carry inflectional markers, there is no constraint on the coreference of any arguments. The identification of the referents is resolved by the context alone. In my Yakkha corpus, the S or A of the converbal clause is not controlled by the main clause S or A argument in 42.9% of the cases. An example is given in (26).

(26) *u-ppa=ŋa tha men-dok-le nasa-lapmana=nuŋ*
3SG.POSS-father=ERG knowledge NEG-get-CVB fish-rod=COM

phurluŋ khet-uks-u-ci=hoŋ hoŋma=be
small_basket carry_off-PRF-3.P[PST]-3NSG.P=SEQ river=LOC

khy-a-ma.
go[3SG]-PST-PRF
'Without his father noticing, he (the son) carried off the fishing net and the basket and went to the river.' [01_leg_07.210]

A rather unexpected finding is that the negative converbal clause can be turned into an adnominal modifier by means of the nominalizers =na and =ha. This possibility is not attested for the other converbal clauses.

(27) a. *men-sen-siʔ-le=na mendhwak.*
NEG-clean-V2.PREVENT-CVB=NMLZ.SG goat
'an uncastrated goat' [31_mat_01.071]

b. *u-luŋ men-da-le=na piccha.*
3SG.POSS-leg NEG-come-CVB=NMLZ.SG child
'the child that cannot walk yet'

As for operator scope, the scope of negation includes the link between the clauses, and is thus over the whole sentence ([neg.A and B]NEG), as was illustrated in example (25a) above.

The illocutionary operators have scope over the whole sentence as well ([neg.A and B]ILLOC) and, as we have already seen for the other converbs, the converbal clause often attracts focus. In example (28a), a question uttered when someone fell down, the event stated in the main clause is presupposed; the focus of the question lies on *lambu mensoʔle*. Example (28b) illustrates that the converbal clause may contain presupposed information as well; it is taken from a discussion about learning methods in which the speaker stresses the importance of listening for learning.

(28) a. *lambu   men-soʔ-le   lam-a-ga=na?*
way   NEG-look-CVB   walk-PST-2=NMLZ.SG
'Did you walk without watching the road?'

b. *meŋ-khem-le   i=ya*
NEG-listen-CVB   what=NMLZ.NSG
nis-wa-m=ha?
know-NPST-1PL.A[3.P]=NMLZ.NSG
'What will we know without listening?'

In (29a), the converbal clause states a (negative) condition for the deontically modalized main clause: the event in the main clause has to happen within a time span specified by the converbal clause, which can be paraphrased by 'as long as not (X)'. The deontic modality has scope over the whole sentence, and the negative converbal clause is even focussed on. The condition it contains is integral to the requirement stated. Similarly, in (29b) a, the converbal clause stands in a conditional relation to the main clause. Optionally, the Nepali postposition *samma* 'until' can be added to the converbal clause to emphasize this.

(29) a. *om   me-leŋ-le   las-a=hoŋ   pheri   to*
bright   NEG-become-CVB   return[3SG]-SBJV=SEQ   again   up
thithi   em-diʔ-ma=bu.
upright   stand-V2.GIVE-INF[DEONT]=REP
'Before the daylight, it (the rock) had to return and stand upright again (they say).'   [37_nrr_07.051]

b. *bagdata   men-nak-le   samma,   ...*
marriage_finalization   NEG-ask-CVB   until   ...
'As long as the Bagdata (ritual) is not asked for, (the marriage is not finalized).'   [26_tra_02.030]

Constituents within the clause may carry focus markers. Consider example (30), with the interrogative pronoun being focussed on by the additive focus particle =*ca*, that results in the exhaustive negation "any" in combination with the negative converb.

(30)   *kanciŋ i=ca   meŋ-ka-le   sok-khusa=se*
       1DU   what=ADD   NEG-say-CVB look-RECIP=RESTR

       ca-ya-ŋ-ci-ŋ.
       eat.AUX-PST-EXCL-DU-EXCL
       'Without saying anything, we just looked at each other.'   [40_leg_08.070]

14.7 Comitative clause linkage in =*nuŋ*

Comitative clause linkage is the semantically least specified clause linkage type. It covers a wide functional range, specifying the manner, time span or some other circumstance under which the main event proceeds. The marker =*nuŋ* is homophonous with the comitative case marker, thus conforming to a common Tibeto-Burman tendency of utilizing case markers as clause linkage markers. This clause linkage type is rather rare in the present corpus.

The comitative clause linkage is not only semantically rather underspecified, but it is not quite restricted in formal terms either. The clitic =*nuŋ* may attach to uninflected stems (see (31a)), to infinitives (see (31b) and (c)), or to inflected verbs (see (31d)), yielding more or less similar manner or circumstantial readings, paraphrasable by 'in a way that' (as distinct from causal or consecutive 'so that').

There are no constraints on coreference. In (31a), the referents of the S and A arguments, respectively, are not identical, while they are in (31b). The example in (31a) could alternatively be expressed by the negative converb construction discussed in §14.6.

(31)   a.   *kaniŋ   asen   men-ni=nuŋ*
           1PL[ERG] yesterday NEG-know=COM.CL

           men-ni=nuŋ=ca   isisi   leks-a-ma=ha.
           NEG-know=COM.CL=ADD   ugly   happen[3SG]-PST-PRF=NMLZ.NSG
           'Yesterday, without us noticing, too, something bad has happened.'
                                               [41_leg_09.064]

     b.   *kam=ca   cok-ma   haʔlo   mimik,   ya-ma=nuŋ!*
           work=ADD do-INF   EXCLA   a_little be_able-INF=COM.CL
           'One also has to work, man — at least a little (in a way that one manages to do it/as much as one can)!'   [28_cvs_04.326]

c. *a-pum*　　　　　　*si-ma=nuŋ*　　　*uŋ-wa.*
　　1SG.POSS-grandfather　kill-INF=COM.CL　drink-NPST[3.P]
　　'My grandpa drinks in a way that will make him drunk (i.e., too much).'

d. *khaʔniŋgo*　*liŋkha*　*ekdam*　　　　*cog-a-nuŋ*
　　but　　　　a_clan　very_much　do[3SG]-SBJV=COM.CL
　　cog-a-nuŋ　　　　　　*bis*　　*wora*　*khibak=ca*
　　do[3SG]-SBJV=COM.CL　twenty　CLF　rope=ADD
　　ipt-i-ci
　　twist[3SG.A]-COMPL-3NSG.P
　　'But the Linkha man, diligently (working and working) made twenty ropes, too.'　　　　　　　　　　　　　　　　　[11_nrr_01.008]

Comitative clauses, if inflected at all, are always in the subjunctive; indicative morphology (tense/aspect marking) is not expressed on them. Yakkha has two sets of subjunctives (cf. §8.5), both used in various irrealis contexts and in subordinate clauses. The first set (the Nonpast Subjunctive) is marked by the absence of any marking except person; it is also found in independent adhortative and optative clauses. The second set is in most cases identical to the past indicative paradigm, and is hence called Past Subjunctive. It is found in adverbial clauses and in counterfactuals. The difference between the two sets becomes evident in comitative clause linkage, too: the temporal reference of the main clause determines which set has to be used. In (32a) with nonpast reference, the Nonpast Subjunctive applies, while in (32b) with past reference the Past Subjunctive applies (the stem-final /s/ in (32b) surfaces only before vowels).

(32)　a.　*ka*　　　　*kucuma*　*kha=nuŋ*
　　　　　1SG[ERG]　dog　　　be_satisfied[SBJV;3SG]=COM.CL
　　　　　pi-wa-ŋ=ha.
　　　　　give-NPST[3.P]-1SG.A=NMLZ.NSG
　　　　　'I will feed the dog sufficiently (in a way that it will be satisfied).'

　　　b.　*ka*　　　　*kucuma*　*khas-a=nuŋ*
　　　　　1SG[ERG]　dog　　　be_satisfied[3SG]-SBJV=COM.CL
　　　　　pi-ŋ=ha.
　　　　　give[PST;3.P]-1SG.A=NMLZ.NSG
　　　　　'I fed the dog sufficiently (in a way that it was satisfied).'

The clause is not only reduced with regard to the tense/mood distinction; sentence-level markers and the main clause nominalization are not possible either.

Adverbial clauses in *=nuŋ* may also translate into 'as long as' (Nepali: V-*in-jhel*). This usage results in a less tight kind of clause linkage, as reflected by its scope properties (see below). Comitative clauses with an 'as long as' reading are always inflected for the subjunctive. The nonpast indicative is not possible in (33), even though the proposition in the adverbial clause (i.e., 'you are in Tumok') has realis status.

(33) *tumok=pe   wa-ci-ga=nuŋ   cuwa   uŋ-a-c-u.*
      Tumok=LOC   live[SBJV]-DU-2=COM.CL   beer   drink-IMP-DU-3.P
      'As long as you live in Tumok, drink millet beer.'

The comitative is also used to derive lexical adverbs. Attached to uninflected stems of (ingressive-)stative verbs, the marker creates adverbs and predicative adjectives, such as *cinuŋ* 'cold, chilly', *nunuŋ* 'well', *limnuŋ* 'sweet(ly)' or *neknuŋ* 'softly' in (34). Some fossilized adverbs are found as well: they look like inflected verbs to which the comitative is added, for instance *ŋkhumdinuŋ* 'not tasty', but corresponding verbs are not available synchronically (see also Chapter 6).

(34) *khyu   nek=nuŋ   leŋ-me.*
      curry_sauce   be_soft=COM   become[3SG]-NPST
      'The curry will become soft.'   [28_cvs_04.054]

The different semantic possibilities of the comitative clause linkage result in different scope and focus options, too. In the manner or circumstance reading, the negation scope covers the whole complex clause, and the adverbial clause attracts focus, in the same way as the converbal clauses discussed above (see (35a)).

If, however, the clause has the reading 'as long as', the negation has scope over the main clause only, and consequently, it cannot reach into the adverbial clause (compare the intended interpretation with the only possible interpretation in (35b)). This shows that one marker can participate in two very different kinds of clause linkage. In this particular case, the inflectional properties of the verb (infinitive vs. inflected for the subjunctive) match nicely with the (overall vs. main clause only) operator scope and focus properties.

(35) a. *si-ma–nuŋ   ŋ-uŋ-wa-ŋa-n–ha.*
          kill-INF=COM.CL   NEG-drink-npst[3.P]-1sg.A=nmlz.nsg
          'I will not drink in a way that I get drunk.'
      b. *hiŋ-ŋa=nuŋ   curuk*
          survive-1SG[SBJV]=COM.CL   cigarette

ŋ-uŋ-wa-ŋa-n=na.
NEG-smoke-NPST-1SG.A[3.P]-NEG=NMLZ.SG
**'I will not smoke cigarettes for my whole life. (i.e., 'I will stop in
some years.')' only:
'As long as I live, I will not smoke cigarettes.'*[13]

The illocutionary operators are assumed to show the same divide with regard
to the two different readings of adverbial clauses in *=nuŋ*. Compare example
(33) above with the deontic clause (36). Unfortunately, the current data set does
not contain examples of imperatives or questions containing adverbial clauses
in *=nuŋ* to back up this assumption, because this clause linkage type is comparatively rare in the corpus.

(36)   *si-ma=nuŋ*   *mẽ-uŋ-ma.*
         kill-INF=COM.CL   NEG-drink-INF[DEONT]
         'One should not drink in a way that one gets drunk.'

14.8 Conditional clauses in *bhoŋ*

Conditional clauses spell out circumstances that have to apply for the proposition
in the main clause to hold true. The conjunction *bhoŋ* (carrying its own stress)
may link finite clauses or infinitival conditional clauses to a main clause. It is also
employed in complemental clauses (see §15.2) and in purpose clauses (see §14.9
below). The dependent clauses it marks are larger than converbial clauses, and
also larger than the *=nuŋ*-clauses discussed above: conditional clauses contain
inflected verbs in subjunctive or indicative mood, and in contrast to the comitative clause linkage the verbs may even carry the nominalizing clitics *=na* and
=ha.

Conditional clauses can be split into those containing realis conditions, those
containing irrealis conditions and those containing general or habitual conditions. This is also reflected in their distinct formal properties: realis conditions
can show indicative morphology (tense/aspect markers, see (37)), with the nonpast indicative if the condition holds at the time of speaking. Irrealis conditions
(both hypothetical and counterfactual) are always marked for the past subjunctive (see (38)). Generic and habitual conditional clauses, i.e., those without specified referents, may be in the infinitive (see (38c)). Most of the examples in the
corpus are in the Past Subjunctive, i.e., irrealis conditionals are more frequent in

---

[13] The main reading of the verb *uŋma* is 'drink', but it can also refer to consuming other substances, as for instance smoking cigarettes or water-pipes (*hukka*).

discourse than realis conditionals (cf. Genetti (2007: 463) for the same observation in Dolakha Newar). Conditional clauses may also have a temporal reading in Yakkha.

(37) a. *Kamala=ŋa*   *mi*   *tupt-wa=na*   *bhoŋ*
      Kamala=ERG   fire   light-NPST[3.P]=NMLZ.SG   COND
      tupt-u-ni.
      burn-3.P-OPT
      'If Kamala lights the fire, may she do it (I do not care).'

    b. *batti*   *n-da-me-n=na.*   *wa-ni*
      electricity   NEG-come[3SG]-NPST-NEG=NMLZ.SG   exist[SBJV]-OPT
      haʔlo!   *n-da-me-n=na*   *bhoŋ,*
      EXCLA   NEG-come[3SG]-NPST-NEG=NMLZ.SG   COND
      n-da-nin-ni   *haʔlo!*
      NEG-come[3SG]-NEG-OPT   EXCLA
      'The electricity does not come. It's alright! If it does not come, may it not come, then!'

    c. *a-cya*   *lambu=be*   *pham-di-meʔ=na*
      1SG.POSS-child   way=LOC   entangle-V2.GIVE-NPST=NMLZ.SG
      bhoŋ,   ...
      COND
      'When my child gets confused on the road, ...'   [01_leg_07.072]
      (The speaker is expecting it to happen; it comes true later in the story.)

(38) a. *kamala=ŋa*   *mi*   *tupt-u*   *bhoŋ*   *hand-wa=na.*
      Kamala=ERG   fire   light-3.P[SBJV]   COND   burn-NPST[3.P]
      'If Kamala lights the fire, it will burn.'

    b. *ka*   *mas-a-bhy-a-ŋ*   *bhoŋ,*   ...
      1SG   get_lost-SBJV-V2.GIVE-SBJV-1SG   COND
      'In case I get lost, ...'   [18_nrr_03.016]
      (The speaker is not expecting it to happen; it does not come true.)

    c. *chep-ma*   *bhoŋ*   *m-muʔ-ni-me-n=ha.*
      write-INF   COND   NEG-forget-COMPL[3SG]-NPST=NMLZ.NSG
      men-chep-ma   *bhoŋ*   *muʔ-ni-me=ha.*
      NEG-write-INF   COND   forget-COMPL[3SG]-NPST=NMLZ.NSG
      'If one writes it down, one will not forget it. If one does not write it down, one will forget it.'[14]

---

[14] This clause could also read as 'if we write it down, ...', as detransitivized clauses may also refer to first person nonsingular agents, see §11.3.1.

Since conditional clauses contain inflected verbs, they may have their own value for polarity (39a). Negative polarity on the main verb can either have scope over the main clause only (see (39a)) or over the whole sentence (see (39b), here with the conditional clause attracting the focus of the negation).

(39)   a.   *paŋ=be*   *ta-meʔ-ma*   *n-yas-u-ga-n*
             house=LOC   arrive-CAUS-INF   NEG-be_able-3.P-2.A-NEG[SBJV]
             bhoŋ,   *aniŋ=ga=ca*   *n-leŋ-me-n,*
             COND   1PL.EXCL=GEN=ADD   NEG-be-NPST[3SG]-NEG
             ŋ=ga=ca   *n-leŋ-me-n.*
             2SG.POSS=GEN=ADD   NEG-be-NPST[3SG]-NEG
             'If you cannot bring it home, it will neither be ours nor yours.'
                                              [37_nrr_07.015]

       b.   *a-hoʔma=ci*   *ŋ-gy-a*   *bhoŋ*   *sidhak*
             1SG.POSS-cough=NSG   3PL-come_up-SBJV   COND   medicine
             n-ja-wa-ŋa-n=ha.
             NEG-eat-NPST-1SG-NEG=NMLZ.NSG
             'I don't take medicine when I have a cough (but when I have a cold).'

Illocutionary force operators generally have scope over the whole sentence, with the conditional clause specifying the question, assertion or command contained in the main clause.

(40)   a.   *wandik=ŋa*   *njiŋ-phaŋ*   *phalumba*
             tomorrow=INS   2DU.POSS-FyB   fourth_born_male
             ta-ya   *bhoŋ*   *i*   *lum-me-c-u-ga=na?*
             come[3SG]-SBJV   COND   what   tell-NPST-DU-3.P-2=NMLZ.SG
             'If your uncle Phalumba comes tomorrow, what will you tell him?'
                                            [40_leg_08.028]

       b.   *ucun*   *n-leks-a-n*   *bhoŋ*   *pheri*
             nice   NEG-become-SBJV-NEG   COND   again
             chept-u-so.
             write-3.P-V2.SEE[IMP]
             'If it does not turn out nice, try and write again.'

Since conditionals provide a background against which the main clause unfolds, it is not surprising that the particle *=ko* that marks topical constituents is often found on conditional clauses (41).

(41) *n-da-ci*   *bhoŋ=go*   *im-m=ha=ci*
      3PL.A-bring-3NSG.P   COND=TOP   buy-INF[DEONT]=NMLZ.NSG=NSG
      lai,   *ca-m=ha=ci!*
      EXCLA   eat-INF[DEONT]=NMLZ.NSG=NSG
      'If they bring them (fish), we have to buy some, we have to eat them!'
      [13_cvs_02.077]

Despite the inherent topicality of conditionals, many conditional clauses may host focus markers as well, both restrictive *=se* (expressing that this is the only condition under which the main clause obtains) or additive *=ca* (expressing that the condition is added to all conceivable conditions). Examples can be found in (42). Additive focus on conditional clauses may yield a concessive reading, but the standard way of expressing a concessive is by a combination of the sequential marker *=hoŋ* and additive focus particle *=ca* (see §14.11 below).

(42) a. *ŋ-khot-a-n*   *bhoŋ=se*   *kaniŋ*   *mimik*
          NEG-be_enough[3SG]-SBJV-NEG   COND=RESTR   1PL   a_little
          in-u-ca-wa-m-ŋ=ha.
          buy-3.P-V2.EAT-NPST-1PL-EXCL=NMLZ.NSG
          'Only if it is not enough, we buy some.'   [28_cvs_04.038]

      b. *ka*   *m-ma-ya-ŋa-n*   *bhoŋ=ca*   *sondu=ŋa*   *nda*
          1SG   NEG-exist-SBJV-1SG-NEG   COND=ADD   Sondu=ERG   2SG
          sukha=ŋa   *hiŋ-me-ka=na.*
          happiness=INS   survive-NPST-2=NMLZ.SG
          'Even if I am no more, Sondu, you will survive easily.'
          [01_leg_07.193]

      c. *aspatal=be*   *kheʔ-ma*   *bhoŋ=ca,*   *heʔne*
          hospital=LOC   carry_off-INF[DEONT]   COND=ADD   where
          kheʔ-ma=na?
          carry_off-INF[DEONT]=NMLZ.SG
          'Even if we have to take him to a hospital, where to take him?' (i.e., there is no hospital)   [36_cvs_06.175]

      d. *wandik*   *nniŋ-cya=ci,*   *jʌnma*   *n-jog-a*   *bhoŋ=ca*
          tomorrw   2PL.POSS-child=NSG   birth   3PL-do-SBJV   COND=ADD
          aphno-aphno   *paisa=ŋa*   *hiŋ-m=ha=ci.*
          own-own   money=INS   raise-INF=NMLZ.NSG=NSG
          'Later, when your children are born, too, you have to raise them with your own money.'   [28_cvs_04.141]

Example (42c) is an example of a 'speech-act conditional' (Thompson, Longacre & Hwang 2007: 267). Speech-act conditionals do not primarily relate to the content of the main clause, but to the fact that the act of communication as such is taking place, as, e.g., in 'In case you did not know, she got married'. Thus, by definition, in speech-act conditionals the illocutionary force has scope only over the main clause. Another example is shown in (43).

(43) *jeppa   cok-ma   bhoŋ   i=ha=ca   im-ma*
      true   do-INF   COND   what=NMLZ.NSG=ADD   buy-INF
      por-a   n-joŋ-me-ŋa-n.
      have_to-NATIV   NEG-do-NPST-1SG-NEG
      'To be honest, I do not have to buy anything.'   [28_cvs_04.187]

It is generally possible for constituents inside adverbial clauses to be focussed on. It is my impression that emphatic markers and constituent focus (e.g., by *=se*, *=maŋ* and *=ca*, see Chapter 17), such as in (44), are more often found in the group of inflected adverbial clauses, such as conditional clauses and sequential clauses, than in converbal clauses.

(44) a.   *a-hoʔma=ci=se   ŋ-gy-a   bhoŋ   sidhak*
           1SG.POSS-cough=NSG=RESTR   3PL-come_up   COND   medicine
           n-j-wa-ŋa-n=ha.
           NEG-eat-NPST[3.P]-1SG.A-NEG=NMLZ.NSG
           'When I am just coughing, I do not take medicine.'

      b.   *eko=se   ŋ-ab-u   bhoŋ,   yapmi*
           one=RESTR   3PL.A-shoot-3.P[SBJV]   COND   person
           sy-a-ma=na   miʔ-ma=na.
           die-PST-PRF=NMLZ.SG   think-INF[DEONT]=NMLZ.SG
           'If they fire just once, one has to consider that someone has died.'
                                                                [29_cvs_05.044]

      c.   *nna,   nani,   nna   luŋkhwak=maŋ   khet-wa-ga=na*
           that   girl   that   stone=EMPH   carry_off-NPST-2=NMLZ.SG
           bhoŋ,   seʔni=ŋa   naʔmasek   lam-ma.
           COND   night=INS   night_time   walk=INF[DEONT]
           'This stone, child, if you take away this very stone, you have to walk at night.'   [37_nrr_07.012]

      d.   *ŋkhiŋ=ca   n-leks-a-n   bhoŋ,   ...*
           that_much=ADD   NEG-become[3]-SBJV-NEG   COND
           'If that much is not possible either, ...'   [37_nrr_07.094]

14.9 Purpose clauses in *bhoŋ*

In addition to conditional finite relations, clauses marked by *bhoŋ* may also express purposes, intentions, cognitive reasons and goals, or states of mind in general (see Bickel 1993 for a similar observation in Belhare). Purpose clauses frequently have optative finite forms, as if they were a direct quote from the subject of the main clause (see (45a) and (45b)). Example (45c), however, shows that the purpose clause can also take the perspective of the speaker. Purpose clauses may also be marked for indicative mood (see (46a)), or have deontic finite forms (see (46b)).

The formal similarity between purposive and speech or thought representation structures (see §15.2.2) can be explained by the etymological origin of the marker *bhoŋ*. It is assumed that, as in Belhare (Bickel 1993), it developed from a combination of the reportative marker *=pu* and the sequential marker *hoŋ*.[15] Since the reportative marker *=pu* is a clitic and gets voiced after vowels, this also explains why *bhoŋ* has a voiced initial despite being an independent word with regard to stress.

(45) a.   *nam   phen-ni   bhoŋ,   nam=bhaŋ*
           sun   shine[3SG;SBJV]-OPT   PURP   sun=ABL
           leŋ-ma=na;   wasik   ta-ni   bhoŋ
           turn-INF[DEONT]=NMLZ.SG   rain   come[3SG;SBJV]-OPT   PURP
           wasik=phaŋ   luŋkhwak   leŋ-ma=na.
           rain=ABL   stone   turn-INF[DEONT]=NMLZ.SG
           'In order for the sun to shine, it (the stone) has to be turned away
           from the sun. In order for the rain to come, the stone has to be turned
           away from the rain.'   [37_nrr_07.116–7]

      b.   *yaks-u-ni   bhoŋ*
           strike-3.P-OPT   COND
           lept-u-ris-u-ŋ=na.
           throw-3.P-V2.PLACE-3.P[PST]-1SG.A=NMLZ.SG
           'I threw it at him, so that it would hit him.'

      c.   *ap-ŋa-ni   bhoŋ   ka-ya-ŋ=na.*
           come-1SG-OPT   PURP   call-PST-1SG=NMLZ.SG
           'He called me, so that I would come.'

---

[15] Bickel (1993) mentions the contracted form [muŋ] in Belhare, combined of the quotative marker *mu* (an allomorph of *-bu ~ -phu*, which is cognate with Yakkha *=pu*), and the ablative/sequential marker *huŋ* (cognate to Yakkha *=hoŋ*).

Purpose clauses have the same internal structure as complement clauses, but they function differently in that they adverbially modify the main clause, and hence are optional, whereas complement clauses function as obligatory arguments, without which the main clause would be incomplete. In (46a), the purpose clause contains quoted speech, which is evident from the use of variables such as the speech-act participant pronoun *nniŋda* and the deictic adverb *nhe*. The conjunction *bhoŋ* in (46a) is ambiguous between a purpose marker and a quotative marker. Parellel structures with a purely quotative function of *bhoŋ* can also be found (see (46b), translated with *are* in Nepali).

(46) a. *nniŋda   nhe   wa-ma*
          2PL[ERG] here   live-INF
          n-dokt-wa-m-ga-n=ha   *bhoŋ*
          NEG-get_to_do-NPST-2PL.A[3.P]-2-NEG=NMLZ.NSG   PURP
          ikt-haks-a-ma-c-u-ci.
          chase-V2.SEND-PST-PRF-DU-3.P-3NSG.P
          'You will not get the chance to live here!, (they [dual] said) and chased them away.' OR
          'They chased them away, so that they would not get the opportunity to live there.'   [22_nrr_05.012–3]

      b. *haku   miyaŋ   ŋkha   yabenpekhuwa=ci=le*
          now   a_little those   healer=NSG=CTR
          soʔ-meʔ-ma=ci=em   *bhoŋ*   *yabenpekhuwa=ci=ja*
          look-CAUS-INF[DEONT]=NSG=ALT   QUOT   healer=NSG=ADD
          n-soʔ-met-uks-u-ci.
          3PL.A-look-CAUS-PRF-3.P-3NSG.P
          'Now we better show the matter to those healers; (they said) and they also showed it to the healers.'   [22_nrr_05.072]

Finally, clauses marked by *bhoŋ* are also found with main verbs such as *soʔma* 'look', *kuma* 'wait' and *yokma* 'search', illustrated in (47). The activity in the main clause is done not in order to achieve whatever is expressed in the purpose clause, but with the goal to acquire knowledge or to achieve a state of mind about the proposition in the purpose clause. These clauses always contain indirect speech or questions (see also (45c) for another example of indirect speech). The perspective is anchored in the speaker and the speech situation, not in the subject of the clause. In (47a), if the perspective of the subject had been taken, the verb *tayamacuha* should have been *tayamacugha* 'how much have you brought'.

(47) a. *paŋ=be*   *a-ma=ŋa*   *ikhiŋ*
house=LOC 1SG.POSS-mother=ERG how_much

ta-ya-ma-c-u=ha   *bhoŋ*   *khesup*
bring-PST-PRF-DU-3.P=NMLZ.NC PURP bag

so=niŋa.
look-[3.P;PST]=CTMP
'At home, when mother looked into the bag to see how much we had brought, ...'   [40_leg_08.025]

    b. *m-ba=ŋa*   *nasa* *ta-wa-ci=ha*   *bhoŋ*
2SG.POSS-father=ERG fish bring-NPST-3NSG.P=NMLZ.NSG PURP

ku-ma=ŋa   *ku-ma=ŋa!*
wait-INF[DEONT]=ERG.CL wait-INF[DEONT]=ERG.CL
'Because I have to wait and wait for your father to bring the fish!'   [01_leg_07.205]

    c. *kucuma* *heʔne* *waiʔ=na*   *bhoŋ*
dog   where exist[NPST;3SG]=NMLZ.SG PURP

yok-ma-si-me-ŋ=na.
search-INF-AUX.PROG-NPST-1SG=NMLZ.SG
'I am looking for the dog (where the dog is).'

    d. *jal* *hetne* *het-u=na*   *bhoŋ*   *hoŋma=ga*
net where get_stuck-3.P=NMLZ.SG REP/PURP river=GEN

u-lap-ulap   *lukt-a-ma.*
3SG.POSS-wing3SG.POSS-wing run[3SG]-PST-PRF
'He ran along the river bank (in order to see) where the net got stuck.'   [01_leg_07.216]

14.10 Sequential clause linkage and narrative clause-chaining in =*hoŋ*

The sequential marker =*hoŋ* indicates that the dependent clause event and the main clause event take place in a temporal sequence. This clause linkage marker is attached to the inflected verb (without =*na* or =*ha*) or to an infinitival form (see, e.g., example (51a)). Sequential clauses can be in the indicative or in the subjunctive. There is no constraint on the corefence of arguments, but the S/A arguments are shared in 60.8% of the occurrences in the corpus (see (48)). Center-embedding is attested only marginally (2.0% of 307 sequential clauses), shown in (49a) and (b). Center-embedding can be attested semantically or via the case

marking of the arguments. In (49a), the dual pronoun belongs to the last two
verbs, while the sequential clause with *tupma* 'meet' has plural reference. In
(49b), the subject is in the unmarked nominative that can only come from the
intransitive main verb, and hence the transitive sequential clause must be center-
embedded. Since overt arguments are rare, one cannot always assess the variable
of center-embeddedness in the data. As (48b) and (49b) have already shown, the
sequential clause may also entail a consecutive reading; (49c) is another example
illustrating this.

(48) a. *nam   lom-me=hoŋ*   *photo   khic-a*
         sun   come_out-NPST[3SG]=SEQ   photo   press-NATIV
         cog-u-m.
         do-3.P-1PL.A[SBJV]
         'Let us take photos when the sun comes out.'

      b. *nam=ŋa   heco=hoŋ,*   *liŋkha   sarap*
         sun=ERG   win[PST;3.P]=SEQ   Linkha   spell
         pi=na.
         give[PST;3.P]=NMLZ.SG
         'As the sun had won, it put a spell on the Linkha man.'
                                                                    [11_nrr_01.020]

      c. *nna   ti?wa=go*   *majhya   paghyam=ŋa*
         that   pheasant=TOP   a_title   old_man=ERG
         napt-het-a-ŋ=hoŋ   *kobeŋ-kobeŋ*
         snatch-V2.CARRY.OFF-PST-1SG.P=SEQ   continously-REDUP
         lam-a-khy-a,   ...
         walk[3SG]-PST-V2.GO-PST
         'That old Majhya snatched the pheasant from me and left quickly, ...'
                                                                    [40_leg_08.037]

      d. *mela=be   [...]   suku=ŋa*   *u-ppa*
         fair=LOC   [...]   Suku=ERG   3SG.POSS-father
         u-ma=ci=ca   *mund-y-uks-u-ci=hoŋ*
         3SG.POSS-mother=NSG=ADD   forget-COMPL-PRF-3.P-3NSG.P=SEQ
         phaps-a-khy-a-ma.
         entangle[3SG]-PST-V2.PST-PST-PRF
         'In the fun fair [...], Suku forgot her parents and got lost.'
                                                                    [01_leg_07.152]

(49) a. *kanciŋ   to   tub-i=hoŋ*
         1DU   up   meet-1PL[PST]=SEQ

uks-a-ŋ-ci-ŋ=hoŋ   *yo*
come_down-PST-EXCL-DU-EXCL=SEQ   over_there
tas-a-ŋ-c-u-ŋ=ba.
arrive-PST-EXCL-DU-3.P-EXCL=EMPH
'After we (plural) had met, we (dual) went down and then we (dual) arrived over there.'   [36_cvs_06.395]

b.   *paghyam=ca*   *piccha*   *nis-uks-u=hoŋ*
     old_man=ADD   child   see-PRF-3.P=SEQ
     cond-a-sy-a-ma.
     be_happy[3SG]-PST-MDDL-PST-PRF
     'The old man was happy, too, when he saw the child.' [01_leg_07.296]

c.   *chippakekek*   *nis-u-ŋ=hoŋ*   *yamyam*
     disgusting   see-3.P[PST]-1SG.A=SEQ   [eating]hesitantly
     ca-ŋ=ha.
     eat[PST]-1SG.A=NMLZ.NC
     'It smelled awfully, and so I ate hesitantly.'

Deriving from its sequential semantics, a secondary function can be observed as well: clauses marked by *=hoŋ* can also express chains of coordinated events in narratives, a function comparable to the 'narrative converb' (Nedjalkov 1995). Some examples are shown in (50). The clause-initial conjunction *nhaŋ(a)* has a very similar function, and is historically derived from a demonstrative and the sequential marker. As (50b) shows, *=hoŋ* is not restricted to verbal hosts. It may attach to adverbs, nouns and demonstratives in non-verbal clauses (i.e., to predicates of copular clauses).[16]

(50)   a.   *nhaŋ*   *ŋ-und-wa-ci=hoŋ*   *pheri,*
          and_then   3PL.A-pull-NPST-3NSG.P=SEQ   again
          haiko=na=be   *ŋ-khe-me=ha=ci.*
          other=NMLZ.SG=LOC   3PL-go-NPST=NMLZ.NSG=NSG
          'They go a bit further and then they pull them (the fish) out.'
                                            [13_cvs_02.13]

    b.   *nhaŋ*   *hattabatta*   *lukt-ab-a=hoŋ*
          and_then   hastily   run-V2.COME-PST[3SG]=SEQ
          muccok=hoŋ   *paŋ=be*   *ta-ya,*   *nhaŋa*
          lifting_lightly=SEQ   house=LOC   come-PST[3SG],   and_then

---

[16] The marker can, not function as a nominal coordinator. Nouns are coordinated by the comitative marker =nuŋ, though.

paŋ=be=hoŋ   *pheri*   *lukt-ab-a=hoŋ*   *sidhak*
house=LOC=SEQ   again   run-V2.COME-PST[3SG]=SEQ   medicine
end-a-bhy-a-ŋ=ba.
apply-PST-V2.GIVE-PST-1SG.P=EMPH
'Then, he came running quickly, he lifted me up, and came to the house, and then, as (we were) in the house, he came running again and applied medicine (on my wounds).'   [13_cvs_02.053–54]

c.   *ka=ca*   *om*   *mit-a-ŋ=hoŋ*   *n-sy-a=ha*
     1SG=ADD   yes   think-PST-1SG=SEQ   3PL-die-PST=NMLZ.NSG
     wa=ci   *solok*   *ta-ŋ-ci-ŋ.*
     chicken=NSG   immediately   bring[PST]-1SG.A-3NSG.P-1SG.A
     'I agreed and quickly brought the dead chicken.'   [40_leg_08.072]

The scopeof negation is less restricted than in the converbal clauses. It may reach over the whole sentence, or be restricted to the main clause. The first possibility is shown in (51a), with the focus of the negation attracted by the sequential clause. Pure main clause scope can be found in sentences like (51b).

(51)   a.   *cama*   *ca-ma=hoŋ*   *sidhak*   *men-ja-ma,*
           food   eat-INF=SEQ   medicine   NEG-eatINF[DEONT]
           ondaŋ=se   *ca-ma.*
           before=RESTR   eat-INF[DEONT]
           'You don't have to take this medicine after eating, but before.'

      b.   *hiʔwa*   *u-yin*   *ind-wa=ci=hoŋ*   *na*
           air   3SG.POSS-egg   lay-NPST=3NSGP=SEQ   this
           u-yin=go   *m-beŋ-me-n.*
           3SG.POSS-egg=TOP   NEG-break-NPST[3SG]-NEG
           'After he has laid his eggs in the air, this egg does not break.'
                                                [21_nrr_04.040]

For illocutionary operators all configurations are possible, and some sentences are even ambiguous, as (52a). In addition, coordinative scope can be found, with the illocutionary force applying to each subclause separately (see the second reading of (52a), and (52b)).[17] Note that for the coordinative reading in imperatives the verb of the clause marked with =hoŋ has to be in subjunctive mood. The imperative *lab-u=hoŋ* is not possible in (52b).

---

[17] Coordinative scope has proven to be difficult to distinguish from overall scope in most cases, and was thus disregarded for the classification of clause linkage types here.

(52) a. *kamniwak   sori   yuŋ-i=hoŋ   uŋ-u-m.*
          friend   together   sit-1PL=SEQ   drink-3.P-1pl.A[sbjv]
          '(We) friends having sat down together, let us drink.' OR
          'Let us friends sit down together and drink!'

      b. *nda   cattu=nuŋ   lab-u-g=hoŋ   tokhaʔla*
          2SG   firmly   grab-3.P-2SG.A[SBJV]=SEQ   upwards
          ky-a!
          come_up-IMP
          'Grab it firmly and come up!'   [01_leg_07.329]

An example of main clause scope is given in (53a). Here, the first part of the
sentence is uttered as a statement in surprise and it thus does not fall under the
scope of the question in the main clause. In (53b), though, the question word is
part of the sequential clause, and the main clause is presupposed, as the question
is not about whether the addressee survived, but how he was able to hold such
a thin rope.

(53) a. *sondu   khaʔla=na   cuŋ=be   tek   me-waʔ-le   jal*
          Sondu   like_this=NMLZ   cold=LOC   clothes   NEG-wear-CVB   net
          kapt-uks-u-g=hoŋ   hetnaŋ   ta-e-ka=na?
          carry-PRF-3.P-2.A=SEQ   where_from   come-NPST-2=NMLZ.SG
          'Sondu, without clothes in this cold and carrying this net – where do
          you come from?'   [01_leg_07.232]

      b. *khaʔla=na   mi=na   khibak=ŋa   imin*
          like_this=NMLZS.G   small=NMLZ.SG   rope=ERG   how
          tapt-a-g=hoŋ   hiŋ-a-ga=na?
          hold-PST-2=SEQ   survive-PST-2=NMLZ.SG
          'How did you survive, holding such a thin rope?' (literally: 'You
          survived, holding such a thin rope HOW?')   [01_leg_07.343]

The sequential clause may also get focussed on as a whole, for instance by the
restrictive focus particle, shown in example (54) from a conversation.

(54) a. *heʔniŋ   lam-me-ci-g=ha?*
          when   walk-NPST-DU-2=NMLZ.NSG
          'When will you (dual) set off?'

      b. *cama   ca-i-wa-ŋ=hoŋ=se*
          rice   eat-1PL-NPST-EXCL=SEQ=RESTR

lam-me-ŋ-ci-ŋ=ha.
walk-NPST-EXCL-DU-EXCL=NMLZ.NSG
'We (dual) will set off only after we (all) had our meal.'

The coordinative reading of *=hoŋ* is also employed in a narrative strategy to build up continuity, known as 'tail-head linkage' (Ebert 2003b: 39). The previous clause, or just the verb, is repeated in a sequential clause, before adding new information in the main clause, as illustrated in (55).

(55)   *ŋkhoŋ=ca*   *a-chik*   *ekt-a=na*
       afterwards=ADD   1SG.POSS-anger   make_break-PST=NMLZ.SG
       belak=ŋa   *esap-esap*   *than-ma*   *yas-a-ŋ.*   *to*
       time=INS   swiftly-swiftly   climb-INF   be_able-PST-1SG   up
       than-a-by-a-ŋ=hoŋ   *khaʔla*   *so-ŋ=niŋa=go*
       climb-PST-V2.GIVE-PST-1SG=SEQ   like_this   look[PST]-1SG.A=CTMP=TOP
       eko   *maŋpha=na*   *hoŋ*   *nis-u-ŋ.*
       one   huge=NMLZ.SG   hole   see[PST]-3.P-1SG.A
       'Nevertheless, as I was so angry, that I managed to climb up. When I had climbed up into the tree and looked, I saw a large hole.' [42_leg_10.022–3]

14.11 Concessive clauses in *=hoŋca*

It is a crosslinguistically common pattern for concessive clauses to be constructed by means of an additive focus marker or a scalar operator (König 1993: 980). Yak-kha employs this strategy, too, combining the sequential clause linkage marker *=hoŋ* (see above) with the additive focus marker *=ca* (see Chapter 17.2.2), as shown in (56).[18] Concessive adverbial clauses indicate that the condition expressed in the adverbial clause is in contrast to the expected conditions, or that the condition is not relevant for the assertion to be true. In (56a) the concessive is employed together with another converb (cotemporal *-saŋ*): this shows that *=hoŋ* has lost its sequential meaning in concessive clauses.

(56)   a.   *ropa*   *lamdhaŋ=be*   *cayoŋwa*   *lin-ca-saŋ=hoŋ=ca*
            paddy_field   field=LOC   food   plant-V2.EAT-SIM=SEQ=ADD
            cama=ŋa   *khot-u-co-nes-uks-u-ci.*
            food=ERG   be_enough-3.P-V2.EAT-V2.LAY-PRF-3.P-3NSG.P
            'Even though they ate what they planted in the field, the food was enough for them.'   [01_leg_07.063]

---

[18] Occasionally, the cotemporal clause linkage marker *niŋ* is found in concessive clauses, too.

b.   *marej   end-a=hoŋ=ca   khumdu   sa.*
      pepper   insert[3SG]-PST=SEQ=ADD   tasty   COP.PST[3]
      'Even though pepper was added, it was tasty.'

c.   *yok-ma=bu,   cek-ma=i*
      search-INF[DEONT]=REP   speak-INF=EMPH
      men-ni-ma=hoŋ=ca   ceŋ-soʔ-ma=bu.
      NEG-know-INF=SEQ=ADD   speak-V2.LOOK-INF[DEONT]=REP
      'One has to search for it (the language). Even though one does not
      know it, one has to try and speak, she said.'   [07_sng_01.11]

In §14.8, speech-act conditionals have been introduced (Thompson, Longacre & Hwang 2007). The same phenomenon is also found with concessive clauses. In (57), the speaker excuses himself for talking about sensitive topics despite the fact that women are present.

(57)   *nhe,   mamu   wanne=hoŋ=ca,   baru   khaʔla*
      here   girl   exist[3;NPST]=SEQ=ADD   instead   like_this
      cok-ma=na,   nna,   lakhe
      co-INF[DEONT]=NMLZ.SG   that   castrated
      coŋ-siʔ-ma=na.
      do-V2.PREVENT-INF[DEONT]=NMLZ.SG
      'Here - even though women are present - instead, one should do it like
      this, one should castrate them.'   [28_cvs_04.228]

Related to concessive clauses are *exhaustive* clauses. They contain a question word functioning as a pro-form that may stand for the greatest conceivable temporal extension in (58a) and for any conceivable location in (58b). Such clauses can either be marked just by the additive focus marker, or by the concessive =hoŋca.

(58)   *ikhiŋ   kus-u=ca   mima   n-lond-a-ma-n.*
      how_much   wait-3.P=ADD   mouse   NEG-come_out-PST-PRF-NEG
      'However much it waited, the mouse did not come out.'   [04_leg_03.008]

(58)   *heʔne   khe-i-ga=hoŋ=ca   [...]   ka=ca   hakt-a-ŋ   au.*
      where   go-2PL-2=SEQ=ADD   [...]   1SG=ADD   send-IMP-1SG.P   INSIST
      'Wherever you go, (...) send (a message) to me too.'   [01_leg_07.276]

14.12 Cotemporal linkage in *=niŋ(a)*

The cotemporal marker=*niŋ* ~ =*niŋa* combines clauses that refer to events that happen at the same time, but that do not necessarily have coreferential S or A arguments. The two forms occur in free variation; no phonological or functional motivation for the alternation could be found. The event in the main clause generally unfolds against the background provided by the adverbial clause, as, e.g., in (59). Given its semantics, it is not surprising that the marker may host the topic particle =*go* (see (59b)). The adverbial clause can be inflected for either one of the subjunctives (see §8.5), but also for different tenses in the indicative mood. Generic statements are in the infinitive, as in (59a).

As in the sequential construction, the S and A arguments do not have to be coreferential (see (59)), but in 37% of the clauses they are. Center-embedding is as rare as in the sequential clause linkage pattern, but it is technically possible.

(59) a.   *uthamlaŋ*   *uimalaŋ*   *lam-ma=niŋa*   *laŋ=ci*
           steeply_uphill   steeply_downhill walk-INF=CTMP leg=NSG
           n-sa-ma=ha=ci.
           3PL-become.PST-PRF=NMLZ.NSG=NSG
           'While walking steeply uphill and downhill, the legs got stronger.'

    b.   *thawa=bhaŋ* *to* *ŋ-khy-ama=niŋ=go*   *mamu* *nnhe=maŋ*
           ladder=ABL   up 3PL-go-PRF=CTMP=TOP   girl   there=EMPH
           wet=na=bu.
           exist[3SG]=REP
           'As they have gone up on the ladder, the girl is right there!'
                                                  [22_nrr_05.111]

The scope properties are similar to those of the sequential clauses. With regard to negation, overall and main clause scope are possible. Overall scope is shown in (60a), and main clause scope in (60b), which acquires a causal reading in addition to the basic cotemporal one.

(60) a.   *ta-ya-ŋ-ci-ŋ=niŋ*   *cama*
           come-PST-EXCL-DU-EXCL=CTMP   food
           n-ni-n=ha.
           NEG-cook[PST;3.P]-NEG=NMLZ.NSG
           'She wasn't preparing food when we came.'

    b.   *pyak=ŋa*   *m-phat-uks-u=niŋa,*   *Tikule=ŋa*
           many=ERG   3PL.A-help-PRF-3.P=CTMP Tikule=ERG

i=ya=ca   *cokla*   *cok-ma*   *por-a*
what=NSG=ADD   work   do-INF   must-NATIV
n-jog-ama-n.
NEG-do-PRF[3SG]-NEG
'As so many helped him, Tikule did not have to do anything.'

[01_leg_07.019]

14.13 Counterfactual clauses in *=niŋ(go)bi* or *=hoŋ(go)bi*

Counterfactual clauses are marked mostly by *=niŋ* for cotemporal clauses and occasionally by *=hoŋ* for sequential clauses. The adverbial clause can be infinitival or inflected for the subjunctive, and is often marked by the topic particle *=ko* (voiced [go] in intervocalic and postnasal position, see §3.5.1). Furthermore, both the adverbial clause and the main clause host the irrealis marker *=pi* ([bi] due to the voicing rule). Clauses as in (61) can only have a counterfactual reading (i.e., it is established knowledge at the time of speaking that the condition does not obtain); they cannot be understood hypothetically. The irrealis marker, however, also occurs in hypothetical statements.

(61)   a.   *ka*   *nis-u-ŋ=niŋ=bi*   *ikhiŋ*
            1SG[ERG]   know-3.P[SBJV]-1SG.A=CTMP=IRR   how_much
            lu-ŋ=bi.
            tell-1SG.A[3.P;SBJV]=IRR
            'If I knew it, how much would I tell!'

    b.   *diana=ca*   *piʔ-ma=hoŋ=go=bi*
            Diana=ADD   give-INF=SEQ=TOP=IRR
            cond-a-sy-a=bi=ba!
            be_happy-SBJV-MDDL-SBJV[3SG]=IRR=EMPH
            'After giving them to Diana too, she would have been happy!'

                                              [13_cvs_02.075]

    c.   *encho=maŋ*   *jal*   *lep-ma*   *cind-a-ŋ-ga=niŋ=bi*
            long_ago=EMPH   net   throw-INF   teach-PST-1SG.P-2.A=CTMP=IRR
            hen   *tuʔkhi*   *n-ja-ya-ŋa-n*   *loppi.*
            today   trouble   NEG-eat-SBJV-1SG-NEG   probably
            'If we had gone, I would have sent it to you.'   [01_leg_07.252]

    d.   *nniŋ=ga*   *ten*   *a-sap*
            2PL=GEN   village   1SG.POSS-[STEM]

n-thakt-u-n=niŋ=go=bi,   ka
NEG-like-3.P-NEG=CTMP=TOP=IRR   1SG

n-da-ya-ŋa-n=bi.
NEG-come-PST-1SG-NEG=IRR

'If I did not like your village, I would not have come here.'

14.14 Interruptive clauses in *=lo*

The clause linkage marker *=lo* does not figure prominently in the current corpus. It signals that a certain event takes place within the time span of another event, often interrupting it (see (62a)), or having an effect contrary to the one expected (see (62b)). The verb in the adverbial clause often includes the inceptive V2 -*heks* (see Chapter 10), which signifies that the action has just begun and has not yet been not completed (see (62a) and (62b)). With telic verbs, this implies that the event has not reached its end point yet (62c). The marker is probably cognate with a comitative marker found, e.g., in Belhare and Bantawa, which is also employed in clause linkage in Belhare (Bickel 1993; Doornenbal 2009). As the examples are limited for this kind of clause linkage, the description of this clause linkage strategy cannot go into further detail.

(62)   a.   *a-ppa,*   *eh,*   *a-ppa!*   *cekt-heks-a=lo*
           1SG.POSS-father   he   1SG.POSS-father   talk-V2.CUT-PST=ITP

           swak   *wa-ya-by-ama.*
           silent   be-PST-V2.GIVE-PRF[3SG]

           'He started calling: Father, hey, father!, when he suddenly fell silent.'
                                                 [01_leg_07.179]

     b.   *jal*   *so-heks-u=lo*   *mas-a-by-ama.*
           net   watch-V2.CUT-3.P=ITP   lose-PST-V2.GIVE-PRF[SBJV]

           'As he was about to watch the net, it got lost.'   [01_leg_07.217]

     c.   *tokhaʔla*   *khem-me,*   *to*   *khem-meʔ=lo*   *pheri*
           upwards   go-NPST[3SG]   up   go-NPST[3SG]=ITP   again

           heko=na=ga   *u-cya*   *leŋ-me.*
           other=NMLZ.SG=GEN   3SG.POSS-child   become-NPST[3SG]

           'It flies up, and within the time it flies up, again this other one has a child (egg).'   [21_nrr_04.046]

15 Complementation

Yakkha has a number of verbs that embed clausal complements. These complement-taking verbs (CTPS, cf. Noonan 2007) license several complement constructions, defined by the type of the embedded clause. The most salient formal distinction can be drawn between infinitival clauses and inflected clauses.[1] A typical infinitival complement construction is shown in (1a). Inflected complement clauses show person, tense/aspect, mood inflection (indicative or subjunctive) and the nominalizing clitics =na or =ha (see (1b), cf. §13.3). In the case of embedded direct speech they may show any marking that is found on independent clauses as well, for instance the imperative (see (1c)).

(1)   a.   *ka   khe?-ma   mit-a-ŋ-na.*
          1SG   go-INF   think-PST-1SG=NMLZ.SG
          'I want to go.'

    b.   *nda   lam-me-ka=na   mi-nuŋ-nen=na.*
          2SG   return-NPST-2=NMLZ.SG   think-PRF-1>2=NMLZ.SG
          'I thought that you will come back.'

    c.   *haku   bagdata=ca   py-a-ŋ-ni-ŋ   bhoŋ*
          now   finalization_of_marriage=ADD   give-IMP-1SG-PL-1SG   COMP

          eko   binti   bisa   cog-wa-ci.
          one   request   request   make-NPST-3NSG.P
          '"Now give me the *bagdata*, too!" she requests from them.'[2]

                                                  [26_tra_02.019]

---

[1] I deliberately avoid the terms *finite* and *nonfinite* here, since finiteness is a problematic concept. The defining criteria are different across languages and across theoretical frameworks. In this case, finiteness would only be defined by the presence or absence of the verbal inflection, as inflected complement clauses are less finite than independent clauses. They lack many features such as clause-final marking for evidentiality or mirativity, certain mood inflections like the imperative, and detached positions. The infinitival clauses, on the other hand, are potentially equal to finite clauses in Yakkha: in one infinitival complement construction the main verb is optional (the deontic construction), so that the infinitive can present a full (deontic) predication (see §15.1.7).

[2] The form *pyaŋniŋ* is more complex than expected from the Tumok data (see §8.5). The speaker's natal home is in Hombong village.

Table 15.1 provides an overview of the complement-taking predicates of Yak-kha. They are grouped according to the inflectional features of the embedded clauses and according to their semantics. Noonan (2007: 120) lists the following semantic classes of complement-taking predicates: utterance predicates, propositional attitude predicates, pretense predicates, comment (factitive) predicates, predicates of knowledge or acquisition of knowledge, predicates of fearing, desiderative predicates, manipulative predicates, modal predicates, achievement predicates, phasal predicates and predicates of perception. In Yakkha, inflected complement clauses occur with utterance predicates, propositional attitude predicates and with predicates of perception. Infinitival complement clauses occur with a broader semantic range of CTPs, as Table 15.1 shows.

Most complement-taking verbs may also take nominal arguments, e.g., *tokma*, which can mean 'get something' or 'get to do something'. In addition to the complement-taking verbs, there are also some nouns that can embed clausal complements, such as *ceʔya* 'talk, matter' or *kisiʔma* 'fear'.

Many complement constructions, particularly those with infinitival complements, are characterized by the referential identity between an argument of the embedded clause and an argument of the matrix clause. This may be reflected by leaving an argument unexpressed in one clause (Equi-deletion). Traditionally, complement constructions with shared arguments are divided into raising and control constructions.[3] In control constructions, the shared argument belongs to both clauses semantically, whereas in raising constructions the shared argument belongs to the embedded clause semantically, despite being coded as argument of the main clause. Hence, in raising constructions an "unraised" alternative expressing the same propositional content is usually available, while in control constructions, there is only one option.

The CTPs taking infinitival complements are discussed in §15.1, the verbs and nouns that take inflected complement clauses are dealt with in §15.2.

15.1 Infinitival complement clauses

15.1.1 Overview

In this section I discuss all constructions that follow the basic pattern of an infinitive followed by an inflected verb. I found 20 predicates that occur with embedded infinitives in Yakkha.

---

[3] Arguments can be shared with respect to morphological marking, agreement or constituency properties, following Serdobolskaya's definition of raising (Serdobolskaya 2009: 278).

Table 15.1: Overview of complement-taking predicates

INFINITIVAL COMPLEMENT	INFLECTED COMPLEMENT
PHASAL	
tarokma 'begin'	
lepnima 'stop, abandon'	
tama 'be time to' (lit. 'come')	
UTTERANCE PREDICATES	
	kama 'say'
	luʔma 'tell'
	chimma 'ask'
	yokmeʔma 'tell (about something)'
PROPOSITIONAL ATTITUDE, DESIDERATIVE, EXPERIENTIAL	
miʔma 'like doing, want' (lit. 'think')	*miʔma* 'think, hope, remember'
kaŋma 'give in, surrender' (lit. 'fall')	*yemma ~ emma* 'agree (to propositions)'
POSS-*niŋsaŋ puŋma* 'have enough, be fed up'	*consiʔma* 'be happy about'
sukma 'intend, aim'	*kuma* 'wait, expect'
leŋma 'be acceptable, be alright'	POSS-*niŋwa wama* 'hope'
kisiʔma 'be afraid'	*niŋwa huŋma* 'decide collectively'
PERCEPTION, COGNITION, KNOWLEDGE	
nima 'know how to do'	*nima* 'see/get to know'
muʔnima 'forget to do'	*muʔnima* 'forget about something'
	khemma 'hear'
	eʔma 'have the impression that'
MODALS	
yama 'be able'	
(copula/zero) 'have to'	
cokma 'try' (lit. 'do')	
ACHIEVEMENT	
tokma 'get to do' (lit. 'get')	
PRETENSE	
loʔwa cokma 'pretend'	
PERMISSIVE, ASSISTIVE (S-TO-P)	
piʔma 'allow' (lit. 'give')	
phaʔma 'help doing'	
cimma 'teach'	
soʔmeʔma 'show'	

Infinitival complement clauses are marked by the infinitive *-ma* to which, optionally, the genitive marker *=ga* may attach (see (2)). Other inflectional categories are not possible on these clauses. Apart from these basic features, the behavior of the various verbs that embed infinitives is far from homogenous, as will be shown below.

(2) a. *ka   khe?-ma(=ga)   cog-a-ŋ=na.*
         1SG   go-INF(=GEN)   do-PST-1SG=NMLZ.SG
         'I tried to go.'

     b. *kucuma=ŋa ka   ha?-ma(=ga)   sukt-a-ŋ=na.*
         dog=ERG   1SG   bite-INF(=GEN) aim[3SG.A]-PST-1SG.P=NMLZ.SG
         'The dog intended to bite me.'

The embedded infinitive depends on the main verb for all inflectional categories. One construction (expressing deontic modality) is exceptional in this respect, though (cf. §15.1.7). In this construction, the nonsingular marker *=ci* attaches to the infinitive when the object has third person nonsingular reference. The marker is aligned with the primary object (compare the intransitive example (3a) with transitive (3b) and ditransitive (3c)).

(3) a. *yapmi   paŋ-paŋ=be   nak-saŋ   khe?-m=ha.*
         people house-house=LOC   ask-SIM   go-INF[DEONT]=NMLZ.NSG
         'The people have to go from house to house, asking (for food).' (S)
                                                            [14_nrr_02.029]

     b. *thim-m=ha=ci.*
         scold-INF[DEONT]=NMLZ.NSG=NSG
         'They (the young people) have to be scolded.' (P)

     c. *wa=ci   pi?-m=ha=ci.*
         chicken=NSG   give-INF[DEONT]=NMLZ.NSG=NSG
         'It has to be given to the chicken.' (G)

The complement-taking verbs can be distinguished according to their valency and their argument realization. Some matrix verbs always have intransitive morphology, some always have transitive morphology, and some verbs assimilate to the valency of their embedded predicates. According to this, the agreement properties have the potential to differ. Yakkha infinitival complement constructions show long distance agreement (LDA), i.e., the matrix verb shows agreement with an argument of the embedded clause. This is illustrated by example (2b) above: the constituent *ka* '1sg' is the P argument of the embedded clause and triggers object agreement in the matrix verb *sukma* 'intend'. LDA is common for

Kiranti languages; it has been described, e.g., for Belhare (Bickel & Nichols 2001; Bickel 2004a) and for Puma (Schackow 2008). An overview of the infinitival complement types and their properties is provided in Table 15.2–15.4 below. In the following sections, these properties will be treated in detail.

The case assignment has to be determined independently from the agreement properties. In the majority of the complement-taking verbs, the case assignment for the embedded arguments comes from the embedded verb. This means that in cases of shared reference it is not necessarily the embedded argument that is omitted, but rather the matrix argument (discussed below). Such structures are known as backward control, and received attention in the literature on control phenomena especially after an article on the Nakh-Dagestanian language Tsez by Polinsky & Potsdam (2002).

Thus, in several infinitival complement constructions the arguments show relations to both clauses simultaneously, so that the whole structure is better analyzed as monoclausal rather than as matrix clause and embedded clause.[4] This is the case when, for instance, case is assigned by the embedded verb, but agreement is triggered on the main verb.[5]

Table 15.2: Argument realization in infinitival complement constructions

VERB	MORPH. VALENCY	ARGU- MENTS	CASE OF OVERT A	AGREEMENT EMB. ARG.	AGREEMENT MATR. SLOT
leŋma 'be alright'		1	by emb. V	[S/A/P] [clause]	→S or →S[3sg]
tama 'be time to'	intrans.	1	n.d.	[clause]	→S[3sg]
copula/zero 'have to'		1	by emb. V	[S/P]	→S
				[1/2]	→S

---

[4] See Haspelmath (1999) for a discussion on clause union in the Nakh-Dagestanian language Godoberi.

[5] Yakkha also has a periphrastic imperfective construction that has developed from an infinitival complement construction, see §8.4.

Table 15.3: Argument realization in infinitival complement constructions

VERB	MORPH. VALENCY	ARGU- MENTS	CASE OF OVERT A	AGREEMENT EMB. ARG.	MATR. SLOT
yama 'be able'		2	by emb. V	[S]	→S
mi?ma 'want'	as emb. V	2	by emb. V	[A]	→A
cokma 'try'		2	by emb. V	[P]	→P
niŋsaŋ puŋma 'be fed up'	as emb. V	2	n.d.	[A] [P] [clause]	→A →P →S[3sg]
sukma 'aim, intend'		2	by emb. V	[S/A]	→A
tarokma 'begin'		2	by emb. V	[P]	→P
lepnima 'stop'	trans.	2	by emb. V	[clause]	→P[3sg]
tokma 'get to do'		2	by emb. V		
mu?nima 'forget'		2	n.d.		
kaŋma 'agree, give in'	intrans.	2	n.d.	[S/A/P]	→S

15.1.2 Predicates with variable valency

Some complement-taking verbs assimilate in valency to the embedded verb. If the embedded verb is intransitive, the matrix verb shows intransitive agreement morphology; if the embedded verb is transitive, the matrix verb shows transitive agreement morphology; compare, for instance, intransitive (4a) with transitive (4b). The verbs *yama* 'be able', *mi?ma* 'like doing' and *cokma* 'try' belong to this class. The S/A arguments of embedded and matrix verb have to be coreferential. Meanings like 'I want him to go' cannot be expressed by this construction. These predicates exhibit backward control. The S/A arguments are case-marked

Table 15.4: Argument realization in infinitival complement constructions

VERB	MORPH. VALENCY	ARGUMENTS	CASE OF OVERT A	AGREEMENT EMB. ARG.	AGREEMENT MATR. SLOT
pi?ma 'allow'		3		[S/A]	→P
pha?ma 'help doing'	ditrans.	3	by matrix V		
cimma 'teach'		3			
so?me?ma 'show'		3			

according to the properties of the embedded verb, i.e., nominative with intransitive verbs and ergative with transitive verbs. This indicates that the overtly realized arguments are those of the embedded verb.

The verb *yama* is a modal verb, expressing abilities, as opposed to *tokma*, which expresses the possibility of an event as determined by other circumstances or participants. Example (4a) shows an intransitive complement clause. The respective transitive form *nyaswaŋanna* (supposing "dummy" object inflection of third person singular) would be ungrammatical here. Example (4b) and (4c) show transitive complement clauses. Both arguments trigger agreement in the matrix verb, and case is assigned by the embedded verb (notice the ergative in (4c)). In (4d), a three-argument verb from the double object class is embedded. The person inflection of the matrix verb is analogous to the inflection that is usually found in the embedded verb *so?me?ma* 'show', aligned with the primary object.

(4) a. *ka   nda=ma?niŋ   hiŋ-ma*
         1SG   2SG=without   survive-INF
         n-ya-me-ŋa-n=na.
         NEG-be_able-NPST-1SG-NEG=NMLZ.SG
         'I cannot survive without you.'

    b. *ŋkha   (...)   them-ma*
         those (...)   lift-INF
         n-yas-uks-u-n-ci-ni-n.
         NEG-be_able-PRF[PST]-3.P-NEG-3NSG.P-3PL.A-NEG
         'They could not lift those (stones).'   [37_nrr_07.029]

c.   *na   mamu=ŋa   luŋkhwak   pok-ma*
     this   girl=ERG   stone   wake_up-INF
     n-yas-u-n.
     NEG-be_able[3SG.A]-3.P[PST]-NEG
     'This girl was not able to wake up the stone.'   [37_nrr_07.036]

d.   *ka   nda   a-den   soʔ-meʔ-ma*
     1SG[ERG]   2SG   1SG.POSS-village show-INF
     ya-meʔ-nen=na.
     be_able-NPST-1>2=NMLZ.SG
     ' I can show you my village.'

When *yama* is negated, occasionally an alternative infinitive marker *-sa* is found, as in (5). It is only attested with *yama*.

(5)   *kanciŋ   i=ca   ka-sa   y-yas-a-n-ci-ŋa-n.*
      1DU   what=ADD   say-INF   NEG-be_able-PST-NEG-DU-EXCL-NEG
      'We could not say anything.'   [40_leg_08.027]

Example (6) and (7) illustrate the same properties for the verbs *miʔma* 'want' (literally 'think') and *cokma* 'try' (literally 'do').

(6)   a.   *paŋ=be   ap-ma   mit-a-ma-ŋ=na.*
           house=LOC   come-INF   like-PST-PRF-1SG=NMLZ.SG
           'I want to come home.' (intransitive)   [01_leg_07.096]

      b.   *suman=ŋa   limlim   inca-ma   mit-uks-u.*
           Suman=ERG   sweets   buy-INF   like[3SG.A]-PRF-3.P[PST]
           'Suman wanted to buy sweets.' (transitive)   [01_leg_07.040]

(7)   a.   *siŋ=be   thaŋ-ma=ga   cog-a-ŋ.*
           tree=LOC   climb-INF=GEN   try-PST-1SG
           'I tried to climb the tree.' (intransitive)   [42_leg_10.020]

      b.   *ŋkha   them-ma   n-jog-uks-u-ci.*
           those   lift-INF   3PL.A-try-PRF-3.P[PST]-3NSG.P
           'They tried to lift those (stones).' (transitive)   [37_nrr_07.029]

The agreement pattern with the embedded object may also apply when the agreement-triggering arguments and the embedded verb are not overt, as example (8) from a conversation illustrates.

(8)   *khuʔ-nen?*   –   *khatniŋgo*
      carry-1>2[SBJV]   –   but

n-yas-wa-ŋ-ga-n=na!
NEG-be_able-NPST-1SG.P-2SG.A-NEG=NMLZ.SG
A: 'Shall I carry you?' B: 'But you can't!'

The verb *niŋsaŋ puŋma* 'have enough, lose interest', an experiencer-as-possessor predicate (cf. §9.2) may also alternate in valency. In most cases, it is intransitively inflected, invariably with third person singular inflection (9a). With transitive embedded verbs, however, it may optionally mirror the inflection of the embedded verb (9b).

(9) a. *nda=nuŋ kon-ca-ma   a-niŋsaŋ*
        2SG=COM   walk-V2.EAT-INF 1SG.POSS-[STEM]
        puŋ-a-by-a=na!   *ikhiŋ*
        lose_interest[3SG]-PST-V2.GIVE-PST=NMLZ.SG   how_much
        koʔ-ma=le   *haʔlo!?*
        walk-INF[DEONT]=CTR   EXCLA
        'I have enough of walking with you! How much do we have to walk?!'
    b. *kha   philim=ci (soʔ-ma)   a-niŋsaŋ*
        THOSE film=NSG   (watch-INF) 1SG.POSS-[STEM]
        puŋ-y-uks-u-ŋ-ci-ŋ=ha.
        lose_interest-COMPL-PRF-3.P[PST]-[N]-3NSG.P-1SG.A=NMLZ.NSG
        'I have enough of (watching) those films.'

15.1.3 Invariably transitive predicates

Some complement-taking verbs always show transitive person inflection. Both subject and object of embedded transitive verbs are indexed on the matrix verb. When intransitive verbs are embedded, the embedded S argument triggers transitive subject agreement in the matrix verb, while the object agreement is default third person singular. Verbs belonging to this class are *tokma* 'get to do', *tarokma* 'begin', *sukma* 'aim, intend', *lepnima* 'stop, abandon' and *muʔnima* 'forget'. Except for *tarokma* all verbs may also take nominal complements.

Example (10) illustrates this pattern with the verb *tokma*. It expresses possibilities that are determined by other participants or conditioned by outer circumstances beyond the power and control of the subject (S or A). When three-argument verbs are embedded, the person marking on the matrix verb is analogous to the person marking usually found on the embedded verb (see (10b) from the double object class). The long distance agreement is obligatory, as evidenced by ungrammatical (10c), where the number features of the embedded object and the person inflection of the matrix verb do not match.

(10) a. *nda   nhe   uŋ-ma*
　　　　　2SG   here   come_down-INF
　　　　　n-dokt-wa-ga-n=na.
　　　　　NEG-get-NPST[3.P]-2SG.A-NEG=NMLZ.SG
　　　　　'You will not get the chance to come down here (i.e., we will not let
　　　　　you come down here).'　　　　　　　　　　　　[21_nrr_04.035]

　　　 b. *ka   kamniwak=ci   sandisa   khuʔ-ma*
　　　　　1SG[ERG]   friend=NSG   present   bring-INF
　　　　　tokt-u-ŋ-ci-ŋ=ha.
　　　　　get-3.P[PST]-1SG.A-3NSG.P-1SG.A=NMLZ.NSG
　　　　　'I got the chance to bring my friends presents.'

　　　 c. **ka   muŋ=ci   im-ma   tokt-u-ŋ.*
　　　　　1SG[ERG]   mushroom=NSG   buy-INF   get-3.P-1SG.A
　　　　　Intended: 'I got the chance to buy mushrooms.' (correct: *imma tok-
　　　　　tuŋciŋ*)

Example (11) shows the transitive agreement with the embedded object for the
verb *tarokma* 'begin'. In (11a), the verbal person marking is the only hint given
on the number of the object argument, as the nonsingular marker on the noun
is optional and often omitted, in this case because of the unspecific reference
of the argument *yakpuca*. Example (11b) and (11c) serve to show that *tarokma* is
not restricted to verbs with intentional agents. Case is assigned by the embedded
verb, since the subjects of embedded intransitive verbs are in the nominative and
not in the ergative.

(11) a. *yakpuca   yok-ma   tarokt-a-ma-c-u-ci.*
　　　　　porcupine   search-INF   begin-PST-PRF-DU.A-3.P-3NSG.P
　　　　　'They (dual) began to look for porcupines.'　　　[22_nrr_05.014]

　　　 b. *khap   khap-ma=niŋa=go   chiŋdaŋ   khoŋ-ma,   khap*
　　　　　roof   cover-INF=CTMP=TOP   main_pillar   collapse-INF   roof
　　　　　yoŋ-ma   tarokt-uks-u.
　　　　　shake-INF   begin[3SG.A]-PRF-3.P[PST]
　　　　　'While (Tumhang) made the roof, the pillar began to collapse, the
　　　　　roof began to shake.'　　　　　　　　　　　　[27_nrr_06.031]

　　　 c. *nna   mamu=ga   o-phok   tuk-ma*
　　　　　that   girl=GEN   3SG.POSS-stomach   hurt-INF
　　　　　tarokt-uks-u.
　　　　　begin[3SG.A]-PRF-3.P[PST]
　　　　　'That girl's stomach began to hurt.'　　　　　[37_nrr_07.020]

Another member of this class is the phasal verb *lepnima* 'stop, abandon' (see (12)). The verb consists of two stems: the lexical stem *lept* 'throw' and the marker *ni ~ i* contributing completive semantics. This verb indicates the terminal point of an event, regardless of whether they are activities or states (as in (12a)), or actual or habitual (as (12b) shows). The embedded object triggers object agreement on the matrix verb.

(12)   a.   *a-nabhuk   hup-ma*
            1SG.POSS-nose   be_blocked-INF
            n-lept-i?-wa-n=na.
            NEG-stop[3SG.A]-COMPL-NPST[3.P]-NEG=NMLZ.SG
            'My nose continues to be blocked.'
       b.   *ka   uŋci   cim-ma*
            1SG[ERG]   3NSG   teach-INF
            lept-i-ŋ-ci-ŋ=ha.
            stop-COMPL-C-3NSG.P-1SG.A=NMLZ.NSG
            'I stopped teaching them.'

As with *tarokma* above, the semantics of *lepnima* do not imply conscious decisions and actions, as both sentences in (13) show. Given the etymological relation to the lexical verb *lepma* 'throw', this is an unexpected finding.

(13)   a.   *paŋ   yoŋ-ma   lept-i-uks-u.*
            house   shake-INF   stop[3SG.A]-COMPL-PRF-3.P[PST]
            'The house stopped shaking.'   [27_nrr_06.036]
       b.   *luŋdaŋ   lupluŋ=be   hom-ma   n-lept-i-ci.*
            cave   den=LOC   fit_into-INF   3PL.A-stop-COMPL[PST]-3NSG.P
            'They did not fit into caves and dens any more.'   [27_nrr_06.004]

15.1.4 Three-argument constructions

Complement-taking verbs with assistive or permissive semantics such as *pha?ma* 'help', *pi?ma* 'give' ('allow'), *cimma* 'teach' and *so?me?ma* 'show' follow a pattern where the G argument of the matrix clause has identical reference to the subject of the embedded clause. In other words, the matrix G argument controls the reference of the embedded S or A argument. The patients of teaching, allowing etc. are arguments of the matrix clause; hence, the agreement is not optional. For instance, a form like *so?metuŋna* (1>3) would not be acceptable in (14b). These verbs realize their arguments according to the double object frame, i.e., the nominal G argument triggers object agreement on the verb and the embedded clause has the role of the T argument (14). An example from natural speech is provided in (14c).

(14) a. *im-ma   pim-meʔ-nen=na.*
          sleep-INF   give-NPST-1>2=NMLZ.SG
          'I allow you to sleep.'

      b. *kondarik   ok-ma   soʔmeʔ-meʔ-nen=na.*
          spade   dig-INF   show-NPST-1>2=NMLZ.SG
          'I will show you how to plough.'

      c. *na   yakkha=ga   ceʔyamumma   ghak   heko=ci=ŋa*
          this Yakkha=GEN   speech   all   other=NSG=ERG
          ŋ-khus-het-u,   cek-meʔ-ma
          3PL.A-steal-V2.CARRY.OFF-3.P[PST]   talk-CAUS-INF
          m-bi-n-ci-nin=niŋa,   ...
          3PL.A-give-NEG-3NSG.P-3PL.A=CTMP
          'When this language of the Yakkha people was all taken away by the others, when they did not allow them to speak it ...' [18_nrr_03.006]

All verbs of this class can have either nominal or infinitival complements, as exemplified with *cimma* 'teach' in (15).

(15) a. *kamala=ŋa   ka   yakkha   ceʔya*
          K.=ERG   1SG   Yakkha   language
          cind-a-ŋ=na.
          teach[3SG.A]-PST-1SG.P=NMLZ.SG
          'Kamala taught me the Yakka language.'

      b. *kei-lak-ma   cim-meʔnen=na.*
          drum-dance-INF   teach-NPST-1>2=NMLZ.SG
          'I will teach you to dance the drum dance.'

15.1.5 The intransitively inflected verb *kaŋma* 'agree, give in'

The verb *kaŋma* 'agree, be willing to, give in' (lit.: 'fall') always shows intransitive person inflection, regardless of the valency of the embedded verb. Hence, there is only one agreement slot and (at least) two potential candidates to trigger agreement when transitive verbs are embedded. For this verb, the choice of the agreement triggering argument is determined by pragmatics, not by syntax. It shows agreement with whatever argument of the embedded clause is more salient in the current stretch of discourse (see (16)). This is also the case for the subject-complement construction with the matrix verb *leŋma* 'be all right' (cf.

§15.1.6 below). With certain embedded verbs, agreement with A is pragmatically more common (e.g., with *cama* 'eat'), while with other verbs agreement with P is more common (e.g., with *came?ma* 'feed'). Interestingly, A arguments in the ergative case are not allowed with this complement-taking verb, indicating that the matrix S argument controls the embedded arguments.

This pragmatically conditioned behavior stands in contrast to Chintang and Belhare, where certain complement-taking verbs are restricted to P arguments alone, following a purely syntactic constraint (Bickel & Nichols 2001; Bickel et al. 2010).

(16) a.   *picha   im-ma   ŋ-gaŋ-me-n=na.*
           child   sleep-INF   NEG-agree[3SG]-NPST-NEG=NMLZ.SG
           'The child is not willing to sleep.' (S)

      b.   *lukt-a-khy-a=ŋ,   chu?-ma*
           run[3SG]-PST-V2.GO-PST=SEQ   tie-INF
           ŋ-gaks-a-n=oŋ,   ...
           NEG-agree[3SG]-PST-NEG=SEQ
           'As it (the cow) ran away, as was not willing to be tied, ...' (P)
                                                       [11_nrr_01.011]

      c.   *ka   uŋ   pha?-ma   ŋ-gaks-a-ŋa-n=na.*
           1SG   3SG help-INF   NEG-agree-PST-1SG-NEG=NMLZ.SG
           'I was not willing to help him.' (A)

15.1.6 Subject complement constructions

Two verbs, namely *tama* 'be time to' (lit.: 'come') and *leŋma* 'be allright, be accepted' (lit.: 'become'), take the whole proposition as their sole argument, usually showing third person singular person marking regardless of the referential properties of the embedded arguments, as shown in (17). This type of complement construction is referred to as subject complement construction.

(17) a.   *uŋ   mit-a: haku   eko   paŋ   cok-ma*
           3SG   think[3SG]-PST: now   one   house make-INF
           ta-ya=na.
           come[3SG]-PST=NMLZ.SG
           'He thought: Now the time has come to build a house.'
                                                       [27_nrr_06.006]

      b.   *yun-ma   leŋ-me?=n=em*
           sit_down-INF   be_allright[3SG]-NPST=NMLZ.SG=ALT

> *n-leŋ-me-n=n=em?*
> NEG-be_allright[3SG]-NPST-NEG=NMLZ.SG=ALT
> 'Is it allright to sit down (or is it not alright)?'

c. *liŋkha=ci   honliŋwa   ca-ma*
   a_clan=NSG a_kind_of_fish eat-INF
   n-leŋ-me-n=na.
   NEG-be_allright[3SG]-NPST-NEG=NMLZ.SG
   'The Linkhas are not allowed to eat the Honglingwa fish.'

It is also possible that one embedded argument gets raised and triggers agreement on the matrix verb (compare (18a) and (18b)).

(18) a. *n-dokhumak   im-ma*
          2SG.POSS-alone sleep-INF
          n-leŋ-me-n=na.
          NEG-be_allright[3SG]-NPST-NEG=NMLZ.SG

      b. *n-dokhumak   im-ma*
          2SG.POSS-alone sleep-INF
          n-leŋ-me-ka-n=na.
          NEG-be_allright-NPST-2SG-NEG=NMLZ.SG
          Both: 'You should not sleep alone.'

When transitive verbs are embedded, the choice of which argument to raise is determined by pragmatics, i.e., by the question which argument is pragmatically more salient (19).[6] Thus, transitive embedded clauses are potentially ambiguous, when there is no overt A argument in the ergative (see (19b)). Such ambiguities are resolved by context.

(19) a. *kaniŋ kha   siau=ci   ca-ma*
          1PL   these apple=NSG eat-INF
          n-leŋ-me=ha=ci.
          NEG-be_all_right-NPST=NMLZ.NSG=NSG
          'We are not allowed to eat these apples.' (P)

      b. *ka   mok-ma n-leŋ-meʔ-ŋa-n=na!*
          1SG[ERG/NOM?] beat-INF NEG-be_allright-NPST-1SG=NMLZ.SG
          'It is not allright to beat me!' (P) OR
          'I should not beat (others).' (A)

---

[6] Information structure has not been studied in depth for Yakkha yet. An argument can be raised either when the discourse is about that argument (i.e., the topic), but also when the reference of that argument is singled out against other possible referents (i.e., focus).

The verb *leŋma* does not only occur with infinitival complements. It can be found following non-embedded structures such as converbal clauses (see (20a)), and it is also found with nominal objects (see (20b)), where it basically just means 'be, become'. *leŋma* does not only express social acceptability, but also personal attitudes (see (20c)). The clause providing the context for the expressed attitude is marked with a sequential marker followed by the additive focus particle, so that the clause acquires a concessive reading. The verb *leŋma* in the third person singular nonpast inflection (*leŋmeʔna*) has also developed into a fixed expression 'It's allright'.

(20) a. *ceʔya=ŋa=se*   *ŋ-khas-iʔ-wa-n=na,*
         language=ERG=RESTR   NEG-be_full-1PL-NPST-NEG=NMLZ.SG,

         cama   *men-ja-le*   *n-leŋ-me-n=na.*
         food   NEG-eat-CVB   NEG-be_alright[3SG]-NPST-NEG=NMLZ.SG
         'One will not be satisfied just by talking; there is no way but to eat food.'

     b. *paŋ=be*   *ta-meʔ-ma*   *n-yas-u-ga-n*   *bhoŋ,*
         house=LOC   arrive-CAUS-INF   NEG-be_able-3.P-2SG.A-NEG   COND

         aniŋga=ca   *n-leŋ-me-n,*
         1P.EXCL.POSS=ADD   NEG-be_alright[3SG]-NPST-NEG

         ŋga=ca   *n-leŋ-me-n.*
         2SG.POSS=ADD   NEG-be_alright[3SG]-NPST-NEG
         'If you cannot bring it (the stone) home, it will neither belong to us nor to you.'   [37_nrr_07.013]

     c. *ka*   *sa*   *matniŋ=hoŋ=ca*   *leŋ-meʔ-ŋa=na.*
         1SG   meat   without=SEQ=ADD   be_alright-NPST-1SG=NMLZ.SG
         'I am fine also/even without (eating) meat.'

15.1.7 The Necessitative construction

15.1.7.1 Introduction

Yakkha has an infinitival construction that expresses necessities, either with a deontic or with a dynamic reading. Deontic modality is understood as the expression of a moral obligation of an event, as assessed by the speaker or by someone else, if one reports on someone else's assessments of a situation (following the distinctions made, e.g., in Nuyts 2006: 2 or in Van linden 2012: 12). In dynamic readings, the expressed necessity is not grounded in the attitudes of the speaker, but in the external circumstances of a situation. This construction is henceforth

referred to as the Necessitative Construction, since the deontic/dynamic distinction does not have syntactic consequences.

In most cases, this construction simply consists of an infinitive to which one
of the nominalizing clitics is added (either =*ha* or =*na*, see (21a)).[7] Alternatively,
the infinitive can also be followed by a copular auxiliary.[8] This is found when
the argument is singled out pragmatically, which is tentatively analyzed as focus here (21b). The auxiliary is obligatory in scenarios with first or second person
objects. Although the occurrence of the auxiliary in this construction is conditioned by reference and pragmatics, it exhibits an interesting alignment pattern
that is conditioned by syntactic roles and referential properties of the arguments
(for details cf. below). Both verbs constitute a tightly-knit unit in the Necessitative Construction. Formally, it is thus rather a simple clause consisting of an
infinitive and an auxiliary.

(21) a. *ka   khe?-ma=na.*
          1SG go-INF[DEONT]=NMLZ.SG
      b. *ka   khe?-ma   ŋan.*
          1SG go-INF[DEONT]   COP.1SG
          Both: 'I have to go.'

The following examples provide an overview of the different readings that the
Necessitative Construction may have. The dynamic reading is exemplified in
(22). Here, the conditions for the necessity of the event lie in the circumstances
of the situation: in the fact that people are starving in (22a), and in the fact that
the stone should not get wet in (22b), both from mythical narratives. Deontic
examples are shown in (23). It is straightforward that both utterances express the
attitude of the speakers. What these examples also show is that the infinitives in
this construction can be inflected by the nonsingular marker =*ci* when the object
has nonsingular number (see (23), also mentioned above). In three-argument
constructions of the double-object frame, the G argument triggers =*ci* (23c).

(22) a. *wasik ta-ni   bhoŋ   wasik=phaŋ luŋkhwak*
          rain   come[3SG]-OPT   COND   rain=ABL   stone
          leŋ-ma=na.
          turn_over-INF[DEONT]=NMLZ.NSG
          'In case it rains, one has to turn the stone away from the rain.'
          [37_nrr_07.112]

---

[7] See §13.3.3 for the functions and etymology of these nominalizers.
[8] See §8.7 for the forms of the copula. The third person present affirmative is zero.

b. *yapmi   paŋ-paŋ=be   nak-saŋ   kheʔ-m=ha.*
   people   house-house=LOC   ask-SIM   go-INF[DEONT]=NMLZ.NSG
   'The people have to go from house to house, asking (for food).'

   [14_nrr_02.029]

(23) a. *nna=haŋ=maŋ   kaniŋ=ca   eŋ=ga   pama=ci*
         that=ABL=EMPH   1PL=ADD   1PL.INCL.POSS=GEN   parents=NSG
         pyak   luŋma·   tuk-ma=ha=ci.
         much   liver   pour-INF[DEONT]=NMLZ.NSG=NSG
         'So that is why we too have to love our parents very much.'

         [01_leg_07.086]

   b. *thim-m=ha=ci.*
      scold-INF[DEONT]=NMLZ.NSG=NSG
      'They (the young people) have to be scolded.'

   c. *wa=ci   piʔ-m=ha=ci.*
      chicken=NSG   give-INF[DEONT]=NMLZ.NSG=NSG
      'It has to be given to the chicken.' (G)

It is not uncommon for constructions expressing deontic modality to develop further meanings. A directive speech act is shown in (24a). The directive is somewhat related to the expression of an attitude, with the difference lying not in the semantics, but in the type of speech act (assertion vs. command). At least one example, taken from a narrative, also points towards an evidential usage of the Necessitative Construction (24b). The context of this utterance is that a king named Helihang is said to have set out to search for the lost language of the Yakkha people. Before doing so, he erected a marble stele at the foot of Mount Kumbhakarna, in order to let his people know whether he was still alive. As long as this stele does not topple over, the people shall know that he is still alive, searching for their language. This example provides a bridging context between deontic and epistemic modality, as one can read it in two ways: either the people infer from the stele standing upright that their king is still alive (epistemic modality), or the people know that they are expected to think that he is still alive, as he told them so when he departed on his search for the language (deontic modality).

(24) a. *ŋkha=ci   ham-biʔ-ma=ci,*
         those=NSG   distribute-V2.GIVE-INF[DEONT]=NSG
         ŋ-ga-ya=oŋ,   ...
         3PL-say-PST=SEQ
         'After they said: It has to be distributed among those (who do not have food), ...'

         [14_nrr_02.031]

b. *nna   cen   wai?=na=ŋa   haku=ca   kaniŋ   i*
   that upright be[3SG]=NMLZ.SG=ERG   now=ADD   1PL   what
   mi?=m=ha   baŋniŋ: ...
   think-INF=NMLZ.NSG   about
   'Since that (stele) stands upright, what we have to think even now:
   ...'   [18_nrr_03.031]

The negated forms of this construction, marked by prefix *men-*, express the
necessity for an event not to happen (see (25a) and (25b)). The deontic meaning
has scope over the negation, not the other way around. Negating the necessity of
an event is expressed by a construction involving a Nepali loan *parnu* 'fall/have
to' and the light verb *cokma* 'do' (25c). The negation of the infinitive is formally
different from the negation in the verbal inflection, and identical to the negation
in another uninflected form, the negative converb.

(25) a. *nhaŋ   cautara=ca   men-jok-m=ha=ci,*
          and_then   resting_place=ADD   NEG-make-INF=NMLZ.NSG=NSG
          barpipal=ca   men-lip-m=ha=ci.
          fig_tree=ADD   NEG-plant-INF=NMLZ.NSG=NSG
          'And neither are they allowed to build resting places, nor to plant
          bar pipal trees.'   [11_nrr_01.017]
      b. *chubuk=ka   caleppa=chen   isa=ŋa=ca   he?niŋ=ca*
          ashes=GEN   bread=TOP   who=ERG=ADD   when=ADD
          men-ja-ma=na.
          NEG-eat-INF[DEONT]=NMLZ.SG
          'No one should ever have to eat the bread made of ashes.'
                                                          [40_leg_08.082]
      c. *iha=ca   im-ma   por-a   n-joŋ-me-ŋa-n.*
          what=ADD   buy-INF   have_to-NATIV   NEG-do-NPST-1SG-NEG
          'I do not have to buy anything.'   [28_cvs_04.187]

15.1.7.2 Alignment patterns

After the basic morphological and semantic properties have been introduced, let
us now turn to the argument realization in this construction. I will show how the
nominalizing clitics attaching to the infinitive are aligned and how the copular
auxiliary is aligned.

Table 15.5 shows the distribution of the two constructions over participant
scenarios. The default option in my Yakkha corpus is the construction without

Table 15.5: Two options of the Necessitative Construction

A>P	1	2	3
1	–	INF+COP	INF+COP or INF
2	INF+COP	–	INF+COP or INF
3-ERG	INF+COP	INF+COP	INF

the auxiliary.[9] In scenarios with third person acting on third, it is the only option. In scenarios with first or second person objects, however, only the construction with the auxiliary is acceptable.

Table 15.6 shows the suppletive inflectional paradigm of the copula (present, affirmative). The forms resemble the agreement suffixes in the verbal inflection, so that I assume that there was a phonologically light stem in a earlier stage that got lost over time.[10] In the past paradigms, there is a stem *sa*, and the person inflection is regular (see §8.7), but in the present forms the stem is zero. This copula does not have infinitival forms. An equational copula as such does not belong to the general morphological profile of Kiranti languages (Bickel 1999c: 276). What is crucial for the following discussion of the data is that the copula has only one agreement slot.

Table 15.6: Inflection of the copular auxiliary (present indicative, affirmative)

	1.EXCL	1.INCL	2
SG	*ŋan*		*gan*
DU	*nciŋan*	*ncin*	*ncigan*
PL	*siŋan*	*sin*	*sigan*

---

[9] As for the auxiliary, elicited paradigms from different speakers on various occasions and plenty examples from unrecorded spontaneous discourse exist to illustrate its alignment.

[10] Related person suffixes in Yakkha are *-ŋ(a)* for first person (exclusive), *-ka* ~ *-ga* for second person, and *-ci* for the dual. The initial /s/ of the plural forms and the dual forms starting in *nci* cannot be related to the agreement morphology of Yakkha. Limbu though, the eastern neighbour of Yakkha, has a 3nsg object agreement marker *-si* (van Driem 1987: 76).

As for the agreement of the auxiliary, with intransitive verbs it simply agrees with the embedded S argument, as shown in example (26a) below. If transitive verbs are embedded, the agreement exhibits a combination of hierarchical[11] and ergative alignment,[12] as shown schematically in Table 15.7. Since there are no forms for the third person, non-local scenarios (3>3) are always marked just by the infinitive and the nominalizers (=na or =ha).

Table 15.7: Alignment in the Neccessitative Construction

A>P	1/2	3
1/2	P	A
3- ERG	P	-

In mixed scenarios (either 3>SAP or SAP>3) the speech-act participant rules out third person (i.e., hierarchical agreement; compare (26b) with (26c) and (26d)).

(26) a. *nda ap-ma   gan.*
         2SG go-INF[DEONT] COP.2SG
         'You have to come.'

     b. *ka uŋci soʔ-ma   ŋan.*
         1SG 3NSG watch-INF[DEONT] COP.1SG
         'I have to watch them.' (SAP>3: A)

     c. *uŋ=ŋa nda soʔ-ma   gan.*
         3S=ERG 2SG watch-INF[DEONT] COP.2SG
         'He has to watch you.' (3>SAP: P)

     d. *uŋ=ŋa ka soʔ-ma   ŋan.*
         3S=ERG 1SG watch-INF[DEONT] COP.1SG
         'He has to watch me.' (3>SAP: P)

In local scenarios (SAP>SAP), the copula always agrees with the P argument, as illustrated by (27). This is a rigid syntactic constraint; the agreement is not ma-

---

[11] Hierarchical alignment is the 'morphological and syntactic treatment of arguments according to their relative ranking on the referential (...) hierarchies' (Siewierska 1998: 10). With reference to agreement, this means that 'access to inflectional slots for subject and/or object is based on person, number, and/or animacy rather than (or no less than) on syntactic relations' (Nichols 1992: 66).

[12] Ergative alignment is given when S and P arguments are treated alike and differently from A arguments.

nipulable by changes in the information structure. There is no context in which a clause like (27a) could mean 'you have to watch me'. Comparing local scenarios to intransitive verbs, we can see that S and P are treated alike and differently from A arguments. Hence, this is a case of ergative alignment. Ergativity in complement constructions has also been found in the neighboring languages Belhare (Bickel 2004a; Bickel & Nichols 2001) and Chintang (Bickel et al. 2010). Still, it is crosslinguistically pretty quirky in complement constructions, or at least it is not documented well enough, which has even led linguists like Dixon (1994: 135) to the conclusion that complement clauses are universally accusatively aligned.

(27) a. *ka   nda   soʔ-ma   gan.*
          1SG   2SG   watch-INF[DEONT]   COP.2SG
          'I have to watch you.' (SAP>SAP: P)
      b. *nda   ka   soʔ-ma   ŋan.*
          2SG   1SG   watch-INF[DEONT]   COP.1SG
          'You have to watch me.' (SAP>SAP: P)

Table 15.8 summarizes the copula forms in the Necessitative Construction. It shows the hierarchical alignment according to an SAP>3 hierarchy, and in local (SAP>SAP) scenarios, it shows the ergative alignment. Some alternations between speakers should be mentioned. For one speaker (out of four) not the whole paradigm was possible. The brackets indicate those forms that were rejected and replaced by the construction without the copula. A possible explanation for the rejection of these forms could be a face-preserving strategy. Explicit reference to a second person agent or a first person patient is avoided in necessitative contexts. Scenarios with a second person A and with a first person P are socially sensitive (e.g., 'You have to [give/serve/help] us.'), and therefore speakers prefer to leave reference to any participant unexpressed. An exception to this strategy are those scenarios where both actants have singular number and are thus clearly identifiable anyway. The avoidance of explicit reference to first person nonsingular patients as a face-preserving strategy is not surprising at all in light of the verbal inflectional paradigms of Yakkha (cf. §11.3.1.3 for details and a possible historical scenario). However, avoiding reference to a second person agent is innovative and limited to this construction.

The following examples illustrate the alignment in verbs of the double object class by means of *piʔma* 'give', which is usually aligned with the primary object (treating G identically to the P of monotransitive verbs). This is also reflected in the Necessitative Construction. In mixed scenarios it is always the speech-act participant that triggers agreement in the auxiliary according to a referential

Table 15.8: Complete paradigm of the auxiliary in the Necessitative Construction

A>P/G	1SG	1DU	1PL	2SG	2DU	2PL	3
1SG							ŋan
1DU.EX				gan	ncigan	sigan	nciŋan
1PL.EX							siŋan
1DU.IN							ncin
1PL.IN							sin
8-8 2SG	ŋan						(gan)
2DU	(ŋan)	(nciŋan)	(siŋan)				(ncigan)
2PL	(ŋan)						(sigan)
3SG	ŋan	(nciŋan/	(siŋan/	gan	ncigan	sigan	
3NSG	(ŋan)	ncin)	sin)				

hierarchy [SAP>3], as examples (28a) and (28b) show. In local scenarios it is the G argument that triggers the agreement, as examples (28c) and (28d) illustrate. Thus, we have again a combination of reference-based and role-based alignment.

(28) a. uŋ=ŋa   ka   cuwa piʔ-ma   ŋan.
          3NSG=ERG 1SG beer give-INF[DEONT] COP.1SG
          'He has to give me beer.' (3>SAP: G)

      b. ka   uŋci cuwa piʔ-ma   ŋan.
          1SG[ERG] 3NSG beer give-INF[DEONT] COP.1SG
          'I have to give them beer.' (SAP>3: A)

      c. ka   njiŋda cuwa piʔ-ma   cigan.
          1SG[ERG] 2DU   beer give-INF[DEONT] COP.2DU
          'I have to give you beer.' (SAP>SAP: G)

      d. nda   ka   cuwa piʔ-ma   ŋan.
          2SG[ERG] 1SG beer give-INF[DEONT] COP.1SG
          'You have to give me beer.' (SAP>SAP: G)

If the reasoning behind hierarchical alignment systems is transferred to the objects of three-argument verbs, as e.g., suggested in Haspelmath (2004b), Malchukov, Haspelmath & Comrie (2010a), and Siewierska (2003), one should also find hierarchical alignment of person marking with respect to the T and the G of three-argument verbs. The expected, typical ditransitive scenario contains a referentially high G argument and a referentially low T argument. The interesting question is what happens when this relation is reversed, i.e., when the T argument is higher on a referential hierarchy than the G argument. This is illustrated by the verb *soʔmeʔma* 'show' (see (29)). If T is a speech-act participant and G is a third person, the auxiliary indexes T instead of G, and G shows a strong tendency to receive locative case marking. The locative case marking is expectable, as "the construction which is more marked in terms of the direction of information flow should also be more marked formally" (Comrie 1989: 128).

(29) *ka*   *nda*   *appa-ama=be*   *soʔmeʔ-ma* *gan.*
      1SG[ERG]   2SG[NOM]   mother-father=LOC   show-INF   COP.2SG
      'I have to show you to my parents.' (T[SAP]→G[3])

The infinitival form of the lexical verb in the Necessitative Construction usually hosts one of the nominalizing clitics. Their function is best described as focus or lending authority to the assertion (cf. §13.3.3). Let us now turn to their alignment.

There are two different alignment patterns, depending on whether we are dealing with the construction with or without the auxiliary. The construction without the auxiliary is found only when the P argument has third person reference, because the auxiliary is obligatory in scenarios with first or second person P arguments. The alignment here is clearly ergative, as shown in Table 15.9 and in example (30). The choice of =*na* vs. =*ha* is conditioned by the number of the S argument in intransitive environments (for all persons) and by the number of the (third person) P argument in transitive environments.

(30) a. *kaniŋ* *kheʔ-m=ha,*   *nhaŋa*   *hum-se*
         1PL   go-INF[DEONT]=NMLZ.NSG   and_then   bury-SUP
         kheʔ-ma=na.
         carry_off-INF[DEONT]=NMLZ.SG
         'We have to go, and we have to carry him off to bury him.' (P=sg)
                                                                        [29_cvs_05.049]

      b. *na*   *khibum*   *imin*   *kaŋ-nhaŋ-ma=na,*   ...
         this   cotton_ball   how   drop-V2.SEND-INF=NMLZ.SG
         'As for how this cotton ball has to be dropped, ...' (P=sg)
                                                                        [22_nrr_05.092]

c. *kha?niŋgo, kaniŋ=go   cekci=be   ni?-m=ha.*
    but   1PL[ERG]=TOP iron=LOC fry-INF[DEONT]=NMLZ.NSG
    'But we have to fry (bread) in something made of iron.' (P=nsg/mass)
    [29_cvs_05.075]

Table 15.9: Alignment of the nominalizers, construction without auxiliary

A>P(=S)	3SG	3NSG
1	=na	=ha
2	=na	=ha
3	=na	=ha

The picture is slightly more complex in the construction with the auxiliary. It is summarized in Table 15.10. When the lexical verb is intransitive, first and second person subjects always trigger =ha (see also (31)). In transitive verbs, first and second person P arguments also trigger =ha, again resulting in ergative alignment, since speech-act participant S and P arguments are treated identically, but differently from A arguments.

(31) *ka   hoŋkoŋ   khe?-m=ha   ŋan.*
      1SG Hong_Kong go-INF[DEONT]=NMLZ.NSG COP.1SG
      'I have to go to Hong Kong.'

Table 15.10: Alignment of the nominalizers, construction with auxiliary

A>P/G	1	2	3SG	3NSG	S
1sg			=na		=ha
1NSG.EXCL		=ha	=ha		=ha
1NSG.INCL					=ha
2SG			=na		=ha
2NSG	=ha		=ha		=ha
3SG	=ha	=ha	=na		=na
3NSG				=ha	=ha

The singular clitic =*na* is only found when a singular A acts on a third person singular P argument. As soon as one participant, no matter which one, has nonsingular reference, =*ha* attaches to the infinitive, illustrated here with 1SG.A acting on 3.SG/NSGP in (32) and with 1PL.A acting on 3.SG/NSGP in (33). This is a hierarchical pattern, according to a number hierarchy [nsg>sg].

(32) a. *ka*   *na*   *sambakhi*   *ca-ma=na*   *ŋan.*
          1SG[ERG]   this   potato   eat-INF=NMLZ.SG   COP.1SG
          'I have to eat this potato.'

      b. *ka*   *kha*   *sambakhi(=ci)*   *ca-m=ha*   *ŋan.*
          1SG[ERG]   these   potato=NSG   eat-INF=NMLZ.NSG   COP.1SG
          'I have to eat these potatoes.'

(33) a. *kaniŋ*   *na*   *phʌrsi*   *ca-m=ha*   *siŋan.*
          1PL[ERG]   this   pumpkin   eat-INF=NMLZ.NSG   COP.1PL.EXCL
          'We have to eat this pumpkin.'

      b. *kaniŋ*   *kha*   *sambakhi(=ci)*   *ca-m=ha*
          1PL[ERG]   these   potato=NSG   eat-INF=NMLZ.NSG
          siŋan.
          COP.1PL.EXCL
          'We have to eat these potatoes.'

15.1.7.3 Comparative notes and discussion

The alignment in the Necessitative Construction is centered around two factors: person (SAP) and syntactic role (P), and the question of which selection principle applies is conditioned by different scenarios: speech-act participant reference is the relevant factor in mixed scenarios, and P is the relevant factor in local scenarios.

The person marking in regular verbs supports this reasoning, as the alignment is more consistent across the columns (representing P) than across the rows (representing A) in the paradigm (cf. Schackow 2012a). Speech-act participant markers are aligned differently from the third person markers. SAP markers show ergative or hierarchical alignment, while the third person is largely aligned accusatively. As I have shown above, the alignment of the nominalizing clitics =*na* and =*ha* is sensitive to participant scenarios. The distribution of tense-marking allomorphs is scenario-based too (cf. §8.4). The distinction between speech-act participants and third persons figures as a factor in other constructions: the ergative case is not overtly marked on first and second person pronouns, and the verbal inflection has person markers that have underspecified speech-act participant reference, e.g., -*m* (for first and second person plural A arguments), -*i* (for first and second person plural S and P arguments). Hence, although the alignment of the Necessitative Construction is unique, the selection principles leading to this pattern can also be found in other domains of the grammar of Yakkha. Alignment splits serve as scenario classifiers in Yakkha (cf. also Bickel 1992 on Belhare).[13]

Hierarchical patterns are a common feature in other Tibeto-Burman languages that show person marking, too, e.g., in Rawang, Kham and in many of the Kiranti languages (cf. DeLancey 1989b: 317, LaPolla 1992: 311, LaPolla 2003: 30, LaPolla 2007, Ebert 1987: 473, DeLancey 2011b: 1, Watters 2002: 398). The particular pattern that was found in Yakkha has been attested, with varying degrees of transparency, in Tibeto-Burman languages of various geographic origins and sub-branches, reaching back to Tangut sources as early as the 12th century (Kepping 1975; 1994). Watters (2002), who compared the person marking system of the Kham dialects with person marking in other Tibeto-Burman languages, found hierarchical patterns in Gyarong, Nocte and Western Kiranti languages with SAP outranking third person and, crucially, with a preference for the object in conflicting scenarios (Nagano 1984, cited in Watters 2002: 388). The alignment in the Yakkha Necessitative Construction also resembles Proto-Tibeto-Burman agreement as reconstructed in DeLancey (1989b), who characterizes the system as "a split ergative agreement pattern in which agreement is always with a 1st or 2nd person argument in preference to 3rd person, regardless of which is subject or object." (DeLancey 1989b: 317).[14]

A potentially interesting side note in this respect is that the same alignment split (ergative and hierarchical, conditioned by a distinction of speech-act participant vs. third person) is also found in the verbal agreement of the Caucasian

---

[13] In search for a Yakkha-internal explanation of the pattern at hand it is tempting to attribute the hierarchical alignment to the defective paradigm of the copula: the absence of third person forms provides an empty slot that is filled by the material marking a speech-act participant. The absence of third person forms cannot, however, explain the entire picture. Firstly, it does not account for the fact that the copula is obligatory when the object is a speech-act participant, but not when the subject is a speech-act participant. Secondly, there are also traces of hierarchical alignment in the verbal paradigm, although there are markers for the third person available. Scenarios of a 3.A>2.P type, for instance, largely neglect reference to the third person A argument (cf. §8.2). Finally, it cannot explain the ergative alignment in local scenarios, i.e., why it is always the object that is indexed on the verb in these scenarios.

[14] As noted earlier, Tibeto-Burman reconstruction and subgrouping are far from being settled, see, e.g., Thurgood (1984); DeLancey (1989b; 2010; 2011b); LaPolla (1992; 2012); Jacques (2012a). Under the assumption that a sub-branch *Rung* exists (see the references from Thurgood and LaPolla), those Tibeto-Burman languages showing agreement would be related on a lower level than Proto-Tibeto-Burman.

(Nakh-Daghestanian) language Dargwa (Zúñiga 2007: 208). The pattern is neither a one-off case, nor is it restricted to Tibeto-Burman. Of course, more cross-linguistic data would be necessary to be able to corroborate any functional-typological explanation for this alignment split. Indeed, it would be exciting to discover that this pattern is more widespread than assumed at this stage. According to Serdobolskaya (2009), referential properties also play a role in raising constructions in some Uralic, Turkic and Mongolic languages languages, and she tentatively suggests this to be an areal feature. More data on other languages could help to answer the question if this feature really has an areal distribution.

On a final note, the auxiliary in the Necessitative Construction is often replaced by the third person form of the Nepali auxiliary *pʌrnu* 'fall/have to', as shown in (34). In this calqued structure, the peculiar alignment pattern of the Necessitative Construction gets lost.

(34) *kʌhile-kʌhile   mamu=ŋa=ca   taʔ-ma=ci   pʌrchʌ.*
      sometimes   girl=ERG=ADD   bring-INF=NSG   HAS_TO
      'Sometimes, the girl has to bring them (further wives), too.'
      [06_cvs_01.044]

15.2 Inflected complement clauses

Inflected complement clauses are found with predicates of cognition like *nima* 'see, get to know', *khemma* 'hear', *miʔma* 'think, hope, consider, like' (see §15.2.1) and utterance predicates such as *luʔma* 'tell, say', *yokmepma* 'tell (about)', *chimma* 'ask' (see §15.2.2). Table 15.1 (on page 465) provides the list of all complement-taking predicates that embed clauses with inflected verbs in Yakkha.

Complement clauses in Yakkha distinguish direct speech and indirect speech. In case of indirect speech, the clauses contain nominalized inflected verbs. In case of direct speech, the verbs are able to express the full range of verbal categories found in independent clauses. Some types of complement clauses are marked by the conjunction *bhoŋ* that also functions as a marker of conditional clauses, direct speech and purpose clauses. The latter seem to have developed out of clauses containing direct speech (see §14.9). Some complement-taking verbs are polysemous, their semantics depending on whether they occur with an infinitival or with an inflected complement. The verb *miʔma*, for instance, means 'like (doing)' with infinitival complements but 'think, hope, consider' with inflected complements. The verb *nima* means 'know (how to do)' with infinitival complements, but 'see, get to know' with inflected complements. Some nouns may embed propositions as well, by means of the complementizer *baŋna/baŋha* (cf. §15.2.3).

15.2.1 Predicates of cognition and experience

The complement-taking predicates of cognition can be further classified into predicates of knowledge, perception, experience and propositional attitude. The most common predicate embedding inflected complements is *nima* 'to see or get to know something', exemplified in (35). The embedded verb is mostly in one of the indicative past tenses and has to carry one of the nominalizers *=na* or *=ha* (cf. Chapter 13). The embedded subject obligatorily triggers agreement both on the embedded verb and on the main verb. On the main verb, it triggers object marking (see (35b)). This can be explained from a semantic perspective: perceiving that a person is doing something implies perceiving that person. The argument realization in the complement clause is identical to that of independent clauses. The subject of the embedded clause receives ergative case marking when the embedded verb is transitive, although the A argument simultaneously triggers object agreement on the matrix verb.

The perspective in complement clauses is that of the speaker, and the zero point is the speech situation; hence the embedded clause contains indirect speech or indirect questions.

(35) a. *khy-a-ma=hoŋ*   *so-ks-u=niŋa*   *eko*   *yapmi*
          go-PST-PRF=SEQ   watch-PRF-3.P[PST]=CTMP   one   person
          bhirik=pe   *het-u=na*   *nis-uks-u.*
          cliff=LOC   get_stuck-3.P[PST]=NMLZ.SG   see-PRF-3.P[PST]
          'He went there, and when he looked, he saw a man caught in a cliff.'
          [01_leg_07.319]

      b. *ka*   *uŋci=ŋa*   *toŋba*
          1SG[ERG]   3NSG=ERG   beer
          ŋ-uŋ-ma-si-a=ha=ci
          3PL-drink-INF-IPFV-PST=NMLZ.NSG=NSG
          nis-u-ŋ-ci-ŋ=ha.
          see-3.P[PST]-1SG.A-3NSG.P-1SG.A=NMLZ.NSG
          'I saw that they were drinking beer.'

Other verbs of this kind are *miʔma* 'think, consider, hope' and the propositional attitude verb *eʔma* 'perceive, have impression', shown in (36) and (37a) respectively. Complement clauses embedded to *eʔma* can also be marked by the

equative case *loʔa* 'like' (see (37b)). This marker is also used in equative constructions, where it subcategorizes nouns (NPs) and adjectives. Again, one can see
that the embedded subject is cross-referenced by subject marking on the embedded verb and by object marking on the main verb. The form **etuŋna* (assuming
third person singular "dummy" object agreement) would be ungrammatical in
(37b) and (37c).

(36) a. *nda   cama   ca-ya-ga=na   mi-nuŋ-nen=na.*
     2SG[ERG] rice   eat-PST-2=NMLZ.SG think-PRF-1>2=NMLZ.SG
     'I have thought you ate the rice.'

    b. *ŋkhatniŋ=ŋa   ka=ca   sy-a=na   mit-a.*
     that_time=INS 1SG=ADD die[3SG]-PST=NMLZ.SG think-IMP[1.P]
     'At that time, consider me dead (think that I am dead), too.'
                                           [18_nrr_03.018]

(37) a. *mi   mi=na   et-u-ŋ=na,*
     fire small=NMLZ.SG perceive-3.P[PST]-1SG.A=NMLZ.SG,
     khatniŋgo   ma   leks-a-bhoks-a=na.
     but   big   become[3SG]-PST-V2.SPLIT-PST=NMLZ.SG
     'It seemed to me that the fire was small, but suddenly it flamed up.'

    b. *haŋ=ha   c wu=g=hu   loʔa*
     be_spicy=NMLZ.NC eat-NPST-2.A[3.P]=NMLZ.NC like
     eʔ-nen=na.
     perceive[PST]-1>2=NMLZ.SG
     'It seems to me that you eat spicy things.' OR 'You seem to me like
     someone who eats spicy things.'

    c. *pyak   ŋ-waiʔ=ya   loʔa*
     many 3SG-exist=NMLZ.NSG like
     et-u-ŋ-ci-ŋ=ha,   khatniŋgo
     perceive-3.P[PST]-1SG.A-3NSG.P-1SG.A=NMLZ.NSG but
     m-man=ha=ci!
     NEG-COP[NEG]=NMLZ.NSG=NSG
     'It seemed to me that there were many, but there were none!'

When the embedded clause has hypothetical or irrealis status, it is in the optative, and the main verb *miʔma* 'think' acquires the reading 'hope'.

(38) *hakt-a-ŋ-ga-ni   bhoŋ   mit-a-masa-ŋ=na.*
    send-SBJV-1SG.P-2-OPT COMP think-PST-PST.PRF-1SG=NMLZ.SG
    'I had hoped that you would send me something.'

Another use of *bhoŋ* is marking complements of experiential verbs like *con-si?ma* 'be happy' and verbs like *niŋwa hupma* 'make a plan together, decide collectively'. In such sentences, the embedded clause contains direct speech, with the full range of inflectional categories on the embedded verb. The speaker shifts the perspective to the subject of the embedded clause (see, e.g., first person singular A in (39a), hortative mood in (39b)), interrogative mood (39c)). The literal translation of (39a) would be 'He rejoiced: I saved another man's life!'.

(39) a. *lamdikpa cahi yapmi hiŋ-u-ŋ=na*   *bhoŋ*
    traveller TOP person save[PST]-3.P-1SG.A=NMLZ.SG COMP
    cond-a-sy-a-ma.
    be_happy[3SG]-PST-MDDL-PST-PRF
    'The traveller was happy that he saved another person's life.'
                      [01_leg_07.331]

   b. *yaŋchalumba a-phu=nuŋ*   *khi khon-se*
    third-born_boy 1SG.POSS-elder_brother=COM yam dig-SUP
    puŋda=be khe-ci   bhoŋ niŋwa
    jungle=LOC go-DU[SBJV] COMP mind
    hupt-a-ŋ-c-u-ŋ.
    unite-PST-EXCL-DU-3.P-EXCL
    'So my third-born brother and I decided to go to the jungle to dig yams.'   [40_leg_08.006]

   c. *haku imin nak-ma=ci*   *bhoŋ, uŋci-niŋwa*
    now how ask-INF[DEONT]=NSG COMP 3NSG.POSS-mind
    ŋ-hupt-u.
    3PL.A-unite-3.P[PST]
    'They decided about how to ask them (for food).'   [14_nrr_02.14]

Since some complement-taking predicates are also able to take nominal objects, they yield a potential ambiguity of interpretations as inflected complement clauses or circumnominal relative clauses (see also Bickel (1999c: 272), Noonan 2007: 120, 143): the two propositions 'I hear the one who is singing' and 'I hear that someone is singing' refer to exactly the same situation in the world. The sentences in example (40) are potentially ambiguous, and there is no structural difference that could resolve the ambiguity (see also §13.3.1.2). It seems that internally headed relative clauses have developed out of complements of perception verbs and were then extended analogically to other kinds of verbs which rule out a complement reading, such as *tumma* 'find', allowing only nominal arguments.

(40) a.   *nna ten=be=ha=nuŋ*   *waleŋ*
           that village=LOC=NMLZ.NSG=COM   Waleng
           ten=be=ha   *kholoŋba=ci chem-khusa uŋ-khusa*
           village=LOC=NMLZ.NSG guests=NSG tease-RECIP pull-RECIP
           n-ja-ya   *nis-u-ŋ-ci-ŋ.*
           3PL-EAT.AUX-PST.NMLZ.NSG see[PST]-3.P-1SG.A-3NSG.P-1SG.A
           'I saw the people of the village and the guests teasing and pulling
           each other (jokingly in a dance).' OR
           'I saw how the people of the village and the guests were teasing and
           pulling each other (jokingly in a dance).'   [41_leg_09.017]

     b.   *ka haŋcaŋcaŋ chu-ya-ŋ=na*   *nis-a-ma.*
           1SG dangling   hang-PST-1SG=NMLZ.SG see-PST-PRF[3A;1.P]
           'They saw me dangling (there).' OR
           'They saw how I dangled there.'   [42_leg_10.040]

15.2.2 Utterance predicates

Utterance predicates distinguish between predocates that embed indirect speech (as already introduced in the predicates of cognition) and those that embed direct speech. Some verbs may occur with both indirect speech and direct speech, for instance *miʔma* 'think'. Predicates embedding indirect speech or indirect questions are, for instance, *yokmeʔma* 'tell (about)' and *khemmeʔma* 'tell, make hear' (see (41)), while direct speech is embedded mainly by the predicates *kama* 'say, call' and *luʔma* 'tell'.

    The complement clauses of both types of utterance predicates can be marked by *bhoŋ*, the complementizer that is also found as a quotative marker and as conjunction on purpose clauses and conditional clauses.[15] This complementizer is frequently found in clauses containing indirect speech and indirect questions (see (41)), and rarely on clauses containing direct speech (see (42e)).

(41) a.   *ak=ka*   *kamniwak=ci, ka isa om, isa om*
           1SG.POSS=GEN friend=NSG   1SG who COP who COP
           bhoŋ uŋci=ŋa=ca   *n-yokme-me-ka-nin.*
           COMP 3NSG=ERG=ADD   NEG-tell_about-NPST-2-PL.NEG
           'My friends, they will also not tell you who I am.'   [14_nrr_02.25]

     b.   *philm=be=cen haku i=ya*   *i=ya*
           film=LOC=TOP now what=NMLZ.NC what=NMLZ.NC

---

[15] These uses of *bhoŋ* are parallel to the functional distribution of the Nepali conjunction *bhʌne*.

cok-ma-sy-a=na   *bhoŋ*
do-INF-AUX.PROG[3SG]-PST=NMLZ.SG   COMP
khem-meʔ-meʔ-nen=ba,   *ani.*
hear-CAUS-NPST-1>2=EMPH   aunt
'I will tell you now what he was doing in the film, auntie.'

[34_pea_04.007]

c.   *nna*   *cuʔlumphi* *isa=ŋa*   *thukt-u=na*   *bhoŋ*
      that   stele   who=ERG   erect-3.P[PST]=NMLZ.SG COMP
    pyak *pyak* *yapmi=ci=nuŋ*   *ceʔya*
     many   many   people=NSG=COM   matter
    leks-a=ha.
    become[3SG]-PST=NMLZ.NC
    'Many people have discussed who erected that stele.'

[18_nrr_03.002–3]

Direct speech (quotes) may show the full range of tense, aspect and modal marking, and also any type of illocutionary force marking, clause-final exclamative particles and the like. The person marking on the embedded verb follows the perspective of the embedded subject, not the perspective of the speaker. Direct speech is generally embedded without any complementizer, as shown in the following examples, where *kama* 'say', *luʔma* 'tell', *miʔma* 'think' and *chimma* 'ask' function as matrix verbs (see (42)), and note that (42e) presents an exceptional case without *bhoŋ*).

(42)   a. *khamba=ŋa* *a-tokhumak*   *yep-ma*
        pillar=ERG   1SG.POSS-alone   stand-INF
        n-ya-me-ŋa-n=na   *ka-saŋ*
        NEG-be_able-NPST-1SG-NEG=NMLZ.SG   say-SIM
        por-a-khy-a=na.
        fall[3SG]-PST-V2.GO-PST=NMLZ.SG
        'I cannot stand alone, said the pillar and fell down.'   [27_nrr_06.17]

   b. *heko=ha*   *nwak=ci=ŋa*   *haku* *nda* *nhe*
       other=NMLZ.NSG bird=NSG=ERG   now   2SG here
       uŋ-ma   *n-dokt-wa-ga-n=na*
       come_down-INF   NEG-get_to_do-NPST-2.A[3.P]-NEG=NMLZ.SG
       n-lu-ks-u.
       3PL.A-tell-PRF-3.P[PST]
       'The other birds told him: Now you will not get the chance to come down here any more.'   [21_nrr_04.035]

c. *hetne=le   ta-ʔi=ya   m-mit-a-ma=hoŋ   uŋci*
where=CTR   come-1PL=NMLZ.NSG   3PL-think-PST-PRF=SEQ   3NSG
m-maks-a-by-a-ma=ca.
3PL-be_surprised-PST-V2.GIVE-PST-PRF=ADD
'They also wondered: Where on earth did we arrive?' [22_nrr_05.30]

d. *hetniŋ-hetniŋ   om=em   men=em*
sometimes   yes=ALT   no=ALT
mit-wa-m=ha.
think-NPST[3.P]-1PL.A=NMLZ.NC
'Sometimes we think: Is it (true) or not?'

e. *nani,   i=na   yubak?,   n-chimd-uks-u.*
child   what=NMLZ.SG   property   3PL.A-ask-PRF-3.P[PST]
'Child, what thing (do you want)?, they asked her.'   [37_nrr_07.006]

f. *imin   kaniŋ   cin-a   cok-meʔ-nen-in?   bhoŋ*
how   1PL   recognize-NATIV   do-NPST-1>2-2PL   QUOT
elaba=ci=ŋa   n-lu-ks-u-ci.
a_clan=NSG=ERG   3PL.A-tell-PRF-3.P[PST]-3NSG.P
'How will we recognize you?, asked the Elabas (people of Elaba clan).'
[39_nrr_08.11]

In a few cases, the reportative particle *=bu* is also found on embedded speech
(see (43a) for direct speech, and (43b) which could be either direct or indirect
speech).

(43)   a. *por-a   cog-a=bu   lu-ya-n-u-m.*
study-NATIV   do-IMP=REP   tell-IMP-PL-3.P-2.A
'Tell him to study.' ('Tell him: study!')   [01_leg_07.094]

b. *kham=be=ca   n-yuŋ-me-n,   siŋ=be=ca*
earth=LOC=ADD   NEG-live[3SG]-NPST-NEG   tree=LOC=ADD
man,   hiʔwa=ga   hiʔwa   wait=na=bu
NEG.COP   air=GEN   air   exist[NPST;3]=NMLZ.SG=REP
ŋ-ga-me.
3PL-say-NPST
'It is neither living on the ground nor in the trees, it just lives in the
air, they say.'   [21_nrr_04.052]

Example (44) serves to illustrate that question words remain in situ in direct
speech; they are not extracted. Semantically, the question word belongs to the
embedded clause because it is an argument of *khuʔma* 'bring'. It is, however, the
focus of the question and hence appears as question word. The particle *=le* serves

as contrastive focus marker, and it emphasizes the cluelessness of the speaker in questions and his eagerness to get to know the answer.

(44) *nda   ka   ina=le   khut-a-ŋ   ly-a-ŋ-ga=na?*
      2SG[ERG] 1SG   what=CTR   bring-IMP-1SG   tell-PST-1SG.P-2.A=NMLZ.SG
      'What did you tell me to bring?'

15.2.3 Complement-taking nouns

Nouns can embed finite complement clauses via the use of the complementizers *baŋna* (if the head noun has singular number) and *baŋha* (if the head noun has nonsingular number or non-countable reference).

Example (45a) shows how *baŋna* links propositions to a head noun from the semantic domain of saying. In (45b) the head noun is from the experiential domain. As (45c) illustrates, the complement clause can be of considerable length and complexity. Narratives often conclude with a structure as shown in (45d).

(45) a. *na   chuʔlumphi   helihaŋ=ŋa   thukt-u=na*
          this stele   Helihang=ERG   erect-3.P[PST]=NMLZ.SG
          baŋna   ceʔya
          COMP   matter
          'the matter about how/when this stele was erected by Helihang'
                                                              [18_nrr_03.004]
      b. *a-ma=ŋa   moŋ-meʔ=ha   baŋna*
          1SG.POSS-mother=ERG   beat-NPST[1.P]=NMLZ.NSG   COMP
          kisiʔma=ŋa
          fear=ERG
          'out of fear that my mother would beat us'   [40_leg_08.030]
      c. *nhaŋroŋ-hoknam=be   me-wasiʔ-le   me-wacek-le   cameŋba*
          a_festival=LOC   NEG-wash-CVB   NEG-wash-CVB   food
          ca-ma   bhoŋ   samba-nwak   leks-iʔ-wa,   phak
          eat-INF   COND   vulture   become-1PL-NPST   pig
          men-semeʔ-le   ca-ya   bhoŋ   phak   loʔwa   pombrekpa,
          NEG-greet-CVB   eat-SBJV   COND   pig   like   lazy
          chippakeppa   leks-iʔ-wa   baŋna   eko
          disgusting   become-1PL-NPST   COMPL   one
          lu-yukt-a=na   ceʔya   wɛʔ=na.
          tell-V2.PUT-3.P=NMLZ.SG   story   exist[3SG]=NMLZ.SG
          'We have a saying that during Maghe Sankranti, if we eat without

bathing, we will become a vulture, and if we eat without bowing down to the pig, we will become lazy and disgusting like a pig.'

[40_leg_08.047]

d. *nnakha   laluban   phaluban=ci   ŋkha*
those   Lalubang   Phalubang=NSG   those

liŋkha=ci   iya   ŋ-wa-ya,   ŋkha=ci   ghak
Linkha_person=NSG   what   3PL-exist-SBJV   those=NSG   all

eko   n-leks-a=bu   baŋna   taplik   om.
one   3PL-become-PST=REP   COMPL   story   COP

'Those Lalubang and Phalubang, those Linkhas, whatever happens, they all became one (they say), (this) is what the story is about.'

[22_nrr_05.134]

Such structures do not necessarily need a head noun, as example (46) shows.

(46)   *keŋ-khuwa   u-thap-ka   kolem=na   sumphak*
bear_fruit-NMLZ   3SG.POSS-plant=GEN   smooth=NMLZ.SG   leaf

baŋna   na=maŋ   om.
comp   this=EMPH   COP

'This is what it means if we say: the high-yielding plant has smooth leaves.'[16]   [01_leg_07.236]

The complementizer is not only used to embed clauses, it may also link names to a head noun, translating as 'called' or 'so-called' (see (47a) and (47b)). As (47c) shows, this structure does not necessarily need a nominal head either. The phrase marked by *baŋna* has nominal properties, like a headless relative clause. It can, for instance, host the nonsingular marker =*ci* and case markers. This shows again how complementation and nominalization are related in Yakkha (see Chapter 13).[17]

(47)   a.   *eko   selele-phelele   baŋna   nwak*
one   Selele-Phelele   so-called   bird
'the bird called Selele-Phelele'   [21_nrr_04.001]

    b.   *haŋsewa   baŋha   yakkha=ci*
Hangsewa   COMP   Yakkha_person=NSG
'the Yakkha people called Hangsewa (a clan name)'   [39_nrr_08.06]

---

[16] From the Nepali saying: *hune biruwāko cillo pāt*, for people who show a promising behavior from an early age on.

[17] Etymologically, the complementizer can be deconstructed into a root *baŋ* (of unknown origin) and the nominalizers =*na* and =*ha*.

c. *jalangaja,   mendenbarik   baŋna=be*
Jalan-Gaja   Mendenbarik   so-called=LOC
'in a place called Jalan Gaja, Mendenbarik (in Malaysia)'

[13_cvs_02.063]

16 Connectives on the text level

This chapter deals with connectives on the text level. These are invariable particles that introduce grammatically independent sentences, but refer back to the
content of the previous sentence (or sentences). These connectives are always
sentence-initial. Some of them are also deictic temporal adverbs. They indicate
relationships of temporal sequence, cotemporality, causality or negativity. Many
of these particles look as if they have been calqued upon Nepali connectives such
as *kinabhane* 'because' or *tyaspachi* 'afterwards, and then'. Another possibility
is that both languages follow a more general areal pattern. Other clause linkage
markers occur clause-finally in Yakkha, as described in Chapters 13, 14 and 15.

16.1 Sequential connectives

Sequential connectives have developed from demonstratives (*na, kha, ŋkha*) to
which the sequential clause linkage marker *=hoŋ* has been added, exactly like
the Nepali connective *tyas-pachi*. The following forms have been found, and are
translatable with 'after this', 'after that', or more generally with 'and' or 'and
then': *nhaŋ (na-hoŋ), khoŋ (kha-hoŋ)* and *ŋkhoŋ (ŋkha-hoŋ)*. It is likely that the
form *nnhaŋ* exists, too, but as these forms are utterend sentence-initially and
usually in very fast speech, such a distinction could not be established reliably.
Examples are shown in (1) and (2). The connective *nhaŋ* is by far the most frequent one, featuring 230 occurrences in the corpus (of 3012 clauses), while *ŋkhoŋ*
is found only 17 times and *khoŋ* is found no more than 38 times. Occasionally,
nhaŋ occurs as *nhaŋŋa*, marked by the instrumental marker in his function of
indicating the time of an event.

(1) a. *uŋ=ŋa*   *pheri,*   *lu,*   *maiti=ci=be,*   *ka*   *haku*
         3SG=ERG   again   INIT   natal_home=NSG=LOC   1SG   now
         bagdata=ca
         marriage_finalization=ADD
         nakt-wa-ŋ-ci-ŋ=ha   *bhoŋ=cen*   *eko*
         ask-NPST-1SG.A-3NSG.P-1SG.A=NMLZ.NSG   COMPL=TOP   one

> ```
> ce?ya      cekt-wa.                  khoŋ        bagdata
> matter     speak-NPST[3A;3.P]   and_then    marriage_finalization
> nak-se     khe-me?=na.
> ask-SUP    go[3]-NPST=NMLZ.SG
> ```
> 'She says: Well, now I will ask my parents for my *bagdata*, too. And
> she goes to ask for the bagdata.'[1]   [26_tra_02.011–2]

b. ```
    ah.   ŋkhoŋ   i   n-jog-u=ha?
    yes   and_then what   3PL-do-3.P[PST]=NMLZ.NC
    ```
    'Yes. And what did they do then?'                         [20_pea_02.011]

c.  ```
    luŋkhwak   hoŋ-ma                     pʌrne,      nhaŋ   khibak=ca
    stone      hole_outINF[DEONT]   having_to   and    rope=ADD
    ip-ni-ma                         pʌrne       sa=bu.
    twist-COMPL-INF[DEONT]   having_to   COP.PST[3]=REP
    ```
    'He had to hole out a grinding stone, and he had to complete making
    a rope, too, it is said.'   [11_nrr_01.007–8]

The temporal ablative *nhaŋto* derived from the most frequent sequential connective *nhaŋ*. Its literal meaning is 'and then up'. This connective is also found
with complements (see §5.2.3), referring to a point in time when an ongoing event
has started. The event or activity does not necessarily have to go on at the time of
speaking. The connective only signifies the initial boundary, as in English 'from
then on'. An example is provided in (2).

(2) ```
     nhaŋto,   garo   n-cheŋd-et-wa=na,
     from_then_on   terace   3PL.A-mason-V2.CARRY.OFF-NPST=NMLZ.SG
     tokha?la.
     upwards
     ```
     'From then on, they mason the terrace, upwards.'          [31_mat_01.093]

## 16.2 Cotemporal connectives

The cotemporal connectives *kha?niŋ* and *ŋkha?niŋ* ~ *nnakha?niŋ* are constructed
of deictic adverbs based on demonstratives and the cotemporal adverbial clause
linkage marker, *=niŋ* (see (3)).

---

[1] The *bagdata* ritual belongs to the marriage custom; see §2.2.2.5.
     ```

(3) ŋkhaʔniŋ   eko   paŋ=ca   m-ma-ya-n=niŋa   tumhaŋ=ŋa
     that_time one   house=ADD   NEG-COP-PST-NEG=CTMP   Tumhang=ERG

     paŋ   cog-uks-u.
     house   make-PRF-3.P
     'At that time, when there was not even a single house, Tumhang built a
     house.'   [27_nrr_06.038]

16.3 Adversative connectives

Cotemporal connectives have developed into an adversative connective, indicating that the propositional content of the clause stands in contradiction or in contrast to some previous content, or that it restricts the previous information in
some way. Their structure is transparent. They are cotemporal connectives marked by the standard topic marker *=ko*. In (4a) the speaker ponders about arranged
marriages. The sentence, about a hypothetical groom, stands in contrast to an earlier (hypothetical) statement that he might leave a good impression or talk nicely.
Example (4b) is self-explanatory.

(4) a. khaʔniŋgo   imin=na,   imin=na,   i=na
         but   how=NMLZ.SG   how=NMLZ.SG   what=NMLZ.SG

         tha?
         information
         'But how, how will he (a hypothetical husband) be, how to know?'
                                                          [36_cvs_06.336]

     b. kha   liŋkha=ci=ŋa   camyoŋba   i=ya=go
         these   Linkha=NSG=ERG   food   some=NMLZ.NC=TOP

         m-bi-ci,   khaʔniŋ=go   phophop=na
         3PL.A-give-3NGS.P   but   upside_down=NMLZ.SG

         sumphak,   sumphak   phophop   n-jog-uks-u=hoŋ=se
         leaf   leaf   upside_down   3PL.A-do-PRF-3.P=SEQ=RESTR

         camyoŋba   m-by-uks-u-ci.
         food   3PL.A-give-PRF-3NGS.P
         'These Linkhas gave them some food, but they gave it to them only
         after turning the leaf plates upside-down.'   [22_ɯɪɾ_05.047–8]

16.4 Causal connectives

The connective *ijaŋbaŋniŋ* 'because' is used for causal clause linkage. It is constructed in parallel to the Nepali *kina bhʌne*, out of the interrogative word *ijaŋ* 'why' and the textual topic marker *baŋniŋ* (see Chapter 17). An example is provided in (5).

(5)   *ŋkhaʔniŋgo   ka   con-si-saŋ,   ijaŋbaŋniŋ   nna*
      but   1SG   be_happy-MDDL-SIM   because   that
      len=bhaŋto=maŋ   ka   heʔniŋ=ca   chocholaplap
      day=TEMP.ABL=EMPH   1SG   when=ADD   naughty
      n-jog-a-ŋa-n.
      NEG-do-PST-1SG-NEG
      'But I was happy, because from that day on I never did mischievous things again.'   [42_leg_10.053]

16.5 The connective of negative effect

The connective *manhoŋ* (also *manoŋ*, *manuŋ*) stands at the beginning of clauses that contain information about what happens when a previously mentioned condition has not been fulfilled, like English 'if not' or 'otherwise' (see (6)). It can be decomposed into the negated existential copula *man* and the sequential clause linkage marker *=hoŋ*.

(6)   a.   *nhaŋ,   henca-khuba=cen   yakkha   om,   man=hoŋ,*
           and_then   win-NMLZ=TOP   Yakkha_person   COP   if_not
           me-henca-khuba   men=na.
           NEG-win-NMLZ=TOP   NEG.COP[3]=NMLZ.SG
           'Then, the winner is Yakkha; otherwise, the loser, he is not.'
                                                                           [39_nrr_08.17]
      b.   *ah,   manhoŋ,   adhi   barkha   khiŋ*
           yes   if_not   half   year   this_much
           khoʔ-ni-me.
           be_enough-COMPL-NPST[3SG]
           'Otherwise (if the harvest is not enough), we can survive for as much as half a year.'   [28_cvs_04.042]

17 Discourse particles and interjections

This chapter provides an overview of operators on the discourse level. Syntactically speaking they are optional, but of course omitting them does not make sense from a discourse perspective. Particles are invariant morphemes and not part of the inflectional paradigm of the verb or the noun. Some particles attach to phrases (potentially including adverbial clauses), others attach to the end of a sentence and accordingly, their scope properties have the potential to differ (see Table 17.1 for an overview). It should be noted that the term *particle* does not make any statements about their nature, apart from the fact that they are uninflected. The operators discussed here can be phonologically bound, free, or have variable phonological status. Some of them can also be stacked to arrive at more specific discourse functions, which in some cases leads to new, phonologically unbound forms. The functions of the particles include indicating topicalized or focussed constituents of the sentence (cf. §17.1 and §17.2). Other particles rather have scope over a section of discourse that is bigger than one sentence, most prominently *baŋniŋ*. Some particles indicate the source of information (evidentiality markers) and the assessment of the speaker regarding the likelihood or reliability of a piece of information (epistemic markers). They are discussed, together with a marker of mirativity, in §17.3. Exclamative particles are the topic of §17.4. Further particles discussed here are the marker of alternatives, the marker of truth-value questions, the vocative and the insistive particles in §17.5. This chapter also contains an overview of the interjections found in Yakkha (§17.6). Two further markers with discourse function have been discussed at length in §13.3.3: the nominalizing clitics =na and =ha.

Rarely, markers from Nepali are used as well, such as emphatic *ni*, the initiative *lu*, and the probability particle *hola* (paraphrasable with 'probably'). They are not discussed here. The only markers from Nepali that are found frequently enough to be considered in this discussion are the contrastive topic particle (see §17.1) and the mirative marker (see §17.3).

This chapter has the character of a descriptive overview, providing merely impressionistic conclusions. It does not present a theory of discourse marking in Yakkha, as an in-depth discourse analysis has not been undertaken for Yakkha yet.

Table 17.1: Overview of discourse particles

PARTICLE	FUNCTION	DOMAIN
=ko ~ =go	topic	phrase, adv. clause
=chen	contrastive topic	phrase
baŋniŋ	textual topic, quotative	adv. clause
=se	restrictive focus	phrase, adv. clause
=ca	additive focus	phrase, adv. clause
=pa ~ =ba	emphasis	sentence
=i	emphasis	sentence
=le	contrastive focus	phrase
=maŋ	emphasis	phrase
=pu ~ =bu	reportative	phrase, emb. clause
loppi	probability/hypothetical	sentence
=pi ~ =bi	irrealis	clause
rahecha	mirative	sentence
lai	exclamative	sentence
=ʔlo	exclamative	sentence
hau	exclamative	sentence
=em	alternation	clause
i	truth-value question	sentence
=u	vocative	phrase
au	insistive	sentence

17.1 Topic

17.1.1 The particle *=ko ~ =go*

The topic particle *=ko ~ =go* (alternation conditioned by the voicing rule, cf. §3.5.1) marks the constituent in the sentence about which a question or assertion is made, and is thus only found once in a sentence. It attaches to constituents of any kind (see (1)), including adverbial clauses (see (2)). In (1a), *=go* attaches to a possessive pronoun that refers to the protagonist of a narrative. The constituent marked for topic does not have to be given in a certain stretch of discourse; in (1b) for instance, the topic of the sentence is a newly introduced discourse topic. In (1c) the assertion is made about a certain time that is expressed by an adverbial.

(1) a. *uk=ka=go*   *pik=ci* *wai-sa=bu.*
   3SG.POSS=GEN=TOP COW=NSG exist-PST.PRF=REP
   'He had cows.'   [11_nrr_01.005]

  b. *a-pum=go*   *nu=na*   *hola*
   1SG.POSS-grandfather=TOP get_well[3SG]=NMLZ.SG probably
   ni?
   PTCL
   'The grandfather is fine, most probably?'[1]   [06_cvs_01.083]

  c. *he?nasen=go* *n-lit-a-ma-n=ha.*
   thesedays=TOP NEG-plant[3SG]-PST-PRF-NEG=NMLZ.NC
   'These days it has not been planted.'   [36_cvs_06.094]

(2) a. *nhe* *nis-u-ŋ=niŋ=go*   *pako* *sa=na.*
   here see[PST]-3.P-1SG.A=CTMP=GO old COP.PST[3SG]=NMLZ.SG
   'When I had seen him here, he was (already) old.' [06_cvs_01.088]

  b. *wa=ci*   *ŋ-ga-ya=hoŋ=go*   *om*
   chicken=NSG 3PL-call-PST=SEQ=TOP bright
   leks-a-khy-a.
   become[3]-PST-V2.GO-PST
   'The cocks crowed, and the day started.'   [37_nrr_07.028]

  c. *massina=ci* *bhoŋ=go,* *massina=ca* *ŋ-und-wa=ci.*
   small=NSG COND=TOP small=ADD 3PL.A-pull-NPST-3NSG.P
   'If they (the fish) are small, they also pull them out.' [13_cvs_02.021]

The constituent marked by *=ko* comes sentence-initially (see (1) and (2)), or in a detached position. Example (3) shows a right-dislocated topic in an afterthought which is marked by *=ko* that was probably uttered to correct the plural marking of the verb to dual in the pronoun. The same is illustrated below by (4b) and (4c).

(3) *haku* *i=ya*   *ka-m*   *ha?lo,* *kanciŋ=go?*
  now what=NMLZ.SG say-1PL.A[SBJV] EXCLA 1DU=TOP
  'Now what shall we say, I mean, the two of us?'   [13_cvs_02.54]

The topic particle is also involved in a fixed construction, where the finite main verb is preceded by its infinitival form, which is marked by the topic particle. This grammatical construction implies that a restriction applies to the propositional content expressed in the sentence (see the examples in (4)). In example (4a), people discuss where one could purchase fish, and that even though a certain

---

[1] *hola* and *ni* are Nepali particles and they do not occur frequently (yet), so they are not discussed further here.

household might have fish, they probably do not have enough to sell them to others. The question in (4c) implies that things could have been worse, as the talk is about an arranged marriage. The construction does not only occur with verbs, but also with other word classes in predicative function (see (4d)). The same structure occurs in Nepali with the infinitive in -*nu* and the topic marker *ta*.

(4) a. *yo   gumba=ci=ge=ca   wa-ma=go*
         across   Gumba=NSG=LOC=ADD   exist-INF=TOP
         wam-me=ha,   ...
         exist[3SG]-NPST=NMLZ.NSG
         'Gumba's family over there has some (fish), (but ...)'   [13_cvs_02.057]

    b. *we=ppa,   wa-ma=go,   ca-ma*
         exist[3SG;NPST]=EMPH   exist-INF=TOP   food
         khoblek.   cama=ŋa   ŋ-khom-me-n.
         eating_up_at_once   food=ERG   NEG-be_enough[1.P]-NPST-NEG
         'There is, there is food, (but) it is eaten up quickly. We do not have enough food.'   [28_cvs_04.169–70]

    c. *nhaŋ   cekt-a-ci=ha,   cek-ma=go?*
         and_then   speak-PST-DU=NMLZ.NSG   speak-INF=TOP
         'And then they talked, at least?' (bride and groom)   [36_cvs_06.289]

    d. *khumdu=go   khumdu,   khatniŋgo   haŋ=ha.*
         tasty=TOP   tasty,   but   spicy=NMLZ.NC
         'It is tasty, but spicy.'

The topic particle is also part of the lexicalized adversative clause-initial connective *khatniŋgo/ŋkhatniŋgo* 'but', which historically is a combination of a temporal adverb meaning 'at this/that time' and the topic marker.

17.1.2 The contrastive topic particle =*chen* (from Nepali)

In addition to the Yakkha topic marker =*ko*, the particle =*chen* (with a freely alternating allomorph [cen]), a borrowed form of the Nepali particle *cāhĩ*, can be employed (see §3.3). It has a stronger reading, marking contrastive topics in contexts where the speaker switches the topic or singles out one constituent (about which an assertion is made) against other constituents, as shown in (5a). In (5b), the protagonists of the story are marked by =*chen*, because the preceding content was about the people who chased them away. In contrast to =*ko*, =*chen* is restricted to constituents of clauses; it is not found on adverbial clauses.

(5) a.   *imin lak-m=ha   baŋniŋ, ka=chen na*
        how   dance-INF=NMLZ.NSG about   1SG=TOP this

        doku=hoŋ=be   u-me-ŋ,   [...]   nniŋda lakt-a-ni.
        basket=INSIDE=LOC enter-NPST-1SG   [...]   2PL   dance-IMP-PL

        'As for how to dance, I will climb into this basket, [...] and you (plural)
        will dance.'   [14_nrr_02.28–9]

    b.   *nhaŋ   khaci lalubaŋ=nuŋ   phalubaŋ=chen   khali*
        and_then these Lalubang=COM   Phalubang=TOP only

        puŋda=e   kheʔ-m=ha.
        forest=LOC go-INF[DEONT]=NMLZ.NSG

        'And then, those (guys) Lalubang and Phalubang only had the option
        to go to the forest.'   [22_nrr_05.045]

17.1.3 The quotative and textual topic particle *baŋniŋ*

This particle marks the question or topic that a broader section of discourse is
about (see (6)). The particle constitutes a stress domain by itself. The voiced initial
could be a reflex of its formerly bound nature. Yakkha also has a complementizer
baŋna, embedding clauses to nouns, sometimes also translating as 'so-called'. Although the origin of *baŋ* is not clear, it looks as if a root of an utterance predicate
has been nominalized to yield *baŋna*, and the cotemporal adverbial clause linkage marker *=niŋ* (see §14.12) has been added to the same root to yield *baŋniŋ*.
In fact, the particle in (6c) has the function of marking direct speech in much
the same function as *bhoŋ* in purpose clauses and utterance predicates (see §14.9
and 15.2.2). In clauses with *bhoŋ* as a quotative marker, the subject of the main
clause and the source of the utterance are coreferential. This is not the case for
speech marked by *baŋniŋ*, as (6c) clearly shows. This example also shows that it
is possible for the topic marker *=ko* to attach to *baŋniŋ*.

(6) a.   *nna   ceŋ   waiʔ=na=ŋa   haku=ca   kaniŋ i*
        that   upright be[3SG]=NMLZ.SG=ERG now=ADD 1PL   what

        miʔ=m=ha   baŋniŋ: ...
        think-INF[DEONT]=NMLZ.NSG about

        'As that (stele) stands upright, what we have to think even now: ...'
                                     [18_nrr_03.031]

    b.   *liŋkha=ŋa=bu   i=ya   i=ya*
        a_clan=ERG=REP what=NMLZ.NC what=NMLZ.NC

> *men-jok-ma*   *baŋniŋ:*   ...
> NEG-do-INF[DEONT]   about
> 'As for what things the Linkha clan is not allowed to do, ...'
>
>   [11_nrr_01.022]

    c.   *maŋcwa=le apt-u*   *baŋniŋ=go i=ha=le*
         water=CTR   bring-IMP   QUOT=TOP   what=NMLZ.NC=CTR
         kheps-uks-u=ha?
         hear-PRF-3.P=NMLZ.NC
         'When we told her to fetch water, what the heck did she understand?'

                                                      [42_leg_10.045]

17.2 Focus and emphasis

17.2.1 The restrictive focus particle *=se*

Restrictive focus is expressed by the particle *=se*. It is attached to the constituent it focusses on. A sentence with a constituent being focussed by the restrictive marker expresses that out of a given set only this constituent fulfills the necessary condition for the proposition to be true. The restrictive focus marker thus has a semantic impact on the sentence, and does not merely add emphasis (see also König 1993).

(7)   a.   *ka=go*   *na*   *mamu*   *hen=se*
            1SG=TOP   this   girl   today=RESTR
            nis-u-ŋ=na!
            know-3.P[PST]-1SG.A=NMLZ.SG
            'But I saw this girl only today!'

       b.   *hoŋkhiŋ=se.*
            that_much=RESTR
            'That much only.'   [11_nrr_01.42]

       c.   *yakkhaba=ga=se*   *cekt-uks-u-m.*
            Yakkha_person=GEN=RESTR   speak-PRF-3.P[PST]-1PL.A
            'We have only talked in the language of the Yakkha people.'

                                                    [36_cvs_06.609]

     The restrictive focus marker can also be found on adverbial clauses (see (8a)), and also inside adverbial clauses, as the focus domain generally extends into subordinate clauses in Yakkha (see (8b)).

(8)　a.　*sumphak　phophop　　　　n-jog-uks-u=hoŋ=se　　　camyoŋba*
　　　　　leaf　　　upside_down　NEG-do-PRF-3.P=SEQ=RESTR　food
　　　　　m-by-uks-u-ci.
　　　　　3PL.A-give-PRF-3.P[PST]-3NSG.P
　　　　　'They gave the food to them only after turning the leaf-plates upside-
　　　　　down.'

　　　b.　*nna　mʌndata=se　　　　　m-bi-wa-ci=nuŋ*
　　　　　that　marriage_custom=RESTR　3PL.A-give-NPST-3NSG.P=COM.CL
　　　　　samma　cahĩ,　...
　　　　　until　　TOP
　　　　　'And as long as only the Mandata is given, ... (the wife does not belong
　　　　　to the husband's side).'　　　　　　　　　　　　　　　[26_tra_02.007]

The marker *=se* is also found in a construction that expresses very urgent requests or imperatives. In such constructions, an infinitival form, marked by the
restrictive focus particle, precedes the inflected verb, as shown in (9).

(9)　*oe　　chiŋdaŋ　oe=maŋ,　　nda　yep-ma=se*
　　　ADDR　pillar　　ADDR=EMPH　2SG　stand-INF=RESTR
　　　yeb-a-sy-a!
　　　stand-IMP-MDDL-IMP
　　　'Oh, pillar, oh, if you only stood upright!'　　　　　　　[27_nrr_06.023]

17.2.2　The additive focus particle *=ca*

Additive focus is marked by the clitic *=ca*.[2] This marker expresses that content
is added to some presupposed or previously activated content, or that some participant is included to the presupposed set of participants, as illustrated by (10).
The marker attaches to constituents of any type, including adverbial clauses, as
will be shown below.

(10)　a.　*nda=nuŋ　ka=ca　　khe-me-ŋ=na.*
　　　　　2SG=COM　1SG=ADD　go-NPST-1SG=NMLZ.SG
　　　　　'I will also go with you.'

　　　b.　*kaniŋ=ca　yakkha　siŋan.*
　　　　　1PL=ADD　Yakkha　COP.1PL.EXCL
　　　　　'We are also Yakkha people.'　　　　　　　　　　　　[39_nrr_08.08]

---

[2] In related languages, the cognate of this marker has aspirated /ch/ initially (e.g., in Bantawa
and Belhare Doornenbal 2009; Bickel 2003).

c.   *encho=ca*   *ta-ya-ma=ga=na.*
      some_time_ago=ADD   come-PST-2=NMLZ.SG
      'You have come before, too.'   [28_cvs_04.164]

The additive focus particle may also be attached to question words, yielding pro-forms that include all conceivable referents and thus have an exhaustive or 'free-choice'[3] reading 'any' or 'ever', as in (11). In this function, the additive focus particle is often combined with the sequential clause linkage marker *=hoŋ* (see (11b) and (c) and the following paragraph).

(11) a. *hetna=ca*   *tihar*   *ta-meʔ=niŋa,*   *na*
        which=ADD   a_hindu_festival come[3SG]-NPST=CTMP this
        uŋci=ga   *yad=be*   *khaʔla,*   *nniŋda*
        3NSG=GEN   remembrance=LOC like_this   2PL
        lakt-a-ni.
        dance-IMP-PL.IMP
        'Whichever Tihar day comes, dance like this, in memory of them (goddess Sangdangrangma and her companions).'[4]   [14_nrr_02.37]
    b. *na*   *makhur=na*   *caleppa* *hen*   *imin=hoŋ=ca*
        this   black=NMLZ.SG   bread   today   how=SEQ=ADD
        ca-ma=na.
        eat-INF[DEONT]=NMLZ.SG
        'This black bread has to be eaten today, by all means.'
                                 [40_leg_08.056]
    c. *i=ya=hoŋ=ca*   *cok-ma* *yas-wa-g=ha.*
        what=NMLZ.NC=SEQ=ADD do-INF   be_able-NPST-2=NMLZ.NC
        'You can achieve anything.'   [01_leg_07.031]
    d. *iʔbeniŋ=ca*
        what_time=ADD
        'at any time'   [13_cvs_02.005]

Scalar notions, translatable with 'even', can also be marked by *=ca* (see the example in (12)), but constituents with a scalar reading are rare in the corpus. Such notions are expressed in concessive clauses increasingly (see §14.11), marked by

---

[3] See König (1993: 980).

[4] Narrative 14 is about a Yakkha goddess called *Saŋdaŋraŋma*, also called *Dokeni*. Tihar is the Hindu festival of the goddess Laksmi, celebrated in October or November, and this celebration has been transformed to a Yakkha celebration in the Yakkha cultural sphere. The Hindu goddess of fortune, wealth and prosperity *Lakṣmī* is identified with *Saŋdaŋraŋma*.

the related particle =*honca*, which is a combination of sequential clause linkage marker and additive particle (see (12c)). In (12c) the scalar reading is combined with restrictive focus 'even if only'.

(12) a. *jammai, kha yamuŋ=ca, ghak heŋ-nhaŋ-ma.*
          all   this beard=ADD all   cut-V2.SEND-INF[DEONT]
          'All (hair), even this beard, one has to cut off all of it (while mourning).'

                                                                [29_cvs_05.058]

      b. *ucun=na   yapmi=ca   ucun   n-nis-wa-m-nin.*
          nice=NMLZ.SG   person=ADD   nice   NEG-see-NPST-1PL.A-3PL.NEG
          'Even nice people will seem ugly to us (if we are forced to marry them).'   [36_cvs_06.330]

      c. *liŋkha=ga   teʔmaŋa=se=honca,*   ...
          a_clan=GEN   clan_sister=RESTR=SEQ=ADD
          'Even if it is only a Linkha sister (as opposed to a Linkha sister who will marry a Limbukhim guy), ...'   [37_nrr_07.095]

In a pattern that is common in the languages of South Asia (and possibly beyond), the additive focus marker is employed together with verbal negation to express exhaustive negation (i.e., to the greatest conceivable extent), which is often paraphrasable with English 'any'. In this function, it is typically attached to interrogative words, as shown in (13).

(13) a. *ka   hetniŋ=ca   m-man-diʔ-ŋa-n=na.*
          1SG when=ADD   NEG-get_lost-V2.GIVE-1SG-NEG=NMLZ.SG
          'I would never get lost.'   [18_nrr_03.015]

      b. *hou,   ka   eko=ca   m-pham-me-ŋ-ga-n!*
          EXCLA 1SG one=ADD   NEG-help-NPST-1SG.P-2.A-NEG
          i=na=le?
          what=NMLZ.SG=CTR
          'Man, you do not help me even with one (word, line); what is going on?' (a complaint uttered while singing a song)   [07_sng_01.16]

17.2.3 The emphatic particle =*pa* ~ =*ba*

The emphatic particle =*pa* is typically attached to the inflected verb or to other sentence-final elements, like the dislocated phrase in (14a). The function of this marker is to indicate that the hearer should be aware of the propositional content already, or to emphasize its truth, paraphrasable with German 'doch', or

English 'of course'. The particle is found on assertions (affirmative and negated), imperatives, hortatives and permissive questions, but never on content or truth-value questions (see (14)). In assertions, it occus mutually exclusive with the nominalizers =na and =ha in sentence-final position. Its function seems similar to these nominalizers, except for its occurrence on imperatives and hortatives, and its absence on the above-mentioned question types (see the ungrammatical examples in (15)). Etymologically, the particle might have developed from the nominalizer =pa.

(14) a. *a-ppa=ŋa*   *et-u-ci=ba,*
       1SG.POSS-father=ERG   apply[3SG.A;PST]-3.P-3NSG.P=EMPH
       samundra=be=pa.
       ocean=LOC=EMPH
       'My father used them (the fishing rods), in the ocean.'
                                                          [13_cvs_02.024]

     b. *nhe,*   *uk=ka*   *u-cya=ci*   *mohan=ŋa*
       here   3SG.POSS=GEN   3SG.POSS-child=NSG   Mohan=ERG
       hiŋ-ma=ci=ba.
       support-INF[DEONT]=NSG=EMPH
       'Here, her children, of course Mohan has to care for them.'
                                                           [28_cvs_04.145]

     c. *kucuma=ŋa*   *co-i-ks-u=ha?*   *khem=ba!*
       dog=ERG   eat-COMPL-PRF-3.P=NMLZ.NC   before=EMPH
       A: 'Did the dog eat up?' B: 'Already before!'

(15) a. **man=ba?*
       EXIST.NEG[3]=EMPH
       Intended: 'There is none?'

     b. **khiŋ=ba?*
       this_much=EMPH
       Intended: 'This much?'

     c. **heʔna*   *khy-a=ba?*
       where   go[3SG]-PST=EMPH
       Intended: 'Where did he go?'

Example (16) shows =pa ~ =ba in permissive questions. Here, it implies that the speaker expects a positive answer (see (16)). In imperatives, the marker is employed to make commands and requests more polite, occurring in a fixed sequence of the focus marker =i (often realized as [e]) and =ba (see (17)).

(16) a. *ca-ŋ-so-ŋ=ba?*
          eat[3.P]-1SG.A-V2.LOOK[3.P]-1SG.A[SBJV]=EMPH
          'May I try and eat it?'   [17_cvs_03.301]

      b. *na=be   yuŋ-ma   leŋ-me=pa?*
          this=LOC   sit-INF   be_alright[3SG]-NPST=EMPH
          'Is it allowed to sit here?'

(17) a. *yokmet-a-ŋ=eba.*
          tell-IMP-1SG.P=EMPH
          'Please tell me about it.'   [19_pea_01.005]

      b. *co=eba.*
          eat[IMP]=EMPH
          'Please eat it.'

The emphatic particle *=pa* also frequently combines with other particles. The particles *=le* and *=ba* are combined in a fixed expression that is shown in (18a). It can attach to the emphatic particle *=maŋ* and to the restrictive focus particle *=se* when it attaches to constituents in predicative function.

(18) a. *i=na=le=ba*
          what=NMLZ.SG=CTR=EMPH
          'watchamacallit, what to say'

      b. *mi=na=maŋ=ba!*
          small=NMLZ.SG=EMPH=EMPH
          'It is so small!'   [36_cvs_06.225]

      c. *hen   khiŋ   se=ppa.*
          today   this_much   RESTR=EMPH
          'Today it is this much only.'

17.2.4 The emphatic particle *=i*

The emphatic particle *=i* is frequently found in assertions that emphasize the truth value of some propositional content (see (19)), usually following the clause-final nominalizers *=na* and *=ha* (see §13.3.3), but never attaching to clauses that are marked by *=pa*. The focus particle is most likely related to the phonologically unbound question marker *i* that occurs in truth-value questions (see below).

(19) a. *kha?la,   eŋ=ga   ce?ya=i*
          like_this   1PL.POSS=GEN   language=EMPH
          chak=ha=i,   chak=ha!
          difficult=NMLZ.NC=EMPH   difficult=NMLZ.NC
          'It is like this, our language is difficult, difficult.'   [36_cvs_06.544]

      b. *menna=i,   paip   cok-se   khe-me-ŋ=na=i.*
          COP.NEG=FOC,   pipe   join-SUP   go-NPST-1SG=NMLZ.SG=EMPH
          'No, I will go to fix the pipe.'

This particle is also found in a negative construction with an infinitival form preceding the finite verb. The construction expresses exhaustive negation 'not at all'.

(20) a. *pheŋ-ma=i   m-pheks-a-ma-n=na.*
          plough-INF=EMPH   NEG-plough[3SG]-PST-PRF-NEG=NMLZ.SG
          'It is not ploughed at all.'   [06_cvs_01.081]

      b. *ka   ni-ma=i*
          1SG[ERG]   know-INF=EMPH
          n-nis-wa-ŋa-n=na.
          NEG-know-NPST-1SG.A[3.P]-NEG=NMLZ.SG
          'I do not know (any songs) at all.'   [06_cvs_01.104]

      c. *ni-ma=i   men-ni-ma=na   yapmi=be?*
          know-INF=EMPH   NEG-know-INF=NMLZ.SG   person=LOC
          '(Getting married) to a person one does not know at all?'
                                                                    [36_cvs_06.325]

17.2.5 The contrastive focus particle =le

The particle *=le* carries a strongly contrastive notion. It is functionally equal to the Nepali particle *po*, which indicates that some new information stands in a strong contrast to the expectations, or was not part of the presupposed knowledge (see (21a)). Thus, it expresses a certain amount of surprise on part of the speaker. The particle is often accompanied by the mirative *rahecha ~ raecha* (borrowed from Nepali), and the functions of both markers are indeed related. The particle is not restricted to marking contrastive information from the perspective of the speaker. In (21b), the assertion stands in contrast to the adressee's expectations, as this assertion belongs to an argument about a particular patch of farming ground.

(21) a. *are,   he?ne   khy-a-ŋ=na=lai,*   *ka?   lambu=go*
          oh!?   where   go-PST-1SG=NMLZ.SG=EXCLA   1SG   way=TOP
          na?mo=le   sa=na.
          down_here=CTR   COP.PST[3SG]=NMLZ.SG
          'Holy crackers, where did I go? The way was down here!'
                                                                         [28_cvs_04.027]

      b. *na=go   aniŋ=ga=le   kham!*
          this=TOP   1PL.INCL.POSS=GEN=CTR   ground
          '(But) this is our ground!'   [22_nrr_05.007]

      c. *ka=go   a-sap=le   thakt-wa-ŋ=na.*
          1SG=TOP   1SG.POSS-[STEM]=CTR   like-NPST[3.P]-1SG.A=NMLZ.SG
          'But I like it (in contrast to the other people present).'

As one can see in the examples in (22), the marker also occurs in questions, marking the constituent that is focussed on. The marker expresses that the speaker is particularly clueless about the possible answer, i.e., that nothing is presupposed. In (22a), the speaker mistook the image quality of the Pear Story film (Chafe 1980) for snow. In (22b), the protagonists of the narrative arrived in some unknown place after fleeing from their enemies.

(22) a. *hiuŋ=le   wai-sa=em   i=le   wai-sa=em?*
          snow=CTR   exist[3SG]-PST=ALT   what=CTR   exist[3SG]-PST=ALT
          'Was there snow, or what was it?'   [19_pea_01.004]

      b. *he?ne=le   ta-i=ya   m-mit-a-ma=hoŋ   uŋci*
          where=CTR   come-1PL=NMLZ.NSG   3PL-think-PST-PRF=SEQ   3NSG
          m-maks-a-by-a-ma=ca.
          3PL-be_surprised-PST-V2.GIVE-PST-PRF=ADD
          'They were surprised, wondering: Where in the world did we arrive?'
                                                                         [22_nrr_05.030]

17.2.6 The emphatic particle *=maŋ*

The particle *=maŋ* is another emphatic marker, as the examples in (23) illustrate. It attaches to constituents of any kind, whether arguments or adverbs or clause-initial conjunctions. It is paraphrasable with 'just' or 'right' in English, but its function is not fully understood yet.

(23) a. *i   cok-ma?   yakkha   ten=be   kha?la=maŋ!*
          what   do-INF   Yakkha   village=LOC   like_this=EMPH
          'What to do? After all, it is just like this in a Yakkha village!'

b.   *nhaŋ=ŋa=maŋ*   *ŋ-ikt-haks-u,*   ...
      and_then=INS=EMPH   3PL.A-chase-V2.SEND-3.P[PST],   ...
      'And right then, they chased him away, ...'   [18_nrr_03.011]

c.   *nna* *jeppa=maŋ*   *eko*   *mem-muʔ-ni-ma=na*   *len*
      that   really=EMPH   one   NEG-forget-COMPL-INF=NMLZ.SG   day
      sa-ya.
      COP.PST[3SG]
      'That really was an unforgettable day.'   [41_leg_09.069]

d.   *ma,*   *na=ci=ga*   *niŋwa=maŋ*   *om.*
      mother   sister=NSG=GEN   mind=EMPH   COP
      'Of course, it is just the concern/love of my mother and my sister.'[5]
                                         [42_leg_10.048]

17.3 Epistemic, evidential and mirative markers

The criterion for a marker to be classified as epistemic is that it expresses the commitment of the speaker to the reality of an event. Evidential markers, on , purely indicate the source of the information (Cornillie 2009). Yakkha distinguishes evidential and epistemic markers. Furthermore, the notion of mirativity has to be distinguished from both evidentiality and epistemic modality. It expresses the unexpected status of some information (DeLancey 1997).

17.3.1 The reportative particle *=pu ~ =bu*

The reportative particle conveys a purely evidential notion: the source of the information is not the speaker but someone else. The source of information can be either unspecific (translating as 'It is said.', see (24)) or a specific, quotable source, as in (25). The particle is frequently found in narrations of legends and myths, as they are a prime example of hearsay knowledge. It mostly occurs sentence-finally; it usually attaches to the finite verb, but it can also attach to any other constituent (including adverbial clauses, see (24c)), also more than once per sentence (see (25b)).

---

[5] Context: a child pondering about being scolded for doing dangerous things. This example is exceptional in not displaying the obligatory possessive marking that is usually found on kinship terms. The reason might be that both participants are highly topical in the narrative, and had been mentioned several times before.

(24) a.   *nam wandik=ŋa   lom-meʔ=niŋa   kam*
        sun   tomorrow=INS   come.out[3SG]-NPST=CTMP work
        cok-ni-ma   sa=bu.
        do-COMPL-INF   COP.PST=REP
        'It is said that he had to have the work completed when the sun
        would rise on the next day.'   [11_nrr_01.007]

     b.   *nna puŋdaraŋma=cen,   eko   maŋme*
        that forest_goddess=TOP one   eagle
        leks-a-ma=na=bu.
        become[3SG]-PST-PRF=NMLZ.SG=REP
        'That forest goddess, she became an eagle, it is said.' [22_nrr_05.108]

     c.   *u-milak   khokt-a-by-a   bhoŋ=bu,   ŋkha*
        3SG.POSS-tail cut-SBJV[3SG]-V2.GIVE-SBJV COND=REP that
        desan-masan   n-da-ya,
        scary_ghosts   3PL-come-SBJV
        n-nis-wa-n-ci-n=ha=bu.
        NEG-see-NPST-NEG-3NSG.P-NEG=NMLZ.NSG=REP
        'If one cuts their (the dogs') tails, they do not see the scary ghosts
        coming, it is said.'   [28_cvs_04.213]

(25) a.   *lu,   abo,   hamro yakkha, eh,   aniŋ=ga*
        INIT, now our   Yakkha, oh,   1PL.EXCL=GEN
        ceʔya=ŋ=bu   chem   lum-biʔ-ma=na=lai.
        matter=INS=REP   song tell-V2.GIVE-INF=NMLZ.SG=EXCLA
        'Alright, in our Yakkha, oh [switching to Yakkha], now we have to
        sing a song in our language, she said.'   [06_cvs_01.102]

     b.   *a-na=bu   khe-meʔ=na=bu.*
        1SG.POSS-sister=REP go[3SG]-NPST=NMLZ.SG=REP
        'My sister has to go, she (my sister) says.'   [36_cvs_06.558]

In (25a), the constituent that is marked by =*bu* is in focus. The speaker remembers that she was asked to sing a song in her language, and not in Nepali, and hence she puts the reportative marker on the focussed constituent *aniŋga ceʔyaŋ(a)* 'in our language'.

Occasionally, the reportative marker =*bu* is followed by an utterance predicate, as in (26). Its occurrence is, however, not obligatory on complements of predicates that embed speech in Yakkha (cf. §15.2.2).

(26) *hi?wa=ga* *hi?wa* *wait=na=bu* *ŋ-gam-me.*
      wind=GEN wind exist[NPST;3SG]=NMLZ.SG=REP 3PL-say-NPST
      'They say that he only lives in the air.' [21_nrr_04.052]

17.3.2 The probability particle *loppi*

This particle expresses that the speaker assesses the content of the proposition to be likely, but not an established fact, very much like the English adverbs 'maybe', 'probably', 'possibly'. It generally comes sentence-finally. Etymologically, it is a combination of the marker *lo*[6] and the irrealis particle *=pi* (see below). Examples are provided in (27). This particle is also found in questions (see (27b)) and in counterfactual clauses (see §14.13).

(27) a. *kathmandu=ko* *men=na* *loppi,*
          Kathmandu=TOP NEG.COP[3SG]=NMLZ.SG probably
          men=na.
          NEG.COP[3SG]=NMLZ.SG
          'It was probably not in Kathmandu [pondering] - no.' [36_cvs_06.311]
      b. *bappura* *isa=ga* *u-cya* *loppi?*
          poor_thing who=GEN 3SG.POSS-child probably
          'Poor thing, whose child could it possibly be?' [01_leg_07.292]

17.3.3 The irrealis particle *=pi ~ =bi*

The marker *=pi* (realized as [bi] after nasals and after vowels) is found mostly on counterfactual conditional clauses, but also on hypothetical clauses. In counterfactual clauses, it attaches to the inflected verb of the main clause and to the clause linkage marker of the subordinate clause, either cotemporal *=niŋ(a)* or sequential *=hoŋ*. There actually are sequences of clause linkage marker, topic particle *=ko* and irrealis marker *=pi*, in all examples in (28). The verbs in counterfactual clauses are always marked for the Past Subjunctive (see §8.5).

(28) a. *ḍiana=ca* *pi?-ma=hoŋ=go=bi*
          Diana=ADD give-INF[DEONT]=SEQ=TOP=IRR
          cond-a-sy-a=bi=ba! *khatniŋgo*
          be_happy[3SG]-SBJV-MDDL-SBJV=IRR=EMPH but

---

[6] Synchronically, it only exists as a clause linkage marker in Yakkha, see §14.14. In Belhare, there are a comitative marker *lok* and a focus marker *(k)olo* that could be related to Yakkha *lo* (Bickel 2003).

    man-nin!
    NEG.COP-3PL
    'We would have had to give them (fish) to Diana, too, she would have
    been happy! But there aren't any.'   [13_cvs_02.056]

b.   *nniŋ=ga*   *ten*   *a-sap*
    2PL.POSS=GEN   village   1SG.POSS-[STEM]
    n-thakt-u-ŋ=niŋ=go=bi,   *ka*
    NEG-like-3.P-1SG.A[SBJV]=CTMP=TOP=IRR   1SG
    n-da-ya-ŋa-n=bi.
    NEG-come-SBJV-1SG-NEG=IRR
    'If I had not liked your village, I would not have come.'

c.   *ŋ-gind-a-by-a-masa-n=niŋ=go=bi*
    NEG-rot-SBJV-V2.GIVE-SBJV-PST.PRF-NEG=CTMP=TOP=IRR
    ikhiŋ   *n-leks-a=bi!*
    how_many   3PL-become-SBJV=IRR
    'If they (the apples) were not rotten, how many would we have!'

The particle *=pi* does not only occur on counterfactual clauses. It can also mark clauses referring to hypothetical situations where it expresses the speaker's assessment about the unlikelihood of an event. In example (29), the hypothetical situation that it will rain stands in opposition to the more likely, but also yet unrealized scenario of a hail storm, as judged by the speaker. In this example, the particle expresses the speaker's assessment of the likelihood of an event. The speaker is 99 percent sure that it will hail and thus uses a counterfactual clause for the proposition that contains the event of raining.

(29)   *wasik=se*   *ta-ya=hoŋ=go=bi,*   *ucun*   *leks-a*
      rain=RESTR   come[3SG]-SBJV=SEQ=TOP=IRR   nice   become[3SG]-SBJV
      sa=bi,   *khatniŋgo* *phom* *ta-meʔ=na*
      COP.SBJV=IRR   but   hail   come[3SG]-NPST=NMLZ.SG
      loppi.
      probably
      'If it just rained, it would have been nice, but it there will probably be hail.'

The interaction between the irrealis marker and the clause linkage markers it attaches to is nicely illustrated by the following clausal minimal pair of hypothetical and counterfactual information in (30). Both sentences are inflected for the Past Subjunctive (which is in many forms homophonous with the past tense), but the clause linkage marker *=niŋ* in (30a) establishes a simultaneous relation between the clauses while *=hoŋ* (30b) establishes a sequential relation, indicating that the event must have occurred prior to the main clause, and thereby implying that it has not been realized.

(30)   a.   *makalu   nis-u-ŋ=niŋ=go=bi*
            Makalu   see-3.P-1SG.A[SBJV]=CTMP=TOP=IRR
            cond-a-sy-a-ŋ=bi.
            be_happy-SBJV-MDDL-SBJV-1SG=IRR
            'If I could see Mt. Makalu, I would be happy.'

       b.   *makalu   nis-u-ŋ=hoŋ=go=bi*
            Makalu   see-3.P-1SG.A[SBJV]=SEQ=TOP=IRR
            cond-a-sy-a-ŋ=bi.
            be_happy-SBJV-MDDL-SBJV-1SG=IRR
            'If I had seen Mt. Makalu, I would have been happy.'

17.3.4 The mirative particle *rahecha* (from Nepali)

The Nepali mirative *rʌhechʌ ~ raicha*,[7] was borrowed into Yakkha and is used as a sentence-final marker of surprise about the propositional content, for instance when the speaker shares newly discovered information. In (31a), the speaker discovers that something must be wrong with the water pipe. In (31b) the speaker remembers something that she had not been aware of at first, only after someone reminded her.

(31)   a.   *maŋcwa   mi=na   rahecha.*
            water   small=NMLZ.SG   MIR
            'The water got less.'   [13_cvs_02.071]

       b.   *ka   ŋkhaʔla   bhoŋ   tutunnhe   bhauju=ghe*
            1SG   like_that   COND   up_there   sister-in-law=LOC
            wa-ya-masa-ŋ=na   raecha,   tunnhe=ba.
            exist-PST-PST.PRF-1SG=NMLZ.SG   MIR   up_there=EMPH
            'If it is like that, I had been uphill, at my sister-in-law's place, I see, uphill.'   [36_cvs_06.399]

Mirativity in Yakkha is not restricted to surprise at the time of speaking, and it does not just indicate the speaker's surprise. The mirative particle is frequently found in narratives, where the notion of unexpectedness either relates to some

---

[7] Diachronically, it is a perfective form of the verb *rahanu* 'to remain'.

point in the time line of the story or to the hearer's state of mind, as the one who tells the story can rarely be surprised of what he tells himself. The function or the mirative marker in narratives rather is to draw the attention of the hearer to the plot than to signal surprise. Further examples from narratives are provided in (32). In (32c), the speaker reports about the events she saw in the Pear Story film (Chafe 1980).

(32) a. *cokcoki-netham=be, eko maḍa oṭemma kham*
          star-bed=LOC   one big   plain   ground
          wait=na   rahecha.
          exist[3SG;NPST]=NMLZ.SG   MIR
          'In the place called Bed of Stars, there is a huge plain area!'
                                                          [37_nrr_07.049]

      b. *pak=na   baŋna   mi=na   phalubaŋ,   na*
          younger=NMLZ.SG called small=NMLZ.SG Phalubang   this
          huture   sa-ma   raecha.
          a_clan   COP.PST-PRF   MIR
          'The younger one, the smaller one, Phalubhang, he was a Huture.'
                                                          [22_nrr_05.074]

      c. *khus-het-u=ha   raicha.*
          steal-V2.CARRY.OFF-3.P[PST]=NMLZ.NSG   MIR
          'He stole them and carried them off!'   [20_pea_02.015]

As these examples have shown, the mirative prefers nominalized sentences as hosts (see §13.3.3). Another marker often found together with the mirative is the focus marker *=le* (see above) that signals contrast to presupposed content, or the absence of presupposed content.

17.4 Exclamatives

17.4.1 The exclamative particle *lai*

The function of the sentence-level particle *lai* (always in sentence-final position) is to add a certain vigor and force to assertions and exclamations (see (33)), to rhetorical questions as in (34a), and to deontic statements, as in (34b). It can in most cases be paraphrased with the Nepali particle *ni*, or with English 'just' and 'of course'. It bears its own stress, but it can also be cliticized in fast speech.

(33) a. *ikhiŋ*   *chiʔ=na*   *yapmi* *lai!*
      how_much greedy=NMLZ.SG person EXCLA
      'What a greedy person!'

    b. *om*   *lai!*
      COP   EMPH
      'Yes, of course!'

    c. *koi*   *khaʔla*   *lai!*
      some like_this EXCLA
      'Some are just like this!'   [13_cvs_02.10]

(34) a. *A: hetne* *wei-ka=na?*   - *B: paŋ=be*   *lai.*
      A: where live[NPST]-2=NMLZ.SG - B: house=LOC EXCLA
      tuʔkhi *ca=se* *i*   *kheʔ-ma* *lai?*
      trouble eat-SUP what go=INF   EXCLA
      'A: Where do you live? - B: Just at home. Why should I go to suffer (in a marriage)?!'

    b. *n-da-ci*   *bhoŋ=go*
      3PL.A-bring-3NSG.P[SBJV] COND=TOP
      im-m=ha=ci   *lai,*
      buy-INF[DEONT]=NMLZ.NSG=NSG   EXCLA
      ca-m=ha=ci!
      eat-INF[DEONT]=NMLZ.NSG=NSG
      'If they bring some (fish), we would definitely have to buy and eat them!'   [13_cvs_02.056]

17.4.2 The exclamative particle *=ʔlo*

The particle *=ʔlo* is used frequently in colloquial speech, signalling a certain lack of patience on the side of the speaker, and possibly also a frustrative notion. It occurs in assertions, imperatives, and questions alike. The marker is always bound, attaching to the sentence-final constituent, which is often another discourse particle, such as *=ha* (see §13.3.3), emphatic *=ba* or contrastive *=le* (see (35)). When *=ʔlo* attaches to other particles, the resulting units become independent words regarding stress (e.g., *haʔlo, baʔlo, leʔlo/laʔlo*, which are always stressed on the first syllable), but not with regard to the voicing rule. The most commonly heard particle is *haʔlo* (see (35b)).

(35) a. *i=ʔlo?*
      what=EXCLA
      'What (the heck)?' (also used as a filler, like 'watchamacallit')

b. *wa-ni*   *haʔlo.*   *n-da-me-n=na*
    exist[3SG]-OPT   EXCLA   NEG-come[3SG]-NPST-NEG=NMLZ.SG
    bhoŋ,   *n-da-nin-ni*   *haʔlo!*
    COND   NEG-come[3SG]-NEG-OPT   EXCLA
    'It is alright! If it (the electricity) does not come, may it not come!'

c. *pi-haks-a*   *baʔlo!*
    give-V2.SEND-PST[3A;1.P]   EXCLA
    'They just gave me away in marriage(, so what)!?'   [06_cvs_01.042]

d. *pi-m-ci-m*   *baʔlo,*   *ŋ-ga-ya-ma=hoŋ,*   ...
    give-1PL.A-3NSG.P-1PL.A[SBJV]   EXCLA   3PL-say-PST-PRF=SEQ
    'Then let us give it to them eventually, they said, and ...'
    [22_nrr_05.131]

e. *ta-met-u-ŋ*   *baʔlo!*   *ka=go*
    come-CAUS-3.P[PST]-1SG.A   EXCLA   1SG=TOP
    jokor   *leʔlo.*
    self-deciding_person   EXCLA
    'Of course I brought her (the second wife)! I can decide for myself!'
    [06_cvs_01.077]

There is a dialectal variety of *=ʔlo, =kho*, which can, for instance, be found in the dialect spoken in Ankhinbhuin village (see (36)).

(36) *hetnaŋ*   *tae-ka=na*   *lai*   *kho?*
      where_from   come[NPST]-2=NMLZ.SG   EMPH   EXCLA
      'Where on earth did you come from?'

As (37) shows, the complex exclamative particles are also found in combination with the mirative.

(37) *n-so-ks-u-n=na*   *rahecha*   *baʔlo!*
      NEG-see-PRF-3.P-NEG=NMLZ.SG   MIR   EXCLA
      'Oh, he has not seen it!'   [34_pea_04.039]

17.4.3 The exclamative *hau ~ =(a)u*

Another exclamative particle is *hau*. It is generally found at the end of a sentence, turning assertions into exclamations (see (38)). Judging from the available examples, it also carries a mirative notion, expressing that the speaker is emotionally involved by making a discovery. It generally bears its own stress, but it can also occur cliticized, thus reduced to mere [au] or even just [u].

Occasionally, the particle is also found at the beginning of sentences in order to draw the attention of the hearer to the propositional content, for instance when the topic is changed (39a), or when an exciting discovery has been made, as in (39b).

(38)   a.   *sal=go*   *mund-i-ŋ=na=i*   *hau!*
               year=TOP   forget-COMPL-1SG.A=NMLZ.SG=EMPH   EXCLA
               'I just forgot the year (of my birth), ha!'   [06_cvs_01.034]

       b.   *taŋkheŋ*   *ka-ya=na*   *hau!*
               sky   call[3SG]-PST=NMLZ.SG   EXCLA
               'It thundered!'   [13_cvs_02.062]

       c.   *mun-nhe*   *sombare*   *daju=ge*
               down_here   Sombar   brother=LOC
               ŋ-waiʔ=ya-ci=bu   *hau,*   *jeppa!*
               3PL-exist=NMLZ.NSG=NSG=REP   EXCLA   really
               'Down here at brother Sombar's house they have them (fish) for sale,
               I have heard, really!'   [13_cvs_02.057]

(39)   a.   *hau,*   *salle=be*   *heʔne*   *wei-ka=na?*
               EXCLA   Salle=LOC   where   exist-2=NMLZ.SG
               'Hey, where in Salle do you live?'   [06_cvs_01.090]

       b.   *hau,*   *kha=go,*   *eŋ=ga*   *yapmi*   *loʔa=ci=ca!*
               EXCLA   these=TOP   1PL.INCL.POSS=GEN   person   like=NSG=ADD
               'Really, they are like our people, too!'   [22_nrr_05.044]

17.5 Further particles

17.5.1 The alternative particle *=em*

If the speaker relates two alternative propositional contents, two clauses are juxtaposed and equally marked by the particle *=em*, as shown in (40). The marker may be fused with the preceding material, e.g., with *=na* to [nem] (see (40c)) or with *=le* to [lem] (see (41a)).

(40)   a.   *lag=ha=em*   *lim=ha=em?*
               salty=NMLZ.NC=ALT   sweet=NMLZ.NC=ALT
               'Is it (the tea) salty or sweet?'

       b.   *hetniŋ*   *hetniŋ*   *om=em*   *men=em*
               when   when   COP=ALT   COP.NEG=ALT

> *mit-wa-m=ha.*
> think-NPST[3.P]-1PL.A=NMLZ.NC
> 'Sometimes we think: is it true or not?'

c. *khumdu=n=em ŋkhumdi=n=em?*
   tasty=NMLZ.SG=ALT not_tasty=NMLZ.SG=ALT
   'Is it tasty or not?' [36_cvs_06.244]

d. *cek-met-u-m-ci-m-ga=m,*
   talk-CAUS-3.P[PST]-2PL.A-3NSG.P-2PL.A-2=ALT
   n-jek-met-u-m-ci-m-ga-n=ha=m?
   NEG-talk-CAUS-3.P[PST]-2PL.A-3NSG.P-2PL.A-2-NEG=NMLZ.NSG=ALT
   'Did you make them (prospective bride and groom) talk or not?'
   [36_cvs_06.323]

The particle is thus not only found in alternation questions; it can also express uncertainty, or a lack of knowledge (see (41)).

(41) a. *na=le=m, lambu, heʔne lambu? na!*
       this=CTR=ALT way where way this
       'Is this the road, where is the road? This one!' [36_cvs_06.216]

   b. *i luʔ-ni-me=he=m?*
      what tell-COMPL-NPST=NMLZ.NC=ALT
      'What will he possibly tell (us)?' [36_cvs_06.343]

   c. *dharan=be waisa-ci-ga=em, hetne waisa-ci-ga haʔlo?*
      Dharan=LOC COP.PST-DU-2=ALT where COP.PST-DU-2 EXCLA
      'Or were you in Dharan; where were you, then?' [36_cvs_06.315]

17.5.2 The question particle *i*

The question particle *i* marks truth-value questions, as in (42). In most cases, the clause it attaches to is nominalized by *=na* or *=ha*. The marker may carry its own stress, but it also occurs phonologically bound, the alternation probably just being conditioned by fast speech. If it occurs independently, a glottal stop is prothesized, as it typically is in vowel-initial words in Yakkha. The marker is most likely etymologically related to the (bound) emphatic marker *=i* that has been described above.

(42) a. *raksi=ŋa sis-a-ga=na=i?*
       liquor=ERG kill[3SG.A]-PST-2.P=NMLZ.SG=Q
       'Are you drunk?'

b. *ka i?*
1SG Q
'I?'

c. *yakthu i?*
enough Q
'Did you have enough?' [36_cvs_06.248]

d. *nis-u-ga=na=i?*
know-3.P[PST]-2.A=NMLZ.SG=Q
'Do you know it?'

17.5.3 The insistive particle *(a)u*

The insistive particle is found on imperatives and on hortatives, adding force and emphasis to these speech acts (see (43)). Possibly related to this marker is a vocative that is found occasionally, as shown in (44).

(43) a. *ah, so-se ab-a-ci, au?*
yes look-SUP come-IMP-DU INSIST
'Yes, please come to look (at the bride), will you?' [36_cvs_06.416]

b. *lu, haku=chen pog-i, au?*
alright now=TOP raise-1PL[SBJV] INSIST
'Alright, now let us get up, will we?' [36_cvs_06.556]

(44) *a-na=u!*
1SG.POSS-eZ=VOC
'He, sister!'

17.6 Interjections

Yakkha has a closed class of interjections, such as *hoʔi*, *bhela* and *yakthu* (all meaning 'Enough!'), *om* 'yes', *menna/manna* 'no' (identificational and existential, respectively), and *issaŋ*, the latter being pronounced with a rising intonation. It stands for 'I do not know' or 'I have no idea', just like the Nepali interjection *khoi*. Examples are provided in (45). Interjections are usually employed as sentence replacements, but in Yakkha it is still possible to additionally express a topic, as in (45a). The affirmative and the negative interjections also have copular function (see also §8.7 and 11.1.11). Interjections, like sentences, can host further discourse particles such as in (45d). In the Ankhinbhuin dialect, *om* has an alternant *ommi*.

(45)   a.   *ka=ca*   *ho?i.*
              1SG=ADD   enough
              'I also had enough.'

      b.   *yakthu=i?*
              enough=Q
              'Did you have enough?'

      c.   *men=na,*   *nna=maŋ!*
              COP.NEG=NMLZ.SG   that=EMPH
              'No, it is that one!'

      d.   *he?ne*   *khet-u*   *ha?lo,* *issaŋ* *la?lo!*
              where   carry_off-3.P[PST]   EXCLA IGN   EXCLA
              'Where did he take it - I have no idea!'   [20_pea_02.031]

      e.   *om=ba!*
              yes=EMPH
              'Yes, of course!'

A particle *lu* (borrowed from Nepali) can be found sentence-initially (see example (25a)) or replacing sentences. It is employed to initiate an action, both in commands and in hortatives.

There is no expression for 'thank you' in Yakkha. Common greetings are *sewayo*, and *seme?nenna*, which is the verb 'greet' with 1>2 inflection 'I greet you'.

Geomorphic interjections, prompting the addressee to look in a particular direction (*tu* for 'Look uphill!', *mu* for 'Look downhill!' and *yu* for 'Look over there!') have been discussed in §7.3.

Appendix

Appendix A: Texts

The owl and I

This text is a written personal narrative by Shantila Jimi (Kathmandu/Tumok).

(1) *phopciba=nuŋ   ka*
owl=COM   1SG
The owl and I

(2) *pyak   encho   ka   miya   sa-ya-ŋ=niŋa   pyak*
very   long_time_ago   1SG   little   COP.PST-PST-1SG=CTMP   very
chocholaplap   cok-khuba   saŋ.
mischievous   do-NMLZ   COP.PST.1SG
Long time ago, when I was little, I was very mischievous.

(3) *i   len=ga   ceʔya   om,   aniŋ=ga   yo*
one   day=gen   matter   COP   1PL.EXCL.POSS=GEN   across
taŋŋoca   weʔ=na   lamdhaŋ=be   ka,   a-ma=nuŋ
Tangoca_field   be=NMLZ.SG   field=LOC   1SG   1SG.POSS-mother=COM
a-na   leks-i-ŋ=hoŋ,   phekme   ok-se
1SG.POSS-elder_sister   be-1PL-EXCL=SEQ   vetch   dig_up-SUP
khe-i-ŋ.
go-1PL-EXCL
This is about one day, my mother, my elder sister and I went to dig our field to plant lentils, there at the Tangoca field.

(4) *kaniŋ   kondarik=ci=ca*
1PL[ERG]   spade_with_long_handle=NSG=ADD
khet-u-m-ci-m-ŋa=hoŋ   lamdhaŋ=be
take_along-3.P-1PL.A-3NSG.P-1PL.A-EXCL=SEQ   field=LOC
khe-i-ŋ.
go-1PL-EXCL
We also took some spades with us and went to the field.

(5) nna   lamdhaŋ   paŋ=bhaŋ   ta-ma   maŋpha   maŋdu
    that   field   house=ABL   come-INF   much   far
    sa-ya.
    COP.PST-PST[3SG]
    The field was quite far from our house.

(6) kaniŋ   lamdhaŋ=be   tas-u-m-ŋa-hoŋ   phekme
    1PL[ERG]   field=LOC   arrive-3.P[PST]-1PL.A-EXCL=SEQ   vetch
    ok-saŋ   khe-i=niŋa   nam=ŋa   tuknuŋ   pho-ya.
    dig_up-SIM   go-1PL=CTMP   sun=ERG   thoroughly   [sun]burn-PST[3SG]
    When we arrived at the field and began to dig the weed, the sun burnt
    down on us mercilessly.

(7) ŋkhaʔniŋgo   nna=be   namciʔmaŋ   heʔne=ca
    but   that=LOC   shady   where=ADD
    m-ma-ya-n.
    NEG-COP.NEG -PST[3SG]-NEG
    But there was no shady place.

(8) ŋkhaʔniŋ   kaniŋ   whaŋma   pirik-pirik   leks-i-ŋ=hoŋ
    that_time 1PL   sweat   running   become-1PL-EXCL=SEQ
    ibebe   wepma   si-i-ŋ.
    too_much   thirst   die-1PL -EXCL
    At that time we were covered in sweat, and we were very thirsty.

(9) nnakha=he   maŋcwa=ca   m-ma-ya-n.
    that=LOC   water=ADD   NEG-COP.NEG-PST[3SG]-NEG
    There was no water, too.

(10) nna   lamdhaŋ=ga   yorok=ŋa   eko   mina   hoŋma   wa-ya.
     that   field=GEN   across=INS   one   small   river   exist-PST[3SG]
     There was a small stream, a bit farther from the field.

(11) ka   a-ma=ŋa   khaʔla   ly-a-ŋ:
     1SG   1SG.POSS-mother=ERG   like_this   say-PST-1SG.P
     Mother told me like this:

(12) phuama,   hoŋma=be   khy-a-g=hoŋ   ci=ha
     last-born_girl   river=LOC go-SBJV-2=SEQ be_cold=NMLZ.NC
     maŋcwa   apt-u   au!
     water   bring-3.P[IMP]   EXCLA
     Daughter, go to the stream and bring some cold water, would you?

(13)   *nhaŋa*   *ka=ca*   *leks-a=ba*   *ka-saŋ*
     and_then   1SG=ADD   be-PST[3SG]=EMPH   say-SIM
     con-si-saŋ   *u-yaŋdhaŋ*   *eko*   *a-muk=ŋa*
     be_happy-MDDL-SIM   3SG.POSS-pot   one   1SG.POSS-hand=INS
     phok-phok   *mok-saŋ*   *khet-u-ŋ=hoŋ*
     drumming_sound   beat-SIM   take_along-3.P[PST]-1SG.A=SEQ
     maŋcwa   *tap-se*   *hoŋma=be*   *khy-a-ŋ.*
     water   take-SUP   river=LOC   go-PST-1SG
     And I responded: 'Okay', and went happily to the stream to fetch water,
     holding the pot and drumming it with one hand.

(14)   *khe?-ma-sy-a=niŋa*   *lamdhaŋ=ga*   *mi?yaŋ*   *yorok=ŋa*
     go-INF-AUX.PROG-PST=CTMP   field=GEN   little   over_there=INS
     tas-uks-a-ŋ=na.
     arrive-PRF-PST[3.P]-1SG.A=NMLZ.SG
     On the way, I came to a place a little further away from the field.

(15)   *ŋkha?niŋ*   *eko*   *khokpu=ga*   *u-thap=ka*
     that_time   one   fig_tree=GEN   3SG.POSS-plant=GEN
     u-sam=be   *usa*
     3SG.POSS-lower_part=LOC   fruit
     keks-a-masa=ha   *nis-u-ŋ.*
     bear_fruit-PST[3SG]-PST.PRF =NMLZ.NSG   see-3.P[PST]-1SG.A
     Then, I saw some fruits hanging from the lower branches of a fig tree.

(16)   *ka*   *ŋkha*   *usa*   *sem-ca-ma*   *mit-u-ŋ,*
     1SG[ERG]   those   fruit   pluck-V2.EAT-INF   want-3.P[PST]-1SG.A
     ŋkhoŋ   *sem-saŋ*   *ekhumdu-ekhumdu*
     thus   pluck-SIM   delicious
     co-het-u-ŋ.
     eat-V2.CARRY.OFF-3.P[PST]-1SG.A
     I wanted to pluck and eat the fruits, and so I did pluck them and ate them,
     enjoying their taste.

(17)   *usa*   *sem-saŋ*   *u-sam=be*
     fruit   pluck-SIM   3SG.POSS-under=LOC
     cu-ma-sy-a-ŋ=niŋ   *thapthum=be*
     eat-INF-AUX.PROG-PST-1SG=CTMP   cluelessness=LOC
     u-thap=phaŋ   *a-muk=pe*   *makhur=ha*
     3SG.POSS-plant=ABL   1SG.POSS-arm=LOC   black=NMLZ.NC

waghui   *loʔwa* *ṭhwaŋ*   *nam-khuba*
chicken_droppings   like   smelling_awful_suddenly   smell-NMLZ
a-yuks-a.
fall-V2.COME.DOWN-PST[3SG]
While I was eating under the tree, without me noticing, something black, smelling awfully like chicken droppings, dropped on my hand.

(18)   *i=ha*   *a-yuks-a=ha*   *bhoŋ*
        what=NMLZ.NC   fall-V2.COME.DOWN-PST[3SG]=NMLZ.NC   COMP
        khaʔla   *siŋ=choŋ=be*   *so-ŋ=niŋa=go,*   *phopciba=le*
        like_this   tree=TOP=LOC   look-1SG.A=CTMP=TOP   owl=CONTR
        weʔ=na!
        be[3SG]=NMLZ.SG
        When I looked up into the tree what had fallen down, there is an owl!

(19)   *nna*   *phopciba*   *siliklik*   *a-chik*
        that   owl   fuming_at_sth   1SG.POSS-anger
        ekt-u-get-u.
        be_angry-3.P-V2.BRING.UP-3.P[PST]
        That owl made me really angry.

(20)   *lap-ma=ga*   *bhoŋ*   *khokpu=ga*   *siŋ=be*   *thaŋ-ma=ga*
        catch-INF=GEN   PURP   fig_tree=GEN   tree=LOC   climb-INF=GEN
        cog-a-ŋ.
        try-PST-1SG
        I tried to climb the tree to catch it.

(21)   *ŋkhaʔniŋo*   *nna*   *siŋ*   *maḍa*   *sa-ya.*
        but   that   tree   big   COP.PST -PST[3SG]
        But the tree was huge.

(22)   *ŋkhoŋ=ca*   *a-chik*   *ekt-a=na*   *belak=ŋa*
        thus=ADD   1SG.POSS-anger   be_angry-PST[3SG]=NMLZ.SG   time=INS
        esap-esap   *thaŋ-ma*   *yas-a-ŋ.*
        swiftly   climb-INF   be_able-PST-1SG
        Nevertheless, as I was so angry that I managed to climb up.

(23)   *to*   *thaŋ-a-by-a-ŋ=hoŋ*   *khaʔla*   *so-ŋ=niŋa=go*
        up   climb-PST-V2.GIVE-PST-1SG=SEQ   like_this   look-1SG.A=CTMP=TOP
        eko   *maŋpha=na*   *hoŋ*   *nis-u-ŋ.*
        one   much=NMLZ.SG   hole   see-3.P[PST]-1SG.A
        When I had climbed up into the tree and looked, I saw a large hole.

(24) *nhaŋa*   *phopciba* *lap-ma=go*   *men=na,*   *nna*
      and_then   owl   catch-INF=TOP   NEG.COP=NMLZ.SG that
      hoŋ=be   *i=ha=le*   *we?=na*   *bhoŋ*
      hole=LOC   what=NMLZ.NC=CONTR   be[3SG]=NMLZ.SG COMP
      so?-ma   *mit-het-u-ŋ.*
      look-INF   want-V2.CARRY.OFF-3.P[PST]-1SG.A
      Then, I wanted to see what was in the hole, even more than I wanted to
      catch the owl.

(25) *ŋkhoŋ* *nna* *hoŋ=be*   *so-ŋ,*   *nna=be=go*
      thus   that hole=LOC   look-[3.P;PST]-1SG.A, that=LOC=TOP
      phopciba=ga *hop=le*   *waisa!*
      owl=GEN   nest=CONTR   COP.PST[3]
      Then I looked into that hole, and there was an owl's nest!

(26) *nna*   *o-hop=pe=go*   *hicci* *u-in=ci=ca*
      that   3SG.POSS-nest=LOC=TOP   two   3SG.POSS-egg=NSG=ADD
      ŋ-wa-ya.
      3PL-be-PST
      In that nest there were two eggs, too.

(27) *ŋkha*   *u-in=ci*   *taŋ-se*   *bhoŋ* *a-muk*
      those   3SG.POSS-egg=NSG   take_out-SUP   PURP   1SG.POSS-hand
      end-u-ŋ=niŋa=go   *phopciba* *piciŋgelek-piciŋgelek*
      insert-3.P[PST]-1SG.A=CTMP=TOP   owl   shrieking_loudly
      ok-saŋ   *pes-a-ra-ya.*
      peck-SIM   fly-PST-V2.COME-PST[3SG]
      When I put my hand into the nest to take out the eggs, the owl flew to-
      wards me, screeching; it wanted to peck me.

(28) *nhaŋa*   *a-ţukhuruk=pe*   *pok=hoŋ*   *pok*
      and_then   1SG.POSS-head=LOC pecking_sound=SEQ   pecking_sound
      og-a-ŋ.
      peck-PST-1SG.P
      Then it began to peck me on my head.

(29) *ka*   *tuknuŋ*   *kisit-a-ŋ=hoŋ*   *mo*
      1SG   thoroughly   be_afraid-PST-1SG=SEQ   down
      uŋ-ma=ga   *cog-a-ŋ=niŋa=go*   *a-laŋ=ŋa*
      come_down-INF=GEN   try-PST-1SG=CTMP=TOP   1SG.POSS-foot=INS

tu-ŋ=na   *siŋ=ga*   *whak*   *ţek*
step_on-1SG.A[3.P;PST]=NMLZ.SG   tree=GEN   branch   breaking_sound
eg-a.
break-PST[3SG]
I was really afraid, and when I tried to get down from the tree, the branch
on which I stood cracked.

(30)   *ka*   *seŋ*
       1SG   falling_sound
       kaks-a-kh-eks-a-sa-ŋ=na.
       fall_down-PST-V2.GO-V2.CUT-PST-PST.PRF-1SG=NMLZ.SG
       I was about to fall down.

(31)   *heko=na*   *whak=pe*   *a-tek*   *het-u=hoŋ*
       other=NMLZ.SG   branch=LOC   1SG.POSS-clothes   hang-3.P[PST]=SEQ
       ka   *haŋcaŋcaŋ*   *chu-ya-ŋ.*
       1SG   dangling   hang-PST-1SG
       My clothes got caught on another branch, and then I was dangling there.

(32)   *chu-ya-ŋ=niŋa=ca*   *phopciba=ŋa*   *ok-ma*
       hang-PST-1SG=CTMP=ADD   owl=ERG   peck-INF
       n-lept-i-ya-ŋa-n.
       NEG-give_up-COMPL[TR]-PST-1SG.P-NEG
       Even then, the owl would not stop pecking me.

(33)   *ak=ka*   *a-ţukhuruk=pe*   *tuknuŋ*   *og-a-ŋ,*
       1SG.POSS=GEN   1SG.POSS-head=LOC   thoroughly   peck-PST-1SG.P
       heli=ca   *lond-a,*   *nhaŋa*   *a-sa*
       blood=ADD   come.out-PST[3SG],   and_then   1SG.POSS-flesh
       tuknuŋ   *tug-a.*
       thoroughly   hurt-PST[3SG]
       It pecked me on my head, painfully; and I was bleeding, too, and it hurt
       so much.

(34)   *ka=ca*   *phopciba*   *iŋ-nhaŋ-ma=ga*   *cog-a-ŋ,*
       1SG[ERG]=ADD   owl   chase-V2.SEND-INF=GEN   do-PST[3.P]-1SG.A
       ŋkhaʔniŋgo   *ka*   *i=ha=ca*   *a-niŋwa=be*
       but   1SG   what=NMLZ.NC=ADD   1SG.POSS-mind=LOC
       ŋ-as-het-u-ŋa-n,   *a-lawa=ŋa*
       NEG-understand-V2.CARRY.OFF-3.P[PST]-1SG.A-NEG,   1SG.POSS-soul=ERG

na?-ya-masa-ŋ.
leave-V2.LEAVE-PST.PRF-1SG.P
I also tried to scare off the owl, but then I do not know anything more, because I was frozen in shock.

(35) yo   a-ma=nuŋ   a-na=ŋa=chen
      over_there   1SG.POSS-mother=COM   1SG.POSS-elder_sister=ERG=TOP
      he?ne khy-a=na   bhoŋ ibebe   yog-a-ma.
      where go-PST[3SG]=NMLZ.SG   comp everywhere   look_for-PST-PRF
      My mother and my sister came looking where I had gone.

(36) hoŋma potik yok-saŋ   ta-ya-ma-ci=niŋ=go   ka
      river side   search-SIM come-PST-PRF-DU=CTMP=TOP   1SG
      haŋcaŋcaŋ chu-ya-ŋ=na   nis-a-ma.
      dangling   hang-PST-1SG=NMLZ.SG   see-PST-PRF
      Looking for me at the riverside, they saw me hanging there.

(37) nhaŋa   uŋci   hani   hani   ta-ya-ma-ci=hoŋ   ka
      and_then   3NSG   quickly   quickly   come-PST-PRF-DU=SEQ   1SG
      lab-a-ma.
      seize-PST-PRF
      So they came quickly and got me down.

(38) ŋkhiŋ   belak=be   phopciba=ca   ok-saŋ   hop=pe
      that_much   time=LOC   owl=ADD   shriek-SIM   nest=LOC
      pes-a-khy-a-ma.
      fly-PST-V2.GO-PST[3SG]-PRF
      That time, the owl, too, flew away to its nest, screeching.

(39) hakhok=ŋa   ka   cend-a-ky-a-ŋ=hoŋ
      later=INS   1SG   wake_up-PST-V2.COME.UP-PST-1SG=SEQ
      so-ŋ=niŋa=go   ka   luŋkhwak   choŋ=be
      look-1SG.A[3.P;PST]=CTMP=TOP   1SG   stone   on_top=LOC
      ips-a-masa.
      sleep-PST-PST.PRF
      Later, when I woke up and looked around, I had been sleeping on a rock.

(40) nhaŋa   a-ma=nuŋ   a-na=ŋa   ka
      and_then   1SG.POSS-mother=COM   1SG.POSS-elder_sister=ERG 1SG
      lab-a-masa.
      grab-PST-PST.PRF[1.P]
      Then, my mother and my sister grabbed me.

(41) *maŋcwa=le*   *apt-u*   *baŋniŋ=go*
     water=CONTR   bring-3.P[IMP]   talking_about=TOP
     i=ha=e   *kheps-uks-u=ha?*
     what=NMLZ.NC=CONTR   hear-PRF-3.P[PST]=NMLZ.NC
     When we told you to bring water, what did you hear?

(42) *imin=hoŋ* *ollobak* *n-sy-a-ga-n=na!*
     how=SEQ   almost   NEG-die-PST-2-NEG=NMLZ.SG
     Somehow you did not die, but almost!

(43) *lu-saŋ*   *thind-a*   *ka*   *ebbebe*   *kisit-a-ŋ*
     say-SIM   scold-PST[1.P]   1SG   shivering_in_fear   be_afraid-PST-1SG
     khoŋ   *ghwa-ghwa*   *hab-a-ŋ.*
     and_then   bawling_sound   cry-PST-1SG
     Saying so, they scolded me, and I was scared and bawled out loudly.

(44) *ma,*   *na=ci=ga*   *niŋwa=maŋ*   *om.*
     mother   elder_sister=NSG=GEN   love=EMPH   COP
     Of course my mother and my sister loved me.

(45) *hakhok=ŋa=go* *lem-saŋ*   *kha?la*   *lu-ya:*   *picchanacha*
     later=INS=TOP   persuade-SIM   like_this   say-PST[1.P]   child
     leŋ-ma=hoŋ *pyak* *chocholaplap* *men-jok-ma=ha.*
     be-INF=SEQ   very   mischievous   NEG-do-INF[DEONT]=NMLZ.NSG
     Later, convincing me, they said the following: 'Children should not be naughty.'

(46) *jeppa* *nna* *len* *ka*   *a-ma=nuŋ*
     true   that   day   1SG[ERG]   1SG.POSS-mother=COM
     a-na=ga   *ce?ya*
     1SG.POSS-elder_sister=GEN   word
     y-yen-u-ŋa-n=na=ŋa   *ollobak* *paro=be*
     NEG-obey-3.P[PST]-1SG.A-NEG=NMLZ.SG=ERG.CL   almost   heaven=LOC
     tas-u-ŋ=na.
     reach-3.P[PST]-1SG.A=NMLZ.SG
     Really, that day, because I did not listen to my mother and sister, I had almost gone to heaven.

(47) *a-ma=nuŋ*   *a-na=ŋa*
     1SG.POSS-mother=COM   1SG.POSS-elder_sister=ERG
     y-yog-a-n-niŋ=bi   *ka*   *hensen*
     NEG-look_for-PST[1.P]-NEG=CTMP=IRR   1SG   nowadays

ŋ-wa-ya-ŋa-n=bi.
NEG-be-PST-1SG-NEG=IRR
If my mother and sister had not looked for me, I would not be here now.

(48) ŋkhaʔniŋgo ka con-si-saŋ, ijaŋ baŋniŋ nna len
but 1SG be_happy-MDDL-SIM why about that day
bhaŋto=maŋ ka heʔniŋ=ca chocholaplap n-jog-a-ŋa-n.
from_on=EMPH 1SG when=ADD mischievous NEG-do-PST-1SG-NEG
But I was happy, because from that day on, I never did mischievous things
again.

(49) ka haʔniŋ tumha=ci=ga ceʔya=ca yem-ma
1SG COMPAR be_ripe=NMLZ.NSG=NSG=GEN word=ADD obey-INF
tarokt-u-ŋ.
start-3.P[PST]-1SG.A
I began to be obedient to my elders.

(50) hensen=ca phopciba ka-ya=na kheps-wa-ŋ
nowadays=ADD owl call-PST[3SG]=NMLZ.SG hear-NPST-1SG.A
ki a-niŋwa imin-imin coŋ-meʔ=na.
or 1SG.POSS-mind how-how do-NPST=NMLZ.SG
Even now, when I hear the sound of an owl, I get a strange feeling.

(51) a-ʈukhuruk=pe og-a-ŋ=na loʔwa
1SG.POSS-head=LOC peck-PST-1SG.P=NMLZ.SG like
en-si-me-ŋ=na.
perceive-MDDL-NPST-1SG=NMLZ.SG
It feels like it is still pecking me on the head.

The Namthalungma rocks

This text is an oral narrative of a mythological story. The speaker is Magman Jimi
Linkha (Tumok).

(1) eko liŋkha=ga teʔma canuwa=be
one a_clan=gen clan_sister Canuwa=LOC
thaŋ-khy-a-ma=na rahecha.
go_away_in_marriage-V2.GO-PST[3SG]-PRF=NMLZ.SG MIR
One Linkha sister went away to Canuwa village in marriage.

(2) *canuwa limbukhim=ci=ga taŋme, liŋkha=ci=ga*
Canuwa a_clan=NSG=GEN daughter-in-law, a_clan=NSG=GEN
teʔma bagdata nak-se mamliŋ
clan_sister finalization_of_marriage ask_for-SUP Mamling
ta-ya-ma.
come-PST[3SG]-PRF
A daughter-in-law of the Limbukhims, a Linkha clan sister, came to Mamling to ask for the bagdata.

(3) *mamliŋ=be o-cheba=ci, u-ppa,*
Mamling=LOC 3SG.POSS-male_clan_relatives=NSG, 3SG.POSS-father,
u-pum=ci=ŋa, ghak, i=ha=we, ŋkha
3SG.POSS-grandfather=NSG=ERG, all, what=NMLZ.NC=LOC, that
ghak m-b-hyaks-uks-u.
all 3PL.A-give-V2.SEND-PRF-3.P[PST]
In Mamling, her father, the grandfathers, everybody, they gave away everything to her.

(4) *ŋkhaʔniŋgo nna mamu=ŋa: ka, na, eko=chen ka*
but that girl=ERG 1SG[ERG] this one=TOP 1SG[ERG]
mit-u-ŋ=na,
want-3.P[PST]-1SG.A=NMLZ.SG
But that girl (said): 'I want one certain thing.'

(5) *saman py-haks-a, na yubak py-haks-a*
property give-V2.SEND-IMP[1.P] this thing give-V2.SEND-IMP[1.P]
lu-ks-u-ci
tell-PRF-3.P[PST]-3NSG.P
She told them: 'Please send these things with us.'

(6) *nani, i=na yubak? n-chimd-uks-u.*
child, what=NMLZ.SG thing 3PL.A-ask-PRF-3.P[PST]
'Child, what thing?', they asked her.

(7) *ka na eko luŋkhwak=chen py-haks-a*
1SG this one stone=TOP give-V2.SEND-IMP[1.P]
lu-ks-u-ci, mamu=ŋa.
tell-PRF-3.P[PST]-3NSG.P girl=ERG
'Send this one stone with me', she told them, the girl.

(8) *na=go   nda   khe?-ma   n-yas-wa-ga-n,   na*
this=TOP 2SG[ERG] carry_off-INF NEG-be_able-NPST-2-NEG this
ŋ-khet-u-n.
NEG-carry_off-3.P[IMP]-NEG
'This one, you cannot carry it off, do not carry it off.'

(9) *aniŋ=ga=ca   na   encho   nhaŋto*
1PL.EXCL.POSS=GEN=ADD this long_time_ago since
wen=ne,   na   ŋ-khet-u-n
exist[3SG]=NMLZ.SG, this NEG-carry_off-3.P[IMP]-NEG
n-lu-ks-u.
3PL.A-tell-PRF-3.P[PST]
'It is ours since times immemorial, do not take it', they told her.

(10) *mamu=ga   u-niŋwa   ŋ-gaks-a-ma-n.*
girl=GEN 3SG.POSS-mind NEG-fall_down-PST-PRF-NEG
The girl did not give in.

(11) *na   tuknuŋ   u-niŋwa   tug-a-ma,   ka   na*
this completely 3SG.POSS-mind have_pain-PST[3SG]-PRF 1SG this
meŋ-khe?-le,   na   luŋkhwak   meŋ-khe?-le
NEG-carry_off-CVB, this stone NEG-carry_off-CVB
ŋ-khe-me-ŋa-n=na   lu-ks-u-ci.
3PL-go-NPST-1SG-NEG=NMLZ.SG tell-PRF-3.P[PST]-3NSG.P
She was so sad; 'I will not go without taking this stone with me', she told
them.

(12) *nna,   nani,   nna   luŋkhwak=maŋ   khet-wa-ga=na*
that child that stone=EMPH carry_off-NPST-2=NMLZ.SG
bhoŋ,   se?ni=ŋa   na?masek   lam-ma.
COND, night_time=INS night_time walk-INF[DEONT]
'This stone, child, if you take away this stone, you have to walk at night.'

(13) *se?ni=ŋa   se?namphok=pe,   he?ne=ca   me-yuŋ-ma=ga*
night_time=INS whole_night=LOC, where=ADD NEG-put-INF=GEN
m-baŋ=be   ta-met-i.
2SG.POSS-house=LOC reach-CAUS-COMPL[IMP]
'At night, the whole night, without putting it anywhere, deliver it at your
home.'

(14) *manhoŋ*   *n-leŋ-me-n=na*
otherwise NEG-become-NPST[3SG]-NEG=NMLZ.SG
n-lu-ks-u.
3PL.A-tell-PRF-3.P[PST]
'Otherwise, it will not be (yours)', they told her.

(15) *paŋ=be*   *ta-me?-ma*   *n-yas-u-ga-n*   *bhoŋ,*
house=LOC arrive-CAUS-INF NEG-be_able-3.P[SBJV]-2-NEG COND
aniŋ=ga=ca   *n-leŋ-me-n,*   *ŋa=ca*
1PL.EXCL.POSS=GEN=ADD NEG-become-NPST[3SG]-NEG your=ADD
n-leŋ-me-n   *n-lu-ks-u=niŋa,*   *na*
NEG-become-NPST[3SG]-NEG 3PL.A-tell-PRF-3.P[PST]=CTMP this
mamu i   *ka-ya-ma=na:*   *ka*
girl what say-PST[3SG]-PRF=NMLZ.SG 1SG[ERG]
ta-met-wa-ŋ=na   *ka-ya-ma.*
bring-CAUS-NPST-1SG.A=NMLZ.SG say-PST[3SG]-PRF
When they told her: 'If you cannot deliver it home, it will neither be ours nor yours', what this girl said, she said: 'I will bring it home.'

(16) *na*   *mamliŋ*   *baŋna*   *luŋkhwak*
this Mamling so-called stone
m-b-hyaks-uks-u.
3PL.A-give-V2.SEND-PRF-3.P[PST]
They gave that so-called Mamling stone to her.

(17) *bagdata*   *nak-se=ha*
finalization_of_marriage ask_for-SUP=NMLZ.NSG
a-kamnibak=ci=ŋa   *nnakha* *luŋkhwak=ha*   *i=ha*
1SG.POSS-friend=NSG=ERG that   stone=NMLZ.NC what=NMLZ.NC
ghak *ŋ-khu-ks-u.*
all   3PL.A-carry-PRF-3.P[PST]
'My friends (who came) in order to ask for the Bagdata, they carry all that belongs to this stone.'

(18) *eko=ŋa*   *eko* *luŋkhwak,* *heko=na=ŋa*   *eko* *luŋkhwak,*
one=ERG one stone   other=NMLZ.SG=ERG one stone
heko=na=ŋa   *eko* *luŋkhwak.*
other=NMLZ.SG=ERG one stone
One (took) one stone, another one (took) one stone, another one (took) one stone.

(19) *heko=ha=ci=ŋa*   *i=ha*   *i=ha*
other=NMLZ.NSG=NSG=ERG   what=NMLZ.NC   what=NMLZ.NC
m-bi-ks-a,   *ŋkha*   *ghak*   *ŋ-kho-het-u.*
3PL.A-give-PST.PRF   that   all   3PL.A-carry-V2.CARRY.OFF-3.P[PST]
They carried off everything that the others had given her.

(20) *nhaŋa*   *yo,*   *mulgaun=be*   *n-das-uks-u,*
and_then   across   Mulgaun=LOC   3PL.A-reach-PRF-3.P[PST]
coilikha=be,   *coilikha*   *ʈhaun=ko*   *nam.*
Coilikha=LOC   Coilikha   place=TOP   name
And then they arrived on the other side, in Mulgaun, in Coilikha, Coilikha
is the name of the place.

(21) *coilikha=be*   *n-das-u=niŋa,*   *nna*   *mamu=ga*
Coilikha=LOC   3PL.A-arrive-3.P[PST]=CTMP,   that   girl=GEN
o-phok   *tuk-ma*   *tarokt-uks-u.*
3SG.POSS-stomach   hurt-INF   start-PRF-3.P[PST]
When they arrived in Coilikha, that girl's stomach began to hurt.

(22) *nna*   *o-phok*   *tug-a-ma=hoŋ,*   *pakha*
that   3SG.POSS-stomach   hurt-PST[3SG]-PRF=SEQ,   outside
yuŋ-a-ma.
sit_down-PST[3SG]-PRF
As her stomach hurt, she went to the toilet.

(23) *pakha=ca*   *yuŋ-a-ma.*
outside=ADD   sit_down-PST[3SG]-PRF
She also went to the toilet.

(24) *nna*   *khatniŋ=ŋa,*   *pakha=ca*   *lom-ma*   *cog-a-ma,*
that   this_time=INS,   outside=ADD   come_out-INF   try-PST[3SG]-PRF,
u-hi   *lom-ma=ca*   *cog-a-ma,*
3SG.POSS-stool   come_out-INF=ADD   try-PST[3SG]-PRF
That time, she felt like vomiting and shitting.

(25) *ŋkhatniŋgo*   *n-lond-a-n.*
but   NEG-come_out-PST[3SG]-NEG
But it did not come out.

(26) *kus-uks-u,*   *kus-uks-u,*
wait_for-PRF-3.P[PST],   wait_for-prf-3.P[pst],
kus-u-lo=be   *wa=ci*
wait_for-3.P[PST]-INT.CL=LOC   chicken=NSG

ŋ-ga-ya-by-a-ma.
3PL-speak-PST-V2.GIVE-PST-PRF
She waited and waited, and while she waited, the cocks already crowed.

(27) *wa=ci*   *ŋ-ga-ya=hoŋ=go*   *om*
chicken=NSG   3PL-speak-PST=SEQ=TOP   bright
leks-a-khy-a
become-PST-V2.GO-PST[3SG]
As the cocks crowed, it had already dawned.

(28) *ŋkhiŋ-belak*   *wa=ci,*   *wa=ci*   *ŋ-ga-ya=niŋa*
that_much-time   chicken=NSG   chicken=NSG   3PL-speak-PST=CTMP
eko=ŋa=cen   *sui*   *lukt-u-get-uks-u,*   *eko*
one=ERG=TOP   quickly   run-3.P-V2.BRING.UP-PRF-3.P   one
luŋkhwak   *uthamalaŋ,*   *limbukhim=ŋa.*
stone   steeply_uphill   a_clan=ERG
At that time, while the cocks crowed, one ran up with the stone, steeply uphill, one Limbukhim guy.

(29) *eko=na*   *lukt-u-get-u=hoŋ*   *to,*   *okhyu,*
one=NMLZ.SG   run-3.P[PST]-V2.BRING.UP-3.P[PST]=SEQ   up   Okhyu
mulgaun=be   *ta-uks-u.*
Mulgaun=LOC   bring-PRF-3.P[PST]
As he ran up with one stone, he brought it there to Mulgaun, to Okhyu.

(30) *na*   *heko=ha=ci=ŋa,*   *na*   *mo=na*   *luŋkhwak,*
this   other=NMLZ.NSG=NSG=ERG   this   down=NMLZ.SG   stone
heko=ha   *luŋkhwak*
other=NMLZ.NSG   stone
n-yuks-u-sa-ci=ha.
3PL.A-keep-3.P[PST]-PST.PRF-3NSG.P=NMLZ.NSG
The others, the lower stones, they had put the other stones down there.

(31) *ŋkha*   *them-ma*   *n-jog-uks-u-ci,*   *them-ma*
those   lift-INF   3PL.A-try-PRF-3.P[PST]-3NSG.P   lift-INF
n-yas-uks-u-n-ci-nin.
NEG-be_able-PRF-3.P[PST]-NEG-3NSG.P-3PL.NEG
They tried to lift them up, but they could not lift them up.

(32) *them-ma   n-yas-u-n-ci-nin,*   *nna=ga*
lift-INF   NEG-be_able-3.P[PST]-NEG-3NSG.P-3PL.NEG   that=GEN
lenlen   ips-a-m=ha,   *luŋkhwak.*
lying_horizontally   sleep-PST[3SG]-PRF=NMLZ.NSG   stone
They could not lift them up, the stones were lying (sleeping) there.

(33) *kha   pok-ma   n-yas-uks-u-n-ci-nin.*
these   wake_up-INF   NEG-be_able-PRF-3.P[PST]-NEG-3NSG.P-3PL.NEG
They could not wake them up.

(34) *nna=be   sum=ci   luŋkhwak   ŋ-wa-ya-ci.*
that=LOC   three=NSG   stone   3PL-exist-PST-3NSG.P
There were three stones.

(35) *eko   lenlen,   eko,   ŋkha   sum=ci   sum=ci,*
one   lying_horizontally   one   those   three=NSG   three=NSG
carpaʈe=ci.
four-sided=NSG
One was lying there hugely, those three, the four-sided stones.

(36) *nnakha   luŋkhwak=ci   pok-ma*
those   stone=NSG   wake_up-INF
n-yas-uks-u-n-ci-nin,   *ŋkhaʔla   uŋci*
NEG-be_able-PRF-3.P[PST]-NEG-3NSG.P-3PL.NEG,   like_that   3NSG
yo   canuwa=be   ŋ-khy-a.
across   Canuwa=LOC   3PL-go-PST
They could not place those stones upright, and like that (i.e., without the stones), they went over there, to Canuwa.

(37) *canuwa   ŋ-khy-a=hoŋ,   heksaŋ   i   leks-a   baŋniŋ,*
Canuwa   3PL-go-PST=SEQ   later   what   happen-PST[3SG]   about
na,   jaba,   na   mamu=ŋa   luŋkhwak   pok-ma
this   when   this   girl=ERG   stone   wake_up-INF
n-yas-u-n,   ŋkhiŋ-belak=ŋa   na   canuwa,
NEG-be_able-3.P[PST]-NEG   that_much-time=INS   this   Canuwa
canuwa   men=na,   mulgaun,   mulgaun=ga   to,
Canuwa   NEG.COP=NMLZ.SG   Mulgaun   Mulgaun=GEN   up
okhyu=be   to   ʈhuŋkha=be   eko   luŋkhwak
Okhyu=LOC   up   steep_slope=LOC   one   stone
waiʔ=na,   dewan   ɖhuŋga   baŋna.
exist[3SG]=NMLZ.SG   Dewan   stone   so-called

As they had gone to Canuwa, about what happened later, when the girl could not place the stone upright, at that time, this, Canuwa, not Canuwa, Mulgaun, above Mulgaun, in Okhyu, in that steep place, there is one rock, called Dewan stone.

(38) *nna   dewan   ḍhuŋga   baŋna   luŋkhwak   sahro   cancan*
    that   Dewan   stone   so-called stone   very   high

    sa-ma=na,   *pyak   cancan,   ikhiŋ*   *cancan,   nna*
    COP.PST-PRF=NMLZ.SG much high   how_much high   that

    cancan=na=bhaŋ   so?-ma=niŋa,   mo   oṭemma,   mʌdes   ghak
    high=NMLZ.SG=ABL look-INF=CTMP down plains   plains   all

    ota=ha=bu.
    be_visible-PST[3SG]=NMLZ.NC=REP

That Dewan stone was really high, it was very high, so high; when one looked down from this high place, the plains, the Tarai, everything was visible, they say.

(39) *nnakha   ghak   ot-a-ma,*   *mo,   nna,*
    that   all   be_visible-PST[3SG]-PRF down   that

    saptakosi=ga   *u-lap=pe*   *tori*
    a_river_confluence=GEN 3SG.POSS-side=LOC mustard

    phet-a=ha=ca   *ot=ha=bu,*   *nna=bhaŋ.*
    bloom-PST=NMLZ.NC=ADD be_visible=NMLZ.NC=REP that=ABL

All was visible, below, even the mustard blooming on the shores of the Saptakosi was visible, from there.

(40) *nna   mamu=ŋa,   nna   mamu=ŋa   nna   luŋkhwak*
    that   girl=ERG   that   girl=ERG   that   stone

    khet-u=na   *din   i*
    carry_off-3.P[PST]=NMLZ.SG day what

    leks-a-ma=na   *baŋniŋ,   haku   heko=na*
    happen-PST[3SG]-PRF=NMLZ.SG about now   other=NMLZ.SG

    taplik   tum-si-me?=na   *nna=be.*
    story   find-MDDL-NPST[3SG]=NMLZ.SG that=LOC

As for what happened on the day when the girl took away the stone, another story can be found, inside that (story).

(41) *na   dewan   ḍhuŋga   l-wa=na,*   *mulgaun=be?=na*
    this   Dewan   stone   call-NPST=NMLZ.SG Mulgaun=LOC=NMLZ.SG

    dewan   ḍhuŋga,   na   cancan=na   luŋkhwak,   uŋ
    Dewan   stone   this   high=NMLZ.SG stone   3SG

sadhai=ca,	*i=na*		*ŋ-gam-my-a,*	*yaksigum,*
always=ADD	what=NMLZ.SG	3PL-call-NPST=NMLZ.NC		place_to_meet

yaksigum	*khy-a=na=bu.*
place_to_meet	go-PST[3SG]=NMLZ.SG=REP

They called that high rock the Dewan stone of Mulgaun; that high rock, it was always, what do they call it – Yaksigum – it always went to the Yaksigum.

(42)
yaksigum	*heʔne*	*khy-a=na*		*baŋniŋ*	*uŋ*
place_to_meet	where	go-PST[3SG]=NMLZ.SG		about	3SG

cokcokinetham=be	*khy-a=na=bu*
a_mythical_place=LOC	go-PST[3SG]=NMLZ.SG=REP

And about where it went, it went to the place called Bed of Stars, it is said.

(43)
cokcokinetham=be,	*eko*	*maḍa*	*oṭemma*	*kham*
a_mythical_place=LOC	one	big	plains	ground

wait=na		*rahecha!*
exist[3SG]=NMLZ.SG		MIR

In the Bed of Stars, there is a huge plain area!

(44)
nna	*kham=be*	*naʔmasek=ŋa*		*uŋ*	*yaksigum*
that	ground=loc	evening_time=INS		3SG	place_to_meet

khy-a.
go-PST[3SG]

And at night he went to that place, to the Yaksigum.

(45)
om	*me-leŋ-le*	*las-a=hoŋ*		*pheri*	*to*
bright	NEG-become-CVB	return-PST[3SG]=SEQ		again	up

thithi	*em-diʔ-ma=bu*
standing_upright	stand-V2.GIVE-INF[DEONT]=REP

Before sunrise, it had to return and stand upright again.

(46)
nhaŋ	*wandik=ŋa=ca*	*yaksigum*	*khy-a,*	*om*
and_then	later=INS=ADD	place_to_meet	go-PST[3SG]	bright

me-leŋ-le	*ap-ma=hoŋ*		*thithi*
NEG-become-CVB	come.LEVEL-INF[DEONT]=SEQ		standing_upright

em-diʔ-m=ha.
stand-V2.GIVE-INF[DEONT]–NMLZ.NC

The next day it went to the Yaksigum again; it had to come back and stand upright again before sunrise.

(47)   *yapmi=ci*   *ni-ma*   *haksaŋ*   *aghi*   *thithi*
        person=NSG   see-INF   COMPAR   before   standing_upright
        em-diʔ-ma   *sa=na.*
        stand-V2.GIVE-INF[DEONT]   COP.PST=NMLZ.SG
        It had to stand upright before people would see it.

(48)   *ŋkhaʔniŋgo*   *na*   *mamliŋ=bhaŋ*   *khy-a=na*   *mamu*
        but   this   Mamling=ABL   go-PST[3SG]=NMLZ.SG   girl
        jʌbʌ   *pakha*   *yuŋ-a,*   *pakha*   *yuŋ-a=hoŋ*
        when   outside   sit-PST[3SG]   outside   sit_down-PST[3SG]=SEQ
        uk=ka   *o-phok*   *tug-a,*   *luŋkhwak*
        3SG.POSS=GEN   3SG.POSS-stomach   hurt-PST[3SG]   stone
        them-ma   *n-yas-u-n-ci-n.*
        lift-INF   NEG-be_able-3.P[PST]-NEG-3NSG.P-NEG
        But the girl that had gone from Mamling, when she sat outside (to vomit
        and shit), as she sat outside, her stomach was aching, she could not lift
        up the stones.

(49)   *wa=ci*   *ŋ-ga-ya-by-a=ha.*
        chicken=NSG   3PL-speak-PST-V2.GIVE-PST=NMLZ.NSG
        The cocks had already crowed.

(50)   *ŋkhiŋ-belak=ŋa*   *nna*   *dewan*   *ḍhuŋga*
        that_much-time=INS   that   Dewan   stone
        n-l-wa=na   *luŋkhwak=ca,*   *eko*   *maʔniŋ*
        3PL.A-call-NPST=NMLZ.SG   stone=ADD   one   without
        yororo   *cicaŋgalik*
        falling_and_tearing_along   in_somersaults
        kaks-a-khy-a-ma.
        fall_down-PST-V2.GO-PST[3SG]-PRF
        At that time, that stone called Dewan stone, too, it fell down tearing ev-
        erything along, just like that.

(51)   *cicaŋgalik*   *kaks-a-khy-a-ma,*   *nna*
        in_somersaults   fall_down-PST-V2.GO-PST[3SG]-PRF   that
        cokcokinetham   *n-l-wa=na*   *kham=ca*
        a_mythical_place   3PL.A-call-NPST=NMLZ.SG   ground=ADD
        uptakham   *luptakham*   *leks-a-khy-a-ma.*
        landslide   landslide   happen-PST-V2.GO-PST[3SG]-PRF
        It fell down in somersaults, that place called Bed of Stars also slid down,
        there was a landslide, burying the ground.

(52) *pahiro   khy-a-ma.*
landslide go-PST[3SG]-PRF
There was a landslide.

(53) *upt-a-khy-a-ma,   nnakha=ci, mo   luŋkhwak=ca*
collapse-PST-V2.GO-PST[3SG]-PRF that=NSG   down   stone=ADD
kheʔ-ma   n-yas-u-nin.
carry_off-INF 3PL.A-be_able-3.P[PST]-3PL.NEG
There was a landslide, and they had not managed to carry off the lower
stones, too.

(54) *dewan   ɖhuŋga=ca kaks-a-khy-a,*
Dewan   stone=ADD   fall_down-PST-V2.GO-PST[3SG]
The Dewan stone fell down.

(55) *cokcokinetham=ca   upt-a-khy-a.*
a_mythical_place=ADD   collapse-PST-V2.GO-PST[3SG]
The Bed of Stars collapsed, too.

(56) *nhaŋ   heksaŋ yo   paŋ=go   n-das-u.*
and_then later   across house=TOP 3PL.A-reach-3.P[PST]
Then, later, they reached the house on the other side.

(57) *paŋ   n-das-u,   nhaŋ   ŋ-wa-ya=hoŋ,   heksaŋ*
house   3PL.A-reach-3.P[PST]   and_then 3PL-live-PST=SEQ   later
i   leks-a   baŋniŋ na   luŋkhwak mo
what happen-PST[3SG]   about   this stone   down
puŋda=e   ŋkhaʔla   wa-ya,   ŋkha   namthaluŋma=ci,
jungle=LOC like_that   exist-PST[3SG] those Namthalungma=NSG
u-maita=haŋ   ŋ-khet-u=ci=ha
3SG.POSS-natal_home=ABL   3PL.A-carry_off-3.P[PST]-3NSG.P=NMLZ.NC
luŋkhwak=ci,   ŋkha,   ŋkhaʔla   ŋ-wa-ya=niŋa
stone=NSG   those   in_that_way   3PL-live-PST=CTMP
uŋci-niŋwa   tug-a-ma   rahecha!
3NSG.POSS-mind hurt-PST[3SG]-PRF   MIR
They reached the house, and as they were there, as for what happened
later, this stone was down there in the jungle, those Namthalungma stones,
the stones they had carried away from her maternal home, as they lived
like that, they were sad!

(58)   *uŋci-niŋwa*   *ŋkha*   *luŋkhwak=ga*   *u-niŋwa*
        3NSG.POSS-mind   those   stone=GEN   3SG.POSS-mind
        tug-a-ma=hoŋ,   *ten=be*   *picha=ci*
        hurt-PST[3SG]-PRF=SEQ   village=LOC   child=NSG
        o-phok=ŋa   *saʔ-m=ha,*   *ghau*   *pok-ma,*
        3SG.POSS-stomach=ERG   churn-INF=NMLZ.NC   wound   infest-INF
        wha,   *wha*   *leŋ-ma=ha,*   *nhaŋ*
        septic_wound   septic_wound   happen-INF=NMLZ.NC   and_then
        koi   *koi*   *sulemwalem*   *leŋ-khe-khuba,*   *mam=ha*
        some   some   head_hanging_down   become-V2.GO-NMLZ   big
        yapmi=ci=ga,   *u-niŋwa*   *meʔniŋ,*   *das*
        person=NSG=GEN   3SG.POSS-mind   without   mental_strength
        men-da-ma=ga   *ŋ-wa-ya-ghond-a-ma.*
        NEG-come-INF=GEN   3PL-live-PST-V2.ROAM-PST-PRF
        As they were sad, as those stones were sad, the children in the village, their stomachs hurt, wounds appeared on them, then, some of them becoming like wilted flowers, the adults, too, they walked around without mental strength.

(59)   *na*   *i*   *leksa,*   *m-mit-a-ma,*   *yapmi=ci.*
        this   what   happen-PST[3SG]   3PL-think-PST-PRF   person=NSG
        'What happened to this place?' the people thought.

(60)   *ŋkhaʔniŋa*   *ikhiŋ*   *leks-a-by-a,*   *wasik=ca*
        that_time   how_much   happen-PST-V2.GIVE-PST[3SG]   rain=ADD
        n-da-me-n=na.
        NEG-come-NPST[3SG]-NEG=NMLZ.SG
        And then, how many (bad things) happened, it does not rain, too.

(61)   *wasik*   *n-da-me-n=niŋa*   *nam*
        rain   NEG-come-NPST[3SG]-NEG=CTMP   sun
        phen-a=na   *phen-a=na,*
        shine-PST[3SG]=NMLZ.SG   shine-PST[3SG]=NMLZ.SG,
        phen-a-nes-a=na.
        shine-PST-V2.LAY-PST[3SG]=NMLZ.SG
        It does not rain, the sun was shining and shining, it kept shining.

(62)   *wasik*   *ta-ya-khy-a*   *bhoŋ*   *ghak*   *i=ha*
        rain   come-PST-V2.GO-PST[3SG]   COND   all   what=NMLZ.NC

yaŋ-kheʔ-ma-gari,   *ghak*
flush-V2.TAKE.ALONG-INF-ADVLZ   all
yaŋ-het-i=nuŋ=ga   *wasik*   *ta-ya-ma.*
flush-V2.CARRY.OFF-COMPL=COM=GEN   rain   come-PST[3SG]-PRF
And when it rained, it rained so much that everything was taken along
by the water.

(63)   *na*   *wasik=le,*   *wasik*   *ta-ya=na=ca*   *la-ma*
         this   rain=CONTR   rain   come-PST[3SG]=NMLZ.SG=ADD   return-INF
         n-nis-u-n,   *nam*   *phen-a=na=ca*   *ucun*
         NEG-know-3.P[PST]-NEG   sun   shine-PST[3SG]=NMLZ.SG=ADD   good
         phen-a=na,   *phen-a=na*
         shine-PST[3SG]=NMLZ.SG   shine-PST[3SG]=NMLZ.SG
         phen-a=na   *leks-a,*   *lan-siʔ-ma*
         shine-PST[3SG]=NMLZ.SG   happen-PST[3SG]   return-MDDL-INF
         n-nis-u-n.
         NEG-see-3.P[PST]-NEG
         This rain, it rained, and did not know how to stop, the sun was shining,
         it happened that it shone nicely, it did not know how to stop.

(64)   *haku*   *i*   *cogi*   *ŋ-ga-ya-ma*   *nnakha*   *mulgaun=be,*
         now   what   do-1PL[SBJV]   3PL-say-PST-PRF   those   Mulgaun=LOC
         okhyu=be=ha   *yapmi=ci.*
         Okhyu=LOC=NMLZ.NSG   person=NSG
         Now what shall we do, said the people from Mulgaun, from Okhyu.

(65)   *ŋkhaʔniŋa,*   *eh,*   *nna=go*   *haʔlo*   *namthaluŋma=beʔ=na*
         that_time   oh   that=TOP   excla   Namthalungma=LOC=NMLZ.SG
         luŋkhwak   *leʔlo!*
         stone   CONTR.EMPH
         At that time, this, gee, it is the stone of Namthalung!

(66)   *namthaluŋma=beʔ=na*   *luŋkhwak*   *nhe*   *ket-a-ma*
         Namthalung=LOC=NMLZ.SG   stone   here   bring_up-PST[3SG]-PRF
         eko.
         one
         One of the Namthalum stones was brought here!

(67)   *na*   *eko=ŋa=go*   *thend-u-get-uks-a=ba,*   *nna,*
         this   one=ERG=TOP   lift-3.P[PST]-V2.BRING.UP-PST.PRF=EMPH   that

> om   leks-a=niŋa,
> bright   become-PST[3SG]=CTMP
> Someone had carried it up, while it was getting bright.

(68)   wa   ka-ya=na,   ka-ya=na,
       chicken   say-PST[3SG]=NMLZ.SG   say-PST[3SG]=NMLZ.SG
       thithi
       standing_upright
       end-u-ghet-uks-u=na   luŋkhwak
       insert-3.P[PST]-V2.TAKE.ALONG-PRF-3.P[PST]=NMLZ.SG   stone
       ceŋ   to   ten=be   wai?=na   haku=ca.
       upright   up   village=LOC   exist[3SG]=NMLZ.SG   now=ADD
       The cocks crowed, and someone placed the stone there upright; it is there,
       up high in the village, even now.

(69)   maḍa   luŋkhwak   om.
       big   stone   COP
       It is a big stone.

(70)   nna   ket-uks-u.
       that   bring_up-PRF-3.P[PST]
       He brought it up there.

(71)   haku   na=be   laŋ=ci   muk=ci   wa-siŋ-khe?-ma=ci.
       now   this=LOC   leg=NSG   hand=NSG   wash-V2.GO-INF[DEONT]=NSG
       Now, at this place, one has to go there having washed one's feet and
       hands.

(72)   nhaŋa   mo   khe?-ma=hoŋ   thak-m=ha=ci.
       and_then   down   go-INF=SEQ   worship-INF[DEONT]=NMLZ.NSG=NSG
       And then, after going down, one has to worship and pray.

(73)   nna=ca   isa=ŋa   thak-ma=na   baŋniŋ,
       that=ADD   who=ERG   worship-INF[DEONT]=NMLZ.SG   about
       liŋkha=ga   te?ma=ŋa   thak-ma=na,
       a_clan=GEN   clan_sister=ERG   worship-INF[DEONT]=NMLZ.SG
       ŋkhiŋ=ca   n-leks-a-n   bhoŋ,   liŋkha=ga
       that_much=ADD   NEG-become-SBJV[3SG]-NEG   COND   a_clan=GEN
       o-te?ma=ŋa,   limbukhim-ga   u-taŋmek
       3SG.POSS-clan_sister=ERG   a_clan=GEN   3SG.POSS-daughter-in-law
       leŋ-khuba=ŋa,
       become-NMLZ=ERG

Now about who has to do the worship, a Linkha clan sister has to do the worship, and if that much is not possible, a Linkha sister, a prospective Limbukhim daughter-in-law.

(74) *ŋkhiŋ=ca* *n-leks-a-n* *bhoŋ,* *liŋkha=ga*
      that_much=ADD NEG-happen-SBJV[3SG]-NEG COND a_clan=GEN
      teʔma=ŋa=se=hoŋ=ca *leŋ-meʔ=na,*
      clan_sister=ERG=RESTR=SEQ=ADD be_alright-NPST[3SG]=NMLZ.SG
      thaŋ-meŋ-khe-leʔ=na=hoŋ=ca,
      go_away_in_marriage-NEG-go-CVB=NMLZ.SG=SEQ=ADD
      If that much is not possible, it is also alright if it is only a Linkha sister, even if she is not going to marry.

(75) *thak-ma=na* *ŋ-ga-ya-ma=hoŋ* *ŋ-khy-a-ma.*
      worship-INF[DEONT]=NMLZ.SG 3PL-say-PST-PRF=SEQ 3PL-go-PST-PRF
      She has to do the worship, they said, and went (the people of the girl's maternal home).

(76) *haku* *imin* *thak-ma=na* *ŋ-ga-ya=niŋa,*
      now how worship-INF[DEONT]=NMLZ.SG 3PL-say-PST=CTMP
      As they said how to do the worship,

(77) *liŋkha=ga* *mamu=ŋa,* *liŋkha* *mamu=ŋa* *thakt-uks-u.*
      a_clan=GEN girl=ERG a_clan girl=ERG worship-PRF-3.P[PST]
      a Linkha girl did the worship.

(78) *tuknuŋ* *nam* *phen-a=niŋa* *kaniŋ=go* *cinuŋ=le*
      completely sun shine-PST[3SG]=CTMP 1PL=TOP cold=CONTR
      cah-a=ba *cog-i-ŋ.*
      need-NATIV=EMPH do-1PL[SBJV]-EXCL
      When the sun was shining so much, though we need cold climate.

(79) *miyaŋ* *taŋkhyaŋ* *mopmop* *cok-t-a-by-a*
      little sky a_little_cloudy do-BEN-IMP-V2.GIVE-IMP[1.P]
      miʔyaŋ *cinuŋ* *cok-t-a-by-a,* *ka-saŋ* *cuwa*
      little cold do-BEN-IMP-V2.GIVE-IMP[1.P] say-SIM beer
      wahe-saŋ, *samphi* *wahe-saŋ,* *nna*
      offer[to_deity]-SIM ginger offer[to_deity]-SIM that
      n-thakt-uks-u, *nna* *thakma=se*
      3PL.A-worship-PRF-3.P[PST] that worship-INF=RESTR
      n-darokt-u=na,
      3PL.A-start-3.P[PST]=NMLZ.SG

Saying: 'Please cover the sky a little for us, please make it a bit chilly for us!', offering beer, offering ginger, they worshipped that stone, and just when they started to worship,

(80) *n-darokt-uksa=niŋa   wasik   ta-ma   tarokt-uks-u.*
3PL.A-start-PST.PRF=CTMP   rain   come-INF   start-PRF-3.P[PST]
when they started (worshipping), it started to rain.

(81) *nhaŋ   uŋci   ŋ-gy-a=hoŋ   wasik*
and_then   3NSG   3PL-come_up-PST=SEQ   rain
ta-ya-by-a,   ucun   leks-a.
come-PST-V2.GIVE-PST[3SG]   good   become-PST[3SG]
And when they came up (from the place of the stones), it was raining for them, it became nice.

(82) *heksaŋ   pheri   nam,   wasik=se   tuknuŋ   ta-ya=hoŋ,*
behind   again   sun   rain=RESTR thoroughly come-PST[3SG]=SEQ
tuknuŋ   wasik   ta-ya,   haku   i   cok-ma,
thoroughly rain   come-PST[3SG]   now   what   do-INF
ŋ-ga-ya-ma.
3PL-say-PST-PRF
Later though, as sun and rain got worse again, it rained quite a lot; 'Now what to do?', they said.

(83) *pheri   ŋkhaʔniŋ=ca,   haku,   pheri   na   liŋkha=ga   teʔma,*
again   that_time=ADD   now   again   this   a_clan=GEN   clan_sister
limbukhim=ga   taŋmeʔ=ŋa,   nna
a_clan=GEN   daughter-in-law=ERG   that
thak-ma=na   ŋ-ga-ya-ma.
worship-INF[DEONT]=NMLZ.SG   3PL-say-PST-PRF
At that time, again, that Linkha girl, the daughter-in-law of the Limbukhims, she has to do the worship, they said.

(84) *imin   thak-ma,   eh,   na,   haku,   na   wasik*
how   worship-INF[DEONT]   oh   this   now   this   rain
la-ni   bhoŋ   thak-ma=na   ŋ-ga-ya-ma
return-OPT   PURP   worship-INF[DEONT]=NMLZ.SG   3PL-say-PST-PRF
haiko=ha=ci=ŋa.
other=NMLZ.NSG=NSG=ERG
As for how to worship, now, in order for the rain to go back, one has to do the worship, the others said.

(85) na   wasik   la-ni   bhoŋ   imin   thak-ma=na
      this   rain   return-OPT   purp   how   worship-INF[DEONT]=NMLZ.SG
      baŋniŋ, lu,   nam,   ikhiŋ   miʔwa
      about   INIT   sun   how_much   tear
      hond-end-u-g=ha,   haku=go   nam=ca
      uncover-V2.INSERT-3.P[PST]-2=NMLZ.NSG now=TOP   sun=ADD
      hond-end-u   ka-saŋ   n-thakt-uks-u.
      uncover-V2.INSERT-3.P[PST]   say-SIM   3PL.A-worship-PRF-3.P[PST]
      For that rain to stop, as for how one has to do the worship: 'Oh, Sun [false
      start], how many tears you (the sky) have dropped, now also make the
      sun come out!' they said, and did the worship.

(86) nhaŋ   nam   phen-a-ma.
      and_then   sun   shine-PST[3SG]-PRF
      And the sun shone.

(87) ŋkhaʔniŋa   nna   luŋkhwak=pu   cilleŋ
      that_time   that   stone=REP   lying_on_the_back
      walleŋ   leŋ-ma   sa=na=bu.
      lying_on_the_front   overturn-INF[DEONT]   COP.PST=NMLZ.SG=REP
      Thus, that stone had to be turned around to the back and to the front.

(88) nna=be   sum=ci   luŋkhwak   ŋ-wa-ya,   eko
      that=LOC   three=NSG   stone   3PL-exist-PST   one
      namthaluŋma,   eko   lalaluŋma,   heko=na=ga
      Namthalungma   one   Lalalungma   other=NMLZ.SG=GEN
      u-niŋ   i=na=ʔlo,   ka=ca
      3SG.POSS-name   what=NMLZ.SG=EXCLA   1SG[ERG]=ADD
      mund-i-ŋ.
      forget-COMPL-1SG.A
      There were three stones, one was Namthalungma, one Lalalungma, and
      the name of the other stone – what – I forgot it, too.

(89) nnakha   luŋkhwak=ci   leŋ-ma=ci=bu,   nam
      those   stone=NSG   overturn-INF[DEONT]=NSG=REP   sun
      phen-ni   bhoŋ,   nam=bhaŋ   leŋ-ma=na,
      shinc-OPT purp   sun=ABL   overturn-INF[DEONT]=NMLZ.SG
      These stones have to be turned around, in order for the sun to shine, they
      have to be turned away from the sun.

(90)   *wasik   ta-ni   bhoŋ   wasik=phaŋ   luŋkhwak*
            rain   come-OPT   comp   rain=ABL   stone
            leŋ-ma=na.
            overturn-INF[DEONT]=NMLZ.SG
            In order for the rain to come, they had to be turned away from the rain.

(91)   *ŋkha   mamu=ci=ŋa   ŋkha   luŋkhwak*
            those   girl=NSG=ERG   those   stone
            n-leks-u-ci=ha=bu,   *hensen   ŋkha*
            3PL.A-overturn-3.P[PST]-3NSG.P=NMLZ.NSG=REP   nowadays   those
            munthum=ca   *mamu=ci=ŋa   isa=ŋa=ca*
            oral_ritual_tradition=ADD   GIRL=NSG=ERG   who=ERG=ADD
            n-nis-wa=nin.
            NEG-know-NPST-3PL.NEG
            Those girls have turned around those stones, it is said, even today, even though none of the girls know our ritual tradition.

(92)   *nna   luŋkhwak=ca   ghak   yaksaŋ=ŋa   kham=ŋa*
            that   stone=ADD   all   grass=ERG   soil=ERG
            lumd-y-uks-u
            bury-COMPL-PRF-3.P[PST]
            Those stones are covered by grass and earth (nowadays).

(93)   *ŋkha   luŋkhwak=ci   ŋ-waiʔ=ya,   okhyu=be,   mo*
            those   stone=NSG   3PL-exist=NMLZ.NSG   Okhyu=LOC   down
            coilikha=be,
            Coilikha=LOC
            Those stones are there, in Okhyu, down there, in Coilikha.

(94)   *nnakha   luŋkhwak=ci=maŋ   n-l-wa=ci=ha*
            those   stone=NSG=EMPH   3PL.A-call-NPST-3NSG.P=NMLZ.NSG
            sum=ci   namthaluŋma.
            three=NSG   Namthalungma
            Those stones are called the three Namthalungma rocks.

(95)   *hoŋkha=ci=ga   na   tablik   om.*
            those_very=NSG=GEN   this   story   COP
            This is their story.

The Linkha man's bet with the sun

This text is an oral narrative of a commonly known legend. The speaker is Dhan Kumari Jimi (Tumok).

(1)　　*luʔ-ma=na,*　　　　　　　*eko*　*aniŋ=ga*　　　　　*liŋkha=ga.*
　　　　tell-INF[DEONT]=NMLZ.SG　one　1DU.EXCL.POSS=GEN　a_clan=GEN
　　　　It has to be told, one (story) about our Linkha clan.

(2)　　*aniŋ=ga*　　　　　　*liŋkha=ga*　*uhile*　　　　　*utpatti*
　　　　1DU.EXCL.POSS=GEN　a_clan=GEN　long_time_ago　origin
　　　　mamliŋ=be　*leks-a=na=bu.*
　　　　Mamling=LOC　happen-PST[3SG]=NMLZ.SG=REP
　　　　Our Linkha clan originated long ago in Mamling, they say.

(3)　　*mamliŋ=bhaŋ*　*wan=ne*　　　　*uhile*　　　　　*liŋkha=ci*
　　　　Mamling=ABL　exist[3SG]=NMLZ.SG　long_time_ago　a_clan=NSG
　　　　nam=nuŋ　*bagari*　*n-jog-a,*　　*ŋ-ga-ya,*　　*bagari.*
　　　　SUN=COM　bet　3PL-do-PST　3PL-say-PST　bet
　　　　The Linkhas from Mamling, long ago they had a bet with the sun, they said, a bet.

(4)　　*bagari*　*n-joga,*　　　*nhaŋ*　　*bagari*　*n-jog-a=niŋa,*　　*nna*
　　　　bet　3PL-do-PST　and_then　bet　3PL-do-PST=CTMP　that
　　　　liŋkha=ga,　*uk=ka*　　　　*u-pik=ci*　　　　　*waisa=bu,*
　　　　a_clan=GEN　3SG.POSS=GEN　3SG.POSS-cow=NSG　COP.PST[3]=REP
　　　　nhaŋ　　　*pik=ci*　　*chuʔ-ni-ma*　　　　　　*pʌrne,*　　　*luŋkhwak*
　　　　and_then　cow=NSG　tie-COMPL-INF[DEONT]　having_to　stone
　　　　hoŋ-ma　　　　　*pʌrne,*　　　*nhaŋ*　　　*khibak=ca*
　　　　make_hole-INF[DEONT]　having_to　and_then　rope=ADD
　　　　ip-ni-ma　　　　　　*pʌrne*　　　*sa=bu.*
　　　　twist-COMPL-INF[DEONT]　having_to　COP.PST=REP
　　　　They made a bet, and as they made a bet, that Linkha, he had cows, it is said, and he had to tie the cows, he had to hole out a stone, and he had to complete making a rope, too, it is said.

(5)　　*nam*　*a-ya=niŋa,*　　　　　　*uŋci=ga*　　　　　*hon=na*
　　　　sun　descend-PST[3SG]=CTMP　3NSG.POSS=GEN　that_very=NMLZ.SG
　　　　leks-a,　　　　　*ceʔya.*
　　　　happen-PST[3SG]　matter
　　　　During sunset, they settled that matter.

(6) nhaŋ   nam   wandikŋa lom-meʔ=niŋa   hoŋkhiŋ
    and_then sun   next_day come_out-NPST[3SG]=CTMP that_much
    cok-ni-ma   pʌrne   sa=bu.
    do-COMPL-INF[DEONT]   having_to   COP.PST=REP
    And then, during the dawn of the next day, all that work had to be finished,
    it is said.

(7) khaʔniŋgo liŋkha   ekdam cog-a=nuŋ   cog-a=nuŋ,
    but   a_clan   very   do-PST[3SG]=COM.CL   do-PST[3SG]=COM.CL
    hakok=ŋa   bis   wora, ikhiŋ,   khibak=ca
    later=INS twenty   CLF   how_many   rope=ADD
    ipt-i-ci,   ka-ya=na   anusar.
    twist-COMPL-3NSG.P   say-PST[3SG]=NMLZ.SG   according_to
    But the Linkha, he worked and worked, he wove twenty ropes, according
    to what had been said.

(8) nhaŋ,   luŋkhwak=ca hoks-i,   nhaŋ
    and_then   stone=ADD   make_hole-COMPL[3.P]   and_then
    luŋkhwak   hoks-i=hoŋ,   nhaŋ   pik=ca
    stone   make_hole-COMPL[3.P]=SEQ   and_then cow=ADD
    chuʔ-i-ci=niŋa=go,   eko=chen=go
    tie-COMPL-3NSG.P=CTMP=TOP   one=TOP=TOP
    lukt-a-khy-a=na=bu,   pik,   goru.
    run-PST-V2.GO-PST[3SG]=NMLZ.SG=REP   cow   buffalo
    And then he also completed holing out the stone, and as he completed
    holing out the stone, then, while he completed tying the cows, one cow,
    one of them ran away, it is said. A cow, a buffalo.

(9) lukt-a-khy-a=hoŋ,   chuʔ-ma   ŋ-gaks-a-n=oŋ,
    run-PST-V2.GO-PST[3SG]=SEQ   tie-INF   NEG-accept-PST[3SG]-NEG=SEQ
    nhaŋ   nna   wa   bhale   ka-ya-khy-a.
    and_then that   chicken   rooster call-PST-V2.GO-PST[3SG]
    It ran away, it was not willing to be tied; and then the cock already crowed.

(10) wa   bhale   ka-ya=hoŋ,   ekchin=ŋa   pheri
     chicken   rooster call-PST[3SG]=SEQ   one_moment=INS   again
     nam=ca   lond-a-by-a,   nhaŋ   liŋkha
     sun=ADD   come_out-PST-V2.GIVE-PST[3SG]   and_then a_clan
     baji=be   har-a   cog-a=na.
     bet=LOC   lose-NATIV   do-PST[3SG]=NMLZ.SG
     As the cock crowed, in one moment the sun came out, too, and so the
     Linkha lost in the bet.

(11)   *har-a*   *cog-a=na,*   *i=na*   *om,* *har-a*
      lose-NATIV   do-NATIV=NMLZ.SG what=NMLZ.SG cop lose-NATIV
      cog-a,   *nam=ŋa*   *he=co,*   *nam=ŋa*
      do-PST[3SG]   sun=ERG win-V2.EAT[3.P;PST] sun=ERG
      he-co=hoŋ,   *liŋkha* *sarap* *pi=na.*
      win-V2.EAT[3.P;PST]=SEQ a_clan spell give[3.A;3.P]=NMLZ.SG
      He lost, what is it (comment to herself), he lost, the sun won, and as the
      sun won, it put a spell on the Linkha.

(12)   *gali,*   *thind-u=na.*
      swearwords,   rant_at-3.P[PST]=NMLZ.SG
      It cursed him, and scolded him.

(13)   *nhaŋ*   *issi=ya*   *ce?ya*   *lu=hoŋ,*   *liŋkha=ŋa=bu*
      and_then bad=NMLZ.NC matter tell=SEQ a_clan=ERG=REP
      i=ya   *i=ya*   *men-jok-ma*   *baŋniŋ:*
      what=NMLZ.NC what=NMLZ.NC NEG-do-INF[DEONT] about
      And then it said ugly things, and as for what the Linkha was not allowed
      to do:

(14)   *purba-pʌṭi* *dailo*   *me-hiŋ-ma=na,*
      east-side   door   NEG-turn-INF[DEONT]=NMLZ.SG
      He shall not turn he door to the East.

(15)   *purba-pʌṭi* *dailo*   *hiŋ-ma=niŋa*   *ucun*
      east-side   door   turn-INF=CTMP good
      n-leŋ-me-n.
      NEG-become-NPST[3SG]-NEG
      It is not good when they turn the door to the East.

(16)   *nhaŋ*   *cautara=ca*   *men-jok-m=ha=ci,*
      and_then resting_place=ADD NEG-do-INF[DEONT]=NMLZ.NSG=NSG
      bʌrpipʌl=ca   *men-li?-m=ha=ci.*
      banyan_tree=ADD NEG-plant-INF[DEONT]=NMLZ.NSG=NSG
      And they shall neither build resting places, nor plant banyan trees.

(17)   *nhaŋ*   *yoŋ=be=ca*   *me?-im-ma=ci=bu,*
      and_then cradle=LOC=ADD NEG-put_to_sleep-INF[DEONT]=NSG=REP
      liŋkha=ci=ga.
      a_clan=NSG=GEN
      They shall not put them into in a bamboo cradle, too, the Linkha's (children).

(18) *hoŋkhaʔla   hoŋkhaʔla   leks-a=hoŋ,*   *liŋkha=ci=ŋa*
      like_that   like_that   become-PST[3SG]=SEQ   a_clan=NSG=ERG
      ŋkha   n-jog-wa-nin.
      that   NEG-do-NPST-3PL.NEG
      As it became like that, the Linkhas do not do that.

(19) *uŋci   uhile*   *nam=ŋa=bu   u-chik*
      3NSG   long_time_ago   sun=ERG=REP   3SG.POSS-hate
      ekt-u-ci=hoŋ   *thin,*   *gali*
      hate-3.P[PST]-3NSG.P=SEQ   [false.start],   swearword
      pi-ci=ya,   *eŋ=ga*   *ceʔya=ŋ*   *sarab*
      give-3NSG.P=NMLZ.NSG,   1PL.INCL.POSS=GEN   language=INS   spell
      pi-ci=ya   *leks-a.*
      give-3NSG.P=NMLZ.NSG   become-PST[3SG]
      Since the sun got angry at them long ago, it cursed them, it happened that
      it put a spell on them, in our language.

(20) *hoŋkhiŋ=maŋ*   *loppi=ni.*
      that_much=EMPH   perhaps=EMPH
      Just that much, probably.

(21) *nhaŋ*   *eko=bu,*   *mo=na   tala=ca*
      and_then   one=REP   down   floor=ADD
      me-wa-m=ha=bu,   *mo=na   tala   to*
      NEG-live-INF[DEONT]=NMLZ.NSG=REP   lower   floor   up
      wa-ma=na   *ucun=na,*   *mo*   *wa-ma=na*
      live-INF=NMLZ.SG   good=NMLZ.SG   down   live-INF=NMLZ.SG
      issiʔ=na=bu,   *mo,*   *u-laŋ-tala=be.*
      bad=NMLZ.SG=REP   down   3SG.POSS-leg-floor=LOC
      And one thing, they say: the Linkhas shall not live on the ground floor,
      too, it is said; living above is good, living below is bad, on the ground
      floor.

(22) *liŋkha=ci=ga*   *lagi,   hoŋkhaʔla=oŋ,   hoŋkhiŋ=se.*
      a_clan=NSG=GEN   for   like_that=SEQ   that_much=RESTR
      For the Linkhas, like that, that much only.

Appendix B: Yakkha kinship terms

The two charts on the following pages show the kinship system for the own family and in-laws.

The following further terms are used:

- great-grandparents: *cottu*

- great-great-grandparents: *kektu*

- great-grandchildren: *sapsik, khopsik*

- great-great-grandchildren: *poʔloŋ*

- great-great-great-grandchildren: *joʔloŋ*

Own family

apum father's father
amum father's mother
apum mother's father
amum mother's mother

ani mother's elder brother's wife
akhedniba mother's elder brother's son
akonba mother's elder brother
akhednima mother's elder brother's daughter

ayem father's elder brother's wife
aphu, anancha father's elder brother's son (e, y)
ayep father's elder brother
ama, anancha father's elder brother's daughter (e, y)

anpekpma elder brother's wife
aecha elder brother's son
aphu elder brother
aecha elder brother's daughter

ayep mother's elder sister's husband
anapmiba mother's elder sister's son
ayem mother's elder sister
anapmima mother's elder sister's daughter

akku father's elder sister's husband
akhedniba father's elder sister's son
ani father's elder sister
akhednima father's elder sister's daughter

anpakpo/anpekpha elder sister's husband
acya elder sister's son
ana elder sister
acya elder sister's daughter

tayme son's wife
acya baba son
yapmen tayme son's son's wife
yapmen son's son

appa father
ama mother

hiphubu-ma husband/wife
EGO

ayapmen son's daughter
yapmen tabhaŋ son's daughter's husband

akonma mother's younger sister
apaŋ mother's younger sister's husband
anapmima mother's younger sister's daughter
anapmiba mother's younger sister's son

ani mother's younger brother's wife
aphaŋ mother's younger sister's husband
akhedniba mother's younger brother's son
akonba mother's younger brother
akhednima mother's younger brother's daughter

achim father's younger brother's wife
akku father's younger sister's husband
apha, anancha father's younger brother's son (e, y)
aphaŋ father's younger brother
ana, anancha father's younger brother's daughter (e, y)
akhedniba father's younger sister's son
akhednima father's younger sister's daughter
ani father's younger sister

tayme younger brother's wife
tabhaŋ younger sister's husband
aecha younger brother's son
anancha younger brother
aecha younger brother's daughter
acya younger sister's son
anancha younger sister
acya younger sister's daughter

tabhaŋ daughter's husband
acya mamu daughter
acya daughter's son

yapmen tabhaŋ daughter's daughter's husband
yapmen tayme daughter's son's wife
yapmen daughter's son
yapmen tabhaŋ daughter's daughter's husband
ayapmen daughter's daughter

562

In-laws

apumamba — spouse's father's father
amamamma — spouse's father's mother
apumamba — spouse's mother's father
amamamma — spouse's mother's mother

aninamma — spouse's mother's elder brother's wife
khoknibu-anpteyba, khoknibu-aphanamba — spouse's mother's elder brother's son (y, e)
akopnamba — spouse's mother's elder brother
aninamma — spouse's mother's younger brother's wife
akopnamba — spouse's mother's younger brother
khoknibu-anpteyba, khoknibu-ananamma — spouse's mother's younger brother's daughter (y, e)

ayempamba — spouse's mother's elder sister's husband
oyemamma — spouse's mother's elder sister
anpteyba, ananamma — spouse's mother's elder sister's son (y, e)
nupinima-anpteyma, nupinima-ananamma — spouse's mother's elder sister's daughter (y, e)

akopnamma — spouse's mother's younger sister
aphapnamba — spouse's mother's younger sister's husband
anpteyba, ananamma — spouse's mother's younger sister's son (y, e)
apteyma, ananamma — spouse's mother's younger sister's daughter (y, e)

oyemamba — spouse's father's elder brother's wife
khoknibu-anpteyba, khoknibu-aphanamba — spouse's father's elder brother's son (y, e)
oyempamba — spouse's father's elder brother
aphapnamba — spouse's father's younger brother
apteyma, ananamma — spouse's father's younger brother's daughter (y, e)

akkunamba — spouse's father's elder sister's husband
aninamma — spouse's father's elder sister
anpteyba, ananamma — spouse's father's elder sister's son (y, e)
akkunamba — spouse's father's younger sister's husband
aphapnamba — spouse's father's younger sister
khoknibu-anpteyba, khoknibu-aphanamba — spouse's father's younger sister's son (y, e)

oyemamba — spouse's father's elder brother's wife
oyempamba — spouse's father's elder brother
khoknibu-anpteyba, khoknibu-ananamma — spouse's father's elder sister's daughter (y, e)
khoknibu-anpteyba, khoknibu-aphanamba — spouse's father's elder sister's son (y, e)

anamba — spouse's father
anamma — spouse's mother

ayeopimama/ana — husband's/wife's elder brother's wife
aphanamba/onap — husband's/wife's elder brother
ananamma/ana — husband's/wife's elder sister
aphu/onap — husband's/wife's elder sister's husband

ayeopimamancha/ananba — husband's/wife's younger brother's wife
apptenba/apap — husband's/wife's younger brother
aph/onap — husband's/wife's younger sister's husband
ayopim — husband's/wife's younger sister

aecha — spouse's elder brother's son
aecha — spouse's elder brother's daughter
aisaba — spouse's elder sister's son
aisama — spouse's elder sister's daughter

aecha — spouse's younger brother's son
aecha — spouse's younger brother's daughter
aisaba — spouse's younger sister's son
aisama — spouse's younger sister's daughter

hiphbubu, hiphbuma — husband/wife
EGO

acya bubu — son
tapme — son's wife
acya mama — daughter
tabbup — daughter's husband

yapmen tapme — son's son's wife
yapmen tabbup — son's daughter's husband
yapmen — son's son
ayeopmen — son's daughter

yapmen tapme — daughter's son's wife
yapmen tabbup — daughter's daughter's husband
ayeopmen — daughter's son
ayeopmen — daughter's daughter

563

Appendix C: Index of Yakkha formatives

MARKER	FUNCTION	SECTION
a-	possessive prefix, 1SG	4.2
-a	past	8.4
-a	imperative, subjunctive	8.5
-a	nativizer on loans	8.8
-a ~ -na	function verb, 'leave'	10.2.18
-ap	function verb, 'come'	10.2.10
-apt	function verb, 'bring'	10.2.11
anciŋ-	possessive prefix, 1DU.EXCL	4.2
aniŋ-	possessive prefix, 1PL.EXCL	4.2
au	initiative particle	17.4
baŋna	complementizer	15.2.3
baŋha	complementizer	15.2.3
baŋniŋ	textual topic, quotative	17.1
-bhes	function verb, 'deliver'	10.2.13
-bhoks ~ -bhoŋ	function verb, 'split'	10.2.21
bhoŋ	conditional, complementizer, quotative	15.2, 14.8, 14.9
-ca	function verb, middle, reflexive	10.2.3, 11.3.4
ca	auxiliary, reciprocal	11.3.4
=ca	additive focus	17.2, 14.11
=chen	topic	17.1
-ci ~ -cin	dual (verbal)	8.2
-ci	3 nonsingular P (verbal)	8.2
=ci	nonsingular (nominal)	5.2.1
-eba	polite imperative	8.5
=em	alternation particle	17.5.1
eN-	possessive prefix, 1PL.INCL	4.2
-end	function verb, 'insert'	10.2.14
enciŋ-	possessive prefix, 1DU.INCL	4.2
=ge ~ =ghe	locative	5.2.2

MARKER	FUNCTION	SECTION
-get	function verb, 'bring up'	10.2.15
=gaŋ ~ =ghaŋ	ablative	5.2.2
-ghet ~ -het	function verb, 'carry off'	10.2.17
-ghond	function verb, 'roam'	10.2.23
=ha ~ =ya	nominalizer, NSG/NC	13.3
-haks ~ -nhaŋ	function verb, 'send'	10.2.16
haksaŋ	comparative	5.2.3
haʔniŋ	comparative	5.2.3
-heks	function verb, 'cut'	10.2.22
=hoŋ	sequential clause linkage	14.10, 14.11
=hoŋca	concessive clause linkage	14.11
hau	exclamative	17.4
=i	sentential focus	17.2
i	question marker	17.5.2
-i ~ -ni	completive	8.4.5, 10.2.2
-i ~ -in	1PL, 2PL (verbal)	8.2
-ka	2nd person (verbal)	8.2
=ka	genitive	5.2.2, 14.3
=khaʔla	directional, manner	5.2.3
-kheʔ	function verb, 'go'	10.2.5
-khuba	nominalizer	13.2
-khusa	reciprocal marker	11.3.4
=ko	topic	17.1
=lai	exclamative	17.4
=le	contrastive focus	17.2
-les	suffix of knowledge or ability	8.8
-lo	interruptive clause linkage	14.14
loppi	probability	17.3
-loʔa	equative	5.2.3
-m	1PL.A>3, 2PL.A>3	8.2
-ma	infinitive	8.9, 15.1, 14.3, 14.4
-ma	event numeral, 'times'	4.5.2
-ma	nominalizer	13.1
-ma ~ -mi	perfect	8.4
=maŋ	emphatic particle	17.2
-masa ~ -misi	past perfect	8.4
maʔniŋ	privative	5.2.3

MARKER	FUNCTION	SECTION
meN-	negation	8.3
meN-...-le	negative converb	14.6
-met	causative	11.3.2
-meʔ	nonpast	8.4
N-	negation (verbal)	8.3
N-	3PL	8.2
N-	possessive prefix, 2SG	4.2
-n	negation	8.3
=na	nominalizer, SG	13.3
-nen	1>2 (verbal)	8.2
-nes	function verb, 'lay'	10.2.19
-nhaŋto	temporal ablative	5.2.3
-ni	optative	8.5
-nin	plural and negation (verbal)	8.3, 8.2
njiŋ-	possessive prefix, 2DU	4.2
=niŋ ~ =niŋa	cotemporal clause linkage	14.12
=niŋgobi	counterfactual clause linkage	14.13
nniŋ-	possessive prefix, 2PL	4.2
=nuŋ	comitative case and clause linkage	5.2.2, 14.7
-ŋ ~ -ŋa	1SG, EXCL	8.2
=ŋa	ergative case and clause linkage	5.2.2, 14.4
-pa	nominalizer	13.1
=pa	sentential focus	17.2
-paŋ	numeral classifier	4.5.2
=pe	locative	5.2.2
=phaŋ	ablative	5.2.2
=pi	irrealis	17.3
-piʔ	function verb, 'give'	10.2.1, 11.3.3
=pu	reportative marker	17.3
rahecha	mirative	17.3
-raʔ	function verb, 'come'	10.2.6
-raʔ	function verb, 'bring'	10.2.7
-ris	function verb, 'place'	10.2.12
-sa	infinitive	8.9, 15.1
-saŋ	simultaneous converb	14.5
-se	supine converb	14.2
=se	restrictive focus	17.2

MARKER	FUNCTION	SECTION
-siʔ	progressive	8.4.3
-siʔ	middle	10.2.4, 11.3.6
-siʔ	function verb, 'avoid'	10.2.24
-soʔ	function verb, 'look'	10.2.25
-t	benefactive	11.3.3
u-	possessive prefix, 3SG	4.2
-u	3.P (verbal)	8.2
=u	vocative	17.5
-uks	function verb, 'come down'	10.2.8
-uks ~ -nuŋ	perfect	8.4
-uks ~ -nuŋ	function verb, continuative	10.2.20
-uks ~ -uksa	past perfect	8.4
-ukt	function verb, 'bring down'	10.2.9
uŋci-	possessive prefix, 3NSG	4.2
-wa	nonpast	8.4
=ʔlo	exclamative	17.4

References

Aikhenvald, Alexandra J. 2006. Serial verb constructions in typological perspective. In Alexandra Y. Aikhenvald & R. M. W. Dixon (eds.), *Serial verb constructions: A cross-linguistic typology*, 1–68. Oxford: Oxford University Press.

Allen, Nicholas J. 1972. The vertical dimension in Thulung classification. *Journal of the Anthropological Society of Oxford* 3. 81–94.

Allen, Nicholas J. 1975. *Sketch of Thulung grammar* (Cornell University East Asia Papers 6). Ithaca, N.Y.: Cornell University.

Andrews, Avery D. 1985. The major functions of the noun phrase. In Timothy Shopen (ed.), *Language typology and syntactic description*, vol. 1, 62–145. Cambridge: Cambridge University Press.

Berlin, Brent & Paul Kay. 1969. *Basic color terms*. Berkeley: University of Chicago Press.

Beyer, Stephan V. 1992. *The Classical Tibetan language*. Delhi: Sri Satguru Publications.

Bhaskararao, Peri & Karumuri Venkata Subbarao (eds.). 2004. *Non-nominative subjects* (Typological Studies in Language 60/61). Amsterdam: Benjamins.

Bickel, Balthasar. 1991. *Typologische Grundlagen der Satzverkettung*. Zürich: ASAS.

Bickel, Balthasar. 1992. Motivations of scenario classes: Belhare and Kham. Paper presented at the 25th International Conference on Sino-Tibetan Language and Linguistics, Berkeley, October 14–18, 1992.

Bickel, Balthasar. 1993. Belhare subordination and the theory of topic. In Karen H. Ebert (ed.), *Studies in clause linkage*, 23–55. Zürich: ASAS.

Bickel, Balthasar. 1994. Mapping operations in spatial deixis and the typology of reference frames. Working Paper No. 31, Max-Planck-Research Group in Cognitive Anthropology.

Bickel, Balthasar. 1995. In the vestibule of meaning: Transitivity inversion as a morphological phenomenon. *Studies in Language* 19. 73–127.

Bickel, Balthasar. 1996. *Aspect, mood, and time in Belhare. Studies in the semantics-pragmatics interface of a Himalayan language* (ASAS 15). Zurich: Seminar für Allgemeine Sprachwissenschaft.

Bickel, Balthasar. 1997a. Dictionary of the Belhare language: Belhare–English–Nepali. Electronic database at the Sino-Tibetan Etymological Dictionary and Thesaurus Project, University of California at Berkeley.

Bickel, Balthasar. 1997b. Spatial operations in deixis, cognition, and culture: Where to orient oneself in Belhare. In Jan Nuyts & Eric Pederson (eds.), *Language and conceptualization*, 46–83. Cambridge: Cambridge University Press.

Bickel, Balthasar. 1997c. The possessive of experience in Belhare. In David Bradley (ed.), *Tibeto-Burman languages of the Himalayas* (Papers in South-East Asian Linguistics 14), 135–155. A-86. Canberra: Pacific Linguistics, the Australian National University.

Bickel, Balthasar. 1998. *Rhythm and feet in Belhare morphology.* http://roa.rutgers.edu/article/view/297.

Bickel, Balthasar. 1999a. Cultural formalism and spatial language in Belhara. In Balthasar Bickel & Martin Gaenszle (eds.), *Himalayan space: Cultural horizons and practices*, 75–104. Zürich: Völkerkundemuseum der Universität Zürich.

Bickel, Balthasar. 1999b. Grammatical relations, agreement, and genetic stability. Ms., University of California, Berkeley. http://www.uni-leipzig.de/~bickel/research/papers.

Bickel, Balthasar. 1999c. Nominalization and focus constructions in some Kiranti languages. In Yogendra P. Yadava & Warren W. Glover (eds.), *Topics in Nepalese linguistics*, 271–296. Kathmandu: Royal Nepal Academy.

Bickel, Balthasar. 1999d. Principles of event framing: Genetic stability in grammar and discourse. Ms., University of California, Berkeley. http://www.uni-leipzig.de/~bickel/research/papers.

Bickel, Balthasar. 2000. On the syntax of agreement in Tibeto-Burman. *Studies in Language* 24. 583–609.

Bickel, Balthasar. 2001. Deictic transposition and referential practice in Belhare. *Journal of Linguistic Anthropology* 10. 224–247.

Bickel, Balthasar. 2003. Belhare. In Graham Thurgood & Randy J. LaPolla (eds.), *The Sino-Tibetan languages*, 546–70. London: Routledge.

Bickel, Balthasar. 2004a. Hidden syntax in Belhare. In Anju Saxena (ed.), *Himalayan languages, past and present*, 141–190. Berlin: Mouton de Gruyter.

Bickel, Balthasar. 2004b. The syntax of experiencers in the Himalayas. In Peri Bhaskararao & Karumuri Venkata Subbarao (eds.), *Non-nominative subjects*, 77–112. Amsterdam: Benjamins.

Bickel, Balthasar. 2005. On the typological variables of relativization. Paper presented at the Workshop on the typology, acquisition, and processing of relative clauses, Max Planck Institute for Evolutionary Anthropology, June 11, 2005.

Bickel, Balthasar. 2008. *Kiranti: An introduction.* Seminar handout, Universität Leipzig.

Bickel, Balthasar. 2010. Capturing particulars and universals in clause linkage: A multivariate analysis. In Isabelle Bril (ed.), *Clause linking and clause hierarchy – syntax and pragmatics,* vol. 121 (Studies in Language Companion Series), 51–101. Amsterdam: Benjamins.

Bickel, Balthasar. 2011a. Grammatical relations typology. In Jae Jung Song (ed.), *The Oxford Handbook of Language Typology,* 399–444. Oxford: Oxford University Press.

Bickel, Balthasar. 2011b. Multivariate typology and field linguistics: A case study on detransitivization in Kiranti (Sino-Tibetan). In Peter Austin, Oliver Bond, Lutz Marten & David Nathan (eds.), *Proceedings of the conference on language documentation and linguistic theory 3,* 3–13. London, SOAS.

Bickel, Balthasar & Martin Gaenszle. 1999. Introduction: Cultural horizons and practices in Himalayan space. In Balthasar Bickel & Martin Gaenszle (eds.), *Himalayan space: Cultural horizons and practices,* 9–27. Zürich: Völkerkunde-museum der Universität Zürich.

Bickel, Balthasar & Martin Gaenszle. 2005. Generics as first person undergoers and the political history of the Southern Kirant. Paper presented at the 11th Himalayan Languages Symposium, Bangkok, December 6–9, 2005.

Bickel, Balthasar & Martin Gaenszle. 2015. First person objects, antipassives, and the political history of the Southern Kirant. *Journal of South Asian Languages and Linguistics* 2(1). 63–86.

Bickel, Balthasar & Johanna Nichols. 2001. Syntactic ergativity in light verb complements. *Proceedings of the 27th Annual Meeting of the Berkeley Linguistics Society* 27. 39–52.

Bickel, Balthasar & Johanna Nichols. 2005. Obligatory Possessive Inflection. In Martin Haspelmath, Matthew Dryer, David Gil & Bernard Comrie (eds.), *The World Atlas of Language Structures,* 242 – 245. Oxford: Oxford University Press.

Bickel, Balthasar & Johanna Nichols. 2007. Inflectional morphology. In Timothy Shopen (ed.), *Language typology and syntactic description,* 169–240. Cambridge: Cambridge University Press (Revised second edition).

Bickel, Balthasar, Goma Banjade, Martin Gaenszle, Elena Lieven, Netra Paudyal, Arjun Rai, Ichchha P. Rai, Manoj Rai, Novel K. Rai, Shree Kumar Rai, Vishnu S. Rai, Narayan P. Gautam (Sharma), Sabine Stoll & Mark Turin. 2006. The Chintang and Puma corpus. DOBES Multi-media Corpus, www.mpi.nl/DOBES.

Bickel, Balthasar, Goma Banjade, Martin Gaenszle, Elena Lieven, Netra Paudyal, Iccha Rai, Manoj Rai, Novel K. Rai & Sabine Stoll. 2007a. Free prefix ordering in Chintang. *Language* 83. 43–73.

Bickel, Balthasar, Martin Gaenszle, Arjun Rai, Prem Dhoj Rai, Shree Kumar Rai, Vishnu S. Rai & Narayan P. Sharma (Gautam). 2007b. Two ways of suspending object agreement in Puma: Between incorporation, antipassivization, and optional agreement. *Himalayan Linguistics* 7. 1–18.

Bickel, Balthasar, Martin Gaenszle, Arjun Rai, Shree Kumar Rai, Vishnu S. Rai, Diana Schackow, Sabine Günther & Narayan P. Gautam (Sharma). 2009. *Puma-Nepali-English Dictionary*. Kathmandu: Chintang & Puma Documentation Project.

Bickel, Balthasar, Manoj Rai, Netra Paudyal, Goma Banjade, Toya Nath Bhatta, Martin Gaenszle, Elena Lieven, Iccha Purna Rai, Novel K. Rai & Sabine Stoll. 2010. The syntax of three-argument verbs in Chintang and Belhare (Southeastern Kiranti). In Andrej Malchukov, Martin Haspelmath & Bernard Comrie (eds.), *Studies in ditransitive constructions*, 285–307. Berlin: Mouton de Gruyter.

Bierkandt, Lennart & Diana Schackow. Submitted. Operator scope in clause linkage typology and a case study on Yakkha adverbial clauses. Ms.

Bohnemeyer, Jürgen, Melissa Bowerman & Penelope Brown. 2010. Cut and break clips. In Stephen C. Levinson & Nicholas J. Enfield (eds.), *Manual for the field season 2001*, 90–96. Nijmegen: Max Planck Institute for Psycholinguistics. http://fieldmanuals.mpi.nl/volumes/2001/cut-and-break-clips/,accessedonJuly15, 2012.

Bohnemeyer, Jürgen, Nicholas J. Enfield, James Essegbey, Iraide Ibarretxe-Antuñano, Sotaro Kita, Friederike Lüpke & Felix K. Ameka. 2007. Principles of event segmentation in language: The case of motion events. *Language* 83. 495–532.

Bradley, David (ed.). 1997. *Tibeto-Burman languages of the Himalayas* (Papers in South-East Asian Linguistics 14). Canberra: Australian National University.

Brown, Lea. 2001. *A grammar of Nias Selatan*. Sydney: University of Sydney PhD thesis.

Brown, Penelope & Stephen C. Levinson. 1993. "Uphill" and "downhill" in Tzeltal. *Journal of Linguistic Anthropology* 3(1). 46–74.

Bühler, Karl. 1934. *Sprachtheorie. Die Darstellungsfunktion der Sprache*. Jena: Gustav Fischer.

Butt, Miriam. 1995. *The structure of complex predicates in Urdu*. Stanford: CSLI.

Butt, Miriam. 1997. Complex predicates in Urdu. In Alex Alsina, Joan Bresnan & Peter Sells (eds.), *Complex predicates* (CSLI Lecture Notes 64), 107–149. Stanford: CSLI Publications.

Butt, Miriam. 2010. The light verb jungle: Still hacking away. In Mengistu Amberber, Brett Baker & Mark Harvey (eds.), *Complex predicates: Cross-linguistic perspectives on event-structure*, 48–78. Cambridge: Cambridge University Press.

Caplan, Lionel. 1970. *Land and social change in East of Nepal: A study of Hindu-tribal relations*. Berkeley: University of California Press.

Caughley, Ross C. 1997. Semantically related vowel gradation in Sunwar and Chepang. *Papers in Southeast Asian Linguistics* 14. 95–101.

Central Bureau of Statistics, Nepal. 2001. *Population census report*.

Chafe, Wallace. 1980. *The pear stories: Cognitive, cultural, and linguistic aspects of narrative production*. Norwood, NJ: Ablex.

Chemjong, Iman Singh. 1967. *History and culture of the Kirat people*. Vol. 1 & 2. Kathmandu: Tumeng Hang.

Comrie, Bernard. 1989. *Language universals and linguistic typology*. 2nd edition. Chicago: University of Chicago Press.

Cornillie, Bert. 2009. Evidentiality and epistemic modality: On the close relationship of two different categories. *Functions of language* 16(1). 32–44.

Coupe, Alexander. 2007. *A grammar or Mongsen Ao*. Berlin & Boston: Mouton de Gruyter.

Creissels, Denis. 2014. P-lability and radical p-alignment. *Linguistics* 52(4). Leonid Kulikov & Nikolaos Lavidas (eds.). 911–944.

Cristofaro, Sonia. 2003. *Subordination*. Oxford: Oxford University Press.

Dahal, Dilli Ram. 1985. *An ethnographic study of social change among the Athpahariya Rais of Dhankuta*. Kirtipur: Centre for Nepal & Asian Studies.

DeLancey, Scott. 1981. The category of direction in Tibeto-Burman. *Linguistics of the Tibeto-Burman Area* 6(1). 83–101.

DeLancey, Scott. 1985. Etymological notes on Tibeto-Burman case particles. *Linguistics of the Tibeto-Burman Area* 8(1). 59–77.

DeLancey, Scott. 1989a. Relativization and nominalization in Tibeto-Burman. Ms., University of Oregon.

DeLancey, Scott. 1989b. Verb agreement in Proto-Tibeto-Burman. *Bulletin of the School of Oriental and African Studies* 52. 315–333.

DeLancey, Scott. 1991. The origin of verb serialization in modern Tibetan. *Studies in Language* 15. 1–23.

DeLancey, Scott. 1997. Mirativity: The grammatical marking of unexpected information. *Linguistic Typology* 1. 33–52.

DeLancey, Scott. 1999. Relativization in Tibetan. In Yogendra P. Yadava & Warren G. Glover (eds.), *Topics in Nepalese linguistics*, 231–249. Kathmandu: Royal Nepal Academy.

DeLancey, Scott. 2002. Relativization and nominalization in Bodic. In *Proceedings of the twenty-eighth annual meeting of the Berkeley Linguistics Society: Special session on Tibeto-Burman and Southeast Asian linguistics*, vol. 28, 55–72.

DeLancey, Scott. 2010. Towards a history of verb agreement in Tibeto-Burman. *Himalayan Linguistics* 9.1. 1–39.

DeLancey, Scott. 2011a. Finite structures from clausal nominalization in Tibeto-Burman. In Foong Ha Yap, Karen Grunow-Hårsta & Janick Wrona (eds.), *Nominalization in Asian languages: Diachronic and typological perspectives* (Typological Studies in Language Series), 343–360. Amsterdam: John Benjamins.

DeLancey, Scott. 2011b. Notes on verb agreement prefixes in Tibeto-Burman. *Himalayan Linguistics* 10(1). 1–29.

DeLancey, Scott. 2011c. "Optional" "Ergativity" in Tibeto-Burman languages. *Linguistics of the Tibeto-Burman Area* 34(2). 9—20.

Dewan, Gopal, Anupa Dewan, Santa Dewan & Jimi Radha. 2059 B.S. *Opchyongme (Palam Rang)*. Kirat Yakkha Chumma, Dharan, Sunsari.

Diewald, Gabriele. 2010. On some problem areas in grammaticalization studies. In Katerina Stathi, Elke Gehweiler & Ekkehard König (eds.), *Grammaticalization: Current views and issues*, 379. Amsterdam: Benjamins.

Dirksmeyer, Tyko. 2008. Spatial deixis in Chintang: Aspects of a grammar of space. MA thesis, University of Leipzig. Leipzig.

Dixon, R. M. W. 1994. *Ergativity*. Cambridge: Cambridge University Press.

Doornenbal, Marius A. 2008. Nominalization in Bantawa. *Linguistics of the Tibeto-Burman Area* 31.2. 67–95.

Doornenbal, Marius A. 2009. *A grammar of Bantawa. Grammar, paradigm tables, glossary and texts of a Rai language of Eastern Nepal*. Utrecht: LOT Publications.

van Driem, George. 1987. *A grammar of Limbu*. Berlin: Mouton de Gruyter.

van Driem, George. 1989. Reflexes of the Tibeto-Burman *-t directive suffix in dumi Rai. In David Bradley, Eugénie J. A. Henderson & Martine Mazaudon (eds.), *Prosodic analysis and Asian linguistics: To honour R. K. Sprigg* (Pacific Linguistics 104), 157–167. C. Canberra: Australian National University, Research School of Pacific Studies, Dept. of Linguistics.

van Driem, George. 1990. The fall and rise of the phoneme /r/ in Eastern Kiranti: Sound change in Tibeto-Burman. *Bulletin of the School of Oriental and African Studies* 53. 83–86.

van Driem, George. 1991. Tangut verbal agreement and the patient category in Tibeto-Burman. *Bulletin of the School of Oriental and Asian Studies* 54. 520–534.

van Driem, George. 1993a. *A grammar of Dumi*. Berlin: Mouton de Gruyter.

van Driem, George. 1993b. Einige Bemerkungen zum Aspekt im Limbu. *Linguistische Berichte* 148. 483–89.

van Driem, George. 1994. The Yakkha verb: Interpretation and analysis of the Omruwa material (a Kiranti language of Eastern Nepal). *Bulletin of the School of Oriental and African Studies* 57. 347–355.

van Driem, George. 1997. A new analysis of the Limbu verb. In David Bradley (ed.), *Tibeto-Burman languages of the Himalayas*, 157–173. Canberra: Australian National University.

van Driem, George. 2001. *Languages of the Himalayas: An ethnolinguistic handbook of the Greater Himalayan Region, containing an introduction to the Symbiotic Theory of Language.* Leiden: Brill.

van Driem, George & Irene Davids. 1985. Limbu kinship terminology. *Kailash* 12. 115–156.

Dryer, Matthew S. 1986. Primary objects, secondary objects, and antidative. *Language* 62. 808–845.

Dryer, Matthew S. 2007. Clause types. In Timothy Shopen (ed.), *Language typology and syntactic description [2nd edition]*, vol. 1, 224–275. Cambridge: Cambridge University Press.

Durie, Mark. 1997. Grammatical structures in verb serialization. In Alex Alsina, Miriam Butt & Peter Sells (eds.), *Complex predicates* (CSLI Lecture Notes 64), 289–354. Stanford: CSLI Publications.

Ebert, Karen H. 1987. Grammatical marking of speech act participants. *Journal of Pragmatics* 11. 473–482.

Ebert, Karen H. 1990. On the evidence for the relationship Kiranti-rung. *Linguistics of the Tibeto-Burman Area* 13. 57–78.

Ebert, Karen H. 1991. Inverse and pseudo-inverse prefixes in Kiranti languages: Evidence from Belhare, Athpare and Dungmali. *Linguistics of the Tibeto-Burman Area* 14. 73–92.

Ebert, Karen H. 1993. Kiranti subordination in the south Asian areal context. In Karen H. Ebert (ed.), *Studies in clause linkage*, 83–110. Zürich: Arbeiten des Seminars für Allgemeine Sprachwissenschaft.

Ebert, Karen H. 1994. *The structure of Kiranti languages.* Zürich: Arbeiten des Seminars für Allgemeine Sprachwissenschaft.

Ebert, Karen H. 1997a. *A grammar of Athpare* (Lincom Studies in Asian Linguistics 1). München: LINCOM Europa.

Ebert, Karen H. 1997b. *Camling (Chamling).* München: LINCOM.

Ebert, Karen H. 1999a. Nonfinite verbs in Kiranti languages – an areal perspective. In Yogendra P. Yadava & Warren W. Glover (eds.), *Topics in Nepalese Linguistics*, 371–-400. Kathmandu: Royal Nepal Academy.

Ebert, Karen H. 1999b. The up–down dimension in Rai grammar and mythology. In Balthasar Bickel & Martin Gaenszle (eds.), *Himalayan space: Cultural horizons and practices*, 109–140. Zürich: Völkerkundemuseum der Universität Zürich.

Ebert, Karen H. 2003a. Camling. In Graham Thurgood & Randy LaPolla (eds.), *The Sino-Tibetan languages*, 533–545. London: Routledge.

Ebert, Karen H. 2003b. Equivalents of 'conjunctive participles' in Kiranti languages. In Tej Ratna Kansakar & Mark Turin (eds.), *Themes in Himalayan languages and linguistics*, 27–48. Heidelberg & Kathmandu: South Asia Institute & Tribhuvan University.

Ebert, Karen H. 2003c. Kiranti languages: An overview. In Graham Thurgood & Randy LaPolla (eds.), *The Sino-Tibetan languages*, 505–517. London: Routledge.

Enfield, Nick J. 2006. Heterosemy and the grammar-lexicon-tradeoff. In Felix K. Ameka, Alan Dench & Nicholas Evans (eds.), *Catching language: The standing challenge of grammar writing*, 297–320. Berlin: Mouton de Gruyter.

Evans, Nicholas D. 2007. Insubordination and its uses. In Irina Nikolaeva (ed.), *Finiteness: Theoretical and empirical foundations*, 366–431. Oxford: Oxford University Press.

Fabb, Nigel. 2001. Compounding. In Andrew Spencer & Arnold M. Zwicky (eds.), *Handbook of morphology*, 66–74. Oxford: Blackwell.

Fillmore, Carl J. 1971 (1997). *Lectures on deixis* (CSLI Lecture Notes 65). Stanford, CA: CSLI Publications.

Foley, William A. 2010. Events and serial verb constructions. In Mengistu Amberber, Brett Baker & Mark Harvey (eds.), *Complex predicates. Cross-linguistic perspectives on event structure*, 79–109. New York: Cambridge University Press.

Foley, William A. & Robert D. Van Valin. 1984. *Functional syntax and universal grammar*. Cambridge: Cambridge University Press.

Gaenszle, Martin. 1999. Travelling up – travelling down: The vertical dimension in Mewahang Rai ritual journeys. In Balthasar Bickel & Martin Gaenszle (eds.), *Himalayan space: Cultural horizons and practices*, 145–174. Zürich: Völkerkundemuseum der Universität Zürich.

Gaenszle, Martin. 2000. *Origins and migrations: Kinship, mythology, and ethnic identity among the Mewahang Rai of East Nepal*. Kathmandu: Mandala Book Point.

Gaenszle, Martin. 2002. Countering the great traditions: Remakings of the Kiranti past. In Axel Harneit-Sievers (ed.), *A place in the world: New local historiographies from Africa and South Asia*, 331–346. Leiden, Boston, Köln: Brill.

Gaenszle, Martin. 2012. Where the waters dry up: The place of origin in Rai myth and ritual. In Toni Huber & Stuart Blackburn (eds.), *Origins and migrations in the extended Eastern Himalayas*, 33–48. Leiden: Brill.

Gaenszle, Martin. in prep. Redefining Kiranti religion in contemporary Nepal. In David Gellner, Sondra Hausner & Chiara Letizia (eds.), *The state of religion in a non-religous state: Discourses and practices in the secular republic of Nepal*. New Delhi: Oxford University Press.

Gaenszle, Martin, Balthasar Bickel, Goma Banjade, Elena Lieven, Netra Paudyal, Ichchha P. Rai, Manoj Rai, Novel K. Rai & Sabine Stoll. 2005. Worshipping the king god: A preliminary analysis of Chintang ritual language in the invocation of Rajdeu. In Yogendra P. Yadava, Govinda Bhattarai, Ram Raj Lohani, Balaram Prasain & Krishna Parajuli (eds.), *Contemporary issues in Nepalese linguistics*, 33–47. Kathmandu: Linguistic Society of Nepal.

Gaenszle, Martin, Balthasar Bickel, Narayan P. Gautam (Sharma), Judith Pettigrew, Diana Schackow, Arjun Rai & Shree K. Rai. 2011. Binomials and the noun-to-verb ratio in Puma Rai ritual speech. *Anthropological Linguistics* 53. 365–382.

Genetti, Carol. 1986. The development of subordinators from postpositions in Bodic languages. *Proceedings of the 12th Annual Meeting of the Berkeley Linguistics Society* 12. 387–400.

Genetti, Carol. 1991. From postposition to subordinator in Newari. In Elizabeth Closs Traugott & Bernd Heine (eds.), *Approaches to grammaticalization, vol. Ii*, 227–255. Amsterdam: Benjamins.

Genetti, Carol. 1992. Semantic and grammatical categories of relative clause morphology in the languages of Nepal. *Studies in Language* 16. 405–427.

Genetti, Carol. 2007. *A grammar of Dolakha Newar*. Berlin: Mouton de Gruyter.

Genetti, Carol, A. R. Coupe, Ellen Bartee, Kristine Hildebrand & You-Jing Lin. 2008. Syntactic aspects of nominalization in five Tibeto-Burman languages of the Himalayan area. *Linguistics of the Tibeto-Burman Area* 31.2. 97–139.

Givón, Talmy. 1976. Topic, pronoun, and grammatical agreement. In Charles N. Li (ed.), *Subject and topic*, 149–188. New York: Academic Press.

Givón, Talmy. 1991. Some substantive issues concerning verb serialization: Grammatical vs. Cognitive packaging. In Claire Lefebvre (ed.), *Serial verbs: Grammatical, comparative and cognitive perspectives*, 137–184. Amsterdam: John Benjamins.

Grierson, George A. 1909. *Tibeto-burman family, part i, general introduction, specimens of the Tibetan dialects, the Himalayan dialects and the North Assam group.* (Linguistic Survey of India III). Calcutta: Superintendent of Government Printing, India.

Gvozdanović, Jadranka. 1987. How synchrony of a language reveals its diachrony (principles of analysis and classification). *Folia Linguistica Historica, Acta Societatis Linguisticae Europae* VIII(1–2). 421–445.

Haiman, John & Sandra A. Thompson. 1984. "Subordination" in universal grammar. *Proceedings of the Tenth Annual Meeting of the Berkeley Linguistics Society* 10. 510–523.

Hall, T. Alan. 2000. *Phonologie.* Berlin: Walter de Gruyter.

Handschuh, Corinna. 2011. *A typology of marked-s languages.* University of Leipzig PhD thesis.

Hardman, Charlotte E. 1981. The psychology of conformity and self-expression among the Lohorung Rai of East Nepal. In Paul Heelas & Andrew Lock (eds.), *Indigenous psychologies: The anthropology of the self,* 161–180. London: Academic Press.

Hardman, Charlotte E. 1990. *Conformity and self-expression: A study of the Lohorung Rai of East Nepal.* School of Oriental & African Studies, London PhD thesis.

Hardman, Charlotte E. 2000. *Other worlds. Notions of self and emotion among the Lohorung Rai.* Oxford, New York: Berg.

Haspelmath, Martin. 1993. More on the typology of inchoative/causative verb alternations. In Bernard Comrie & Maria Polinsky (eds.), *Causatives and transitivity,* vol. 23 (Studies in Language Companion Series), 87–120. Amsterdam: Benjamins.

Haspelmath, Martin. 1995. The converb as a cross-linguistically valid category. In Martin Haspelmath & Ekkehard König (eds.), *Converbs in cross-linguistic perspective,* 1–55. Berlin: Mouton de Gruyter.

Haspelmath, Martin. 1997. *Indefinite pronouns* (Oxford Studies in Typology and Linguistic Theory). Oxford: Oxford University Press.

Haspelmath, Martin. 1999. Long-distance agreement in Godoberi (Daghestanian). *Folia Linguistica* 33. 131–151.

Haspelmath, Martin. 2002. *Understanding morphology* (Understanding Language Series). London: Hodder Arnold.

Haspelmath, Martin. 2004a. Coordinating constructions: An overview. In Martin Haspelmath (ed.), *Coordinating constructions,* 3–40. Amsterdam: John Benjamins.

Haspelmath, Martin. 2004b. Explaining the ditransitive person-role constraint: A usage-based approach. *Constructions* 2. 1–71.

Haspelmath, Martin. 2005. Argument marking in ditransitive alignment types. *Linguistic Discovery* 3. 1–21.

Haspelmath, Martin. 2007. Ditransitive alignment splits and inverse alignment. *Functions of Language* 14(1). (special issue on ditransitives, guest edited by Anna Siewierska), 79–102.

Haspelmath, Martin. 2009. Terminology of case. In Andrew Spencer Andrej Malchukov (ed.), *Handbook of case*, chap. 33, 505–517. Oxford: Oxford University Press.

Haspelmath, Martin & Thomas Müller-Bardey. 2004. Valency change. In Gert Booij, Christian Lehmann & Joachim Mugdan (eds.), *Morphologie / morphology. Ein internationales Handbuch zur Flexion und Wortbildung/ An International Handbook on Inflection and Word-Formation*, chap. 107, 1130–1145. Berlin: De Gruyter.

Heine, Bernd & Tania Kuteva. 2002. *World lexicon of grammaticalization.* Cambridge: Cambridge University Press.

Hildebrandt, Kristine. 2007. Prosodic and grammatical domains in Limbu. *Himalayan Linguistics Journal* 8. 1–34.

Hill, Nathan W. 2014. A note on voicing alternations in the Tibetan verbal system. *Transactions of the Philological Society* 112(1). 1–4.

Himmelmann, Nikolaus P. 2004. Lexicalization and grammaticization: Opposite or orthogonal? In Walter Bisang, Nikolaus P. Himmelmann & Björn Wiemer (eds.), *What makes grammaticalization: A look from its fringes and its components*, 21–42. Berlin: De Gruyter.

Hodgson, Brian Houghton. 1857. Comparative vocabulary of the languages of the broken tribes of Nepal. *Journal of the Asiatic Society of Bengal* 26(5). (Reprinted 1880 in Miscellaneous Essays Relating to Indian Subjects, Vol. 1. London: Trubner and Co., 161–215), 317–71.

Hook, Peter Edwin. 1991. The Emergence of Perfective Aspect in Indo-Aryan languages. In Elizabeth Closs Traugott & Bernd Heine (eds.), *Approaches to grammaticalization* (Typological Studies in Language), 59–90. Amsterdam: Benjamins.

Hook, Peter Edwin & Prashant Pardeshi. 2009. The semantic evolution of EAT-expressions: Ways and byways. In John Newman (ed.), *The linguistics of eating and drinking*, vol. 84 (Typological Studies in Language), 153–172. Amsterdam: Benjamins.

Hopper, Paul J. & Sandra A. Thompson. 1980. Transitivity in grammar and discourse. *Language* 56. 251–299.

References

Hopper, Paul J. & Elizabeth Closs Traugott. 1993. *Grammaticalization.* Cambridge: Cambridge University Press.

Horn, Laurence R. 1989. *A natural history of negation.* Chicago: The University of Chicago Press.

Hyslop, Gwendolyn. 2011. *A grammar of Kurtöp.* University of Oregon PhD thesis.

Jackendoff, Ray. 1983. *Semantics and cognition.* Cambridge, Mass.: MIT Press.

Jacques, Guillaume. 2012a. Agreement morphology: The case of Rgyalrongic and Kiranti. *Language and Linguistics* 13. 86–113.

Jacques, Guillaume. 2012b. An internal reconstruction of Tibetan stem alternations. *Transactions of the Philological Society* 110. 212–224.

Jespersen, Otto. 1904. *Lehrbuch der Phonetik.* Leipzig: Teubner.

Jespersen, Otto. 1965. *A modern English grammar on historical principles.* Vol. VI. London: George Ellen & Unwin Ltd.

Jimi, Indira, Visvakaji Kongren & Manita Jimi. 2009. *Engka Yakkha cheptap 1.* Sanothimi, Bhaktapur: Siksa tatha Khelkud Mantralaya.

Jimi, Indira, Visvakaji Kongren & Manita Jimi. 2010. *Engka Yakkha cheptap 2.* Sanothimi, Bhaktapur: Siksa tatha Khelkud Mantralaya.

Kansakar, Tej Ratna. 2005. Classical Newar verbal morphology and grammaticalization in classical and modern Newar. *Himalayan Linguistics* 3. 1–21.

Kazenin, Konstantin I. 2001. Verbal reflexives and the middle voice. In Martin Haspelmath, Ekkehard König, Wulf Oesterreicher & Wolfgang Raible (eds.), *Language typology and language universals,* vol. 2 (Handbücher zur Sprach- und Kommunikationswissenschaft 20), chap. 68, 916–927. Berlin: De Gruyter.

Keenan, Edward L. & Matthew S. Dryer. 2007. Passive in the world's languages. In Timothy Shopen (ed.), *Language typology and syntactic description,* vol. 1, chap. 6, 325–361. New York: Cambridge University Press.

Kemmer, Suzanne. 1993. *The middle voice* (Typological Studies in Language 23). Amsterdam: Benjamins.

Kepping, Ksenia Borisovna. 1975. Subject and object agreement in the Tangut verb. *Linguistics of the Tibeto-Burman Area* 2.2. 219–31.

Kepping, Ksenia Borisovna. 1994. The conjugation of the Tangut verb. *Bulletin of the School of Oriental and Asian Studies* 57. 339–346.

Kongren, Ramji. 2007a. *Yakkha jatiko samskar ra samskriti (yakkha indigenous people's tradition and culture).* Kathmandu: Kirat Yakkha Chumma, Indigenous Peoples Yakkha Organization.

Kongren, Ramji. 2007b. *Yakkha-nepali-english dictionary.* Kathmandu: Kirat Yakkha Chumma, Indigenous Peoples Yakkha Organization.

König, Ekkehard. 1993. Focus particles. In J. Jacobs, A. von Stechow, W. Sternefeld & T. Vennemann (eds.), *Syntax: Ein internationales Handbuch zeitgenössischer Forschung*, 978–987. Berlin, Boston: De Gruyter Mouton.

König, Ekkehard & Peter Siemund. 2007. Speech act distinctions in grammar. In Timothy Shopen (ed.), *Language typology and syntactic description*, 2nd edn., vol. 1: Clause Structure, 267–324. Camdrige, UK: Cambridge University Press.

Lahaussois, Aimée. 2002. *Aspects of the grammar of Thulung Rai: An endangered Himalayan language*. Berkeley: University of California PhD thesis.

Lahaussois, Aimée. 2003. *Aspects of the grammar of Thulung Rai: An endangered Himalayan language*. Ann Arbor: UMI Publications.

LaPolla, Randy J. 1992. On the dating and nature of verb agreement in Tibeto-Burman. *Bulletin of the School of Oriental and African Studies* 55. 298–315.

LaPolla, Randy J. 1995. 'Ergative' marking in Tibeto-Burman. In Yoshio Nishi, James A. Matisoff & Yasuhiko Nagano (eds.), *New horizons in Tibeto-Burman morphosyntax* (Senri Ethnological Studies 41), 189–228. Osaka, Japan: National Museum of Ethnology.

LaPolla, Randy J. 1996. Middle voice marking in Tibeto-Burman. *Pan-Asiatic Linguistics: Proceedings of the Fourth International Symposium on Languages and Linguistics* 5. Bangkok: Mahidol University, 1940–54.

LaPolla, Randy J. 2001. The role of migration and language contact in the development of the Sino-Tibetan language family. In Alexandra Y. Aikhenvald & Robert M. W. Dixon (eds.), *Areal diffusion and genetic inheritance: Problems in comparative linguistics*, 225–254. Oxford: Oxford University Press.

LaPolla, Randy J. 2003. Overview of Sino-Tibetan morphosyntax. In Graham Thurgood & Randy J. Lapolla (eds.), *The Sino-Tibetan languages* (Routledge Language Family Series), chap. 2, 22–42. London & New York: Routledge.

LaPolla, Randy J. 2007. Hierarchical person marking in the Rawang language. Paper presented at the 40th International Conference on Sino-Tibetan Languages and Linguistics, Harbin, China.

LaPolla, Randy J. 2012. Comments on methodology and evidence in Sino-Tibetan comparative linguistics. *Language and Linguistics* 13.1. 117–132.

Lehmann, Christian. 1984. *Der Relativsatz*. Tübingen: Narr.

Lehmann, Christian. 1988. Towards a typology of clause linkage. In John Haiman & Sandra A. Thompson (eds.), *Clause combining in grammar and discourse*, 181–226. Amsterdam: Benjamins.

Lehmann, Christian. 2002. *Thoughts on grammaticalization (second, revised edition)* (Arbeitspapiere des Seminars für Sprachwissenschaft der Universität Erfurt). Erfurt: Seminar für Sprachwissenschaft, Universität Erfurt.

Letuchiy, Alexander. 2009. Towards a typology of labile verbs: Lability vs. Derivation. In Alexandre Arkhipov & Patience Epps (eds.), *New challenges in typology.
Transcending the boundaries and refining the distinctions*, 223–244. Berlin: Mouton de Gruyter.

Levin, Beth. 1993. *English verb classes and alternations: A preliminary survey.* Chicago: The University of Chicago Press.

Levin, Beth & Malka Rappaport Hovav. 2005. *Argument realization.* Cambridge:
Cambridge University Press.

Levinson, Stephen C. & David P. Wilkins (eds.). 2006. *Grammars of space: Explo-
rations in cognitive diversity* (Language Culture and Cognition 6). Cambridge,
UK: Cambridge University Press.

Lewis, M. Paul, Gary F. Simons & Charles D. Fennig. 2015. *Ethnologue: Languages
of the World.* SIL International. http://www.ethnologue.com.

Li, Chao. 2007. Split ergativity and split intransitivity in Nepali. *Lingua* 117. 1462–
1482.

Lichtenberk, Frantisek. 1991. On the gradualness of grammaticalization. In Elizabeth Closs Traugott & Bernd Heine (eds.), *Approaches to grammaticalization*,
37–80. Amsterdam: John Benjamins.

Linkha, Magman. 2012. छुबुक्का चालेप्पा *[The bread of ashes].* Mother Tongue Center
Nepal (UNM).

Linkha, Magman. 2067 B.S. *Yakkha jati ek parichaya.*

Linkha, Magman & Bam Dewan. 2064 B.S. *Yakkha ce'ya sikla: Prarambhik Yakkha
sabda samgraha.* Sunsari: Kirat Yakkha Chumma, Indigenous Peoples Yakkha
Organization.

Linkha, Ram Kumar. 2013. *A comparative study of Yakkha and English kinship
terms.* Tribhuvan University, Janta Multiple Campus, School of Education MA
thesis.

Lyons, John. 1969. *Introduction to theoretical linguistics.* Cambridge: Cambridge
University Press.

Malchukov, Andrej. 2008. Split intransitives, experiencer objects, 'transimper-
sonal constructions': (re-)establishing the connection. In Mark Donohue &
Søren Wichmann (eds.), *The typology of semantic alignment*, 76–100. New York:
Oxford University Press.

Malchukov, Andrej & Bernard Comrie (eds.). 2015. *Valency classes in the world's
languages. Vol 1: Introducing the framework, and case studies from Africa and
Eurasia.* Berlin: De Gruyter Mouton.

Malchukov, Andrej, Martin Haspelmath & Bernard Comrie. 2010a. Ditransitive
constructions: A typological overview. In Andrej Malchukov, Martin Haspel-

math & Bernard Comrie (eds.), *Studies in ditransitive constructions*, 1–36. Berlin: De Gruyter.

Malchukov, Andrej, Martin Haspelmath & Bernard Comrie (eds.). 2010b. *Studies in ditransitive constructions*. Berlin: De Gruyter.

Manandhar, Narayan P. 2002. *Plants and people of Nepal*. Portland, Oregon: Timber Press.

Masica, Colin. 2001. The definition and significance of linguistic areas: Methods, pitfalls, and possibilities (with special reference to the validity of South Asia as a linguistic area). In Peri Bhaskararao & Karumuri Venkata Subbarao (eds.), *Tokyo symposium on south Asian languages: Contact, convergence, and typology [= the yearbook of south Asian languages and linguistics 2001]*, 205–267. New Delhi: Sage Publications.

Matisoff, James A. 1969. Verb concatenation in Lahu: The syntax and semantics of 'simple' juxtaposition in Lahu. *Acta Linguistica Hafniensia* 12. 69–120.

Matisoff, James A. 1972. Lahu nominalization, relativization, and genitivization. In John P. Kimball (ed.), *Syntax and semantics, vol. 1*, 237–57. New York: Academic Press.

Matisoff, James A. 1986. Hearts and minds in South-East Asian languages and English: An essay in the comparative lexical semantics of psycho-collocations. *Cahiers de linguistique asie-orientale* 15. 5–57.

Matisoff, James A. 1990a. Bulging monosyllables: Areal tendencies in South East Asian diachrony. *Proceedings of the Sixteenth Annual Meeting of the Berkeley Linguistics Society* 16. 343–359.

Matisoff, James A. 1990b. On megalocomparison. *Language* 66. 106–120.

Matisoff, James A. 2003. *Handbook of Proto-Tibeto-Burman: System and philosophy of Sino-Tibetan reconstruction*. Berkeley: University of California Press.

Matthews, David. 1984. *A course in Nepali*. London: School of Oriental & African Studies.

McGregor, William B. 2009. Typology of ergativity. *Language and Linguistics Compass* 3(1). 480–508.

Michailovsky, Boyd. 1985. Tibeto-Burman dental suffixes: Evidence from Limbu. In Graham Thurgood, James A. Matisoff & David Bradley (eds.), *Linguistics of the Sino-Tibetan Area: The state of the art*, 363–375. Canberra: Pacific Linguistics.

Michailovsky, Boyd. 1994. Manner vs. Place of articulation in the Kiranti initial stops. In Hajime Kitamura, Tatsuo Nishida & Yasuhiko Nagano (eds.), *Current issues in Sino-Tibetan linguistics*, 766–772. Osaka: National Museum of Ethnology.

Michailovsky, Boyd. 2003. Hayu. In Graham Thurgood & Randy LaPolla (eds.), *The Sino-Tibetan languages*, 518–532. London: Routledge.

Miller, Amy. 2001. *A grammar of Jamul Tiipay*. Berlin: Mouton de Gruyter.

Montaut, Annie. 2004. *A grammar of Hindi*. München: Lincom Europa.

Mosel, Ulrike. 2006. Grammaticography: The art and craft of grammar writing. In Felix K. Ameka, Alan Dench & Nicholas Evans (eds.), *Catching language: The standing challenge of grammar writing*, 41–68. Berlin: De Gruyter Mouton.

Næss, Åshild. 2007. *Prototypical transitivity*. Amsterdam: Benjamins.

Næss, Åshild. 2009. How transitive are eat and drink verbs? In John Newman (ed.), *The linguistics of eating and drinking*, vol. 84 (Typologial Studies in Language), 27–43. Amsterdam: Benjamins.

Nagano, Yasuhiko. 1984. *A historical study of the rGyarong verb system*. Tokyo: Seishido.

Nedjalkov, Vladimir P. 1995. Some typological parameters of converbs. In Martin Haspelmath & Ekkehard König (eds.), *Converbs in cross-linguistic perspective*, 97–136. Berlin: Mouton de Gruyter.

Nespital, Helmut. 1997. *Hindi kriya-kosa: Containing all simple and compound verbs, their lexical equivalents in English and illustrations of their usage*. Allahabad: Lokbharati Prakasan.

Newman, John. 2009. A cross-linguistic overview of 'eat' and 'drink'. In John Newman (ed.), *The linguistics of eating and drinking*, vol. 84 (Typological Studies in Language), 1–26. Amsterdam: Benjamins.

Nichols, Johanna. 1992. *Language diversity in space and time*. Chicago: The University of Chicago Press.

Noonan, Michael. 1997. Versatile nominalization. In Joan Bybee, John Haiman & Sandra A. Thompson (eds.), *Essays on language function and language type. Dedicated to Talmy Givón*, 373–394. Amsterdam: Benjamins.

Noonan, Michael. 2007. Complementation. In Timothy Shopen (ed.), *Language typology and syntactic description, vol. Ii: Complex constructions*, 52–150. Cambridge: Cambridge University Press.

Noonan, Michael & Teresa Fanego. 2008. Nominalizations in Bodic languages. In María José López-Couso & Elena Seoane (eds.), *Rethinking grammaticalization: New perspectives for the twenty-first century*, 219–238. Amsterdam: Benjamins.

Nuyts, Jan. 2006. Modality: Overview and linguistic issues. In William Frawley (ed.), *The expression of modality*, 1–26. Berlin: Mouton De Gruyter.

Opgenort, Jean Robert. 2004. *A grammar of Wambule*. Leiden: Brill.

Peterson, John. 2010. *A grammar of Kharia: A South Munda language* (Brill's Studies in South and Southwest Asian Languages). Leiden & Boston: Brill Academic Publishing.

Pokharel, Madhav P. 1999. Compound verbs in Nepali. In Yogendra P. Yadava & Warren W. Glover (eds.), *Topics in Nepalese linguistics*, 185–208. Kamaladi, Kathmandu: Royal Nepal Academy.

Polinsky, Maria & Bernard Comrie. 1999. Agreement in Tsez. *Folia Linguistica* 33. 109–130.

Polinsky, Maria & Eric Potsdam. 2002. Backward control. *Linguistic Inquiry* 33. 245–282.

Pradhan, Kumar. 1991. *The Gorkha conquests*. Calcutta: Oxford University Press.

Pramodini, Devi Nameirakpam. 2010. EAT expressions in Manipuri. *Language in India* 10. 1–15.

Rai, Arjun. 2011. *Nature, culture and the adaptation of the Yakkhas*. Kirtipur, Kathmandu: Tribhuvan University, Central Department of Sociology & Anthropology MA thesis.

Rai, Novel K. 1984. A descriptive study of Bantawa. Ph.D. dissertation, Deccan College Post-Graduate Research Institute, Pune (India).

Rai, Novel K. & Werner Winter. 1997. Triplicated verbal adjuncts in Bantawa. In David Bradley (ed.), *Tibeto-burman languages of the Himalayas*, 135–155. Canberra: Pacific Linguistics (A-86).

Rai, Novel K., Balthasar Bickel, Martin Gaenszle, Elena Lieven, Netra Paudyal, Ichchha P. Rai, Manoj Rai & Sabine Stoll. 2005. Triplication and ideophones in Chintang. In Yogendra P. Yadava (ed.), *Current issues in Nepalese linguistics*, 205–209. Kirtipur: Linguistic Society of Nepal.

Rai, Novel K., Manoj Rai, Netra P. Paudyal, Robert Schikowski, Balthasar Bickel, Sabine Stoll, Martin Gaenszle, Goma Banjade, Ichchha P. Rai, Toya N. Bhatta, Sebastian Sauppe, Rikhi Maya Rai, Janak Kumari Rai, Las Kumari Rai, Durga Bahadur Rai, Ganesh Rai, Dayaram Rai, Durga Kumari Rai, Anita Rai, Candra Kumari Rai, Shanti Maya Rai, Ravindra Kumar Rai, Judy Pettigrew & Tyko Dirksmeyer. 2011. *Chintang-Nepali-English dictionary with grammar*. Kathmandu: Chintang Language Research Program.

Rapacha, Syankarelu Lal, Bag-Ayagyami Yalungcha & Amar Tumyahang. 2008. *Indo-Nepal Kiranti bhasaharu.* Kathmandu: Kirantivigyan Adhyayan Samsthan.

Read, Alfred Frank Charles. 1934. *Balti grammar*. London: The Royal Asiatic Society.

Russell, Andrew J. 1992. *The Yakha: Culture, environment and development in East Nepal.* Oxford University PhD thesis.

Russell, Andrew J. 1997. Identity management and cultural change: Religion and politics amongst the Yakkha. In David N. Gellner, Joanna Pfaff-Czarnecka & John Whelpton (eds.), *Nationalism and ethnicity in a Hindu kingdom: The politics of culture in contemporary Nepal*, 325–350. Amsterdam: Harwood Academic Publishers.

Russell, Andrew J. 2000. The missing and the met: Routing Clifford amongst the Yakha in Nepal and NE India. *Journeys* 1. 86–113.

Russell, Andrew J. 2004. Traditions in transition: Sanskritization and Yakkhafication in East Nepal. *History and Anthropology* 15(3). 251–61.

Russell, Andrew J. 2007. Writing travelling cultures: Travel and ethnography amongst the Yakkha of East Nepal. *Ethnos* 72(3). 361–382.

Russell, Andrew J. 2010. Perceptions of forests among the Yakkha of East Nepal: Exploring the social and cultural context. In A. Guneratne (ed.), *Culture and the environment in the Himalaya*, 61–78. London: Routledge.

Rutgers, Roland. 1998. *Yamphu: Grammar, texts, and lexicon*. Leiden: CNWS Publications.

Saxena, Anju. 1992. *Finite verb morphology in Tibeto-Kinnauri*. University of Oregon PhD thesis.

Schackow, Diana. 2008. Clause linkage in Puma (Kiranti). MA. thesis, Department of Linguistics, University of Leipzig. Leipzig.

Schackow, Diana. 2012a. Grammatical relations in Yakkha. Paper presented at the 45th Meeting of the Societas Linguistica Europaea, Stockholm.

Schackow, Diana. 2012b. Referential hierarchy effects in three-argument constructions in Yakkha. *Linguistic Discovery* 10.3 3(10). 148–173.

Schackow, Diana, Balthasar Bickel, Shree Kumar Rai, Narayan Sharma (Gautam), Arjun Rai & Martin Gaenszle. 2012. Morphosyntactic properties and scope behavior of 'subordinate' clauses in Puma (kiranti). In Volker Gast & Holger Diessel (eds.), *Clause-linkage in cross-linguistic perspective* (Trends in Linguistics), 105–126. Berlin: De Gruyter Mouton.

Schiering, René, Kristine Hildebrandt & Balthasar Bickel. 2010. The prosodic word is not universal, but emergent. *Journal of Linguistics* 46. 657–709.

Schikowski, Robert. 2012. Chintang morphology. MS, University of Zürich.

Schikowski, Robert. 2013. *Object-conditioned differential marking in Chintang and Nepali*. University of Zürich PhD thesis.

Schikowski, Robert, Balthasar Bickel & Netra Prasad Paudyal. 2015. Flexible valency in Chintang. In Andrej Malchukov & Bernard Comrie (eds.), *Valency classes in the world's languages. Vol 1: Introducing the framework, and case studies from Africa and Eurasia*, 669–708. Berlin: De Gruyter Mouton.

Schlemmer, Grégoire. 2003/2004. New past for the sake of a better future: Re-inventing the history of the kirant in East Nepal. *European Bulletin of Himalayan Research* 25/26. 119–144.

Schultze-Berndt, Eva. 2006. Taking a closer look at function verbs: Lexicon, grammar, or both. In Felix K. Ameka, Alan Dench & Nicholas Evans (eds.), *Catching Language: The standing challenge of grammar writing*, 359–392. Berlin: Mouton de Gruyter.

Selkirk, E. 1984. On the major class features and syllable theory. In M. Aronoff & R. T. Oehrle (eds.), *Language and sound structure*, 107–136. Cambridge: MIT Press.

Serdobolskaya, Natalia. 2009. Towards the typology of raising: A functional approach. In Patience Epps & Alexandre Archipov (eds.), *New challenges in typology* (Trends in Linguistics), 269–294. Berlin: Mouton the Gruyter.

Shafer, Robert. 1974. *Introduction to Sino-Tibetan.* Wiesbaden: Harrassowitz.

Sharma (Gautam), Narayan P. 2005. *Case markers in Puma.* Paper presented at the 26th Annual Conference of the Linguistic Society of Nepal, Kathmandu.

Siewierska, Anna. 1998. On nominal and verbal person marking. *Linguistic Typology* 2. 1–56.

Siewierska, Anna. 2003. Person agreement and the determination of alignment. *Transactions of the Philological Society* 2(101). 339–370.

Siewierska, Anna. 2011. Person marking. In Jae Jung Song (ed.), *The Oxford Handbook of Linguistic Typology*, 322–345. Oxford: Oxford University Press.

Silverstein, Michael. 1976. Hierarchy of features and ergativity. In Robert M. W. Dixon (ed.), *Grammatical categories in Australian languages*, 112–171. New Jersey: Humanities Press.

Sprigg, R. K. 1985. The Limbu s-final and t-final verb roots. *Linguistics of the Tibeto-Burman Area* 8. 1–35.

Subba, T B. 1999. *Politics of culture.* Chennai: Orient Longman.

Svensén, Bo. 2009. *A handbook of lexicography: The theory and practice of dictionary-making.* Cambridge: Cambridge University Press.

Tamang, Jyoti Prakash. 2010. *Himalayan fermented foods. Microbiology, nutrition and ethnic values.* Boca Raton, FL: Taylor & Francis Group.

Tesnière, Lucien. 1959. *Éléments de syntaxe structurale.* Paris: Klincksieck.

Thompson, Sandra A., Robert E. Longacre & Shin Ja J. Hwang. 2007. Adverbial clauses. In Timothy Shopen (ed.), *Language typology and syntactic description*, vol. 2, 237–300. Cambridge, UK: Cambridge.

Thurgood, Graham. 1984. The Rung languages: A major new Tibeto-Burman sub-group. *Proceedings of the 10th Annual Meeting of the Berkeley Linguistics Society* 10. 338–349.

Toba, Sueyoshi, Ingrid Toba & Novel K. Rai. 2005. *Diversity and endangerment of languages in Nepal* (UNESCO Kathmandu Series of Monographs and Working Papers 7). Kathmandu: United Nations Educational, Scientific & Cultural Organization, Kathmandu Office.

Tolsma, Gerard. 1999. *A grammar of Kulung*. University of Leiden PhD thesis.

Tournadre, Nicolas. 1991. The rhetorical use of the Tibetan ergative. *Linguistics of the Tibeto-Burman Area* 14. 93–107.

Turin, Mark. 2007. *Linguistic diversity and the preservation of endangered languages: A case study from Nepal*. Tech. rep. Kathmandu: International Centre for Integrated Mountain Development (ICIMOD).

Turner, Ralph Lilley. 1931. *A comparative and etymological dictionary of the Nepali language*. Reprint New Delhi: Allied Publishers Ltd. 1980.

Van linden, An. 2012. *Modal adjectives: English deontic and evaluative constructions in synchrony and diachrony*. Berlin: Mouton the Gruyter.

Van Valin, Robert D. & David P. Wilkins. 1996. The case for 'effector': Case roles, agents, and agentivity revisited. In Masayoshi Shibatani & Sandra A. Thompson (eds.), *Grammatical constructions*, 289–322. Oxford: Oxford University Press.

Vincent, Nigel. 2013. Conative. *Linguistic Typology* 17(2). 269–290.

Watters, David E. 2002. *A grammar of Kham*. Cambridge: Cambridge University Press.

Watters, David E. 2008. Nominalization in the Kiranti and Central Himalayish languages of Nepal. *Linguistics of the Tibeto-Burman Area* 31(2). [Special Issue on Nominalization], ed. by Coupe, Alexander, 21–44.

Wegener, Claudia. 2012. *A grammar of Savosavo*. Berlin & Boston: de Gruyter Mouton.

Whelpton, John. 2005. *A history of Nepal*. Cambridge, UK: Cambridge University Press.

Winter, Werner, Gerd Hansson, Alfons Weidert & Bickram Ingwaba Subba. 1996. *A synoptic glossary of Athpare, Belhare and Yakkha*. Unterschleissheim, München: Lincom Europa.

Wittenburg, Peter & Han Sloetjes. 2008. Annotation by category – elan and iso dcr. In *Proceedings of the 6th international conference on language resources and evaluation (lrec)*.

Witzlack-Makarevich, Alena. 2010. *Typological variation in grammatical relations.* University of Leipzig PhD thesis.

Witzlack-Makarevich, Alena, Taras Zakharko, Lennart Bierkandt & Balthasar Bickel. 2011. Decomposing hierarchical alignment: Participant scenarios as conditions on alignment. Paper presented at the 44th Annual Meeting of the Societas Linguistica Europaea. Universidad de la Rioja, Logroño, Spain, 8–11 September.

Woodbury, Anthony C. 1985. Noun phrase, nominal sentence, and clause in Central Alaskan Yup'ik Eskimo. In Johanna Nichols & Anthony C. Woodbury (eds.), *Grammar inside and outside the clause,* 61–88. Cambridge: Cambridge University Press.

Wälchli, Bernhard. 2005. *Co-compounds and natural coordnation.* Cambridge: Cambridge University Press.

Yakkha, Ajaya Jimee. 2012a. चासुवाबे *[At the Udhauli Festival].* Mother Tongue Center Nepal (UNM).

Yakkha, Shantila Jimee. 2012b. फोप्चिबा नुइ का *[The owl and I].* Mother Tongue Center Nepal (UNM).

Yap, Foong Ha & Karen Grunow-Hårsta. 2010. Non-referential uses of nominalization constructions: Asian perspectives. *Language and Linguistics Compass* 4(12). 1154–1175.

Yap, Foong Ha & Iwasaki Shoichi. 1998. The emergence of 'give' passives in East and Southeast Asian languages. In Mark Alves, Paul Sidwell & David Gil (eds.), *Papers from the Eighth Annual Meeting of the Southeast Asian Linguistics Society SEALS VIII,* 193–208. Canberra: Pacific Linguistics.

Zimmermann, Eva. 2012. Affix copying in Kiranti. In Enrico Boone, Kathrin Linke & Maartje Schulpen (eds.), *Proceedings of the ConSOLE XIX,* 343–367. Leiden: Leiden University.

Zúñiga, Fernando. 2007. From the typology of inversion to the typology of alignment. In Matti Miestamo & Bernhard Wälchli (eds.), *New challenges in typology: Broadening the horizons and redefining the foundations.* 199–221. Berlin: Mouton de Gruyter.

Name index

Language index

Subject index